Primary school people

Beginning to teach in a primary school means establishing a whole set of relationships – with one's class of course, but also with the other adults who work in the school. These include teachers and teaching assistants, support staff of various kinds, from the visiting educational psychologist to the essential school secretary, and parents, both as helpers in the school and as the major influences on their children's lives outside school.

This book is designed to give students and newly qualified teachers a taste of what they can expect, and to help them to get the most out of these relationships both for themselves and for their children. Throughout, it draws upon the experiences of new teachers, often in their own words, but it also uses the voices of other 'primary school people' to offer differing perspectives. Throughout, the text is supported by points for discussion, questionnaires and check-lists to help new teachers to define and analyse their own situation.

Jean Mills and **Richard W. Mills** are both experienced teachers who work at Westhill College, Birmingham, where Jean is Senior Lecturer in Education and Richard is Principal Lecturer and Head of the English Department. They have published widely, including *Bilingualism in the Primary School* (Routledge, 1993).

Primary school people

Getting to know your colleagues

Edited by Jean Mills and
Richard W. Mills

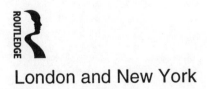

London and New York

First published 1995
by Routledge
11 New Fetter Lane, London EC4P 4EE

Simultaneously published in the USA and Canada
by Routledge
29 West 35th Street, New York, NY 10001

© 1995 Jean Mills and Richard W. Mills

Typeset in Palatino by LaserScript, Mitcham, Surrey
Printed and bound in Great Britain by
TJ Press (Padstow) Ltd, Padstow, Cornwall

British Library Cataloguing in Publication Data
A catalogue record for this book is available from the British Library

Library of Congress Cataloging in Publication Data
A catalogue record for this book has been requested

ISBN 0–415–11396–2

Contents

Contributors

Andrew Coates is Head of Creative Arts at Westhill College of Higher Education, Birmingham. He is a practising artist who exhibits widely and often uses his work as the basis for curriculum projects in primary schools. Since 1987 he has been chair of the joint governing body of an infant and junior school.

June Dunkley is an experienced primary school teacher and Deputy Head of a nursery and infants school in the West Midlands. Research into the role of the school nurse formed the basis of her dissertation for a further degree.

Gill Hackett taught for a number of years in West Midlands primary schools, holding posts of responsibility for language and special needs, before becoming an Advisory Teacher for Primary English. She is presently Senior Lecturer in Education at Westhill College, Birmingham.

Ann Lance spent twenty years teaching in inner-city primary schools, including nine as a Headteacher. This was followed by a period of secondment to the National Primary Centre for research in a number of areas, including that of mentoring. She is currently a Senior Lecturer in Education at Westhill College, Birmingham.

Jane Leadbetter is currently Senior Educational Psychologist in a major city, having taught for a number of years in an East Midlands High School. Her particular interests include behaviour management in schools and pre-school assessment. She is joint author of *Special Children: Meeting the Challenge in the Primary School*, Cassell.

Nabela Mann is in her third year of teaching in a culturally diverse inner-city primary school, where she has responsibility for the Reception Class of four- to five-year-old children. She is currently engaged in Masters Degree research into the bilingual development of young children.

Jean Mills has taught since the 1970s in nursery, infant and junior schools in England and lectured in Higher Education in Canada and Australia. Author of several articles and books, including *Bilingualism in the Primary School: A Handbook for Teachers*, Routledge, she was formerly Deputy of a Language Support Service in a large Local Authority, and is currently Senior Lecturer in Education at Westhill College, Birmingham.

Richard W. Mills taught for ten years in English schools before moving into Teacher Education. Having lectured in Pakistan and Australia, he is currently Principal Lecturer, Head of the English Department, and Bachelor of Humanities Co-ordinator at Westhill College, Birmingham. He is the author/editor of some twenty books on education, including *Observing Children in the Primary Classroom*, Routledge.

Jane Officer has worked in city schools for twenty years, mainly in the areas of special education, special needs and support for both learning and behavioural difficulties. Latterly, she has been employed as an advisory teacher with the Schools' Psychological Service.

Jane Powell has several years' teaching experience in primary schools as a language support teacher and Home–School Liaison Teacher. She was Area Co-ordinator of a team of HSL teachers and is currently Deputy Head of an inner-city infants school.

Chris Rush entered the profession as a mature student and is now in her sixth year of teaching. Her curriculum responsibilities have included mathematics, music, humanities, science and assessment. She is currently Deputy Head in a West of England infant school.

Wendie Wildman is a newly qualified teacher, in her first year at a four-hundred-strong suburban junior and infant school, having Art and Design as a specialist interest. She currently has charge of a Key Stage 2, Year Five class (9–10 years). In her second year she will take on responsibility for the Expressive Arts, to include drama and dance.

Roger Woods is currently Principal Lecturer, Head of the Education Department, and Initial Teacher Training Co-ordinator at Westhill College, Birmingham. He has taught in primary schools in England and Nepal, serving as class teacher, Deputy and Headteacher.

Acknowledgements

We wish to record our special thanks to our contributor colleagues for their committed and conscientious involvement. We are glad to acknowledge the other various contributions of children, teachers, non-teaching professionals and parents, whose words are recorded verbatim or whose ideas have added to our understanding.

The National Primary Centre (NPC) readily agreed to extracts being included from its publications *Brace Yourself* and *Practice to Share*. The Editor of the *Strategies* journal, Helen Hancock, was similarly very helpful in permitting extracts from Barrie Pinfield's article.

Particular thanks are due to present and past students for their positive involvement. Sometimes this is quite substantial; sometimes it is reflected merely by a single comment. In each case the material they provide adds an immediacy and a sense of real context which are crucial.

Several key players in this drama have disguised identities, to protect them and their institutions. They know who they are and we are very conscious of their contributions.

Finally, the book is dedicated to Joan and Sallie, former school secretaries.

Jean Mills and Richard W. Mills

Introduction

Jean Mills and Richard W. Mills

'I was surprised by the number of people who came into my classroom in the course of the day. I wasn't quite sure what my position was, in relation to theirs. This had to be negotiated quickly . . . . Few new teachers have the confidence to carry out such negotiations in front of their class.'

(Newly qualified teacher, *The Teacher*, September 1993)

This book has been written for new teachers and for students in teacher-training, whether they are in college/university departments, or under some other placement scheme. It will also, we hope, be useful for middle and senior management staff in school and, indeed, for some of those other adults whose involvement in the community of the school is rarely found described in such books.

This was our starting point. We reflected on the usual valuable advice given to students and new teachers about National Curriculum coverage; about lesson planning and evaluation; about differentiation of task; about management and organisation. One large area seemed to be missing or only briefly touched on. This was the area of developing personal and professional relationships, not merely with children, but with all those adults whose working lives are, somehow, related to the well-being of the children (see Biott, 1990; Bourne and McPake, 1991; Mortimore *et al.*, 1993; Thomas, 1992).

Some of these adults will work full-time in one school, others part-time in several schools; some will be on the permanent pay roll, others will have only a proportionate involvement; some will always be on the school premises, others in and out through the week; some will be trained, others untrained; most will be paid, some (i.e. parents) will not. If a school is a community of children and adults, then it follows that the significance of the network of relationships between the new teacher and all others needs to be recognised and utilised.

Accordingly, the notion of partnership is crucial.

In some cases (e.g. with caretaker, secretary, meals assistant, cleaning staff, governor), it may merely be sufficient for community morale for their work to be known and appreciated. Some of these roles occupy whole chapters in this book; some are included from time to time, wherever appropriate. In other cases (e.g. Special Needs co-ordinator, Home–School Liaison teacher, educational psychologist, nurse, Headteacher, lunch-time supervisor, speech therapist, social worker, child and family therapist, special attachment person), a knowledge of when and how they can help may be invaluable. In other cases still (e.g. classroom assistant, post holder, mentor, Section 11 teacher, neighbouring/team teaching colleague), the highest degree of co-operation and collaboration is essential.

Little of this will be really effective, of course, unless it is built on a real partnership between class teacher and parents, and such a crucial relationship is frequently explored throughout this book.

For many decades after the introduction of compulsory education, schools were regarded as teacher territory. Indeed, in some schools the division between home and school was reinforced by a painted or chalked line in the playground which parents were not supposed to cross. However, since the 1960s a variety of reports and accompanying research have urged teachers to strengthen the links between home and school (see Edwards and Redfern, 1988:11).

The process has been two-way. Not only have parents become more aware of a school's curriculum and ethos, but schools themselves have appreciated issues that affect the lives of their children and have acknowledged the skills that parents and the wider community have to offer. This has led to many other developments, such as parents working in classrooms; parents using knowledge and expertise for the school's benefit; the employment of Home–School Liaison teachers and link workers; the development of community rooms, toy libraries, playgroups in school.

Such a shift in thinking does not happen overnight. Much hard work and thought have gone into developing and maintaining these relationships on both sides. There are varieties of home–school partnerships (see Bastiani, 1989 and Long, 1983). In particular, there is increasing evidence that involving parents in the formal education of their children leads to significant gains in attainment (see Tizard *et al.*, 1988).

Successful classroom partnerships, whether between teacher and parent or between teacher and other professional, require certain skills and qualities, such as:

- good interpersonal relationships, sensitivity, openness, trust, tact, empathy;
- good preparation with understood and shared objectives;
- negotiation of collaborative ventures;

- clear ongoing guidance and mutual evaluation;
- mutual recognition of skills, background, knowledge, attitudes;
- appreciation of each other's strengths and weaknesses;
- willingness to share roles and territory occasionally;
- retention of personal integrity.

All of us, not only students on teaching practice and newly qualified teachers, need to be able to demonstrate these skills and abilities if we are to work successfully in partnership with others who have a stake in the shared enterprise. All stages along the polarities of youth–age, experience–inexperience, flexibility–inflexibility need to be acknowledged and reckoned with.

This book attempts to show how particular individuals approach the issue of collaborative endeavour. We believe that such a personal, case study approach offers a practical and accessible way in for most teachers and other professionals. All our contributors work, directly or indirectly, in partnership with others in the education service. We know that, sometimes, things can, and do, go wrong; that relationships break down; that friction can occur and be damaging. Nevertheless, the tone of the book throughout is positive. The problems, such as they are, exist to be overcome. They will be, given management commitment and participation of all associative staff in shared aims.

We end on such a note, with a brief exchange between eight-year-old Louise and her teacher, as follows:

Louise: Do you like working here?
Teacher: Yes I do. It's never boring because something different happens every day, and something usually makes us laugh.

REFERENCES

Bastiani, J. (1989) *Working with Parents*, Windsor: NFER-Nelson.
Biott, C. (1990) *Semi-Detached Teachers: Building Support and Advisory Relationships in the Classroom*, Basingstoke: Falmer.
Bourne, J. and McPake, J. (1991) *Partnership Teaching: An In-Service Pack for Schools*, London: HMSO.
Edwards, V. and Redfern, A. (1988) *At Home in School. Parental Participation in Primary Education*, London: Routledge.
Long, R. (1983) *Developing Parental Involvement in Primary Schools*, London: Macmillan.
Mortimore, P., Mortimore, J. and Thomas, H. (1994) *Managing Associative Staff*, London: Paul Chapman.
Thomas, G. (1992) *Effective Classroom Teamwork*, London: Routledge.
Tizard, B., Blatchford, P., Burke, J., Farquhar, C. and Plewis, I. (1988) *Young Children in the Inner City*, London: Laurence Erlbaum.

Part I

New encounters

Chapter 1

Getting to know you

*Section I: Richard W. Mills, with material from
Wendie Wildman*
*Section II: Richard W. Mills, with material from
Nabela Mann*

EDITORS' INTRODUCTION

This chapter sets out to locate the book in the real world of children and adults, in the belief that a glimpse into someone else's world, however brief and individual, reaches parts which statistics and graphs and large scale surveys do not reach, valuable as such material may be.

Section I monitors the experience of a newly qualified teacher (NQT) as she moves from student on teaching practice to fully fledged teacher, actually getting paid for her work. Snatches of comment and report show her coming to terms with this situation; learning to find her way about; meeting new teaching and non-teaching colleagues; getting to know her class of boys and girls; experiencing panic at the thought of meeting their parents.

What is conveyed is not exactly 'booming, buzzing confusion', but it is fairly hectic and helter-skelter, as impressions made by different people crowd in upon her consciousness. The intention is deliberate, for subsequent chapters of the book pick up these initial encounters and deal at more length with the significance of such professional relationships.

Section II is complementary, with information from another (newish) teacher – viz. in her second year – about getting to know her children. This time the setting is the infants department but the principles are the same anywhere. She learns about her boys and girls by watching their interaction during class; by studying their academic and medical records; by observing them in a range of contexts; by assessing their work; by listening to what colleagues say about them; by meeting their parents. She selects three of them in order to give a reasonably rounded picture of how they appear in school.

In all of this, she is drawing on the lessons learned in training: of the skills of analysis and observation; of the judgement involved in assessment and evaluation; of the tact and sensitivity required for good management and organisation. For this reason, the chapter forms a bridge between the world of teaching practice and the first teaching appointment.

Section I: Adults

Richard W. Mills, with material from Wendie Wildman

> Parents have been banned from our school trips because of their swearing and bad behaviour.
>
> (A junior school teacher)

Meeting, and learning about, your future colleagues is part of the exciting and daunting task of beginning work in a new place. In our context it applies to students on teaching practice, newly qualified teachers, and experienced teachers changing post. Later in this book you will read about a Headteacher's perspective. Here the intention is to see things from the point of view of an NQT. Let us first of all imagine that our newcomer received, in her briefing documents, the following sheet (which closely mirrors, apart from the names, an authentic list):

Staffing and organisation

Teaching staff

	A.F. Dykes	Headteacher
	G.G. Chamberlain	Deputy Headteacher
Class 1	H. Mitchell	Year 6 Co-ordinator/Adviser on Information Technology
Class 2	P. Judges	Mathematics
Class 3	A. Cotterill	Science and Technology
Class 4	B. Smith	Year 5 Co-ordinator/Adviser on Multi-Cultural Matters
Class 5	H. Dennis	History and Geography
Class 6	S. Feldman	Art and Display/English Responsibilities
Class 7	D. Taylor	Library and Resources/Girls' Games/ Swimming
Class 8	H. Hobbes	Year 4 Co-ordinator/RE/Stock
Class 9	V. Elwood	Off-site Education
Class 10	F. Padley	English

Class 11	W. Vaziljevic	Year 3 Co-ordinator/PE/Health Education
Class 12	J. Dutton	History and Geography
	L. Shenstone	Special Needs
	M. Filey	LSS
	S. Poole	LSS
	J. Hurley	NNEB

Non-teaching staff

M. Biddle	Senior Secretary
A. Parker	Asst. Sec. (Temp)
J. Doyle	Caretaker
J. West	Cleaner
M. Fairley	Cleaner
A. Coggins	Cleaner
J. Colder	Principal Lunchtime Supervisor
E. Jones	Senior Supervisor
L. Jackson	MSA
J. Tucker	MSA
M. Thomas	MSA
L. Kennes	MSA
G. Howe	MSA
A. Bartle	MSA
W. Statham	MSA
P. Swann	Senior Servery Assistant
C. Raybould	SA
F. Bell	SA
S. Hodgkins	SA
N. Foggin	Crossing Warden

Such a list might provoke many questions:

- Who is male and who is female?
- What is, or are, LSS, MSA, SA?
- Do class numbers refer to rooms, or ages, or are they random?
- How do you pronounce Vaziljevic?
- Why do the Head and Deputy have two initials and everyone else only one?
- What is 'Off-site education'?
- Do I get stock from H. Hobbes or M. Biddle?
- Are there two posts for History and Geography?
- Does the Special Needs teacher have a class?
- Who looks after English, S. Feldman or F. Padley?
- Which cleaner will do my room?

Some of these questions may be important; some may be trivial. But how does one tell the difference? In any event, is it more important to get to know the children or the staff?

The fact is, of course, that it is important to get to know both staff and children as soon as you can. The more you do, the more you realise the inadequacies of such a list as that above, which indicates nothing of the relationships between colleagues, formal and informal; nothing of the history of that network of relationships; nothing of the precise roles and functions of each person. The moral, then, for a newcomer is to get out of the classroom, when that is possible, and move around the school regularly so as to become recognisable (and to recognise others) in the corridors, in the playground, at the gate, as well as in the staff room.

What follows now are extracts from the notes of an NQT engaged in this very task of getting to know the routines and rituals of her classroom and school, and the adults who work there. While Section II of this chapter addresses the issue of learning about the children, this section assumes such developing knowledge as a background to other encounters.

Key Stage 2 teacher, Wendie Wildman, in her first half-term of teaching at a suburban primary school, writes as follows:

Time-table

Who tells you, or helps you, to prepare for developing a time-table? The thought of creating my own was quite daunting.

On 1st September, Teacher Day, after a lengthy staff meeting, we returned to our classrooms to sort things out. The TV Co-ordinator was the first to come round, with a list of possible programmes that linked with my curriculum. With my fellow Year Group teacher, Alison, we decided to use two programmes:

1 Good Health, covering PSME
2 Earth in Space, covering Science.

Since we would watch both programmes live (why?), they were fixed on our time-table.

Then the PE Co-ordinator came around with Hall times. We would be swimming after Christmas, for the whole of the Spring Term, and so that time would need to be avoided when booking Hall times, so that the children would not lose a PE period.

Art and Craft had to be where we have a long afternoon with no assembly. That was Friday.

Assemblies are on Monday and Wednesday, 2.30 – 2.50 p.m.; on Tuesday 3.05 – 3.25 p.m.; Thursday 2.30 – 2.50 p.m.; Friday, with hymn practice, 9.00 – 9.30 a.m.

Then the rest! Well, that was simply a case of following the appropriate curriculum percentages of time, as dictated by the National Curriculum and the school. Oh! I nearly forgot. Then the Music Room time-table came around, making my Fridays a day for the Arts.

Registers

After spending some time in school with a Year Five class before the summer hols, I had gathered a number of tips about filling in registers. When I returned, I found that the registers had changed to pink MIR computer sheets. This caused problems for most of the staff, not just me, so that was a great relief. It takes some time getting name pronunciation right, and establishing a 'please do not disturb' routine.

Notes/registration

I find every morning my desk covered in money, notes, pictures, slips etc. A big shock – how on earth do you get through a register when someone's bringing all these things your way?

Collecting money

All children must bring dinner money, school fund and trip money in to me in an envelope labelled with the child's name, what the money is for, class, and amount. These go to our fab Secretary, Jan, who opens them and deals with the change, which is returned in another envelope and labelled. What a dream! This is a great relief and takes the responsibility off our shoulders.

Our dinner and attendance registers are placed in our pigeon holes every morning to be collected. Dinners go straight away and registers in the afternoon.

Trips

I have planned a trip with two other members of staff for my children to go to see *The Nutcracker* ballet. We all contributed to the construction of the parents' letter and devised a small book recording the class names, payments, return of parents' acceptance slips. Talking of letters, we were told by the Head that for parents' evening meetings all members of staff wrote their own letters and made their own arrangements. This was a daunting prospect for me, but with some guidance from my fellow Year Group teacher, I managed it. I was quite proud of it at the time, but have since noticed two errors.

Parents' evening

This has got to be one of the most frightening moments in my life. I had organised two meetings, one at 6.15 p.m. and the other at 7.15 p.m., and I decided to stay at school all day until they arrived. I had spent the entire weekend worrying about what clothes to wear; what to say; what to do with my hair. It was almost like getting ready for a first date!

To aid my presentation, my fellow Year Five teacher, Alison, had explained how she always prepared a small booklet for the parents to refer to during a presentation and to take away with them. This seemed like a useful task, but how could I possibly find the time to produce such a booklet? In the end, it took several lunch-times and the whole weekend, but I was pleased with the end product, as was my mentor. In fact the booklet was a godsend, for I no longer felt I was going to be alone in my meetings. It gave me a real sense of security, something in black and white to fall back on.

The staff had told me that parents would want to suss me out. This made me feel both nervous but, at the same time, prepared, which sounds quite strange. I wanted the parents to know that our jobs overlapped and complemented each other, so that each child received the best from both of us.

The level of language worried me. How to be professional but human, and NOT patronising. I decided to use minimal jargon and to do without constant quotations from DFE policy and bumph. They wanted to know about their child, not about the Education Department.

Originally, the fact that I might be caught out on the National Curriculum, or school policy, was one of my biggest fears, but I decided that honesty was the best policy. It's a point that I feel all NQTs should remember. If you bluff, you'll never learn anything, and a lesson I've learnt is that, most of the time, your colleagues don't expect you to know everything. After all, they've probably been teaching as long as you've been living.

For THE EVENT I used a cue card to guide me through. My headings were:

- Welcome. Thanks for coming. Good opportunity to meet.
- How 5J operates: teamwork; class unity and support.
- My main aims – encourage independence/involve chn. in decision making.
- Rewards: merit stamps/charts.
- Pet hates: rudeness and telling lies.
- Stress on language, maths, topic work and assessing chn.
- Any questions?

On the day, my mentor informed me that she would not be sitting in with me, but would hang around in the corridor. At first I was panic-stricken but, after the shock, I realised that it was a compliment.

As I started talking to the assembled parents (c. 30), I can recall one moment I feel I will never forget. I remember looking round the room and thinking, 'Wow! Are all these people really listening, agreeing, accepting me?'

At the end of the evening a lot of the parents thanked me for being so informative, and assured me of their support. I felt I was on such a high, as if I'd won first prize in a major competition and it all seemed so silly how I'd worried before. I have recruited two mums to listen to readers and have produced record books for them to use and me to check on.

I record my closing speech for posterity:

I would finally like to finish off by saying that this is our classroom. It belongs to all of us – you, the children, and me. I would like to think that you will always feel welcome in this room and that any problem you have, you can come in and discuss it with me. So please feel free to come in any time.

From my vast experience (two parents' meetings), I offer my tips to others:

- be honest;
- be yourself;
- be well prepared;
- try to see things from the parents' point of view;
- be positive; and
- show your enjoyment.

Final note on parents

The experience of meeting the parents all together made me realise just how important they are. I feel that it would be beneficial in training if we had time dedicated to inviting parents into college to discuss their hopes and fears, and their expectations of us as teachers, social workers, substitute parents. In fact, partners.

Dinner supervisors

Mrs Bates has just started this academic year, as I have, and we get along very well. During wet lunch times we organise joint ventures. For instance, she brought in card and paper and we arranged a competition for the children to design and make a spooky Hallowe'en mask. The class judged the competition later that afternoon; the mask that elicited the greatest gasp of horror was the winner. We've also organised a Christmas card competition, with Mrs Bates donating three prizes for the winners. It certainly brightened up a miserable hour and I appreciated her kindness and thought. A good dinner supervisor, like Mrs Bates, is worth her weight in gold and certainly makes my job much easier after a wet lunch. In the Infants there's one dinner supervisor per class and in the Juniors one per year group.

Photographer

Never reckon (as I did) on teaching a crucial lesson when the school photographers are in. Children going in and out of the classroom means that there is a fair amount of disruption, no matter how organised it is. We have a classroom assistant going around calling the children and collecting family groups together.

For the staff photo we all decided to surprise the Head and Deputy by putting on fancy dress when we turned up for the photo.

NNEBs/classroom assistants

Each Junior teacher has an assistant for one whole lesson every week and one whole lesson alternate weeks.

Gillian Spinks is an extension of me; the other half I so often want to split myself into. Her two main interests are her family and her Open University study of Art. She told me that most teachers used her ability to mount and display work, but that seemed to me such a waste of valuable class time. So I arranged with Gill to join me on alternate afternoon sessions to team teach Craft Design and Technology. I use the first session of the week she is out as a design lesson, so that we are both together for the practical lesson, to make sure every child gets off to a good start.

For my regular slot, I asked Gill if she would work with my SEN group in Language, to give them extra support and confidence. She does this, with work on short story reading; comprehension; dictation; spelling; discussion. The group of five children sometimes go out with Gill into the library or they work at a table in the classroom. All five are developing well and Gill informs me of any concerns, so that we develop a two-pronged attack. Without that extra 1 hour 15 minutes those 'famous five' (as we call them) would have even more problems, and without Gill, both the class and I would suffer.

Caretaker and cleaners

Mrs Hazel Dillen is our caretaker and has her own room in the Annexe building. I've not yet had much dealing with her, but I intend to use her as part of a safety project we are doing later in the term. I want her to talk about safety in the school. She's great with the children and always has time to talk with you about a classroom problem.

Rita, my class cleaner, is wonderful. On the first day she asked me about the best day to clean the children's desks. We agreed on Friday night, after Art, for obvious reasons. We arranged, too, that the children would put their chairs on their desks at the end of each day but Friday, to make sweeping easier, and leave them down for Friday. Such a routine may seem trivial to a teacher, but it isn't. Not for Rita, anyway. Incidentally, she never complains and often compliments me on the state of the room. I always give her notice of any days when we may be more messy than usual.

School nurse

I have only met her once, but she seems approachable and friendly enough. The staff have told me how good she is talking to the children about Health Education, so I'm sure I'll sign her up at some point.

The secretary

The biggest, best, and most useful shoulder to cry on.

Jan Baines is like another part of me and without her professionalism I could have made far more mistakes than I have. She's guided me on the organisation of money collecting (including giving me tins) and advised about consent forms, photographs and trips. She's suggested I keep copies of all letters I send out, both for my own records and also for occasions when children lose them. Whenever I collect money I inform Jan that it's coming in and she tells me how she'd like it organised. This communication is essential to avoid mistakes.

She takes and passes on messages; deals with free dinner forms; sorts out registers; has a wealth of useful contact telephone numbers; is a mine of school information. She is a GEM. Oh! and she'll also tell you when it's possible to see the Head!

CONCLUSIONS

What can be learned from Wendie's experience? Is it possible to draw some general conclusions from the findings of one person?

This whole book is built on the premise that we can gain enormous insight into the reality of class and school life by homing in on the worlds of particular individuals, and that such specific detail can assist us in two ways. It can alert us to possible ways of doing things which we would not have otherwise thought of, and it can provide case study examples from which general principles may emerge. What are the principles to be drawn from Wendie Wildman's first few months as a newly qualified teacher?

- However good your teacher-training might have been, it can only ever be a part preparation for the full-time, permanent role of qualified teacher. The training continues in the job (and the concept of perpetual staff development is now becoming established in education).
- Negotiation with colleagues is needed and calls for collaborative skills of a high order:

    (i)   for time-table planning (as with the subject co-ordinators);
    (ii) for curriculum planning (as with the classroom assistant);
    (iii) for learning from those more experienced (as with the secretary);
    (iv) for awareness of the strengths of others (as with the dinner supervisors. Chapter 2, Appendix 3 is concerned with the training of such supervisors).

- The job is now for real, with genuine responsibility resting on your shoulders. This applies not only to the children's learning, for which the buck stops with you, but also for administrative tasks (registers); for collecting money (dinner/trips); for bureaucracy (all those desk notes).
- You are constantly called on to make quick judgements (e.g. about what is significant and insignificant; about what action to take in disputes; about how to deal with a multitude of calls on your time and attention).
- You need to get around and meet people. As a relatively extrovert

person, Wendie does not find this difficult. How would a more intro-
verted student or new teacher manage?

- Again, Wendie is in a well-organised, very supportive school. Suppose
  you are not? What skills will you need to be able to negotiate tricky
  situations, where little help, apparently, is available?
- What kind of 'contract' will you hope to establish with children and
  their parents? Have you given much thought to such a concept?
- How aware of your language are you? Do you modify it appropriately
  to fit the context, avoiding jargon with parents, on the one hand, and
  incomprehension by children, on the other?
- Perhaps above all, are you prepared to learn? As Wendie points out,
  one needs to be totally honest and ready to admit ignorance by adopting a positive approach and a preparedness to be helped by others,
  whoever they are. This, of course, applies to us all, children, parents
  and teachers. But real learning involves empathy as well as facts;
  insight, as well as knowledge.

Here, as an example, is a glimpse of the understanding available to
children in another school (not Wendie's), when they interviewed one of
their cleaning staff and asked her about the job . . . . What was the best
part? . . . What was the worst part? . . . Did she like the children? When
one of the children asked Mrs Nellis what she thought about as she
cleaned their classroom, this is what she said:

> Well, I've been usually thinking about what I'm going to get for tea
> today and tomorrow. Sometimes I think about people that I know,
> perhaps are ill, you know, think about them, or if they've lost anyone.
> Think about them also, so we could say a silent prayer, which has
> happened just recently to me.

Section II: Children

Richard W. Mills, with material from Nabela Mann

> *Are you her boyfriend? Have you got a gold tooth?*
> (7-year-old girl on first meeting an adult visitor to her classroom)

This book is largely about working with adults in the primary school, and
many of the glimpsed encounters touched on in Section I of this chapter
will be developed throughout the succeeding chapters. In such a way, the
potential value of knowing how to capitalise on all available adult resources will be explored.

However, no book on such a subject would be acceptable without
substantial reference to the children for whom all these resources are

being mobilised. In any event, what is uppermost in the minds of students and new teachers are questions about the children, not about the adults: 'What will they be like?' 'Will they be well behaved?' 'Will I be able to cope?' 'Are there any non-readers?' 'Will they like me?'

Such questions will be heartfelt but they are, at this stage, inevitably vague and unfocused. They address the class as a group; they do not differentiate. Once the teaching practice student or new teacher has met the class, it will cease to be a block of teaching fodder, an amorphous lump; it will become a collection of individual boys and girls, each with their own personalities, habits, idiosyncrasies. That, after all, is what makes the job so interesting.

Accordingly, this section of the opening chapter addresses the issue of how a recently qualified teacher gets to know her children and focuses on the degree and quality of that knowledge.

Nabela Mann is now in her second year of teaching. Towards the end of her first year, she collated her thoughts and records of the Year Two (aged 6–7) children whom she had taught for that year. Her knowledge of each boy and girl had, of course, been accumulating since the very first encounter and even, in some cases, prior to that, by word of mouth from colleagues before the Autumn Term started. One has to weigh such 'knowledge' carefully: children react differently to different teachers; information may be partial; circumstances may change, and so forth.

How, then, did Nabela acquire detailed views on her children?

- By consulting the register and school records, she found dates of birth; details of family members; information about illnesses and hospital-isation.
- By talking with parents and their former teacher, she learned about parental attitudes and relationships with school.
- By talking informally with the children, she discovered something of their cultural background, their interests and hobbies, their personality.
- By observing the children in the classroom and at play, she was able to make judgements about their attitudes to school and to each other.
- By assessing their work, she was able to pin-point their levels of achievement on appropriate National Curriculum scales. (In each case, samples of the children's work across a range of curriculum areas were retained in individual folders.)

Such knowledge is never static; records are, in one sense, out of date as soon as written; the situation is changing and information is cumulative. Their main purpose is not as archive material. It is, rather, as a means of sharpening the awareness of the teacher, so that each child may be treated and taught in the most appropriate way. Teachers who are also parents have early learnt the need for differentiation. Contrary to the glib maxim that we should treat all children alike, we should, I believe, treat each one differently, if we are to be fair to all. In this way, record keeping is not an end product but, rather, part of the teaching process, a tool for improving one's classroom work.

Here, then, is material provided by one newly qualified teacher, at the end of her first year. It is in the form of:

- *General summary* about the school and class (i.e. a brief 'situation analysis');
- *Outline information*, in chart form, of five boys and girls; and
- *Specific detail*, in prose form, about another three children.

General summary

The primary school, of some 200 children, is situated in an inner-city area of high unemployment. Those parents who are in employment work as shopkeepers, taxi drivers, seamstresses, factory or post office staff.

The environment is multi-ethnic and multi-faith, with the majority of families being of Asian origin, having forged integral links between England and the sub-continent. Thus, second generation children have been offered a rich cultural heritage. Many have been brought up in a mother tongue other than English, their predominant first language being Punjabi, followed by Urdu.

As one would expect, therefore, there are many local places of worship and of religious or linguistic instruction which the children of the school attend. Many go straight after school to the local mosque to receive instruction about Islam and to learn to read and write Arabic, in preparation for tackling the Holy Koran. Others visit the gurdwara or temple, either to read Punjabi or simply with their families for the religious and cultural experience.

My class of 29 children are aged between six and seven years. Although the children appear to be of similar age and educational experience, in fact, each one emerges as an individual. More of this later.

The children get on very well together and the various social sub-groups exist for mutual help, rather than to exclude others. The class is stable; there is little falling-out between friends. The children are generally sympathetic and considerate towards one another. In Year One the children were used to a very child-centred approach to learning. There was much 'hands-on' experience and closely planned discovery learning within small groups. As they seemed to have gained so much from this, I decided to continue in a similar manner.

Hence, curriculum topics are taught via topics laid down in our school's yearly Development Plan. This enables the curriculum areas to be taught in a meaningful context, with children either in small groups, pairs, whole class, or one-to-one, as the activity and circumstances require.

The class have had a five-week experience with teaching practice students. In addition, they are used to working alongside other adults. For example, the EST (English Support Teacher) is in each day, as is the bilingual nursery nurse to take six children at the end of afternoon school for a group activity. The predominant mother tongue is Punjabi and since I am multilingual in English, Punjabi and Urdu, I tend to use whatever language is appropriate to support the children's learning. Although the children receive bilingual experiences openly, they appear less comfortable about making use of their mother tongues orally.

Generally, the class are a delight to teach because each child is a unique individual.

Outline information

Reena d.o.b. 15-9-85	
Family background	Mother, father, 1-yr baby brother, two sisters, 5 yrs and 12 yrs
Relationship of teacher with parents	Have seen little of parents since older sister collects her from school. Open discussion with them at parents' evening
Culture, religion, mother tongue	Hindu, Punjabi, goes to temple for celebrations
Attendance/illness	Good school attendance, except four week trip to India
Interests/hobbies	Helping sister in kitchen; reading magazines
Personality	Extrovert, happy, talkative, confident, loving; has many friends
National Curriculum Levels	
Maths	Number 2. Other areas 2
English	Reading 3. Writing: working to 3. Speaking/listening 3
Science	2
Foundation subjects	Working to 3

Harpinder d.o.b. 23.10.85	
Family background	Mother, father, two brothers 13 and 16
Relationship of teacher with parents	Good rapport with mum; speaks to me in Punjabi. Often chats at the end of the day
Culture, religion, mother tongue	Sikh. Punjabi. Attends Punjabi language classes at school
Attendance/illness	Excellent attendance
Interests/hobbies	Watching cartoons; drawing; reading interesting books
Personality	Very confident, bubbly, sensitive; enjoys working in a group
National Curriculum Levels	
Maths	Number: working to 3. Other areas, working to 3
English	Working to 4 (reading); 3 (writing); 3 (speaking and listening)
Science	3
Foundation subjects	3

Sharon d.o.b. 18.11.85	
Family background	Mum and dad live separately. 5-yr-old brother
Relationship of teacher with parents	See very little of mum as Sharon is normally picked up by taxi or a social worker
Culture, religion, mother tongue	Christian. English
Attendance/illness	Sickle cell sufferer. Has been hospitalised several times. Dietary restrictions
Interests/hobbies	Colouring, writing, drawing, reading stories
Personality	Quiet, caring, sociable, helpful; has a close circle of friends

National Curriculum Levels	
Maths	Number 2. Other areas 2
English	Reading 3; writing working to 3; sp./list. 3
Science	2
Foundation subjects	2

Ijas d.o.b. 16.03.86	
Family background	Mother, father, 8-yr-old sister
Relationship of teacher with parents	Mother comes in to school and chats in Punjabi about her problems
Culture, religion, mother tongue	Muslim. Punjabi. Visits mosque for religious and linguistic instruction
Attendance/illness	Poor attendance. Mum often keeps him at home to go shopping or visiting
Interests/hobbies	Visiting his friend's house; colouring; playing football
Personality	Always smiling and cheerful; positive attitude; needs help with most areas of learning
National Curriculum Levels	
Maths	Number working to 2. Other areas 1
English	Reading 1; writing 1; sp./list. 2
Science	Working to 2
Foundation subjects	Working to 2

Doreen d.o.b. 14.12.85	
Family background	Mother, stepfather; 8-yr-old brother; 9-yr-old sister; two stepbrothers; two stepsisters

Relationship of teacher with parents	Mother very chatty and often makes me cakes; gives the class tadpoles, sweets, etc.
Culture, religion, mother tongue	African Caribbean. Christian. English
Attendance/illness	Excellent attendance
Interests/hobbies	Playing on the computer; reading books; seeing friends
Personality ·	Shy, polite, industrious, sensitive, helpful
National Curriculum Levels	
Maths	Number 2. Other areas 2
English	Reading 3; writing working to 3; sp./list. 3
Science	3
Foundation subjects	3

Specific detail

Here are three more children in the class. In each case I've attached a loose 'title' to them, but I'm well aware of the potential dangers in labelling. The brief description merely highlights a distinguishing feature; it doesn't encapsulate the whole person. With each of them it's impossible to do justice to all aspects of their personality and attainment and the various aspects that influence their lives. Why should we assume they are less complicated than we are ourselves?

Jason, a boy with behaviour problems

Soon after entering school Jason developed a very destructive attitude towards the furniture and building, and became very malicious towards his peers and members of staff. His Year One teacher made it her key aim to help socialise him and settle him down in the classroom, where his immaturity stood out in stark contrast to his peers.

After I first met him in Year Two, I learned from a nursery colleague that Jason's behaviour had changed drastically since the arrival of his baby brother some two years earlier. Up to that point he had all the attention to himself; now he felt left out.

Reluctant to apply himself to any task unless carefully supervised, he would resort to becoming loud, boisterous and aggressive in the classroom. He would scribble on others' books and hide their work. He would flick pencils and rubbers around the room, and bang the table to get attention.

The task was to change the negative reinforcement to something positive. Accordingly, the support teacher and I decided that we would so organise ourselves that, for at least five minutes for each of the three sessions in the day (i.e. morning; after break; afternoon), I would work with Jason one-to-one so that he could briefly become the centre of attention in an activity related to the curriculum. This had positive results and he displayed a great hidden ability to grasp concepts quickly. It soon became evident that what he really lacked was self-confidence and my efforts were directed towards raising his self-esteem.

Naturally, the one-to-one attention could not last for ever and, in the Spring Term, I began to wean him off this and encourage him to work in a small friendship group. Not surprisingly, he initially displayed an unwillingness to share and co-operate, since he preferred to dominate and control the activity. Clearly, his attention-seeking had now been transferred from teacher to small group. Accordingly, I intervened on a regular basis, but less and less as time went by.

In the third term Jason became able to work reasonably well in a group and more willing to be *equally* involved. However, despite having come a great way towards modifying his unacceptable behaviour, we have still not solved the matter for he is still particularly difficult with the dinner supervisors whom he either ignores, or is rude to, or struggles with physically.

Our strategy for coping with this was to devise some kind of dinner-time reward (in the form of a star board), whereby particularly good behaviour during, say, a wet dinner-time, would be acknowledged by a star awarded in assembly. Within seven weeks of the start of this system, Jason was rewarded with a star, so we feel we are making some slow progress. We (i.e. the dinner supervisor, Jason and I) now review his behaviour each week. Some weeks appear worse than others, but the foundations of progress have been laid.

With regard to Jason's academic achievement, it's clear from his written work that he possesses a vivid imagination which he is able to implement in a story structure. He has the ability now to become absorbed in a task and to cut out all distractions. He relishes positive attention and praise given by those in authority. He has a greater sense of personal accomplishment and, in consequence, his self-esteem has been raised, and he now has a more positive approach to his learning.

Zaman, a very able boy

He is a happy, confident child, with a very positive self-image and the friendship of his peers. Many of his qualities are strong ones because he believes in his own potential. He has encouraging parents who often work alongside him. He is eager to learn and easily stimulated by new and original challenges.

Zaman's passion for books is clear when one hears him read extracts from his favourite Roald Dahl books since they are read with clarity, expression, fluency and, above all, complete comprehension. Along with books, he also loves American wrestling on television, and action-packed videos. His powers of observation are considerable and he spent forty-five minutes drawing the Muslim prayer mat I had taken in, being quite engrossed in the intricate detail of the design. Perhaps this somehow linked with his recent visit to Saudi Arabia to see his working father.

Sustained concentration is the hallmark of all his activities. He sets himself high standards and enjoys receiving praise and tangible rewards from his teachers and peers. At one point he distinctly felt that he was superior to others in the class and this resulted in a period when he did not work to his full potential. However, he came out of that phase when he realised that one or two children were catching up on him.

Zaman's potential extends beyond the classroom since he visits a mosque regularly where he is learning not only to read and write Urdu but also to read Arabic.

Noreen, a very sociable girl

Much of Noreen's time in school is spent chatting with her peers and me about a whole variety of topics. She always has a piece of news to share during our initial morning conversations. If ever she feels overlooked, she will ensure that, the next day, she brings in an object, or a letter, or a photograph, or a painting, which can't be ignored.

She is a happy, settled, extremely lively child who relishes all forms of attention. She often leaves her work to give me a hug and to tell me how much she loves me. She has many friends, both inside and outside school. She always has someone around her and, while working, will chat away merrily, and often sing to herself while engaged on a task. Since one of her uncles is a singer in a local band, Noreen attends many parties and social functions, and this, perhaps, accounts for her sociable nature and her singing.

She displays a comfortable understanding of the aspects of learning that we have encountered. In maths, for instance, she has a good basic understanding of number, but she can become confused when she meets with new concepts. Consequently, she requires continual reinforcement of previously acquired skills before moving on. This is why she is still working on the early stages of tens and units addition, as opposed to working with more sophisticated number skills, as some of her peers are doing.

Understandably, the oral, rather than written, versions of her stories more easily reveal her vivid imagination. She often tires of planning and, hence, her work can be rushed or appear as if little thought had gone into it. On the other hand, her enjoyment of everything even manages to come through all the repetition, as in this piece:

> I enjoyed playing in the playground. And I like Miss Mann because she is fune. And now we are gowing to Miss Kents class and I am gun to Miss Mann. And I like Miss Hall and Miss Tucker. And I like conservation because its fune and my school and my school is fune. Then I went to Miss Kents class and I am gowing to the sweg puhoo and it is fun.

CONCLUSIONS

These are only three out of the twenty-nine children in the class and much more could have been written about each of the three (including the danger of gender stereotyping). Nevertheless, what principles can be drawn from the first year of Nabela's teaching career, in terms of treatment of individual children?

• The use of theory to illuminate and underpin practice

In the case of Jason, a deliberate policy of positive reinforcement was pursued and found to be successful. Along with this is the positive approach that problems are there to be solved and not merely identified.

• Understanding of personal and domestic background

There was an awareness of how position in the family and how the changing network of family relationships can affect children's school lives. Implicit in this is the concept that home and school are inextricably linked and that each requires knowledge of the other.

• Collaborative strategy

Nabela worked with whichever colleague was most relevant: the support teacher to enable an element of one-to-one contact within the classroom;

the dinner supervisor to improve behaviour during break-time. Such an arrangement is based on mutual respect between adult colleagues, along with the awareness that the academic learning and personal well-being of children cannot be separated, and that the school has responsibility for both.

- Acceptance of children

Underpinning this attitude is the knowledge that patience and understanding are required to permit maturity to develop reasonably. At the same time, there is the clear understanding that teaching involves changing the behaviour of individual children, both for their own sakes and for the sake of others in the class.

- Variation of grouping and teaching methods

There is recognition that, ultimately, children need to be able to operate independently, in pairs, in small groups, as a larger grouping – both during their school careers and in later life – and so all roads lead to this end. Underlying this, too, is the knowledge that different kinds of language are required in different contexts and that different sets of social encounter provide a valuable range of challenges and experiences.

- Celebration of personality and culture

Implicit in this notion is the rich concept of diversity, whether of background, language, way of life or character. Thus, the intellectual potential and cultural experience of Zaman is noted, alongside the sociability and comradeship of Noreen.

The children in this class clearly have many benefits, and seem to recognise this. Here, finally, are the words of another class member, Sanjay:

> Class 2 is a good class because you do lots of good work. I like Miss Mann because she is cond to me. I like my frend Kamil because he donts not scat at me. In PE I like them games. I lovd about the watre cycle. My fist taske is the rain forest becusre I went to now how animal becoming extinct. A elephants is becoming extinct becarse people are biting the elephants tuck.

Chapter 2

Help is at hand
Section I: Roger Woods
Section II: Ann Lance
Section III: Roger Woods

EDITORS' INTRODUCTION

This book outlines the wide range of adults whom new teachers are likely to encounter and work with, in varying capacities. However, who will be the most significant on first taking up an appointment? The choice may be individual, but it is likely to be either the teaching colleague with whom one is most closely involved, or the Headteacher, who has such an enormous influence on the ethos, attitudes and routines of the school.

Accordingly, this chapter seeks to address the issue of contact with both these major influences, the mentor and the Headteacher.

It is clear from first-hand evidence that new teachers are overwhelmed by a mass of apparently trivial administration. Experienced staff who can recall such a feeling in their early years, or those in whom the quality of empathy is not strained, will be more likely to understand the bewilderment of new colleagues trying to cope with competing demands. It must be the same in many a job, however good the training. There must always be a gap between prior practice and actual practice, and good Headteachers and mentors will be sensitive to this.

Section I recalls and records the initial responses of new teachers to classroom and school life in an account which complements the individual experience of Wendie Wildman in the first chapter. Section III links those early anxieties and uncertainties with the help given by designated mentors. Lying between these two sections is Section II – an account from the perspective of a Headteacher who can recall events both from her own start in teaching and from having seen many new teachers through their induction period.

What emerges is that, whether in the role of Head or mentor, the same personal and professional qualities are required. Partners at any level need to trust each other; to respect each other's confidentiality. They need to build up rapport in a mutually supportive way, with regular meetings and routines. Whether they have one, or thirty-one, years' experience, they are colleagues engaged in the same enterprise for the benefit of their children.

Section I: Views of newly qualified teachers

Roger Woods

> I find every morning my desk covered in money, notes, pictures, slips, etc.'
>
> (NQT)

As Chapter 1 indicated, newly qualified teachers, who may have trained for up to four years, will have learned and practised a great many things as Teaching Practice students in several different schools. They will have a comprehensive understanding of the National Curriculum Key Stage for which they were training. They will have considered classroom management issues; cross-curricular themes; ways of presenting material and encouraging learning in children; school structures and rituals; the education system. While teacher training courses are very demanding, and require students to shoulder a considerable amount of professional responsibility, the transition between college and school inevitably brings fresh challenges to a new teacher. Assuming responsibility for a class of your own involves taking all kinds of decisions and making judgements for which there has been no real opportunity to practise.

Wendie Wildman, in Chapter 1, described her encounters with new colleagues and other adults. The new teachers I interviewed concentrated on learning the school procedures and getting to grips with the curriculum. They had all just finished doing Bachelor of Education degrees or Post Graduate Certificates at different institutions. All of them were anxious about getting things right and doing their best for the children in their charge. They were all emphatic that there was a great deal for them to learn.

Jonathan, interviewed after two weeks in his first post at a junior and infant school, said:

> There's so much to learn. Things like how to label children's books. How to organise the room. When you've been in a teacher's class on teaching practice, the teacher has done all that, or if you want to change something, she'll give you advice. When you get into your room on your own and you know that you have 32 children coming, needing everything to be organised for them, it's quite different. I seem to have been asking everyone who comes in to the classroom for ideas and suggestions. My room was decorated over the summer and I've had new furniture, so I've been arranging it and asking people: 'What do you think about this? What do you think about that?'

These might seem small things. Some of Jonathan's queries could be easily dealt with. Jane, another NQT in her first month of teaching, commented:

> The decisions are often fairly little things, like: What books do I put their work in? What shall I put on the front of a book? How are we going to organise the library? Shall I have monitors? What shall I do with work that's finished? It's all stuff that someone on teaching practice can easily tell you about, but when you start work in your own classroom there's no one there even to know that you're not sure what to do.

David, looking back on his first days of teaching after successfully completing his first year in school, was asked to recall how he felt about taking over his first class:

> The thing you really need to get to grips with after leaving college is organising your room. After the Summer holidays you arrive and the chairs are stacked up in one corner and the desks are stacked up in another corner. A trolley comes around that gives you pencils and pens and books and you just sort of stand there amazed and think, well, what am I going to do now? For the first week I kept wondering how I could check pencils, which always seemed to be going missing.

These sorts of decisions are to do with management and organisation. They range from fairly simple but nevertheless important ones like the labelling of children's books to ones which place a heavy burden of responsibility on the new teacher.
David again:

> Just getting used to running your own class places a lot of responsibility on you. I had a computer in my class and I had to make sure it was always locked away every night. There's no one else who would do it and I wouldn't have been popular if it had been stolen.

The responsibility for expensive equipment must be challenging, but the responsibility for comparatively small amounts of money can bring its own problems. Lisa, interviewed after two weeks in her first job, said:

> Handling money was something new. I have to collect biscuit money. Children pay 50p per week every Monday and I have to keep an account of where the money's going, and who's paid. It seems a small thing but it's easy to get muddled.

Irmah, at the same stage but in a different school, commented:

> Just having to be responsible for money is a new thing, and if any money goes missing you have to deal with that.

Jonathan again:

> Selling crisps can be a hassle at first. Knowing who pays and who doesn't. Then there's money for book clubs.

Money was something that concerned all the new teachers I talked to. In addition to these questions about routine management concerns there were issues which arose out of the curriculum.

Samreena, after three weeks in post, noted:

> I had questions about the level of children's work. In the first few days I wanted to know whether the work I was getting from them was at the right sort of level, or whether they were taking advantage of me because I was new.

Jane had similar anxieties:

> The job is so serious. I'm really responsible for my children. Teaching practice is different. If after six weeks the children haven't learned anything, it's been a waste of six weeks, but *only* six weeks. Now, it's for real.

These professional responsibilities aren't simply owed to the children, but to their parents. This is an issue which features prominently in this book, and it is an area which concerned all the new teachers I talked to.

Samreena:

> How do you develop a relationship with parents? I've had parents in the classroom and I've talked my way through, but some sort of guidance about how to relate to parents is necessary.

Irmah, likewise:

> It's a big responsibility talking to parents about their children. It's especially difficult when you're new to the school, and to the job. I wasn't sure whether parents should first go to the Head. You're not sure what you should tell parents about things or whether children can take books home. I've never been to a parents' evening and I'm a bit anxious about that, too.

(Readers will recall Wendie Wildman's anxieties at her first parents' evening.)

These are immediate concerns, apparent when NQTs first begin work. Other concerns arising as the job progresses will be highlighted presently. Fortunately, each of these newly qualified teachers had a mentor to guide and support them. This is the case for every new teacher in school. All schools are expected to adopt a system whereby each newly qualified teacher is partnered with a designated member of staff whose role includes helping them to sort out the answers to the sorts of things listed above. Such a person is called a mentor. There are various views as to what a mentor should or shouldn't do, and there will be lots of differences in the ways in which mentors work with their partners.

This will be the substance of Section III. Meanwhile, how does a Headteacher view the task of inducting new colleagues into her school and into the profession?

Section II: A Headteacher's perspective

Ann Lance

Every student and newly qualified teacher has expectations of the Headteacher of the school in which they are about to undertake their school experience, or embark on their new career. I hope this section of the book will help to give such newcomers to the profession an idea about how they may be perceived by the Headteacher of the establishment which they are about to join. What are the expectations which the Head is likely to have of them? What support can they reasonably expect? How can they make a positive impression in their early days as a teacher? Will the Head remember how it feels to be on the threshold of a career?

EARLIER MEMORIES

In the dim and distant past I can remember being a student, and if I try very hard can conjure up in my memory a picture of the Headteacher of the school where I carried out my final teaching practice. He was a very effusive character who went out of his way to welcome us as a group of students, and I have vivid memories of his assemblies which were full of humour and warmth. I can also remember with even greater clarity my experiences as a new member of staff in my first post, and I have very great respect for the Headteacher who encouraged me through that challenging year.

Remembering very vividly my own experience as a newly appointed teacher in the early 1970s, I have always been acutely aware of the important watershed at which people have arrived, both personally and professionally, when they take up their first post in a school.

It was a time of change in my life. Having lived away from home for a number of years I had to readjust to family life at home again. Having only experienced teaching as a student, I found myself fully fledged, as it were, on paper, but not too sure about my own ability to be a 'real' teacher. I remember parents approaching me on the first day, asking for support or guidance about matters concerning their children, and wondering how I was expected to know. I couldn't even fill in the register with any great confidence, because I hadn't had any experience of this before. I had never before set up a classroom from scratch because, as a student, I had always begun my practices some weeks into the term, and had never realised how much hard work went into creating interest corners, making displays for the classroom, organising the resources.

All newly appointed staff find themselves in this state of flux when they embark on their career. Some have had to move to an unfamiliar place and set up in a flat or house. For others there is a great contrast between their final year at college where they were, perhaps, engaged in their dissertation, and this different form of rigour. The contrast of the differing cultures of 'student life' and the 'school world' takes some getting used to.

Many students find themselves separated from their partner because they have not been able to find employment in the same location, and this can place them under great strain. Some mature students, who are starting their career from their home base where they have an established family commitment, have to adjust to a situation which has less flexibility than they have grown accustomed to.

For teaching practice students, school experience also makes demands which they do not face in the course of their lives in college. They need to consider their dress and appearance in a different light. This does not mean that they are required to turn up at school in suits from Marks & Spencer, but it does mean careful consideration about appropriate dress, which contrasts with the expectation in their college role. It may also involve them in travelling some distance to the school in which they are placed, and this has implications for making an earlier start each morning. Long-term planning of lessons and the immediate everyday chores of classroom organisation and marking have to be crammed into hectic days in school, and evenings of commitment back at home or college.

Having outlined the challenges which face the student or newly qualified teacher, let me draw on my experiences in order to introduce the perspective of a Headteacher.

Between 1984 and 1993, I was in charge of a large urban primary school and, in that capacity, I encountered many students and newly qualified staff who came to engage in school experience, or to take up their first post. I was acutely aware of the responsibility which rested upon my shoulders to ensure that they got off to the best possible start. This was not only for their good, but also in the best interests of the children.

Let's consider, then, some of the issues which the Headteacher needs to address to ensure the successful induction of a student or a new teacher.

FIRST ENCOUNTERS

The Head will want to ensure that you are welcomed warmly to the school, and will often do so personally. Sometimes this is not possible. As a student you may feel rebuffed by this, and think that it signifies a lack of interest or concern on the part of the Head. I suggest you suspend your judgement. The duties of the Headteacher in the 1990s go well beyond the paternalistic role which was more traditional in years gone by. It may well be that s/he is involved in a meeting concerned with the financial management of the school or in some other crucial encounter. Most Heads would prefer to welcome new staff to being locked behind closed doors with a financial assistant and a computer, but the reality is that they sometimes have no choice but to deal with such matters. If this coincides with your arrival at the school, and you are met by the Deputy Headteacher, it would be wrong to assume that you are not considered to be important. You may well have some cause for concern if the Headteacher is never visible, but don't assume that will be the case on the strength of their absence on your arrival!

The Head will also want other members of the staff team to make you feel at home and welcome you into their classrooms. It is very reassuring for newcomers to a school if their arrival is known to all members of staff; if the school secretary is expecting you and greets you in a friendly manner; if the teachers you meet are positive about your presence and welcome you to the team. This is very likely to happen when you visit your school for the first time.

However, you could be unfortunate and have a less welcoming experience. Schools are very dynamic institutions, and even where the best-laid plans are made, arrangements are sometimes overlooked. The needs of children and their parents must be met as a priority, and sometimes the arrival of visitors coincides with an unexpected event concerning a child or children. Like the Head, other teaching colleagues may be unable to attend to you immediately. In such circumstances, you must expect to take a back seat.

Again, if you don't receive the red carpet treatment from the school on your arrival, don't jump to conclusions about the school's attitude towards you as a new member of staff. Of course, if no one speaks to you in the ensuing weeks, you will know that your initial impressions were not ill-founded, but this isn't likely to happen. Teachers are generally very affable and supportive towards new colleagues, and this is not surprising in a caring profession. They welcome new people and the skills, personalities and ideas which they bring into their school. They will, however, expect you to have the confidence to acknowledge their welcome, so it is a good idea for you to consider how you can best sell yourself on this first visit, without giving the impression that you think you know it all before you start! One new applicant wrote on his application form: 'I know I have a lot to give to the teaching profession'. Well, so he had, but he could have phrased it rather differently, as he readily acknowledged at his interview.

The Head will want you to gain a good impression of the atmosphere created in the school in relation to work displayed in classrooms and corridors. Most primary schools are beacons of excellence in this respect, but it is possible that you will arrive at a point when the physical environment of the school is not at its best. While this may signify that display is an area which does not carry a high priority, it might also relate to particular circumstances which are currently affecting the situation, such as building work or redecoration. So, again, keep your eyes and ears open, but guard your tongue, for you must also be realistic and acknowledge that individual teachers have different strengths and weaknesses. While stimulating displays in a classroom are often the hallmark of a good practitioner, some teachers have greater strengths in other areas. Be aware that you may be observing a display which is made up entirely of children's work, and has, indeed, been presented by children. It may not look as professional as some other teacher-inspired displays, but is it less acceptable for that?

The Head will want you to feel confident that the curriculum is well organised and resourced within the school, and that it is broad and balanced in its content. To reinforce this you may well be given documentation which explains the curriculum policies within the school. If you do receive such documents, make sure that you keep them carefully and read them at the earliest possible opportunity, making a mental note to match the assertions with your observations over a period of time. One teaching practice student returned to her college after her first visit to school, convinced that the school had no resources at all; after three more visits, she was impressed with the range available. Her mistake had been to assume that they would all be together in one place. They were, in fact, widely dispersed, so as to be more easily accessible to those who needed them, as our student came to realise.

All being well, you will observe a range of curriculum activities on your initial visit but, if you don't, beware of assuming that they do not happen within the school. You may be looking around at a time when they are less in evidence than at other points in the week. Perhaps a major project has just come to an end. Perhaps key teachers are out of school on an in-service course. Perhaps ... perhaps .... Again, the message for you is to reserve your judgement.

The Head will want you to see positive interaction between parents and the school. You can look for evidence of the school's commitment to parental involvement by noting their presence in classroom as helpers. You might well see a Parents' Information Board, from which you can glean evidence of the type of communication which exists between the school and its community. There may be a school community room, which will also flag up the school's commitment in this area. If you have the opportunity to visit the nursery unit, or the reception classes, you will be able to make judgements about the way in which the teachers interact with the parents. How positive, for instance, is the body language? What evidence is there of a partnership between teachers and parents, for the good of the children? How open is the access to the school for parents and visitors? You need to be aware, in this regard, that some schools have particular reasons for being cautious about entrance to the school, and might therefore confine admission to one particular door, and that, perhaps, with a bell or a key padlock. The safety of the children is paramount in such arrangements.

Incidentally, do not judge a person, book or school by external appearance. In the case of the latter, many a forbidding Victorian facade, with scuffed doors and paint peeling off the window frames, in my experience conceals a wonderfully warm, decorated, and attractive and welcoming interior.

FIRST DAY

When a new member of staff arrives at the school, whether as a student or newly qualified teacher, as soon as the school day begins they are 'on stage'. The children will arrive in school with the clear expectation that their 'new teacher' will be *au fait* with the school system, will know all the routines and will have the situation under control. Indeed, parents may well approach them either to greet them, or to ask a question, or perhaps to supply some information of a medical or routine nature. 'Can you make sure Nathan gets his inhaler at lunch-time, please?' 'Do you allow crisps at play time?' 'How much is dinner money?' 'Shelley gets headaches in writing lessons'.

Just as one tries to plan for all eventualities in lesson preparation, so one can anticipate many issues that may arise with parents and be prepared for them.

INFORMATION

It is not possible to memorise every routine concerning the school organisation in advance of the first day. However, it is important that Headteachers give all new staff, and especially new recruits to the profession, a supply of information which will ease their arrival, and help pupils and their parents to feel confident at their first meeting. Some of the following points of information may be more crucial for the newly qualified teacher but others are equally necessary for students on teaching practice:

- starting and finishing times; break, lunch and Assembly times;
- guidelines for completing the register;

- routines for collecting children from the playground;
- procedures for wearing and storage of clothes;
- guidance for outside visits to library, swimming baths;
- arrangements for PE apparatus and hall;
- a class timetable;
- instructions about collecting money for lunch, snacks, trips; and
- rules about break-time snacks.

While some of these may seem trivial to the outsider, experienced teachers know just how important it is to have daily classroom routines sewn up, otherwise behavioural difficulties may arise. After all, children will become bored and likely to be disruptive if routine activities take longer than they should.

SUPPORT

Although some information can be given in written form, it is important that the Head ensures that human support is provided for new staff. This, indeed, is the premise behind this book, which stresses the collaborative nature of school life. The new teacher, or teaching practice student, will need support from a whole range of people, which includes the non-teaching staff as well as teachers. As we have seen earlier, the list is potentially large and includes the following:

- a mentor;
- a classroom assistant;
- a school governor;
- the school secretary;
- the building services supervisor (caretaker/school keeper/janitor);
- a Year Group colleague;
- support staff (e.g. language support, Special Needs);
- the cleaners;
- the Deputy Headteacher;
- parents;
- a curriculum post holder;
- meals staff; and
- lunchtime supervisors (see Appendix 3).

This will only happen if the Headteacher alerts the support staff to the needs of the newcomer, and also builds meeting times into the routine to enable them to collaborate and make relationships. It is important for students and new members of staff to recognise that they will not be alone in needing support from these colleagues. All of us do.

BEYOND THE FIRST DAY

If the Head has been successful in nurturing the new staff through the first day, s/he cannot sit back and become complacent. Good teachers set themselves very high standards and run the risk of 'burn out' if they are not carefully guided. There are some days when an NQT or student who has obviously had a difficult day needs to be sent home when the school day has finished, rather than staying behind for hours after the children have left. Good Headteachers have high expectations of staff, but, equally, they need to recognise the signs of stress which begin to creep in when inexperienced and sometimes over-anxious staff don't get the balance quite right.

One of the traps which some new teachers fall into is that of pushing themselves flat out in a number of directions until they collapse. This is an ineffective way of working and can have a number of negative results:

- the teacher's enthusiasm and sense of commitment may suffer;
- the relationship with pupils may deteriorate;
- small problems may escalate out of all proportion;
- teachers may become physically ill.

This is not a healthy way forward. It is a question of pace. Old-timers in the profession become adept at working to their limits, maintaining interests beyond school, and surviving to the last day of term. (They then go home and collapse!) Teachers who capture the imagination of their pupils do not spend all their waking hours making workcards. They work very hard both during and beyond the school day, but they also find time to enjoy leisure activities which reflect their interests. They fire the imagination of their pupils because they organise their lives to maintain a balance between their work in school and at home, while still reserving time for themselves.

A CAUTION FOR NQTS

New members to the profession often charge at their first term in the manner of a student on a six-week teaching experience. This does not work, partly for reasons I have discussed above concerning pace, but also because the role is no longer that of a student. It is that of a full-time, fully paid, member of the teaching establishment. NQTs are expected to fulfil the responsibilities of members of a teaching team, with all that is implicit in that role. Expectations are placed upon them which they may not have experienced on teaching practices. These may include the following items:

- playground duty;
- broad responsibility throughout the school at all times;
- class and school assemblies;

- class visits out of school during the day;
- extracurricular activities;
- curriculum working parties and staff training days; and
- contact with parents, both on a day-to-day basis and at formal meetings.

The Headteacher needs to be aware of this increased level of expectation facing new teachers. There may well be areas about which the NQT feels least confident, through lack of experience. The reservations which may be felt by new staff may not always be openly expressed. Sometimes they internalise their feelings because they do not want to lose face. They may be aware, too, that reservations can be perceived by other staff as signs of a lack of commitment or as some kind of incapacity. What is clear is that the Headteacher has a major responsibility to ensure that all the staff help to play a part in the induction of new people. They do not need to molly-coddle the new colleague (whether teacher or ancillary staff member), but they can provide different levels of support when appropriate.

PEOPLE WHO CAN HELP

Newly qualified teachers need to prepare themselves for the times when they will need help. Embarking on a career is a challenging time and those who think they can go it alone are unlikely to succeed in getting through the first term. In this situation the NQT will need different people and different times for different types of support. In order to celebrate success, or discuss problems about school, it could be one of a range of people within the system: from the Deputy Head to the schools adviser; from the school secretary to a curriculum area leader; from the teacher next door to the official mentor.

But it is also vital for individuals to set up a network of support for themselves outside their professional life. It is important to identify people with whom successes can be shared, who will lend a sympathetic ear, and who will have an interest in school life. Friends, partners, family members, colleagues in other schools, students sharing accommodation, could all be possible sources of support in this respect.

REAPING THE BENEFITS

Headteacher support for new teachers and students is vitally important. Time and effort spent in assisting new (and prospective) colleagues is a very worthwhile investment. Where Headteachers neglect this process of nurturing, they run the risk of having to restore the shattered confidence of a new teacher, or losing a potential member of the profession. The wise Head, therefore, builds a system of support into the induction of new members of staff and students, thus increasing their chances of achieving success.

I hope that your experience as a student or newly qualified teacher will be a positive one. This comment from a teacher who embarked on her career in 1993 may be a source of encouragement for you:

I don't think I've ever worked so hard in my life. But I've made it through my first year, and now I know I'm a proper teacher. Seeing the progress that children have made, and getting positive feedback at parents' evening, has made it all worth while.

Section III: Mentor to the rescue

Roger Woods

The two previous sections viewed events from the perspectives of new-comers and old hands. Section III now enlarges on the role that the NQT's mentor can play during the crucial first year.

The school is a large city primary. There are over twenty classes and, as in other large schools, staff turnover is higher than in a small primary school, simply because there are more teachers who get promoted or leave for other reasons. When the Probationary Year was discontinued, the Headteacher welcomed the opportunity to implement a mentoring scheme for NQTs because she felt that a well-organised scheme of induction would benefit them personally and would also benefit the profession by improving the retention rate of new teachers.

Seven teachers have joined the staff as NQTs over the last three years and the school has developed a comprehensive mentoring programme. Three experienced teachers have been on mentor-training courses (see Appendix 2) and each NQT for the past two years has been allocated a mentor on taking up post. One of these mentors is Anne, who has taught in the school for two years and has curriculum responsibility for English. She is a promoted teacher and a member of the school's senior manage-ment team. Anne has not been on a formal mentor-training course, but she has supported newly qualified staff members in other schools in which she has taught.

This is the first time she has acted as a mentor in this school. Her mentee is Moira – a new teacher taking a Year Four class. Anne first met Moira in the Summer Term while the latter was still a student studying for her Bachelor of Education degree. Moira had arranged to visit the school for a day and the Headteacher had covered Anne's class for an hour so that they could meet. At this first meeting Anne showed Moira around the school and explained the ground rules of their relationship. This would include communication by phone if either had any questions, queries or comments about beginning work in the school. A few calls were exchanged and they met again twice before school started in September.

Anne called in to Moira's classroom before school on the first morning of the term to check that everything was prepared and ready for the class. She called back at playtime and accompanied Moira to the staff room. In doing this, Anne was not only giving moral support by introducing Moira to the company of colleagues; she was also emphasising to those colleagues that she was Moira's mentor and had a responsibility for her. Because the Autumn Term began on a Thursday there were only two school days in the first week and Anne managed to call in twice more to Moira's classroom, both times when she was teaching. Anne knew that Moira would be occupied and unable to give her time, but she wanted to know something about the climate of the classroom, and a couple of spontaneous brief visits told her a good deal.

They met after school on the Monday of the second week of term for an hour and a half. This meeting had been arranged well before term started and would be the first of a series of regular Monday meetings. Anne thought that it was very important to have a formal arrangement to meet regularly. If she and Moira agreed to meet on an informal basis, as the need arose, Anne feared that they would not meet, that there would always be more pressing and immediate needs. As Anne noted:

> If you don't arrange to meet, formally, then you'll keep saying 'Have you got time tomorrow?' and you'll find that you can't make it tomorrow.

Only by establishing their relationship on a professional footing would vital opportunities not be missed. Anne planned from the start, therefore, to meet Moira every week at the same time throughout the first term. They would review the need for weekly meetings in the second term, but whatever they decided about how often to meet, Anne would propose that meetings were scheduled, rather than left to chance.

In the meetings Anne would discuss issues which Moira wished to focus on. These would be the sorts of issues indicated by the new teachers in Section I, namely, questions about organisation; policy and management; rituals and procedures; contact with other adults. Queries about the curriculum content could arise, but since Moira planned her work in a Key Stage cluster group with two other teachers, Anne would provide support in a slightly different way.

The first meeting involved helping Moira to prioritise and plan her day-to-day work. In the second meeting, a week later, they spent time discussing individual children in Moira's class, and Anne made suggestions about how to handle situations which could arise. Moira broached the subject of parents and how to involve their help at home and in the classroom. Anne discussed coming in to observe Moira in the classroom and work with her for a morning in the following week. Anne understood that Moira might have felt a little apprehensive at this, which was why she delayed such a visit until the third week of term. Anne closed the meeting by reassuring Moira and counselling her not to try too much too quickly.

Anne tried to visit Moira in her classroom each day for the first few days of term. In that early part of the scheme and their relationship, these were brief visits. Anne had her own class to teach but she was anxious to put Moira at her ease. She waited until their relationship had developed before arranging a formal observation session of Moira in her classroom. Anne felt that teaching could be a very isolated job and wanted to support and encourage Moira without threatening her. Popping into Moira's classroom before the children arrived in the morning, or visiting during the working day to confirm an arrangement or check whether Moira had everything she needed, worked well. In the third week of the term, Anne's class was taken for half a working day by the Headteacher to release her to spend time in Moira's classroom.

That was for a morning session to work on a planned programme which they had devised together. Anne expected to be able to respond better to Moira's needs after seeing her teach and work with the class. She could tell that Moira was fairly nervous about the experience, and she tried to make her presence in the room as unthreatening as she could, by innocuously pursuing work with children. Anne did not sit at the back of the room and observe Moira's practice. The two of them had arranged that Anne would take a maths group while Moira was doing writing with the other groups. They discussed the morning's progress at playtime and again at lunch-time. Anne was able to give Moira some advice about her approach to some children and they had a valuable conversation about how Moira formed the groups in the classroom. This was useful, but Anne felt that the most important feature of the exercise was that their relationship had been consolidated and that she could use such opportunities to observe Moira working to help her develop in the future. Moira was very positive about the experience:

> I was nervous at first – it was a bit like waiting for a college supervisor to come on teaching practice. Everything seemed to go wrong, too, but I got an awful lot out of it in the end. Anne was so reassuring when we talked afterwards and gave me a good idea about how to organise the start of the day.

Anne thinks that Moira must be able to trust her for the scheme to work. If a mentor is not trusted by the newly qualified teacher then the relationship can founder and not be productive. For Anne this trust takes two forms – one, that anything the newly qualified teacher says will be held in strict confidence, and two, that the mentor must be a professional 'supporter' rather than someone who appraises performance. This will be especially important if the newly qualified teacher is on a short-term contract.

The subject of trust and confidentiality was raised by a number of NQTs I talked to and will be discussed later. It is an important one because Anne will have to write a report on Moira for the Headteacher. This report will be discussed by the LEA adviser who oversees the school. Anne has discussed this with Moira, but it is one feature of their arrangement which she is a little uncertain about. On the other hand, one very positive feature that Anne appreciates is that Moira has the confidence to take the initiative and ask for things, make suggestions and evaluate the advice she receives – both from her mentor and from other colleagues.

SOME COMMENTS FROM TEACHERS WHO HAVE BEEN THROUGH THE SCHEME

Mentoring schemes proliferate. The arrangements for ending the Probationary Year determined that all new teachers should work with a mentor throughout the first year of teaching. This model of induction into the teaching profession is not new since mentoring schemes have been in operation in a variety of forms for some time (see Hagger *et al.*, 1993). Section I introduced the topic by reporting the voices of teachers at the very beginning of their careers. In this, Section III, I want to look at a group of teachers who have recently completed their first year of teaching. From this some conclusions about good practice will be drawn and some pointers as to how to make the best use of the scheme will be identified.

I interviewed Alan at the beginning of his second year of teaching. He had established a positive relationship with his mentor from the start:

> If it hadn't been for the mentor I had, I'd have left teaching after the first half-term. When I started off I felt clueless about SPMG maths – I'd never been in a school which used it before. It was arranged that Gill had some non-contact time and she came in and helped me to get sorted out. Gill showed me how to sort my groups out and helped me to arrange the room.

This is a very practical instance of the mentor as *teacher*. It requires some considerable resourcing to allow a mentor to have the opportunity to work alongside the person being inducted, but the expense must be borne if it produces effective results, as it seems to do. Perhaps, more importantly, a mentor can help a new teacher cope with the big change from college to school and the stress that any new teacher is likely to suffer, which has been addressed in Section II. In Alan's words:

> By about three or four weeks into the first term I'd got to the point

where I thought I couldn't do it any more. I was so tired. It's such a shock having to get up early every day and get to school prepared and ready. It's not like teaching practice where you might have some free time, or you know it's going to end soon. They (colleagues) used to keep telling me to relax, but I couldn't. The little bit of non-contact time I had was so good for me. Gill, my mentor, was brilliant. She arranged for people to give me a little bit of support, so I had the English post holder and the Science post holder to come in and do a lesson with me.

I asked Alan whether he had been able to share his feelings with Gill:

Yes. We got on really well. She was so reassuring. She said,' Don't worry. Everyone feels like that at some point, and when you get past that point you'll be fine.' If Gill hadn't said that to me, I'd have packed it in. When I had the half-term holiday I considered not going back.

This echoes the thoughts of the Headteacher in Anne and Moira's school, and in Section II of this chapter, that a successful mentoring scheme might help retain teachers in the profession. The experience of others who, likewise, had finished their first year of teaching, touches on the same issue. Thus Baljinder, interviewed at the end of her first year of teaching, noted:

When I first started I tried to do too much. I plunged into everything straightaway – the topic work and the reading and the maths, and I was obviously being too ambitious. I can see it now, but at the time I went to Barbara, my mentor, and said 'It's just not working.' Her advice was to relax a bit and take a few weeks to find out the range of ability in the class first of all and work out how I wanted to be with children and to get them used to me. That was the most useful bit of advice I had, because until then I was building up this frustration with the job and myself, thinking, I just can't do it.

Revealing feelings of incompetence is a sensitive and difficult thing to do. Many of the teachers I talked to recognised such feelings. Being able to share such feelings with their mentors was clearly important to Alan and Baljinder. It doesn't take a year in school to appreciate this. Moira, after three weeks in school as an NQT, said:

I feel under pressure all the time. Anne's given me tremendous advice about taking things slowly and sorting out one thing at a time, but I still feel sometimes that I can't cope. I want to be able to talk to my mentor about this without feeling that other teachers, or even the Head, will get to hear about it.

Alan admitted:

I was at a point when I wasn't too bothered about who knew I was having problems coping. You feel better talking to someone who you know won't go and tell the Head whatever you've said though.

The rapport that can grow between the two partners in the relationship would be threatened by any breach of confidence. A teacher who has undertaken to induct a new entrant to the profession might be well advised to adopt the protective stance shown by Anne to Moira – where, for example, Anne accompanied Moira to the staff room on the first day of term. This protective attitude will have numerous opportunities to express itself. The NQT is likely to be appraised and the mentor will have to support him or her through that process, while possibly even taking part in the assessment. Tracy, having just finished her first year of teaching, was grateful to her mentor for the way she was supported in dealings with the LEA adviser. She said:

My mentor really helped me to prepare for the adviser's visit. She put in extra time and helped me make sure my room was ready and went over lesson plans with me. The adviser coming in my classroom was very different to my mentor being in the room with me. Everything was planned down to the last minute and I have to say that I don't teach like that normally – but my mentor knew that.

This highlights the fact that NQTs have other forms of support in school, apart from their mentors. NQTs can expect occasional visits from LEA advisers and, in addition, a strong LEA will operate an induction programme for NQTs which is likely to involve a limited number of training days when NQTs from different schools will be called together.

A SUMMARY OF GOOD PRACTICE

Individuals differ and relationships forged between different people follow different courses. What suits one mentoring partnership might not suit another. Moira and Anne were becoming friends through their professional partnership. Moira, while a little nervous at first of Anne working in her classroom, was positive about the experience and even welcoming. Baljinder, however, while having a great regard for her mentor, didn't enjoy the time her mentor spent with her in the classroom:

I didn't like it at all. It was worse than being back at college and having a TP (teaching practice) supervisor coming in. I knew why she wanted to come in but I never got to like it.

Interestingly, Baljinder and her mentor did not meet on a regular basis, but were happy to meet informally, which was something that all the other pairs were anxious to avoid doing. While all the partnerships I have reported differ, there are some fairly constant features of good practice to consider:

1 Confidentiality;
2 Careful selection of mentors;
3 Trust;
4 Regular meetings; and
5 The involvement of other colleagues.

Confidentiality

The one feature of a successful mentoring partnership voiced by all – mentors and NQTs – was confidentiality. The discussions that take place must be absolutely confidential to the partnership. New entrants to teaching are likely to face occasions of doubt and uncertainty when they question, like Alan, whether they will even continue. Feelings of doubt and uncertainty so early in one's career are disturbing and alarming, but by no means unusual. The NQT will benefit from being able to discuss these with the mentor, but will be unlikely to speak frankly if it is felt that other colleagues and authority figures are going to be privy to comments made in the heat of the moment, or when under stress.

This issue is complicated by the fact that many mentors may have to contribute to a report on the NQT at the end of the year or even on a termly basis. While it would be unrealistic to expect all mentor pairings to develop as friendships, an honest rapport between the partners is likely to be more effective than a grudging and half-hearted tolerance of each other.

Careful selection of mentors

The partnerships discussed above all had a quality of respect between the partners. The respect on the part of the NQT for his or her mentor will in part depend on a sense of confidence that the mentor can help. It is for this reason that mentors are generally experienced teachers who have gained wisdom of the school world. There is some tension here, for the NQT must not be overawed by authority, or anxious about appraisal. For such reasons it might be best for a Headteacher to avoid being a mentor.

Compatibility of personality can never be guaranteed, but is marvellous where it occurs. For this reason, some schools allow new teachers to choose their own mentors, on the basis of a brief acquaintance. While it might sound an ideal solution, in fact it can bring its own problems. New teachers who make their own choice, only to discover a little later that they have made a mistake, are in a worse situation than those whose choice is made for them. Where there is clear incompatibility of personality between mentor and mentee, changes need to be made swiftly for the benefit of all concerned. Age difference might be thought a barrier to good communication, but this does not necessarily follow. Successful mentoring partnerships, like successful marriages, can overcome all sorts of differences.

Trust

A new entrant must have confidence that the mentor has sufficient relevant experience to be able to help. The mentor is in a position of considerable privilege and there must be mutual respect if the two are going to work effectively together. The NQTs mentioned above were helped by their mentors. Their questions were answered and their queries dealt with. This quality of trust will depend on the advice offered being good advice, given in a spirit of genuine professional and personal concern.

The quality of empathy needs to be exercised on both sides. While the new teacher may, initially, be a little overawed by someone with twenty years' experience, the older colleague may well be reflecting on the new-comer's assumed grasp of current thinking and recent developments.

So much for selection and pairing. What of procedures?

Regular meetings

Formal meetings to underpin casual encounters, at least during the early stages of the year, are likely to prove productive. Informal contact is fine, but teachers' lives are busy and there are always likely to be other things which will be more urgent. If there does appear to be nothing to meet about, it is easy to postpone an arrangement.

While formal agendas are probably inappropriate, some mutually understood check-list is helpful so as to focus attention. Such headings might include:

- reactions to individual children;
- lesson planning and evaluation;
- catering for individual differences and special needs;
- behavioural and management issues;
- assessing children and reporting to parents;
- school policies and procedures; and
- updating on National Curriculum.

The involvement of other colleagues

The mentor must be respected by other colleagues and in a position to command their attention. Alan's mentor secured the services of various co-ordinators to help him get to grips with the organisation of the curriculum. Moira's mentor introduced her to colleagues and encouraged her to approach others. Samreena's mentor encouraged her to seek a network of relationships within the staff room.

The moral here is that, while a good mentor is precious, the mentor must not be precious about the role, but must see it as enabling and liberating. In such a way, the relationship ideally moves from dependency to interdependence.

CONCLUSION

The first year of teaching will be full of challenges and opportunities. We speak of 'induction programmes' for new entrants because we know that, however well trained by college or university, new entrants have special and particular needs. As a newly qualified teacher there will be much to assimilate and accommodate to. The success of the first year in teaching can be enhanced by a positive relationship with an experienced teacher – a mentor. This relationship can be constructed by both parties, as long as both take it seriously and both have a stake in it.

REFERENCES

Hagger, H., Burn, K. and McIntyre, D. (1993) *The School Mentor Handbook*, London: Kogan Page.
Lance, A. (1992) *Brace Yourself*, Oxford: National Primary Centre.
National Primary Centre (1993) *Practice to Share: Lunchtime*, Oxford.
Traquair, N. (1994) *The Open Door: What Makes Mentoring Work*, Oxford: National Primary Centre.
Wilkin, M. (ed.) (1992) *Mentoring in Schools*, London: Kogan Page.

Appendix 1: Resources

Newcomers to a school, whether student or NQT, cannot be expected to operate successfully without appropriate resources, and it is the responsibility of the Head of the school to ensure that classroom equipment is available, and subject to an efficient system of distribution. Access to centrally stored resources must be explained to staff at the outset, and part of a Head's role is to ensure that staff members who have responsibility for such equipment are alerted to the possible needs of new teachers and students. Equally, new members of staff must recognise the need to acquaint themselves with the particular system in the school, and have confidence to approach appropriate staff members to help them with this. Students may need to establish what they can reasonably expect from the school in terms of photocopying, for instance. Some schools may be happy for them to have free access to such facilities, but in other establish-ments there may be more stringent rules about printing.

It is helpful if new teachers and students have a clear idea of the essential equipment which is required in a classroom, because in this way they can identify any 'missing links' in advance of their requirement during an activity or lesson. Sometimes anxious teachers buy equipment which is actually available in school, because they haven't been made aware of available stock. It's amazing how much equipment is necessary as basic stock in a classroom. This is a list which was put together by the staff of a primary school. Do you think they were being ambitious or realistic?

crayons (wax)	sellotape	dictionaries
crayons (pencil)	drawing pins	thesaurus
paints	paper clips	class books (fiction & non-fiction)
paint brushes (assorted)	hole punch	reading books
paint trays	Tipp-ex	project resources
glue spreaders/brushes	lined paper	work books/folders
glue pots	plain paper	Notes of Guidance
water pots	scrap paper	Record/Assessment materials
newspaper	sugar paper	Current project notes
pencils	card	National Curriculum folders
pens	calculators	time-table
rulers	maths equipment	clock
rubbers	games	mop/bucket
felt pens	construction equipment	dustpan and brush
scissors	wet play activities	broom
teacher's scissors	world map	tape recorder
sharpeners	Europe/UK map	board rubber
stapler	atlases	board ruler
gun tacker	timeline	Pritt stick
Blutack	baskets/trays – storage	

Source: Lance, A. (1992) *Brace Yourself*, Oxford: National Primary Centre.

Appendix 2: A mentor – NQT agreement

(With acknowledgement to Gail Vaughan-Hodkinson)

NQTs will be provided with:

- a mentor;
- regular non-contact time;
- opportunities to meet mentor;
- access to Local Education Authority training days;
- access to local support groups;
- paperwork requirements; and
- the opportunity to visit other schools.

NQTs will receive a log book containing:

- guidance notes;
- statements of entitlement for NQTs;
- school policy documents;
- pro forma to record details of NQT/mentor meetings;
- pro forma to record LEA training days;
- pro forma to note assistance from local support groups;
- record of observational visits by Headteacher;
- record of observational visit by adviser;
- lesson plans, with half-term evaluations and aims; and
- miscellaneous notes and pro forma.

NQTs will be expected to:

- participate fully in the induction programme;
- keep a log of support given by mentor, Headteacher and others;
- discuss appropriate use of non-teaching time with mentor;
- show mentor written records of planning for the needs of all children;
- seek advice from mentor about management and organisation and school policy;
- arrange with mentor observation sessions of colleagues' teaching;
- arrange with mentor observational visits to other schools; and
- seek advice of mentor about playing a full part in the life of school and community.

Mentors will be required to:

- remain up to date on school and LEA policies;
- provide support and advice, as appropriate, to NQTs;
- determine individual personal and professional needs of NQT;
- oversee NQT's log book, record keeping, lesson preparation, evaluations;
- observe NQT teaching and managing children in other contexts;
- arrange collaborative teaching with NQT and/or observation of own lessons;
- liaise with colleagues and schools on behalf of NQT;
- liaise with Headteacher and adviser regarding NQT's progress;
- determine with NQT which information is confidential and which is public.

Appendix 3: Lunch-time supervisors

Good lunch-time/dinner-time supervisors, as we saw in the opening chapter, can play a genuinely collaborative role with mainstream teachers, provided that they share similar aims and approaches. The supervisor who sees herself as screaming jailer is hardly likely to fit this role and all require appropriate training.

What follows now are extracts from a National Primary Centre document designed to address this training issue, and printed here with their kind permission.

Lunch-time supervisors are not well paid. They can be interviewed on a Friday and be working the next week. They are on duty during a part of the day when the children in their charge are most 'free'. Teachers will know that managing such 'freedom' requires considerable skill and initiative. To be sustainable and effective, such initiatives must be part of a properly resourced whole-school approach. Lunch-time supervisors are 'significant' adults. They should feel part of a team, with a common understanding of the organisation, values and vision of the school, and with a shared commitment to improving the quality of care.

Training and awareness of role requirements

Such training needs to address the issues of:

- their responsibility for safety and supervision procedures
- first aid and medical routines
- fire regulations
- relevant school policies
- manner towards the children
- strategies for control and building positive relationships
- gender and racial awareness
- contact with parents
- relationship with classroom teachers
- organisation and provision for wet lunch-time breaks.

The following way forward is offered by one Headteacher, who writes:

In our school, the staff were concerned that there was more unruly behaviour at lunch-time than at any other time of the day. The lunch-time supervisors' methods of control often seemed to escalate undesirable noise levels and behaviour patterns, and these often spilt over into the afternoon teaching session and had a detrimental effect on the children's learning. There was little communication between teaching staff and supervisors; we were mutually wary of one another.

Discussion among interested teachers led to the Deputy Head producing a booklet for the lunch-time supervisors, containing ideas of what to do with the children at lunch-time, particularly on wet days.

Another member of staff went on duty with the supervisors and then held a meeting with them afterwards to gather ideas and suggestions and to listen to their problems.

These two initiatives have been followed by the establishment of a monthly meeting between the Deputy Head and representatives of the lunch-time supervisors.

It is early days yet, but a major bonus has been a significant improvement in the relationships between the lunch-time supervisors and the teaching staff. For the supervisors, having a proper channel of communication and being drawn into consultation and planning has benefited their self-image.

Some of the long-term suggestions, such as better wet lunch-time resources and more outdoor games and toy provision, have still to be implemented and will mean extra responsibility for the supervisors, but the goodwill is now there.

The essential features of the improvements to date have been the re-establishment of a dialogue between supervisors and teachers, the willingness of members of the teaching staff to set aside a small amount of time to address the lunch-time problems and the high degree of co-operation which supervisors have shown.

Source: South Area Teachers Project Group (1993) *Practice to Share. The Management of Children's Behavioural Needs*, Oxford: National Primary Centre.

Part II

Other teachers as colleagues

Chapter 3

The role of a post holder

Section I: Gill Hackett
SectionII: Chris Rush

EDITORS' INTRODUCTION

Since the 1988 Education Act, perhaps the adage 'Every teacher is a teacher of English' should be replaced with 'Every teacher has an area of responsibility'. Many new teachers in primary schools will now have oversight for an aspect of the curriculum very early in their careers and this development is highly relevant in the debate about the nature of teacher-training. Can primary school teachers be both generalist and specialist? Can breadth and depth be maintained, side by side? Major areas, such as assessment, Special Needs, and the core curriculum subjects of English, Maths and Science will, most probably, be in the hands of a senior member of staff, although one can never be sure of this since choice of particular post holders – and disposition of curriculum responsibilities – will depend on many factors.

This chapter is in two sections. Section I gives an overview of the situation and outlines the duties of one such post holder for English. Section II describes some of the early experiences of a mature teacher new to her role as Maths post holder. Any new teacher reviewing the list of activities both engaged and the different roles entailed, might well feel daunted, while recognising that one develops such expertise with experience. Like the authors, most post holders will also have oversight of a class, with the usual preparation and planning which that entails and, in addition, may be members of the school's management team. In fact, this is one way in which the concept of 'middle management' has entered the primary school, namely, via a tier in effect below the status of Head and Deputy but nevertheless carrying substantial responsibility.

Such post holders will have administration and paperwork. They will need to keep abreast of curriculum developments in their area to provide specialist expertise. Above all, they will be sources of support and advice for colleagues in the ways recounted below.

Section I: An overview

Gill Hackett

Pupil: There is three lamp-posts.
Teacher: If I say, 'There *are* three lamp-posts, ' does that sound better?
Pupil: No.

8.05 a.m.

Mrs Andrew's car draws into the school playground. Resisting the temp-
tation to boil the staff-room kettle, she goes immediately to her junior
school classroom. There is some last-minute preparation for the day's
activities to be done, but first she needs a quiet half-hour to complete the
orders for resources for the next year. The school secretary has been
pressing her for these for the past week and she needs to check a few
catalogue numbers and then to ensure that she has not overspent.

Once this paperwork is complete she is able to prepare for the
children's arrival. Mrs Andrew likes her classroom to be well organised
and to present a working environment for her nine-year-olds as soon as
they arrive, so she checks that everything they will need is at hand. She
glances at her watch. Five minutes to the bell. A colleague calls in to ask
for advice. As always on these occasions Mrs Andrew would like to be
able to sort things out at once but has learnt that this is not always
possible and suggests a lunch-time meeting on the following day when
she will have had time for reflection.

8.55 a.m.

The class is escorted from the playground into the classroom. They are
familiar with Mrs Andrew's routines and settle quickly to the 'quiet
activities' she insists upon while she conducts the early morning business
of the classroom. Registers are taken, money for a class visit is collected
and a few minor issues are dealt with.

9.10 a.m.

Assembly time and Mrs Andrew clutches a pile of books as she makes her
way to the school hall with her class. She has asked the Headteacher for a
few minutes at the end of assembly to talk to the children about the
forthcoming 'Book Week' she has organised. Her enthusiasm is infectious
as she describes the wide range of activities that will be taking place and
whets the children's appetites by showing new books and by reading
extracts from some of them. Organisation of this event has involved Mrs

Andrew in a great deal of extra work, but it has become a regular feature of the school year and she is looking forward to it.

9.30 a.m.

Back in the classroom, the children gather on the carpet for an introduction to the session. Until mid-morning break they will be engaged in a range of Mathematics activities and these few minutes are used to ensure that each group knows exactly what to do. As soon as they are all busy Mrs Andrew joins the group she has planned to work with. She is able to spend most of her time concentrating her attention in this way, having planned a number of activities for other groups that can be pursued with a greater degree of independence, although from time to time she visits each group to check on their progress.

10.40 a.m.

Mrs Andrew is not on playground duty so is able to enjoy her cup of coffee. As in most staff-rooms the conversation turns inevitably to some aspect of school life and, on this occasion, staff are sharing their concerns about Paul's lack of progress as a reader. Because it is her responsibility to have an overview of both English and Special Needs, Mrs Andrew is already aware of the problem and feels that she may soon have to request specialist help from the local authority. For the moment, however, she must dash to the telephone to check that the Book Fair materials will be arriving on time.

10.55 – 12.00 noon

This is one of the occasions in the week when Mrs Andrew is time-tabled to teach as a subject specialist. For the past year the school has been trialling a more specialised approach to teaching with the older children, whereby a proportion of their work in English, Mathematics and Science has been taught by the respective post holders. On this particular morning Mrs Andrew is taking a Drama lesson with a Year Six class. They have been studying Tudor and Stuart times as a History-focused project and today they are dramatising scenes relating to the Great Plague. The children are responsive and very much involved in their roles. Mrs Andrew notes how valuable Drama has been in enabling a number of children, who otherwise might be thought of as less able to make significant contributions, to be imaginatively involved, and to demonstrate the extent of their knowledge and understanding of this period of history.

12.00 – 1.10 p.m.

The lunch break is usually a busy time for Mrs Andrew.

On several days a week she is involved in lunch-time activities or clubs but today she has a meeting with the school's senior management team, of which she is a member. She has been leading a working party that has been reviewing approaches to and resources for reading in the school and the time has come to discuss ways in which proposed changes may be implemented. The review has formed part of the school's ongoing development plan and so has been identified as a priority for professional development in the coming year.

It is decided that the initiatives will be introduced through a training day and a series of staff meetings with an additional meeting for parents. It will be Mrs Andrew's responsibility to organise these and she is already thinking about the support she will hope to harness both from colleagues and from the LEA advisory service. She has learnt from past experience that the successful implementation of new initiatives can hinge crucially on the way they are introduced to the staff.

1.10 – 3.30 p.m.

Mrs Andrew spends the afternoon with her own class teaching her own subject specialism, English. She believes that it is an important part of her role as post holder to be demonstrating in her own practice the kind of approaches she wishes to see employed in the school. It is not unusual to see reading, writing and talk all going on at the same time in her room and to see the children engaged in lively and purposeful language activities.

On this particular afternoon they are nearing the completion of work that has focused on a favourite book and which will form part of an exhibition for Book Week. Some of the children are redrafting sections of a story they have written themselves as a sequel to the book; others are using the word-processor to make a final draft of completed chapters. Another group has written a dramatisation of part of the story and is occupied with a rehearsal of their scene. Maps, games and illustrations inspired by the book are all at varying stages of completion. Mrs Andrew's role this afternoon is mainly that of a consultant, with children turning to her, or to each other, for advice. She finds that, when they are working independently in this way, she is able to make many useful observations and assessments of their progress.

3.30 p.m.

Once the children have departed, Mrs Andrew, like most teachers, makes some preparations for the next day and catches up on her marking and record-keeping. If possible she likes to reflect on the events of the day. Today this time is restricted as she has to attend a course at the local Teachers' Centre. As post holder she recognises the importance of her own professional development and welcomes the opportunity to extend her own knowledge and expertise, and to share experiences with colleagues throughout the Local Authority. At the end of a long day it is sometimes hard to maintain this enthusiasm; she hopes that the course will prove worth while and that it will help her to plan forthcoming school INSET.

And so ends a typical school day for Mrs Andrew. Let us review her activities. She has:

- taught her own class;
- ordered language materials on behalf of the school;
- checked a budget;
- arranged to advise a colleague;
- played a major role in the school Assembly;
- organised a Book Week;
- discussed the special needs of one child;
- considered help from outside agencies;
- taught her specialist subject to another class;
- noted the particular contribution of certain less able children;
- participated in a senior management team meeting on approaches to reading;
- considered the planning of an INSET training day;
- offered an English-teaching model within her own classroom;
- done her marking, record-keeping, and preparations for the next day; and
- attended a local Teachers' Centre course after school.

Whereas, at one time, Mrs Andrew's post holder duties might have been little more than nominal and could have consisted mainly of ordering books, this is no longer the case. The post holder now has very real responsibility as leader for a curriculum and as consultant to both staff and parents.

POST HOLDER AS LEADER

Recent changes in education, including the introduction of the National Curriculum, have had a significant impact on post holders, making their role a crucial one in primary schools. In their preparation for the implementation of these changes, schools were encouraged to delegate curriculum leadership (NCC, 1989) and the old image of the entirely autonomous teacher working alone with the classroom door closed has gone for ever.

It is now accepted that each aspect of school life must be effectively managed to ensure that all children have access to a broad and balanced curriculum. The status and experience of each post holder can vary enormously, however, both within a school and from school to school. Some may be relatively junior members of staff; others may be Heads or Deputies. In small schools several posts may be held by one person; in large schools responsibilities will be shared. While, in an ideal world, each post holder would be an enthusiastic specialist, in reality some staff may have accepted roles that they would not have chosen freely.

The status of certain subject areas is also a significant factor as the core National Curriculum subjects of English, Maths and Science are, understandably, given high priority in schools and are, therefore, likely to be awarded the highest allowances and status. These post holders are more likely than others to be members of the school's senior management team. All subjects of the National Curriculum will be part of someone's responsibility but wider or cross-curricular responsibilities must also be covered by each staff. These might include RE; assessment and its associated recording and reporting; special educational needs; the co-ordination of a Year Group or Key Stage. The possible permutations are almost limitless and it is not always easy for newly appointed staff to discover exactly who is responsible for what. A school prospectus or staff handbook is helpful, and one can, of course, always ask.

Although the scope of any particular post will vary considerably from school to school there can be no question that the role of the post holder is of crucial importance and that the related duties consume a significant amount of time for many teachers. In many primary schools the post holder may have little, if any, non-contact time to pursue the duties.

This makes the task of ensuring a broad and balanced curriculum, and a coherent and planned approach to all aspects of school life, even more difficult. It can only be achieved through the development of whole school policies that incorporate within them the aims and objectives of all aspects of the curriculum. Each post holder has a significant role in ensuring that the relevant section of such a policy is written, that it is regularly reviewed, and that it reflects current staff thinking, while allowing scope for possible future developments.

A great deal of advice is produced at both national and local levels to assist schools in the formulation of policies both for the National Curriculum and for wider aspects of the curriculum of a school. The *Handbook for the Inspection of Schools* (OFSTED, 1992), containing the criteria that will inform all future inspections, is readily available and likely to be an important point of reference.

While drawing on such sources, however, policy statements must be documents that are written for a specific individual school; which reflect the thinking of a particular staff; which show the ways in which statutory requirements are to be interpreted and implemented for a particular group of children. Such statements should be personal, specific and identifiable, rather than impersonal, vague and transferable.

The designated post holder clearly has a crucial leadership role to play in the formulation and recording of policy and, in order to be able to perform the role adequately, must ensure that his/her own professional development is not neglected. Policies are frequently developed within the context of a working party that needs such specialist leadership. In most schools it is likely that, at any given time, a review of some policy or other is in progress, so there is usually an opportunity for new members of staff to become involved. One assumes that most post holders would warmly welcome offers of involvement from NQTs.

All teachers, whether newly qualified or highly experienced, will be involved in staff training days and it is here that post holder leadership qualities will be clearly in evidence. It is at such INSET sessions that written policies have to be translated into action, which inevitably involves change. While this may be perceived by experienced colleagues as threatening, NQTs, ignorant of a previous regime, will accept the procedure as normal, since they will be unaware of any change involved.

Schools are required to produce carefully constructed development plans in which priorities are identified (Hargreaves *et al.*, 1989). Closure days for training provide the opportunity for the necessary programmes to take place and NQTs, fresh from training or other experience, can make their own unique contribution.

Support, however, is reciprocal and, increasingly, a teamwork approach is the norm. In this respect, the NQT can expect some classroom help from post holders. It has become increasingly common in recent years for post holders to be released from class teaching responsibilities at specific times in the week in order to be deployed in this way. This has proved to be a most effective means of ensuring curriculum development and has enabled post holders to lead by example.

The introduction of aspects of the National Curriculum that appeared threatening to many primary teachers, such as science and technology, was often most successfully accomplished where the respective post holders were able to work alongside less confident colleagues. The scope for one teacher to be free to give such support is clearly limited in primary schools where, particularly in small schools, there is little flexibility in staffing, but many post holders feel that it is impossible to lead effectively unless they are able to do so. Even where such practice is made possible it may be that post holders must take their turn, with priority given to areas in which staff feel less confident or where new developments are taking place and which have been identified in the school development plan. Particular subjects or year groups may be targeted or such support may be provided as part of an induction for newly qualified teachers.

Although some staff may at first have felt threatened by the presence of a colleague, 'the expert', in their classrooms, the benefits of working collaboratively are soon apparent. Newly qualified staff, like students in training, may initially feel uncomfortable and may worry about displaying their own performance, but these fears should be quickly allayed. The opportunity, if offered, to work with and learn from an experienced colleague with expertise in a specific area should be welcomed. It is almost always beneficial for teachers and children.

Though the practice of classroom support is fairly well established, it is still relatively rare to encounter truly specialist teaching in primary schools where traditionally each member of staff has been expected to teach the whole range of the curriculum to one class. The introduction of the National Curriculum, particularly at Key Stage 2 where the content of some subjects is vast, has, however, caused many schools to consider carefully whether it is possible or indeed desirable for every teacher to have the necessary knowledge and expertise to teach all subjects in the required depth. Alexander *et al.* (1992) encouraged schools to consider deploying post holders as specialists or semi-specialists, particularly towards the end of Key Stage 2, and at the present time we are seeing an increasing number who are willing to experiment. The core subjects of English, Mathematics and Science are often first to be treated in this way.

Follow-up reports (NCC, 1993; OFSTED, 1993) have repeated the suggestion that schools should consider flexible strategies for the deployment of staff and, if the trend continues, NQTs are even more likely to find that at least some of their class time-table is to be taken over by a post holder. There can, of course, be considerable benefits in deploying staff as specialists, bringing, as they do, both expertise and enthusiasm to a subject. The opportunity to work in this way has been welcomed by many post holders while others regret the amount of time they lose with their own classes. NQTs may find that they have the opportunity to observe the specialist at work but, for the most part, staff whose classes are being taught by a post holder will be expected to 'swap' and may find themselves teaching a range of lessons with a number of different classes. In all cases where classes are taught by more than one person the need for liaison becomes very important. That, indeed, is a key theme of this book since issues of continuity and progression are particularly significant.

The same recent reports on curriculum organisation and classroom practice have also suggested that placing children into streams or sets may be more effective than mixed ability teaching. This practice is still alien to most primary teachers but newly qualified staff should be aware that they may find themselves in a school that is experimenting in this way. The planning of the work of such groupings is likely then to form an extended part of the work of the subject post holder. In any event, no teacher on appointment to a staff should be surprised to find a wider range of organisation than might have been encountered in the past.

THE POST HOLDER AS CONSULTANT

The role of the post holder has now become very much that of specialist consultant to whom colleagues can turn for help and advice. Much consultation will be informal and on an ad hoc basis, and NQTs will usually find that such help is readily available. It is no longer assumed that every primary teacher is a specialist in all areas of the curriculum and even the most experienced members of staff will now take it for granted that they regularly need to seek advice, so there need be no fear that to do so will be interpreted as a sign of weakness. Post holders are able to suggest appropriate content, assist with planning schemes of work or particular lessons, and advise on suitable resources. NQTs should remember, however, that these responsibilities are almost always held in addition to a full teaching time-table and not assume that post holders can always be available on demand.

Such individual help as is offered would be in the context of school-wide policies and practice and, in order to achieve such an overview, it is not uncommon for post holders to monitor the termly or half-termly plans of each teacher. Such monitoring may be in addition to, or instead of, the Headteacher's scrutiny. In such a way, the post holder has a clearer picture of his/her area of responsibility across the school than ever before. For NQTs this knowledge can be invaluable.

It will be much in evidence with regard to children with special educational needs. The designated co-ordinator will be expected to have specific expertise and will be able to play a part in the diagnosis of difficulties and in the planning of appropriate learning experiences. Subject post holders, however, would also expect to be called upon to suggest approaches and resources, and most will welcome inquiries from NQTs who are concerned about weak children in their class.

One of the ways in which a post holder is most relied upon by colleagues is indeed as an adviser on the choice and use of resources. He or she knows exactly what is available both within the school and from other sources and has probably been responsible for selecting and ordering the appropriate stock. A considerable degree of delegation now means that most post holders will be managing a portion of the school's budget. Specific percentages of the available total are often allocated to each curriculum area, but there is often a great deal of flexibility from year to year so that additional finance can be made available to support a particular focus or initiative.

Post holders may be sympathetic to individual requests but it is rare that funding is generous enough to allow for expensive individual idiosyncrasies, especially if these do not support established practice. Many post holders consult with colleagues on a regular basis and certainly where a major new initiative is planned, perhaps to refurbish the library or to introduce a published scheme, when all staff are likely to have the opportunity to make suggestions and place requests.

The classification and storage of resources is usually also part of a post of special responsibility. Some resources may be centrally stored while some may be located in separate classrooms. The establishment and maintenance of a resource area may take up a considerable amount of time and the hard-pressed post holder will often welcome an offer of help from a newly appointed colleague. Wherever resources are located the post holder will be responsible for ensuring their accessibility and main-tenance and will be able to advise newly qualified teachers as to what is available and appropriate. Some scarce resources may have to be allo-cated to classes on a rota basis or may need to be requested in advance or signed for. The smooth running of the classroom and the successful completion of a lesson so often depend on having the right resources at the right time, and enlisting the help of the post holder to ensure that this can happen is therefore a wise move.

While books and equipment are very important resources, it must not be forgotten that the most valuable resources of all are the people who work with children. Part-time support staff, non-teaching assistants and parents are all to be found in schools, providing extensive support to class teachers. Indeed, that is the key theme of this book and all staff, including NQTs, will seek information in this regard, as they will for resources available in the wider community, such as libraries, museums and art galleries or from the Local Education Authority or neighbouring colleges. He or she will be able to suggest places to visit and people who can be invited into school.

In such a way, the post holder may be perceived as the public face of his/her areas of responsibility. This may involve specialist contact with parents or liaison with visitors, outside agencies or local authority advisers, librarians or educational psychologists. It may also mean, at times, addressing meetings of parents or governors.

So many and varied are the duties of a post holder that newly qualified teachers could be forgiven for thinking that they can expect to meet Wonder Woman and Superman rolled into one. While the reality will be a bit less glamorous, the help given, if not so dramatic (i.e. saving the world from destruction), should nevertheless be appropriate, positive and encouraging. And remember, the NQTs and students of today are the post holders of tomorrow. In which regard, Appendix 1 will provide some awareness raising.

REFERENCES

Alexander, R., Rose, J. and Woodhead, C. (1992) *Curriculum Organisation and Classroom Practice in Primary Schools*, a discussion paper, London: Department of Education and Science.

Hargreaves, D.H., Hopkins, D., Leask, M., Connolly, J. and Robinson, P. (1989) *Planning for School Development*, London: Department of Education and Science.

National Curriculum Council (1989) *A Framework for the Primary Curriculum*, York: NCC.

—— (1993) *The National Curriculum at Key Stages 1 and 2*, York: NCC.

Office for Standards in Education (OFSTED) (1992) *The Handbook for the Inspection of Schools*, London: OFSTED.

—— (1993) *Curriculum Organisation and Classroom Practice in Primary Schools*, a follow-up report, London: OFSTED.

Section II: In the hot seat

Chris Rush

In September 1992, I became Maths co-ordinator, following the promotion of the previous post holder to another school. I had no particular qualifications, expertise or experience for this role, other than a willingness to do my best for the staff and children. Indeed, had I been as aware then of the range of responsibilities (see Appendix 2) as I subsequently became, I should have been distinctly alarmed.

My former responsibility had been for planning, assessment and record-keeping, and, at the time of appointment, I was organising a training day in these areas. It was an easy decision to focus on Maths and, particularly, the issues involved in MA1 and MA9. Staff were asked to select evidence from their children's Maths work, for purposes of assessment and recording.

During the course of that day, it became apparent that Key Stage 2 teachers had a very different conception of MA1 and MA9 from that held by Key Stage 1 teachers. Immediate tasks, then, were to reconcile these attitudes while, at the same time, looking at MA1 provision within the school, and continuing the change from Nuffield Maths to Heinemann Maths. In this respect, we wanted to offer the children problem-solving activities to develop their thinking, rather than have them drudge their way through the 'two pages a day' treadmill.

Accordingly, I worked with lower school staff on building up resources; allocating materials to specific age groups; discussing teaching methods; regularly reviewing our procedures. We made good progress but insufficient materials forestalled total success and I did not feel that I was able to do enough to help colleagues who lacked adequate resources, despite setting up a central pool of teacher-focused Maths materials.

Many Maths ideas for this central pool came from a DFE 20-day course for Maths co-ordinators that I attended, and formed the core of much of our school INSET sessions. Materials were produced by all colleagues and fed into the central collection. Particularly valuable was the Maths games library for children, and the sets of loop cards produced by the part-time Special Needs teacher for individual children who needed help. Labelling and matching materials for each key Maths concept was as time-consuming as it was valuable.

During the year I was able to give support to individual colleagues, either with ideas for specific Maths concepts, or help with individual children. I also felt that I was able to organise resources for them, and to order anything they particularly needed. However, I did feel that I only responded to specific requests from staff, rather than initiate support in the classroom. I had intended to use my non-contact time to offer support in a variety of ways in each classroom, but other pressures meant that I only visited another classroom when I was especially asked to do so.

One of these pressures was that involving parents. Our school policy was to be as open as possible to sharing curriculum approaches with parents and, accordingly, four meetings were held on Maths alone, following careful preparation in staff meetings, all of which was my responsibility, although many colleagues were involved.

By the Summer Term, most of the tasks set down in the Institution Development Plan (IDP) had either been accomplished or were well under way.

LOOKING BACK

Reflecting on my first year as a Maths post holder, I feel that the person who benefited most was me! I certainly learned more about the teaching of Maths, and my own ability and confidence in this curriculum area developed considerably. I spent much time thinking about relevant issues that I had not considered before. I had a greater awareness of resources and a wider range of skills and techniques to use in my own classroom, as well as throughout the school.

With regard to the 20 points outlined in Appendix 2, I can honestly report some modest degrees of success with sixteen of them. I missed out on 7, 8, 14, 15, 18, 20. Above all, I feel that my own classroom needs to be further developed, so as to offer a model to colleagues as a central focus for Maths activities. I need regular and interactive Maths displays around the room, with further development of the Maths area within the room, and with encouragement to colleagues and parents to browse through packs and articles and books on display.

LOOKING FORWARD

Although the experiences of the last year leave me more confident to tackle the role of Maths post holder in a new school, I realise that there will be much to do, and that I will not be able to do it all at once. The pressures of being a teacher in a new environment, however experienced one is, are quite immense and I shall have the added responsibilities of being a new Deputy Head. I will also have responsibility for music, an area of the curriculum which is high on the IDP. So all my aims need to be prioritised.

First and foremost, I intend to do my best to set a good example of mathematical practice in my own classroom, from the very beginning, and have regular and active Maths displays around the room. This was a task left incomplete at my previous school. I have already set up a Maths area in the room and am pleased with how it looks. I have also set up a teacher-resources area in the room, where my colleagues can browse through the mass of materials which we have accumulated.

Another high priority is to talk with the staff about how they see the Maths curriculum now, and what they think we need to consider for the future. I suspect that I will need to initiate change and I would like this to be as painless as possible and, ideally, needs-led. (Do I really want to be cast in the Heroine-Innovator role?)

There are no central storage areas in this split-site school, so one important task is to ascertain precisely what we have and where it is. One thing I am aware of is that the school has an excellent Maths games library. This has been in existence some time and, in fact, become a model for neighbouring schools to copy. Parents come into school each week to help their children choose a game to play at home. This is marvellous and may help to supplement the investigational and problem-solving activities within the Nuffield Maths Scheme which is currently operated and, in my view, is rather lacking in crucial aspects.

This will be my first experience of teaching in an infants school and I intend to use my junior experience to establish good relationships throughout what will become, in time, one primary school. Only on the basis of good, amicable, professional and personal relationships between all who work in a school can the children's best interests be served.

Appendix 1: How important are they?

1 Circle the number that indicates the importance you place on each of the aspects of the role of the post holder with particular reference to the newly qualified teacher.

1 Very important $\Rightarrow$ 5 Not important

- Source of information about school policies.   1 2 3 4 5
- Help in planning my schemes.   1 2 3 4 5
- Classroom support.   1 2 3 4 5
- Specialist teaching in my classroom.   1 2 3 4 5
- Monitoring my planning.   1 2 3 4 5
- Advice about resources.   1 2 3 4 5
- Guidance with assessment.   1 2 3 4 5
- Help in providing for pupils with special educational needs. 1 2 3 4 5

2 You would like to acquire an item of equipment that is not currently used by the school. When you approach the appropriate post holder she is not immediately enthusiastic. Would you:

   a) Arrange a time to meet her when you can explain the merits of the equipment in detail?
   b) Complain to the Deputy Head that you are not being supported?
   c) Buy the resource yourself and hope to demonstrate its successful use in your classroom?
   d) Attempt to rally support among your colleagues?
   e) Give up! She probably knows best.

3 A post holder suggests that she works alongside you in your classroom for one morning a week. Do you:

   a) Welcome it as a sharing of the load?
   b) Suspect that she may be checking up on you?
   c) Hope to pick up some tips that will enhance your own teaching?
   d) Invite her to collaborate with you in the planning of the sessions?
   e) Quickly change your original plans?

4 There is one area of the curriculum that you find particularly difficult to manage. Do you:

   a) Ask for advice before you begin your planning?
   b) Buy a book?
   c) Try to rearrange your time-table to avoid teaching it as far as possible?
   d) Write up your forecast notes for the Headteacher and hope for the best?
   e) Inquire whether you could observe the post holder teaching?

Appendix 2: Maths, a number of roles

Barry Pinfield (1992), working with a group of in-service teachers, devised the following areas of responsibility for a Maths post holder:

1 To develop, with the whole school, a Maths policy that offers agreed objectives; embraces a school Maths scheme; allows for a regular review of strengths and weaknesses in policy or scheme.

2 To develop a workable system of assessment and record-keeping with all colleagues.

3 To decide on measures that provide balance, continuity and progression in Maths, and to encourage forward planning for these.

4 To encourage an enthusiastic and positive approach to Maths.

5 To be responsible for the organisation of existing resources.

6 To support colleagues in their teaching, especially those who are lacking in confidence, or are new and inexperienced, or on supply.

7 To develop cross-phase links from nursery through to secondary schools.

8 To encourage cross-curricular links within the school by developing themes that give scope to Maths work.

9 To ensure that all colleagues are aware of the individual needs of children, and that special cases are catered for.

10 To update resources in the light of new ideas and developments.

11 To provide appropriate INSET for colleagues that encourages their own and the post holder's development.

12 To encourage parental support for what is going on in the classroom, and parental awareness of the National Curriculum, and to report to parents on the development of their children.

13 To work towards liaison with other post holders, LEA and other agencies.

14 To liaise with governors and ensure that they are conversant with recent developments and new requirements in Maths teaching.

15 To encourage the display of Maths work throughout the school.

16 To keep up to date with Maths issues, new documents and publications, and other developments, and ensure dissemination to colleagues.

17 To support teachers involved in SATs and encourage dissemination of their experience.

18 To encourage links with industry and commerce.

19 To attend courses and meetings related to Maths.

20 To reach agreement on a job description.

Source: Pinfield, B. (1992) 'Maths monitor', *Strategies*, Vol. 2, No. 2.

Chapter 4

Special needs

Section I: Jane Officer

Section II: Jane Leadbetter

EDITORS' INTRODUCTION

The Special Needs teacher (Section I) and the educational psychologist (Section II) are placed side by side in this section. The first will work mainly in the school, of course; the second will usually come from a centrally maintained Local Education Authority team, one of the few groups of professionals that LEAs are still required to retain. In other ways, the roles of SEN teachers and the educational psychologist may well overlap. They will liaise over certain children with learning and/or behavioural difficulties, and they will collaborate with mainstream colleagues in devising programmes for individual boys and girls. The SEN teacher will help colleagues to differentiate work and to implement a model of assessment through teaching. The educational psychologist, in contrast, will work with several schools, in a range from nursery to secondary, and provide further support for teachers in terms of staff development courses, reviews of current practice and assessment and monitoring.

The changing face of Special Needs provision in mainstream schools over the past few years reflects the many changes in education itself. These changes have been dramatic and far reaching. Issues related to assessment and intervention are highlighted as the National Curriculum becomes more familiar and the educational attainments of children are recorded in more formal ways than previously. Children with special needs are entitled to full access to the curriculum and teachers are responsible for ensuring that all children are taught in a way that allows them to learn, what are now, mandatory tasks. This can be a daunting job for any teacher, especially new and inexperienced teachers, but the advent of the National Curriculum and the changes in Special Needs legislation over the past fifteen years has led to many positive initiatives and changes in attitudes and practice which can only benefit children with special needs.

Section I focuses on:

- many positive changes in policy and practice;
- the role of the Special Needs teacher;

- the role of the class teacher; and
- practical suggestions and ideas for collaborative work.

Section I: The teacher

Jane Officer

> There's one lesson they don't have to sit down and do with him, and that's art. He likes art.
>
> (Parent of eight-year-old boy)

LEGISLATIVE CHANGES

The Warnock Report of 1979, the subsequent Education Acts of 1981 and 1988 and the Code of Practice on the Identification and Assessment of Special Educational Needs, May 1994, confirm the needs, rights and changing concept of special educational needs over the last fifteen years. This can only be good for children, their parents and schools as *all* children are entitled now, by law, to access to the National Curriculum. The most recent legislation makes it clear that the class teacher is central to the processes involved in ensuring that any children in his/her class identified as having a special need are taught in the most effective and appropriate way for their unique needs. Although this may sound daunting, the legislation makes it clear that any intervention and support process should take place within a whole school framework; with the full understanding and support of parents; with specific responsibilities allocated to the Headteacher, Special Needs teacher and any outside professionals involved.

Unfortunately, the resources required to meet many of the legal requirements are not universally available and this will mean that the ability to cater appropriately for special needs will vary from school to school, and area to area. Even so, with a positive approach from all staff involved, and a whole-school commitment to supporting children within a structured framework, many needs can be met within the classroom.

WHAT IS A SPECIAL EDUCATIONAL NEED?

A special need may cover a whole range of difficulties and differing levels of difficulties. The concept of a continuum of need was introduced by the Warnock Report in 1979 and continues to be regarded as useful. The need may be:

- emotional or behavioural;
- a specific disability or a learning difficulty; and
- permanent or transitory.

It is estimated that up to 20 per cent of all children experience a special need at some time in their school life and the majority of these are transitory requiring the minimum of input. Examples of this sort of need could be the upset, withdrawn child who has experienced the death of a relative or even a family pet, and needs comfort and time to talk through the feelings of loss. Or the child who has been in hospital for removal of tonsils, which had previously affected learning in school. Other children have greater and more long-term needs which, clearly, require more and longer intervention.

The underlying principle is one of recognising *individual requirements* and ensuring that these are met within the available resources. About 2 per cent of children are said to have special needs which require long-term assessment and provision, probably with the protection of a Statement of Needs which details the resources and teaching arrangements necessary to meet them. Some of these children will remain in mainstream schools with extra support.

The main concern in primary schools, of both class teachers and Special Needs teachers, are children deemed to have a learning difficulty. How is such a learning difficulty defined? It is reckoned that a child has a learning difficulty if s/he:

1   Has a significantly greater difficulty in learning than the majority of children of the same age.
2   Has a disability which prevents or hinders the child from making full use of educational facilities provided for children of the same age.
3   Is under 5 and falls within the definition of (a) or (b) above or would do if special education provision were now made.

(Education Act 1993, section 156)

Clearly, the first definition is most commonly encountered in mainstream primary schools. It is also the least specific. This has the advantage of being interpreted in a flexible way depending upon the class or school. It can also have the disadvantage of identifying large numbers of children with learning difficulties within a classroom! Schools in certain affluent suburbs may consider that children reading only at their chronological age have a 'learning difficulty', while an inner-city school, with a daunting range of poverty driven social problems, may identify up to 50 per cent of their children as having 'learning difficulties.' These are matters of debate and discussion both within the school and beyond. The concept of 'need' is both relative and conditional upon context and circumstances.

Children with a home language different from English should not be considered as having a learning difficulty as such, but they do, clearly, have a need, both to become competent in English and also to maintain their first language. The main principle to be followed is that Special Needs teaching is no different from other good teaching; it involves careful planning for specific pupils, using appropriate methods and materials, at a conceptual level which can be comprehended, and in a positive and supportive atmosphere. Such a formula for success is available to all teachers and can be learnt with time, experience and good staff development.

Teachers newly arriving in primary schools have a great deal to learn, quickly. Some do so via an induction programme, however sketchy. Others learn in advance from sessions with mentors, as outlined in Chapter 2. Most learn while actually involved in doing the job, and although this is probably the most effective way of learning, some errors could be avoided by careful scrutiny of documentation. Many schools provide a file of necessary information and the best of these packages are written from a real, personal context. All such staff handbooks should include comprehensive details of the school's policies and procedures. Among these policies it is a statutory requirement to include a Special Needs Policy, with clear guidelines for identification, assessment and intervention procedures. Responsibilities of class teachers, Special Needs teachers/co-ordinators, Headteacher, parents and governors should be listed alongside the procedures for involving both parents and outside professionals as necessary.

Current legislation aims to clarify schools' procedures for identifying, assessing, teaching and evaluating the cycle of intervention which aims to alleviate the special need. The complete process is seen as a five-stage model in which the class teacher remains the key figure. The role of the Special Needs teacher/co-ordinator is to ensure that the process is carried through appropriately, in the best interests of the child and with the full co-operation and involvement of parents. The process allows for an exit from the process at any appropriate point so allowing for the principle of a continuum of need. Briefly, the five-stage process is as follows:

Stages 1, 2 and 3 are school-based. Stages 4 and 5 are shared with the Local Education Authority. Headteachers are certain to be involved by Stage 3 but, more probably, will be involved much earlier and, in many schools, at the first Stage:

Stage 1 Class teacher identifies a child's special educational needs and, consulting the school's SEN co-ordinator/teacher, gathers information and takes whatever initial action is appropriate.

Stage 2 The school's SEN co-ordinator/teacher takes lead responsibility for planning and managing any required Special Needs provision, working in close liaison with the class teacher.

Stage 3 Class teacher and SEN co-ordinator/teacher are supported from outside the school by LEA and other agencies.

Stage 4 The LEA considers the need for a statutory assessment and, if appropriate, makes a multi-disciplinary assessment.

Stage 5 The LEA considers the need for a statement of special educational needs (see Appendix 2) and, if appropriate, makes such a statement, with arrangements for monitoring and review.

THE ROLE OF THE SPECIAL NEEDS TEACHER IN SCHOOL

The role of the Special Needs teacher in primary schools has been changing over the last ten years or so in response to changing concepts and principles. Most schools cannot afford the services of a teacher solely to take charge of SEN and the general pattern is for an experienced class teacher to assume the responsibility of Special Needs co-ordinator. Often the responsibilities have to be met within the school day without time allocation and this further reinforces the need to establish efficient procedures for meeting children's needs, especially within the classroom. The responsibilities of the Special Needs teacher/co-ordinator were laid down in the Code (May 1994) as:

1 the day-to-day operation of the school's SEN policy;
2 advising class teachers;
3 taking the lead in managing pupils at Stages 2 and 3;
4 updating and overseeing the records of all pupils with special educational needs and working with parents of such children; and
5 liaising with outside agencies including the educational psychology service and other support agencies, medical, social and voluntary organisations.

A legislative framework for special needs is to be welcomed, if it leads to a more accountable approach in schools than is sometimes the case. With a structure in place, schools should be enabled to develop effective and efficient ways to help all children. However, many schools need to debate the range of attitudes and concepts relating to the children they teach before deciding on the model of good practice they wish to adopt and embed in the school's Special Needs policy. A co-operative, whole-school approach, with commonly shared aims, goals and positive attitudes, creates an atmosphere where teaching and learning can develop and change in response to individual needs.

WITHDRAWAL OR IN-CLASS SUPPORT?

In the past, most Special Needs teaching was seen as something 'different'; it happened out of the classroom and was the province of a teacher who had skills that no one else on the staff possessed. Children were withdrawn, either singly or in groups, and were taught certain skills and information which was intended to enable them to integrate back into their class.

Critics of this approach pointed out that, while the children were being withdrawn, they were being deprived of certain parts of the mainstream curriculum and it was also more difficult for them to reintegrate, especially if the skills taught outside the classroom were not reinforced in the classroom, but were seen as something quite separate. The logic of withdrawal assumed that those selected would either make progress at a much faster rate than the others or that the others would be standing still, educationally speaking, and merely awaiting the return of their classmates. Moreover, in the absence of clear assessment procedures, it was often a moot point as to which children were deemed to need withdrawal support.

The arrival of the National Curriculum, with its emphasis on access to learning for all children, has made it more difficult to justify children being regularly taught outside the classroom when they are likely to miss essential teaching and learning opportunities. However, many schools do operate a successful withdrawal system, for very limited periods of time, for teaching basic skills to children who need the time and attention as individuals or in small groups. The essence of a successful withdrawal system is joint decision-making and feedback between class and SEN teacher and an assessment and evaluation process which ensures that progress is monitored and recorded in such a way that the class teacher can reinforce it.

Using the Special Needs teacher as a support within the classroom has found favour more recently. The terms of the support need to be clearly negotiated between the class and Special Needs teacher, with joint decisions on approach and attitude; on the degree of shared knowledge and responsibility; on aims and objectives; on lesson content, teaching strategies and methods of assessment. That is a key premise of collaborative work and one that underpins every chapter in this book. Good support teaching does not mean that the SEN teacher works with the weakest group of children only, or on a different task from the rest of the class. It should be team teaching at its best. It is an opportunity for the class teacher to work with the children whom she knows need extra help and it is an opportunity for colleagues to work together, observe and discuss what works well, what needs changing, and how best to develop children's skills.

IDENTIFICATION OF SPECIAL NEEDS

Finding a definition of a 'special need' is fraught with difficulty. The use of norm-referenced tests in basic subjects, such as a standardised reading or spelling test, does not give information which is useful to the class teacher faced with a child who is having difficulty in learning to read or spell. They merely confirm what is already known and result in labelling the child in question as a 'poor reader'. Although the National Curriculum and teacher's assessment will highlight those children having difficulties in certain areas, in themselves they can offer no remedies or courses for action. However, the NC assessment should highlight for teachers an important principle in identifying special needs: they reveal themselves in a specific context.

For example, children who are failing to read while engaged with the school's reading scheme may learn to read through science in which they are especially interested. Other children may be poor at maths in the classroom, but have no difficulty spending money at the school shop and getting the correct change! We are all, as adults, aware of how proficient most of today's children are with video and computer technology. By comparison, many of us are appropriately rated as 'slow learners'. In such a case, the children are very familiar with the context; we are not. Therefore, the identification of a special need or learning difficulty should take into account a range of contexts, experiences and skills. The most useful and efficient way to assess the skills of those children who are a source of concern to the teacher is by a process of assessment through teaching, not through separated and discrete testing.

Assessment through teaching requires that the teacher identifies:

1 a skill to be taught and learnt;
2 a way of teaching that skill; and
3 a means to evaluate whether the skill has been learnt.

The starting point for assessment is to:

- check what the child already knows in the identified skill area;
- decide what to teach next and in what sequence;
- choose a range of teaching strategies to meet the intended target skill; and
- set a realistic review date to evaluate the outcomes of the teaching programme.

Such a process enables teachers to gather useful information and to use their teaching skills within the classroom, where the transferability, or specificity, of newly acquired skills can be observed and reinforced.

An example of assessment through teaching would be a common primary class concern. For instance, class teacher Ms England is concerned that eight-year-old Jason's spelling of many common words is poor, when compared with most of the children in her class. She is considering ways to improve it. Firstly, she informally discusses her concerns with the SEN co-ordinator, whose first suggestion is that she check out which common words Jason can spell accurately. Ms England also tells Jason's mother of her concerns and her intended course of action.

Ms England then arranges for Jason to spend ten minutes with her at dinner-time to check if he can spell twelve common English words. She assures him that it is not a test, but a way of helping him to spell better. She finds that he can spell four of the words accurately and is almost correct with five more. She decides to teach Jason the eight words in two groups of four and sets a review date for three weeks' time. Ms England arranges to see Jason for five minutes each dinner-time and, using a variety of teaching strategies, teaches him the first four words. She also talks to his mother and asks if she, too, will help him at home and she gives teaching suggestions. After four weeks, Jason can spell all but one of the words accurately and Ms England notices that Jason is now spelling those words accurately in his story writing. The outcome is discussed with the SEN co-ordinator and Jason's mother and, as he has really enjoyed the teaching and is highly motivated, it is decided to teach him a further twenty words over the next six weeks in groups of five words at a time.

This model of assessment through teaching can be used to assess and teach many skills across the curriculum as it allows the teacher to develop and use a whole range of teaching and learning strategies and is entirely compatible with the requirements of the National Curriculum for assessment as a continuous process. The structure of the process has good generalisation potential. Furthermore, it gives good and positive feedback to both pupils and teacher, and provides quality information. However, it must also be labelled time-consuming and labour-intensive.

Nevertheless, the model can be adapted for use with a group or whole class of children provided that clear aims and objectives are set by the teacher and made clear to the children.

An example of this use of the model would be Mr Gould, who is planning a lesson on the Roman invasion of Britain for his Year Four class. He has two aims:

1 that the children will work co-operatively, in pairs; and
2 that they will begin to have some understanding of how it feels to be invaded by a foreign army.

His objectives are:

1 that the children will discuss the material he provides; and
2 that they will write a newspaper article account of the invasion from the British point of view.

Accordingly, Mr Gould collects a series of current newspaper items and, in pairs, the children discuss the headlines and learn something of the structure and tone of a typical article. They practise writing a headline and first paragraph of a particular incident. Feedback to the class from each pair enables Mr Gould to assess what he needs to teach; which strategies to use over the series of lessons; which children may need differentiated materials. Assessment and evaluation can be made of the outcome of the stated aims and objectives, as well as of the quality of the work produced. Decisions can then be made on which skills and processes need to be taught next.

DIFFERENTIATION FOR SPECIAL NEEDS IN THE CLASSROOM

The children in any classroom possess a range of skills at different levels and in different areas. The challenge of providing adequately for all of them is a concern for every teacher, however experienced. National Curriculum pressures and constraints have to be the first consideration in any classroom. In order to meet the needs of all children, differentiation is a daily necessity. The needs can be met in two ways: differentiation by preparing a range of different materials and differentiation by the outcomes from commonly used material.

Differentiation by task implies that the teacher should know each child's skills across the curriculum and prepare separate materials for groups or individual pupils dependent on their current skills in each area. Material prepared must relate to the aims and objectives of the lesson overall in order to be able to assess its outcomes.

If, for example, the aim of the lesson is to 'teach the children that different cloud formations give rise to different weather patterns' and the objectives are 'to discuss, match and label pictures of clouds following a whole class discussion', the different materials for each group need to match the overall aims and objectives and differ only in the complexity of the language and task. Giving the weaker children weather pictures to colour in, for example, is not ensuring access to that part of the curriculum being taught.

Differentiation by outcomes implies that all the children are to learn and work from the same source material or worksheets and each child is assessed on the outcome of that work. This process requires careful planning by the teacher, but once the skill is mastered it can make life in the classroom considerably easier.

Aims and objectives need to be clear and simple and the material prepared to meet the lesson's intentions. If, for example, Mrs Tempest is teaching her Year Three class about maps she might decide to prepare a lesson with two objectives:

1 the children will discuss a map of an island, in pairs, and find features, following co-ordinates; and
2 they will add some features following co-ordinate instructions.

She might start the lesson with a discussion and a class activity on co-ordinates and then organise them to work in mixed pairs. Part One of a prepared worksheet would be an exercise similar to one done as a class exercise for *all* the children to complete. Part Two of the worksheet would ask the children to draw their own map and incorporate features in certain co-ordinates. Part Three would tell the children to write an account of the process of preparing a map in this way and to describe co-ordinates. Differentiation by outcomes would involve assessing how far each child progressed on the tasks. *All* children complete Part One; *most* children complete Part Two; *some* children complete Part Three. All have been pursuing the same aims and objectives.

Grouping children to undertake these tasks, whether by input or outcomes, needs to be flexible according to the task. Children learning to spell the same words are best taught together as they can interact and reinforce each other through games etc. For most activities though, a mixture of abilities in a group enables the sharing of skills and it can include elements of peer tutoring so that children can learn from each other, given good models and a sharing of strengths and weaknesses. Recording outcomes in the classroom needs to include expected outcomes as well as those things which occur unexpectedly. Keeping a book in which observations can be written down as they occur is the simplest way to record significant, if unexpected, events. This can run alongside the school's official assessment and recording process.

Keeping accurate and detailed records of all children's progress in the classroom enables both the class teacher and SEN teacher to make decisions on any further action required. The process of ongoing assessment through teaching provides information which may be used if outside professional help is requested. Patterns and rates of learning over time will be recorded and will provide a basis for any professional discussion.

BEHAVIOURAL PROBLEMS IN THE CLASSROOM

Behavioural problems may occur as a result of a learning difficulty or a disability, such as a hearing or sight problem. They may also occur as a result of home problems. All these avenues need to be explored and weighed. The SEN teacher may suggest a particular programme of support for the child in the classroom and the same principles of assessment, teaching and evaluating are followed as for a learning difficulty. For example, a child's aggressive behaviour may be a response to being called names by his peers; it may be part of domestic patterning in that his father hits his mother; it may be frustration born of an inability to hear what the teacher is saying; it may be anger at being unable to cope with the work set. Finding the cause of the behaviour is the starting point to dealing with it.

CONCLUSION

Supporting children with special needs in classrooms can be rewarding. Systems to assess, teach and evaluate progress are essential and a whole-school approach will ensure that all staff are aware of the processes and resources available. Teaching children with learning difficulties requires the same skills as any other quality teaching, such as sensitivity, judgement, tact, empathy, understanding, patience, flexibility, good sense. The changing role of the Special Needs teacher over the last few years and the arrival of the National Curriculum ensure that all children have access to the whole range of skills and information. All children are special; many will need extra support during their school life. These needs are, almost always, best met in the classroom, with their teacher and their peers, and with information and back-up from home, as Appendix 1 indicates (see p. 87).

Section II: The educational psychologist

Jane Leadbetter

Within a busy primary school, there are many visitors who come and go: sales representatives; Local Education Authority personnel; sites, buildings and maintenance staff; parents; medical people; teachers and children from other schools; overseas experts; college students and tutors; young people on work experience. Many of the school's teachers, particularly those new to the profession, or new to that school, may have little idea of the identity or role of these visitors. Indeed, some may carry a certain mystique, and it is in this category that many would place the educational psychologist.

Even if the visit is announced on the staff notice board, the very word 'psychologist' has something of an alienating effect, and if a code is used, (as will be the case throughout this part of the chapter), such as 'EP' or 'ed. psych.', this may be even more confusing to NQTs. More unnerving for inexperienced staff might be the news that this mysterious figure, the ed. psych., is coming to sit in on one of their lessons or to assess a child within their class.

A more relaxed, and potentially more informative, introduction might occur if the ed. psych. is a familiar figure and has, perhaps, been involved in workshops with school staff or in running some in-service training. At such an encounter a new teacher might sit in on discussions with other teachers at the school, learning the language and procedures of such a meeting, and absorbing, in a non-threatening context, something of the professional relationship within which a case study is developed. The effect, perhaps, would also be to de-mystify the role of ed. psych. and to make it apparent that all professionals have their various contributions to make, in a collaborative context of partnership.

This section of Chapter 4 attempts to explain something of the approach and training of EPs; to define their relationships with practising teachers, particularly Special Needs co-ordinators; to give examples of the type of work commonly undertaken in primary schools.

With which children, then, might an EP be involved in a primary school?

A CHILD WITH LEARNING DIFFICULTIES

Depending on the amount of time the EP can spend in a school and the frequency of their visits, the EP may intervene at a range of levels with a child who has some form of learning difficulty. In many cases, the identification of children who are failing to progress satisfactorily is initiated by their class teacher, in consultation with the Special Needs co-ordinator in the school (see Section I). Normally, the chain of communication and response would be: teacher to SEN co-ordinator to Headteacher to EP. A first course of action, and one which could be entirely internal to the school, would be to check records to see whether the child is known to other services, particularly the school health service. In this way the school seeks to be assured that the child's sight, hearing and general health are satisfactory. Many a learning or behavioural difficulty can be attributed, at least initially, to some medical condition.

In the absence of a medical diagnosis, an early option is to discuss referral to a particular aid service such as specialist support teachers, speech therapists or social work agencies. Here the EP can often make proposals which the school staff would not be in a position to make, and which may be quite appropriate to help the child.

If the class teacher and SEN co-ordinator are unsure about how to plan individual work programmes for a particular child, the EP may well do some detailed planning with them, looking at what the child is currently able to do, jointly setting realistic targets, and looking at the most effective way of teaching particular skills. Once the teachers have implemented such a programme for several weeks, the EP would normally be involved in reviewing the child's progress and advising on the next set of targets.

For some children this level of intervention may not prove enough and their rate of progress or the complex nature of their problems may mean that the EP will want to see the child individually to undertake more detailed assessment. This may involve more in-depth curriculum-based assessment, perhaps involving the analysis of their decoding skills in reading, or of the problem-solving strategies they use when undertaking number work. It may also involve testing the child's cognitive skills by using intelligence tests which can provide information about other aspects of the child's performance or ability. This may include a distinction between their non-verbal skills (such as coding skills, spatial awareness) and more verbally based skills (such as comprehension tasks, vocabulary tests). Very often the EP will select from a range of materials and approaches depending on the nature of the problems and the information s/he is trying to ascertain.

Any information gained from such an assessment should provide useful directions to aid the teacher's planning. However, for some children, it may also indicate more long-term or complex learning difficulties and, in such a case, it may be that a 'formal' or 'statutory' assessment needs to be made, in the child's best interests. This is commonly referred to as 'statementing' and teachers may be aware that some children in their school hold 'statements' which detail their special educational needs and also the special educational provision which the local authority decides that the child requires.

The process by which a statement is obtained (see Appendix 2) involves seeking written advice from a number of sources about the child who is being assessed. These include:

- the child's parents;
- the child itself;
- a teacher who has recently taught the child;
- doctor; and
- an EP.

All such advice is gathered in by the LEA officer who initiated the assessment, within strict time limits, and a decision is then made as to whether or not a statement will be issued. Parents have rights of appeal at various stages of an assessment, should they be unhappy with any aspects of the procedure or with any suggested outcomes. The Code of Practice lays down, in great detail, the specific requirements of any statutory assessment.

A CHILD PRESENTING BEHAVIOURAL DIFFICULTIES

Many children are referred to EPs because their behaviour is causing concern, sometimes within the classroom, sometimes outside the class in less structured periods and sometimes in all settings. At the early stages of concern, as in the previous example, the child's name may be raised with the EP in order to discuss the obvious problems and to obtain some 'low level' advice. This may include analysing what has, and has not, been effective in managing the child's behaviour in the past and the rewards and sanctions which are available to the pupil.

A common course of action may be for the EP to sit in the class for a period of time, simply observing all the interactions within the classroom but particularly focusing on the behaviour of the pupil in question. From such observations feedback and advice can be given to the teacher about a range of factors, including:

- the layout of the room;
- the positioning and demeanour of the child;
- the apparent relationship between the child and its peers and teacher;
- the class routines and rules;
- the language and tone of the teacher;
- the lesson planning, content, and differentiation of tasks and materials.

Many of these factors are keys to reducing overall disruption in classes and therefore increasing the teacher's control and consequently the potential for learning.

Within some well-run, orderly classes there are children who find it very difficult to conform and who may require specific programmes which are designed to manage or modify aspects of their behaviour. Depending on the child's age, the EP may want to see him or her individually. For younger children it may be possible to ascertain their view of the current situation and of their own behaviour. However, it may often be very difficult for them to express their feelings or any reasons behind their behaviour, even if they knew them. Using a range of methods, perhaps involving games, drawing or tests, it is sometimes possible to gain insight into the motivating factors behind a child's behaviour. For older children, it may be that this type of initial assessment can be taken further, over a number of visits, involving counselling or further exploration of the problems and potential solutions.

As with assessments of learning difficulties, it is vital that the psychologist aims to provide the teacher with some insight, guidance or advice on handling the child in the future. In some cases it is appropriate for specific behaviour management programmes to be implemented. This may involve deciding which behaviours need to be changed; specifying what it is that the child is required to do; determining what rewards are on offer if the child meets agreed targets; identifying what sanctions will be used if the child does not comply. Recording mechanisms, such as star charts, progress sheets, home-school books or contracts, are powerful devices for improving, as well as monitoring, children's behaviour.

If a child's behaviour is extremely disruptive (see Appendix 1), or if their emotional state is making learning impossible for them, it may be that further, more 'formal', assessment is needed, in order to assess the extent of their special educational needs and to decide whether or not any special educational provision is necessary. While such an assessment is taking place, the EP, the class teacher and the SEN co-ordinator are often still working together to find effective ways of managing the child's behaviour.

TRAINING AND BACKGROUND OF EPs

The two typical cases described above have made reference to the type of approaches and the methods which EPs commonly employ. As in any profession, there is a wide spectrum of views and practices within educational psychology and these will influence the way in which an individual EP construes a problem and how they subsequently intervene. However, the training and qualifications required to become an EP are strictly regulated and all contain some common core components.

Many EPs have a first degree in Psychology or have a major component of their degree in Psychology. Others have 'boosted' the amount of psychology in their initial qualifications by taking additional first degrees or degree components. The amount of psychology studied has to meet requirements set by the British Psychological Society (BPS).

A second component is a minimum of two years' teaching experience, which usually entails acquiring a teaching qualification. Finally, it is necessary to complete successfully a professional training course, which is usually for at least one full-time year and which results in an MA. In this way it is hoped that the two disciplines of Psychology and Education are brought together to produce a psychologist who is experienced and competent in working within the field of education. For this reason, teachers should have confidence that EPs can see issues and people from the perspective of the classroom and the school, and not in isolation as 'interesting cases.'

What are the EP's roles and responsibilities within Local Education Authorities?

Although not all EPs are employed by LEAs, it is currently the case for the majority. At the present time, they are one of the few groups of professionals that LEAs are required to retain centrally and whose services cannot therefore be delegated to schools. This central retention is due, to a great extent, to the fact that EPs have had statutory duties under the Education Act (1981), since it was implemented in 1983.

The Education Act (1993) and the ensuing Code of Practice (1994) reiterate the central role of EPs in the early stages of the identification and assessment of children with special educational needs and confirms their statutory function in providing advice to the LEA, once it has been agreed that a formal assessment of a child will be undertaken. In many LEAs, the EPs are the officers who attend annual reviews of statemented children in special and mainstream schools and who can monitor the effectiveness of the provision in meeting a child's needs.

As officers of an LEA, EPs will therefore be prescribed certain mandatory duties. However, many EPs, as we shall see in the next section, feel they can work most effectively by developing relationships with the schools they cover and thereby influencing and improving the lives of a greater number of children. In the final analysis, it is the individual child and the family who are the clients for an EP and it is towards their best interests that an EP must always work.

This complex triangle of roles and responsibilities means that the EP is often an important mediator between the needs and the wishes of the child and family, the school, and the LEA. It is here that the skills of a psychologist are particularly important.

COMMON WAYS OF WORKING IN PRIMARY SCHOOLS

Patterns of service delivery

Across the country, different local authorities employ varying numbers of EPs and, although the recommended ratio is one EP to 5,000 children, many authorities employ far fewer than this. The size of the patch, together with the statutory and local requirements laid upon EPs, are two key factors that determine the level and type of work that EPs can undertake in schools. Although there is no prescribed method of service delivery, a common pattern is as follows.

Most EPs are allocated a range of schools, often geographically based, which include nursery schools, primary and secondary schools and some special schools or units. Depending on the number of schools and their other responsibilities, EPs will divide their time according to locally agreed formulae. They will then visit their schools regularly and begin to build up a network of contacts and a range of knowledge.

In primary schools this may begin with a planning meeting with the Headteacher and the SEN co-ordinator. At such a meeting, the amount of EP time available and the school's priorities for development may be discussed and then negotiation about the type of work may begin. In some schools Heads may prefer to use all the EP's time to advise teachers and to become involved with individual pupils, whereas another school may feel there are no pressing individual problems with which they require help, but they want to review their reading or behaviour policy and would like help in implementing new systems. These are two ends of a spectrum and usually Heads prefer to have access to casework and advisory work alongside development work and in-service training.

Thus, a pattern may emerge where an EP might spend the first part of a series of regular visits in discussion with the Special Needs co-ordinator (see Section I) about a range of children. Some of these may be at very early stages, where class teachers have registered concerns and are implementing programmes within the classroom. Other children may be receiving extra help and individualised educational programmes from the Special Needs co-ordinator or from visiting support services. A further group may be personally known to the EP who may be monitoring their progress.

Another common activity, during a regular primary school visit, is to talk to class teachers who have children they are concerned about and to observe in classrooms. The EP may also need to remove a child from class to work with them individually. If in-service training or development work is planned then a meeting with the Head, Deputies and relevant curriculum co-ordinators may be included in a visit.

PARENTAL INVOLVEMENT

It is important to note that the role of parents is vital at every stage of concern about a child who is experiencing difficulties (see Appendix I). Most schools do routinely discuss with the child's parents any difficulties that arise, as soon as this is possible. However, if this has not been done beforehand, it should be when outside agencies are being consulted. Although most EPs are happy to give general advice on individual pupils and are entitled to do so, it is good practice for schools to inform parents when this is happening and to seek their approval. Certainly, before a child is seen individually by an EP, parental consent would need to be gained. Without this, the EP would be unable to work individually with a child. Seeking parental consent is only the first step, however.

Most programmes of intervention, whether they are primarily focused on behaviour or learning, will be more effective if they receive backing and reinforcement from home. Therefore, parental co-operation is vital. To achieve this, parents need to be informed of what is happening with their child. This is true both at an early stage, where their child may be receiving modified programmes of work, and at much later stages, where formal assessment and alternative forms of provision may be under consideration.

Psychologists can sometimes play an important role in bringing parents and school closer together, particularly if disagreement or dispute has arisen. Often EPs will carry out a home visit to gain information about the child's behaviour at home or about the parents' perception of their child's difficulties. Parents might find it easier to discuss their worries and dissatisfactions with someone who is not from the school, but who is, nevertheless, familiar with their particular situation. For some parents, being on their own territory and not in the Headteacher's room also helps.

On occasion, an EP's work on behalf of primary school children extends beyond school, home, parents, in other ways. For some children a range of professionals may be involved and this will necessitate consultation and communication with such colleagues, often leading to case conferences. If alternative placements are being used for a child on a temporary or part-time basis then the EP will need to visit these settings and be in regular contact with them. If special school provision of some kind is under consideration for a child, then the EP may need to visit, check out, or set up visits for others in order to expedite a placement.

Finally, if a child needs to be provisionally placed elsewhere, or is permanently excluded during a formal assessment, then the EP will continue to be involved in the procedure even though the child is no longer on roll at the primary school. Therefore, for one child, the amount of direct work undertaken by the EP within that school may only be a small proportion of the overall work undertaken on that case.

What other groups of children do EPs work with?

Although this book is concerned with people in primary schools, EPs are in rather different positions from others as they have roles and responsibilities across a wide age range and with respect to a large number of different groups of children. This has advantages and disadvantages but, on the whole, it tends to add to the expertise of the EP and therefore should improve the quality of service that they are able to give.

It is useful for new teachers to know where the interests and expertise of their visiting EP lie so that they may tap into this where necessary and also so that they may be aware of the range or breadth of the job. Teachers who feel overwhelmed by children (or even one child) with learning and/or behaviour difficulties can feel neglected by EPs. Being able fully to appreciate the enormous case load and the exacting responsibilities borne by many such psychologists will assist understanding on both sides.

PRE-SCHOOL CHILDREN

EPs are involved with children from the age of two upwards. Children who have a diagnosed condition or who experience developmental delay, for whatever reason, may need to undergo a formal assessment in order to identify their special educational needs. EPs are involved in multi-disciplinary assessments and fulfil a key role in advising on the type of placement most suitable for each child. They also visit nursery schools and classes and day nurseries, particularly where there are children with special educational needs.

OTHER SPECIAL CONCERNS

Children with sensory impairment

EPs regularly visit schools and units for children who are blind or partially sighted, and also those schools and units which provide for children who are deaf or who have partial hearing. They are also involved in initial assessment and advising on placement for such children.

Children with physical difficulties

Many children with minor physical difficulties cope with little help or adaptation in mainstream schools. Others require more help and may need placement in units or schools that have specialist resources and specialist staff. EPs are called in to give advice in such situations and to contribute to assessments.

Children with general, specific and severe learning difficulties

As we have seen earlier in this chapter, EPs are involved with many children who have some form of learning difficulty. This is often of a general or moderate nature, which can be helped either within mainstream schools or within special schools or units. However, some children do have more specific learning difficulties which may only affect certain aspects of their performance, i.e. their reading or spelling. Such children are sometimes termed 'dyslexic' or exhibiting 'specific learning difficulties'. EPs are regularly involved in assessment and programme planning for these children. There are also many children who experience severe learning difficulties and these children require very careful assessment to decide on their placement.

Children with speech and language difficulties

The language development of some children is delayed and specific programmes are required to ensure that they improve as rapidly as possible. Other children suffer from disordered language which will affect their educational progress. EPs are involved in assessing, monitoring and advising such children and, in this, may include temporary or part-time placement in specialist language units or schools.

Children with emotional and behavioural difficulties

As we have seen earlier in this chapter, many of the children referred to EPs have some form of emotional or behavioural difficulty. If their placement in a mainstream school cannot be sustained they may need to be placed in a special school or unit, sometimes residentially, for a short or long period of time. Again, EPs have a specific role in this process.

Secondary age pupils

Most EPs cover a range of schools, and this will naturally include secondary schools. Although some aspects of the work are different in primary and secondary schools (particularly the number of staff with whom it is necessary to communicate), by and large the approach is similar and so the pattern of service delivery is likely to be similar.

BEHAVIOUR MANAGEMENT

Not surprisingly, many EPs run courses on behaviour management and related issues. This may include:

- developing whole-school policies;
- improving teacher–pupil communication;
- setting up home–school record books; and
- case study and simulation activities.

(See Luton *et al.*, 1991, for a host of suggestions.)

There are also, in some schools, teacher support groups which were set up to help teachers to share problems and solutions, particularly concerning behaviour difficulties. Psychologists are often involved in these and they can be very successful (see Hibbert *et al.*, 1992). Bullying and stress management are other related areas where psychologists can often contribute to in-school courses and policy development (see Besag, 1989).

CURRICULUM DEVELOPMENT

Prior to the introduction of the National Curriculum, EPs were often involved with teachers in modifying, differentiating and task-analysing curriculum areas in order to make them more accessible to children with learning difficulties. With a renewed interest in children with special needs apparent, due to their prominence in the Education Act (1993) and the Code of Practice (1994), it is likely that this type of work will have a higher profile. More specifically, EPs become involved in helping to set up reading programmes in school using a variety of methodologies such as:

- Direct Instruction (see Englemann, 1980);
- Paired Reading and Peer Tutoring (see Topping and Wolfendale, 1986; Topping, 1988); and
- Reading Recovery (see Clay, 1985).

STRESS MANAGEMENT

In some Local Education Authorities the EP's expertise is used in supporting staff in a variety of ways. This may be by providing a different ear to listen to teachers; by giving practical advice to senior management; by running support groups for staff and parents; by looking directly at issues of stress management. Some schools have felt that running courses for teachers in time and stress management saves both time and undue stress in the short and long term.

CONCLUSIONS

Alongside the array of other people with whom a primary school teacher comes into contact, the EP may seem marginal, transient and distant. It is unfortunate if this is the case and EPs should strive to avoid this. However, class teachers can take some steps to ensure that their needs are met as fully as possible and, in short, to ensure that they get the best out of their visiting EP. Here are some pointers for NQTs, which will assist effective communication:

- Find out how often and when the EP visits your school.
- Talk to the key person involved with the EP, i.e. the Special Needs co-ordinator, Deputy or Headteacher, about ways of making best use of the EP's time.
- If there is a particular issue or child to discuss with your EP, talk it over first with key colleagues in your school.
- In consultation with the school's senior management, ensure either that you have met the relevant parents or that you have talked with colleagues who have done so.
- If possible, ask for cover to be arranged for the class in order that an uninterrupted consultation can occur.
- Ensure that as much basic written information as possible is available and that you have read it carefully.
- Be as clear and objective as possible when describing individual pupils or specific situations and when defining problems.
- Accept that the EP will need to undertake a certain amount of data collection before a sensible opinion can be formed. If practical advice is not given automatically, then ask for some. (It may only be possible for the EP to give interim, low-level advice to begin with.)
- Ensure that any agreed plans or programmes are implemented as effectively as possible and record all outcomes.
- On the EP's next visit, give feedback information, as accurately and honestly as possible, on the progress of any agreed action plans.

As in any professional relationship, it takes time to build up confidence and trust. However, in many schools where EPs have worked successfully over a period of time, they can become an important part of the support structure.

REFERENCES AND FURTHER READING

Ainscow, M. and Florek, A. (eds) (1989) *Special Educational Needs: Towards a Whole School Approach*, London: David Fulton.
Besag, V. (1989) *Bullies and their Victims in Schools: A Guide to Understanding and Management*, Milton Keynes: Open University Press.

Clay, Marie M. (1985) *The Early Detection of Reading Difficulties* (3rd edn), Auckland: Heinemann.

Department of Education and Science (1981) *Education Act*, London: HMSO.

Department for Education (1993) *Education Act*, London: HMSO.

—— (1994) *Code of Practice. The Identification and Assessment of Children with Special Educational Needs*, London: HMSO.

Englemann, S. (1980) *Direct Instruction*, New Jersey: Educational Technology Publications Inc.

Hibbert, K.A., Powell, J., Stow, L.M. and Stringer, P.H. (1992) *Understanding and Managing Difficult Behaviour. Establishing Staff Support Groups*, Newcastle-upon-Tyne: Psychology Consultancy in Education.

Leadbetter, J. and Leadbetter, P. (1993) *Special Children. Meeting the Challenge in the Primary School*, London: Cassell.

Lindsay, G and Miller, A. (eds) (1991) *Psychological Services for Primary Schools*, Harlow: Longman.

Luton, K., Booth, G., Leadbetter, J., Tee, G. and Wallace, F. (1991) *Positive Strategies for Behaviour Management*, Windsor: NFER Nelson.

Topping, K. and Wolfendale, S. (eds) (1986) *Parental Involvement in Children's Reading*, London: Croom Helm.

Topping, K. (1988) *The Peer-Tutoring Handbook. Promoting Co-operative Learning*, London: Croom Helm.

Appendix 1: Establishing a profile

(Richard W. Mills, with material from Marie Nation)

As indicated at the end of the chapter, dealing adequately with special educational needs involves defining what we mean; observing a particular child in a particular context; gaining other information about that child from appropriate sources; planning a suitable programme of support and help with the collaboration of all concerned.

This appendix charts some of these stages from the point of view of a newly qualified teacher.

STAGE ONE: IDENTIFICATION

In the term preceding her appointment to a mainstream primary school, our new teacher was able to observe the Year Three class which would become her Year Four class (i.e. children aged eight years) in the new academic year. Five children were pointed out to her by the Class Three teacher as in need of special help. These children were:

- Billy – a child already being seen for severe emotional and social behaviour difficulties by the educational psychologist. Described as a delicate boy who needs a lot of love and affection.
- Adam – a child regarded as having fairly typical learning difficulties, compounded by poor speech. Vague, muddled and behind with his

work. Being helped regularly in his own classroom by a learning support teacher.

- Vanessa – a child with sickle cell anaemia and a heart condition which had involved long periods of hospitalisation. Excluded, for her own good, from physical education and swimming.
- Paula – a child with behavioural difficulties. Short temper; hurts other children; acts before she thinks; described as having a 'strange self-image.' Regularly visited at school by a member of the Behaviour Support Team.
- Christopher – a child with a visual impairment thought to affect his academic work and behaviour. Visited weekly by a teacher from the Unit for Visually Impaired Children.

STAGE TWO: OBSERVATION

In time, our new teacher would develop her knowledge of all these children, along with the other 26 in her class. However, to begin with, she selected one child for particular attention and, given the fortunate circumstances, not only of having time for observations and interviews but also being aided by collaborative and supportive future colleagues, was able to build up a useful picture which would help her for the forthcoming term and year. Here are extracts from her brief observation notes on Billy, recorded at different times:

Silent reading (ten minutes) – did not read the book in front of him at all. Remained in his seat but spent his time flicking through the pages; gazing around the classroom; playing with objects on the table; talking to several of his classmates; counting the pages of his book. Later observation of Billy reading with his support teacher, in a one-to-one situation, showed him to be much more settled and to be concentrating well.

Art (fifteen minutes) – remained on task all the time. Stayed at his table; spoke to his neighbours appropriately. Interactions with others were all task-related. Final painting was of a good standard. Obviously enjoys Art.

Physical Education (thirty-five minutes) – unusually withdrawn and unco-operative. Preferred to sit at the side of the hall and watch, sucking his thumb, rather than join in.

Maths (twenty-five minutes) – desultory interest in a worksheet on symbols. Preferred to doodle on sheet, rather than answer questions. Ended by folding sheet many times.

Assembly (fifteen minutes) – sat cross-legged on floor fiddling with his shoes for much of the time. Made reasonable attempt to join in singing.

Drama (twenty minutes) – Billy's outburst ruined much of the lesson. He attempted to inflict injury on himself in numerous ways, including biting, pulling hair, kicking, punching and generally throwing himself about. Class teacher fully occupied in trying to restrain him. Rest of the class not at all put out. Normality restored on return to classroom from hall.

Break-time (fifteen minutes) – took a new boy under his wing and spent the whole of the time walking round with him and talking.

Billy clearly has severe social and emotional behavioural difficulties and can be very volatile. He is supported by an in-school advisory support teacher for 50 per cent of the school time-table. So serious are his problems that he visits a child psychiatrist (not educational psychologist) for out-of-school support and treatment.

STAGE THREE: PARENTAL INTERVIEW EXTRACTS

Interviewer (I):   What problems does Billy have at school?

Mrs C: His main problem is that he finds difficulty in concentrating and sticking onto one subject. You can talk to him and he'll talk to you and then, suddenly, he'll just change the subject. They can't get him to sit down for very long.

I: When do you think he's at his best in school?

Mrs C: When he's working with Mrs Day. He gets more done then.

I: Do you feel he gets enough attention or too much attention in the classroom?

Mrs C: It's hard to say really, because of how he is and the paddies he throws. He's one of those children that thrives on attention. You have to be very careful how you work the attention around him, if you know what I mean. He can be very manipulative. He can get you to do what he wants to do and sort of suggest that it's your idea, sort of thing.

I: You don't feel that, if he was left to get on with his own devices, he'd get more done?

Mrs C: No. He has to have that support, that back-up. You have to make it look like it's his idea. The same thing as he does to you.

I: Is he different at home?

Mrs C: No. He's a proper live-wire at home. He's never still, and if he can't find anything to do to pass the time, he'll start winding his brother and sister up. You know, tormenting them and really bugging them, basically. Nine times out of ten, we can get him to do something that he likes to do, like drawing.

I: Do you feel that you're involved enough in Billy's education? Does the school tell you what's happening?

Mrs C: Yes. I'm lucky really. I've had a very good relationship with the school. If he's naughty, because the school knows the problems that Billy's had at home, with his father and us splitting up, they've been very understanding with him. They've always told me what they're thinking of doing with him. If they're going to try different ways of getting him to work, they always tell me. I see his class teacher at least once a week, even if it's only for a couple of minutes, just to see if he's alright. That keeps him happy because he knows we're talking about him.

I: Is the school doing enough to help Billy?

Mrs C: Yes. They've given me so much back-up. Not just with my son's problems but with my problems as well, because they know that my problems affect my son. They've given me probably 110 per cent back-up. There's been time when it's come a very close call to whether he's excluded from school because of his behaviour. When I told the Headteacher what had been going on at home with my ex-husband, he said, 'Right. Well, we'll sit down and we'll talk about it again.' Rather than push Billy out even more, rejection like, he's been there.

I: So he's making sure that home and school interact, isn't he?

Mrs C: Well, they must do. Billy's home life affects his school life a great deal. Me and my husband have been split up now for nearly seven years and ever since I had Billy his dad has never really bothered with him. There's been times when he's come over and said to him, 'Don't come near me, you're not coming with me, you're nothing to do with me.' Having said that, Billy still yearns, if you like, to see his dad. I haven't stopped him seeing him and, as long as they want to see him, they can, but I've had to go to court to get an injunction because he was coming over and causing an argument and saying all sorts of things in front of the kids.

I: Is it alright for me to talk about this with Billy?

Mrs C: Yes, if he mentions it first. He's very open. He does talk to Mrs Day and to his class teacher. He says, 'Can I go and tidy the book corner?' And she's told me that it's almost as if when he's tidying the books he's tidying his mind. After he's tidied up a bit, then he'll go and talk to her about what's bothering him. I'm not bothered who he talks to, as long as he's telling somebody, because I know I'll get to find out and help him.

I: Right. We'll take things step by step, and slowly, to prevent upsetting him.

Notes The key points for me which emerged from our conversations were:

• the strength of the partnership between Mrs Carter and the school;
• the crucial roles played by Mrs Day, the class teacher and the Headteacher;

- the home background details, as a partial explanation of Billy's behaviour;
- knowing something about Mrs Carter's own problems;
- Mrs Carter's own insights into the situation;
- the overwhelming feeling that we're all trying to do our best for Billy, despite the fact that he can drive us to distraction; and
- the daunting realisation that I'll soon be a key player in this drama. Eeek!

Appendix 2: Making a statement

(Jean Mills)

As the chapter and the 1994 Code indicate, written advice is assembled from several sources when children are being considered for statements of special educational need. Below are examples of the kinds of information which might be included. Each would, of course, give the child's name: (Angela Smith); date of birth: (19.3.89); address; names of parent(s) or guardian(s); present placement: (Park Road Reception Class); date of admission.

Parental representations and evidence

We would like Angela to stay at Park Road School. She has been very happy there and the staff know her well and have helped her a great deal. She gets on with the other children and moves about the building without difficulty.

Medical report (extracts)

Dr J. Roberts, consultant community paediatrician.
Special difficulties (over and above general health check):

1 Impaired vision – wears spectacles; attends ophthalmology out-patients.
2 Mild hearing impairment – further assessment at Park Road. Should be seen at six monthly intervals by school nurse and medical officer. School advised about seating.

Educational advice

Mrs D. Marner, teacher, Park Road Reception Class.

Parental Involvement

This referral was discussed with Angela's parents towards the end of her first year at school. They are concerned that she should have the best education possible in a 'normal' school.

Other agencies involved: Mrs C. Foster, teacher of the visually impaired; Visiting Teacher Service.

Related factors

We have discovered that Angela has very poor vision and this is now hindering further progress.

Current skills

Number/Maths: Can count to five without help. Can sort with help according to colour but not shape. Can grade five rings in size. With prompting, can match a lotto board.

Language: Has improved since wearing glasses every day. Is now using more than two/three word phrases. Articulation is mostly clear. Can follow simple instructions and is beginning to respond to stories, songs and rhymes.

Fine and gross motor skills: Is now able to ride a bike unaided and use the slide. Walks up/down stairs unaided, two feet per tread. Throws a small ball over arm, can run and stop, avoiding obstacles when wearing glasses. Can walk on tiptoe, cannot jump. Can thread beads onto a string. Is beginning to use crayons, scissors, pencils, appropriately. Uses right hand mostly. Can complete two piece jigsaw.

Attention skills: Easily becomes distracted, but periods of attention getting longer.

Self-help: Can go to the toilet unaided. Needs help with fastenings and laces.

Social skills: Improving. Now approaches other children and talks to them. Will play in the home corner and shop.

Comments: Angela learns best in one-to-one situations on an individual programme related to her needs. Has lost many days through illness.

Visiting teacher's report – visual handicap

Mrs C. Foster, teacher of the visually handicapped. Information from the Eye Department, East Park Hospital:

Angela is extremely myopic (short-sighted) in the left eye, less so in the right. Angela has nystagmus (a wobbling of the eyes which affects the ability to focus) and a right convergent squint. School advised about seating.

Observations (see school report)

Scanning: Angela can scan a group of six objects and find one the same from a group in a one-to-one teaching situation and with constant encouragement.

Near vision: Can see and pick up 'hundreds and thousands' beads. Usually works close to tasks.

Distance vision: Can identify 5 cm models up to 2 metres. Kay Picture Test indicates she can see at 6 metres what a normally sighted person can see at 60 metres.

Comments: Angela is a very short-sighted child who has missed out on much incidental learning in her early years. There are gaps in her experience and knowledge. She tires quickly as looking is hard work for her, and concentration flags. She needs opportunities to explore a wide range of everyday objects.

Psychological advice (extracts)

Janet Brown, senior psychologist.

Sensory: Angela has diminished hearing assessed at 40 db loss. This should be constantly monitored. Severe impairment of vision in both eyes.

Summary of skills: Angela does not enjoy PE and is hesitant in her movements. However, she is independent in known environments and moves about confidently. She is friendly towards adults and shows pride in her achievements. Angela is working towards recognition of letters and practises copying with help. Her writing is large but well formed.

Summary of current difficulties: Angela has a learning delay due largely to visual impairment, but with an element of general learning difficulties and possible hearing difficulties.

Summary of needs: Angela needs an individualised curriculum with small steps that will take account of her visual and learning difficulties. There should be close monitoring of her progress and a specialist curriculum for increased mobility and appropriate low vision aids.

Conclusions/recommendations: A school with facilities for children with visual difficulties with a structured curriculum. I would recommend that she is given a statement of special educational needs.

Statement of special educational needs

Angela's statement might include the following information:

Assessment of need: In identifying Angela's special educational needs the suthority has taken into account the views of the parents and the advice which has been submitted towards the assessment. Angela has a learning delay largely due to visual impairment, but with an element of general learning difficulties and possible hearing difficulties (see DFE, 1994: 85 for all the information prescribed by the Regulations).

Special provision

This should include:

1 Individualised programmes of work that will take account of her visual and learning difficulties, concentrating on literacy, number and language development. Specific aims and objectives to be identified.
2 Specialist curriculum for increased mobility.
3 Small group teaching with opportunities for individual attention.
4 Access to aids and facilities for children with a visual impairment.
5 Close liaison between school staff and home.
6 The School Medical Officer is requested to review her hearing regularly.

It would appear that Angela's needs might be met either by the Local Education Authority agreeing to employ a Special Needs assistant, in addition to the support from the Visiting Teacher Service, or by arranging transport for Angela to attend a school nearby, which has more facilities for children with visual impairment.

Appendix 3: Identification and assessment of special needs

(Jane Officer)

Flow chart to illustrate Stages 1, 2 and 3 (school-based), according to the Code (1994)

PRE-STAGE 1
(class teacher)

concern(s)

⇓

take action

⇓

review

⇓

exit or

⇓

STAGE 1
class teacher with support from SEN co-ordinator
headteacher and parents involved at all times

collect information
ATs, class records, observations, known health problems,
parents' perceptions, child's perceptions

⇓

Assessment of needs
immediate concerns
wider concerns and assets

⇓

Decision-making
continue as present
seek further advice
set individual teaching programme with aims, objectives, criteria
and strategies

⇓

Review
effectiveness of the plan
updated information
progress made

⇓

Future action
difficulties resolved   difficulties remain?

⇓   ⇓

Exit   Stage 2

STAGE 2
SEN co-ordinator takes the lead with class teacher

review all information from Stage 1
seek new information from agencies involved with the child

⇓

Assessment of needs
based on
information from Stage 1, new information at Stage 2

⇓

Decision-making
seek further advice and/or
draw up new educational plan

⇓

Individual education plan
curricular needs (setting objectives, criteria, monitoring and recording)
teaching requirements (strategies, materials, group size, timing of
supports)

⇓

Review date
may be within half a term/must be within a term;
teachers, parents, support staff involved and invited

⇓

Outcomes

⇓   ⇓   ⇓

child continues at Stage 2   child reverts to Stage 1   child moves to Stage 3

STAGE 3
school asks for external specialist help
trigger for Stage 3 is **either** a decision at a Stage 2 review **or** an initial
concern where early intensive intervention with outside support is
immediately necessary, following discussions between teacher, parents,
Headteacher and SEN co-ordinator

Roles and responsibilities are shared
SEN co-ordinator, class teacher, peripatetic teachers, educational
psychologist, health services, social services, etc.

Information required
all information from Stages 1 and 2 and report from Stage 2 review
SEN co-ordinator should discuss all information with parents, collect
and date their views and agreement to action at Stage 3

⇓

Assessment of needs
appropriate specialists take the lead in assessing needs
educational psychology service plays key role in assessing, planning
and reviewing provision

⇓

Decision-making
advice from other agencies and specialists
SEN co-ordinator and external specialist draw up teaching plan; specific
targets are set and monitored; parents informed of teaching
arrangements

⇓

Review
may be within a half-term/must be within a term; support staff,
parents, invited and involved; convened by SEN co-ordinator
focus on progress made, effectiveness of teaching plan, updated
information and advice, whether child should be referred for
statutory assessment

⇓

Outcome of review

⇓   ⇓   ⇓

child continues at Stage 3   ⇓   child reverts to Stage 2

⇓

child is referred for statutory assessment
(Stages 4 and 5)

Chapter 5

The work of a home–school liaison teacher

Jane Powell

EDITORS' INTRODUCTION

This chapter concerns a teacher who may be from the school, but is not necessarily in it all the time; who may be working in the local community, but is not necessarily from it. She (and it is often 'she' in a primary school) is variously described as the Home–School Liaison Teacher (HSLT), Cultural Liaison Officer, Community Education Teacher or Outreach Worker. The designation depends on the Local Education Authority involved, and there may be slight differences in the way each of these professional roles will be carried out.

What all such teachers will share is the maintenance of communications and relationships between the homes of the children and the school. As part of their regular commitment, the teachers will usually work with mainstream colleagues. For the other part, their role may be quite diverse, but it will always have as its focus the enhancement of children's learning through a development of home–community–school links.

A brief historical survey locates the role within that area of debate concerned with deficit models of experience, culture and language; with what were formerly called 'Educational Priority Areas'; with the child-centred philosophy of the Plowden Report, and compensatory provision.

Nevertheless, on account of her experience and time-table flexibility, the HSLT can be a vital source of information for an NQT about the locality, and about children's homes, parents and cultural background. Provision of HSLTs will be mainly in inner-city urban areas, partly because these have been identified as major areas of social deprivation, and partly for the positive reason of building links within fairly anonymous areas, with a view to encouraging greater participation of parents in the life of the school. While this may be so, one must be wary of stereotypes. There can be anonymity and poverty in rural and suburban areas, too.

As the chapter shows, wider community contacts are invaluable, wherever the school is situated, for curriculum projects and in providing genuine experiences in the form of visitors and outings. The nature of the two-way exchange needs to be appreciated. Modern primary schools are an integral part of their local community, not an oasis in the middle of it.

I'm an integral part of the school's flotsam.

(Gill, HSLT)

Monday a.m.

Meet parents as they bring their children to school and remind them about the workshop this afternoon.
Prepare tea for after Assembly, and then, when Assembly ends, take class while Head and class teacher speak to parents informally in staffroom.
Drop into play-group and English class to see parents involved, and speak to two local residents who have come in to hear readers.
Write a fund-raising application to raise money for our Toy Library.

Monday p.m.

Prepare for workshop on ways of supporting children's reading, then take the class while the teacher speaks to the group.
After school continue to make costumes for our carnival troupe with parents and children.

Tuesday a.m.

Visit local bus garage with Y5 class as part of our 'Transport' topic, and as a follow-up from a talk by a parent about his job as a bus driver.

Tuesday p.m.

Home visits to take reports to parents who did not attend parents' evening, and to invite a number to come into school to meet their child's teacher and discuss the report. Follow-up on parents who missed the workshop on reading, but said that they wanted to find out what had taken place.

Tuesday evening

Attend a residents' association meeting to discuss our efforts to get a crossing placed on a road next to the school.

Wednesday a.m.

Open and run Toy Library.
Take a parent and child to visit a special school that the child may attend.
Join in local Community Lunch to make contact with community groups in the area.

Wednesday p.m.

Prepare questions with reception class that the children will ask moms when we take groups out to visit women in their homes and at work in the local community for a topic on 'Work' and 'Jobs our Moms do'.
Take part in a Friends of the School meeting to plan our Summer Festival.

Thursday a.m.

Meet two teaching practice students. Talk about HSL work and take them round the school and the catchment area.

Thursday p.m.

Take another small group of Key Stage 2 children to local library for more material on our transport project.
Catch up on administration.

Friday a.m.

Assist with Year Three class Assembly in hall. Greet parents before and after, organising children to serve tea in the community room.
Take opportunity to talk informally with mothers to be visited by reception children on the 'Work' topic.
Review session on week's work with Head and Deputy.

Friday p.m.

Attend training session with other HSLTs on LEA community project on 'Developing the School Environment.'

It will be clear from the above schedule that the role of the Home–School Liaison Teacher (HSLT) is both interesting and diversified. Clearly, the axis of home–school is the major focus, but there is no single model for the work of HSLTs. In fact, the diversity is reflected in the titles they have been given: HSLTs/workers; cultural liaison staff; community education teachers. Despite variations in the role, the main task for these specialist teachers has been the improvement of the relationship and communications between home and school, as a means of enhancing pupil achievement.

As there is no blueprint for what constitutes good home–school relations or parental involvement, schools involved in trying to develop this area of their work may be approaching it from a wide variety of perspectives depending on the experiences, interests, needs and priorities of both school and parents. This will be reflected in the practice of the HSLT, and this invariably includes home visiting; small group mainstream teaching; pre-school provision; adult education; initiatives to encourage parents to come into the classroom or help their children at home; liaison with other agencies.

As a brief introduction to the work of the HSLT, this chapter will give an historical perspective on the development of the ideas around parental involvement in school, and the teachers whose role has been to focus on this area. It will then outline a number of activities that HSLTs may be involved with, and will end by looking at ways in which an NQT, or teacher who is new to a school, may be able to work with, or link into, the work of the HSLT.

HISTORICAL BACKGROUND

For much of the period since the introduction of compulsory schooling in Britain, education was regarded as the exclusive domain of teachers. They were seen to have sole responsibility for the education of children while parents had little or no role to play in this process once children had begun their schooling. There was a clear division between home and school 'marked symbolically by the white line in the playground which parents were not expected to cross' (Edwards and Redfern, 1988: 1). Although there were attempts to develop relationships between the two, these remained small-scale and isolated initiatives. Since the early 1960s, however, a number of reports have encouraged schools to examine the ways in which they interact with parents, in order to improve their home–school links and to develop a greater understanding.

For instance, the Newsom Report, *Half Our Future* (Central Advisory Council for Education, 1963), emphasised the need to acknowledge that the two spheres of home and school could not operate effectively in isolation from each other:

> The schools cannot do the job alone, and parents cannot delegate their responsibility for guiding their children. Many situations would be helped simply by the schools knowing more of the home circumstances and the parents knowing more of what goes on in school.
>
> (Central Advisory Council for Education, 1963: 71)

Four years after this report, the major influence on the practice of developing home–school relations was published. The Plowden Report, *Children and their Primary Schools* (1967), was based on large-scale research into the relationships between home background and educational achievement, and on the increasing number of initiatives by teachers to bring home and school closer together. It meant that, for the first time, there was official acceptance of the importance of including parents in their children's education. Plowden's recommendations were based on a straightforward sequence of cause and effect, namely school programmes to raise parental awareness leading, in turn, to enhanced pupil attainment. The Report proposed that all schools should have a programme for contact with children's homes, to include:

1　a regular system for the Head and class teacher to meet parents before the child enters;
2　arrangements for more formal private talks, preferably twice a year;
3　open days to be held at times chosen to enable parents to attend;
4　parents to be given booklets prepared by the schools to inform them in their choice of schools and the education children would receive;
5　written reports on children to be made at least once a year and the child's work seen by parents; and
6　special efforts to make contact with parents who do not visit the schools.

Although the Plowden Report made quite radical recommendations, and has remained the major influence on the study and practice of home–school relations in Britain, 'it also drew on many aspects of the conventional wisdom of the day which were subsequently questioned and found to be lacking' (Edwards and Redfern, 1988:11).

At the time the report was published, there was a widely held view that working-class children's level of achievement was adversely affected by a lack of parental interest and by the family's negative or neutral attitude towards education, which overrode other effects of school or community. Plowden concluded, therefore, that if working-class parents could be encouraged to show a greater interest and level of participation in their children's education, then the school performance of their children would be enhanced. The report did not take account of the ways in which the material, social and economic circumstances of the family may affect attitudes and involvement.

Such an approach was based on a deficit model of the working-class family, and a stereotyped view of social class, with the responsibility for the poor educational performance of many working-class children blamed on the perceived deficiencies in the families themselves rather than elsewhere. 'The evidence concerning under-achievement of working-class pupils and more recently, the under-achievement of black pupils, has been interpreted in terms of cultural deprivation, cultural difference and cultural oppression' (Williams, 1985: 333).

Such a view also perpetuated 'the parent stereotypes of staffroom mythology and folklore, with parents (particularly working-class parents) seen as a largely passive, ignorant and undifferentiated body, with a limited interest in their children's schooling, needing the enlightenment from initiatives taken by knowledgeable professionals' (Bastiani, 1987: 94). Although this deficit model has been challenged and frequently discredited since that time, the idea that part of the teacher's role was to compensate for disadvantage and 'make good' deficiencies that children bring to school has still had a powerful effect.

Compensatory ideologies stressed the importance of encouraging the families of children who were not succeeding at school to be more like those who were. The criteria that Plowden used to measure positive parental attitudes to school, which were associated with school achievement, were, to a large extent, linked to middle-class behaviour patterns. The criteria by which parents' attitudes were judged was both class-biased and ethnocentric, and variations from that norm were regarded as deficiencies, rather than accepted as valid differences.

The arrival of large numbers of black settlers in Britain coincided with the increasingly popular view of working-class family life as disadvantaged and deprived, and this label was rapidly extended to include them (Edwards, 1988).

Although schools cannot compensate for the inequalities of society, Plowden thinking, and the 'Headstart' programmes in the USA, have all been based on the premise that compensatory provision and an interventionist approach can lead to more equalised opportunities in school. However, if the material and economic situation of pupils remains the same, the long-term effects of these policies will be of only limited success.

Acknowledging this, however, does not take responsibility from the school, and should not leave teachers 'feeling absolved from their professional responsibility to educate all children effectively, . . . more research in America is now focusing on successful schooling rather than ineffective homes' (Tomlinson, 1984: 15).

The Plowden Report had recommended the setting up of Educational Priority Areas (EPAs), and the Halsey Report was an account of the action research project into their work. The research aimed to raise educational standards and extra teachers were employed to increase the efforts to involve parents in the education of their children. It moved on from Plowden by seeing curriculum development as one of the essential elements in its development programme. 'A more relevant curriculum based on the child's immediate surroundings and experience could stimulate learning and therefore improve skills as well as being enjoyable in itself and increasing his knowledge of, and involvement in, the community' (Halsey, 1972: 137).

Tizard *et al.* found that, even after fifteen years, there was still a lack of consensus as to what constituted parental involvement in school:

> To some teachers, it meant the active presence of parents within the school . . . . To others, it implied that parents were involved in the management and decision-making processes. . . . Still others meant little more by the term than that parents were energetic and generous in raising funds.
>
> (Tizard *et al.*, 1981: 4)

The authors found that the different interpretations could be related to ideas about which group the involvement was intended to benefit: the teachers, parents or children. The strategies adopted would also be affected by the way in which the school regarded the parents. If a deficit model was adopted there would be a 'top down' approach, with the professionals passing information to the parents, but failing to acknowledge the expertise of the community. It would emphasise negative rather than positive experiences and would not lead to the pupils' background and culture being reflected in the curriculum. If, however, the school had come to recognise and value the skills and expertise which existed within the community, it would need to begin to develop new ways of enhancing parental involvement, as well as examining the implications this had for curriculum development.

In more recent years there has been a much greater interest in the development of positive links between parents, the community and schools, and this is reflected in the growing numbers of books on the subject (see Further Reading, p. 109).

Whether or not they have a HSLT, schools have come to realise the importance of a two-way communication process with parents and the community so that the school is more aware of, and responsive to, the issues that affect parents and the needs of pupils. In turn, parents are more aware of what is taking place in schools and are therefore more equipped to support their children's learning. The more informed parents are, the more confident they will be to take part in the life of the school, to ask questions, and to put forward their views. This may be done informally at casual encounters or more formally, either through their representatives on the governing body or at the annual governors–parents meeting.

Parents, then, are increasingly seen as contributors to the school by sharing their skills, knowledge and resources. This enables them to be viewed in a more complementary role as partners with teachers, and to have their contributions acknowledged, valued and built on through a curriculum made more relevant to the particular needs of their children.

To bring this about, the school needs to re-examine that curriculum as a means of utilising these resources and, in turn, to open up its resources for use by the community. For this to happen, teachers need to be willing to become more familiar with the children's backgrounds, and acknowledge that parents and the community have a wide range of skills, interests and knowledge to complement those of the teachers. In such a way, Plowden's child-centred philosophy is richly enhanced.

With the introduction of the National Curriculum, the development of improved home–school links may be seen as yet another additional pressure that teachers have to take account of. However, key elements of the National Curriculum include:

> The principle that each pupil should have a broad and balanced curriculum which is also relevant to his or her particular needs . . . .
> That principle must be reflected in the curriculum of every pupil. . . .
> The curriculum must also serve to develop the pupil as an individual, as a member of society and as a future adult member of the community with a range of personal and social opportunities and responsibilities.
>
> (DES, 1989)

This means that the development of closer links with the community can be presented in terms of implementing the National Curriculum more effectively by utilising community resources and relating the curriculum to the experiences of pupils and parents, while at the same time fulfilling another of its aims, that of keeping parents better informed of what is taking place in school. Such an approach is also good child-centred practice, as it aims to start from, and build on, the child's experience. How much better if the class teacher can bring a subject to life by using the child's experiences and language and by showing the value the school attaches to such things by using them in the classroom. For this to be really effective, however, the whole school needs to be involved. The approach needs to permeate all areas of school life, with the issues being addressed by every teacher following a written policy. Those schools with a HSLT are well placed to implement the policy, within the context of the School Development Plan.

Home–School Liaison Teachers were initially seen as problem-solvers, as missionaries charged with the task of educating families who, it was felt, lacked the necessary skills to encourage their children to succeed in school. Such a view of the parents and the community meant that their skills and experiences remained unacknowledged by the school. Since then, however, there has been a considerable change in the way the home backgrounds and languages of working-class and black children are regarded by schools; multi-cultural/anti-racist educational ideas have influenced the practice of many teachers, who have come to hold positive attitudes:

The negative notion of cultural deprivation, built into early versions of compensatory intervention, is rejected in favour of a positive definition of the educational potential of home, neighbourhood and local culture. The emphasis is, therefore, on active educational partnership at the local level, the importance of which is now widely recognised at all levels of this compulsory education system.

(Martin, 1987: 25)

CURRENT PRACTICE

What, then, might a newly qualified teacher expect to find in a school which either has a HSLT or which takes seriously its responsibility within and towards the local community?

Job descriptions vary, but the major purpose of the role is to link home and school, and encourage/increase parental involvement by extending parents' knowledge and understanding of school practices and the part they have to play in their child's development, so that they can use their skills to support his/her learning as a way of enhancing achievement.

The way in which different home–school links practitioners approach their work will be determined, to a great extent, by the details of their job descriptions. These might include:

- encouraging parents to become more involved in the life of the school and their children's learning through home visiting and the development of appropriate information and material, and the setting up of parents' groups, workshops, and classes for adults;
- building closer links with the community and organisations in the area;
- enhancing teachers' awareness of parental contributions to the education of their children, supporting them in their efforts to involve parents in school life, and encouraging them to use external resources which exist in the community in their classrooms; and
- supporting whole school change through policy development and the sharing of good practice.

While such premises may underpin the job description of any HSLT, each will act according to personal strengths and school requirements. In any event, little could be achieved by one person acting alone and any individual needs the back-up and support of the school management team and of the whole staff. The presence of a HSLT does not absolve other teachers, including NQTs, from their community and family responsibility; it merely serves as a focus for that endeavour (see Wolfendale, 1992: 74).

Any HSLT new to a school would initially be involved in discovering:

- the initiatives that the school had already taken to extend parental involvement;
- how parents were informed about the curriculum;
- how they were involved in their children's learning in and out of school;
- how the community was involved in the school;
- how these resources were used in the curriculum, and what parents said they wanted;
- whether there was a Parent Teacher Association and, if so, how it functioned;
- which existing staff had most experience of the parents and the community; and
- who were the most appropriate people to make contact with.

Having discovered this information, the new HSLT may then move on to find out what people would like to happen. This information may be sought both informally and through a more formalised audit using a set of questions or a questionnaire for staff and parents. An activity for individual teachers may be to ask them to log their interactions with parents:

1 Which parents did you speak to yesterday, and what about?
  a)
  b)
  c)
  d)
2 How often do you normally communicate with parents during the school day?
  a) number of times:
  b) face-to-face; by phone; letter; message; any other.
3 How many parents of the children in your class do you recognise by sight?
4 How many of those parents do you know by name?

Note that the purpose of such a questionnaire is not only to elicit information, but also to alert colleagues to possible action.

From the information gained, the HSLT should be able to see the most appropriate points on which to focus her attention, while attempting to identify the factors which may constrain or enable the implementation of any initiatives. These may include:

- the school's ethos;
- the degree of support likely from the Head and staff;
- the school's previous HSLT experience;
- the existing level of parental involvement;

- the school building – its accessibility; how welcoming it appears; whether there is a waiting area, community room, space for parents in school;
- the school's catchment area – do parents have to travel from long distances or have little experience of coming out unaccompanied?; and
- the size of the budget available for implementing initiatives.

Some activities encourage initial contact between home and school: a jumble or car boot sale or other fund-raising event; trips; assemblies with coffee to follow; parents' evenings. Others develop those contacts or focus them on a particular issue:

- the introduction of a PTA;
- curriculum and pastoral workshops (e.g. on Reading, Maths, Science, computers, or behaviour, truancy, social education);
- environmental awareness raising (for instance, one particularly extrovert HSLT came to school dressed in an enormous dinosaur costume and gallumped around the playground 'eating' litter);
- home learning activities (for example, the use of commercially produced schemes such as 'Pact' for Reading; 'Impact' for Maths; 'Ships' for Science);
- help in classes (for example, with reading, art work, cookery, games, technology, topic work: for a project on the Second World War, one grandparent offered her experiences as 'Genuine Evacuee');
- assistance with extracurricular activities (such as visits, residential experience, clubs, sports teams); and
- adult education classes (e.g. literacy; English as a Second Language; Keep Fit; assertiveness; 'Fight Stress with Aerobics').

The HSLT's responsibility is to build on existing strengths and develop new initiatives, as appropriate. Parental involvement should not, however, always be equated with the number of adults in school; it is often more concerned with building a sense of belonging and of feeling valued, so that parents believe that their skills and contributions are acknowledged and acted upon by the school. An example of this is parental involvement in learning at home, which is an expanding area. It develops communication between home and school and enables parents to participate to a greater extent in their children's learning but may not necessarily result in their being seen in school any more often.

Whatever forms the involvement takes, all mainstream teachers and volunteer parents need to be quite clear of their respective roles, or where responsibilities start and stop. It is here that the HSLT may have a contribution to make, in an informal manner, to accompany the more formal guidance at meetings and through letters. As part of her home visits (e.g. to inform of good work; meet new parents; advise on special needs; advertise events; explain procedures), she is often able to develop the kind of informal yet professional relationship which is invaluable. On occasions, she may take a mainstream teacher with her, and it ought to be part of the induction programme of all NQTs to make half a dozen such home visits, with a more experienced partner. In such a way, the worlds of home and school come together, to the benefit of all. In any event, many HSLTs have a teaching commitment of up to 50 per cent and need to see the unity inherent in their dual role.

In following her own teaching role and in acting collaboratively in planning work with colleagues, the HSLT will become aware of, and pass on information about, a wide range of provision in the local area. Such contacts may include:

- other educational establishments;
- recreational/sports establishments and community centres;
- community/residents' groups;
- advice centres and support agencies;
- health centres and health workers;
- city departments – neighbourhood offices, social services, urban renewal, environmental services, road safety;
- police, fire, ambulance services;
- religious groups;
- councillors and the MP;
- the library; and
- shops and industry.

The HSLT may share material with her immediate teaching partners, but may also act as a resource provider for other teachers. Depending on her experience and areas of expertise, she may also be able to provide in-service training for staff about her role and the ways in which she is able to support colleagues in their efforts to increase parental involvement.

Schools who are able to employ a Home–School Liaison Teacher are fortunate. Those less endowed will need to find other ways in which to strengthen their relationships with home and parents. There may be no HSLT, but the functions of one remain. Experienced teachers are well aware of this, but it takes time for many newly qualified teachers to see beyond the immediate concerns of their classroom. That is understandable. However, when they do reach out into the local community, with the guidance of colleagues, their pupils will become real people, with real homes and real other lives. Realising this, they will be better teachers.

FURTHER READING

Atkin, J. and Bastiani, J. (1988) *Listening to Parents*, London: Croom Helm.
Bastiani, J. (1989) *Working with Parents: A Whole-School Approach*, Windsor: NFER-Nelson.

Edwards, V. and Redfern, A. (1988) *At Home in School: Parent Participation in Primary Education*, London: Routledge.
Griffiths, A. and Hamilton, D. (1987) *Learning at Home: The Parent, Teacher, Child Alliance*, London: Cedar.
Stacey, M. (1991) *Parents and Teachers Together*, Milton Keynes: OUP.
Wolfendale, S. (1992) *Empowering Parents and Teachers*, London: Cassell.

REFERENCES

Bastiani, J. (ed.) (1987) *Parents and Teachers: Perspectives on Home–School Relations*, Windsor: NFER-Nelson.
Central Advisory Council for Education (England) (1963) *Half Our Future*, London: HMSO.
DES (1989) *From Policy to Practice*, London: HMSO.
Edwards, V. and Redfern, A. (1988) *At Home in School: Parent Participation in Primary Education*, London: Routledge.
Halsey, A.H. (ed.) (1972) *Educational Priority*, Vol. 1, London: DES/HMSO.
Martin, I. (1987) 'Community education: towards a theoretical analysis' in G. Allen and J. Bastiani (eds) *Community Education: An Agenda for Educational Reform*, Milton Keynes: OUP.
Plowden Report (1967) *Children and Their Primary Schools*, London: HMSO.
Tizard, B., Mortimore, J. and Burchell, B. (1981) Involving Parents in Nursery and Infant Schools: A Source Book for Teachers, London: Grant McIntyre.
Tomlinson, S. (1984) *Home and School in Multicultural Britain*, London: Batsford.
Williams, J. (1985) 'Redefining Institutional Racism', *Ethnic and Racial Studies* 8, 3, July.
Wolfendale, S. (1992) *Empowering Parents and Teachers*, London: Cassell.

Part III

Other adults as colleagues

Chapter 6

A classroom assistant

Jean Mills

EDITORS' INTRODUCTION

As other chapters in this book indicate, it is not unusual, from time to time, to find more than one adult in a classroom full of children. Some of these people are fully qualified professionals, such as NNEBs (certificated by the Nursery Nurse Examination Board) or special needs care assistants to help disabled children. Some are there by virtue of experience and personal qualities, such as parents, voluntary workers, secondary school pupils on work experience. Some are students in training, whether for teaching itself or for child care or social services. The point here is that, while all could be regarded as classroom assistants, they each have different skills and abilities and needs and, above all, backgrounds. It is this background, whether of educational qualification or practical expertise, which needs to be taken into account during negotiations to determine the nature of the work undertaken. A newly qualified teacher may find herself working alongside an older, more mature, assistant colleague, and may need to adjust to such teamwork.

This chapter describes the work of a classroom assistant who performs all the usual tasks, but has additional skills.

Mrs Virdi offers the extra dimension of being bilingual (in English and Punjabi). The intention of the chapter is not only to show how such specific expertise may be used, but also to suggest that many other classroom assistants may have particular interests and talents which could benefit children's education but which may be overlooked in the concentration on everyday skills. All classroom assistants need social, interpersonal, manual skills; some may have specific knowledge of archaeology, book-binding, computers, cookery, music, painting; most have detailed knowledge of the school locality, history and clientele.

Here is a perspective on this issue, through the work of Mrs Virdi, a 36-year-old woman of East African origin, working with Mrs Holmes, a 25-year-old teacher in her first year of teaching.

We need to have respect for each other. They're the qualified teacher and I'm the classroom assistant. I've got twenty years' experience. I'll respect them, but they must respect me.

(Jean Reynolds)

The setting is a medium-sized primary school in the suburb of a large city. The immediate area of the school consists of large, three-storey, late Victorian houses, most of which are smart and in a good state of repair. The school, dating from the 1970s, is one-storey, designed in a semi-open plan, with shared painting and water areas between classrooms. With such a style of architecture, collaboration between teachers is not only desirable but virtually inevitable.

I am here to spend the morning with Mrs Virdi, the bilingual classroom assistant (BCA). Mrs Virdi has worked at the school for two years, having completed the Bilingual Communicators' course at a local college of further education. She came to England from East Africa in 1968 when she was 11, and is bilingual in Punjabi and English.

It is now 9.10 a.m. on a dry autumn day, three weeks before Christmas. Here in the reception class Mrs Holmes, the class teacher, and Mrs Virdi are greeting children on arrival. It is a joint activity and the two adults work in concert. Mrs Holmes sits in the book area, near her desk, and children are settling themselves on the mat by her. Mrs Virdi is acting as gatekeeper, standing at the edge of the classroom area and collecting the children's reading books, commenting to each one as she does so.

'Come on, Daniel, you're late. Go and sit down . . . . You're going to do lots of work today . . . . Janice, you've got your book . . . . Come on, Joshua and Sandeep. Ah, not now, we're not in the PE hall now.'

She chats in Punjabi to parents and to children while collecting money, but comments in English to Mrs Holmes, 'Mommy's gone away some-where, dad told me.' She fastens a child's hair, saying, 'Tikka?' ('OK?'), as she finishes.

Mrs Holmes calls the children to order, 'If you're not sitting nicely I don't think Mrs Virdi will choose you', and says to Mrs Virdi, in a tone indicating non-public use of voice, 'Three's enough, I think.' The state-ment is a combination of injunction and suggestion which, by its apparent open-endedness, would not offend. This highlights the sensitivity needed by adult colleagues in their communications with each other, so that neither feels unduly threatened or powerless.

Mrs Virdi takes two girls (Hanifa and Asha) and a boy (Sundeep) to the painting area, where they will make collage figures of themselves on card, using material from a bag of scraps, while the rest of the class goes to Assembly.

As she works with the children Mrs Virdi moves smoothly between

English and Punjabi, interspersing instructions and specific teaching points, as this extract indicates (Punjabi is in italics).

Mrs Virdi (MV):   *Face. It's a face, isn't it?*
Child (C):   (nods).
MV: *What sort of things are there on a face?*
C: Eyes.
MV: There's eyes. *What else is there?*
C: Nose.
MV: *There's a nose. Hanifa, what else is there?*
C: Mouth.
MV: Mouth, well done. *Mouth isn't it?* (Note 'mouth' also translates as 'face' in Punjabi.)
C: (nods).
MV: *What's a face/mouth?*
C: (points).
MV: Yes. *OK, first let us make all our things. Wait a minute, where's the black pen? I'll go and get the black pen.* What colour's this?
C: Black.
MV: Black. *What do you call this in Punjabi? Do you know what you call it in Punjabi? What do you call it? What colour is it? Like this. If we write with this, which colour will it make?*
C: Green.
MV: *OK, what colour is this? This is* brown. *What colour is this?*
C: Black.
MV: Black black. *Black, isn't it? What do you call it in Punjabi?*
C: (whispers) *Black.*
MV: *Black,* that's right. *OK* now, can you draw me all the things you see on a face? You just say the thing.
C: Eyes.
MV: Eyes.
C: Nose.
MV: Nose.
C: Mouth.
MV: Mouth. Nicely, because this is for, we're going to put it on a card, so Deepa *make it nice, nice, OK? Make it nice. Where the eyes, where are we going to put the eyes? One eye here. . .*
C: *Here, here, here.*
MV: *Yes, one eye here, one eye here.*
C: Mouth, neck, neck, neck.
MV: *This is* the neck *isn't it?* The neck will *come here on the face,* under the face. Deepa, you make it.

At other times, as here, incidental conversation about the children's lives occurs.

C: *I went doctor.*
MV: *What happened? Did you go to the doctor?*
C: (nods).
MV: *And what did your doctor do? Did he check your ear?*
C: (nods).
MV: *Are your ears alright?*
C: (indistinct, child explains about the doctor).
MV: *And what did you say?*
C: (muffled).
MV: *Who went with you?*
C: Nobody.
MV: Nobody went?
C: No. What's this?
MV: Have you done that? Now what colour trousers do you want to wear?

The rest of the class now returns from Assembly, ahead of Mrs Holmes, and Mrs Virdi again reinforces the positive code of the school, while continuing with her group, 'Walk, please. Let's see who's sitting down really nicely. Oh, Amal, well done.'

While Mrs Holmes sits the children on the mat to practise Christmas songs, Mrs Virdi finishes the collages with Hanifa, Asha and Sundeep, explaining to children from the next class who pass by, 'Do you know what we're making?'.

C: A man.
MV: No, we're making all the children in our class. We're going to make shoes and clothes.

Sundeep finishes and Mrs Virdi points out the parts of the picture, which shows his clothes, his skin, hair and shoes, saying to him, 'Can you put it up there to dry?'. As Asha and Hanifa finish, the group copies the rest of the class in singing 'Over all the roof tops', 'Jingle Bells', and 'When Santa got stuck up the chimney'. Asha shows me her finished card and smiles shyly, to be followed by Hanifa, who has noticed this spare adult. Under the direction of Mrs Virdi they tidy up and wash, and Mrs Virdi puts the painting corner back in order.

It is now 10 o'clock and Mrs Virdi sits with another four children who are writing their own stories in small booklets made with two pieces of paper stapled together in the middle. She asks each child in turn for their story. For one, it is Fireman Sam; for another, a jungle with dragons. Two of the less confident children ask for help with drawing their pictures, and, in fact, later Mrs Virdi holds the hand of one and helps him.

As before, Mrs Virdi fulfils several tasks at once. She talks to Sandeep about her story, discovering that it is about the jungle. What kind of jungle is it? One with big trees. Later we discover that this dragon has been ill but, 'He's alright now.'

MV: How did he get alright?
C: Mommy. (So Mrs Virdi writes a sentence in the child's book: 'Mommy helped the dragon to get better.')

However, on the next page there is a television. Mrs Virdi: 'I thought you said he was in the jungle?' 'No on television,' is the reply. Mrs Virdi's enquiry, 'Is he happy now?', helps Sandeep produce the last sentence for the book: 'The dragon is happy and watching television.'

Similarly, with other children in her group Mrs Virdi draws out the story using Punjabi. Thus, to me Sandeep can only indicate that her story is about a shop. To Mrs Virdi, on the other hand, it is revealed that Sandeep went shopping with her mother and bought lots of different foods, such as rice, daal, tomatoes, peas, rice crispies, baked beans, onions. She puts the title: '"Going shopping", by Sandeep'. This is clear evidence of how the specific knowledge or expertise of an assistant can sometimes add that extra dimension to classroom work.

At the same time, other children from different groups approach Mrs Virdi to show her what they are doing. So, Sarita comes with a plastic flower she has made. Mrs Virdi comments: 'Oh, Sarita, what's that? Lovely. Go and make a different flower.' Ranjit arrives: 'Mrs Virdi, look what I made, an aeroplane.' Mrs Virdi's reply, 'You went to India, didn't you?' leads to a short conversation about the aeroplane Ranjit went on.

It is now break-time and Mrs Virdi, from her position with her group, encourages children to tidy up the plastic shapes and sort out the hospital role-playing area, while exhorting the writing group to colour in their pictures for crisp time so they can continue after play.

Mrs Virdi then leaves for the staff room to have a short break and to make tea. Whoever makes staff-room tea and coffee is bound to be popular; many classroom assistants do this job, but some schools vary the procedure on grounds of fairness and maximising contact with children. The way in which any school organises such matters reveals much about its hierarchical structure. What are perceived as ancillary tasks can denote the status of those who perform them.

During playtime, while the teachers have their break, Mrs Virdi is available for first aid for playground casualties. However, since accidents often happen inconveniently, this can be a task for all teachers at some time or another, even though a specific person has been identified. Again, each school will have its own procedures, both for location of medical equipment and nominated personnel. Each member of staff needs to know all the ground rules.

At this point, Mrs Virdi and I discuss her role in school and her use of her mother tongue.

In line with general school policy that a mother tongue should be valued, Mrs Virdi felt that 'on the ground' she decided when it was most appropriate. Therefore, she continually adjusted according to the situation and the child. She pointed out to me that Sundeep had insisted on replying to her Punjabi with English, and speculated that possibly this was due to his embarrassment, not wanting to be different from other children. As a result, for some children their ability in their mother tongue was declining because of their perception of the importance of English. Over time, this would inevitably result in cultural loss.

For herself, she felt it was important to highlight the value of Punjabi in school by using lettering and having books in Punjabi available so that the children realised that their language was not inferior. New children were surprised and pleased to meet someone they could immediately communicate with. When asked if she received in-service training, it emerged that Mrs Virdi was not appointed under Section 11 (whereby the government pays a substantial part of the salaries of professionals working with New Commonwealth people). Consequently, she was, in fact, outside the LEA's in-service arrangements. This would be in line with HMI findings that a BCA's expertise was usually acquired through induction or on-the-job training (1992:2). In Mrs Virdi's case she also had her Certificate as a Bilingual Communicator.

As far as planning went, Mrs Virdi stated that Mrs Holmes discussed with her in the morning what they would do, either on a daily basis, or picking up the work from the previous day. She now felt so used to the situation that 'it has become natural to me to fit in everything'. The amount of planning which classroom assistants are involved in varies from school to school and time to time. Some assistants would merely respond to direction; others would take part in negotiations.

It is now 11.05 a.m. and the children come back in. Memoona, Sandeep, Waqas and Zubair return to the table with Mrs Virdi and continue writing their books. Mrs Virdi talks in Punjabi to the boy who wanted help with his drawing, and supports him by questions and prompts, holding his pencil with him, feeding in vocabulary for parts of the body in English and Punjabi. In spite of this, Sandeep interrupts her in English, saying: 'Look, I done now. I done it, Mrs Virdi.' Mrs Virdi switches to English to reply, 'Oh, well done, that's lovely. What about finishing this writing? You didn't finish this writing. Do you think you can be very clever and finish that as well? . . . I'll give you a pencil.' She comments on Sandeep's drawing: 'You're not rubbing like that. You're being very careful. You're not going outside the lines.' Sandeep replies: 'I'm being very careful.' 'You're being very careful and that's good.' The English language repetition is, clearly, not coincidental.

However, when talking about Sandeep's picture, Mrs Virdi uses Punjabi to expand the response, and sums up with an English sentence, 'So you put lots of things in the basket?', and reads the English as she writes: 'We put lots of things in the basket.' Sandeep's book continues, 'There were only a few things left in the shop,' and to Sandeep again, 'Sandeep came back home, heh?'. Helping with the writing, Mrs Virdi uses the formula from a television programme, 'All the way round, up and down again' then switches into Punjabi within which some of the 'Letterland' phrases can be heard . . . 'Dippy Duck'.

Turning to Waqas, she helps him with his Fireman Sam story in a similar way, writing and intoning: '"Fireman Sam", by Waqas. That's Fireman Sam?'. Waqas puts his pencils behind his ears and comments to Mrs Virdi who turns to me to explain, 'He's going to be a carpenter.'

Meanwhile a Sikh boy approaches to have an apron put on and Mrs Virdi speaks to him in Punjabi:

MV:	*Last week you weren't here. Were you not well?*
C:	(shakes his head).
MV:	*What was wrong?* (pause). *What was wrong? Tell me. What was hurting you? What was hurting you?*
C:	(inaudible).
MV:	*Was your stomach hurting? Was your mouth hurting? Were your arms hurting? Were your legs hurting? Tell me where?*
C:	(mumbles).
MV:	*Hey?*
C:	(mumbles).
MV:	*What?*
C:	(mumbles).
MV:	*What was hurting?*
C:	Back.
MV:	*Was your back hurting? Aah, it must still be hurting.*

Turning to me she says in English, 'Did you see that reaction? He's looking at you and I'm asking him in Punjabi. Looking at you, he won't reply in Punjabi: he kept on looking at you and he wouldn't reply.' The adult interpretation of child behaviour is helpful, and in this context very helpful, but not without its dangers; body language can be deceptive.

Mrs Virdi then helps Zubair: '"Fire", by Zubair. What happens to your policeman?'. Zubair: 'He's dead.' She writes for him, and again intersperses English and Punjabi. 'The p-o-l-i-c-e-m-a-n wears a blue hat. Oy, Zubair. *Look. The policeman you know the thief? He goes into the shop, yeah? And then the policeman catches him.* The p-o-l-i-c-e-m-a-n catches the . . . . He puts them in prison? H-e puts, . . . You *look here. I'm doing your work, why are you looking over there? He puts them in jail. So that meant you're right.* The po-lice-man goes home. OK, take your pencil and can you write over my writing?'.

Zubair completes the task and shows his work to Mrs Virdi, who responds: 'Did you do that? It's wonderful. We've been practising our names and he did that by himself. You are getting a very, very clever boy. Well done.' She then takes him, as reward, to put up a point by his name on the class chart. To be really effective, any school policy, and particularly one involving rewards, needs the acceptance and practical endorsement of all staff, teachers and assistants so that there is consistency of approach.

Noticing that one of the children in the hospital is dragging the doctor's coat about the floor, Mrs Virdi comments, 'Nadia, everybody's been walking on that floor. You'll get germs and make all your patients ill. You don't want to do that do you? Can you pick that up, please. Good girl, I'll have it.'

Then she looks at her watch and announces, 'I think it's tidying up time?' The use of 'I think,' mirroring Mrs Holmes' words earlier, indicates a language style common to both teacher and assistant. Where this is not the case, the potential for friction between two adults in the same classroom would be enormous.

Mrs Virdi moves around, exhorting children to tidy up, and, as she does so, begins singing, 'Everybody sit down, sit down, sit down, everybody sit down, sit down, sit down, just like . . . .' Children deserving points are praised and Mrs Virdi becomes surrounded by children showing their work and claiming points. Mrs Virdi goes from table to table tidying up, helping children to pick up counters, and shepherding those who remain towards the carpet, where Mrs Holmes begins counting as an incentive for children to sit down.

'1 . . . 2 . . . 3 . . . 4 . . . 5 . . . . Sundeep, Jamie, everybody looking at me, everybody.' Joshua is rewarded for tucking in his chair, Shaun for trying hard with the tidying up. It is now time to organise the children for dinner. Some are chosen to go to the toilet. Equipment is taken off a child who is fiddling. Then badges are handed out to those who have meat, or no meat, or no beef. The dinner children queue and Mrs Virdi supervises them and the 'home' children on the carpet.

'Sit down properly, show Mrs Holmes. If you talk to me properly I might answer you, Suneal. Please, Narinder, cross your legs. Sit up nicely. Come on, Bonita, show everyone what a nice girl you are.'

Sisters and brothers arrive to collect home children and the last few sit waiting. Waqas traces a letter and, as reinforcement of the 'Letterland' figures, Mrs Virdi asks: 'What letter is that, Waqas?'. 'Annie Apple.' 'How do we do Annie Apple?'. Mrs Holmes joins in, 'How do we do Clever Cat?'.

Zubair's sister takes him off, and Mrs Virdi's question, 'How many sisters is that, Waqas?', leads her and Mrs Holmes into a discussion about the two families and whether Zubair's mother had been in hospital to have a baby or for some other reason, and about Sundeep and how excited he gets. Now Mrs Virdi's own son from another class arrives and her morning ends as she takes him home for lunch.

REFLECTING ON THE MORNING

When I read over this description and asked myself, 'What is Mrs Virdi's role in this classroom?', the first answer was: she enhances the job of the teacher. By this I meant to imply that she improved its value, attractiveness and quality. In the words of HMI, 'non-teaching staff enable . . . teachers to fulfil their professional roles more effectively . . . the work of these staff is so valuable that important aspects of teaching and learning would be curtailed without their help' (1992: viii).

Ideally, of course, that is what one would hope for and, in a variety of ways, this is what Mrs Virdi does. How does it occur and within what parameters does she work? Three at least are apparent:

- the school's policy and ethos;
- Mrs Virdi's role as bilingual assistant; and
- her own personal style.

Linking the three is the notion of interpreter, and in this role she operates in several ways.

First, of course, for several children she is the bridge between home and school; she interprets the world of school for them and their parents; she performs a reciprocal function for the school.

This was literally true at the beginning of the morning, when Mrs Virdi acted as 'gatekeeper', on the threshold of the classroom, enquiring about a mother's absence and new babies. Later, while chatting incidentally, she learned about visits to the doctors, and, at the end of the morning, she and Mrs Holmes pooled information on one particular child.

Obviously, a similar function would be performed by any classroom assistant, particularly since many would live near the school and, therefore, have local knowledge. Mrs Virdi lives within walking distance and her own child, it will be remembered, goes to the school. In such a situation, she would be constantly on the receiving end of all the school's written and oral communications. Moreover, as part of the staff, she would be in the position of needing to respect confidentiality concerning certain staff-room information about local families.

Many classroom assistants would live near their own schools. They would all also carry out such supportive functions as: tidying up; assisting with display; reinforcing discipline; supporting the learning of children. However, for bilingual people, there is an extra dimension. Because they are often called upon to translate for teachers they may experience sensitive or confidential situations. Mrs Virdi herself commented that parents confided in her, and that she had to sort out confusions when information had not been correctly conveyed.

For example, assistants cited situations such as being asked to translate during cases of suspected child abuse, or conveying to parents that their child was to be statemented, with a view to finding a place in a special school. In this latter case, the assistant felt that one difficulty was the Punjabi translation of 'special school' which sounded too severe. Later, a parent had berated the assistant as if she had been part of the decision making. Similarly, assistants may have the experience on Parents' Evening of hearing complaints about the teacher in Punjabi, as the teacher herself waits to be told what is being said. It is not surprising that sometimes, as one assistant pointed out to me, they are apprehensive when they hear the phrase, 'Come and translate', and that they adjust their role accordingly. In the case cited, this was by being neutral, 'staying between the school and the parent'.

In the same way, when acting as the link between the home and the school, BCAs are continually forced into translation choices. How do you translate the phrase 'mathematical concepts'? Again, when trying to persuade a mother to stay with her crying child, you have replaced 'traumatic' with 'upset', have you really adequately conveyed the child's distress?

Dilemmas are frequent. BCAs suggest that they are often the bridge between cultures, whether or not they wish to be. For example, they may have to explain aspects of the education system, particularly for parents of early years children who feel that too much 'playing' goes on. Alternatively, BCAs may well be the only colleagues who have first-hand knowledge of particular cultures, customs, beliefs, dress and diet.

While such information might be invaluable, the difficulty of conveying the nuances of one culture to another should not be underestimated. British-born professionals might like to ask themselves how they might discuss the differences between children living in inner city areas with those in rural areas; the religious dimensions of the conflict in Northern Ireland; or the origins of Christmas customs, without distortion by generalisation or stereotyping.

In the classroom it was clear that Mrs Virdi worked within the ethos and practices of her particular school and reflected its values to the children. So, for example, several times she conveyed the notion that school is for work; that children need to be punctual; that completing work, trying hard, 'sitting nicely', are all praiseworthy; that good effort is rewarded. It was noticeable how many times that morning Mrs Virdi supported the school's positive policy: 'well done . . . lovely . . . clever girl . . . . good boy'.

In such ways, she obviously fulfilled many of the functions traditionally associated with classroom assistants: fitting in with the organisation and management of the class teacher by working to her general instructions; actively endorsing school policies; providing first aid; making tea and coffee. Not having the main responsibility for discipline she reinforced the routines of the classroom, shepherding children onto the carpet, organising tidying up, and so on. She provided physical comfort, tying laces, fixing hair, finding tissues. All such tasks free the teacher but also add to the children's experience of school.

At the same time, Mrs Virdi carried out these functions in her own particular way, which itself had an educational value. She related flexibly to several children at once, matching her responses to their needs. She was calm, polite, good-natured. She corrected and directed children in an oblique way ('I want you to. . . . Why don't you? . . . . Could you do this for me? . . . . Are you going to show me?') that suggests to children a reciprocal relationship of mutual confidence and support. At times, directions sought to extend children's experiences by entering into their fantasy world. Thus, Ranjit was encouraged several times to fly his aeroplane round the classroom to collect more passengers. Nadia was exhorted to pick up her doctor's coat to avoid germs in the hospital.

However, in using her bilingual skills, Mrs Virdi was able to provide experiences that a monolingual English-speaking assistant could not provide. The school's policy of valuing the children's mother tongues was made flesh by her presence. As she said: 'They are surprised and pleased that there is someone who can communicate with them'. Moreover, because of this skill, she took on part of the teacher's role and did so in particular ways. In her words: 'On the ground, I decide when and how to use Punjabi'. She was, thus, making school policy in a way that might not be apparent to monolingual teachers. For example, she matched her use of Punjabi to particular children by:

1 Encouraging lexical transfer of vocabulary items such as colours and parts of the body from English to Punjabi (and vice versa), by embedding the word in a Punjabi phrase ('There's a nose').
2 Directing children's attention to the parallels in each language by such phrases as, 'What do you call this in Punjabi?'.

The hidden message here for the children is that, when two languages operate, there are, therefore, two labels for the same concept. Similarly, such comparisons imply a language learning strategy, that one way to learn is consciously to look for comparisons between languages.

3 Making instructions and explanations more direct and explicit.

It was interesting that the only direct reprimand was in Punjabi: *'You look here! I'm doing your story, why are you looking over there?*. As an example of the hidden curriculum of bilingualism, this occurred unknown to the teacher or myself. (It was discovered later by the Punjabi translator of the audio tape.)

4 Eliciting more complex responses and providing parallel translations.

In the book-making episode the response was often extended in Punjabi, and rephrased in English into written standard form, read out loud to the child as the letters appeared in front of him. In this way a very strong connection was made for the children between the English form and its symbolic representation. Compare my extension of Sandeep's words, 'I went shopping. I crossed the road', which reinforced simple sentence patterns, with what Mrs Virdi elicited, 'There were only a few things left in the shop'.

5 Using Punjabi for more intimate contexts, for example enquiring about visits to the doctor.

Very often choice of language is related to situation and it is more natural, especially for young children, for Punjabi to be the favoured language for home and personal contexts and English for school, academic and formal contexts. Mrs Virdi herself was well aware of socio-linguistic constraints when she pointed out to me the boy who would not reply to her in Punjabi because I was present.

FROM THE PARTICULAR TO THE GENERAL

The morning with Mrs Virdi was, I think, typical of her way of working. It has interest for us, not only because of her evident skill and expertise, but also for the way in which an element of school policy was being made minute by minute. Since monolingual teachers might not know what was being said, aspects of school policy such as how to talk to parents and how to tackle sensitive issues may be created in situ by someone who had not been fully consulted and involved in corporate policy planning. Clearly, there is no problem here where practice matches policy, but it will not always do so.

Because they are relatively scarce, demands on BCAs are often high. They may be expected to make lengthy written translations (in one case of National Curriculum documents), sometimes in their own time, depending on circumstances. The pressures could be considerable given particular language expertise.

However, it could be argued that all classroom assistants experience pressure of some sort. With minimal training, they may be called on to exercise many skills which experienced teachers take for granted. Some older classroom assistants may, indeed, feel they are at least as competent as their newly qualified teacher colleague. It could be irksome to be in that position when the salary, age, qualifications and status differentials are so pronounced.

Indeed, teachers may be unaware of the qualifications assistants possess and the training they have received. As this chapter indicates, different assistants have different strengths to offer a school, and a bilingual person may not operate in the way a special needs assistant, for example, does (see Balshaw, 1991). The key seems to be in finding what each person brings and working with them accordingly.

This can be a particularly valid point for those who have done the two year training for the NNEB (Nursery Nurse Examination Board) certificate. Eileen, for example, compares her role working in an infants school with later experience in a nursery. In the first, 'I was used as a general dogsbody . . . sharpening pencils, photocopying, making tea and coffee. The only contact I had with the children was to listen to readers and supervise art and craft.' In contrast, in the nursery she was 'treated like a valued colleague. We worked as a team to plan lessons, teach, tidy up afterwards, and had our own groups for observation, group work and record keeping. Nursery nurses are employed to work with teachers not for them.' The team-work described by Eileen can extend to community liaison, student supervision, and contribution towards school policies. Not all NNEBs would want such responsibilities but, as she says, 'there's no way of knowing unless you ask', and, one might add, unless teachers know something of the NNEB training and the areas where invaluable help and advice can be provided (see Clark, 1988).

In the cause of harmony and professional effectiveness, each classroom partner clearly needs to respect the integrity of the other. The personal and working partnership achieved by Mrs Holmes and Mrs Virdi offers one successful model.

REFERENCES

Balshaw, M. (1991) *Help in the Classroom*, London: Fulton.
Clark, M. (1988) 'Roles, responsibilities and relationships in the education of the young child', *Educational Review*, Occasional Publication, No. 13.
HMI (1992) *Non-Teaching Staff in Schools*, London: HMSO.

Appendix 1: Guidelines for working with a classroom assistant

The availability and deployment of classroom assistants varies between schools and between Local Education Authorities. You may be lucky enough to have an assistant in your classroom for much of the week, or, she (he) may be time-tabled to work with you for only short periods. In the case of Mrs Virdi, her work covered four areas:

1 Educational (supporting the curriculum);
2 Pastoral (supporting children's social skills and behaviour);
3 Liaison (consulting colleagues about planning and preparation);
4 Ancillary (tidying up, putting out materials, making tea).

(See Balshaw (1991) *Help in the Classroom*, London: Fulton)

Discussion with classroom assistants has highlighted the following areas of dissatisfaction:

• insufficient time for preparation and evaluation of sessions;
• arriving to find the teacher unprepared and having to fit in as best she can;
• being unsure of her role and responsibilities in some classrooms;
• being unsure about disciplining children in front of the teacher;
• needing training in some areas, such as helping children with special needs, assisting with physiotherapy and speech therapy; and
• having most time taken with ancillary tasks such as mixing paint, photocopying, mending reading books, administering first aid.

Whatever your situation, it is helpful to reflect on it so that you make the most of a precious resource, for everyone's benefit: yours, the assistant's, the children's.

The assistant

• What particular personal and professional skills does your assistant have?
• Are you using them to the full?
• Does your assistant live in the local community and have knowledge of the area which could be helpful to you and the school?
• How long has your assistant worked at school? Has she long-standing knowledge and relationships with several families?

School organisation

• What contribution does your assistant make to planning meetings, teacher days, parents' evenings?
• How is your assistant's time-table decided? Does she have any say in how she is deployed throughout the school?
• Does your assistant attend induction meetings or accompany staff on home visits?
• Does your assistant attend training sessions?
• Is she part of the communication system in the school, so that she can keep up with events?
• Do other adults know about her roles and responsibilities, such as: supply teachers, parents, governors, peripatetic teachers?

Classroom organisation

• Has your assistant a job description and a school policy document, to assist with consistency of approach?

- What time can you set aside for discussion and reflection with her?
- Do you need to discuss any of the following ground rules: classroom organisation; classroom procedures; the purpose of activities; expectations; giving appropriate help; correcting mistakes; listening to children reading?
- How is she used to working? Does this suit you both?
- Do you discuss your termly plans and share copies of your weekly forecasts? Can your assistant contribute to these?
- Would your assistant like a base in your classroom to store useful items, or an inviting corner where she can withdraw children to work with them?
- How will you communicate with her when time for discussion is brief?
- Would a jotting pad, where you write out what you have planned for that session, be helpful?
- All assistants (and teachers) become engaged in menial tasks. How will you ensure that there is a balance between these and supporting children's learning?

Supporting children's learning

- How can you best work? When are the best times for one to supervise a group, the other the rest of the class?
- When will your assistant work with all the class on a particular task? Which individual children will she support and why?
- How can your assistant contribute to formal and informal observations and assessment?

Developing a partnership

You may feel apprehensive about having another, possibly much older, adult in your room. Many very experienced teachers feel like this. However, remember the partnership will work best if:

- you feel settled, at ease and confident;
- there is good communication;
- you are well-organised;
- you trust each other, and are prepared to share roles and the children;
- you can both contribute your skills;
- you both exercise tact, diplomacy and sensitivity; and
- you each practise putting yourself in the other's shoes.

Appendix 2: Job description: classroom assistant

Main duties

1 To take small groups to reinforce by repetition and reassurance the teacher's lessons.
2 To improve language skills by spending time with individual children to ensure they understand the language that equips them to deal with classroom routines.
3 To assist the teachers by interpreting the needs of individual children in specific situations.
4 To provide ancillary support, as required by the class teacher, such as: mounting displays; photocopying; making work cards; preparing art and design materials; assisting with cookery sessions.
5 To help integrate children who have recently entered school.
6 To take groups of children at story time.
7 To help maintain the school library stock and other equipment.
8 To listen to children reading and help them understand the content of what they read.
9 To assist the process of home–school liaison.
10 To undertake any other tasks, as required by the class teacher or Headteacher, which will improve the educational opportunities of the children.

Chapter 7

A school secretary

Richard W. Mills

EDITORS' INTRODUCTION

This chapter seeks to explore a role which is little researched and often unremarked, but of crucial significance to the smooth running of any school, large or small. Adopting a case study, blow-by-blow, approach, the chapter monitors and categorises the tasks that one good secretary does in the course of a busy day. She is seen to be at the heart of the administration; to have many dealings with children and teachers; to have a range of contacts with adult visitors to the school; and to be the focal point for face-to-face, telephone and correspondence enquiries. Her interpersonal skills are of a high order, as is the respect in which she is held by all in the school community.

Most first contacts with a school, by whatever means, are often with the secretary, who carries a public relations and receptionist role, particularly with present and prospective parents. For new teachers and, indeed, anyone new to the school, the secretary can be an invaluable source of information regarding current procedures, past history and knowledge of the area. Outside the scope of this chapter, but worth mentioning, is that, increasingly, school secretaries carry major responsibility for administration of the budget, whether the school is managed by the Local Education Authority or is grant maintained. For that reason, if for no other, they will invariably be computer literate and financially aware.

If the experience of one primary school secretary, during one day, is generalisable, then the implications of such an investigation for teacher training, induction and staff development are self-evident. For any community to function effectively, all members need to know as much as possible about the work of each colleague in that community, and this has been a major theme throughout the book.

She gos to evre class and gets the redsistar and she fons your mom up if you are sik.

(Dean)

It is a truth universally acknowledged that a large primary school, in possession of a delegated budget, must be in want of a good secretary.

Whether a twentieth-century Jane Austen would have written such words is debatable, but the sentiment itself is hardly in dispute. A good secretary is invaluable. She (and it is 'she') is not only the first point of contact between the school and the outside world, but also a key person in the smooth running of the whole enterprise.

That being so, it is odd that the role hardly figures in teacher-training courses; that inexperienced teachers seem unaware of the scope of the job; that it rarely features in induction programmes for new staff. Here, for instance, is part of a conversation between two newly qualified teachers (NQTs) and myself:

RWM: You had experience of the secretary, then, on teaching practice?

NQT 1: Not very much. She was someone to send to for photocopying in an emergency or something like that. That was what I was told. Or a telephone message that came in, but I didn't really have very much contact.

RWM: Were you introduced to the secretary? Did you know her name?

NQT 2: Well, I was on teaching practice here, so I knew a little bit about this office before I came. I knew their names and bits about what they did. Mainly, from my point of view, it was money, dinner money, that sort of thing, and passing on messages.

NQT 1: I wasn't introduced to the secretary. In fact, I don't think I even knew where the secretary's office was till I stumbled on it. No, not here. When I was on teaching practice. The Head said he would give us a morning. He said it was very important that we should go in and see what goes on, but he never got round to it. It just never happened.

RWM: What contacts do you have with the secretary? How does her work impinge on yours?

NQT 1: I don't see her very often, unless there's a problem with a child or dinner money, or payment for a course.

NQT 2: Unless she pops into the classroom and gives us letters to give to the children to take home.

NQT 1: Or comes to fetch a child who has to go to the doctor's.

NQT 2: It's usually to do with registers, because I often get them wrong. So I have to go and check at dinner-time to see how many children I'm supposed to have, because they come late, you see. Well, they're not as bad now, but if children come in late and you haven't marked them in the register, usually you have to send them to the office to make sure they get a mark for the day.

NQT 1: The way I organise my Monday mornings is really because I know that I've got to do registers and dinner money and send them down as quickly as I can. So I organise the work so that I'm free to do that, just for the first fifteen minutes.

RWM: So it affects the curriculum in that sense? The children have to work independently?

NQT 2:   Yes. Something that they don't need you for. We're trying anyway to promote more independent learning, so that helps with the collection of registers and that sort of thing.

RWM: Yes. Well, would you say it would be useful for you to spend half a day in the office? Would it merely be interesting or would it be useful?

NQT 1:   I think both. I think the more we know about their job, the better.

RWM: I suppose one could extend that and say it would be useful to spend half a day with the caretaker or school nurse.

NQT 1:   Yes, I think so.

NQT 2:   Yes, especially with the secretary. They've got lots of information in there.

To judge, then, from this exchange, it would appear to at least two NQTs that the school secretary:

• has a store of crucial information;
• is an important person within the organisation of the school;
• makes some impact on curriculum planning;
• is perceived as dealing largely with money, registers, and the needs of individual children;
• is also concerned with less significant administrative matters; and
• could usefully be shadowed.

In order to realise this last possibility, I arranged to spend a day (8.30 – 5.00 p.m.) in a large urban primary school shadowing secretary Sheila. At the start of the day neither of us knew what we had discovered by the end, namely that during seven and a half working hours she had no fewer than ninety-eight different encounters: on average, one every four and a half minutes. Such a schedule might be surprising to newish teachers, but not to those more experienced:

RWM: I'm following Sheila to find out about the work of a secretary.

Experienced teacher: Oh! blimey. I hope you've got your skates on then. It's a busy life.

However, to begin at the beginning.

Andrew Road Primary School has some five hundred children, including an eighty-place nursery with two teachers and two classroom assistants. The culturally diverse intake is in a new building, which in 1973 replaced the former Victorian school, and overlooks the nearby city centre. There are a Headteacher and Deputy; some fourteen class teachers in the Infant and Junior departments; three floating staff (i.e. one Special Needs teacher; one Home–School Liaison teacher; one language support teacher); three further classroom assistants.

Only two teachers have been there longer than Sheila. She has served for eighteen years, having previously worked for a solicitor. Her office, which she shares in the mornings with an assistant, Hilary, is about 3 metres by 5, and looks out through a hatch onto the carpeted entrance foyer, smartly furnished for visitors and one-to-one reading sessions, and dominated by a poster announcing, 'Our True Nationality Is Mankind'. Alongside a collage of photographs of children at work in the school, there is a parental notice board with details about Home–School liaison work; community enterprises; child abuse; school uniform; National Children's Homes; Office of Fair Trading.

Sheila's office is tidily crammed with shelves; photocopier; coffee machine; two computers; two printers; a filing cabinet; a typewriter; a safe; three chairs; three sets of drawers; a table; working surfaces around the walls; two telephones; two footballs; one box of toilet rolls. High on the shelves are boxes relating to LMS (Local Management of Schools); staffing; admissions; school visits; free meals; school nurse; swimming baths; playing fields. One wall of the office is covered with notices relating to Local Education Authority concerns; governing body membership; supply teacher telephone numbers; video collections; city suppliers; calendars; fire notices; time-tables; thank-you letters from parents; product advertisements.

Both the wall and the office itself testify to the breadth of concerns that the secretary's office deals with. Unlike most classrooms whose main interests are curriculum centred, Sheila's work-room speaks of the world out there, the world of commerce, adult negotiations, finance.

A selection of Sheila's ninety-eight separate personal encounters in her office will give a flavour of her work and responsibilities.

1 At 8.30 a.m., on arrival, she meets the Headteacher to divide up the post. The Head opens the letters and Sheila the parcels, checking on her IBM computer database which staff had previously ordered the items.

2 A local authority gardener arrives at the hatch for access to the mower, kept in the school garage. Sheila goes out to find the caretaker. This is one of dozens of excursions she makes throughout the day, many of them to the nearby staff room.

3 Ten-year-old John, carrying a football, brings a form nominating his dad for election as a parent governor. The form is a week late, but Sheila discovers that John's dad has already been nominated anyway.

4 A teacher brings the news that there is a dead chick in the incubator.

7 Two eight-year-olds, Sharon and Tina, bring a tin of crisp money for safekeeping in Sheila's office. The tin has a note indicating the amount (£9.85) and this is immediately checked by Sheila who sends the children back to their classroom with a receipt. (It is worth noting that all teachers find themselves constantly collecting money for a variety of purposes – dinner; biscuits, crisps, fruit, drinks; charity; visits; savings – and need to know the book-keeping procedures.)

Children moving around the school with money or messages or lost property often travel in pairs, for solidarity, between themselves; safety, of the items they carry; security, against the possibility of an adult intruder on the premises.

9 A teacher calls in to say that a child has gone to Leeds for a funeral. Such information has to be entered in a book recording details of children who arrive in school for registration but then leave later in the day. Sheila's book contains a range of teacher explanations for such absence: 'dentist; mother poorly; hospital; going to family party; eye test; clinic X-ray; stomach ache; vaccination; rash; accident to thumb; appointment at new school; Securicor parcel; wet weather; bumped head; speech therapy; visiting father; nosebleed; soiled herself; bumped in eye.' It is not a list for the faint-hearted.

10 A teacher asks, 'Sheila, is the Advisory Service in here?' (looking for the address book): secretary as human Yellow Pages.

14 The mother of Emma and Rita arrives to pay their dinner money and chats briefly with Sheila about the girls, a reminder that the secretary can often be a front-line recipient of news and confidences about children in the school.

15 Seven-year-old Shah-Uddin and Ijas bring a form for the mobile dentist currently on site.

18 The incubator teacher (see item 4) now brings news of an imminent event: 'I can just hear its little squeaking.'

21 Ten-year-old Marita: 'I've just come to tell you I'm here.' She is, but rather late.

For those readers wondering at this point who the anonymous and un-numbered callers are, I can tell you that they are mainly children with marked dinner and attendance registers. Both are important documents, having a direct bearing on school income, numbers, returns, and on the pastoral care of children. Attendance registers are more complex than formerly, with some local authorities requiring completion of an absence category code (see Appendix 1). Whatever the format of the document, secretaries have to maintain complete records.

I should point out, too, that, like all secretaries, Sheila is constantly fielding a variety of telephone calls, alongside the direct personal encounters. For instance:

- John's dad rings about the responsibilities of a parent governor and arranges an interview with the Headteacher.
- Shakil's mother rings to say he is ill and won't be in today.
- Sheila gives advice about income support to a father phoning to ask if he is eligible. (In such a way do secretaries and teachers take on the role of social worker or Citizens' Advice Bureau.)
- Sonny's mother rings about a medical.
- A local Headteacher phones about the appraisal cycle.
- A college asks to speak to the Head about teaching practice placements for its students.
- The school photographer rings to make arrangements.
- A neighbouring secondary school Head phones about transfer.
- An engineer wishes to call to check the boiler.
- A teacher in another school rings for a colleague who is presently unavailable. Sheila advises her to try again during break-time, but takes a message meanwhile.

She comments:

> Sometimes the teachers don't realise that we can't just switch ourselves off and deal with what they want us to deal with. But there's no tension. Oh! God, no. This is a really happy school. This office is a place where they can let off steam. I'm a kind of agony aunt. The staff's really nice. There's only Carol really and that's just a joke. She's always coming in for the liquid paper. Always making mistakes. But it's all good banter.

24 Amy is brought in late by her mother. Sheila to Amy: 'You're not generally quiet like that. You're chatty, aren't you?'

25 Two five-year-olds arrive with biscuit money and information. Oman says: 'We've brought a egg and it's tap tap tappin. It not my birthday yet. It tomorrow.' (It is actually three months hence.) Alice chips in: 'The nursery egg's died.'

27 Two more children with a plastic box of money requiring change for

£10. Sheila: 'This is from our favourite teacher. You always have one that drives you mad, in the nicest possible way.' The secretary's job, clearly, has a great deal to do with money and Sheila regularly takes large sums of money to the local bank, some five minutes away. There is, locally, a termly meeting of secretaries whose schools have fully delegated budgets. The intention is to check financial and other procedures; exchange information about courses; standardise records (e.g. about truancy, whose definition is by no means simple).

28 The Headteacher (who has already been in and out several times) comes with a form about new admissions procedures; confirms a personal order for a book, 'Teaching Children to Play Games'; briefly discusses capitation details and several impending visits.

Sheila likes the range of concerns and tells me:

> I do like that. You get to know members of the public and the outside agencies. There's Sylvia who comes in to test the children's hearing. Every child has a hearing test. Katy comes in to do speech therapy. Alison, the school nurse, tests the eyes and joins in the medicals when the doctor comes in. We now share Joan (Home–School Liaison teacher) with Aster Drive Infants. Oh, that reminds me, I must check David (7), Kerry (4) and Spencer (6) because they just take a walk and the ESW (Education Social Worker) needs to know. Social Services are turning a blind eye. And this area is inner ring. Those kids have just come in sometimes for their dinner and then gone out playing for the rest of the day. And we had a parent mugged in the park only last Friday.

32 A representative from the Prudential Insurance Company calls at the hatch to leave a poster and arrange a training day date with the Head.

35 An experienced teacher pops in to collect some typing. He had done most of it himself (for the School Newsletter) but had not been able to complete it. In any event, his own dot matrix printer could not rival the office's superior model. Sheila is accustomed to doing typing for the staff, but will only oblige when given plenty of notice. Letters are a different matter. On the Head's instructions, all that go out from the school are typed by Sheila, to ensure presentational quality and adequate records. Recent letters include those to do with:

- appointment of a parent governor;
- induction of reception children;
- school closure for a training day;
- child absences;
- governors' meeting;

- beginning of term welcome;
- price of school meals;
- primary to secondary transfer;
- parents' evening;
- possible NALGO industrial action; and
- information about a Safari Park visit.

Alongside the logging of such letter communications (and standardised forms – see Appendix 2, p. 139), a record is kept of all telephone calls; all child admittance details; all expenditure items; all official visitors; all staff absences; all 'Services and Deliveries'. Apart from logging parcel deliveries, the latter includes such items as:

- workman to repair fence;
- replacement of glass in broken window;
- delivery of monitor;
- testing of fire alarms;
- mending of photocopier;
- police constable visit about crime prevention; and
- checking of electric pump in nursery.

38 Eight-year-old Cherie arrives with money for a Safari Park visit. Sheila counts it immediately since Cherie has been told to return to her classroom with the plastic money box. I ask her if she has been to the Safari Park before. She replies, 'No. I've been before.' Rather baffling, that.

39 A pair of six-year-olds come with dinner money, one of them, Sitar, explaining, 'I had sandwiches yesterday. My mommy hadn't got no change.' As before, the amounts are recorded.

During the dinner break the Headteacher speaks about the role of the school secretary:

> All teachers, particularly new ones, need to know the ground rules. You know, about typing letters, making contacts. We put the details in our Staff Handbook, but there's always more you could add – about admin, about money, absences, ESWs (Education Social Workers), medicals, visits. Some Heads are very jealous of their secretaries. Here Sheila has wonderful contact.

69 Eight-year-old Mina comes, for no discernible purpose, and comments, 'This is a good school. You get better chips an that.'

75 A father arrives to give details about his daughter's doctor's appointment. He gives her birth as 3.8.87. Sheila cannot trace the address in her records and it transpires that the family moved two years previously without notifying the school. The new address is now recorded.

78 Two children return the liquid paper. Evidently Carol has been busy again.

79 Sheila is now busy comforting nine-year-old Meras, who feels ill and could only eat one potato for her dinner.

83 The Home–School Liaison teacher calls in to leave her handbag while she goes off to look at the new chick in the nursery.

84 A mother comes to collect her daughter who has had a fainting fit.

85 A representative from Venetian Blind Services is at the hatch to keep his appointment with the Headteacher for giving an estimate. Sheila makes him some coffee while he waits. He shares the foyer with a class-room assistant playing Snap with two infant children.

86 Two workmen from the Council call to see the caretaker.

88 A teacher comes to borrow the A–Z. She is off to a meeting on the National Curriculum.

90 A teacher comes to telephone her Union for information about an LEA reading test.

92 Two nine-year-old boys call to ask about free meals.

93 A father calls to complain that his daughter's T-shirt has been ripped. He is referred to the Head who, in ten minutes, sorts out the matter amicably.

Towards the end of the day a stream of staff call into the office to give trip money; collect forms; ask about keys; pass on messages; bring lost pro-perty; enquire about children.

Some of the foregoing may seem trivial. Perhaps it is, in the grand scheme of things, but one person's trivia is another's essence. Throughout the day Secretary Sheila has dealt with a helter-skelter of varying con-cerns, with unvarying courtesy, pleasantness and good humour. From child to parent, teacher to teacher, adult professional to adult unem-ployed, she has listened sympathetically and responded appropriately.

Few staff would be aware of the totality of Sheila's day (which, in her case, can last, on occasions, to 6.30 p.m. when a child has not been collected and needs either to be taken home or to the local police station). When asked at one point in the morning how many encounters she had already had with different people in her office, one NQT estimated ten; an experienced teacher estimated fifty. There had, in fact, been sixty-five encounters at that stage, with more to come. And all that in addition to the other duties.

These might be categorised, with reference to the numbered encounters listed earlier, by 'Secretary as':

- Banking and administrative clerk (1; 15; 21; 25; 27; 28; 38; 39).
- Friend and therapist (4; 14; 18; 42; 46; 48; 53; 57; 69; 79).
- Receptionist and PRO (3; 24; 32; 45; 50; 64; 85; 86; 93).
- Informant and archivist (3; 9; 10; 55; 75; 92).
- Typist and telephonist (35; 60; 90).
- Organiser and 'go-fer' (43; 49; 78; 83; 84; 88).

The secretary's office is like no other room in school. It is a fixed point in an ever-turning world. It is telephone booth; surgery; reference library; stock cupboard; typing pool; bank; museum store; waiting room. Its chief occupant is always there, available as the focus for an enquiry. The office is apart from the normal activity of teaching, yet it shares with the classroom a constantly changing focus of concerns. It does not have the relaxed camaraderie and ordered untidiness of the average staff room, but it shares a sense of professional humour, sometimes bordering on black comedy. The occupant of such a room plays a vital part in the life of any school and her work needs to be familiar to all, particularly newly qualified teachers.

Appendix 1: Marking the register

Attendance registers are now much more sophisticated than formerly. The NQT not only needs to become familiar with the range of children's names, but also with a system for coding absences which seems complicated, even by GCHQ standards.

Here is one such system. Its value for new teachers will not lie in learning the code, since schools will vary in their systems. What it does do is to alert newcomers to the profession to the wide range of different kinds of authorised absence.

Authorised absence codes

Inside the letter O the following letters should be marked:

B   Receiving part-time and/or temporary education off-site through home teaching or at a Behaviour Support Unit, or other educational establishment.

C   Other circumstances, such as local authority licensed performance; bereavement; court appearance.

D   Awaiting removal from the register (i.e. de-registration).

E   Excluded either permanently or for a fixed or indefinite period, prior to being de-registered. Exclusion on medical grounds.

H   Holiday, for which school has granted leave.

I   Interview.

L   Late.

M   Medical/dental treatment/sickness.

P   Approved sporting activity.

R   Religious observance.

S   Study leave.

V   Educational visit.

W   Work experience.

Z   Exceptional extended holiday absence (e.g. to visit relatives overseas).

Unauthorised absence codes

Ø   Late after close of registration period.

O   Absence unauthorised.

NB: School secretaries will advise new teachers about the procedures for recording weekly and termly absence calculations.

Appendix 2: Educational visits

Each school secretary has a range of forms for various purposes and will give guidance to NQTs about how to complete them. Staff are now very aware of safety requirements and, correspondingly, of the need to prove that every appropriate care has been taken. Here is one such form, which will give a flavour of the necessary bureaucracy.

Destination ....
Date of visit .... a.m. p.m. all day.
LEA informed: Yes. No.
Time of departure from school ....
Time of expected return to school ....
Name of teacher i/c party ....

Other accompanying teachers ....
Other accompanying adults ....
Any others ....
Number of children in party from each class:
  Class .... Boys .... Girls .... Class .... Boys .... Girls ....
  Class .... Boys .... Girls .... Class .... Boys .... Girls ....
  Class .... Boys .... Girls .... Class .... Boys .... Girls ....
Type of transport ....
Name of company ....
Tel. no of company ....
Date of confirmation from company ....
Insurance company used ....
Type of insurance cover ....
Date note of information sent to parents ....
Date note of permission request sent to parents ......
Have all consent returns been received? Yes. No.
(If not, child without consent return may not go on trip except by
special permission of the Headteacher.)
Cost to parent of visit ....
Are children required to bring:
     Packed lunch?   Yes. No.
     Have they been told so?   Yes. No.
Have children been told what to bring and what not to bring? Yes. No.
Has any special clothing (e.g. raincoat) been suggested?   Yes. No.
Have all children been informed of the disciplines involved?   Yes. No.
Have all staff been informed of their responsibilities?   Yes. No.
Has a proper account been kept of all money from children?   Yes. No.
Have all children paid proper amounts?   Yes. No.
Has all work been planned relating to this visit?   Yes. No.

NB: Such a list is not an example of bureaucracy for its own sake, and NQTs should not feel so daunted by it that they intend never to take children anywhere. Parts of the list serve as useful reminders of what to do and not to do. Other parts almost have the status of legal requirements. The key aim is for children and staff to get maximum social and educational enjoyment and profit, in safety.

Chapter 8

Good health to a school nurse

June Dunkley

EDITORS' INTRODUCTION

What image comes to mind when you hear the title 'school nurse'? Unpleasant injections, head inspections, white starchy clothes, forbidding spectacles? On what information are these images based? What do you know about the functions performed by a school nurse?

We will all have our own stereotyped views from childhood but, as this chapter shows, the role is not defined by the caricature just described. Like all the other adults in this book, the school nurse has particular skills and knowledge which can be harnessed. In the account that follows, a Deputy Head describes how she involved her infant school's nurse in a health education topic which, itself, helped to cement an important professional relationship.

This is a clear case of a non-teaching member of the school's associative staff being directly involved in the planning and implementation of a cross-curricular theme within the National Curriculum. The initiative developed from an in-service course attended by the Deputy, but it was within the context of a school already used to working in a multi-disciplinary way and making use of inter-agency initiatives. It was also a school dedicated to partnership with parents and to looking outward at the wider world. In other words, conditions were ideal for such a collaborative venture to flourish.

She tack about our boddy if you don't brush you haie you with get mittens in you haie.

(Five-year-old child)

SETTING THE SCENE

Where do developments in a school's curriculum originate? By attending an in-service course? By reviewing current policy? By building on existing strengths? The particular curriculum development now described involved an outside agent, the school nurse, and included all three elements just mentioned.

The school is a purpose-built infant school which was opened in 1967, and provides: 'a relaxed, caring environment in which children are encouraged to build positively on their strengths, and where expectations of behaviour and learning are high' (LEA Inspection Report, 1990). Since the appointment of the Head and Deputy Head in the late 1980s, the curriculum has undergone review in consultation with the staff, and policy statements and schemes of work encompassing National Curriculum requirements have been produced. The Head and Deputy Head work closely together, and each member of staff is encouraged to contribute towards the collegiate management of the school. The 'open' style of management is reflected in the relaxed, friendly atmosphere. Parents are welcomed into the school on a daily basis, to work alongside staff in the classrooms, as well as attending consultation sessions, assemblies, celebrations and PTA social events. This open-door policy reflects the recognition of parents as first and continuing educators of their children.

As Deputy Head of the school, I have a number of managerial and curricular responsibilities, not least of which is a full-time teaching commitment to a class of twenty-two Year One children. During the Spring Term, 1992, the LEA offered a one-day course for Health Education Guidance, 4–19 years, which I attended. The course was multidisciplinary, with input from the Health and Drugs Liaison Officer, and the Senior Health Education Officer from the Education Unit of a local hospital. The course members represented primary, secondary and special schools, the Police Force (Schools Liaison Department) and the Health Service.

Subsequently I led a series of staff meetings to 'cascade' the information I had gleaned, and to lead staff towards an analysis of provision and presentation of health education matters within school, with a view to improving this provision.

A REVIEW OF CURRENT PRACTICE

As a staff we agreed that the profile of health education needed to be raised, and it was acknowledged that many aspects were covered incidentally as part of the hidden curriculum, or indeed as part of the ongoing programme of school topics. The first step, therefore, was to examine current practice. The school operated a rolling programme of topics, which lasted for one term, each of which had a specific curricular bias of either Science, History or Geography. While having a particular bias, each topic aimed to address cross-curricular issues. Those that lent themselves most readily to the inclusion of health elements were:

- *The Senses*: a Science-based topic, often supported by visiting speakers who had a sensory impairment and who worked with people with disabilities (e.g. the school piano tuner, a familiar figure to the children, usually took part of an Assembly during this topic, leading them to consider life with a visual handicap. A member of the hearing-impaired teaching service would also come into school to demonstrate and teach certain elements of 'signing', perhaps a familiar song or rhyme, and to talk to the children about hearing loss.).
- *Caring*: another Science-based topic, emphasising the correct processes for caring for ourselves, at various stages of development, and also the care of animals and plants at home, in school, and within the wider environment. Road safety, elements of the Country Code and environment issues were all components of this topic.
- *Other Lands:* a topic with a Geographical emphasis, which occurred during the Autumn Term. Children were encouraged to consider similarities and differences between lifestyles, diet, rites of passage, homes, modes of dress, religious beliefs and festivals, etc. In such a way, issues of race and culture were introduced.
- *Change:* had an historical emphasis, beginning with the experiences of the child, requiring photograph evidence of change in ourselves (i.e. from birth to the present), and leading on to change over a period of time (comparing baby photographs of ourselves, our parents, our grandparents, for instance). Diet, sanitation and health provision across the generations served to illustrate both History and health matters.
- *Water:* a Geography-based topic, leading towards consideration of sources of water supply and availability, and thus towards matters of hygiene.

Health education in a very wide sense, as an element of the personal, social and moral education of the individual, was addressed by the ongoing collection of items such as tin foil, used postage stamps, aluminium cans, items in support of the annual 'Blue Peter' appeal, together with active support of National Charity events such as 'Red Nose Day'.

Having carried out the review, we agreed that, at Key Stage 1, it was not appropriate to teach health education as a discrete element of the curriculum, but, rather, that it should continue to be a cross-curricular theme, as outlined by the National Curriculum Council. We also felt that the wider term of 'personal, social and moral education' was more closely aligned to our ethos, with its intention to educate 'the whole child'. With these points in mind, we moved on to consider the following questions:

- What was our understanding of personal, social and moral education with regard to Key Stage 1?
- Which aspects of PSME did we do well?
- Which aspects did we need to improve upon?
- How were these improvements to be implemented?

INTER-AGENCY INITIATIVE

In discussing the responses to these questions it was decided that we should pilot a scheme of inter-agency co-operation, enlisting the help of the school nurse, with whom we had already established a mutually satisfying working relationship. This proposal was based on an earlier successful pattern of in-service meetings.

Previous inter-agency initiatives had involved a team of educational psychologists leading a series of staff meetings to discuss the implications of the Elton Report on behaviour and discipline. All staff, including the dinner supervisors, had attended a series of very informative sessions led by the educational psychologist, considering possible strategies for behaviour modification during playtime and lunch-times, as well as during the more structured sessions within the school day. The presence of 'experts' had added a dimension to the discussions, and the exercise had been well received by the staff.

On another occasion, the dinner supervisors were again invited to join the teaching staff for a series of meetings led by a representative of the Red Cross, who ran a course on basic first aid procedures. On this occasion we also reached out into the community, and invited the leaders of the local playgroup to our meetings.

Building on this past experience the senior management team felt it appropriate to approach the school nurse with a view to discussing our proposals, i.e. to involve her in the classroom and to deliver INSET, with possible involvement in home–school bridge-building too. We were fairly confident that our approach would be met with approval, as the school nurse had been developing her role within the school to encompass parental involvement, though to date this involvement had been limited to work with 'new' parents of the children entering reception, offering advice and information on the available Health Services.

Prior to our proposal, the school nurse had made a point of building relationships with staff, timing her visits to coincide with coffee time in order to meet on an informal basis; she had attended a number of concerts and PTA social functions, again meeting staff and parents in informal situations. Before her 'official' visits to do vision checks, or whatever, with the reception children, she made a point of visiting on a number of occasions, just 'popping in' for a chat, to ensure that when she came in her official capacity, she would be a familiar face to the children, and not a total stranger.

Our instincts turned out to be well founded. On approach, the school nurse agreed to work in the classroom, alongside teaching staff, to promote personal hygiene.

THE ROLE OF A SCHOOL NURSE

Before launching into a description of what we did, I feel it would be helpful to give a brief outline of the career path that our school nurse had followed.

Mrs Susan Keays entered the Health Service in the early 1970s. Having qualified as a State Registered Nurse, she left hospital nursing in the late 1970s in favour of district nursing. The move into school nursing took place in 1990 and, from her own choice, Mrs Keays undertook a school nurses' course at a local polytechnic. Such a course is now fast becoming a requirement, rather than an optional extra, and it is important for us all to realise that the philosophy of such a course emphasises the role of the school nurse as an active force for the promotion of health, not only in the school but also in the wider community, aiming to increase students' understanding of factors influencing the well-being of the child and the potential role of a school nurse.

A third of Mrs Keays' time was spent in 'fieldwork practice'. Six areas of study were presented as inter-related components, rather than discrete elements, and comprised child development; sociology; social psychology; social policy; principles and practice; and considerations relating to provision of care for the child with special needs. Having successfully completed the course, Mrs Keays was able to return to her employing authority as a 'certified' school nurse.

Historically:

> the status of school nursing has suffered from the lack of any statutory provision of specialist training. School nursing is seen as a job with no prospects for nurses who lack ambition; trapping school nurses in a task oriented mould where enormous workloads and lack of opportunity for real contact with the children has made their work frustrating and stultifying.
>
> (Catherine Burns, HVA General Secretary, 1990)

Mrs Keays does not consider that she fits this historical mould, but rather aims towards the more contemporary role as:

> the resource person . . . the interface between home, parents and the health education unit . . . looking beyond the immediate school-age client group, to involve the community as a whole . . . not wishing to usurp the teacher . . . nor to give them free time . . . but . . . to act in accord with the teacher to offer expertise and support for the demands of the National Curriculum.
>
> (Professor Keith Tones, Leeds Polytechnic, Health Education Unit)

It is certainly our experience that the role fulfilled by Mrs Keays equates readily with the criteria defined by Professor Tones.

Mrs Keays is contracted to work a total of 1,040 hours per annum. Theoretically, this part-time work commitment is twenty hours per week; practically the 1,040 hours average out at twenty-three and a half hours per school week, once holiday periods have been deducted. In real terms, however, Mrs Keays works 'flexi' hours, with time allocation being driven by needs. During the period of initial school medical examinations, for example, she may spend anything up to thirty hours in one infant school or department.

In her role as school nurse, Mrs Keays is responsible for four schools, which are situated within a geographical radius of five miles. Three of the four schools are situated within the same 'cluster group', and, in the main, the children transfer *en bloc* from the infant school to the neighbouring junior school and, subsequently, on to the nearby secondary school. The remaining school of the quartet is a primary school, which also incorporates a unit for children with recognised and statemented special educational needs. Of the children on roll at this primary school, approximately 30 per cent transfer to the secondary school.

Mrs Keays allocates her time on a daily, sessional, basis, with the secondary school claiming two sessions due to its number of students. The proposed weekly schedule is submitted to the local Health Centre, which acts as a 'clearing house' for calls, although each Headteacher also has Mrs Keays's home telephone number for use in an emergency.

As a member of the Health Service, Mrs Keays is accountable to her 'professional adviser', who, in turn, reports to the neighbourhood manager. The school nurses have regular meetings with their professional adviser, often in group situations to facilitate a sharing of experience and expertise.

ROLE IN SCHOOL

Contrary to the 1950s and 1960s caricature school nurse image of 'Nitty Nora', in charge of 'nits and naughty bits', the role of the modern school nurse has a far greater and richer compass.

To begin with, she performs a wide range of medically related tasks. When a child enters its Reception Year there is a vision test. A height and weight check is made during the child's Reception Year. These initial screenings are administered before the full school medical, which involves the Community Medical Officer with the school nurse acting as receptionist, administration clerk and friendly, familiar figure, both for the child and for his/her parent(s), thus enabling a potentially strained encounter (being examined by an unknown doctor in the unfamiliar surroundings of the school medical room) to be relatively non-threatening. Any child giving cause for concern with regard to visual and auditory capabilities will be the subject of 'follow-up' screenings during subsequent years until a satisfactory resolution is reached.

During Key Stage 2 it is common for the school nurse to talk to the girls in Year Five, with regard to the onset of menstruation. As part of their programme of sex education, children in Year Six discuss their reactions to a video with their form teacher and the school nurse. During each Autumn Term in Key Stage 2, the school nurse measures the height and weight of each child to enable them to complete the relevant section in their personal journal.

Involvement at Key Stage 3 takes the form of personal, social and moral education, in conjunction with purely 'medical' matters. Individual 'health interviews' are held biannually, with routine height, weight and vision checks being made alongside a general discussion about dietary matters, healthy eating, physical fitness and exercise routines. Confident in the knowledge that their privacy will be respected, the children are given the opportunity to discuss their personal, developmental concerns with a caring adult who has a peripheral interest and involvement with the educational establishment, rather than a more integral involvement as, for instance, their pastoral or form tutor. Friendship groups, peer pressure, problems of initial adjustments, adaptations to life within a secondary school have all been discussed at these biannual interviews with Mrs Keays, and such counselling continues alongside more traditional activities, such as administering rubella and BCG injections.

In addition to her school-based work, Mrs Keays may also be called upon to attend and contribute to case conferences, for example in cases of child abuse or when a child has been proposed for inclusion on the 'At Risk' register. With regard to children who are subject to case conferences, interaction with other agencies may involve representatives from the areas of Education, Health, Social Services, Educational Psychology, Educational Welfare, in addition to the parents and/or 'carers', who also have a legal right to be present at such a conference.

Mrs Keays may also be involved in making home visits, should circumstances dictate. Families with a child in the Special Needs Unit may well gain support from home-based counselling from someone who has awareness of the school situation, in conjunction with an awareness of the physical, medical constraints which are having to be encountered and overcome. On such occasions, the role of school nurse overlaps with that of Home–School Liaison Officer and, where both co-exist in a school, there clearly needs to be consultation and negotiation to avoid potential embarrassment and duplication of effort.

It is customary for the school nurse to receive notification from the Accident and Emergency Department should any child who attends a school within her 'catchment' area have had cause to visit the Department for any reason. The notification is followed up with a telephone call to the parent(s), or, in the case of a student in the secondary sector, with a private interview in the school's medical room. After discussion with adult or child, the school nurse would hope to assess the situation resulting from treatment at the hospital, and offer advice as to any subsequent action that may be needed. In certain circumstances, a home visit may be required.

Notification of 'routine' operations, such as tonsillectomy, appendectomy, insertion of grommets, will also be forwarded to the school nurse, who will 'follow up' the cases in a similar manner. Children who have undergone such surgery are also subject to follow-up medical examination by the Community Medical Officer, who aims to monitor progress. In cases of surgery, or where medical conditions are to be noted, there clearly needs to be appropriate liaison between the school nurse and all relevant teaching and non-teaching staff.

THE INITIATIVE IN ACTION

Having agreed to take part in the project in the classroom, Mrs Keays was anxious to make a start with 'a critical friend'. As she had worked closely with me over the previous two years, in my role as reception teacher, she decided to work with my class first. In preparation for her visit, I told the children that she was coming to talk to them, and asked them what they thought a school nurse had to do. There were a variety of responses:

> She probably operates on people . . . . Last year she weighed us . . . . And she saw how tall we'd grown . . . . She put a patch on my eye . . . . That was to see if you knew your Letterland characters . . . . Yes, I remember, she played that with me too . . . . My mum's a nurse she helps people get better . . . . Does she give them medicine? . . . . Does Mrs Keays give medicine? . . . . Does she do needles? . . . . I don't like needles.

On her arrival, Mrs Keays showed the class a bag, from which she took a hair brush, saying, 'Who can tell me if they used one of these this morning?'. This question was answered with echoes of, 'Me', 'I did', 'I've got a blue one', and other such comments. Mrs Keays told the children how important it was to brush hair night and morning to stop little creatures making their homes in their hair. The children were also told to make sure their brush was kept clean. The children began to discuss nits, and where they came from. One child claimed he had two at home.

The next visual aid to be used was a toothbrush and a tube of toothpaste. There was much discussion regarding colour of brush and brand of paste, as well as the loss of baby teeth, and current exchange rates offered by the tooth fairy. One mummy had wanted to keep the baby tooth, and so had exchanged money with her child, but most children agreed that the best thing was to leave the baby teeth under the pillow, as the tooth fairy needed the teeth . . . to make jewellery for herself . . . to make into new teeth . . . to give to the dentist to make false teeth for nannies and granddads. There was much comparing and wobbling of loose teeth, and then a discussion regarding when best to clean them. Home rules seemed to vary: after breakfast; when I get dressed; at bedtime were all proposed. The children were told that teeth should be cleaned each morning and evening. Teeth should really be cleaned after each meal, but that wasn't always possible.

A toilet roll prompted the inevitable giggles of embarrassment, and there was far more need for adult intervention in gaining descriptions of the correct procedures for toilet routines. It was eventually agreed that everyone should flush the toilet, then wash and dry their hands. The use of soap was discussed, and the fact that thorough drying of hands in school was quite difficult because there are only paper towels, not real ones, as at home.

In drawing the thirty-minute session to a close, Mrs Keays pointed to either a part of her body, or to one of the visual aids she had used, and the children were encouraged to explain how to look after the body part, or when and how to use the selected item.

The children were then given the opportunity to draw and write about anything they had been talking about during the session.

While the children were thus occupied, we adults were able to snatch time to discuss what had been a very well-organised and informative session. I had been afforded the luxury of observing my whole class (something I am rarely able to do, without another adult in the room) and had witnessed the children's skills of interaction and communication, both with peers and an adult. I was able to confirm my assessments of the speaking and listening capabilities of certain individuals, and observe the individual characters within the group, making mental notes of those who contributed a great deal as well as those who chose to remain silent.

I was able to give positive feedback on presentational skills, control and content. We discussed the topic of head lice, and thought that it might be worth stating that, in spite of precautions, nits do like nice clean heads for homes, so if anyone became infested, they need not be upset, because treatments were available. I felt that this was important, as I know that parents were recently horrified that their child had gone home with head lice, and the parents' reaction had been quite upsetting for the child.

The first session was complete. Mrs Keays was relieved and reassured, and I was satisfied that our inter-agency project had been launched in such a positive manner.

A similar format was used in each session, though the length was altered to suit the age range. The nursery and reception children were urged to bring a handkerchief to school, or to use the tissues from the class box if noses needed wiping (at which prompt there was a mini-procession towards the container). The children were also reminded to cover their mouths should they cough or sneeze (inevitably coughs and sneezes were demonstrated). Year One and Year Two classes were equally responsive.

Without exception, the class teachers found the experience well worth while.

The role of observer is a rare luxury for the primary teacher, and one which was valued by my colleagues. It was felt that the reinforcement of messages of basic hygiene could not be overemphasised, and that a three-pronged attack – home, school and nurse – could only be of benefit in the long term.

The entire teaching staff were united in their praise of content and presentation of material. Possible future topics were discussed, with the issue of time-management and other organisational constraints being addressed. The overall feeling was that the topic of health was integral to our work with young children and highly appropriate as our ongoing cross-curricular theme. Thus, it was agreed that personal fitness (linking with transport and locomotion) would be the focus for the Spring Term, and healthy eating (linking with the imminent opening of the school kitchens) for the Summer Term.

HOME–SCHOOL PARTNERSHIP

Each Friday morning there is a 'Family Assembly', to which parents, siblings, friends and neighbours are welcome. The PTA offers crèche facilities, but many parents use the Assembly as a familiarisation exercise for their pre-school children. The Assembly is a celebration of achievements. Children are encouraged to bring into school any awards or certificates they have gained, through attending uniformed organisations such as Boys Brigade or Brownies, for example, or for achievements in the swimming pool or at the local school of dance. Each child with something to 'share' is encouraged to give an explanation of the tasks required to attain the award, thus giving an opportunity for boosting confidence in the area of 'public speaking'. Birthdays are also celebrated, with adults being invited to share their milestones with the children. Achievements for efforts made in school are rewarded with Good Work Certificates during this Assembly, and there is always a great deal of support for the event, with a regular audience/congregation of some fifty families represented each week.

As part of the liaison initiative, Mrs Keays was invited to speak to the parents, following one of the regular Friday Assemblies. The PTA Secretary agreed to take notes of what was said, with Mrs Keays's knowledge and permission. Here is part of her verbatim record, which mirrors the activities described above:

> Last week I went into Mrs Dunkley's class, and took with me a bag of items related to personal hygiene. Each item related to one particular part of the body. I started at the head, and worked down. First out of the bag was a hairbrush, which should be kept clean and washed regularly. Hair should be brushed hard at night and in the morning to deter head-lice. Next out of the bag was a toothbrush and a tube of toothpaste. I talked to the children about brushing their teeth, especially after eating. We all know that's not really practical during a school day, so I stressed the importance of brushing each day, night and morning. Next time I speak to them, I'll tell them how important it is to visit the dentist regularly.

She went on to outline the rest of her talk, telling the audience where else she would visit in the school, and topics she would cover later in the year, finishing with:

> In January and early February, the reception children will be having vision tests, which I'll do with them, and then they'll be having medicals in March. You'll get a letter, telling you all about it, with dates and times on, but if you've got any worries, you know where to find me if you want a chat. I'll be here for the medicals anyway, and it's nothing to worry about.

Immediately following this information session, Mrs Keays joined the parents for the weekly social chat over coffee and biscuits, thus giving an opportunity for further discussion with those people with queries.

In a straw poll of parents I spoke to, I gathered that most people found the input helpful in building a picture of their child's experience in school, and also in breaking down barriers, and building relationships with a professional from the Health Service. The general feeling was one of confidence in and with Mrs Keays.

Perhaps a key point to be made here, in terms of communication with parents, is that if we, as teachers, feel they should know as much as possible about our work with their children, then the same goes for any other adult involvement in the classroom. What do parents know, one wonders, about the involvement of classroom assistants, teaching practice students, peripatetic special needs staff, and so forth?

IN THE CLASSROOM, SPRING AND SUMMER TERMS

Our next topic was transport and locomotion and this was used by Mrs Keays to compare and contrast the car and the human body. The headlights of the car were likened to the eyes of a child, and led to discussions about eye tests, spectacles and blindness.

'The main part inside a car is its engine', said Mrs Keays. 'Who can tell me the name we give to our special engine in here?' (pointing to position of heart).

Having teased out the required response, together with additional information regarding muscles, blood and Valentine's Day, Mrs Keays went on to compare the stomach with a petrol tank, and good food with quality petrol. (Sensibly she left diesel fuel out of the reckoning.) Healthy, clean, well-cared-for feet and close-fitting socks and shoes were compared to the wheels and tyres of vehicles. This latter point led to a great deal of discussion relating to a visit to the school, earlier that week, of a new Range Rover Defender vehicle, with tyre tread of impressive proportions.

In order to involve the children more directly, Mrs Keays showed them how to feel the pulse in their wrists. Some denied they had a pulse. We then went out onto the playground and gave the children the opportunity to run around the playground and then retake their pulse, following strenuous activity. Most discovered their pulses after this, which made its own point. Having experienced a variety of activities, the children returned to the classroom and were presented with a photocopied quiz sheet, which served to reinforce the earlier session.

Mrs Keays repeated similar sessions with the other classes, and again the staff appreciated the efforts she had made to integrate her health input with the ongoing topic. As a bonus, Mrs Keays was able to offer a similar format to the primary school in her catchment area, with equal success.

The final delivery, during the Summer Term, was slightly different, in that it focused on healthy eating and coincided with the opening of the school kitchen. The advantage of this was obvious, in that it linked a relatively abstract concept with something the children could see and touch and walk round. Attention was also drawn to foodstuffs on offer at each class Tuck Shop, and also to the content of recipes encountered during food technology sessions.

FINALLY

Drawing conclusions for this piece of action research is extremely difficult, as I believe that the initiative will continue and, once it gains momentum, I feel sure it will develop and grow into an integral part of our school curriculum. The staff continue to build on links with the community, and to believe in the importance of the 'hidden' issues of PSME. Collaborative planning and delivery is an accepted part of our school process, and involving the school nurse has enhanced the delivery of the curriculum.

The status of the school nurse has undoubtedly been raised by this initiative, both in terms of her own self-esteem and also in terms of her role within the staff room. Relationships between Mrs Keays and the children have blossomed, and parents are, consequently, aware of her increased involvement in the classroom. This, in turn, has enriched the relationship between home and health via the school. Ideally, the children in our care are taking the health promotion messages home and subsequently into the wider community via their own extended families and circles of friends.

From a personal viewpoint, my relationship with colleagues and parents has been strengthened by frank, open, discussions, often regarding sensitive issues. The co-operation and trust I received were gratifying, and reflect the overriding ethos of the school as an open environment where individuals are respected and valued. I identify fully with 'The Lessons Learnt' by King:

> Any account of research is a fragment of indirect autobiography, especially when the writer has been the sole researcher . . . . my experience of the researcher was a rewarding one, both professionally and personally.
>
> (King, 1978)

Having gained my original inspiration in this area back in the Spring Term of 1992, it was gratifying for me to be able to attend one of the last inter-agency courses offered in the LEA in the Spring Term of 1993. The focus of that course was the use of children's literature as a vehicle for delivering health education and already the staff, and the school nurse, have agreed that during the academic year 1993/94 we should, as a school, trial some of the books suggested in order to address issues such as sibling rivalry, bereavement and self-esteem. Once again my colleagues are proving to be open-minded, innovative and co-operative in their attitudes towards curriculum initiatives, and the role of the school nurse has been given the status she has worked hard to achieve.

In concluding this chapter I acknowledge the fortunate position in which I find myself, and would draw the attention of the reader to a quotation from the school's LEA Inspection Report, 1990, replacing the word 'children' with 'individuals', as I believe that the school provides:

> a relaxed caring environment in which *individuals* are encouraged to build positively on their strengths, and where expectations of behaviour and learning are high.

It cannot be denied that each individual is valued, and that certain aims and objectives could equally apply to the adult members of the school community: self-esteem is crucial to all elements of the curriculum, hidden or otherwise, and it is as important to adults as children. It is within this atmosphere that I have been able to work, and to enable this initiative to develop.

FURTHER READING

King, R. (1978) *All Things Bright and Beautiful?*, Chichester: Wiley.
LEA (1978) *Inspection Report* (Solihull), privately circulated.
NCC (1989) *Curriculum Guidance 1. A Framework for the Primary Curriculum*, York: NCC.
——— (1990) *Curriculum Guidance 5: Health Education*, York: NCC.
Nixon, J. (ed.) (1980) *Teachers in Research*, London: Schools Council.
Pollard, A. (1985) *The Social World of the Primary School*, London: Cassell.
Pollard, A. and Tann, S. (1987) *Reflective Teaching in the Primary School*, London: Cassell.
West Midlands RHA (1982) *Health Education in Schools*, Birmingham: Spartan.

Appendix 1: Some responsibilities

The following serve as examples of the wide variety of issues a school nurse may have to deal with.

Head lice

A home visit might be made to discuss the effective treatment of head lice. It is no longer normal practice for every child's head to be examined at the beginning of every term by the school nurse; the responsibility lies with the parents. In spite of receiving literature outlining suitable and effective treatments for dealing with the problem of head lice, some parents find it difficult to cope adequately with such an infestation. In some cases, the Headteacher can make a request for a home visit, especially if there is cause for concern and it is felt that if the problem is discussed on 'home ground' on a one-to-one basis the benefits would be greater than sending home yet another leaflet, or issuing a summons to attend a meeting in school, which would result in unnecessary anxiety, and questioning from peer groups (of both parents and children).

Communicable diseases: meningitis

Incidence of this disease, though rare, not unnaturally causes alarm among parents. If a child is admitted to hospital, representatives from the Area Health Authority in my locality have, in the past, offered support and advice to the parents of the child, discussed the implications with the Headteacher and run an open forum for any parents or members of the local community in order to offer information to address their concerns.

The Headteacher has hosted such meetings to give information and reassurance. Mrs Keays has been kept informed of developments by the Headteacher. Following recovery, Mrs Keays has added her support to that of the organisations more directly concerned with the infection.

Special Needs support

Children may be admitted who have recognised special educational needs because they have been born with particular congenital syndromes, or perhaps mild cerebral palsy. Often, the child's parents may have had a great deal of contact with various and numerous medical, surgical and educational agencies and may be concerned that their child should remain within mainstream education for as long as is possible and appropriate.

Mrs Keays has been involved with families in this situation, adopting a supportive role. Alternatively, in my LEA, children may transfer on the completion of Key Stage 1 from the infant school into the Special Needs Unit at the local primary school. In such cases, Mrs Keays has remained involved, providing continuity, a familiar face in new surroundings, and a professional who was already familiar with case histories. Mrs Keays is also able to supplement the written reports which are sent to the Special Needs Unit. Parents are able to discuss particular concerns with Mrs Keays, who is able to call in local specialists from the school medical team if necessary.

Staff slimming sponsorship

Finally, on a lighter note, as it were, as part of its programme for the expansion of nursery provision, the Local Education Authority agreed to fund the staffing for a nursery unit at our infant school. The Authority also agreed to fund certain alterations to the existing buildings, with the understanding that the school PTA would supplement this basic provision. As a staff, we decided to support the venture and raise money by lowering our combined weight, i.e. we organised a collaborative sponsored slim. The venture was to be monitored, recorded and judged by a neutral individual, and who better to fill the role than Mrs Keays, who conducted an impartial confidential weigh-in within the confines of a school stockroom.

It has to be said that this venture was successful only in the short term. True, we did raise almost £100 in support of the nursery fund, but, sad to say, neither our individual nor our corporate weight loss was maintained. An interesting development to the venture was the parents' group which formed to follow a similar format, i.e. using school facilities on a weekly basis to lose weight while raising money for the nursery fund. Again this venture was financially successful, but not renewed after the Autumn Term opening of the nursery class. It went the way of all flesh.

Chapter 9

Meet a governor

Andrew Coates

EDITORS' INTRODUCTION

It will be rare for students on teaching practice to have any contact with governors, and the first contact that most new teachers have will be at formal interview when they may hardly be able to remember names, let alone functions and responsibilities. The purpose of this chapter is to demystify the role and to indicate something of its growing significance as a result of recent legislation.

Accordingly, the human scale is emphasised. Governors are not represented as distant, aloof dignitaries who descend, *deus ex machina* style, when something has gone wrong or when far-reaching decisions need to be made. Instead they are presented as working people, intent on doing an honest job for the good of the school and everyone in it.

They have major responsibilities and take them very seriously, sometimes dividing duties among them, as appropriate – some to oversee finance and staffing; others, sites and buildings; others, curriculum policy. They are not concerned with the day-to-day running of the school – that is the Headteacher's job – but they are charged in law with ensuring that appropriately agreed policies are carried out. In order to fulfil that role, they need to have mechanisms in place for ensuring that they know what is going on in the school and what is in the minds of parents.

As the chapter shows, they have a mass of material to deal with, much of it arising from new legislation, but their concerns can often be very mundane, and no less significant for that, given the aim of a smoothly running enterprise for the benefit of all children and adults. Such an aim applies to schools within the remit of the Local Education Authority, as much as to grant maintained schools whose finance comes from central government.

The chapter ends with information that will be close to the heart of every newly trained teacher, namely, the governors' role in the appointment of applicants for teaching posts. For those who aim high from the start, there is material not only about the appointment of an NQT, but also of a Headteacher.

When I first became a governor, the subject which had, even by then, been on the agenda for the past two years was the smelly lavatory in the Infants.

(School governor)

Amanda, a secretary in her full-time work, is forceful and ebullient, persuading through laughter and enthusiasm; lab technician David is serious, sometimes ponderous, but invariably informed and reliable; Ruth, youth worker, is quiet and shy – says little, but makes pertinent and incisive comments when confident of her ground, particularly in relation to the welfare of children; geriatric nurse John has a profound concern for the human predicament and is disorganised, vague and often late, but sometimes turning up for meetings a week early; Richard's blunt and business-like manner can be abrasive and he sees his role as that of devil's advocate (as well as local councillor); unemployed Pauline is sophisticated and neat, with a thorough grasp of educational theory and practice; accountant Roger, a financial wizard, is highly articulate with the ability to challenge emotional outburst through reasoned and logical argument; factory manager Clive is, to use his words, 'just a parent'.

Such a group of highly individual, sometimes idiosyncratic, people may be found on any governing body. They are, in fact, to be found on the governing body I have chaired now for several years and which contains sixteen governors in all. Our only common bond is a passionate belief in the value of education and a preparedness to devote valuable time to help ensure that educational provision is of the highest possible standard, and that the lives of our children are enriched.

However, few governors are likely to join the governing body with such high ideals. Concerned parents might well have a burning desire to act on behalf of children and the local community, but they are just as likely to have been persuaded to stand for election by other parents at the school gate. Some might have political allegiances and, initially at least, have their own, thinly disguised, agenda. Co-optees from business, commerce and the caring professions may have grudgingly agreed to join after insistent persuasion by an enthusiastic Headteacher. Nevertheless, this mixed bag of motivations and loyalties, with its variety of skills and values, somehow welds itself into a cohesive and decisive unit, capable of liaising effectively with the Headteacher and senior management of their school, and working in partnership to discharge their duties and deal effectively with the minefield of educational bureaucracy.

The responsibilities of the governing body as specified in the 1988 Education Reform Act and explained in some detail in the DES publication, *School Governors: A Guide to the Law* (1992), are complicated. They range from such issues as the school's curriculum, budget and discipline policy to the production of an annual report and dealing with staff grievances and parents' appeals and complaints. The fact that many governors complete their four-year term of office and often volunteer for a further term would seem to suggest that these responsibilities are taken extremely seriously.

Governors' meetings can be animated, controversial, argumentative or sometimes merely efficient, depending on the nature of the agenda – but they are rarely dull. They must be conducted according to certain formal requirements, as laid down in the School Government Regulations. For instance, every school must hold a meeting at least once every term; the chair and vice-chair are normally elected at the first meeting of the school year; decisions cannot be taken unless a quorum of governors is present; minutes are taken and signed by the chair as an accurate account of what happened; and the clerk (a paid officer) is required to send the agenda to each member at least seven clear days before the meeting.

The sheer complexity of the work makes it necessary for most governing bodies to meet at least twice every term. *Ad hoc* groups may be set up to deal with issues such as writing a job specification for the appointment of a Deputy Headteacher, or negotiating a new job description with the Building Services Supervisor towards a new role as Site Manager. When social events with the PTA and the staff are added to an already considerable list of commitments, Thursday evenings at home become a thing of the past.

A great deal of the business of meetings is routine and can be dealt with quickly and efficiently. A typical agenda will contain:

- a report from the Headteacher detailing the daily running of the school, its staffing, financial position, the curriculum and staff training;
- matters raised by the staff representative; and
- communications received from the Local Education Authority and the Department for Education.

Such matters are not always routine, however. Further information may be required about issues such as the particular needs of a pupil currently being statemented by the educational psychologist, or the precise reasons why another pupil has to be excluded from school. A long debate will examine ways in which the problem of falling rolls can be minimised. Matters raised by the staff, perhaps in respect of vandalism in the car park, or the security of the building and the daytime safety of children following the apprehension of a prowler, will provoke serious and concerned discussion. Suggestions offered to help remedy these concerns will then affect how the budget is spent and savings will have to be made in other areas to help pay for the necessary improvements. Communications from outside bodies, particularly new legislation affecting the curriculum or the government of schools, are often long and difficult. At the same time, a mini publishing boom has accompanied this legislation which offers advice on how to cope with the exigencies of governing. Governors may never fully understand this plethora of literature and it needs to be explained in order that amateur volunteers can come to terms with what is essential.

A routine agenda, however, though mercifully short, is hardly likely to galvanize a meeting. The cement that binds an otherwise amorphous gathering is the potential dispute and the attendant identification of a common enemy. The most extreme instance of such confrontation is the proposed closure or amalgamation of the school by the Local Education Authority. Righteous indignation quickly becomes a considered and serious debate as strategies are rehearsed, modified and finalised, resulting in a measured campaign which expresses the strongest possible support for the school's continuation as a viable unit. Parental support is actively sought, the archives are dredged for evidence which charts the school's past reputation for excellence, and a concise document listing its curriculum strengths, the appropriateness of its location within the community, the quality of its staff and its links with teacher training establishments and in-service training is widely circulated.

It is the kind of information which may be as appropriate for an application for grant maintained status as for a campaign against closure.

Although in the past schools may rarely have been threatened with such extreme demands, governors may perceive a need to examine closely an aspect of their school's management, perhaps as a hedge against potential danger. An instance of this may be the suggestion of merging the infant and junior schools following the resignation of the junior school Headteacher. A range of opinions is sought and choices are examined, in consultation with staff, in relation to possible savings of teachers' salaries and administration costs; increased flexibility in delivering the National Curriculum and the advantage of enhanced curriculum expertise; the special problems imposed by two-site working or the physical constraints of the present building; the special ethos of the schools as perceived by parents and the local community; the particular needs of pupils. Both the course of the discussion and the ultimate decision are carefully minuted as a precise record which can be referred to in case of subsequent repercussions.

Not all the issues confronting the governing body are so momentous, however. When I first became a governor the subject that had, even by then, been on the agenda for the past two years was the smelly lavatory in the Infants, the result of twenty years' misuse by small boys. The battle to solve this distasteful problem by the provision of a new drainage system and floor continued for a further year. Subsequent victory hardly sweetened the feelings of frustration that such a trivial and simple issue could have occupied so much valuable time and necessitated the writing and receiving of so many letters.

Indeed, correspondence between governors and local authority officers, councillors and contractors, perhaps concerning the resurfacing of the playground, the resiting of the car park or the installation of speed ramps, can reach mountainous proportions. This may lessen with the advent of local management of schools, but will never disappear entirely. Nevertheless, tenacity, even at the risk of being branded as 'troublemakers,' would seem to be the one attribute which can achieve a quality, value for money service, and best ensure the safety of children and staff on school premises.

Governors 'are not expected to take detailed decisions about the day-to-day running of the school – that is the role of the Head . . . [who] will discuss all the main aspects of school life with the governors and expect them to offer general guidance' (DES, 1992, s 3, sub-s 2). Similarly, the full governing body need not take every decision; it can delegate a committee, or individual, or Headteacher to take certain decisions on its behalf. Every governing body will have a number of committees (often Finance, Curriculum, Sites and Buildings) and their work is likely to increase as schools become more autonomous.

Financial accountability is a crucial area of concern and a committee, in close liaison with the Headteacher, will devise proper financial procedures for monitoring the budget. Such a committee will determine a range of pay discretions including incentive allowances for teachers and grades for non-teaching staff. A small group of governors must be available to direct whether an excluded pupil should be reinstated, and 'at least three governors should decide whether a member of staff is to be dismissed or recommended for dismissal; a subsequent appeal [being] heard by an equal or greater number of governors' (DES, 1992, s 6, sub-s 14).

Further responsibilities include:

- determining the curriculum policy and ensuring its delivery;
- arriving at a staffing plan and participating in staff appointments;
- making regular inspections of the buildings and grounds; and
- agreeing on the school's aims, values, ethos and priorities.

Governors must also have in place agreed policies on charging for school activities; sex education; homework; school uniform, in addition to a curriculum statement published in the School Development Plan, and staff disciplinary procedures.

The range and complexity of these issues is immense and it cannot be stressed too often that they can only be dealt with effectively by ensuring the full co-operation of the Headteacher and staff, the trained professionals who deal with the complexities and pressures of teaching children and liaising with parents on a daily basis. In the case of County and Controlled schools, the role of the Local Education Authority is crucial in this equation, as considered expert advice is always available, thus enabling governors and Headteacher to do their jobs efficiently.

Much of the work is demanding; some may well be onerous, and I have yet to meet a governor who would relish the job of disciplining a teacher, let alone recommending dismissal on the grounds of misconduct. Nevertheless, there are times during a governor's period of office when problems have to be met head-on.

The teaching staff may justifiably complain that classrooms are not adequately cleaned, litter collections are spasmodic, or the boiler needs to be turned on earlier for Monday morning comfort. These problems require that someone talks them over, perhaps accompanied by a cup of tea or a pint, in order that potential alienation does not exacerbate the issue. A governorship may have to be terminated on the grounds of non-attendance at meetings for a continuous period of more than six months. A parent may complain that the school neglected to respond adequately to an injury, or bullying in the playground, or racial discrimination among pupils. In such cases, a thorough and careful investigation is necessary and the results communicated either by letter or, better still, face-to-face with the party concerned. Anonymous letters – invariably a distasteful method of communicating grievances – will involve the governing body in examining its policy for dealing with complaints and communicating it to parents.

Most of a governor's work, however, is pleasurable and largely self-rewarding in that each shared contribution adds to a growing commitment to the welfare of children and young people, coupled with the knowledge that perhaps the next generation will benefit from that contribution.

Tramping round the school grounds on a Saturday morning can be fun, despite the empty beer cans in the hedge, left after Friday night revels at the local hostelry. The PTA Barbecue Disco can be sheer joy or a miserable cacophony, depending on your age and musical predilections. Nevertheless, whatever your preferences, such occasions provide opportunities for governors, staff and parents to meet on common ground and form those bonds of friendship on which the school may thrive.

Other contacts are possible. Parent governors have been known to hold 'surgeries' in school where parents can air grievances, thus improving communications and enabling the governing body to address problems before they are blown out of proportion. Governors are welcome to visit the school at any time to meet the staff and observe how a skilful and committed teacher works with children in an atmosphere of mutual trust and learning. Some schools have established a 'Rent-a-Gov.' scheme whereby children write to a particular governor and meet in class on occasions. It must be remembered, however, that many governors work during the day and, despite the fact that employers must give them reasonable time to visit their school and perform their duties, employers are not bound to pay for that time, thus limiting the opportunities for such visits.

Special occasions are the 'stuff' on which sound relationships between governors, teachers, ancillary staff and the community are built and thrive. The Harvest Festival with the stage laden with gifts of fruit and vegetables, and attended by parents and Senior Citizens, is a rewarding social and aesthetic experience. The carol concert or the Christmas production of 'Aladdin' (complete with wobbly scenery) will enchant because of the pleasure children show, knowing that their job has been well done. The retirement of the school secretary after thirty-five years, who regales her audience with stories and anecdotes, and who remembers children's parents when they were pupils, is a milestone in the school's history. The leaving presentation of a much-loved teacher can extend a morning Assembly until playtime. I recall one occasion when, after six individually wrapped cups and saucers and a coffee pot had been studiously (and slowly) unwrapped, a parent whispered, 'I'm glad she wasn't given a dinner service.'

Perhaps a more 'serious' means of communication between governors and parents is the Annual Parents' Meeting and the production of an annual report. 'Once a year the governors of every school must hold a meeting for parents so that they can discuss the Annual Report and any other matters connected with the governors' work at the school' (DES, 1992, s 9, sub-s1). All parents of registered pupils must be invited to the meeting, and, if there are at least 20 per cent present, they can pass resolutions on any of the issues discussed.

The writing of the report is time consuming and treated extremely seriously. Each governing body will determine its style and precisely what it should contain, and the authors' contributions are discussed in detail before its publication and transmission to parents. The contents of each report, however, must conform to criteria laid down by the Education (No 2) Act 1986, and will contain a summary of the governors' work during the year; the name of each governor, the date on which his/her term of office comes to an end and whether s/he is a parent, teacher or foundation governor, was co-opted or is *ex officio*; the name and address (this can be the address of the school) of the chair and the clerk; a summary of the latest financial statement, how the money was used and how gifts to the school have been spent; the school's links with the community; and notice of the date, time and place of the Annual Parents' Meeting (Part III, s 30). It may also contain the number of children in the school, curriculum statements, term dates and perhaps a short description of the work of the PTA, particularly if their efforts have resulted in a donation. Secondary schools are required to provide information about public examinations and junior schools must list the secondary schools chosen by Year Six leavers.

This is a lot of information and it is difficult to be brief if each section is to be adequately covered, running the inevitable risk that many parents will find it inaccessible, and even tedious. The largely factual report, therefore, needs to be clearly written, jargon free and presented under defined headings, perhaps adopting a 'something for all' policy, so at least it is possible to focus on a particular area of interest whether that is the school's work and links with the community, or the recently adopted health education policy. Its tone aims to communicate to parents that the school is a caring, energetic and forward-looking establishment, capable of furthering the interests of their children, but without sounding self-congratulatory. A governing body sensitive to the fears that people have when faced with posing a question to a meeting of their peers, will also include a tear-off slip so that it can be presented in their name.

The laudable intention of the meeting, to 'give the whole parent body the opportunity to become more closely involved in the life of the school, to mutual benefit' (DES Circular No 8/86, s 13), has, in my experience, regrettably failed to live up to expectations in many schools. Tea and biscuits are invariably supplied, special curriculum demonstrations are often provided by children and educational videos might be shown – all this in an attempt to enrich the evening by providing another focus to complement the otherwise formal report and subsequent discussion.

Despite these ploys it would seem that parents are unwilling to turn up in large numbers, even though few fail to attend parents' evenings when they have the opportunity to discuss the progress of their own children. Perhaps the underlying problem is that the event is too 'abstract' and, by its nature, is incapable of dealing with specific issues. In mitigation, however, the report is invaluable as it provides a yardstick for future planning. The evening, for those parents who do attend, is an opportunity to meet the governors and staff and discuss issues of mutual concern. Perhaps if parents don't attend, it merely means that they have no major concerns.

In the case of County and Controlled schools, the Local Education Authority employs the school's staff but governors managing a delegated budget have extensive powers and can determine a staffing complement, and whether a member of staff should be replaced. Not all governors need to be involved in interviewing and selecting, however, and the governing body determines which and how many governors will take this responsibility. The appointments procedure is one of their most important duties and a successful appointment at any level is crucial to the future well-being of the school, requiring a great deal of careful planning and preparation. This is the first point of contact between the newly qualified teacher and the governors involved in appointments. It is the latter's responsibility to ensure that the experience, from start to finish, is both friendly and professional.

When appointing a Head or Deputy Headteacher the vacancy must be advertised throughout England and Wales and a selection panel of at least three governors set up. In the case of a vacancy for a Deputy Headteacher, the Headteacher has the right to attend meetings and offer advice. Other teaching appointments may well be the responsibility of the Headteacher and one or more governors as determined by the governing body. In all appointments the Chief Education Officer or a representative can attend meetings and offer professional advice, but only governors are allowed to vote and the Local Education Authority must abide by their decision unless the candidate fails to meet the legal requirements on qualifications or health. It is also against the law to discriminate because of sex, race and ethnic or national origins (DES, 1992, s 14, sub-ss 8–10, 13).

Despite the governors' primacy in these procedures, it would be a foolish governing body which ignored, or failed to seek out, the considered advice of local authority representatives. Indeed, it has been my experience that such advice not only saves work, but also ensures that every eventuality is catered for and that the proceedings run smoothly and conform strictly to the law.

The recruitment process starts as soon as a vacancy occurs and follows a systematic series of operations from determining a job description and person description through to the final interview and subsequent appointment. The appointment of a Headteacher is the entire responsibility of the governing body in liaison with the local authority. The selection of other teachers, including the Deputy Headteacher, must, in my opinion, involve the full participation of the Headteacher who will work with the appointee daily and will be the person most likely fully to understand the needs of the school.

A job description will reflect the nature of the work and its duties and responsibilities in some order of importance. A person specification describes the characteristics of the person required and may be devised under the headings of 'essential' and 'desirable,' so as not to limit the range and quality of applications by being too explicit. These will vary according to the level of the appointment.

Senior management posts require a great deal of experience in education and sound leadership and communication skills. Potential post holders must be capable of planning and implementing a significant aspect of the National Curriculum. Newly qualified teachers need to provide evidence of their commitment to teaching, of successful experiences while in training and, perhaps, of some expertise in a specific area of the curriculum. In such a case, the college reference is an important document and perhaps the only 'objective' evidence for their potential as teachers. (Appendix 1 contains a job description and a person specification for the post of infant school Headteacher as devised by me, in conjunction with the governing body and based on a Local Education Authority approved format.) When applications have been received, a shortlist is determined and references are requested in preparation for the interview.

These complicated procedures are designed to secure the 'right' person for the job. They do not prevent humanity, however, as candidates are invited to see the school and meet the staff and stress is minimised by ensuring a warm and courteous welcome. The interviewing panel may indeed be as nervous as the candidates. Interviews are carefully prepared and candidates are treated equally. Questions are usually devised beforehand and they should be clear, unambiguous and directly related to the requirements of the job – not to extraneous issues or matters associated with a person's sex, marital status or race. This should enable candidates to relax and respond freely, express opinions and make judgements.

When the time comes to reach a decision, each member of the interviewing panel completes his/her assessment of each candidate independently using the criteria agreed at the outset, before comparing notes in open discussion. At the point of selection it is desirable that a consensus has been reached, but, if this proves impossible, a vote is taken. Even at this stage, however, the process is fraught with problems. We have all heard of the person who is a 'good talker' and who 'got the job because s/he interviewed well', and conversely, the person who 'goes to pieces' or who, because of nervousness, appears overconfident, perhaps boastful. Similarly, governors may have shared values about the ethos of the school, thus applying an unintentional bias against certain candidates who 'will fail to fit in'.

Potentially emotive words are also used as judgements of value. Terms such as 'thinking person', 'dynamic', 'open-minded', 'forceful', 'quiet', 'academic', 'liberal', mean different things to different people. We all like to think of ourselves as good judges of human behaviour, however, but we interpret it differently according to our own experience. Perhaps the ability to adjust and change opinions in the light of constructive and reasoned debate is the only way to overcome our prejudice and make the best choice for our school.

Finally, without the good will and co-operation of all teaching and non-teaching staff and parents, the work of the governing body can never be truly effective. Some teachers, particularly those who have recently qualified, may find the seemingly sophisticated and outwardly confident governor intimidating. Perhaps you might like to consider that this outward show masks a mixture of indecision and self-doubt.

REFERENCES

Department of Education and Science (1986) *Education (No 2) Act,* London: HMSO.
—— (1986) *Circular No 8186.*
—— (1992) *School Governors: A Guide to the Law,* London: HMSO.

Appendix 1: Job description for a newly qualified teacher

This post, on the Standard National Scale for salary purposes, is to be performed in accordance with the provisions of the School Teachers' Pay and Conditions Document and within the range of teachers' duties set out in that document.

The post requires you to teach children in the 3–7 age range.

Duties and responsibilities

- Carry out the duties of a school teacher as determined by current and subsequent conditions of service.
- Be responsible to the Headteacher in all matters related to work within the school.
- Deliver a broad and balanced curriculum, which is up to date, relevant to all pupils, and sufficiently flexible to accommodate changing needs and the requirements of the National Curriculum.
- Monitor and evaluate pupils' progress and maintain suitable records.
- Support the Headteacher in providing an equitable range of educational opportunities for all pupils, having regard, as appropriate, to background, culture, gender and special educational needs.
- Support the Headteacher in developing and implementing the agreed aims and policies of the school.
- Work with the Headteacher and staff in sustaining the ethos of the school, which aims to provide a stimulating and caring environment.
- Support the Headteacher in upholding the school discipline policy and its systems for enhancing children's social and pastoral development.
- Support the Headteacher in developing productive relationships with parents and the community.
- Undertake appropriate in-service education and training.

This job description will be revised as and when necessary following appropriate consultation procedures.

Person specification

	Essential	Desirable
Experience	Evidence of successful teaching experience during training.	Evidence of other experience of working with children, i.e. classroom assistant/nursery nurse/ playscheme/summer camp.
Skills and abilities	Ability to work as a member of a team. Evidence that a range of National Curriculum subjects have been studied and understood. Evidence of some understanding of assessing, recording and reporting on children's development and attainment. Some awareness of current developments in primary education. Energy and enthusiasm.	Evidence of some expertise in a National Curriculum subject. Evidence of some expertise in an area which will enhance the life of the school, i.e. ability to play a musical instrument, qualifications in a sporting activity, some fluency in a foreign language.
Training	Willingness to undertake appropriate training.	
Education/ qualifications	Qualified teacher status.	Either a good Honours degree in an area appropriate for the needs of young children, or evidence that a good BA (QTS)/B.Ed. Hons degree will be achieved.
Other	Some understanding of the needs of children from diverse social and economic backgrounds.	

Appendix 2: Job description for a Headteacher

The Headteacher is responsible to the governors and, in the case of county schools, to the Local Education Authority, for the successful administration and organisation of the school and for determining the curriculum provision. She/he will be expected to achieve good working relations with staff and community and to be accountable to governors and the LEA. The duties of the Headteacher are those listed in the School Teachers'

Pay and Conditions Document 1992 and, in particular, those described below (not in order of priority).

Duties and responsibilities

The Headteacher will be expected, in conjunction with the LEA, governors and staff:

- to manage the school in a positive way;
- to institute appropriate mechanisms for consultation and decision-making;
- to make provision for children with special needs;
- to devise appropriate strategies for managing and co-ordinating the work of the school which recognise the needs of children from diverse social and economic backgrounds;
- to formulate the school's aims and to put into practice its objectives through a school development plan;
- to maintain a broad and balanced curriculum which is up-to-date, relevant to all pupils and sufficiently flexible, in relation to the delivery of the school's integrated approach, to accommodate changing needs and the requirements of the National Curriculum;
- to modify the organisation and curriculum in the light of pupil needs, national priorities and local policies;
- to monitor, evaluate and review the quality of provision and standard of teaching, and of pupil progress, and to maintain suitable records;
- to deploy and manage staff and other resources according to the needs of the school;
- to organise appropriate staff development and school based in-service programmes and to ensure there is a programme of counselling for staff concerning their responsibilities and careers;
- to provide appropriate job descriptions to indicate general responsibilities, specific tasks, lines of management and accountability;
- to uphold the school discipline policy and organise systems for the social and pastoral development of pupils to complement their academic work;
- to encourage and develop productive links with parents, the community and other schools in the area;
- to operate and develop the local management of the school in accordance with the scheme approved by the Secretary of State for Education;
- to supervise and participate in arrangements for the Appraisal Scheme; and
- to provide a fair and equitable range of educational opportunities for all pupils irrespective of background, culture, gender and special educational needs.

Person specification

	Essential	Desirable
Experience	Considerable primary management experience (at least two years as Deputy Head or Head in a primary school). Substantial teaching experience in the appropriate age range.	Management experience in the appropriate age range. Significant teaching experience.
Skills and abilities	Ability to lead, organise, motivate and care for the whole school community, in liaison with the staff team. Ability to communicate appropriately with a range of people (pupils, teachers, support staff, parents, governors, members of the wider community). Ability to prioritise and delegate appropriately. Ability to develop and co-ordinate whole-school policies. Ability to monitor, review and evaluate the delivery and development of the curriculum, in relation to the changing requirements of the National Curriculum, and to plan appropriate staff development activities. Energy, enthusiasm, and a positive outlook.	Experience of financial management.
Training	Willingness to undertake appropriate training.	
Education/ qualifications	Qualified teacher status.	Evidence of further appropriate study.
Other	Understanding of the needs of children from diverse social and economic backgrounds, and of those with a variety of special needs.	

Index

Balshaw, M. 125
Bastiani, J. xi, 103
BCA *see* bilingual classroom assistant
Besag, V. 85
bilingual classroom assistant (BCA),
  experience 114–20; pressures on
  124; qualifications 124–5;
  role/function 121–4
Biott, C. x
Bourne, J. and McPake, J. x
British Psychological Society (BPS) 80

caretaker 11, 131
case conferences 147
child psychiatrist 89
children, behavioural difficulties
  78–9, 84; with emotional
  difficulties 84; as individuals 153;
  with learning difficulties 77–8, 84;
  mixed ability 58; with physical
  difficulties 83–4; pre-school 83;
  secondary school 84; under
  achievement with sensory
  impairment 83; with speech and
  language difficulties 84;
  streams/sets 58
children (getting to know them)
  14–15; general summary of
  conditions 15–16; outline
  information 16–19; in practice
  22–3; specific detail 19–22
Children and their Primary Schools
  (1967) 102
classroom, essential equipment 44–5;
  organisation 25–6, 126–7; practice
  58; routines and rituals 6–13
classroom assistants 10–11, 12, 33,
  113–14; and classroom

organisation 126–7; developing
  partnership with 127; experience
  of bilingual assistant 114–20;
  functions of 122–3; job description
  128; as link between home and
  school 122; and planning 118;
  pressures on 124; qualifications
  124–5; role 121–2; and school
  organisation 126; skills of 123–4;
  support for children's learning
  127; work areas 125–6
Clay, Marie M. 85
cleaners 11, 13, 33
Code of Practice (1994) 67, 70, 78, 80,
  85
communicable diseases 154–5
Community Education Teacher
  Outreach Worker *see* Home–School
  Liaison Teacher
Community Medical Officer 146, 148
Cultural Liaison Teacher *see*
  Home–School Liaison Teacher
curriculum, cross-curricular theme
  141, 142–3; development 57, 103,
  141–2; organisation 58; teaching of
  topics 15–16, *see also* National
  Curriculum

Deputy Head 33, 35, 51, 141, 142;
  appointment of 164
dinner supervisor *see* lunch-time
  supervisors

Education Acts 51, 80, 85, 157, 162
Educational Priority Areas (EPAs)
  98, 103
educational psychologist (EP or 'ed.
  psych.') 66, 76–7; and behaviour

Coffee

The Plant and the Product

René Coste

Member of the Academy of Overseas Sciences, France
Tropical Agronomist
Formerly Director of the Coffee and Cacao
Research Institute (IRCC), France

With the collaboration of H Cambrony
Agronomist, specialist in Tropical Agronomy

Translated by Judith N Wolf
with editorial advice from H D Tindall
Emeritus Professor of Tropical Agronomy
Cranfield Institute of Technology, England

MACMILLAN

.ABORATORS AND FRIENDS

t
ier
franchi
beuf

\M

Originally published in 1989 under the title
Caféiers et cafés by
Maisonneuve et Larose, 15 rue Victor-Cousin, 75005 Paris, France.
No responsibility is taken by the holders of the copyright
for any changes to the original French text.

This edition published by THE MACMILLAN PRESS LTD
London and Basingstoke
Associated companies and representatives in Accra,
Auckland, Delhi, Dublin, Gaborone, Hamburg, Harare,
Hong Kong, Kuala Lumpur, Lagos, Manzini, Melbourne,
Mexico City, Nairobi, New York, Singapore, Tokyo

Published in co-operation with the Technical Centre for Agricultural and
Rural Co-operation, PO Box 380, 700 AJ Wageningen, The Netherlands.

ISBN 0–333–57296–3

Phototypeset by Intype, London
Printed in Hong Kong

A catalogue record for this book is available from the British Library

The opinions expressed in this document and the spellings of proper names
and territorial boundaries are solely the responsibility of the author and in
no way involve the official position or the liability of the Technical Centre
for Agricultural and Rural Co-operation.

Cover illustration: Coffee Harvesting (*C. arabica*) in Burundi, Mumirwa (Source: J Deuss)
with background illustration © Phil Brodatz, Dover Publications Inc.

Contents

(iii)

Preface

This book, entitled *Caféiers et Cafés* in French, replaces my earlier work, *Le Caféier*, published in 1968.

I was asked by my friends and publisher to write this new book called *Coffee, the Plant and the Product*, in order to distinguish it from the earlier work and to better emphasise its more comprehensive nature. It is part of a large series of works of which I am the Series Editor, most of which are only available in French, published by Maisonneuve et Larose.

Since 1968, considerable progress has been made on research, be it agronomic, technological, chemical, or physiological. During this 20 year period, knowledge of coffee trees and coffee has increased considerably since the first Brazilian studies which took place more than a century ago. The potential that this knowledge offers with regard to the evolution of coffee growing and technological developments in the use of beans is of major interest. Circumstances throughout the world have also undergone major changes (mainly with regard to the cultivation of robusta in Brazil, the Philippines and Indonesia), concerning production as well as consumption problems. It was therefore considered necessary to perfect and update the earlier work.

The present work, *Coffee, the Plant and the Product*, is a technical book which, although constructed along the same lines as my previous publications (see Bibliography), has been thoroughly restructured, revised and updated, to keep abreast of the knowledge acquired over the past years and the technical inputs that have led to a better exploitation of coffee trees and coffee throughout the world, particularly with regard to genetics, tissue culture, chemistry and physiology.

The structure and arrangement of the work was revised and the bibliography updated to include the principle studies published since the publication of *Le Caféier* in 1968. Despite this agronomic enrichment, its practical impact has been carefully preserved. Coffee growers will find that it contains advice and information of value for the development of their plantations.

I would like to express my deep gratitude to my colleagues and friends who have each helped in this task in the areas of their own specialities, most particularly to H Cambrony for his contribution in the area of agronomy, and in addition E M Lavabre, J C Vincent and R Muller. I would also like to thank Miss J Collot, Head of the Documentation Service of the IRCC, and her colleague, Mrs Boussard.

Many thanks go also to my friend, Mr J P Pinardon, President and Director-General of Editions Maisonneuve et Larose, for his interest in this new work *Coffee, the Plant and the Product*, and to the CTA, for its participation in co-publishing this book.

Paris, 1991
R Coste

Acknowledgements

The author would like to express his gratitude to several firms that manufacture coffee processing equipment for supplying illustrations for this book:
BENTALL   (United Kingdom)
John GORDON   (United Kingdom)
Ferd   GOTHOT (Germany)
NEOTEC   (Hamburg, Germany)
ILLYCAFFE   (Italy)
Figures 78, 81, 86, 87, 89, 90 and 98 are taken from the book *Les caféiers et cafés dans le monde*, by R. Coste, vol. I, 1955; figures 79, 80, 82, 83, 84, 85, 88 and 91 appeared in *Protection des culture de caféiers, cacaoyers et autres plantes pérennes tropicales*, by E.-M. Lavabre, I.F.C.C., 1961.

The Technical Centre for Agricultural and Rural Co-operation (CTA) operates under the Lomé Convention between member States of the European Community and the African, Caribbean and Pacific (ACP) States.

The aim of CTA is to collect, disseminate and facilitate the exchange of information on research, training and innovations in the spheres of agricultural and rural development and extension, for the benefit of the ACP States.

To achieve this aim, CTA:

• commissions and publishes studies;
• organises and supports conferences, workshops and courses;
• supports publications and translations;
• and offers an extensive information service.

Postal address: Postbus 380, 6700 AJ Wageningen, Netherlands
Telephone: 31–0–8380–20484
Telex: 44–30169 CTA NL
Fax: 31–0–8380–31052

1 *Botanical classification*

General information

Coffee is a member of the large Rubiaceae family, within which it constitutes the *Coffea* genus that was created by C. Linnaeus. The coffee tree had previously (1717) been considered to be a Jasmine (*Jasminum arabicum laurifolio*), by A. de Jussieu, who is responsible for its first botanical description. Professor A. Chevalier referred to about 70 species in his systematic grouping in 1929. Since then this figure has increased, with the addition of some new species that have been discovered throughout the world over the past few years, particularly in Madagascar. Explorations conducted recently in Africa will undoubtedly enable this inventory to be further enriched.

Whatever the resources of the woodland flora may be, the two main species exploited in the world at the present time are *Coffea arabica* L. and *Coffea canephora* Pierre. Other species of coffee are being cultivated less extensively, although they are still found in certain countries for various reasons. These are namely *C. liberica* Bull ex Hiern, *C. abeokutae* Cramer, *C. dewevrei* de Wild and Durand and *C. congensis* Froh.

Coffea robusta, which is very widespread, is generally considered to be a variety or form of *C. canephora* whereas, according to A. Chevalier, *C. excelsa*, which is well known in Central Africa, is one of the many strains of *C. dewevrei* de Wild and Durand.

The different species of the *Coffea* genus have very diverse appearances and behaviour. This applies to their development up to the adult stage, starting from the sub-shrub stage when they are a few decimetres tall, until they become 12 to 15 m tall trees, and to the characteristics of their branches, leaves, flowers, fruits, and beans, which are also very disparate. Some of these species, which look very different from cultivated coffee trees, can only be identified with certainty by specialised botanists.

Coffea arabica L.

Coffea arabica is the species that has been known for the longest time and is also the most widespread throughout the world.

It is an evergreen, often multi-stemmed shrub, about 8 to 10 m tall. Its branches are opposite, long, flexible, and rather thin; its habit is semi-erect when young and spreading or pendulous when adult. The leaves are opposite, oval-shaped, acuminate, having a short petiolè with undulating margins and a shiny, slightly crinkled surface. The leaves are between 10 and 15 cm long and 4 to 6 cm wide. White, jasmine-scented flowers, grouped together in the axils of the paired leaves, with two to three cymes, make up whorls of 8 to 15 flowers. Each flower is attached by a short pedicel. A calyx, made up of five small sepals, is above the ovary. The corolla is formed by a long tube which spreads out into five narrow lobes (rarely six). There are usually five stamens, with linear exserted anthers and the pistil is made up of a long style with two fine stigmata which dominate the corolla. The ovary is in the form of a drupe, and is commonly called a cherry. It is ovoid or sub-globulous, red when ripe, 10 to 15 mm wide and 16 to 18 mm long, and consists of a coloured exocarp (skin), a fleshy, yellowish-white mesocarp (pulp) and two beans joined together along their flat sides. When one of the two ovaries aborts, the other develops into an ovoid bean, which is commercially known as a 'peaberry'. Each bean is protected by two coats. The first, the endocarp, is thin with a fibrous texture (parchment) and the second, the perisperm, is a very fine membrane (skin or silverskin) which more or less adheres to the bean. The seed (or bean in commercial language) is yellowish-grey to slate-grey, and is rather bluish or grey-green, depending upon the variety, the method of preparation, the environment, and the amount of time it is stored for. It consists of a corneous endosperm and has a smooth surface, with a more or less rectilinear furrow running along the main axis of the flat side. The embryo is short and is located at the base. It consists of a conical radicle and two cordiform cotyledons (Figs 1, 2, and 3).

The size and shape of the beans differs depending upon the variety, environmental conditions, and cropping practices. On average, they are 10 mm long, 6 to 7 mm wide and 3 to 4 mm thick. They weigh between 0.15 and 0.20 g.

Coffea arabica is not from Arabia, as its name implies, but from Ethiopia (Abyssinia), where it grows in very large stands, on the high plateaux (1300–1900 m). Botanists agree upon its African, rather than Asian origin.

This species, which is autogamous (self-fertilising), has relatively uniform characteristics. Nevertheless, it has given rise to a numer of varieties (hybrids, mutants, etc.), regional types and cultivars, which reflect the influence of the environment.

Among the many varieties of *C. arabica*, the following should be noted: *C. arabica* L **var**. *typica* L. was introduced into Brazil from French Guyana at the beginning of the eighteenth century. It was used in the country's original coffee plantations before the spread of selected varieties which predominate today.

C. arabica **L**. **var**. *amarella* **Chev**. is the result of a mutation of *C. arabica* L. var *typica*, which was discovered in Brazil in the Botucatŭ region (São Paulo). This small shrub with yellow fruits is not very widespread and is considered to be a botanical curiosity (Amarelo Coffee from Botucatŭ).

C. arabica **L**. **var**. *maragogype* **Hort**. is originally from Bahia, and is considered to be a mutation. It is an expansive shrub with large leaves, long

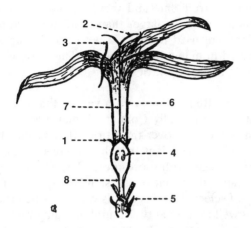

1 calyx

2 stigmata

3 stamens

4 ovaries

5 calicle

6 corolla tube

7 style

8 pedicle

Fig 1   Flower of *C. arabica*, longitudinal section

Fig 2   *C. arabica* flower buds

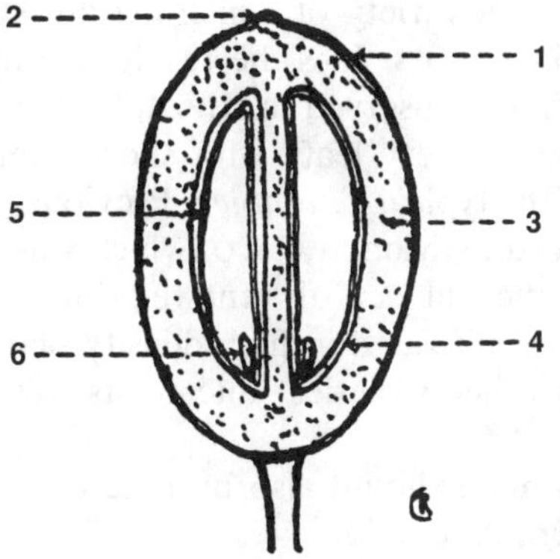

1 epicarp (skin)

2 disc

3 mesocarp (pulp)

4 endocarp

5 seminal tegument

6 embryo

Fig 3   Diagrammatic cross-section of *C. arabica* fruit

internodes, and large fruits. It fruits late and very irregularly; productivity is highly variable. The beans are much larger than those of *C. arabica* var. *typica* (0.25 – 0.30 g). They are used to make a beverage having qualities which are widely appreciated in many different ways. This variety is grown in Brazil and other Latin American countries.

C. arabica **L. var.** *bourbon* **(B. Rodr) Choussy** is a variety that is considered to be a recessive mutant. It is originally from the Indian Ocean island of Reunion and has been introduced all over the world. It is smaller than the typical *C. arabica*, and is a compact plant, which is a consequence of the abundant development of branches with short internodes. The young shoots are green. The bean is smaller than that of the standard species. Brazilian plantations consist largely of selected strains of this variety, which is appreciated for its productivity as well as its quality. Natural breeding with a variety of *C. arabica* imported from Sumatra to Brazil at the end of the last century led to the creation of the **Mundo Novo**. Its strains, which were selected by the Campinas Institute of Agronomy, possess extraordinary qualities with regard to robustness, vigour, and especially productivity.

According to some authorities, another variety, the 'Bourbon Amarello', which is also highly productive, was the result of a natural hybridisation between *C. arabica* var. *amarella* Chev. and *C. arabica* var. *bourbon*. Many selected strains are grown in Brazil.

C. arabica **L. var.** *laurine* **J. L. de Lanessan**, originally from Reunion, is a small shrub which is considered to be a mutation of *C. arabica* var. *Bourbon*. Often called 'Pointed Bourbon', it fruits little, but is highly regarded for the quality of its production.

C. arabica **L.var.** *Mokka* **Cramer** (mutation) is a small coffee tree with many branches, and is not very productive. The small beans are used to make a high quality beverage. It is not grown extensively.

C. arabica **L. var.** *caturra* **KMC** is a variety of which certain strains have been widely appreciated in previous years. It is the result of a mutation of *C. arabica* L. var. *bourbon* which was observed in Brazil. The shrub, which is low-growing and looks dwarfed, is very leafy with short internodes. Its productivity is higher than that of the typical *C. arabica*. Previously cultivated in Brazil, it has since been replaced by Mundo Novo, which was mentioned earlier. However, it has been the subject of renewed interest of late, especially in Colombia. It is being cultivated in high density plantations, to which it lends itself better than other varieties, due to its low branching habit.

The low-growing, dwarfed **Catuai** should also be noted. It is a hybrid between Mundo Novo and Caturra Amarello.

The hybrid of **Timor** should be mentioned. This is a natural hybrid between *C. arabica* and *C. canephora*. It is used in various associations by geneticists who value it for its resistance to *Hemileia vastatrix* and Coffee Berry Disease (CBD).

In addition to the varieties of coffee that are cultivated, there are several others that are used for research only. The following varities of *C. arabica* L. should be noted: var. *myrtifolia* (syn. var. *murta*); var. *culta* Chev.; var. *angustifolia* (Roxb.) Chev.; var. *calycanthema* KMC; var. *cera* KMC; var. *semperflorens* KMC; var. *pendula* Cramer; var. *polysperma* Burck; var. *nana* KMC; var. *rugosa* KMC, etc.

Besides these rather well-defined varieties, *C. arabica* has a great number of cultivars which are the result of the plant's adaptation to environmental conditions. Most coffee-growing regions have one or more typical forms that constitute as many cultivars ('Blue Mountain' for example). However, these characteristics, which are not hereditary, may alter rapidly when the ecological conditions change.

Coffea canephora Pierre

The species *C. canephora* takes second place in the world to *C. arabica*. It is mostly grown in Africa and Indonesia and is also being cultivated quite successfully at the present time in northern Brazil (Bahia, Amazonia, etc.). In this region, the climate, which is hot and humid, is not favourable for growing *C. arabica*. The volume of business generated from this species on the international market has been increasing steadily for half a century, and it may be said that one third of the coffee consumed in the world today originates from this species.

Coffea canephora was discovered in Africa towards the end of the last century. Its natural area of distribution is extremely vast as it grows in the hot, very humid climatic zones that cover most of the western forested region, the Congo Basin and Mayumbe, and extend as far east as the western shores of Lake Victoria.

An evergreen shrub, it grows to a height of 8 to 10 m, and is naturally multi-stemmed. Its branches are long and flexible; the leaves are large (20–35 cm long and 8–15 cm wide), oblong, acuminate, and undulating. The inflorescences are axillary, and consist of one to three whorls, each of which have 15 to 20 white, scented flowers, with corollas of between five and seven petals. Each cluster has a total of several dozen, indeed even as many as a hundred flowers, which develop into very abundant, compact groups of fruits. The latter are either sub-globular or ovoid and are 8 to 16 mm long. The exocarp is red when ripe. The beans are ovoid and although their size varies, they are generally small.

Compared with *C. arabica*, *C. canephora* generally appears to be more vigorous and productive. It is also more robust and less vulnerable to diseases, namely *Hemileia*. The organoleptic qualities of its beverage differ from those of *C. arabica*, but they are also appreciated by many consumers and are widely used for manufacturing instant coffee. The caffeine content is also higher in *C. canephora* than in *C. arabica*.

The species *C. canephora*, which unlike *C. arabica* is cross-fertilised (or self-sterile), includes robustas, Kouilous, Niouli, etc, which are extremely polymorphic forms of coffee, but have a number of common characteristics.

The great diversity of these species and their transitional forms has not made the task of systematic botanists any easier. The species nomenclature is still imprecise.

The most widely cultivated variety (its classification as a variety is contested by some botanists) in the world is **robusta**, which makes up at least 95 per cent of the *C. canephora* plantations. This variety corresponds well to the typical description of the species given earlier. It is not necessary to emphasise its vigour and productivity, both of which are well known.

The cultivation of robusta has increased considerably throughout the world, not only in Africa (Ivory Coast, Congo, Cameroon, Uganda, Angola, etc.), but also in the Far East (India, Indonesia, Philippines, etc.) and Oceania (New Caledonia, etc.).

The **Kouilou** (or **Quillou**) variety, which grows spontaneously in Congo, Gabon, Ivory Coast, etc. is very similar to robusta. This variety, which occurs in various forms, is distinguished from robusta particularly by its longer leaves and smaller fruits and beans. It is cultivated in the Ivory Coast together with robusta, but its advantage over robusta is that it is more drought-resistant. However, the small size of its beans is actually a handicap for its distribution from a commercial point of view. It is also cultivated in Madagascar with typical robusta, and in Ghana, etc. It is known in Brazil by the name 'Conilon'.

The variety **Niaouli** is originaly from Dahomey, and is characterised by a bushy habit. Fruiting is relatively meagre although it does continue throughout the year. However, this is a serious disadvantage as it favours the development of a dangerous bean pest, the berry borer. Its cultivation is limited to Dahomey and Togo and is not very extensive even in those countries.

Finally, there is the so-called **de la Nana** variety, in Central African Republic, which is renowned for its resistance to drought.

Several common *Coffea* varieties are illustrated in Figs 4 to 13.

Other cultivated species

The two main species, *C. arabica* and *C. canephora*, account for at least 99 per cent of the world's coffee. The remainder consists of the production of several species, the interest in which has become very minor with the considerable extension of robusta coffee. These are mainly *C. liberica* Bull. *in* Hiern and *C. abeokutae* Cramer, which are described briefly hereafter:

Coffea liberica **Bull.** *in* **Hiern** grows to a height of 15 to 18 m. Vegetative growth is robust, and it is characterised by large, leathery, leaves (20–35 cm) having long petioles; its flowers, whose corollas have between 5 and 11 lobes,

Fig 4 *Left   C. arabica* coffee trees. Kivu, Zaire (Courtesy: Cours)

Fig 5 *Below   C. excelsa.* Boukoko Station, Central African Republic (Courtesy: Pujol)

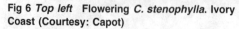

Fig 6 *Top left* Flowering *C. stenophylla*. Ivory Coast (Courtesy: Capot)

Fig 7 *Top Right* Mature *C. liberica*. Reunion (Courtesy: Coste)

Fig 8 *Bottom left* *C. excelsa*. Central African Republic (Courtesy: Dublin)

Fig 9 *Bottom right* *C. mauritiana* branches. Reunion (Courtesy: Foury)

(8)

Fig 10 *C. arabica* fruiting. Madagascar (Courtesy: Cours)

and its large globular fruits, which are grouped together to a maximum of about 10 fruits per cluster. The beans grow to a length of about 18 mm. The quality of the beverage is rather mediocre (Fig 7).

There are many varieties of *C. liberica*, which were grown quite successfully in Africa, tropical Asia, and even in the Americas (Guyana) after the devastation of *C. arabica* plantations due to *Hemeleia* attacks at the end of the last century. However, its cultivation has now been almost completely replaced by *C. robusta*.

Coffea abeokutae **Cramer** is a rather large shrub, with very vigorous leaf production, and a more or less conical habit. This species is extremely variable and exists in several different forms. It seems to be related to either *C. liberica*, or *C. dewevrei* var. *excelsa*. It was widely cultivated in the Ivory Coast, where its production was commercially known by the name 'Gros Indēniē'. A serious disease, tracheomycosis, decimated the plantations about 40 years ago and robusta was grown as a substitute.

Coffea dewevrei **de Wild and Durand** is characterised by the height of the trees, which may be as tall as 15 to 20 m, their vigour and productive ability. The leaves are large (20–40 cm long) and leathery. The fruits, which are red when ripe, are of average size. There are many forms, the main one being referred to as *C. excelsa* Chev., which was discovered in the Upper Chari Basin; there are many stands of this in Sangha and East Cameroon.

Excelsa coffee is of some interest, with its remarkable adaptation to tropical climatic zones with a very pronounced, long, dry season (five to six months). It remained popular in the Central African Republic for that reason, given the possibility of cultivating it in regions with insufficient rainfall which were unsuitable for *C. robusta*. Unfortunately this species is very sensitive to tracheomycosis, which decimates it. It produces coffee of rather irregular quality. It should be noted that the species is still being cultivated in the Far East in Indonesia, North Viet Nam, etc., but on an extremely limited basis (Figs 5 and 8).

The following coffee species still exist, although they are no longer of agricultural interest: *C. stenophylla* G. Don., orginally from West Africa (Fig 6); *C. eugenioides* Moore, originally from the region of the great African lakes (Fig 72); *C. congensis* Frohener, which was found in the areas flooded by the rising of the river in the Congo basin and has the special characteristic of being able to withstand long periods of submersion. A few Indian species should be added to this list, such as *C. bengalensis* Rose., *C. travancorensis* W. and A., *C. wightiana* W. and A., etc.

Finally, this section would not be complete without mentioning the many species of spontaneous coffee in the Mascarenes Islands, and most particularly in Madagascar, a common characteristic being the absence of caffeine in the beans. These are: *C. mogenetii, C. dubardii, C. mauritiana* Lamarck (Fig 9), *C. bertrandii, C. luxifolia, C. farafaganensis, C. vianneyi,* etc.

During recent explorations in Africa, specimens of the species *C. pseudozanguebariae* Br., whose beans are caffeine-free, were collected in forests near Mombasa, Kenya.

The quality of the beverage prepared using these species is unfortunately mediocre at best due to the bitter elements present in the beans. Although this prevents them from being used on their own, there is still the possibility of using them in research on the production of good quality coffee with little or no caffeine other than from the arabicas, through genetic combinations with other cultivated species. However, the research that was being carried out on this extremely interesting topic was interrupted in 1974 for political reasons at the request of the Malagasy government.

Systematic classfication of the *Coffea* genus

This classification seems very complex and confused to the layman. The increase in coffee growing since the beginning of the century, together with the appearance of numerous natural hybrids, mutants, cultivars, etc., poses a problem for these studies. Moreover, extensive deforestation in Africa, where pockets of forest species had previously been found, has undoubtedly already resulted in the loss of species, the absence of which will render the job of the botanist even more difficult.

After the great botanists such as Linnaeus and de Jussieu, several authors studied the systematic classification of the *Coffea* genus. Among the works published, those of Professors Chevalier, de Wildeman, Lebrun, Krug, Porteres, and Leroy will be referred to in this text.

A considerable amount of herbal material has been amassed at the National Museum of Natural History in Paris, and has been significantly enriched over the past few years, namely with the collections of Leroy. Moreover, on-site observations have enabled plant collectors to clarify certain facts.

Can one then hope that a new systematic classification of the genus will soon be established? Such a key to the classification of species, sub-species, cultivars, types, etc., with information on the links between them, would be of enormous value to those working on the improvement of coffee throughout the world.

Species collections and gene banks

Research work has necessitated the establishment of living collections in some research stations. Their components, which are studied and monitored, are used to improve plant material, mainly in hybridising programmes.

Thus in Campinas (Brazil), as in Ruiru (Kenya) and Divo (Ivory Coast), there are quite sizeable botanical collections of coffee species.

Today, the collections found on stations of cultivated and particularly forest species take on considerable importance due to the unfortunate and ever-increasing disappearance of areas of natural stands in the middle of forests, which have themselves been devastated by intensive exploitation.

For 20 years, several organisations have carried out these exploratory missions. The IFCC, ORSTOM, and the National Museum of Natural History in Paris have explored West, Central, and East Africa, including Madagascar and the Mascarenes Islands, with teams of highly qualified experts specialising in the *Coffea* genus. Leroy, assisted by Vianney-Liaud (IFCC), Charrier and his team of specialists from ORSTOM were the driving forces behind this. The living material collected was mostly from the Ivory Coast (Divo Central Station and Man Station) and has already been the subject of many reports. There are no specimens of forest coffee trees from the Mascarenes in these collections.

It is thus particularly urgent to take any action necessary to prevent the destruction of this plant material and to ensure its protection and conservation. It would be highly desirable for a large, international organisation to assume the responsibility, due to the magnitude of this endeavour and its international implications. The possibilities today of conserving this material in 'gene banks', under specified conditions, using laboratory 'in vitro' tissue culture techniques should enable this goal to be achieved.

2 *Ecology*

Ecological factors (climate, soil) have a major effect on coffee because the trees cannot grow if a certain number of conditions are not met. The coffee tree's sensitivity to some of these conditions is such that they may also act as limiting factors. However, short of these limitations, the shrub is quite flexible and capable of adapting to many different ecological situations. Moreover, man steps in if necessary, and puts agronomic research to good use by correcting or reducing unfavourable or marginal environmental effects.

Climatic factors

The major climatic factors are **temperature, water, light**, and **wind**. However, before examining these factors, it would be best to describe the basic climatic characteristics of the regions of origin of the two main species, which will ensure a better understanding of their response to these environments.

Coffea arabica

The natural stands of this species are in Ethiopia, on the high plateaux, at approximate altitudes of 1300 to 1800 m, at northern latitudes of 6° to 9° (Kaffa, Tana, etc.). This region is marked by a dry season that lasts about four to five months. The total annual rainfall is about 1500 to 1800 mm. The average temperature is about 20° to 24°C with low extremes of +4° to +5° and highs of 30° to 31°C. This is clearly a high altitude, temperate, tropical climate with contrasting seasons.

This knowledge helps to explain the difficulties encountered when cultivating this species in lowland, tropical regions with excessive heat and humidity, or with a very different rainfall pattern, either with abundant rainfall, or poor seasonal rainfall distribution. All attempts made to cultivate it in the lower Ivory Coast and the Congo Basin have failed. Experience, together with an awareness of *C. arabica*'s natural environment, indicates that in inter-tropical regions, the species could only prosper in zones where the combination of the altitude and the latitude provide indispensible anti-dotes to unfavourable factors. Such is the case, for example, in East Africa (Kenya, Tanzania) where coffee is planted in terraces between 1300 and 2100 m, and in West Africa on the high plateaux of Cameroon. In Brazil, the main coffee-growing region is located in the states of São Paulo and Paraña. The altitude is lower (between 600 and 800 m), but this is compensated for by its geographical position at low latitudes (20° to 23° south).

Coffea canephora

This species thrives in a typical equatorial climate where the average temperature is between 24° and 26°C, without great variations, with abundant rainfall (at least 2000 mm) distributed over a nine to ten month period, and with atmospheric humidity at a constant level approaching saturation.

Temperature

Temperature is one of the limiting factors in the life of the coffee tree. Generally speaking, no *Coffea* species can survive for any length of time at a temperature nearing 0°C. A distinction should once again be made between *C. arabica* and the other species. *C. arabica*, by its very origin, is better suited to withstand fluctuations in temperature, provided they are not too extreme. In 1975, during the great catastrophic frosts of Paraña in Brazil, the temperature at dawn dropped to between −7° and −8°C in some places. Several million shrubs perished within an hour or two. At a higher temperature (0°C to −2°C), which is not unusual in Paraña during the winter, the foliar tissue and green shoots were killed. This was manifested by almost complete defoliation of the shrubs, and the drying out of the young branches (black tip). Fruiting had been largely localised on the young wood, and the problem had repercussions the following year with an appreciable loss in the harvest. These cold temperatures are sometimes recorded elsewhere in high altitude coffee-growing regions that are either near or bordering the tropics. This situation also occurs on the high plateaux of central and southern Madagascar (alt. 1400–1600 m; lat. 20°–22° south). Drops in temperature, which are even less pronounced than those previously mentioned, result in physiological problems that are reflected in the trees' growth and fruiting.

    C. arabica also suffers badly from increases in temperature above 30°C, especially if the air is dry. Accelerated transpiration dehydrates the tissues. The foliage wilts (wilting point) and if the condition lasts for too long, it turns brown, dries out, and falls. At the first rains, the shrub's nutritional resources are used to rebuild its branches and foliage, to the detriment of fruiting.

    Coffea canephora is much less adaptable to lower temperatures than *C. arabica*. Problems arise as soon as temperatures reach +8° to +10°C. The leaves and fruits do not withstand temperatures below +5° or +6°C, whereas the shrubs perish well before the freezing point is reached. High temperatures are also harmful, especially in an atmosphere with insufficient humidity. The leaves fall and the tips of the branches and buds dry out and die.

The most favourable average temperatures are between 22°C and 26°C, with no very pronounced differences in day and night.

The requirements of other species (*C. liberica, C. excelsa,* etc.) are comparable to those of *C. canephora.* However *C. excelsa,* which originates from regions bordering the savannah, has drought-resistant characteristics, as does the 'de la Nana' variety that was mentioned earlier.

Thorough climatic studies have been carried out in Brazil, namely in Paraña since the catastrophic frosts of 1975 (page 13). The studies concentrated on the topoclimate and microclimate and were done with the help of aerial photographs at scales of 1:50 000 and 1:100 000 (Fig 11).

Topoclimatic studies revolve essentially around the land's relief and configuration, such as small valleys, slopes and their exposure, dominant winds, etc. This information is used when establishing coffee plantations, to reduce the risk of frost.

Fig 11   *C. arabica* plantation after the 1975 frost. Paraña, Brazil (Courtesy: Coste)

Microclimatic studies are concerned with the condition of the land linked with cultural treatments: bare, covered with spontaneous vegetation or cover crops, use of mulch, planting density, windbreaks, pruning system, etc. All elements that have an effect on frost, its location, and its degree of intensitv are included in the studies.

In Brazil, the Development Services have been able to designate the most favourable regions for coffee growing in each state, based on general climatic parameters. For example, there is a very widespread region in Paraña, which is bounded by a frontier line (called the frost line 'linha de geada'), that has been classified as being unsuitable for coffee growing.

Instructions and recommendations are given to planters in each area, based on data collected by topoclimatic and microclimatic surveys.

Water

A Distinction must be established here between **rainfall, atmospheric humidity**, and **dew**.

Rainfall

In terms of importance, rainfall is the second most limiting climatic factor, after the ambient temperatuare. Two inseparably linked elements must be considered: the total amount of rainfall during the year and its monthly, indeed weekly, distribution (rainfall pattern).

It is generally assumed that coffee prospers in regions where rainfall is between 1500 and 1800 mm per year, with a pattern consisting of a few months with little rain or even relative drought, corresponding to the dormant period that precedes the main flowering period. In many coffee-growing regions, the amount of rainfall exceeds this norm (Colombia, Costa Rica, Guatemala, Mexico. Indonesia, Cameroon).

Coffee growing is risky with less than 800 to 1000 mm of annual precipitation, even if it is well distributed, and productivity fluctuates as a result. Irrigation can offset a lack or a poor distribution of rainfall to a certain degree (Kenya, Arabia, Mysore).

The canephoras adapt well to abundant precipitation, exceeding 2000 mm per year (Sumatra, Malaysia).

For all species, the seasonal rhythm of the rains, particularly those that follow the dry season, has a major effect on flowering, fruit setting, and fruiting.

Many individuals have studied the adaptation of certain species of *Coffea* to drought, including Lebrun in Zaire, Magalhaes in Brazil, Josis in Burundi, Amongo in Ghana, and Boyer in the Ivory Coast. In the Ivory Coast, for example, the objective was to produce robusta and Arabusta (hybrid of *C. arabica* × *C. robusta*) coffee trees that could adapt to a dry season lasting four or five months in regions north of the boundaries of that forest. Contrary to what one might have expected, the results showed that the robustas performed better than the arabustas.

Atmospheric humidity

Atmospheric humidity has a pronounced effect on the vegetation of the coffee tree, particularly for species other than *C. arabica*. The intensity of transpiration depends, in fact, upon the atmospheric capacity (vapour tension) and the temperature. In forested regions of the west coast of Africa and the Congo Basin that are hot and very humid, the level of moisture in the air is always very high, approaching saturation. These conditions are particularly favourable to *C. canephora*. However, the species also does well in less humid climates, provided the dry season is shorter.

C. arabica prefers a less humid atmosphere, comparable to that of the sub-temperate Ethiopian high plateaux.

Dew

It is important to note the amount of water supplied by the morning dew, as in certain regions where *C. arabica* is grown, it represents a significant contribution to the amount of water present in the foliage, particularly during the dry season.

Light

In its natural habitat, coffee is found in shaded or semi-shaded situations (clearings, secondary gallery forests, banks of water courses). Its response to light has caused it to be traditionally considered a heliophobic plant, requiring high, somewhat dense cover in a plantation. Later on it will be shown that this shade practice, which was debated for a long time, is generally being abandoned today. It is known, in fact, that coffee trees with high productivity potential (selections) are capable of particularly high yields when they are cultivated intensively without shade.

Wind

Wind is generally harmful to coffee trees as it can break the branches and cause the leaves to fall. In addition to this mechanical effect there is a physiological effect, which is just as important, especially when the winds are hot and dry in nature. The leaves and young shoots wilt and the plant's growth is retarded. The harmful effect of these winds is much more pronounced when the soil-water reserves have been seasonally lessened or exhausted as in light, very permeable soils with little retentive capacity.

Regions that are in the path of cyclones (West Indies, Madagascar, Viet

Nam) are subject to very violent winds which can cause considerable damage to coffee plantations. Both shade and coffee trees may be uprooted and the latter severely damaged. The frequency and violence of the cyclones, together with infection by the fungus *Hemileia*, are the reasons for coffee growing being abandoned in Reunion during the last century.

Remedies for unfavourable ecological and agricultural factors

It is possible to remedy situations with unfavourable ecological factors, although only in a very limited way. For example, by studying mutants, varieties that are resistant to fluctuations in temperature or drought may be created or selected by using plant breeding techniques. This facilitates growing coffee in areas that are on the fringe of their normal ecological environment.

For a long time, either artificial or natural shade was used to control excessive exposure to light. Now mulching is preferred because it keeps the ground moist and prevents it from becoming over-heated. Shade is effective in protecting coffee against low morning temperatures in high altitude regions (Kenya) or against hail. It also makes it possible to maintain a higher level of environmental moisture around the shrubs in dry regions.

Finally, most of the cropping operations (fertilisation, pruning, etc.), as well as erosion control measures on sloping lands, generally have a considerable impact on the environment, and may contribute either to improving it, or to making the shrubs more resistant to adverse factors due to better conditions.

Soil factors

Coffee does not appear to have very specific soil requirements. In fact, it performs just as well in the clay-silicaceous soils of granite origin in the lower Ivory Coast or Cameroon as it does on soils of volcanic origin with diverse characteristics that are encountered all over the world (dolerite, basalt, ash, tufa, etc.), or even on alluvial soils, such as those on the eastern coast of Madagascar.

On the other hand, the texture and depth of the soil are extremely important factors. In fact, the coffee tree is capable of extending its root system considerably. For example, its remarkable underground development in Brazilian soils with average fertility but excellent physical properties is particularly notable. This characteristic enables it to exploit a considerable volume of land and to thus offset a relative lack of fertility. In compact or shallow soils, the taproot remains short and the roots only develop in the upper horizons, at a depth rarely exceeding 0.3 m. Under these conditions, any intensive cultivation clearly requires major fertiliser inputs. On the contrary, in deep, particularly permeable soils, the root system develops to some depth and occupies a considerable volume of soil.

With regard to the pH of the soil, most authors agree that the best conditions are between pH 4.5 and 6.0. While this is undoubtedly true, it is also true that there are magnificent, highly productive coffee plantations on soils that are much less acidic. Indeed they are nearly neutral (pH 7.0). As in many cases, it would be difficult to prove this criterion with complete certainty.

Geographical distribution of the main species

The general distribution of the main coffee species cultivated throughout the world is as follows:

C. arabica

Africa: High altitude zones of Kenya, Tanzania, Uganda, Zaire, Cameroon, Ethiopia, Rwanda, Burundi, Madagascar.

Asia: High altitude zones of Arabia (Yemen), India, the Philippines, Indonesia (Java, Sumatra), Viet Nam.

Central and South America: High altitude zones of Mexico, Guatemala, Honduras, San Salvador, Nicaragua, Costa Rica, Panama, Colombia, Venezuela, Ecuador, Paraguay, Peru.
    Middle altitude zones of Brazil, the Caribbean Islands, etc.

C. canephora

Africa: Low altitude zones of Zaire, Angola, Ivory Coast, Nigeria, Ghana, Central African Republic, Madagascar, Togo.
    Middle altitude zones of Cameroon, Uganda, Tanzania.

Asia: Low and middle altitude zones of Indonesia, India, Philippines, New Caledonia.

Central and South America: Hot, humid regions of northern Brazil.

Other species

Coffea liberica is represented by vestiges of plantations in Africa. Some large estates still exist in Surinam and Indonesia.
    Coffea excelsa has been the object of extension efforts in Central African Republic, to identify resistant types after the destruction caused by trachaeomycosis.
    Coffea abeokutae, the production of which is known in the Ivory Coast by the commercial name of 'Gros Indénié', has now been mostly abandoned in favour of *C. canephora*. The serious damage caused by tracheomycosis is mostly responsible for this situation.

3 Development and physiology

The life of the coffee plant is divided into three main phases. The first is the **growth phase**, which begins when the seed germinates and ends when the plant is fully grown. This phase takes from four to seven years, depending upon the species and environmental conditions. The second is the **productive phase**, which is the longest, spreading over a period of 15 to 25 years. The final phase is that of **physiological decline**, which ends with the death of the plant.

Only the first two phases are taken into account from an agricultural point of view. The logical solution to the decrease in production below the profitability threshold that marks the beginning of the third phase, is to uproot the unproductive shrubs.

The growth phase

The seed and its germination

The seed consists mainly of endosperm, the tissues of which contain starch, fat, reducing sugars, saccharides, tannins and caffeine. It contains about 20 per cent water. There is an embryo at one end with a conical radicle and cordiform cotyledons.

Two coatings cover the endosperm. The first is the **endocarp** or **parchment** of the fruit which is a drupe. The second, which is very fine, is the **seminal tegument** or **testa** (skin).

The ripe, healthy, well-formed seed may germinate as soon as it is harvested, in the absence of a dormancy period, if it is placed in satisfactory environmental conditions, namely humidity, heat and aeration.

The seed absorbs water when placed in a sufficiently moist environment; this being the phenomenon of **imbibition**. Visually, imbibition appears to be an expansion of tissues, but its internal action triggers the metabolic and enzymatic processes that induce germination.

The optimum temperature for the germination of coffee seeds is about 30° to 32°C. Below +10°C, germination is very slow. Its duration mainly

Fig 12 Six week old seedlings of *C. arabica*. Colombia (Courtesy: National Coffee Federation of Colombia)

Fig 13 Seedlings of *C. robusta* in propagators. Ivory Coast (Courtesy: Capot)

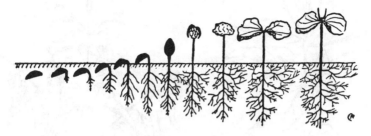

Fig 14 *C. arabica*: stages of development of the seedling

depends on the interaction of two factors: temperature and moisture and, to a lesser degree, the aeration of the environment and its pH.

The first indication that germination is occurring is the appearance of the radicle three or four weeks after sowing (*C. arabica*). 20 to 25 days later, the hypocotyl elongates and carries the seed, which is still covered in its parchment, out of the ground; this is **epigeal** germination. Shortly afterwards, this light covering is detached, and two bracteoles or cotyledonary leaves, which are very different from ordinary leaves, open. These are oval-shaped, and are between 2 and 4 cm in diameter, with undulating edges. At their point of insertion on the plumule there is a dormant axillary bud (Figs 12, 13 and 14).

The terminal bud appears at the same time as the bracteoles. About 10 to 12 weeks after sowing, it rapidly produces two normal, primary leaves. These are opposite, in pairs. The cotyledonary leaves, having completed their nutritional role, then wilt and die.

The root system grows actively during the first weeks of germination. The taproot penetrates deeply and forms a great number of roots and rootlets (Fig 17). Mes studied the relationship between the soil temperature and growth of the roots (*C. arabica*). The optimum is reached between 26°C and 32°C. Franco found through experimentation that soil temperature at root level affects aerial development at 26°C during the day and 20°C at night. Temperatures above 28°C are unfavourable to growth and are lethal above 38°C. The same author also observed an interaction between the temperature of the root system and the transpiration of the coffee tree.

Growth and development

The first plagiotropic branching of the young coffee tree appears four to six weeks after emergence, when the plant has between 5 and 11 pairs of leaves and is 0.20 to 0.30 m high (Figs 15 and 16).

The morphogenesis of *C. canephora* has been the subject of numerous studies. During the first year, in addition to the two buds in the axils of the bracteoles, the coffee tree has three buds per axil at the fourth node, three or four per axil at the fifth and sixth nodes, and four per axil thereafter. In

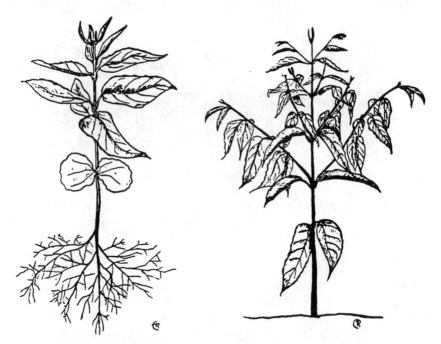

Fig 15 *C. arabica*: young tree at three months

Fig 16 *C. arabica*: young tree at nine months

case of an accident, these buds can give rise to orthotropous replacement axes, arising from the stem of the young coffee tree. It will be shown later that good use has been made of the stem's branching behaviour by Vianney-Liaud in Madagascar, in his original technique of producing rootstock cuttings in the nursery.

Plagiotropic branches are the result of so-called 'extra-axillary' buds or 'heads of series', which are formed at each node, a few millimetres above the 'seriated' buds, which produce the orthotropous axils. Only one bud of this type is formed in the axil of each leaf. The so-called 'primary' plagiotropic branch that it produces cannot therefore be replaced no matter what the age of the shrub may be.

The primary branches also have buds at each node that develop either into secondary plagiotropic branches or flower buds. The former, 'heads of series', form under the same conditions as their counterparts in the vertical axil. The latter develop into flower buds under certain conditions (floral induction) which will be discussed later. Under the same conditions, the secondary branches can give way to tertiary or 'fan' branches.

Primary, plagiotropic branches are opposite in pairs at alternate perpendicular levels along the main axis.

At one year, *C. arabica* will already have produced four to eight levels of primary branches, while at the same age, *C. canephora* will have produced between six and twelve.

The growth of the young coffee tree, triggered by the lengthening of the leading axis and the successive elongation of the related internodes, does not occur at an even pace throughout the year. It is more active during the rainy season and is also greatly affected by environmental conditions; light being a very favourable factor for *C. arabica*.

At two years, the coffee tree will be about one metre in height. It will have several series of branches. Towards the third or fourth year, when it will be about 1.50 to 1.75 m in height, the relationship between the root system and the branching structure determines the balance between the flow of root regulating hormones (cytokinins) and the auxins and gibberellins present in the shoots and leaves, leading to the physiologically mature state of flowering. Axillary buds can thus be induced to flower at favourable times. The coffee tree, at this stage, enters into the second phase of its life.

Productivity phase

Nutritional structures

We will first study the root system, then the shoot system. Mineral nutrition will be examined in Chapter 5 in the section entitled 'Fertilisation'.

The root system

The root system of the mature coffee tree consists of:

- A **taproot**, which is often extensively branched, robust, and generally short (0.3 to 0.5 m), but may grow as long as 1.0 m in deep soils. Its main functions are to provide stability and anchorage and to ensure the supply of water to the plant.
- A number of **secondary roots** which develop from the taproot and grow vertically downwards. The lighter and more penetrable the soil, the deeper they will develop. Their role, together with that of the taproot, is to assist in supplying water to the plant.
- **Lateral roots**, which are generally numerous, develop, often almost horizontally, and are further extended by a network of rootlets. They explore the superficial and richest layers of the soil. Their role is essentially to provide mineral nutrition to the plant (Fig 17).

Many factors affect the development of the underground root network of the coffee tree. Some of them, apart from heredity (species, variety) are soil texture and composition, aeration, drainage, water and mineral resources, and cropping methods.

Several agronomists such as Nutman, have studied the development of the roots of the coffee tree and the distribution of its network. In most cases, they found that over 80 per cent of the roots (sometimes over 90 per cent) are found in the upper soil layer, between the surface and a depth of 0.3

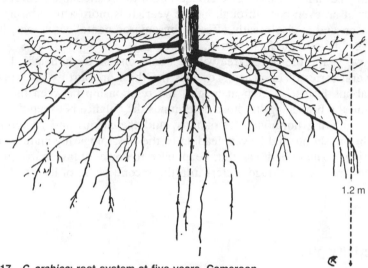

Fig 17   *C. arabica*: root system at five years. Cameroon

Fig 18   *C. robusta*: root system at 3½ years covering approximately 3 m². Yangambi Station, Zaire (Courtesy: Bocquet)

metres. However, in certain soils with exceptional qualities (namely Brazilian terra roxa) the volume of soil exploited by the coffee tree was found to be considerable (about 12 to 15 cm³). On the other hand, in heavy, very moist soils, the superficial root concentration could reach 95 per cent. These facts confirm the ability of the coffee tree to adapt to its environment. The linear development of the roots and rootlets has been recorded in studies carried out by Nutman and others. For example, a total of 22 765 m of root and rootlet length has been recorded for a mature coffee tree (Fig 18).

Fig 19 *C. arabica*: mature root system with twisted taproot. Foumbot, Cameroon
(Courtesy: Gerin)

Fig 20 *C. arabica*: young plants with twisted taproots. Foumbot, Cameroon
(Courtesy: Gerin)

The climate has a marked effect on the development of the superficial
roots and rootlets. If the soil is dry, is excessively exposed to the sun for at
least part of the year, or is subjected to alternating drought and moisture,
the roots and rootlets do not develop close to the soil surface. Using mulch
is a good way to prevent the soil from heating up excessively. In Uganda,
Thomas found three times as many root hairs developing on *C. canephora*
under mulch, compared with the number developing under bare soil conditions. Certain non-competitive cover plants, like *Flemingia congesta*, may
be just as effective (IFCC).

The effect of removing part of the root system has been much debated. It seems that there is no effect on the superficial root hairs when they are only slightly reduced (namely during cropping operations). On the other hand, accidental or deliberate amputation of large lateral roots has been shown to have definite repercussions, such as ensuing nutritional problems. The vibrating harvesting machines that have been used in experiments on some large farms have been abandoned due to the nutritional disorders they provoked. It is also known that a poorly formed taproot (twisted or buckled) shortens the lifespan of the coffee tree (Figs 19 and 20).

There is still not enough known about the biological reactions in the soils around coffee trees, particularly the macro- and microflora and effects on tree growth.

Finally, although it has been proven that there is an interaction between the development of the aerial and underground parts of the plant, details of the physiological process are still unknown.

Nutman showed that leaf transpiration of *C. arabica* occurred at an average day-time rate of 0.4 to 1.23 g H_2O dm^{-2} $hour^{-1}$ per shrub. With a total surface area estimated to be about 400 dm^2, root absorption was the equivalent of 2.5 g cm^{-1} $hour^{-1}$, which is a very low rate.

The shoot system

The framework of the coffee tree essentially consists of a vertical axis, the trunk, and several series of primary branches (Fig 21). The latter bear fruit

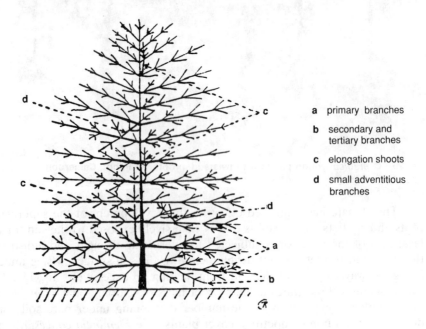

a   primary branches

b   secondary and
    tertiary branches

c   elongation shoots

d   small adventitious
    branches

Fig 21   Typical architecture of the coffee tree

when young, and have secondary renewable branches, which, together with the tertiary branches, provide the mainstay of production. It will be shown in Chapter 5 that single-stem pruning takes full advantage of this growth pattern, whereas multi-stem pruning consists, on the contrary, of mainly exploiting the primary branches, which are periodically rejuvenated by renewing the leaders (trunks).

Ph. de Reffye carried out a mathematical study on the architecture of robustas and the shedding of branches that occurs in coffee trees with a high productivity potential, due to a lack of stability in the shrub structure. This vegetative condition is sometimes accompanied by the breaking of branches due to insufficient wind resistance and a lack of solidity of the woody tissues. The study was completed by Snoeck in attempts to determine the importance of the mineral fertilisation factor. This research is of great interest, together with studies in genetics, with the objective of increasing productivity.

The total foliar surface of a mature coffee tree depends upon the species, its health, light intensity and other environmental conditions. While undertaking research on transpiration, Franco and Inforzato found that the foliar surface of *C. arabica* was between 22 m² and 45 m² depending on the tree characteristics.

In the Ivory Coast, Boyer studied the development of leaves of *C. canephora*. The lifespan is generally between seven and ten months, except in the case of premature leaf fall. It consists of four phases: growth (three to four weeks), cutinisation (four to five weeks), mature state (four to six months) and senescence (three to six weeks).

Leaf renewal has not yet been studied in depth. For *C. arabica*, Rayner in Kenya found that major leaf fall occurred between August and the beginning of November (rainy season), when the plants were about seven or eight months old. Other minor losses occurred during the remainder of the year. No information is available on the behaviour of other species.

On the contrary, the transpiration of coffee trees has been the subject of numerous publications by Nutman, Franco, Inforzato, Ringoet, Pereira, Lemee, Boyer and others.

Boyer carried out some thorough research in the Ivory Coast, which was necessitated by problems of drought-resistance posed by the IFCC. Through experimentation, like Lebrun, he distinguished three different stages during the course of water loss:

1 Stomatal opening, due most likely to the evaporation of a thin film of water on the cuticle.
2 Stomatal closure, which ends in total occlusion when the foliar water deficit reaches between 18 and 30 per cent, as is the case with some varieties of *C. canephora*.
3 Cuticular transpiration. The stomata remain closed, but the leaf dehydrates slowly and steadily, and gradually loses its turgidity until it reaches the wilting point.

Boyer found very different drought-resistant capabilities in two cultivated varieties of *C. canephora*, which were manifested in the ability of the leaf tissues to withstand and resist a high degree of dehydration. The most resistant variety demonstrated swift stomatal closure, less active cuticular transpiration, and a more efficient use of the water supply.

The quantities of water that evaporate from the coffee tree have been calculated by Nutman, Pereira, Franco, and Inforzato for arabicas and by Ringoet for robustas. For arabicas in Brazil, the average daily rate for an unshaded shrub is 6.29 g dm^{-2} day^{-1}, which corresponds to 593 mm of rainfall, or 7273 l per year. A much higher rate was found in East Africa, with 840 mm in Kenya (six-year average).

Ringoet in Yangambi (Zaire) recorded the daily transpiratory rhythm in *C. canephora* and found that in the morning (6:30 to 12:00) the water loss was 45.5 per cent and in the afternoon (12:00 to 17:00) it was 52.6 per cent. The difference of 1.9 per cent represents the nocturnal evaporation.

Brazilian agronomists have studied the effect of low temperatures on the vegetation in particular. An ambient temperature of 0°C to +3°C for several hours was found to induce a discolouration of the leaves by destroying the chloroplasts. The lower the temperature, the faster this occurs. The leaves turn brown and fall. In young plants, a temperature of −2°C causes the base of the stem to become thin due to the death of the outer tissues. This is known in Brazil by the name 'geada de canela'.

Dancer reported a very interesting study on the effect of removing part of the foliage on the growth of the fruits in *C. robusta*. He found that the final weight of the fruits and beans was reduced by 30 per cent, by reducing the number of leaves during the initial stages of development of the fruits. This excision appeared to have little effect when carried out during the maturation period.

Almeida, Matiello and Miguel also found that the defoliation of *C. arabica* was responsible for a loss of fruit. The level of loss was directly related to the percentage of leaves removed (27 per cent with 60 per cent defoliation; 48 per cent with 90 per cent defoliation). This excision is also accompanied by a loss in unit weight of the fruits.

The two preceding studies illustrate the effect that defoliating pathogen attacks may have on production, especially the fungus *Hemileia*.

Light intensity, photosynthesis and photoperiodism

Following Nutman, several other authors have confirmed that the rate of photosynthesis (respiration and carbon assimilation) in the coffee leaf, considered individually, is greater in diffused light than in full light (Franco, Alvim, Sylvain). This rate has also been shown to be greater early in the morning and late in the afternoon than during the hours of high light intensity. In Kenya, for *C. arabica*, the optimum rate of photosynthesis has been recorded at 24°C, decreasing rapidly below 15°C and above 32°C. However, Franco has very rightly observed that this information does not confirm that the coffee tree is ombrophile. In fact, he emphasises the fact that only the shrub's outer leaves are exposed to intense light. Most of the inner foliage is more or less protected from sunlight and is thus located in optimum conditions for photosynthesis. Sylvain and Alvim have verified this fact through experiments. The adaptation of the coffee tree to full sunlight is thus related to its ability to assimilate (Castillo).

This information is extremely important in order to understand why many planters have abandoned shade, based on their own personal observations.

All species of coffee may be considered to be adapted to short days. In their country of origin, as in regions where they are cultivated, the day is between 10½ and 13½ hours long, and about 12 hours long at the equator.

C. arabica is fairly flexible because it is still able to flower even if the day is 14 hours long. However, if it is any longer, floral induction does not occur. No experimental data on this subject are available for other species.

Reproductive functions

Flowering

The first flower buds generally appear towards the third year (with clones, flowering occurs one year earlier), but flowering does not reach its full extent until the fourth or fifth year of growth.

The flower buds arise from the clusters of nodal buds which are located in the leaf axils on plagiotropic branches, and evolve either into secondary branches or flowers, as has already been described.

Floral initiation has been studied by several authors including Cramer, Rayner, Van der Meueln, Cambrony, Moens, and Mes. It occurs from 'undifferentiated bud nodes' (Moens), under complex stimulating actions, which are still not well known. These may include well-defined hormonal balances between auxins, gibberellins and cytokinins, exposure to light, drought, seasonal rotations, differences in diurnal and nocturnal temperature and C/N relationships. Flowering does not exhaust the stock of buds on a node. Some remain dormant and may later evolve into floral cymes or secondary branches (Rayner). Others may originate from embryonic bud tissues.

The coffee inflorescence is a cyme with a very short axis that carries a varying number of flowers (two to nine for *C. arabica*, three to five for *C. excelsa*). Several inflorescences are grouped together in clusters, depending upon the species, nutritional conditions and other factors.

In principle, the flowers form on the one year old wood which is only slightly lignified. However, they more often appear on wood that is already well lignified (one to three years), and more exceptionally on old wood. Thus all adult coffee trees have primary branches with unproductive wood (base of the trunk), productive wood (one or two year old wood and young secondary branches that have developed from it) and green, herbaceous tips that are not yet flower-bearing.

When the flower buds are at a very advanced stage, development is temporarily halted. Their final development and anthesis are generally triggered by rainfall that immediately follows a period of drought. Porteres defined the 'precipitation/flowering threshold' as 'the volume of water received by the soil which is capable of raising and maintaining the state of turgor within the plant being necessary and sufficient enough to trigger flowering'. The amount of this precipitation is between 10 and 35 mm, depending upon the country and the seasonal characteristics. Capot observed that in the Ivory Coast, the flowers of *C. canephora* opened five to seven days after the activating rain, and flowers of the liberio-excelsoids after only five days. He also noticed that the more pronounced the seasonal drought, the greater the level of flowering. The same author noted that in the lower Ivory Coast, in a sub-equatorial climate, the flowers of *C. canephora* appear almost all year round (25 to 50 openings) with 'useful' flowerings (capable of developing into the ripe fruit) from December to February.

Cambrony and Capot studied the floral biology of *C. canephora* in the coastal environment of the Ivory Coast. The main points of their observations regarding anthesis are: the flower blossoms during the night, finishing at about 4.00 or 5.00 am. The style, which is folded in the bud, straightens, while the stigma, which had been joined, separates. The pollen grains are freed from the anthers in the morning and are dispersed by the wind and insects, mainly bees. In the afternoon, the anthers turn brown and shrivel. The white corolla withers, detaches from the ovary, and is retained by the stigma for two or three days before falling off. If pollination has not taken place, the style remains receptive for four or five days.

Several authors have recorded cases of atrophy or floral malformation, particularly in *C. arabica*, namely with so-called star flowers (star, sterretje, estrella, etc.). These anomalies have been attributed to unfavourable meteorological conditions such as excessively hot climate, insufficiently differentiated seasons, insufficient diurnal and nocturnal thermal differences. Whatever the case may be, these flowers are sterile.

Pollen production is considerable. Ferwerda calculated that an adult coffee tree in the plantation receives two and a half million grains of pollen in eight hours from a distance of eight metres. This quantity is more than sufficient to ensure the fertilisation of its approximately 20 000 to 30 000 flowers. The pollen falls on the lower storeys of the coffee tree due to the force of gravity and is also transported by the wind and insects. The number of these disseminating agents, which generally act together, is dependent on the nature of the environment. The wind transports the pollen at varying distances, but stretches of about 100 m have been recorded.

The pollen grains of *C. canephora* are about 0.02 to 0.03 mm in diameter. Those of *C. arabica* are larger and thicker. They take very little time to germinate (one to two hours under favourable conditions) and produce a pollen tube that develops very quickly.

Pollen can be stored for at least three months at a temperature of +6°C.

For a shorter period of storage, a laboratory desiccator may be used with a dehydrating agent such as anhydrous calcium chloride or actigel. Sampling conditions have a considerable effect on the length of storage time (atmospheric humidity, duration of handling, etc.).

Current knowledge on coffee pollen has substantially increased as a result of recent research by Leroy, Lobreau-Callen and Dentan.

The success of pollination is related to the existing weather conditions. Strong rains and violent winds are some of the factors that may be harmful to the process and the proportion of non-fertilised flowers may be very high.

C. arabica is about 90 per cent autogamous (self-fertile) thus a great number of its flowers are fertilised before anthesis, but all the other species are cross-fertilised (self-sterile).

Formerly it was stated that the corolla and stamens dry out and fall off immediately after fertilisation. The pistil then becomes detached. On average, two or three days may elapse between anthesis and the falling off of these floral components.

Fruiting

The fruits develop fairly rapidly during the weeks that follow fertilisation according to Texeira, who claimed that in Brazil, in *C. arabica*, most of the fruits reach half their normal length in about 12 weeks following flowering. However, Capot, in the Ivory Coast, found a different reaction in *C. canephora* with, in contrast, a very minimal, even negligible increase for the first four or five years. This difference in the growth rates is explained by the fact that the fruits of *C. canephora* require three to four months more to reach maturity (Fig 10) than those of *C. arabica*.

The following analysis of the fruit's development (*C. arabica* Catuai amarello) is borrowed from the definitive study by Dentan (*Etude microscopique de développement et de la maturation du grain de café*, C. R. Onzième Colloque ASIC Lomé (Toto), pp. 381–398. Quoted from p. 382.):

'Sixteen-day-old cherries are the size of grape seeds. Inside, the primordium of the two seeds can be observed. The pericarp is relatively large. The cotyledons of the seeds are connected to the pericarp by an easily visible funicle. After 45 days, the seeds have grown noticeably, but towards the 60th day they show their characteristic form. During this time, many cellular divisions may be observed, especially in the outer layers of the cotyledons. Around the 70th day, the central cells begin to elongate and the number of cellular divisions decreases. The growth of the cherries continues normally. At that time the beans are extremely fragile. The cells, which are greatly elongated, display very fine cell walls. It is only on about the 120th day that the cell walls really thicken and become more firm. On about the 190th day, the cherries and beans have reached their definitive size, but they will continue to gain weight until the end of the maturation period.'

The highest level of shedding (young fruit dropping off) is observed in *C arabica* and the other species during the first months of development. The reason for this phenomenon may be defective fertilisation, insect attacks, e.g. *Volumnus, Antestiopsis*, persistent drought, etc. It is also sometimes attributed to physiological problems, the mechanisms of which are not well understood.

During the following months, there may also be a loss of fruit, the cause of which may be nutritional deficiencies, or pathogenic infection.

The period which elapses between the flowering and maturation of fruits varies according to the species and variety. Climatic conditions and cropping practices also have an effect. The average times are as follows:

C. arabica	six to eight months
C. canephora	nine to 11 months
C. excelsa	11 to 12 months
C. liberica	12 to 14 months

Altitude has a moderating effect on maturation. The air temperature drops about 1°C for every 180 m increase in elevation. On the high plateaux of Cameroon, for example, a two-week delay is observed between plantations located at 1100/1200 m and 1600/1700 m. The same was found to be true in Kenya and Latin America. The harvest may occur earlier depending upon the exposure of the slope in mountainous countries.

Coffee fruits are usually dark red when fully ripe (except for some varieties of *C. arabica* which have yellow fruits) and must be harvested at this stage (Chapter 7). This is particularly important for *C. arabica*, the ripe fruits of which fall soon after reaching maturity, contrary to those of *C. canephora* which remain attached for several weeks (Fig 22).

Fruits are often harvested early, when they are still green. This is a common practice at the present time for various reasons (namely theft), and results in weight loss, as the bean is not yet fully developed. A deterioration in the quality also results, mainly because the chemical substances that generate the aroma are either absent or are present in very small amounts in the four to six week period before they are ripe.

Abnormal fruit formations are often observed in the coffee tree such as single seeds (peaberries), multicarpellate, or many seeded fruits (elephant beans). The incidence of peaberries varies depending upon the species, the percentage of hybrids, the age of the plants, and seasonal factors. The presence of an abnormally high proportion of these beans is generally the result of poor fertilisation, possibly due to excessive rain. However, it may also be influenced by the genetic constitution of the plants.

The magnitude of the fruiting is related to various factors: heredity, age, climatic conditions, cropping practices, etc. It may also vary considerably from one year to the next. These factors notwithstanding, the level of production of the coffee tree has been found to fluctuate: there may be a sizeable harvest one year which may be followed by a small harvest the following year. However, it should be noted that differences in the size of the harvests

Fig 22 *C. eugenioides*: fruiting stage. Ivory Coast (Courtesy: Couarn)

are smaller in well-maintained plantations, especially if they are adequately fertilised. These differences are also considerably reduced in highly productive clonal plantations, which receive large quantities of fertiliser.

The productive potential of all species of coffee is extremely variable. Observers have found considerable differences in individual coffee plantations where the harvests were carried out on individual trees over several consecutive years. In Colombia, Gardner found that out of 810 *C. arabica* trees in one plot, 60 per cent of them had had lower than average production for five years. On the other hand, 20 per cent of the plants had provided over 50 per cent of the total harvest.

In Brazil, Filho found considerable cumulative differences in *C. arabica* trees that had been observed for seven consecutive years, between a minimum of 7 kg and a maximum of 66 kg of fruits, which is a tenfold increase.

Findings along the same lines have also been recorded in various countries, namely by the IFCC when candidates for highly productive cutting source plants were being sought in *C. canephora* plantations (Chapter 7). This emphasises the great interest in clonal plantations, at least for this cross-fertilised species.

Phase of physiological decline

The coffee tree has a fairly long period of full productivity. Its duration is influenced by many factors such as the ecological environment, maintenance and cropping techniques, general health.

The first signs of decline are normally apparent after 15 to 20 years of fruiting. These symptoms may appear much earlier in poorly established, badly maintained plantations that are either insufficiently or not fertilised. On the other hand, in the case of well-maintained, rationally managed plantations, the fully productive period may greatly exceed the average.

If the profit from the harvests is not enough to cover cropping costs, and if the age of the shrubs is the only reason for this, the only option is to uproot the plants and, if necessary, to replant after allowing a certain period of time to elapse.

The aging shrub shows the clearest signs of physiological decline. The trunk appears old and distorted and has dried-out branches with sparse foliage; the leaves are chlorotic and sensitive to fungal diseases; fruiting is irregular and fruits fall prematurely. Its root system is generally also in an advanced state of deterioration. Plants eventually die following a long period of senility.

4 *Propagation*

Coffee trees growing in the forest reproduce by means of seeds. These germinate on the spot, at the foot of the shrub, and are also frequently disseminated by birds or small mammals who are fond of the fruit's sugary pulp.

Coffee species may be propagated by seed, and by using routine forestry techniques such as cuttings, grafting, or the use of suckers. Propagation by cuttings is the most commonly used technique. *In vitro* vegetative propagation has also recently been developed.

Propagation by seed

Seeds that are to be sown must come from healthy fruits that have been harvested when fully ripe, preferably from adult shrubs. The productivity of the parent seed plants is not particularly important because this characteristic (or its genetic complex) is unfortunately not easily transmitted (Chapter 8). On the other hand, some of the bean's characteristics (shape, size, etc.) whose transmissability to the progeny has been proven, should be considered. The fruits are pulped by hand (not mechanically) immediately after harvesting. The parchment seeds are spread out to dry on racks, in a shaded, ventilated area. They are then sorted, and all those that are malformed, small, or damaged are eliminated.

The coffee seed is capable of germinating as soon as it is harvested due to the absence of a dormancy period, but its germinative capacity is rather short-lived. It should therefore be planted without too much delay. According to numerous reports on *C. arabica*, after being stored for three months, and under good conditions, the rate of germination falls to 90–98 per cent and during the next two months to about 70–75 per cent. After five months, it is below 50 per cent (20 to 25 per cent after nine months). *Coffea canephora* loses its germinative capacity even more quickly. This deterioration increases rapidly under poor storage conditions, e.g. relatively high temperature and high humidity. The viability of the seeds may be determined by carrying out germination tests periodically.

Many trials have been conducted on methods of coffee seed storage. If certain precautions are taken (moisture content lowered to 10–12 per cent, seeds protected from atmospheric humidity) the germinative capacity can be maintained at a satisfactory level for over six months. Huxley found that excessively rigorous drying (moisture content lowered to less than 8 per cent) and very low temperatures ($-15°$ and $-19°C$) killed the seeds, but refrigeration at temperatures between $+4°$ and $+7°C$ was favourable.

One kilo of seeds contains:

C. arabica	4000 to 5000 seeds
C. canephora	3000 to 3500 seeds

In all cases, the seeds should be stored in their parchment. This covering provides good protection against outside agents, particularly excessive atmospheric humidity.

It is advisable to disinfect the seeds by submerging them in a very diluted copper sulphate solution for a few minutes.

Finally, sealed polythene bags or soldered metal boxes should be used to transport them. Today, the rapidity and efficiency of airline connections makes it possible to send seeds considerable distances under excellent conditions, provided it is ensured that they are placed in the cabin or in heated baggage holds. They should of course be treated for control of pests and diseases before despatch.

Sowing

Sowing can be done either **in situ** (Brazilian system) or **in the seedbed or nursery**, directly in beds, pots, or bags.

Sowing in situ

This is still a common practice in Brazil. The seeds are sown in groups of prepared planting holes 0.4 to 0.5 m deep, at a spacing of 3.0 m × 3.0 m, with three to five seeds per planting hole (two to three holes per group). In principle, only one plant per hole should be allowed to remain after germination. Each group of planting holes will contain two to three coffee trees arranged in a triangular or paired formation. Each group is considered a shrub from an agricultural and statistical point of view. This technique, which is traditional in Brazil, is not rational. It is justified locally because it economises on labour.

Today the recommendations of the CIB (Coffee Institute of Brazil) are as follows:

- 'Mundo Novo' variety: 4 × 2.5 m; 4 × 1 to 2 m with only one or two coffee trees per hole.
- 'Catuai' variety: 3.5 × 2.5 m; 3.5 × 1 to 2 m also with only one or two coffee trees per hole.

Fig 23   Use of the small rule for sowing

Sowing in the seedbed

This is the most rational method. The selected land should be freshly cleared, and the soil very friable and rich in humus. The seedbeds should be 1 m wide and 2 to 4 m long. The soil must be completely loosened to a depth of at least 0.2 m, and well levelled. The seedbed should be protected from excessive exposure to light and strong rains by a cover made of palm leaves and branches. The seeds are either sown broadcast or in close rows at a spacing of 2 to 3 cm (1000 seeds per m^2). It is very important not to place the seeds deeper than 1 or 2 cm as it will affect germination (Fig 23).

The most favourable soil temperature for germination is 28°C to 30°C.

Maintenance consists of frequent watering (except in a very humid climate), weeding, and disease and pest control.

In Latin America, seeds are often germinated in buildings. They are sown in small flat boxes (germinators) which are a few decimetres deep, at a density of 2 kg of seedlings per m^2 (or about 0.5 kg per box). The seeds are removed as soon as the radicle appears and are planted in pots.

The seedlings should not remain in the germinator for more than three to four weeks. They should then be planted out in the nursery at a sufficiently wide spacing (0.25 m to 0.40 m) to allow them to develop into robust, well-developed plants (Fig 13).

The nursery

This is composed of beds that are 1.2 m to 1.5 m wide and several metres long. The soil should be deeply loosened to a depth of 0.35 to 0.40 m and generously fertilised with manure or compost.

The size of the nursery is related to the number of plants required. Based on an average of 20–30 plants per square metre, and considering the area which is occupied by paths, roads and compost heaps. The nursery should cover about 1/100th of the entire area to be planted.

Seedlings raised in the germinator can be transplanted as soon as the cotyledonary leaves open, after rigorous selection and elimination of puny, malformed plants with a twisted taproot. Planting out is done with a gardener's dibber, making sure that the soil is tightly packed around the entire length of the taproot. The most frequent reason for the failure of the vegetative regrowth of seedlings is the presence of air pockets near the roots. The collar must also be in a well-placed position at ground level, preferably slightly above rather than below the original soil level.

If there is too much sunlight, it may be necessary to provide a light cover for the 10 or 15 days that follow planting out. Placing some intertwined palm leaves or branches on either side of the bed is normally sufficient. However, in very sunny regions, 30 to 50 per cent shade has a favourable effect on growth.

Maintenance is limited to light mulching, weeding, watering (in case of prolonged drought), pest and disease control, etc.

The length of time that the plants should remain in the nursery varies depending upon the species cultivated, the time of planting, climatic conditions. Arabicas usually remain in the nursery for about 12 to 15 months. Robustas, having more vigorous vegetative growth, usually remain for six to eight months.

Use of pots and polythene bags

The use of special polythene bags is now very widespread. They are replacing bamboo pots and heavy, cumbersome baskets. The bags, like the pots, have many advantages, such as facilitating transplanting, particularly in areas where the climatic conditions are not very favourable. It is important to use sufficiently deep bags so that the taproot will not become twisted.

The bags (or pots) are filled with compost or good soil that is finely pulverised and well firmed, although not too tightly. The pre-germinated seedlings or plantlets are carefully transferred to the bags, which are placed next to each other in a shaded nursery. The soil is kept sufficiently moist (but not excessively) by watering or better still by spraying with water. It is advisable to split the bags longitudinally (the bottom section included) when they are placed in the planting holes, so that the taproot and other roots are not inhibited in their development by the plastic film, the decomposition of which is uncertain if it is not biodegradable. Bamboo pots and baskets are normally used by small-scale planters (Figs 24 and 25).

Maintenance procedures for plants raised in baskets is the same as described for nurseries: weeding, disease and pest control, replacement of malformed plants, etc.

Fig 24   Cuttings from *C. robusta* in shaded nursery for hardening off. K'Palime Station, Togo (Courtesy: Castaing)

Fig 25   *C. arabica* in polythene bags Foumbot, Cameroon (Courtesy: Bouharmont)

Vegetative propagation

Propagation by cuttings

The technique of propagating coffee species by cuttings has been studied for at least 20 years. It has now been made highly efficient and the results are spectacular, particularly for the species *C. canephora*.

The importance of using this propagation technique for cross-fertilised species lies in the exact reproduction of the coffee tree from which the cuttings were taken (cutting source plant) and the possibility of creating homogenous clonal plantations from trees that have been selected for their attributes, particularly high productivity. It is an undeniable advantage to associate several intercrossed clones in order to have fertile shrubs, as it makes the entire multi-clonal plantation considerably more flexible. This is indispensible for coping with the usual cropping hazards such as climatic variations, sensitivity to certain diseases, pest infestations, etc.

Choosing and preparing cuttings

Only the orthotropic shoots or vertically growing, elongated branches (suckers) can be used to produce a shrub with a normal habit. Cuttings from plagiotropic branches (with semi-erect or horizontal development) produce abnormal, low, creeping trees with a shrubby habit.

The best results are obtained using leafy cuttings with one node. The non-lignified orthotropic branches are taken from the cutting source plant and cut into as many pieces as they have nodes as follows: one cut should be a few centimetres below the node (heel cutting) and the other just above. The terminal part of the shoot that is unsuitable for the operation is eliminated. Each cutting is then split longitudinally by a perpendicular cut made at the level of insertion of the buds, i.e. at the leaf axils (cleaved cutting). Finally, in a second operation, half of the leaf blade is removed in order to limit congestion in the trays and reduce evapotranspiration.

Trials in Madagascar (IFCC) with *C. canephora* proved that the highest percentage of rooting was obtained with cleaved or uncleaved cuttings, with a heel portion 3 to 6 cm long, and with only half of the leaf blade retained. Cuttings without heel portions had a very low percentage of rooting. Those without leaves showed a zero percentage of rooting.

The cuttings are placed in trays called **cutting trays** or **propagators** which resemble gardeners' propagation cases. They are long, cement tanks which are about 0.6 to 0.8 m high and 0.7 m wide, and are divided into sections. The bottom is pierced with drainage holes. The tray is filled with stones up to two thirds of its height; the largest stones being placed on the bottom. A rooting substrate, which is 0.2 to 0.3 m thick, covers them. Each section has a removable, inclined, glass (or better still polythene) cover. The trays are usually set up back to back (Fig 26).

Fig 26 *C. robusta*: arrangement of cuttings in a propagator. Nkolbisson Station, Cameroon (Courtesy: Blaha)

The entire unit is covered with overhead shade (spaced bamboo lattice, boards, plastic screen, etc.) erected at a height of about two metres above the ground, with one metre high panels for lateral protection.

A budding callus forms on the wound, covering the base of the heel cutting two to three weeks after planting. The first roots appear a few days later. After two months, the non-rooted cuttings should be removed (Fig 27).

Once the cutting operation has been completed, its success will depend on a certain number of factors and must often be adapted to suit local conditions. Some of the most important factors are:

Cutting trays

The first cutting trays which were designed, were based on the model of propagators used in Trinidad for propagating cocoa. The design was then simplified, mostly for economic reasons. Experiments were later carried out in the Ivory Coast and Madagascar (IFCC) using semi-rustic installations without propagation cases. The trays were simply covered with a transparent polythene sheet supported by arches (tunnel) and shaded by a bamboo lattice (Fig 28). Basic coverings using sheets of jute which were kept permanently moist also gave interesting results (75 per cent success). Finally, propagation by cuttings inserted in plastic bags, under a translucent polythene sheet, was over 90 per cent successful. However, the technique of bulk propagation is preferred, planting out the cuttings in bags as soon as the roots appear. This gives excellent results and uses the propagators to their best advantage (yield is five times greater).

a and b – root emission

**Fig 27   *C. robusta* cuttings.
Ilaka Station, Madagascar
(Courtesy: Kuehn)**

c and d – root system

Fig 28 *C. robusta*: cuttings under a plastic tunnel. Togo (Courtesy: Partiot)

The trays can hold between 250 and 400 cuttings per square metre. The capacity depends especially on the area of the half-leaves. A square metre of a well-used tank can thus potentially provide 1500 to 2000 rooted cuttings per year.

Light
The level of diffused light falling on the cuttings is a very important factor. It must be adjusted according to the regional and seasonal light intensity. It normally varies between 25 and 60 per cent of the outside light intensity.

The rooting substrate
Many materials have been used, such as sand, peat, compost, coconut fibre, sawdust, coffee parchment; sometimes mixing them together. In the Ivory Coast and Central African Republic, the IFCC uses fine sawdust at a certain stage of decomposition. In Madagascar, the substrate consists of fine riverine sand, and is rather silty. It must be sterilised periodically, either by heat or with a gaseous chemical product.

The temperature of the rooting environment
The average temperature in the propagation cases must be maintained at about 25° to 28°C. If it rises much above this standard temperature, it becomes necessary either to spray the glass panes constantly, to whitewash them with lime-water, or to cover them with damp canvas.

The problems most often encountered are caused by a fall in nocturnal temperature. For example, in Madagascar, *C. canephora* cuttings require a month longer for rooting during the cool season than during the hot season. In Kenya, in high altitude areas it is necessary, due to temperature fluctuations, to heat the *C. arabica* propagators with electric heaters, in order to maintain a temperature of about 24°C.

Root-promoting substances
Many trials have been carried out using root-stimulating substances, dating from the time when the effect of bovine urine was discovered in India, up to the discovery of synthetic hormones like indole acetic acid, α – naphtalenacetic acid, 2–4 dichlorophenoxyacetic acid, indole propionic acid, etc.

These substances stimulate root development. However, the propagation of *C. canephora* by cuttings can now be between 90 and 100 per cent successful without the use of hormones, depending upon the clones used. These products have been practically abandoned in order to simplify the operation and for economic reasons. It is more justifiable to use hormones with *C. arabica*, which is propagated much less easily by cuttings than *C. robusta*. This is a common practice in East Africa.

The nature of the cutting
The first cutting trials began with 20 to 25 cm long orthotropic branches. The technique most commonly used today was discovered only after many trials. This is the **leaf bud cutting**, taken from a semi-lignified branch.

The optimum time of year for propagation by cuttings
The rainy season is the best time of year for propagation by cuttings. *C. arabica* is particularly affected by the seasons. For *C. canephora*, there is little difference in rooting success between the seasons and this operation is possible all the year round.

However, irrigating the trees selected for propagation lengthens the growth period of the suckers, thus making it possible to have a supply of material for cuttings in a satisfactory, turgid state for root production in periods other than the rainy seasons.

Heating the substrate of the propagators (Kenya) also enables the cuttings to continue to root for some time in cooler regions during the winter season (mountains, regions near tropical latitudes), so that a very short period of the year, less than three months, is not suitable for propagation. This time period can be more profitably spent on propagator maintenance and the renewal or disinfection of the substrate.

Transporting cutting material

Portions of branches (and unprepared cuttings) may be conserved for the duration of a journey simply by placing them in sealed polyethylene bags. After 12 to 14 days of conservation, the rooting percentage of the cuttings may be over 90 per cent. It does not appear to be necessary to immerse them in solutions of anti-transpirant.

Specific varietal or clonal potential for propagation by cuttings

The suitability for propagation by cuttings varies according to species and even variety. *C. canephora* propagates very easily, with a success rate varying from 70 per cent to almost 100 per cent, depending upon the clone. Propagation of *C. arabica* requires more care. In the Central African Republic, it was some time before the propagation of the species *C. excelsa*, which is very difficult, was satisfactorily accomplished and it required the use of a synthetic hormone, β indole butyric acid. The percentage of success has been increasing progressively from 17 per cent in the initial stages, to over 70 per cent.

The clonal nursery

The cuttings must remain in propagators for a sufficient amount of time to ensure that they are well rooted.
The percentage rooting of cuttings in the nursery may be as high as 90 to 95 per cent; fully rooted cuttings will have roots 30 mm long with three pairs of leaves. The rooting percentage may only be between 25 and 80 per cent when the cuttings are less developed. With canephoras, 8 to 12 weeks are estimated to be necessary for rooting. With the species *C. excelsa*, the length of stay in the nursery may be up to 24 weeks.

The cuttings are inspected when they come out of the trays and those that are malformed and weak, with poorly developed roots, are discarded. The others are then planted out very carefully in the nursery in beds filled with fertile soil. Shade must also be provided. Plastic bags are also commonly used to raise cuttings. Good results are obtained using a mixture of compost and decomposed sawdust as a substrate. The bags must be placed next to each other in the shaded nursery.

The plants will be sufficiently developed and ready to be transplanted about eight to nine months later. *C. canephora* plants will by then have six to eight pairs of leaves and one to two pairs of branches. Considering the losses that may occur in the shade nursery, a final survival level of 80 per cent is considered to be satisfactory.

The tree nursery

The term tree nursery is used to describe a nursery of clones which have been specially selected and grown for the intensive production of orthotropic branches to be used for cuttings. The best technique for producing erect branches is the bending method of training, which is achieved by bending the young plant (Fig 49).

In Madagascar, a new technique was developed by Vianney-Liaud

(IFCC). It consists of planting out the young coffee trees in a shade nursery at a spacing of 0.25 m × 0.25 m. The plagiotropic branches are systematically removed to favour the formation of orthotropic branches. When the main stem has six to eight pairs of leaves (8–10 months) it is pruned back to the lignified wood, about 0.15 m from the ground, with a pair of leaves remaining at the base. The branch which has been removed will provide a certain number of cuttings. Two orthotropic shoots which will develop from axillary buds will provide a new series of cuttings seven to eight months later. New orthotropic shoots will continue to develop, and, after the same period of time, provide a third series of cuttings. Despite any application of fertilisers or manure, the stock plants will become exhausted after a fourth harvest. They must then be uprooted and replaced after cultivating the land thoroughly and deeply. With this technique, 1000 cuttings per m^2 may be easily produced in less than three years.

This system enables 15 000 to 20 000 plants to be produced per year, with a 30 m^2 area of trays, and 100 m^2 of tree reserve.

In vitro propagation

Coffee tree propagation has benefitted over the past years from basic research undertaken on *in vitro* culture techniques, the results of which have already been extended to many plants from temperate countries.

These new methods are obviously of interest for propagating coffee trees at a much higher rate. This is particularly relevant for cross-fertilised species, as preserving their attributes in the progeny eliminates the need for propagation by seeds.

Work has been carried out by Dublin (IRCC), Staritsky, Sondahl, Custers and other researchers on developing tissue culture using fragments of tissue from stems, leaves, ovaries, stamens and other parts. This results in the production of rooted embryoid plants which, within a few weeks, give rise to plants having a hereditary genetic composition that is, in most cases, exactly the same as that of the plant from which the original tissue was obtained.

Many of these advanced techniques are still at the laboratory stage because they require specific installations, an aseptic environment, access to nutritive substances, hormones, and the supervision of an experienced staff. However, their use in the near future is so promising that it seems appropriate to devote a significant proportion of this chapter to this technology.

In vitro tissue culture for *Coffea* species

Among the new biological technologies, *in vitro* plant tissue culture in artificial culture media offers new ways to vegetatively propagate coffee

(Cambrony, 1984), with a greatly increased propagative potential, compared with the commercial method of horticultural propagation as described previously.

The principle of this *in vitro* method is relatively simple, but it will still require further experimental trial and error with coffee before it can be fully recommended.

It consists of the utilisation of growing media (solid or liquid) of well-established mineral and organic formulations, upon which an **explant**, consisting of an organ or fragment of an organ (stem or branch internode, bud, petiole or blade of a leaf, unripe fruit, embryo, anther, ovule, etc.) of plant tissue, or a cellular mass (cambium, apical meristems, endosperm, etc.) is deposited. This is placed in its entirety, in a glass container of the appropriate size and shape (large test tube, Petri dish) and is subjected to alternating periods of light and dark of varied lengths and often also to variations in temperature.

It must be stressed that all the material and ingredients used must be rigorously disinfected beforehand and all operations except for the final establishment in a normal horticultural environment, must be carried out in filtered air from which all germs have been eliminated. Moreover, the technicians themselves and their clothing must be extremely clean.

The development and growth of the new tissue formed may give way either to a non-organised structure (callus) or an organised structure (embryoid bud), both of which are genetically similar; or a variant of the donor plant, depending upon the physico-chemical conditions of the culture, the number and nature of the sequences used, and the nature of the explant. Increased vegetative reproduction can thus be obtained which may be integrated into a plant improvement programme, depending upon the way the culture is oriented.

Vegetative propagation techniques

True **micropropagation** or *in vitro* tissue culture represents a miniaturisation of the classical horticultural process, in which a fragment of the stem or branch with pre-existing or embryonic buds develops an orthotropic leafy stem, which will in turn be divided into microcuttings. After a period of rooting, the resultant plantlets can be planted out in a normal horticultural environment, and progressively reach a normal size, with a potential for high quality production.

A sophisticated variation of the foregoing procedure is **apical meristem culture** which enables healthy plants to be produced, free of viral infection.

Another variation, **micrografting**, which has been developed in *Citrus* by Navarro and Murashige (1975), resembles the horticultural technique of grafting which has already been used on coffee trees by Vianney-Liaud and is mentioned on page 59.

Finally, there is **somatic embryogenesis** which involves passing from the tissue culture stage through an undifferentiated callus phase, within which an organised embryoid structure may arise which, when planted out in an appropriate environment, will develop into a normal seedling. This structure may be formed either during or after a rather long phase of organogenesis (sometimes even passing through a secondary callus stage).

This last technique offers a reasonably high propagation coefficient of the plant material. This reproduction is only ensured with a somewhat unpredictable degree of variation, which is directly related to the number of cellular regenerations undergone by the original material, in other words, the number of mitoses of the nuclei which take place under very variable conditions.

The study of plant tissue culture has been progressing steadily since the first trials on the regeneration of plant fragments which were conducted by Rechniger in 1893.

Our knowledge of plant physiology has increased, particularly with regard to the effect of hormones (auxins, gibberellins, cytokinins) and their balance in the process of organogenesis (Skoog and Miller, 1957).

The potential practical value of tissue culture was illustrated by the work of Gautheret (1939), followed by that of Morel and Martin (1952) on *Citrus* meristem culture. This practice soon became widespread in the production of many healthy virus-free fruit trees and ornamental plants.

However, it was not until the 1970s that information became available on the micropropagation of coffee trees, when Staritsky obtained good results with the first production of somatic embryos using fragments of young orthotropic stems of *C. canephora*. Then, in 1971, Dublin demonstrated the possibiliity of bud regeneration, using fragments of stem and branch internodes of *C. arabica*. Coovuoco produced many shoots from fragments of orthotropic stems, whereas Colonna developed the *in vitro* culture of mature embryos. Herman and Haas (1975) obtained somatic embryos from fragments of *C. arabica* leaves, and were soon followed by Sharp and Sondahl (1977) who experimented with a very wide range of organ culture: leaf petioles and laminas, stems and unripe fruits, using different species (*C. arabica, C. canephora, C. dewevrei* var *excelsa*) for the production of somatic embryos, passing through the callus phase. Lanaud (1981) was the first to succeed in somatic embryogenesis using *C. canephora* ovules. In the same year, the work of Kartha and Londono on *C. arabica* meristem culture was published. The tissue culture laboratory of the Gerdat Centre in Montpellier also finalised the different methods of *in vitro* vegetative propagation of the Arabusta hybrid, under the direction of Dublin; much of the technical information reported in the following pages has been based on the work of this author.

Some practical aspects of *in vitro* propagation of coffee

Only orthotropic shoots should be used for propagation material in order to obtain a plant with a normal habit.

Micropropagation

Three main sources of propagation material may be used:

1 Plant material from pre-existing buds in the axils of the leaves. Their earlier development, protected by the stipules, leads to the inclusion of bacteria which renders this material difficult to disinfect.

However, it is possible to obtain a sufficient rate of bud development and the production of orthotropic stems by double disinfection and the use of culture solutions. The various materials include saccharose and cytokinins and pre-treatment in a liquid medium favours bud enlargement and the development of the buds into orthotropic stems.

The addition of cysteine to the culture medium, the combined effect of low temperature and darkness, and an increase in the amount of subculturing, all help to combat phenolic oxidations while increasing the rate of growth of the stems.

Moreover, reducing the light intensity encourages the elongation of the internodes; this facilitates their final sectioning into a microcutting.

2 Plant material from latent, rudimentary buds on fragments of internodes of orthotropic stems. Successful experiments have been conducted, using this technique to offset the problem of the disinfection procedure which is necessary in the previous process. Buds of 15 to 20 mm in length appear on the apical surface of the explants and these are placed in a normal position in the culture media with the radicle region submerged in the medium.

The most effective medium has been found to be the mineral medium of 30 K de Margara (1972). In the four to five weeks after placement in the culture medium, there is successive formation of a scar callus (of cambial origin), within which the meristems are differentiated; their numbers depending on the abundance of cytokinin in the medium. These meristems evolve rapidly into leafy buds, then into stems.

Various substances such as cytokinin, saccharose, malt extract, and adenine have a positive effect on the stimulation of latent buds on coffee trees.

The most active cytokinins are Zeatin and Benzyl-amino-purine (BAP). The result of an increase in the concentration of BAP from 1 to 10 mg is:

- an increase in the speed at which the buds appear;
- an increase in the number of buds per explant, without a significant change in the percentage of explants with latent buds;
- a delay in bud development on the stem of the differentiated buds.

If the concentration is too high, there is a reduction in the number of differentiated buds.

When an explant remains in the original medium, only one bud among the differentiated buds on the wound surface develops, to the detriment of the others which die.

The explant may be cut longitudinally into two or four, to increase the yield of the buds. This yield may be further increased by excising and subculturing each differentiated bud in a fresh medium. Under these conditions, a single explant may produce a dozen shoots after four months of culture.

Dublin also observed that 'The position of the internodes on the stem determines the capacity of the explant for bud initiation. Only the last two or three internodes, those closest to the apical meristem, are liable to have this potential for bud initiation.'

There is a limit to the size of the explants. Only the fragments of the internodes that are larger than 10 mm are capable of bud initiation. This concept is reminiscent of the original work of Rechniger, who maintained that the vertical position of the explant in the culture medium determines the optimum rates for bud initiation.

He also noticed that the duration of the callus formation phase that precedes bud emission is significantly shortened (less than 20 days between placing it in the culture and bud differentiation). Moreover, this callus is reduced to only a few layers of cells. It follows, therefore, that there are practically no risks of genetic variations occurring during this brief phase, which thus renders this system of propagation extremely valid in terms of uniform production.

Rechniger stated that 'The differentiated bud emits new leaves and elongates until it forms a stem with a few pairs of leaves. This phase of elongation of these stems is also an important step, because these stems are destined to produce microcuttings. It is thus very useful to accelerate their growth by promoting the elongation of the internodes.'

Several factors may contribute to this acceleration and the elongation of the stem tissues:

- frequent subculturing in a fresh medium at an optimum rate of one per month;
- enrichment of the culture medium with potassium nitrate, saccharose, (50 g/l), and adenine;
- an increase in the size of the culture dish.

Dublin, in fact, found that miniaturisation (short internodes and small leaves) was encouraged by the use of tubes of classical dimensions (25 mm in diameter) which hampered the final operation of producing microcuttings. The increase in the gaseous volume resulting from the use of a larger container enabled development to be accelerated, and more vigorous stems and larger leaves to be obtained.

The optimum temperature for growth is 27°C, and a reduction in light induces the elongation of the internodes.

After harvest, these orthotropic stem tissues are sectioned into microcuttings and replaced in the culture medium.

Dublin states that 'Each microcutting, consisting of a node with two leaves that have been reduced by half and an internode, is placed in a medium enriched with sugar and cytokinin. As a general rule, only one of the axillary buds of the microcutting is allowed to develop, whereas the others are inhibited. Experience shows that forcing all these buds, or those growing from the axils of the small nodes, to develop is not advantageous, since it leads to the formation of spindly shoots that cannot be utilised for continuing the production of microcuttings. The bud develops more rapidly when the microcutting originates from more vigorous shoot tissues, and elongation may begin within 8 to 10 days after placing the microcutting in the culture medium.'

Under optimal cultural conditions, as already specified, each microcutting may produce a new shoot with four to six pairs of leaves after two months of culture.

This shoot may also be sectioned into microcuttings. The original microcutting, subcultured in a fresh medium, will continue to produce new shoot initials which are more numerous and vigorous at each new subculturing, as the volume of the rootstock increases. This procedure can contribute to the true *in vitro* collection of rootstocks for the production of microcuttings compared by Dublin to the creation of germplasm reserves in the classical horticultural procedure of propagation by cuttings.

An estimate shows that, with the production of four or five microcuttings, plus a rootstock, at the end of two months of culture, close to 20 000 cuttings may be obtained from a single cutting after 12 months.

By comparison, in a classical horticultural coffee propagation programme, as practiced in Africa (Ivory Coast, Togo, Cameroon), 24 months may elapse between the time the cutting is taken, through rooting in the cutting tray, development in the nursery, planting in the germplasm collection, and the harvest of 50 to 100 primary cuttings. During the same period of time (24 months), *in vitro* micropropagation may have produced about 5^{12} propagules from a single cutting, or several million cuttings in the case of the F_1 hybrid of *C. arabica* × *C. robusta* which is well known for its vegetative vigour.

The **terminal rooting phase** of the orthotropic shoots obtained at the end of the micropropagation process is also well established. It essentially involves their subculturing in a solid medium with a low mineral concentration to which some β-indole butyric acid (1–2 mg/l) has been added.

This root-promoting hormone may also be applied to the propagules in a concentrated solution (50 mg/l) during a preliminary soaking for 24 hours before planting out. The roots appear after a period of 15 days and the success rate is usually between 95 and 100 per cent.

The rooted cuttings may finally be planted out in a normal nursery substrate as soon as the roots are 0.5 to 1 cm long. Maintaining them in an atmosphere with a high level of humidity, and applying normal phytosanitary precautions should ensure their survival with an excellent percentage take.

In this medium, root development will continue and the dwarf habit of the seedlings will be progressively reduced, as the root system thickens to accommodate a plant consisting of leaves and internodes of normal dimensions.

According to Dublin, a rooted plantlet that is developed enough to be planted in the field can be produced 10 to 12 months after the two-leaved microcuttings are placed in the culture medium. This time period is compared to that necessary for a seed or a normal type of cutting to produce a plant ready for transplanting to the field.

3   Obtaining orthotropic shoots by reversion of the plagiotropic characteristic of branch tissues. This reversion may be obtained by using successive cultures in media which are rich in cytokinin, in association with the development of bud initials which are promoted by the frequent pruning of all plagiotropic growths. This procedure ensures the encouragement of rejuvenation in the original material which also strengthens progressively to form a vigorous, productive rootstock.

Among the shoots that result from these new buds, orthotropic shoots are distinguished from plagiotropic shoots by the position of their leaves; orthotropic shoots having horizontally positioned laminas, untwisted petioles, and a main axis with a vertical habit (displaying negative geotropism). Harvesting these orthotropic shoots and sectioning them into microcuttings initiates the start of a new propagation cycle as in the preceding case.

The interest in using this reversion technique arises particularly from the greater availability of plagiotropic material on all coffee trees used as cutting source plants.

Meristem culture is possible with *Coffea* as Kartha and Londono (1971) have shown, but it is difficult in the initial stages due to the presence of waxy exudates around the terminal buds and the phenolic oxidations that adversely affect the culture medium. The yield is consequently low and the propagative potential inadequate, since the strong apical dominance inhibits the vigorous bud production by the meristem that occurs in other species such as plum trees. Moreover the usefulness in producing healthy, virus-free plants is also limited, as this type of problem occurs rather infrequently in coffee.

Somatic embryogenesis

This system of propagation has been most frequently researched since 1970. Its technology is therefore well documented.

The process begins with a callus phase or a callus-forming phase that occurs in darkness in a medium that is balanced with auxins and cytokinins. It then progresses with a phase of embryoid differentiation, which occurs in the light in an auxin-free medium strengthened with cytokinin. The development is completed by a phase during which the embryos are transformed into plantlets, which are then raised in the nursery (Fig 29).

Fig 29   Arabusta seedling from a somatic embryo (Courtesy: Dublin)

The different methods of production may be presented as follows according to Dublin:

Embryogenesis on sections of young orthotropic stems
This technique, which was the first to be standardised, requires five to seven months before the first embryoids are obtained.

These may appear on the primary callus. They are generally few in number, but they are identical to the original parent material and have distinct root and cotyledonary zones. Two small cotyledonary leaves dominate the latter zone.

These embryos can also be produced on the secondary callus after subculturing the bud growth tissues taken from the primary callus. The yellowish colouring of these second generation calluses clearly distinguishes them from the first which are dark brown. Their embryogenic value is also much greater.

Embryogenesis on sections of young plagiotropic branches
This method has been carried out successfully with *C. arabusta* explants. However, it is necessary to combine regenerative pre-treatments with sequences of somatic embryogenesis in order for it to succeed.

Somatic embryogenesis on leaf tissues
This procedure, which was initiated by Herman and Haas (1975) and Sondahl and Sharp (1977), appears to be very promising.

Its advantage, over the two previously mentioned procedures, is that it can be carried out using an abundantly available, easily renewable material from the parent source plant. The tissues are also easily disinfected and are not subject to phenolic oxidations and diffusions which invade the medium and are responsible for the death of many stem and branch explants.

Its embryogenic value is also enhanced by the fact that somatic embryoids can be produced:

- directly on the original callus on the vein of the leaves, without going through an undifferentiated callus phase. Moreover, this production is very rapid, requiring only two to three months of culture;
- on the primary callus, after the explant stage, sustaining these partially developed calluses in the differentiation medium. This embryogenesis consequently requires more time, i.e. four to five months of culture;
- on the secondary callus, after increasing the amount of auxin in the medium and following the development of a stable, yellowish cellular structure which is highly embryogenic. Over 1000 embryoids have been counted on such a callus in a single test tube. The timeframe for such a culture exceeds five months. Anomolous growth may frequently occur in many of the embryoids that arise from this type of callus, such as preferential growth of a certain zone (root or hypocotyledonary). These inhibitions are usually easily eliminated by re-establishing a better auxin/cytokinin balance in the culture medium. The excess of cytokinin favours the growth of the cotyledonary zone and conversely, the auxin predominance enhances root development at the expense of the cotyledonary zone, which is sometimes reduced to two small excrescences.

Embryogenesis on coffee flower ovaries
This process has resulted from studies by Lanaud (1981) on *C. canephora*, and is also adapted to *C. arabusta*. It can produce embryoids after four to five months of culture and offers the advantage of providing easily accessible explants, a zero infection rate, and a high propagation potential.

Among all these processes for creating somatic embryos, those that take the shortest time and use a moderate number of cellular divisions offer the best guarantee for the genetic conformity of the progenies in relation to the hereditary constitution of the original source plant.

Transformation of somatic embryos into seedlings
Whatever the process of embryogenesis may be, normal, balanced somatic embryos are produced with cotyledonary leaves and well-differentiated hypocotyledonary and root zones. An intermediary culture in a liquid medium is sometimes necessary to regulate an uncoordinated embryogenesis which leads to gaps in the development of the original embryoids and the offspring of the embryoids which they produce.

The normal embryos are then individually subcultured in a so-called development medium, where roots and stems evolve into seedlings with three to four pairs of leaves which may then be transferred to the nursery.

These individual manipulations are delicate and very exacting and the 'plating' method is often preferred. This entails raising a batch of embryoids with a sufficiently developed cotyledonary zone, which are then spread out in a solid, stem-promoting culture medium. This technique succeeds in preferentially producing shoots with three to four pairs of leaves, following a development phase of the cotyledonary leaves, until the normal leaf size of 1 to 2 cm in diameter is attained. These are comparable to those produced by embryos resulting from the germination of normal seeds. This stage of intermediary breeding also constitutes a phase of selection during which the embryoids which are not well formed or are otherwise unsuitable for this type of culture are eliminated.

These shoots, which are the easiest to handle for sampling, are then treated in a rooting medium in a similar way to those resulting from micropropagation techniques.

After root induction, the root, shoot and leaf systems of the plantlets which are formed from somatic embryos rapidly develop after planting out in nursery conditions. The plants can be established in the field after eight to ten months.

Necessary resources

Staff who are trained in applied biology are required to carry out these delicate propagation procedures effectively. Their responsibilities must be planned and supervised by a well-qualified, competent specialist in tissue culture methodology.

Until the beginning of the 1980s, the techniques associated with microcuttings and the embryogenesis of coffee had been carried out under experimental conditions in cell biology research laboratories. However, these techniques will continue to require well-equipped installations, even under industrial conditions, as, for example, where ornamental plant tissue culture is carried out. The resources required include specially equipped buildings and specialised equipment including: **receiving rooms**, for the primary preparation and disinfection of the plant material collected from the field or greenhouses; **workrooms** for microdissection and subculturing in a sterile medium, including equipment such as a laminar flow transfer hood; **rooms for producing explants** with aseptic cabinets and shelves which can be adjusted for light and temperature; **stores** for glassware (test tubes, Petri dishes, or sterilisable plastic containers) and materials for preparing the culture media, together with containers and apparatus that are indispensable to the preparation and/or sterilisation of these media such as scales, water distilling equipment, stoves, various sterilisers; **rooms for final repotting** in nursery substrates, and for the initial growing under controlled conditions before being transferred to greenhouses or ordinary shade nurseries.

It is essential to build screens between 'dirty' rooms and 'clean' rooms in such laboratories and to organise the order of the rooms logically, taking into consideration the sequence of the basic operations required for the recommended culture method. In addition, there must be no uncontrolled air currents, which are carriers of dust and microbes and may contaminate both explants and culture media.

A shower room, with sinks and bathrooms and a dressing room where staff can put on clean laboratory uniforms, would usefully complete such a building.

Of the many materials that are essential in the preparation of culture media, such as those of Murashige and Skook, are the necessary chemicals to prepare these media. The culture centre should also have an adequate supply of minerals such as nitrates, phosphates, sulphates, various trace elements and organic elements such as saccharose, malt extracts, adenine, cysteine and the plant hormones, i.e. cytokinins (BAP Zeatin), auxins (2,4-dichlorophenoxyacetic acid, alpha naphthalene acetic acid, β-indole butyric acid), gibberellins, and gelling substances such as agar-agar). Last but not least, the centre should also stock a range of disinfectants to clean the equipment and the premises, which is also essential for the preparation of healthy explants.

The organisation and layout of the entire premises, equipment and products, as well as the number and quality of the organisers and workers, all revolve around the propagative potential of the plant material. This was previously emphasised in the section on methods of micropropagation, and expanded upon in the section on somatic embryogensis. Most associated buildings will thus be of the same area as those rooms used for producing explants and, in addition, may include annexes used for plant breeding such as greenhouses or nurseries. Provision of rooms for processing and shipping seedlings should also be considered, if the final stages of breeding are to be carried out on the recipient's premises outside the establishment, perhaps at long intercontinental distances. International phytosanitary regulations will not apply in this case as the small, sterile bottles carry healthy microcuttings, embryoids, or seedlings, which are free of pathogenic germs and parasites.

The overall process is highly complex, with numerous operations being involved in the production of several generations of explants and their progeny. Operations must therefore be carefully planned beforehand, and work must be rigorously organised, in order to ensure its financial and technical success.

The potential of tissue culture

The importance of tissue culture for improving plant species is obvious. However, the process really became established with regard to coffee with the **suspended culture in a liquid medium** of cells of stem parenchyma (Sharp, 1968). Experience has shown the possibility of the culture and proliferation of coffee cells in an *in vitro* medium. This approach was later explored by

Waller (1980) and subsequently resulted in the creation of caffeine-enriched lines derived from somatic cells of *C. arabica laurina*.

Coffee cell culture linked with fermentation is a promising direction for the production of a primary material which could be useful in the food industry, cosmetics, and pharmacology. The culture of cells from coffee rootstocks that have been selected for their high chlorogenic acid, trigonellin, and caffeine content also has great potential. However, applying genetics to the selection of coffee material remains the preferred area in which tissue culture could possibly play a successful role, as it could have a very positive effect on the quality of the plant material produced.

In this area, the following has already been realised or is planned in coffee research centres:

1 The conservation of very diversified collections of coffee species and varieties in gene banks. Transport or intercontinental exchanges of microcuttings could be facilitated as a result of this activity since the material could be sent via postal packages of micro test tubes with a solid medium. Phytosanitary requirements for this 'germplasm' (see Chapter 2) would be fully complied with, due to the complete absence of pathogens.

2 Enlarging genetic bases and the propagation of variants: tissue culture has proven to be the potential source of major genetic variations, such as modification of the ploidy (Fig 30), linkage and gene transfers, depending upon the origin of the explants, the composition of the media, the physiochemical procedures followed, and the frequency and duration of subculturing, etc.

The systematic organisation of this variability may entail exerting selection pressure on the cultured material through the culture medium, such as modification of the saline composition and the introduction of toxic factors from pathogenic or parasitic micro-organisms. This will have a favourable affect on the survival of the cells and ultimately the embryoids, possibly producing cells which are tolerant or resistant to this tension. Tissue culture could also be useful for assessing the compatability of stress-resistant varieties with new forms of rootstocks.

3 The creation of haploids by anther culture is an interesting operation which is ultimately aimed at obtaining homozygotic lines directly through chromosomal duplication, using colchicine, of haploid anthers. The creation of homogenous hybrid varieties has already been achieved using diploid coffee trees, beginning with a very small number of natural haploids which have been found in seed-bearing progenies.

4 *In vitro* fertilisation of species or varieties which are incompatible due to the existence of a biological barrier within the flower style, as exists in canephoras and other diploid cross-fertilised coffee species.

Fig 30   *C. canephora*: six
months old, tetraploid,
seedling (Courtesy: Capot)

5   Favouring the survival of interspecific hybrids, by ensuring the culture, after excision, of immature embryos which are prone to early abortion due to an incompatibility with the tissue of the endosperm.

6   Obtaining and propagating somatic hybrids through the fusion of proto-plasts, which could enlarge the genetic base of species and varieties for selection by enabling naturally very distant genes to be incorporated, and making more unlikely genetic combinations possible through the use of plasmides or tumorous tissues. This could produce hybrids which are of interest in the diagnosis of pathogens, or which could be used in the pro-duction of plant vaccines.

Future plans

The 1980s have revealed spectacular innovations in coffee growing. However, a time for reflection and development is still necessary, in order to make judgements based on the possible practical results of their applications and to perfect and finalise the routine industrial processes where required, since these will be essential for the economic application of the new plant material.

The spread of serious pathogens throughout the world (leaf rust, coffee berry disease, etc.), the appearance of new diseases and predators, and the increase in pest damage such as that caused by beetles, leaf miners and nematodes, make it necessary to consider the need for the rapid renewal of varieties that are currently being cultivated, at regional or even national levels, in order to prevent these devastating epidemics. It is within these synergistic aspects of plant improvement that the new high-yielding techniques of vegetative propagation have become so important (see also Chapter 8).

Grafting

Coffee grafting has been practiced for a considerable period of time. One of the applications was to associate the *C. arabica* species, which has a root system that is highly sensitive to nematodes, with *C. liberica*, which is resistant to nematodes. Grafting has also been used to propagate natural hybrids and clones. Until propagation by cuttings was perfected, grafting was the main method of vegetative propagation used in experimental stations. In recent times, its interest has considerably decreased.

The best grafting methods are: simple cleft grafting, top grafting, side grafting, shield budding or grafting, sub-cotyledonary approach grafting.

Grafted cuttings

At the experimental station at Kianjavato, Madagascar, Vianney-Liaud introduced the idea of grafting lignified and semi-lignified wood, collected during explorations in the forest pockets of spontaneous coffee trees in the Mascarenes, onto cuttings of cultivated coffee trees which were in the process of rooting in the propagator, to ensure the survival of the former. The considerable success of this operation resulted in the widespread use of this technique of cleft grafting on to rooting cuttings, sometimes referred to as 'bench grafting', with all species and varieties of coffee.

5 *Agronomy*

In this major chapter, the author has compiled information concerning coffee cultivation in the true sense of the word. The main topics discussed are planting, primary cropping operations and maintenance (excluding phytosanitary problems which are discussed in Chapter 7).

Planting

Coffee is usually established on forest land. Trees are less frequently found in savanna regions as in these areas the soils have been eroded, are generally less fertile, and the climate is generally less favourable, with a long dry season.

Land preparation

The first operation consists of clearing the trees. They are generally burned, despite the drawbacks of this practice in causing the destruction of humus, loss of fertilising elements which are volatilised or leached by the rains and rapid deterioration of the soil which has been extensively exposed. All agronomists have condemned and fought against the use of burning as a management practice for forest land. They recommend a two-step operation. In the first phase, the undergrowth is cut and incinerated, then the large trees are cut. The time that elapses between these operations is used to prepare the soil, and particularly to establish a live cover. The large trees are sold as timber, and of the remaining trees, small branches are heaped together and burned, and trunks and large branches are gathered together in windrows and left to gradually decompose.

The second part of the operation consists of marking out the blocks and plots. The blocks are generally of two to four hectares in size to facilitate the servicing of all the plots, especially with regard to the transport of fertiliser and harvested crops.

Once the land has been prepared, the planter must decide on the plantation design and planting density, and must then proceed to mark out and dig the planting holes.

Plantation design and planting density

The plantation design and the planting density depend upon many factors such as the species, variety or clone to be established, fertility and slope of the land, shade, maintenance methods, i.e. manual or mechanical, pruning system, and harvesting methods used, i.e manual or mechanical.

One of the major agronomical preoccupations is to establish the ideal design and density which will guarantee the best yields for each species. Many trials have been conducted in different countries with the following yield-related considerations:

- Aerial competition (light, aeration);
- Root competition (water, minerals);
- Maintenance and harvesting equipment (namely mechanisation);
- Economics and management costs.

These types of trials are complex and conclusions can only be drawn after several years of observations.

It is known that beyond a certain density, the competition between plants is such that their production declines. However, one may also consider that this singular drop in production can be compensated for, over a certain period of time, by the density of planting. This problem must also be examined from the point of view of the well-being of the plant and as a function of the cost of production. High densities, for example, are considered to be favourable to the development of diseases and the proliferation of pests.

Although the most rational geometric designs are the equilateral triangle and hexagonal formation, square or rectangular designs are preferred (Fig 31) because they are easier to mark out.

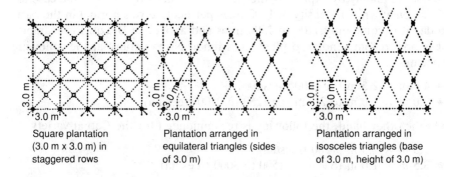

Square plantation
(3.0 m x 3.0 m) in
staggered rows

Plantation arranged in
equilateral triangles (sides
of 3.0 m)

Plantation arranged in
isosceles triangles (base
of 3.0 m, height of 3.0 m)

Fig 31 Plantation designs

Table I illustrates some figures of plantation density in relation to the geometric design and the spacing between the shrubs.

Table 1 Density of the classical plantation according to its geometric design and spacing

Spacing (m)	Approximate number of shrubs (per ha)		
	Square, rectangle, isoceles triangle	Hexagon	Staggered rows
1.80 × 1.80	3000	3450	–
2.00 × 2.00	2500	2875	–
2.50 × 2.50	1600	1840	3200
3.00 × 2.50	1300	–	–
3.00 × 2.50	1100	1270	2200
3.00 × 3.50	930	–	–
3.50 × 3.50	800	920	1600
3.50 × 4.00	700	–	–
4.00 × 4.00	625	720	1250
4.00 × 4.50	550	–	–

For mechanised operations, windrowing the trees that have been cut but not incinerated requires a spacing of 3.0 m to 3.5 m, resulting in the arrangement of the lines in pairs. Later we will see that planting along the contours (singly or in pairs) is advised for land that has a slope of more than 5 per cent.

In older plantations, the most widespread average densities are as follows:

C. arabica   2.0 m × 2.0 m to 3.0 m × 3.0 m;
C. canephora   2.5 m × 2.5 m to 3.5 m × 3.5 m.

Plantation densities have increased noticeably over the past 30 years. The basic reason for revising old traditions is the concept of calculating yield per hectare and not per plant, together with the need to lower the cost price of coffee, mainly by exploiting the land more efficiently. Such is the case for C. arabica: while a density of 1000 trees per hectare was normal in the past, today it is commonly 1200 to 1500 trees and above. In Brazil, for example, it is now recommended to plant the Mundo Novo variety at the following spacings:

- 4.0 m × 2.5 m (or 1000 trees/ha):
- 4.0 m × 1.0 m to 2.0 m (or 1250 to 2500 trees/ha).

On the other hand, the following is recommended for the Catuai variety:

- 3.5 m × 2.5 m (1200 trees/ha);
- 3.5 m × 1.0 m to 2.0 m (1500 to 3000 trees/ha).

For multi-stem pruning of arabica, Bouharmont advises a spacing of 3.0 m × 1.5 m, 2.5 m × 1.8 m, or 2.25 m × 2.0 m, or about 2200 trees/ha, especially for the Java cultivar in Cameroon. Multi-stem pruning is more suitable for use with a reduced spacing. The same author also recommends a density of 2660 to 2900 trees/ha, with spacings of 2.75 m × 1.25 m, 2.50 m × 1.50 m, and 1.90 m × 1.90 m under optimum conditions.

Results from numerous trials conducted by the IFCC with *C. robusta* indicate that the optimum density in the Ivory Coast is about 2000 trees/ha (3.0 m × 1.7 m) with multi-stem pruning. The cumulative production recorded for eight consecutive harvests was 14 453 kg of clean coffee or an annual average of 1932 kg/ha.

The advantage of the design of 3.0 × 1.7 m (2000 trees/ha) is that it is possible to use the interrows for growing food crops such as rain-fed rice, maize, groundnuts, etc. during the first and second years. Moreover, it enables certain operations to be mechanised such as weeding and spraying of chemicals.

High density planting

Recent experiments have been conducted using a new technique which has now been applied in some Latin American countries. It involves **very high density planting**. There are generally over 5000 plants per hectare, and sometimes over 10 000 plants per hectare.

However, this intensive exploitation of coffee trees can only be contemplated using low, so-called dwarf plants, e.g. Caturra or Catimor varieties. Very careful fertilisation techniques must be implemented, particularly when fertiliser is used in large quantities. The presence of the disease caused by *Hemileia* is an obstacle, due to the difficulty in applying protective treatments.

The production of the crop is limited in principle to three to five harvests, or until the shrubs are six or eight years old, a timespan that corresponds to the maximum fruiting potential of the young plants. Beyond this period, the production level shifts rapidly, as it is affected by various adverse constraints. These include root competition, loss of leaves at the base of the trunk, excessive sucker production, and a tendency of the main axis to become etiolated. The result is that this method of exploitation loses all of its yield value. At the end of the cycle, the plantation is either regenerated by stumping or is replanted after uprooting, followed by a fallow period of a year or two.

Yields obtained from high density plantations are very high. Figures have been recorded from 3 tonnes/ha to over 4 tonnes/ha on an annual average of three harvests with Mundo Novo. They are even higher with Caturra.

An interesting experiment was conducted in Colombia at six different ecological sites for five consecutive years on harvests at three densities: 10 000 shrubs/ha (1.0 × 1.0 m), 5000 shrubs/ha (1.42 × 1.42 m) and 2500 shrubs/ha (2.0 × 2.0 m). Three tonnes/ha/year of 12–6–22 fertiliser were applied on each plot in four annual applications.

An analysis of the cumulative results shows that in all cases the best production per unit area was obtained with 10 000 shrubs/ha. It should be mentioned that at this density it is necessary to establish short vegetative cycles of about three to five years only, before proceeding to rejuvenation pruning.

In some plots, the increase in production between 10 000 shrubs/ha and 3500 shrubs/ha is 94 per cent; between 10 000 and 2500 it is 23 per cent: Henao and Mestre-Mestre (1980).

In another Colombian experiment, the density of the shrubs per unit area and fertilisation were combined. Seven plots were selected in seven coffee growing regions at four densities: 1.25 × 1.25 m, or 6410 shrubs/ha; 1.50 × 1.50 m, or 4444 shrubs/ha; 1.75 × 1.75 m or 3268 shrubs/ha; 2.0 × 2.0 m or 2500 shrubs/ha were the criteria. Four doses of 12–12–17 fertiliser were applied in four annual applications, in four different amounts: 200 g, 500 g, 600 g and 800 g per tree, per year.

The result of this experiment, which was conducted over a five-year period, confirm the results already recorded for high densities, for example that the best yields were obtained on the most densely planted plots. The statistical interpretation also proved that an application of 2500 kg of fertiliser per hectare per year was adequate, compared to 3000 kg in the trials: Henao and Arias (1981). Table 2 shows some of the results obtained from an experiment conducted in Brazil by the CIB.

In 1967, this intensive coffee farming technique was initiated in Colombia. Brazil, Kenya, Puerto Rico, Jamaica, the IFCC in Cameroon, Ivory Coast and New Caledonia then followed suit, testing this technique experimentally. The results with *C. arabica* showed that the highest yields were obtained with a density of about 6000 to 6500 trees per hectare (1.25 × 1.25 m) in combination with mineral fertiliser (12–12–17), with the highest quantity being applied at a rate of 800 g per year (or 5000 kg/ha) in several applications. Depending upon the local conditions, these yields varied between 2700 kg/ha/year and 3300 kg/ha/year of clean coffee. The average yield of some plots had risen to 4000 kg/ha/year.

In 1982, Kiara and Nsagi, two authors from the Coffee Research Station of Ruiru, Kenya, published a very interesting study on the production costs of such farms and their profitability. The outcome was that, depending upon the average planting densities of *C. arabia* coffee at the time (1981), the best financial results were obtained with 4000 to 5000 trees/ha, and the optimum would be obtained at about 4000 trees/ha.

Whatever the appeal of these experimental results may be, caution should still be exercised and these results, which are relatively recent, should be further confirmed before being applied and used to make appropriate recommendations.

This technique, which was initiated in Latin America, seems to have evolved in practice. Densities have increased to about 5000 to 6000 shrubs per hectare and the farming cycle has been lengthened, due to the rather high investments that the planter must make: the purchase of plants, land preparation (digging planting holes), planting, fertiliser applications, harvesting, etc. Snoeck (1987) indicated some reservations in a relatively recent report on this subject: 'Very high densities are only suitable for planters with investment possibilities or subsidies. Moreover, these densities are only justified for highly technically oriented plantations where all the inputs are applied at the right time: herbicides, fertilisers, pesticides, pruning . . .'

Table 2 Comparing production according to planting density (five sites)
Average of the first three harvests (*C. arabica*)

Trial site	High density		Traditional density	
	Spacing Density/ha	Coffee Prod./ha	Spacing Density/ha	Coffee Prod./ha
1 *Varginha*	2.0 × 0.5 m 10 000	2750 kg	4.0 × 2.0 m 1250	1060 kg
2 *Varginha*	2.0 × 1.0 m 5 000	2000 kg	4.2 × 1.0 m 2400	1090 kg
3 *Caratinga*	2.0 × 0.5 m 10 000	2935 kg	4.0 × 1.5 m 1650	1055 kg
4 *Maringa*	1.85 × 1.0 m 5 500	2000 kg	3.8 × 1.0 m 2600	1050 kg
5 *Marilandia*	2.0 × 0.5 m 10 000	1115 kg	4.0 × 1.5 m 1650	350 kg

In Costa Rica, agronomists have been practicing new, intensive coffee farming techniques over the last few years on several thousand hectares, combining high densities (7000 plants/ha) with low and high pruning systems, which particularly favour the development of fruiting branches. This technique is applied to varieties of *C. arabica* with a low, dwarf habit. It consists of pruning the main roots, pollarding young plants, very careful fertilisation and shade control. Yields average about 4000 kg/ha.

The potential of this technology is of great interest. The results, mainly those obtained in Costa Rica, attest to the fact that it is still possible to make significant progress in intensive coffee farming. The practice of establishing high density plantations in some countries already shows progress. The setbacks that have been recorded at times should not discourage, but should serve as a reminder that there are still many problems left to be solved. These are mainly in the areas of genetics, physiology, particularly mineral nutrition, and maintenance techniques such as pruning operations. Current, routine, or classical methods (even for African *C. robusta* growing) will undoubtedly be replaced by new intensive farming techniques due to the economic and social requirements of the next century. The new methods will ensure that the world's coffee needs will continue to be met, using smaller areas of land, and that the producers' work will bring higher remuneration through increased profitability.

An in-depth study of the effect of high densities on the *C. arabica* plantation microclimate was undertaken in Kenya (Ruiru station). The main findings were as follows:

- The highest total radiation was recorded in plantations with lower densities (1100 shrubs/ha). Those with high densities (6670 shrubs/ha) showed a reduction in radiation level to a quarter of this figure.
- In high density plantations, soil temperature is maintained at an optimal level (24°C), which is favourable to the water supply. Stomatal transpiration and the temperatures recorded on the leaves illustrate these results. The loss of water from the soil through evaporation decreases in these populations, which is a favourable factor promoting good vegetative growth.

It should be emphasised that this experiment was conducted in plantations located at an altitude of about 1700 m. It is therefore only relevant for comparable situations and only applies to *C. arabica*.

Marking out and preparation for planting

Marking out consists of establishing where each coffee plant will be placed in the rows; a stake being used to mark individual planting stations.

The dimensions of the planting holes must be calculated according to the nature and fertility of the soil and the root development of the young plants. The holes must obviously be larger on clayey, compact, or stony soil than those on friable soil. Soils which have a hard subsoil such as tufa, calcareous or quartz concretions, must be deeply ploughed. The age of the plants is not relevant in this operation. In fact, it is essential to dig holes of normal dimensions, even if the development of the plant at the time of transplanting does not appear to warrant it. The volume of the hole should nevertheless be increased for particularly vigorous coffee trees.

The effect of the size of the holes on yields has been the subject of many trials. Yields are higher with larger holes (0.6 m × 0.6 m × 0.6 m to 0.9 m × 0.9 m × 0.9 m) than with smaller ones (0.3 m × 0.3 m × 0.3 m to 0.4 m × 0.4 m × 0.4 m). The increase in yield is approximately 5 to 10 per cent. The average dimensions should not be less than 0.4 m wide and 0.4 m deep.

Hole excavation was traditionally undertaken manually and the labourers were paid at piece-work rates. On commercial plantations, hole-boring machines with augers are now used which can dig holes that are 0.3 m to 0.7 m in diameter, and 0.5 m to 0.8 m deep. Their work capacity is between 30 and 60 holes per hour.

It is advisable to dig the holes a few weeks before transplanting so that the soil becomes well aerated. In compact, clayey soil, a superficial type of laterisation may occur, and the walls must then be scraped with a spade or hoe at the time of planting to allow the roots of the transplant to penetrate the soil and develop adequately. In this situation, it is preferable to leave the holes open for a minimal amount of time before planting.

A few days before planting the young coffee trees, a basal dressing of fertiliser, compost or manure may be applied. This should be thoroughly mixed with the soil used for filling the holes.

Transplanting

Planting the young coffee plants does not require any particular technical skills, but is a common arboricultural operation which does, however, require some care and attention.

Planting with bare roots

For plants grown in nursery beds as opposed to those grown in pots or plastic bags, the first operation consists of removing the plant from the soil without damaging either the taproot or the lateral root system. Before lifting the plants the soil should be well watered. When the plants have been carefully lifted, by cutting around the ball of roots with a spade, the soil is shaken from the roots and the plants are carefully inspected. This is necessary in order to eliminate all weak, malformed plants or those whose roots are malformed (twisted or buckled taproot etc.). Transplanting a defective plant should be strongly discouraged, since it will have no chance of developing into a healthy, productive shrub (Fig 32).

The young plants should be wrapped in a moist canvas cloth or banana leaves as soon as they are lifted out of the soil so that the roots are not exposed to the sun.

Dipping the roots in slurry made from clay and water when they leave the nursery will favourably affect the establishment of the plant and is

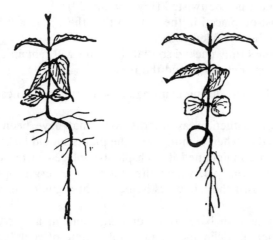

Fig 32 Plants with malformed taproots

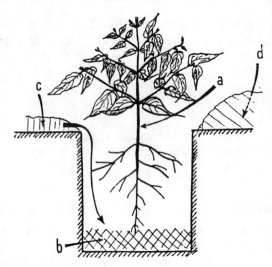

Fig 33   Planting the coffee tree

therefore highly recommended. On the contrary, pruning the plant by removing some of the roots and part of the leaves does not appear to have any beneficial effect on rooting and growth (IFCC). Well developed taproots may be shortened below the point at which the lateral roots emerge.

Two labourers normally work together as a team during planting. One holds the plant in the centre of the planting hole with the taproot vertically extended and the collar placed at, or slightly above, ground level, while the assistant fills in the hole with soil. After it is filled, the surface must be slightly mounded to allow for the sinking which will occur during the first rains (Fig 33).

The main precautions to be taken are:

1 The taproot must not be twisted (Figs 19 and 20).
2 The plant must be placed in the hole so that the collar will be at ground level when the hole is filled with soil.
3 The soil must be firmly packed so that the plant will remain upright; there should be no air pockets around the roots.

Errors which occur during planting are generally due to carelessness or neglect.

Primarily for aesthetic reasons, the rows that have been marked out should be adhered to when planting, and the plants should be evenly spaced. The spacing will be maintained if each plant is placed in the centre of the hole, which is, in principle, where the stake is. A very simple procedure which is used to assist the labourers is the use of a guide rule (Figs 34 and 35).

When planting with bare roots, dipping them in a slurry gives good results if it is done at a climatically favourable time of year (approximately 5 per cent do not take). The advantage in planting with bare roots over the

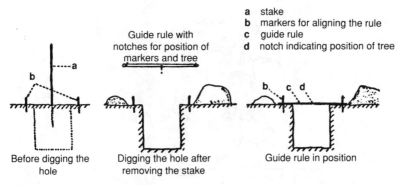

a   stake
b   markers for aligning the rule
c   guide rule
d   notch indicating position of tree

Guide rule with notches for position of markers and tree

b

a

Before digging the hole

Digging the hole after removing the stake

Guide rule in position

Fig 34   Use of the guide rule

Fig 35   Planting the coffee tree using the guide rule

following techniques described is that it enables the roots to be examined.

Experiments have also been conducted in Brazil on large farms using a coffee planting machine that was adapted from a planting machine used for planting *Eucalyptus*.

Planting with a root ball

The plants are removed from the nursery after having been generously watered and the soil is kept in place around the roots with woven straw or banana leaves. The coffee trees are transported on stretchers or in boxes and planted, keeping the ball of soil as intact as possible.

This planting method is facilitated by the use of a 'Java' planter, which is a metal cylinder made from sheet steel which is split longitudinally. It is between 0.15 m and 0.30 m high and 0.10 m to 0.20 m in diameter. At one

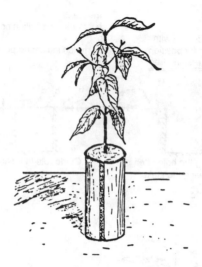

Fig 36   Coffee plant in a 'Java' planter

end of the cylinder, the steel is thinner to facilitate its penetration into the ground and the other end is reinforced by a metal fastener (Fig 36). The tool is pushed into the soil and cuts out a cylinder around the plant. The lateral roots and root hairs may be somewhat damaged, but the taproot will remain intact, which is most important. The planters containing the plants are transported in crates. When planting, the planter should be placed at the centre of the hole at a height which ensures that the collar will be slightly above ground level. The edges of the cylinder are then opened by hand and the cylinder is removed, leaving the plant and the surrounding soil in place. The hole should be filled by firming the soil around the roots as recommended for bare root planting.

The advantage of this system is that it causes the minimum amount of root disturbance to the young plant. However, it does prevent any root examination and requires the transport of relatively heavy and cumbersome material.

Plants raised in baskets, pots or plastic bags

Planting coffee trees that have been raised in baskets, bags, or pots made of plant fibres is a very simple procedure, but they should be placed in the soil carefully to avoid root disturbance. The baskets decompose very quickly and do not inhibit the development of the plants.

However, this cannot be said for the commonly used polythene bags, which are non-degradable. They must be split longitudinally and the bottom opened. It is generally preferable to remove the bags entirely.

An interesting technique, using a ball of compressed soil which is commonly used in European market gardening, was experimented with in coffee growing, with successful results. The most important aspect is the preparation of the substrate which must make the balls of earth quite resistant to watering or movement. It must also be rich and sufficiently porous to ensure that the young coffee plants will develop properly. This substrate generally consists of clay from termite mounds and vegetable compost, with some added straw and fertiliser.

The use of anti-transpirant products may be effective, as experience in Madagascar has shown, for planting with bare roots during the dry and cool seasons.

Stumping

Transplanting over-developed coffee seedlings or cuttings after a lengthy stay in the nursery presents some risks. It is advisable to stump them by pruning at a height of 0.25 to 0.30 m above the collar about 10 days before planting. It is also advisable to reduce the size of the root system by careful pruning.

Time of the year to transplant

The most favourable time of year for transplanting is at the beginning of the rainy season, a few weeks after the first rains, when the atmosphere is sufficiently humid. From planting in the middle of the rainy season the percentage take is often lower, but more importantly, the roots are not always developed enough for the plants to withstand the following dry season.

Post-transplanting operations

In sunny regions, the young coffee trees must be protected for two to three weeks after transplanting to reduce the level of transpiration and promote the vegetative regrowth. A few palm leaves or branches positioned around each plant will provide this protection.

A few weeks after transplanting, any dead plants should be counted and replaced. It is sensible to anticipate this risk by establishing surplus plants in the nursery.

Primary Cropping Operations

Erosion control

It is of prime importance in coffee growing to protect the soil from accelerated degradation and erosion caused by natural agents, particularly rainfall. It is especially necessary in certain areas, mainly because of the configuration of the land, the nature of the soil, and the amount and severity of the rainfall.

The effects of erosion are very obvious: furrows and gullies caused by the moving water, baring of the roots of the shrubs and removal of the top soil. This devastating effect is always accompanied by other forms of soil deterioration which may be less spectacular but are just as serious. These may include removal of humus, leaching of soluble mineral salts and alteration of the physical structure of the soil. Sheet erosion is a very serious condition caused by the already leached silt which has been deprived of organic matter, mineral salts, and clay particles, being carried from the higher parts of the plantations to the lower parts.

Several authors have attempted to calculate the losses of sloping, bare soil due solely to the effects of runoff in areas of Kenya, India and Colombia. They all produced very alarming figures and concluded that it was essential to take appropriate protective measures which may vary depending upon the cropping environment and its vulnerability.

The principal means of control that should be practiced in coffee growing are briefly discussed.

Soil cover

The practice of clean weeding, which consists of removing all spontaneous vegetation in the coffee inter-rows, is being increasingly abandoned. It is now only practiced in countries with relatively low precipitation levels, such as Brazil, despite the fact that it is criticised by the extension services. In regions which are subject to intense precipitation in terms of severity or quantity, it is now common to use a cover crop from the time the coffee plants are established. Previously it was stated that the soil must be conserved by planting a live cover as soon as the forest has been cleared. At the adult stage, when the leaves of the shrubs overlap, protecting the soil in the inter-rows is sufficient. However, this does not exclude the use of other means of protection to prevent intense runoff, if the slope of the land requires it.

The best adapted species of Leguminosae for the region are normally used as a soil cover. Many species which were still being used 10 and 20 years ago have been eliminated as a result of recent experiments. Moreover, other criteria have also been introduced in addition to the qualities which had been recognised for a long time and were expected from these plants, such as easy propagation, vigour, adaptive properties, spread and thickness of the cover. Physiological studies have become necessary to investigate deep rooting, tolerance to drought or the nutritive competition of various cover crops with the coffee.

The most widely used Leguminosae in the world are: *Indigofera endecaphylla* Jacq, *Pueraria javanica* Benth, *Centrosema pubescens* Benth, *Desmodium ovalifolium* Grill & Perr., *Flemingia* sp. *Stylosanthes gracilis, Vigna oligosperma, Mimosa invisa* and *Leucaena* sp.

In the lower Ivory Coast, several experiments (IFCC) conducted with *C. canephora* proved that *Flemingia* was superior to *Tithonia, Stylosanthes, Pueraria*, and *Leucaena*, the natural cover being the control. *Flemingia* is not very competitive, especially if its root system is already well established when the coffee is transplanted. In addition, it accumulates a high content of nitrogen and calcium in the leaves. It is regularly cut down when planted in the inter-rows and the dead leaves are used as a mulch around the coffee trees. Boyer (Fig 37) studied in particular the effect of cover crops used in experiments on the soil's seasonal moisture balance. He concluded that the choice should focus on species with deep taproots which draw water from lower soil levels and also efficiently protect the soil surface, the consequence being a reduction in the drying gradient of the upper horizons of the soil where the greatest activity of the coffee root system is localised. He estimated that *Flemingia* fulfilled these conditions, whereas others, like *Stylosanthes*, *Pueraria*, *Tithonia*, etc. were not recommended in regions where the rainfall was not abundant enough to rapidly restore the soil's natural water reserves. On the other hand, these species, which produce large quantities of green matter, may be used to advantage in very humid regions where the dry season is not extensive. In the Central African Republic, trials have shown the regional value of *Mimosa invisa* and *Pueraria*. These two plants have been maintained for 10 years in trial plots with a minimal amount of maintenance, and have been shown to completely protect the soil against erosion and invasion by graminaceous weeds, particularly *Paspalum*. However, controlling excessive development of *Pueraria* is recommended, in order to prevent it from smothering the coffee trees with its vegetation. In Madagascar, favourable results were obtained with *Vigna oligosperma*. In Cameroon, a cover crop trial conducted over four seasons with *C. robusta* gave the following results (average production of clean coffee): *Flemingia* 1198 kg; *Mimosa*: 1143 kg; *Pueraria*: 1013 kg; Control with natural cover: 859 kg. The statistical interpretation proved that the three cover plants were significantly superior to the control (Figs 38 and 39).

The diversity of these results further proves that there is no ideal cover crop able to adapt to such diverse ecological environments as those in which coffee is established. The choice of cover crop must therefore be based on either the advice of specialists or after comparative trials have been carried out, where some of the most regionally widespread plants are made to compete.

Mulching

Mulching consists of covering the soil with a thick layer of straw, grass, dead weeds or compost and has been practiced for some considerable time in conjunction with coffee growing in Kenya, Kivu and other countries. The excellent results obtained explain why its use is so widespread, particularly in arabica-growing regions.

This inert mulch has many other advantages in addition to erosion control. It creates a thermo-protective screen which reduces water loss from the soil by evaporation and prevents weeds from developing. It is also an excellent source of organic matter (Fig 40).

The usefulness of this practice has been emphasised by numerous experiments, mainly conducted in East Africa, where mulching has become a common practice in arabica plantations. Very deteriorated coffee plantations

Fig 37   *C. arabica* with *Flemingia* cover (Courtesy: Bourharmont)

Fig 38   Collection of 18 month old *C. robusta* with *Pueraria* cover (Courtesy: Liabeuf)

Fig 39   *C. robusta* with *Mimosa* cover (Courtesy: Liabeuf)

Fig 40   Mulch on young coffee trees. Brazilian technique of several plants per planting hole. São Paulo, Brazil (Courtesy: Sylvain)

have been restored by mulching. Pots of plants used for mulch are maintained adjacent to coffee plantations in Kenya.

The effect of mulching on root development has been studied by Bull in Tanzania, using clones of adult *C. arabica*. He found that the mulch had an effect on the roots in the upper layers of the soil in particular. The dry weight of the secondary roots doubled, whereas that of the primary roots increased by 40 per cent.

The effect of mulching on yields has been appreciated by many planters. It is difficult to assess the exact effect given the very diverse conditions: the nature of the mulch and the tonnage per hectare, the environment (climate, soil texture and fertility), cropping practices, etc. It is interesting to note the results of a series of trials conducted with young *C. canephora* in the Ivory Coast (IFCC), shown in Table 3.

Apart from the considerable difference between the harvests of the treated plots and the control, it should be noted that with mulch containing above 80 tonnes of green matter per hectare (*Tithonia* and *Flemingia*), there is no advantage. Moreover, the input of fertiliser in combination with mulch further increases the advantage of the treated plots.

The first results from another trial comparing the effects of mulch and cover crops are shown in Table 4.

Mulching gives the best overall results, followed by clean weeding. With regard to mineral nutrition, mulching may have a pronounced depressive effect on potassium nutrition. On the contrary, mulching improves NPK nutrition.

Table 3   The effect of mulching on *C. canephora* production in the Ivory Coast
Cumulative results from two harvests (kg/ha)

Organic fertiliser	Pruned coffee trees		Multi-stemmed coffee trees during the pruning cycle	
	Without fertiliser	With fertiliser	Without fertiliser	With fertiliser
Light mulch (40 tonnes/ha green matter)	537	592	2221	3357
Moderate mulch (80 tonnes/ha green matter)	737	669	3346	4419
Heavy mulch (120 tonnes/ha green matter)	750	775	2685	4144
Control	233	497	137	2377

Table 4   Soil cover trials (results in kg/ha)

Soil cover	A	B
Mulch	1527	3779
Clean weeding	1469	2932
Pueraria	681	2654
Natural cover	517	2742

Different plants are used as mulches: *Pennisetum purpureum* (Elephant grass), *Panicum maximum*, banana leaves, *Tithonia, Flemingia*. In certain countries such as Kenya, they are cultivated on land adjacent to the coffee plantation. Robinson estimated that in East Africa about 0.8 to 1.6 ha of *Pennisetum purpureum* (Elephant grass) must be cultivated for use as an annual mulch, applied to alternate rows in a 0.5 ha planting of coffee. The same author indicates that *P. purpureum* is capable of yielding 150 tonnes of green matter per hectare (in two cuts). In the Ivory Coast, over 200 tonnes/ha was obtained with *Tithonia* (IFCC).

When using mulch on flat, fertile land, it is advisable to apply it on alternate rows of coffee trees, applying the mulch twice a year so that each row receives at least one dressing of mulch each year. On sloping, eroded land, the mulch should be applied between each row of coffee trees. The optimum time of year for application varies depending upon the rainfall. In regions with two rainy seasons, it should preferably be applied before the long rains. In regions with only one rainy season, the mulch should be applied before the rains if they amount to less than 1000 mm. On the contrary, in regions with over 1000 mm of rainfall, the mulch should be applied before the end of the rains and must be sufficiently liberal to cover the soil until the beginning of the following rainy season.

The nutritional input of mulch obviously depends upon the material used. For example, in Kenya, it was calculated that mulching coffee plantations using alternating rows, at a plant spacing of 3.5 m × 3.5 m, using a quantity of about 15 tonnes to 20 tonnes of dry matter per hectare, provided about 110 kg of nitrogen, 18 kg of phosphorus, 1200 kg of potassium, 18 kg of calcium, and 30 kg of magnesium per hectare. However, it is possible to reduce the amount of mulch used by 50 per cent, especially for maintenance mulching.

Although mulching has many supporters, it also has many critics who rightfully object to its high cost and the serious risk of fire it poses during the dry season. It should also be noted that the use of mulches is discouraged in regions that are sensitive to frost because its presence on the soil during clear nights favours the accumulation of cold air at the base of the coffee trees and limits the effects of convection.

Cropping methods

Certain precautions must be taken in cropping practices in the tropics, especially in hilly regions, in order to observe the basic principles of soil conservation. For example, working the land during the rainy season even with light hoeing should be avoided, especially on sandy or light soils.

Moreover, maintaining the inter-rows of coffee must not be neglected, particularly with regard to weed control. Earlier we saw that under good conditions, cover crops, like mulch, protect the most active superficial soil layers, and prevent weeds from developing. If this technique is not possible, **selected weeding** should be carried out. This consists of maintaining the natural plant cover after eliminating harmful species; the natural cover is then regularly cut. A combined method of weed control consists of strengthening this natural cover by sowing seeds of species of creeping legumes. The key is to ensure a good **permanent ground cover**.

Clean weeding, which has been practiced for a long time, has today been abandoned by most countries with high rainfall.

Contour planting

When the slope of the land exceeds three to five per cent, it is advisable to survey and plant along the contour, alternating the position of the shrubs from one row to the next. This technique includes the maintenance of a soil cover using cover plants, mulch, etc. (Fig 41).

Marking out the contours should not present any major problems. Topographer's equipment is normally used, i.e. a gauge, a clinometer with a colimator, etc. If this equipment is not available, a device made of wood would be suitable. The least complicated is a triangle with a plumbline. One foot of the triangle is fixed at the starting point, the second is moved in the

Fig 41 *C. arabica*: contour planted plantation. Colombia (Courtesy: Colombia Coffee Federation)

approximate direction of the contour line at the same level, until the plumbline falls in the notch which exactly marks half the length of the horizontal bar. A marker is placed there and the equipment is moved, pivoting it on the point that has just been marked. A second marker is planted when the horizontal position is reached, and so on. A gauge with a spirit-level may also be used.

Drainage ditches, protective banks and live hedges

To limit the damage caused by erosion on sloping land, **blind ditches** (oblong closed pits) may be dug at intervals being sited at right angles to the steepest slope. They should be between 0.3 and 0.4 m wide, 0.5 to 0.6 m deep, and a few metres long.

At the end of the rainy season, the pits, which will have become parially filled with soil, are cleaned out. They are then sometimes used to make organic manure by being filled with plant residues; other pits are dug elsewhere. This practice obviously does not affect the basic principle of covering the soil with a cover crop or mulch to prevent erosion but is an additional, optional technique.

In hilly regions where the frequency and severity of the rains are not a serious threat, mounds of earth or **banks** are constructed around each coffee tree as a conservation measure. This is common practice in Brazil.

Hedges must be established to help control erosion on land with a steep gradient. They provide protection which is comparable to that of contour planting, use of ditches, mulching, etc., and can also be used in combination with these practices.

Live hedges for erosion control are arranged along the contours at varying distances from each other depending upon the slope of the land. The cosmopolitan legume, *Leucaena glauca*, is perfectly suitable for this purpose due to its hardy nature. It is easy both to limit the growth of the hedge to a reasonably low height and to suppress its lateral extension by adequate pruning. Also, the *Leucaena* should not be allowed to fruit, to prevent it from propagating in the coffee plantation. Other legumes with an erect habit may also be suitable, for example, *Cassia sophora L., Indigofera suffruticosa* Mill., *Tephrosia candida T., Cajanus cajan.*

Strip cropping

It is also possible to limit the damage from erosion caused by rainfall through strip cropping. This consists of contour planting strips of land with coffee, normally in strips containing three, four or five rows, and cultivating the land in between these sets of rows with cover crops or mulch. They may also be occupied by spontaneous grasses.

These strips should be planted along the contours. Their widths may be irregular or variable and will depend upon the slope, the texture of the soil, rainfall, etc. This method of cultivation should only be adopted on the parts of the farm most liable to erosion.

Terraces

Terraces become a necessity when the land slopes beyond a certain degree. The cost of converting the land to terraces is such that, even when mechanically accomplished, it can only be contemplated under very special conditions and on extremely limited areas of ground. It does not appear necessary to elaborate on designs for terracing within the framework of this book, some of which are illustrated in Figs 42, 43, 44 and 45.

Pruning

General information

The objective of pruning is to provide the coffee plant with a robust, balanced framework and to stimulate the development of some of its branches to provide the maximum production potential.

The architecture of the coffee plant was studied in Chapter 2. However,

Fig 42   Contour terraces. Dschang Station, Cameroon (Courtesy: Coste)

Fig 43   *C. arabica*: young plantation on terraces. Fogo Island, Cape Verde (Courtesy: Lavabre)

Fig 44   Foreground: contour planted *C. arabica*. Background: *C. arabica* under rubber trees. Kajoerras, Indonesia (Courtesy: Cambrony)

Fig 45   Terraces cultivated in *C. arabica*, fruit trees and cereals. Saudi Arabia (Courtesy: Cambrony)

readers should recall that an adult shrub consists of a vertical axis, the trunk (orthotropic formation), which bears a certain number of storeys or series of branches. These are the so-called 'primary' branches, which grow opposite each other in pairs and give rise to 'secondary', then to 'tertiary' branches which are plagiotropic in habit.

Both the trunk and the primary branches make up the main framework. In Chapter 2 we saw that the primary branches are not replaced, contrary to the secondary and tertiary branches which are often renewed, often with excessive proliferation (Fig 21).

It is not long before the natural architectural balance of the young coffee tree becomes altered. This can be caused by the accidental or deliberate loss of primary branches, or by the development of suckers, etc. (Fig 46).

This change in the balance of a coffee tree which is left to grow freely occurs fairly quickly, and is accompanied by a natural elongation of the trunk. This results in the trunk becoming denuded rather quickly at mid-height (loss of poorly fed branches), and gradually losing its primary branches. A few years later, only a few low branches remain, together with a tuft of young branches forming a sort of plume at the top. This is often the appearance of uncultivated coffee trees and shrubs from abandoned plantations which have not been pollarded. The upper storeys become disproportionately longer and form a sort of parasol, which isolates all the other branches from the outside resulting in their death (Fig 47). At this stage, fruiting occurs exclusively on the outside; the inner branches being barren. Production is obviously significantly reduced.

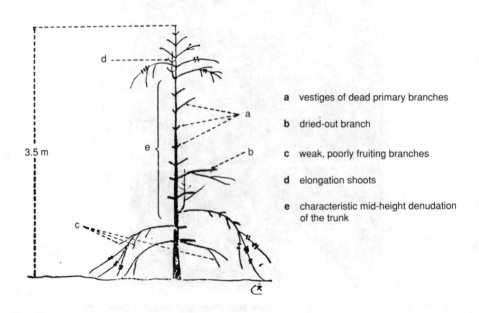

a   vestiges of dead primary branches

b   dried-out branch

c   weak, poorly fruiting branches

d   elongation shoots

e   characteristic mid-height denudation of the trunk

Fig 46   Free-growing coffee tree with a single trunk

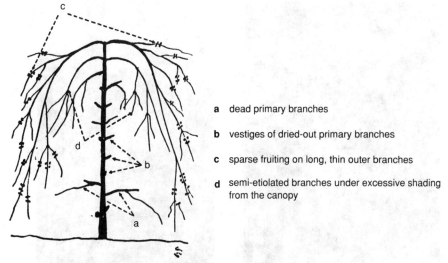

a   dead primary branches

b   vestiges of dried-out primary branches

c   sparse fruiting on long, thin outer branches

d   semi-etiolated branches under excessive shading from the canopy

Fig 47   Free-growing coffee tree showing parasol form

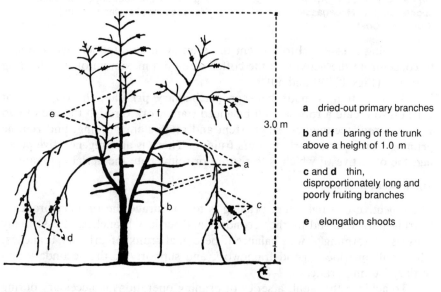

a   dried-out primary branches

b and **f**   baring of the trunk above a height of 1.0 m

c and **d**   thin, disproportionately long and poorly fruiting branches

e   elongation shoots

3.0 m

Fig 48   Free-growing coffee tree showing multi-stemmed form

From the physiological point of view, it may be useful to repeat that, in principle, coffee fruits on one-year old wood. In a young shrub, the primary branches are short and the sap flows easily through them. Fruiting is therefore satisfactory. However, as these branches get longer, the fruiting zone tends to become further removed from the trunk, especially if it is not balanced by the formation of secondary branches. This results in a great proportion of the older wood becoming non-productive.

Fig 49 *C. arabica* growing spontaneously. Madagascar (Courtesy: Coste)

Fig 50 *C. arabica*: unpruned trees. Madagascar (Courtesy: Coste)

Pruning is essential to prevent these unfavourable tendencies, and also to concentrate the activity of the coffee tree on a maximum of fruit-bearing branches (Figs 48, 49 and 50).

A distinction is made between **preliminary pruning**, the objective of which is to create a robust, well-balanced framework through the use of two very different techniques: single-stem and multi-stem pruning, and **routine pruning** which particularly favours fruiting. There is also **regenerative pruning**, the objective of which is to restore or rejuvenate the aerial apparatus.

Single-stem pruning

The objective of single-stem pruning is to encourage the primary branches to fruit first, followed by the secondary and tertiary branches. It essentially consists of forming a well-balanced, perennial trunk of primary branches, which will provide a good framework and support for the secondary and tertiary fruiting branches.

To achieve this goal, a series of pruning operations is necessary during the third or fourth year of growth:

- Removal of the primary branches that are less than 0.20 to 0.25 m from the ground, to promote air circulation around the base of the shrubs;
- Limitation of the number of storeys of primary branches, so that the distance separating them is at least 0.12 to 0.15 m, in order to facilitate aeration and illumination. This must be done very carefully, as these branches, which are essential in the single-stem pruning system, do not regenerate;

- Removal of the secondary branches which develop close to the trunk (0.10 to 0.15 m). This creates a kind of aeration chimney in the centre.
- Removal of all adventitious branches which are unproductive and clutter the shrub unnecessarily (Fig 51).

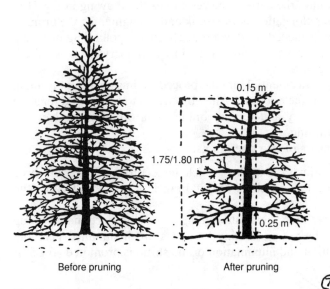

0.15 m

1.75/1.80 m

0.25 m

Before pruning   After pruning

Fig 51   Single-stem pruning: pollarded at 1.8 m

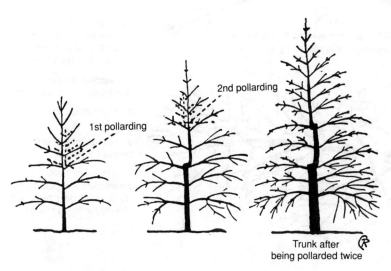

2nd pollarding

1st pollarding

Trunk after
being pollarded twice

Fig 52   Staggered pollarding

The other essential operation in the single-stem pruning system is **pollarding**, which is executed when the coffee tree has reached a certain stage of development; generally at about 1.8 to 2.0 m for arabicas (Fig 51). The main stem is pruned back above a fork and one of the opposing branches is removed to prevent the weight of fruits on opposite branches from splitting the upper part of the trunk. This can frequently occur if this precaution is not taken. After pruning, the coffee tree resembles the drawing in Fig 51b.

Preventing further elongation of the trunk and strengthening the primary branches may also be achieved by staggered, alternate, pollarding of young plants, the first operation being undertaken in the nursery. This is called, 'bayonet' pruning (Fig 52).

Routine pruning is an essential, annual procedure in single-stem pruning and is an integral part of the operation. the objective is to favour and regulate the formation of secondary and tertiary branches in order to produce the required pattern of fruiting.

It essentially consists of two operations:

- tipping back the primary branches which have provided two or three harvests, to induce the development of branches which will carry the following harvest;
- removal of weak shoots and shortening of disproportionately long branches, so that the young fruiting branches are maintained near the trunk and the aeration and illumination of the shrub is promoted (Fig 53).

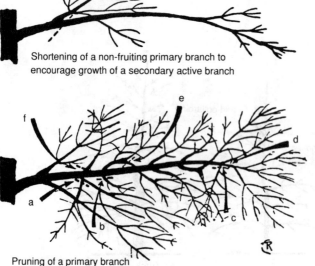

Shortening of a non-fruiting primary branch to encourage growth of a secondary active branch

Pruning of a primary branch

a and **c**   removal of a surplus, badly positioned secondary branch with limited fruiting potential

b   removal of an underdeveloped secondary branch

d   shortening of the primary branch

e   removal of part of the secondary branch

f   removal of a poorly developed secondary branch which is inhibiting the growth of a neighbouring branch

Fig 53   Routine pruning operations

Finally, the framework is modified by **thinning** every three to five years, sometimes rather drastically, to correct a poor balance or uneven distribution of the branches.

Pruning operations are inevitably followed by a proliferation of orthotropic shoots or suckers. It is essential that these are removed periodically.

Single-stem pruning is more suitable for *C. arabica* than for *C. canephora*, which has a natural inclination to form several main branches.

Multi-stem pruning

Multi-stem pruning, as opposed to single-stem pruning, is based exclusively on exploiting the fruiting potential of the primary branches. It consists of inducing the formation of a number of axes or main branches from the basal part of the tree and ensuring their renewal after four or five years of fruiting. In principle, these main shoots are removed once the fruiting of the primary wood is almost exhausted, that is before the secondary branches develop.

Multi-stem pruning consists of two operations; formation of the main leader and renewal of the main branch axes.

Formation of the main leader

The simplest method consists of pruning back the young coffee tree to within 0.25–0.39 m from the ground while retaining some of the basal shoots. However, this presents some problems; the main leader becomes overloaded with suckers and there is insufficient spacing between the shoots. More rational techniques are therefore preferred such as the bending method of training known as 'agobiada' (Fig 54) or the lyre or candelabra (single or double) system.

The bending method of training or **arcure** consists of bending over the stems of the young coffee trees in an arc (40 to 45°) for 12 to 18 months; these branches are normally 0.80 to 1 m in length). The tip is held in place by a wooden peg secured in the ground. Any branches which come into contact with the ground are removed. Numerous orthotropic shoots (suckers) will form as a result of bending over the main leader. Four to six of the most vigorous suckers are retained; a few months later the number being reduced to three to five. The tips of the primaries that have been retained are then pruned (Fig 55). The coffee tree now resembles a curved step of 0.4 to 0.5 m in length (the main leader) from which some suckers are growing (Fig 55). These suckers may be renewed as required, as is described later. The bending method of training is usually carried out on the plantation at the beginning of the rainy season when the plants are growing vigorously.

Training the main leader in the form of a **lyre** or **double lyre** is easily achieved by simple or double pollarding (Fig 56). The use of sticks or spreaders is sometimes required to spread the axes of the main branches. The training for the **candelabra** system is comparable to that for the double lyre.

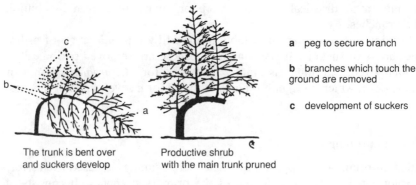

a   peg to secure branch

b   branches which touch the ground are removed

c   development of suckers

The trunk is bent over and suckers develop

Productive shrub with the main trunk pruned

Fig 54   Multi-stem pruning: training for agobiada

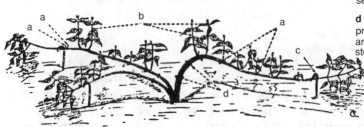

a   pruned suckers

b   developed suckers

c   pegs used to secure the stems

d   position of the primary branches which are removed when the stems are bent

Fig 55   Bending the stems to stimulate the formation of suckers

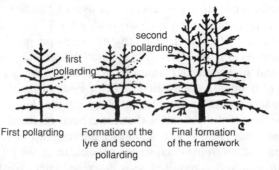

second pollarding

first pollarding

First pollarding

Formation of the lyre and second pollarding

Final formation of the framework

Fig 56   Costa Rica pruning: training for candelabra or double lyre

Renewal of the main branch axes

In whatever form the stem may be trained, the main branch axes are renewed in a similar manner. Each stem consists, in principle, of two, three, or four productive axes bearing a few replacement shoots at various stages of development. Routine pruning simply consists of renewing the primary wood

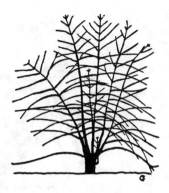

Fig 57   Characteristic shape of a young, multi-stemmed, free-growing coffee tree

which will have become exhausted after three or four harvests, and replacing it with wood of a similar type which is young and potentially productive. This is achieved by removing the old shoots growing from the base and replacing them with the same number of young shoot axes. To provide for future growth, new shoots will be chosen from among those that form later on. Surplus shoots are cut back close to the trunk. (Fig 57).

The renewal cycle may be repeated three, four or even five times annually where the trees are particularly vigorous and productive.

The first harvest is gathered at the end of the second year, but the most productive one is generally obtained during the third year. Subsequently production may decrease, and renewal during the fourth year is usual.

There are several methods of renewing the main shoot axes. An annual rate of renewal of one axis per year is usual. The coffee tree will therefore have one axis which shows decreasing production at a specific time (third or fourth harvest), another which is during production (second or third year), one or two others which are at the beginning of production (first or second year) and various replacement axes at different stages of growth. An exhausted axis is replaced each year so that the tree always has three or four productive axes, although each has a difference in age of one year (Fig 58).

The practice of renewing two axes per year may also be adopted, causing the number of axes replaced each year to be doubled.

Finally, the cycle may be repeated several times per annum, e.g. five or six times with three, four, or five axes of the same age which are all renewable at the same time. In order to avoid severe physiological shock, the two axes selected for their ability to fruit well are retained for one year as 'sapdrawers'. After stumping, new shoots will appear, among which the most robust and suitably located will be retained for the new cycle. The sapdrawers will be removed the following year (Fig 59).

There are sometimes problems associated with encouraging the formation of a sufficient number of shoots. It is therefore advisable to allow maximum air movement and light penetration to the trunk by increasing the distance between the main leaders.

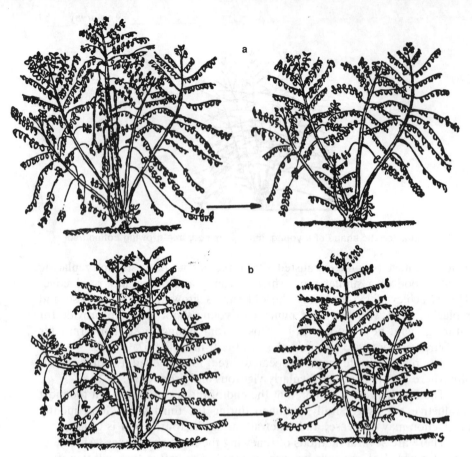

a and **b** Four to six stems are selected, one or two of the exhausted stems are cut back, enabling replacement suckers to develop as a result of improved light penetration

Correct   Incorrect

c The stems must be pruned carefully with a saw; the cut must be clean and directed towards the outside. The use of a machete is not recommended

Fig 58 Annual pruning of the coffee tree (after Capot: The Ivorian Coffee and Cocoa Planter's Calender. IFCC, 1984)

Fig 59 *Opposite* **Rejuvenation or five-yearly pruning of coffee (after Capot: The Ivorian Coffee and Cocoa Planter's Calender. IFCC, 1984)**

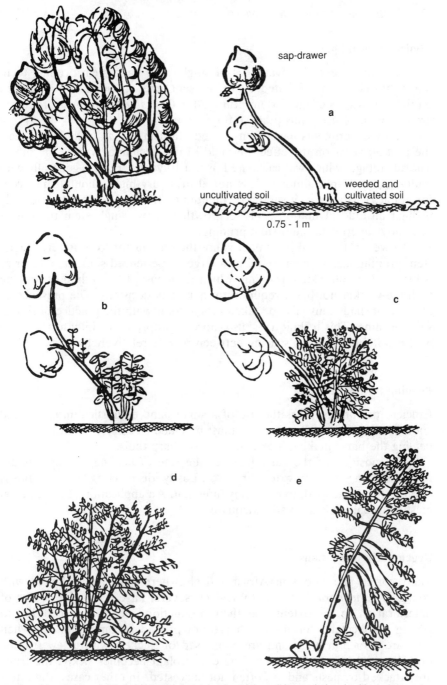

sap-drawer

a

uncultivated soil

weeded and cultivated soil

0.75 - 1 m

b

c

d

e

a A well located, productive sap-drawer is retained, and the soil is weeded and cultivated around the base.   **b** Suckers appear; three to four being retained or five if the shrubs are well spaced. These should arise from the perimeter and at the base of the stump. All other shoots are pruned away. **c** At the end of the year, the suckers will be ready to flower; they are regularly removed and the sap-drawer is pruned after its fruits have been harvested.   **d** At the end of the fifth year, the new stems will have been harvested four times, with three sizeable harvests.   **e** The tree is then stumped, except for one stem which will act as a sap-drawer, and the cycle begins again.

Choice of technique

The advantages and disadvantages of single- and multi-stem pruning techniques have been long debated. At the present time, opinions are still divided on the advantages of multi-stem pruning for *C. arabica*, but most producers are in favour of using this practice for *C. canephora*.

Many experiments have been carried out using *C. arabica* over at least the past 30 years on the effect on yield of one technique versus the other. The advantage, which was calculated over a 10-year period, is generally with multi-stem pruning, although it is not always very high (about 10 per cent for arabica). However, it should be mentioned that in certain cases, namely in high altitude plantations, where growth is slow, single-stem pruning is generally superior to multi-stem pruning.

However, the yield increment is not the only factor to consider. Single-stem pruning management requires a large, experienced staff. Its cost price is higher than multi-stem pruning, which is an easy, fast method of pruning with the worker not being required to make any decisions. The presence or absence of shade must also be taken into account with the practice of single-stem pruning. This technique is also more appropriate for hilly terrain, and is also suitable when the spacing between rows is relatively low.

Pruning technique

Efficient pruning involves the use of a small hand or horticultural saw and good pruning shears. Pruning cuts must be made cleanly, without tearing or peeling the bark; making it essential to use sharp tools.

The position of the cut influences the rate of healing. Stumps should not be left since they may dry out or rot. Lastly, disinfecting large wounds is strongly recommended, to avoid any infection. An application of agricultural mastic or coal-tar is normally adequate.

Regenerative operations

Many coffee plantations in Africa and elsewhere have been planted with young *C. canephora*, but, due to neglect, several have reached a degree of deterioration to the extent that their production does not exceed 100 to 200 kg per hectare. Shrubs which are not pruned become etiolated when they are 4 or 5 m high, and are composed of thickets with a few fruiting branches high up on the shrub. The entire plant becomes sickly, the fruits are attacked by pests and are often not harvested. In other cases, the inter-rows are invaded by plants composed of perennial weeds and harmful grasses such as *Imperata, Paspalum*, etc. Production under such conditions is often nil or of an unmarketable quality.

In order to find out to what extent, and, if feasible, under what conditions restoration was possible and profitable, studies were carried out by

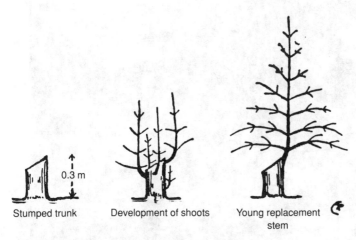

Fig 60 **Stumping of coffee trees**

Fig 61 *C. canephora*: 13 year-old plantation three years after being stumped on a sap-drawer. Ivory Coast (Courtesy: Capot)

Colinet in Rwanda-Burundi, and Capot in the Ivory Coast. The following is a summary of Capot's work.

The first operation is the **stumping** of the tree and selection of a **sap-drawer**. One stem is retained per tree for one year after stumping to act as a sap-drawer (Fig 60). Some of the shoots arising from the stump will be selected (Figs 61, 62 and 63).

Fig 62   *C. robusta* with *Pueraria javanica* cover: three months after stumping (Courtesy: Deuss)

Fig 63   Regeneration of a *C. robusta* plantation which had been stumped eight months earlier. Rwanda (Courtesy: Colinet)

Stumping must be carried out immediately following harvesting. The stems are cut at an oblique angle to a height of 0.25 to 0.30 m. The lower branches are also removed.

The removal of the aerial system causes a physiological and nutritional imbalance to exist; this must be offset by cultivating the soil to a distance of 0.75 to 1.0 m around the stump, at a depth of 0.20 m. Numerous superficial roots will be mutilated during this operation, but they regenerate rapidly. This operation must be executed immediately following stumping.

Regeneration may be adversely affected by the shade which has been encouraged by the excessive elongation of the shoots. Any shade present should therefore be removed if necessary; alternatively the shade trees should be considerably pruned.

Finally, the exposure of the soil to direct sunlight after the removal of the foliage of the coffee trees may encourage the development of certain harmful, light-loving plants, particularly grasses, such as *Paspalum conjugatum, Imperata cylindrica, Digitaria adscendens*, etc. They can be eradicated by weeding around the coffee trees with a machete or hoe. In most cases, the best solution is either to establish a live cover crop such as *Flemingia congesta* and *Pueraria javanica* (Ivory Coast), or to apply a mulch.

The shoots must be selected when they have reached a height of 0.25 to 0.30 m. Six to seven strong, well-formed shoots that are well distributed around the trunk should be retained. The remainder should be pruned close to the trunk. Six to eight weeks later, only four shoots should be retained, the remainder being eliminated.

Retaining four stems of the regenerated coffee trees is normal for plantation densities of 1000 to 1300 trees per ha. At lower densities, it is advisable to select five stems and, at higher densities, this number should be reduced to three. The objective is to obtain a density of 4500 to 5000 stems per hectare.

Placing 'spreaders' which are forked pieces of wood or bamboo slats cut into a 'V' shape at the ends may be a useful and profitable technique for slowing down the growth of the stems. This will enable the pruning cycle to be lengthened by at least one year, and will ensure that the shrub will take on the shape of a flared goblet. This encourages the healthy development of the inner branches and facilitates cultural treatments and harvests.

Maintenance operations consist of sucker removal, maintenance of the soil cover, plant replacements, cultivation of food crops in the inter-rows, such as rice and maize in the first year.

The yield of regenerated plantations will depend on the ages of the coffee trees. The best results are obtained with eight to fifteen-year old shrubs. With older shrubs that are weakened due to a lack of care, the shoots will be poorly formed or insufficient in number. The success of the operation may then be jeopordised. However, in Madagascar, *C. canephora* trees that were over 25 years old and generally deteriorated were fully regenerated; they were, however, located on particularly fertile soils.

During the first year, a transitional harvest will be provided by the sole stem which was conserved as a sap-drawer. It may be as much as 300 to 350 kg per tree which, in many instances, may be higher than those previously obtained. The first main harvest from the four conserved stems may produce 200 to 400 kg/ha, the second, 1200 to 1800 kg/ha and the third, 800 to 1200 kg/ha. The average annual yield of a regenerated coffee plantation under good conditions could be 750 kg/ha of clean coffee. Capot reported that in Uele (Zaire), under very satisfactory ecological conditions, an average of 1500 kg/ha over four years (1000, 600, 3200, and 1300 kg/ha) was obtained with vigorously growing robustas. In Rwanda-Burundi, Colinet obtained average yields of 1150 to 1750 kg/ha with regenerated robusta coffee trees (as opposed to 300 kg/ha previously). It must be stressed that such an increase in production can only be ensured if, in addition to improving the fruiting framework, additional attention is given to the trees in terms of cropping practices such as sucker removal, weeding, fertiliser application and general health care.

Calculated in terms of work days, annual labour costs should be considered for an average of 90 to 150 days/ha, according to Capot. It can therefore be considered to be profitable from the first four-year cycle, including stumping, digging planting holes, establishment of the cover, etc.; operations requiring a considerable amount of work.

The regeneration operations on large plots may be carried out over a period of several years. This is the advice given to small-scale planters in order to avoid too great a variation in production from one year to the next. The plot may be divided, for example, into three, four, or five blocks, one of which is treated per year.

Fig 64   Conversion to multi-stem pruning: replacement stems and shoots

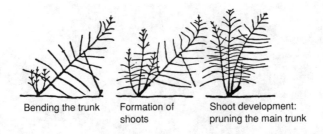

Bending the trunk   Formation of   Shoot development:
                     shoots   pruning the main trunk

Fig 65   Multi-stem pruning: bending the stem to induce the development of suckers

Conversion pruning

The most frequent requirement is to convert trees that have been managed under the single-stem pruning system to multi-stem pruning. If the coffee trees are still young, the so-called **verga** method may be used, which consists of bending over the main leader at an angle of 45°, to induce sucker production. The end is then cut, where there are no shoots. Stumping then follows for adult coffee trees which should be cut back to a height of 0.25 to 0.35 m, after pruning the branches at the base of the trunk to assist in the formation of shoots (Figs 64 and 65).

Another technique, called lateral pruning has been successfully tested in Tanzania. It consists of cutting all the primaries on one half of the shrub in the first year, and the rest in the second year. Under good conditions, shoots develop at the base of the trunk which receives plenty of light and the farmer obtains the benefits of an improved harvest for at least one season.

Shade

General information

The assumption that coffee should be grown in conditions resembling those of their natural habitat has been debated for a long time. Supporters and adversaries of shade have confronted each other with equal conviction in the superiority of their argument. However, it has not been possible to make a comparison between the two cultural systems in most cases, due to the absence of a concrete, scientific definition of the level of light intensity required by the coffee tree for optimum growth and fruiting, and also because the conditions in question such as species or variety, ecology, erosion control, and cropping techniques are extremely varied. Nevertheless, a fairly clear conclusion has now emerged as a result of research work and numerous experiments: shade is favourable for the growth of coffee under certain conditions.

The physiological effect of shade on the coffee tree has been discussed in Chapter 2. It was shown that the rate of photosynthesis was slower under

Fig 66 *C. canephora*: shaded plantation with *Flemingia* cover. Indonesia (Courtesy: Cambrony)

conditions of high light intensity, but it was emphasized that this was only valid for the shrub's outer leaves; those on the inside being shaded by neighbouring leaves (self-shading) and therefore under more favourable conditions for carbon assimilation.

Shade is generally considered to have a moderating effect on floral induction and fruiting. Specialists are very familiar with this concept, and recognise the importance of shade in protecting plantations where the future could be compromised by excessive production in the first years. Shade also reduces evapotranspiration and enables the coffee tree to withstand prolonged periods of drought more easily. This thermo-protection for shrubs also continues through the night and contributes to the avoidance of an excessive drop in temperature; in high-altitude regions, the difference in temperature between the shaded area and the outside environment can be 4° to 5° C. In the top soil layers, a lower temperature prevents the organic matter from decomposing too rapidly.

Shaded soil is less exposed, and is therefore less prone to drying out superficially; this enables the rootlets to continue their nutritive activities. The soil is also less sensitive to erosion caused by rain.

Shade also has a debilitating effect on weeds. In addition, it subdues the intensity of the wind and prolongs the ripening period of fruit.

However, although shade has a favourable effect on yield, it does require additional maintenance work, for example pruning the shade trees to control the size of the canopy. The moisture level maintained favours the development of diseases, and shade trees compete with coffee trees for nutrients, water, and minerals.

It is difficult to judge these favourable and unfavourable factors given the complexity of the relationships which exist between productivity factors and their interdependence in a coffee plantation. Whatever the case may be, it is important to confirm experimental results that agronomists have recorded in various locations regarding the superiority of the production of plantations that are either slightly shaded of completely unshaded.

However, experimental results can also be very disappointing. In fact, if the increased nutritional needs of coffee trees, which are required to ensure a more abundant fruiting, are not met, the resulting physiological imbalance may rapidly reduce them to a state of unfruitfulness. This occurs on many plantations, particularly in Africa in arabica-growing regions with high levels of sunshine.

The requirement of each species with regard to illumination varies tremendously, depending upon the ecological conditions of the growing environment. The intensity and average duration of the illumination, the average temperature and its variations, atmospheric humidity, the length of the dry season, the variation in wind speeds, soil fertility, are some of the many elements that affect the phsyiology of the coffee tree either adversely or favourably.

Porteres has attempted to define and compare the requirements of cultivated species as a function of their ecological environment. His facts do not contradict recent experimental results on the superiority of harvests from unshaded plantations because, in any case, a plantation's productivity will not increase if it is not appropriately managed.

Shade is clearly not essential in cloudy regions where humidity levels are high for most of the year. This is especially valid for coastal forested regions of West Africa, where *C. canephora* is grown. However, the need for shade is more debatable in areas bordering the forested strip, near the savanna, where the illumination is more intense and less diffused. The same holds true in other regions with a high levels of illumination. However, this criterion should not be considered on its own, but in association with other productivity factors such as ecology, cropping techniques, etc.

The effect of climate has been more clearly ascertained for arabica. In East Africa for example, where coffee trees are planted at different altitudes, between 1000–2200 m, local climate conditions are so varied that shade appears to be necessary in some regions, whereas in others its absence has a negligable effect. The suitability of a high canopy must also be considered with regard to possible water competition, as is the case mainly in the eastern part of the high-altitude coffee-growing zones of Kenya, Uganda and Tanzania. At high altitudes, shade may be useful in limiting the drop in temperature at night, which is very noticeable above 2000 m, with potential frost (Kenya, Mexico, etc.).

Shade tree species

The list of species of shade trees used in coffee growing is very long. The following should be noted:

Albizzia lebbeck Benth. (Madagascar, Colombia, Central America),
A. malacocarpa Stand. (Cameroon, Colombia, San Salvador),
A. stipulata Boiv. (Madagascar, Malaysia, Uganda, Congo),
A moluccana Miq., *Deguelia microphylla* Val. (Indonesia, Cameroon),
Erythrina lithosperma (India, Indonesia, West Indies),
E. umbrosa H. B. K. and *E. velutina* Will., *Gliricidia maculata* H. B. K.
    (Central America, Colombia, India, Philippines, East Africa),
Grevillea robusta (Kenya, India),
Inga edulis Mart. (Colombia, West Indies, Far East),
Inga spectabilis (Colombia, Central America),
Leucaena glauca Benth. (India, Indonesia, Philippines, West Africa),
Pithecolobium saman Benth. (East Africa).
All the species mentioned, except for *Grevillea* are Leguminosae (Figs 67
    and 68).

When a coffee plantation is established on forest land, as is generally the case, shade is ensured by a few species of trees which remain uncleared, preferably Leguminosae. It is preferable to choose trees with sparse, spreading foliage which do not have a very extensive root system.

In commercial plantations, shade must be considered from the time the young coffee trees are planted. Shade trees are raised in the nursery and are generally planted at the same time as the coffee trees, although this practice also often involves the establishment of temporary shade (*Tephrosia, Crotallaria, Sesbania*, etc.).

The spacing of the shade trees depends upon the density of the canopy desired. Considerations also include the species of shade tree selected, climate, etc., and may vary greatly for a single species, depending upon regional conditions. Species with marked horizontal branch development should generally be planted at a spacing of 15 to 18 m (*Albizzia stipulata, A. falcata*) as opposed to 12 to 15 m for those with less spreading foliage such as *A. lebbeck* or an even lower spacing of 8 to 12 m for those with a pyramidal or spindle-shaped habit, such as *Grevillea robusta, Erythrina edulis, Cassia siamea*.

The siting of shade trees in the coffee plantation is also determined by the plantation design used for the coffee trees. Shade trees may either be planted in the rows of coffee trees, where they replace the same number of coffee shrubs, or in inter-rows, if maintenance is not mechanised.

Intensive cropping without shade

Much information is available, some of which is of dubious value, regarding intensive coffee growing without shade.

Fig 67 *C. robusta* plantation. Amboin, Angola (Courtesy: da Ponte)

Fig 68 *C. arabica* plantation with shade (*Albizzia malacocarpa*). Baigom, Cameroon (Courtesy: Coste)

In a later section on fertilisation the extraordinarily high yield obtained with selected varieties of *C. arabica*, grown without shade at a high density, will be illustrated. The results of a trial conducted by the Agronomic Institute of Campinas (Brazil) are also of particular interest (Table 5).

In Puerto Rico, several authors recorded the results of an experiment which had the same objective using nine varieties of arabica coffee. All the varieties had a higher yield in the sun than in the shade. Calculated on the basis of three consecutive years, the average yield was 2000 kg/ha without shade, whereas the yield was 40 per cent lower with shade. One tonne of fertiliser 12–6–16 was used each year in three applications.

Table 5   Yield obtained from shaded and unshaded plots at the Agronomic Institute of Campinas (Brazil) (annual average based on five consecutive harvests)

Stations	Yield		Advantage over production without shade (%)
	Shade	Sun	
Campinas	155	279	180
Jari	49	206	420
Mococa	85	182	314
Pindorama	30	203	677
Ribeira Preto	6	147	2450

(Source: Pupo de Moreas, *Culture e adubacâo de caffeiro*)

Favourable findings regarding coffee trees grown without shade have been recorded in San Salvador, Guatemala, Colombia, and elsewhere, in addition to the spectacular results obtained on high-density plantations which were discussed at the beginning of this chapter.

In Central America, shade is nevertheless considered to be a positive element in soil conservation and for water catchment basins. In Venezuela, Costa Rica and Mexico, arabica plantations are generally located at altitudes of 800 to 1500 m in hilly regions where erosion is rightfully considered a serious problem. The shading of coffee plantations is therefore an important factor in successful erosion control.

Agronomists are now confronted with the problem of maximally exploiting the production potential of new selections, which is largely dependent on their being grown in an area which has intense sunshine, together with the necessity to protect the soil with high, shrubby foliage.

A solution may be found in the use of mulch plants with tall stems, such as certain erythrinas, provided they are periodically pruned severely, and their height is limited to approximately 3 m. There are numerous advantages to this method of shading: the increase in illumination raises the level of fertility of the flowers, and therefore productivity, and the mass of green matter from the trimmings provides a mulch which can be used for erosion control and to supply the soil with organic matter. Additionally, the root system of the legume fertilises the soil with nitrogen.

Fig 69 Village plantation of *C. robusta*. Ivory Coast

Muller reported this observation from Costa Rica and recommended further experiments with this technique be conducted in Venezuela and elsewhere in Latin America with erythrinas, and indeed with other mulch-producing plants.

Today, robusta coffee is grown in full sunshine in Africa (Fig 69), with the exception of home gardens where the coffee is planted among banana and other fruit trees. Under these conditions the selected varieties and cultivars can reach very high production levels.

Fertilisation

General information

Coffee is generally regarded as exhausting the soil in which it is grown. For example, the soil on old, abandoned coffee plantations in Brazil must be regenerated before being used for any new agricultural purposes. Knowing which essential elements have been removed during harvesting enables a scientific evaluation to be made regarding which fertilisers are needed in a coffee plantation. Several authors have assessed the needs for N, P, K, Ca, and even minor elements. Catani has reported the quantities of fertilisers used in four years per hectare of coffee (*C. arabica*) in Brazil as being: N: 94.7 kg; P_2O_5: 14.4 kg; K_2O: 116.8 kg; CaO: 76.7 kg; MgO: 25.1 kg. The same author found that in order to produce 1000 kg of fruit per hectare, it was necessary to absorb: N: 15 kg; P_2O_5: 2.5 kg; K_2O: 24 kg; CaO: 2 kg; MgO: 1 kg. Forestier gave the following figures for the production of 1000 kg of clean coffee: N: 30 kg; P_2O_5: 3.75 kg; K_2O: 36.5 kg.

Nitrogen and potassium are considered to be the predominant elements in the nutrition of the coffee tree. This has been confirmed by numerous experiments.

The requirements for different nutrients during the growth period and at various stages of fruiting has been studied for the two main species. For *C. arabica*, Catani and Moraes reported a very marked progression in demand, especially during the third and fourth years of production (Table 6).

Table 6   Total quantities of nutrients absorbed by young coffee trees from the 1st to the 5th years (figures in grammes)

Elements	Age				
	1 yr	2 yrs	3½ yrs	4 yrs	5 yrs
N	1.29	28.27	80.45	84.24	117.47
P_2O_3	0.11	3.67	9.38	9.89	16.33
K_2O	1.43	20.85	85.45	70.88	121.35
CaO	0.63	22.80	64.65	59.61	77.11
MgO	0.32	2.16	22.33	13.18	23.47
Dry matter	76	2665	6103	6748	10 174

(Source: Cantani and Moraes (1958) *Rev. de Agr. Piracicaba*)

Malavolta reported the following results from an analysis of the beans and husks of *C. arabica* in Brazil (Table 7).

Table 7   Analysis of *C. arabica* beans and husks (Brazil)

Element	amount in 60 kg of beans (g)	amount in 30 kg of husks (g)
N	996	525
P	66	42
K	918	1123
Ca	168	126
Mg	96	36
S	78	48
B	0.96	1.02
Cu	0.80	0.54
Mn	1.20	0.87
Zn	0.72	2.10
Fe	3.60	4.50

(Source: Malavolta, *Culture e adubaçâo do cafeeiro*)

Symptoms of deficiencies of mineral elements may be observed on the leaves. After a series of observations of deficient *C. canephora* crops in pots. Franco and Mendes in Brazil, and Loue in the Ivory Coast published studies illustrated with colour plates on the most common deficiencies (N, P, K, Fe, Ca, Mg) in *C. arabica* and *C. canephora*. Nitrogen deficiency, which is the most frequent, was manifested by a uniformly yellow or greenish-yellow colouring of the lamina. A bronzish colour, together with necrotic spots were the symptoms of phosphorous deficiency. A potassium deficiency was shown by a marginal necrosis.

The technique of foliar diagnosis has significantly assisted biochemists in monitoring the evolution of requirements and exposing deficiencies. Foliar diagnosis enables the mineral content of a particular leaf to be determined at any one time. However, given that mineral nutrition is also related to other physiological mechanisms, the information provided by this method is not always related to yield and does not assist in determining the needs for major mineral elements, either in terms of quality or quantity. However, as Forestier has stated, it is a useful technique for monitoring the effect of fertilisers and for testing the impact of outside conditions on nutrition. The symptoms occur for different reasons: they are either dependent upon the coffee tree itself (different distribution of elements depending upon the amount of light to which the leaf is exposed, the age of the bearing shoot, presence of fruit, size), or they may be the result of environmental factors (rainfall, soil type), or even cropping practices (shade, cover, irrigation). Interpreting foliar diagnosis thus requires a good knowledge of all these factors, so that a correlation may be established by analysing elements that can affect both the yield and the mineral nutrition.

This technique enabled an approach to nutritional problems to be established, especially in Africa. It also permitted the approximate fertiliser needs of coffee trees in each ecological region to be estimated in a general but nevertheless useful way. It would be worthwhile to pursue this comprehensive task in more detail in smaller geographic and ecological areas, to give greater clarity of inputs (type, quantities, best times of the year for fertiliser application, etc.).

Organic fertilisers

Studies on fertilising coffee organically began with mulching, which is a very effective but costly technique. **Green manures** should also be mentioned in this context. This practice consists of cultivating several legumes in inter-rows which are hoed in at a certain stage in their development. Suitable species are *Crotalaria, Indigofera sumatrana, Cajanus* and *Tephrosia*. They have a considerable fertilising effect. There is the possibility, however, that their decomposition in the soil will lead to a temporary nitrogen deficiency, due to bacterial activity.

Farmyard manure is used in coffee growing in mixed-farming regions.

The quantity used is 20 to 30 tonnes per hectare, often in a rotational cropping system which may be based on alternate years or a one-year-in-four rotation.

The use of waste from processed coffee in the form of compost is highly recommended where there is a shortage of fertiliser. Preparing a good compost made of coffee pulp is relatively easy; a layer of pulp, 0.25 to 0.30 m in depth alternating with layers of plant waste, soil, compost, etc. The material can be used three to four months after fermentation has begun. It is necessary to keep the compost moist by frequent watering and to turn over the heap once or twice to blend it, in order to obtain a homogenous product.

Mineral fertilisers

Many trials have been conducted in the tropics to determine the nature and quantity of fertilisers required for coffee crops and the best times to apply them. However, only a few may be considered valid, namely those that were carried out under strict experimental conditions and are statistically interpretable. Even so, studying and analysing these results does not provide all the answers to questions concerning coffee fertilisation. In fact, the needs of the coffee tree vary considerably depending upon the species and variety (lines and clones), the age of the shrub, the ecological environment, cropping techniques, etc. Moreover, none of the elements considered acts independently, interactions being the rule, and their complexity renders the search for an answer even more difficult.

With coffee growing in general, even considering the coefficients of utilisation (N: 50%, P: 10%, K: 45%), fertilisers have so far been too strictly calculated based on restoring elements to the soil that have been removed during harvesting, in order to achieve an optimum nutritional balance. However, these concepts may in fact lead to the progressive exhaustion of the soil reserves. Trials have been conducted using large quantities of manure which have greatly exceeded theoretical needs. The results are rather recent, but they confirm this technique by occasionally producing spectacular and highly profitable increases in the harvests. The most likely conclusion is that the losses of mineral elements from tropical soils are much greater than one would imagine, whether it be the result of intensive leaching, being carried to lower levels, a process of immobilisation, or the exchange capacity, etc. Some points that are still unclear will certainly be clarified if we become more educated in the interactions which occur in tropical environments.

Studies on the chemical composition of the coffee tree and its fruits, which were discussed earlier, prove that nitrogen and potassium are essential elements for its nutrition.

Nitrogen

This element plays a leading role in the growth metabolism of coffee and, later on, in the formation of young branches and leaves, particularly in the photosynthetic activity of the latter. Carbohydrate nutrition and fruiting will thus be better ensured and more satisfactory. During periods of drought, this nutrition may be adversely affected, the symptoms being manifested in a yellowing of the foliage and die-back (drying out of the tips of the branches). The same phenomenon may be observed when the coffee tree is overloaded with fruit. The amount of nitrogen in the leaves has been determined by foliar diagnosis in many instances. It may be assumed that the amount present is usually about 2.25 to 3 per cent for adult trees, with the critical level being from 1.8 to 2 per cent.

Potassium

This is the predominant element in the tissues of fruits and beans. It is also present in the main branches of the coffee tree. The average level of potassium in the leaves is 1.8 to 2.2 per cent for a mature plant. Critical levels vary greatly depending upon the species and environmental factors but they are generally between 0.25 and 1.6 per cent.

Other elements

The **phosphoric acid** requirements of the coffee tree are fairly modest. The average level for the leaves of a mature plant is between 0.12 and 0.15 per cent. Symptons of deficiency often appear at much lower levels (0.07 to 0.1 per cent). This element enters into the metabolism, mainly at the time of floral induction and flowering.

   Calcium is also important as are other elements, the symptoms of deficiency appearing below a certain threshold, and being reflected in the vegetation, flowering and fruiting.

   Over the past few years, special attention has been paid to the **minor** or **trace elements**: magnesium, iron, boron, zinc. In serious cases of deficiencies, applications of the deficient element were found to re-establish a suitable level of fertility. However, when dealing with isolated cases, the deficiency found may simply be due to a deficient metabolism for a minor element in the shrub.

   Nitrogen and potassium clearly play a major role in terms of maintaining fertiliser balances. For example, the following are some of the more commonly recommended elements for widely used formulas:

1 *Canephora* coffee (Robusta-Kouilou)

Ivory Coast – per productive tree:
Zone with tertiary sands: 40 g N, 30 g P_2O_5, 100 g K_2O.
Granitic zone: 30/50 g N, 20/40 g P_2O_5, 50–80 g K_2O.
(Source: Loue and Verliere)

Table 8 Fertilising regime for Madagascar – Alluvial soils of the east coast (fertiliser applied per hectare)

Age of trees (years)	Times of the year fertiliser applied	
	March/April	October/November
1	25 kg urea	25 kg urea
2	50 kg urea	50 kg urea
3	100 kg urea	100 kg urea
4	400 kg 20.10.10	400 kg 20.10.10
	> 100 kg kieserite	> 100 kg kieserite

(Source: Snoeck)

Table 9 Fertilising regime for Central African Republic

Age of trees	Quantity applied per tree	Dates of application
Planting year	50 g of ammonium sulphate at 21%	September
2nd year	50 g of ammonium sulphate	April, July, September
	75 g of bicalcium phosphate at 38% (Recommended for the eastern part of the country)	
3rd year	65 g of ammonium sulphate	April, July, September
	75 g of bicalcium phosphate	April
4th year	90 g of ammonium sulphate	April, July, September
	75 g of bicalcium phosphate	April
5th to 7th year	110 g of ammonium sulphate	April, July, September
	75 g of bicalcium phosphate	April
Year of stumping	110 g of ammonium sulphate	April, July, September
	100 g of bicalcium phosphate (Recommended for the eastern part of the country)	April
Years following stumping	110 g of ammonium sulphate	April, July, September
	65 g of potassium chloride at 60%	April, September
	100 g of bicalcium phosphate (Recommended for the eastern part of the country).	April

(Source: Forestier)

2 *Arabica* Coffee

Cameroon (Bamoun country)

100 g of nitrogen per productive tree in four applications: March-April, October-November. A supplement is applied with one moderate application of P_2O_5 (in March) and K_2O (March and October) when foliar diagnosis reveals a deficiency in these elements ($P_2O_5 < 0.15\%$ – $K_2O < 2\%$ in December).

(Source: Benac)

For single applications, ammonium sulphate or the granular form of urea is used as a nitrogen source; bicalcium phosphate or triple superphosphate is used as a phosphoric acid source; potassium chloride is used as a potassium source.

The Brazilians and Hawaiians have researched the input of nitrogen in large quantities in split applications. Franco reported the results obtained in Brazil on a 40-year old arabica plantation with an average production of between 1000 and 1100 kg/ha, where applications of 0.6 kg to 1.8 kg of ammonium sulphate were applied per tree, equivalent to 120 to 380 g N. Responses were highly significant and increasingly pronounced from year to year with increases in yields as follows: 8.4 per cent; 60.7 per cent; 30.9 per cent; 50.3 per cent; and 63.1 per cent. In Puerto Rico, Abruna obtained 2500 kg/ha of coffee by applying 277 kg of N in the form of ammonium sulphate, ammonium nitrate, or urea; supplemented by 340 kg of magnesium sulphate and 680 kg of potassium sulphate. In Hawaii, Cooil harvested an average of 5641 kg/ha of coffee for four years after applying 463 kg of N, 183 kg of P_2O_5 and 2043 kg of formula 10–5–20, amounting to a total of over three tonnes of fertiliser per hectare, with a predominance of nitrogen and potassium.

The IFCC has conducted many experimental trials of this type. The results illustrated in Table 10 were recorded in Cameroon with arabica coffee on volcanic soils, rich in exchangeable bases, with applications containing increasing quantities of nitrogen (IRCC).

**Table 10 Average production (four consecutive years)
(kg of clean coffee/ha/year)**

Ammonium sulphate (kg/ha	Production	
	'Java' arabica	'Caturra' arabica
(Control) 0	281	282
250	606	753
500	1076	957
1000	1465	1593
2000	1415	1670
3000	1197	1844

These and other equally significant results illustrate the spectacular results which may be obtained with split applications of large quantities of nitrogen.

Findings for robusta (Table 11), showed a similar trend (IRCC).

Table 11   Average production (two consecutive years)
(kg of clean coffee/ha/year)

Ammonium sulphate (g/tree)	Production
(Control) 0	2002
500	2493
1000	2701
1500	2606

Table 12 illustrates results obtained from another trial with robusta, combining cover crops of *Pueraria* and applications of nitrogenous fertiliser (ammonium sulphate) (IRCC).

Table 12   Average production (ten consecutive years)
(kg of clean coffee/ha/year)

Ammonium sulphate (g/tree)	*Pueraria*	Natural cover	Average
(Control) 0	611	618	615
250	749	700	724
750	734	976	855
Average	698	765	731

The cover crop did not appear to affect yields significantly, but the highest quantity of fertiliser applied markedly increased production.

The search for the best form of nitrogen for applying to coffee has prompted several experiments by the IRCC. Their results appear in Table 13.

Table 13   Application of nitrogen to *C. robusta*
(kg clean coffee/ha)

Fertiliser	1978	1979	1980	1981	Total
Control	891	2313	1906	2184	7294
Ammonium sulphate	909	2903	3198	2844	9854
Urea	841	2292	2723	2621	8477
Ammonium nitrate	995	2519	2783	3182	9479
Fertiliser 20–10–10	702	2381	2463	2366	7912

(Source: IRCC, 1982)

In the Central African Republic, Forestier also found that *C. robusta* and *C. excelsa* responded extremely well to nitrogenous manure.

Large quantities of nitrogen must be divided into about four to six applications per year, otherwise losses may be considerable.

Given the balance that must exist between the different nutrients, it is inevitable that the response to ever-increasing quantities of nitrogen will be eventually curtailed by limiting factors, requiring a corresponding increase in the level of other elements. However, high aplications of nitrogen may result in a significant increase in yield.

In support of this argument, a report by Forestier on *C. canephora* showed that the application of potassium fertilisers became essential after several harvest in order to balance the nutritional status of the plant and maintain a high level of productivity.

Excellent results were obtained, often using only nitrogenous fertiliser. However, the rapid increase in availability in the soil of other essential elements such as phosphoric acid and potassium make it necessary to give a great deal of attention to these other elements which can be mobilised for nutrition.

Through research conducted over many years in the Ivory Coast, Snoeck, at the IRCC, found that in moderately fertile soil, coffee trees often responded to nitrogen applications very favourably. However, the trees did not react in the same way to other major elements. He also noted that repeated applications of nitrogen led to soil acidification, resulting in losses of some exchangeable bases, and imbalance of K, Ca, Mg and Mg/K.

There is an urgent need to pursue studies on the vital physiological phenomena which are related to the mineral and water nutrition of coffee trees. Research carried out to date, using either plants in tanks fed with controlled nutritive solutions, or through classical field experiments, will not bring about a satisfactory solution or a full understanding of nutritional requirements as long as the knowledge related to these phenomena is inadequate.

In Africa, a great deal of attention has been paid to the mineral nutrition of the highly productive clones of *C. canephora* which have been selected by the IFCC, and which are being increasingly exploited. An annual production of about 2 to 3 tonnes of clean coffee per hectare, with little variation, requires considerable nutritional resources, indeed much more than the richest soil can normally provide. Applying large quantities of fertiliser is therefore essential with this new plant material. Failure to do so may have serious consequences, for example a rapid die-back of the branches may occur.

The highly significant effect of nitrogen and potassium applications after stumping in regeneration operations, giving increases of 25 to 45 per cent, has also been made apparent.

Snoeck (1987) has given details of a computer programme which enables fertiliser needs to be determined, based on obtaining chemical analyses of the soil.

Costs of fertilisers and manure and their profitability

Fertilisers are an important component in the production costs of coffee, given the high price of chemical fertiliser overseas. Fertiliser costs must therefore be incorporated in the general expenditure costs which include transport to the plantation, handling, storage, and finally application.

It is difficult to estimate the increase in the volume of the harvest which results from fertiliser applications in the case of a perennial plantation crop such as coffee, since the effect of the fertiliser does not always show during the first or second years. With the exception of nitrogen, which has a rapid effect, and also serious deficiency symptoms, the effects of potassium and phosphoric acid often only appear later and after repeated applications.

The effect of phosphate and potassium fertilisers on fruiting is often barely visible and weighing the harvested crop is frequently the only valid means of estimating the effect of fertiliser applications. The weight of the fresh fruit and also the yield of the dried beans should be included in these assessments. On commercial plantations, it is recommended that randomly selected plots, which are either unfertilised or have all been given different fertiliser treatments, are used for the control plots.

Estimating the profitability of an exclusively nitrogenous fertiliser is relatively easy, since the effects are shown in the fruiting response as early as the first and second years. For the two other essential elements, it is necessary to observe the development of the vegetative growth of the fertilised plots and also their productivity for at least three to five consecutive years.

In general, all rational fertiliser applications are likely to be profitable. If not, reasons must be found for this situation; these may include insufficient nutrients, an inadequate balance between the elements, inadequate levels of application, unsuitable times or methods of application or the presence of antagonistic elements in the soil.

Maintenance

Cropping methods

The maintenance of a coffee plantation includes fairly frequent weeding during the months that follow transplanting. Previously it was stated that clean weeding is being practiced less and less, with the exception of Brazil, where it is an established tradition. It can be substituted for, either by establishing a cover crop or mulch, or by adopting selective weeding.

Clean weeding requires a lot of hoeing and weeding which is carried out in inter-rows by customary methods; these may be manual, or by the use of draft animals or tractor-drawn equipment.

Herbicides

Many experiments have been carried out regarding the use of herbicides in coffee growing areas using various products. The validity and efficiency of these experiments has often involved the support of producers, particularly on the large plantations.

In Brazil, for example, the Coffee Institute of Brazil (CIB) generally recommends the following products:

- pre-emergence: Diuron, Simazine, MCPB;
- post-emergence: Dalapon, Diquat, Paraquat, MCPA;
- pre- and post-emergence: 2, 4-D.

In the Ivory Coast, the use of herbicides has enabled labour costs to be reduced. The staff necessary for maintenance work has been reduced by 60 to 70 per cent, and the number of cropping practices has been reduced by half compared with traditional manual maintenance. Overall, throughout the year, about 80 per cent is saved on labour in the most successful cases (IRCC).

In Kenya, numerous trials with herbicides have been conducted in arabica plantations. Results show that certain products cannot be used under specific conditions, while others should be prohibited due to the risk of damage to shrubs or to the detrimental flavour they give to the coffee. Some of the best products are 2,4-D, MCPA, and Dalapon. The use of herbicides has now become more expensive then manual or mechanical weeding, but it has the following advantages: it preserves the soil structure, more mulch is produced, and supervision is reduced. However, the elimination of certain perennial grasses has posed a special problem in that two applications of a large quantity of Dalapon may in fact harm young coffee plants.

New products such as Ametryn, Simazine and Diquat have recently been experimented with throughout the world. It is difficult to interpret the results as they vary according to numerous local factors, the knowledge of which is often lacking, such as availability and cost of labour, plant species, rainfall and soil characteristics.

A combination of financial constraints and the organisation of work on the farms has nevertheless made the use of herbicides popular for coffee maintenance. Precautions must be taken when using them to avoid damage to the shrubs and in some instances the neighbouring crops, due to the dissemination of the product by the wind or contamination. Some solutions may be provided for by the use of a plastic cover stretched over sticks, or a hood for spraying herbicides. Moreover, equipment used for herbicide application should not be used for other purposes.

The most commonly used products are listed in Table 14.

Table 14   Some herbicides used in coffee growing

Name	Method of treatment	Effect
2, 4-D amine	Pre- and post-emergence	Effective on all weeds (systemic)
Paraquat	Post-emergence	Effective on all weeds (contact)
Dalapon	Post-emergence	Grass weed control (contact)
Glyphosate	Post-emergence	Grass weed control (systemic)
Diuron	Pre-emergence	Effective on all weeds (nurseries)

Note: the doses to be used are as recommended by the manufacturers.

Mechanisation

Farmers are induced to use herbicides and mechanised maintenance when there is a lack or shortage of labour or where labour costs are high. Coffee growers in some countries, particularly Kenya, have been using light tractors with a small wheelbase for some time. Cutting attachments consist of blades from various models of hoe and the tines of scarifiers. Unfortunately these cropping methods have been found to have certain disadvantages: excessive root damage may occur if operations are carried out too frequently; the soil structure may be altered and erosion may be prompted. Consequently, a return to mechanical weed control methods may become more attractive and is often combined with manual labour.

The types of equipment used for this particular operation include stalk cutters, rotary cutters, shredders, and mowers.

Planting holes may be excavated by mechanical borers on tractors which are capable of excavating between 30 and 60 holes per hour. There is even equipment with self-righting devices for work on hilly terrain.

Some intermediary forms of mechanisation are becoming increasingly popular on family-run or small-scale farms. This has become possible through the development of small, reliable machines with equipment which can be operated by one or two men.

Organised groups of producers have also developed a system for the joint use of equipment by individuals or co-operatives. Some of this equipment includes: chain saws for clearing forests, the periodical stumping of coffee trees and for pruning shade trees if necessary; tree dozers or power-driven cultivators; horticultural tractors with a wide range of tools for cutting weeds and cover crops; manual, mechanical augers capable of digging between 20 and 30 holes per hour; small trailers adapted for use with power driven cultivators for transporting products for processing, fertilisers, harvested crops and also sawn wood when sites have been cleared or pruned.

Small motorised sprayers are also available for pest and disease control operations and together with knapsack sprayers and mist blowers, form a large part of the equipment which helps to increase the planters' resources and reduces labour costs. Brazil illustrates well how a wide and diversified range of material can be adapted to the most common farming practices.

Irrigation

Irrigation is necessary in regions where the dry season is severe and fairly extended. This is common practice in Arabia, (Yemen), Mysore (India), Kenya and Brazil.

Irrigation systems may distribute the water by **gravity** or by means of **sprinklers**. Using gravity, water is initially pumped through pipes to the highest points in the plots and is then allowed to flow over the soil, being channelled from tree to tree along furrows. The rate of flow will depend on the slope of the land. The main disadvantage of this system, which is commonly practiced in the mountains of Yemen, is that superficial erosion may occur, sometimes resulting in severe soil leaching.

Fig 70   Sprinkler irrigation: coffee plantation in São Paulo, Brazil (Courtesy: Sylvain)

With sprinkler irrigation, the water is applied in the form of droplets, which is more akin to natural rainfall and has a beneficial effect on the foliage. This form of irrigation requires an installation which includes a motor pump, a water distribution pipe network, and rotating sprinklers (Figs 70 and 71).

This technique has many advantages: 20 to 40 per cent of the water may be saved, considerably less erosion occurs on sloping lands, and irrigation is possible with coffee planted on flat land which would be difficult to irrigate using the gravity method. Conversely, the expenses involved for purchasing and installing sprinkler equipment are rather high and immediately pose a problem for the profitability of its use.

Irrigating coffee trees may be necessary in order to compensate for insufficient precipitation occurring during the critical period of fruit setting, following flowering. Irrigation can also be carried out on a more regular basis to compensate for long seasonal periods of drought.

Irrigation is justifiable in either case: applying a few millimetres of water during the critical fruiting period may save the harvest, and if the soil is allowed to dry out during seasonal drought periods serious, damage to the coffee plantation may result, necessitating the regeneration of the shrubs.

Numerous studies on sprinkler irrigation have been undertaken, particularly in Brazil and East Africa: most of them on arabica coffee (Table 15). They emphasise the increase in yield which may occur due to irrigation and which may sometimes exceed 100 per cent.

Fig 71 *C. arabica* plantation: motor-drive pump and sprinklers in operation. Babadjou, Cameroon (Courtesy: Muller)

Table 15 Irrigation trial in the Ivory Coast (Divo)
(kg of clean coffee/ha)

Method of irrigation	1980	1981	1982	Total
Control (no irrigation)	677	1224	2260	4161
Sprinkler irrigation 1.2/60 mm* (until June)	1494	2327	3164	6985
Sprinkler irrigation 1.0/60 mm	2231	3328	2726	8285
Sprinkler irrigation 1.0/40 mm	1749	3140	2562	7817
Sprinkler irrigation 1.2/60 mm	2298	3080	2439	7817
Localised sprinkler irrigation using tensiometers	2030	3524	1946	7500

*Crop factor, indicating irrigation deficit (based on evapotranspiration rates from open pan observations and/or tables).
(Source: Activity Report IRCC, 1982)

Table 16 Irrigation trial in the Ivory Coast (Tombokro)
(kg of clean coffee/ha)

Method of irrigation	1973	1974	1975	Total (1975–1982)
Control (no irrigation)	230	1319	3002	15 991
Class A tank	1885	3366	2931	18 758
Tensiometers	2315	4534	2776	19 239

(Source: Activity Report IRCC, 1982)

Little is known, however, of the results of using this technique with robusta. This species is generally grown in very moist climates with shorter periods of water deficiency than those observed in areas where arabica is grown. However, trials carried out in the Ivory Coast by Snoeck, (IRCC) have proved the effectiveness of applying water to robusta according to the readings of tensiometers installed in the upper layer of the soil. Tables 15 and 16 show that in the equatorial region with four seasons, irrigation is an essential factor for the adequate assimilation of fertiliser, particularly during the period of fruit swelling during the short dry season, as it stabilises the shrubs' water balance. A very interesting agronomic trial was conducted on robusta coffee by Rose in a marginal growing region in the Congo. After three years, the trial proved that maintaining soil moisture at a constantly high level during the dry season gave the best results, since the yield more than doubled. Applying water at the time of flowering also had a positive effect, but this was less pronounced. Observers found that coffee trees survived drought periods very well when they were irrigated every 10 days. During the third year of the trial, water consumption (evapotranspiration) was between 3.9 and 4.0 mm per day between July and August, indicating that 40 to 50 mm of water must be applied every 10 days for optimum results.

Trickle irrigation is yet another method of applying the water, consisting of a branched network of plastic pipes of small diameter, arranged in various types of drainage designs. It has proven to be the most economical in terms of water use and is also very effective for the development of the coffee trees. However, it is also the most expensive in terms of investment costs (four to six times the cost of a sprinkler installation). Its use is justified for high value operations, for example seed plots, or when planting coffee trees in climatic zones that are only marginally suitable due to irregular rainfall and limited water resources.

Irrigation methods should be based on experimental data, in which the major factors are the nature of the soil (retention capacity, etc.) and evapotranspiration. Uncontrolled and ill-timed applications of water may do more harm than good, causing erosion, soil leaching, off-season flowering and fungal epidemics. It is therefore vitally important that those who wish to irrigate consult specialised individuals before choosing a system.

Catch crops

Occupying the inter-rows of coffee with food crops when the trees are young is a common practice in Latin America and Africa. In Brazil, sharecropping contracts allow the contractors to cultivate inter-rows of food crops such as maize. In West Africa, robusta plantations are commonly interplanted with cassava, banana, sweet potatoes, etc. This custom is theoretically not compatible with rational coffee production because soil exhaustion is inevitably accelerated, and water competition is increased in many cases. Morever, many of the inter-crops do not cover the ground adequately for the control of erosion. However, since this practice has become commonplace amongst coffee growers some advantage may be gained by advising planters in their choice of interplanted crops. A trial was carried out in the Ivory Coast (Abengourou) to study the effect of traditional food crops such as yam, banana, maize, rice and groundnut in the region in question. The conclusion was that they were not competitive during the first three years of coffee growing, except for plantain, the presence of which considerably reduces yields (Figs 72 and 47). However, beyond the first three years, all inter-row crops generally do compete with coffee and their use must be strongly advised against. This timespan is reduced by a year when the spacing between coffee trees on the plantation is less than 3 m between the rows.

Trials in both East and West Africa have shown that conditions for the success of temporary intercropping which has no competitive effect on the coffee trees basically depend on the use of seedlings from plants that are already adapted to the region's seasonal cycle and ecology. Under these conditions, exploiting the inter-rows profitably is possible without harming the main crop. Such interplanted crops include rice, beans, soybeans, ground-nuts, yams, various vegetables (cabbage, lettuce, potato, etc.), and indeed even cash crops like cotton (Benin, Togo). Planting maize in association with the coffee may be profitable as its yields are very high. However, this is still a controversial practice because the substantial development of maize in dense cultivation results in excessive temporary lateral shade over the young coffee trees, which inhibits normal growth, causing etiolation. However, this is more or less compensated for by the other advantages of maize in providing windbreaks and substantial amounts of mulch from maize stalks and cobs after harvesting.

The technique of growing coffee in hedges, for example as in the many deciduous fruit tree growing areas in Europe and elsewhere, possibly along the contours, with a spacing of at least 4 m between the rows, makes it essential to plant an intermediary crop in the inter-rows, not only to render the unoccupied land profitable, but more importantly to prevent soil erosion.

Companion crops

In some countries, other crops are grown in association with coffee, such as rubber in Uganda, and quinine and papaya in Tanzania. These provide shade for the main crop. This technique has never given satisfactory results. The conclusion is, therefore, that it is more profitable to plant each crop separately in well-defined plots.

One exception is pineapple, which is often grown as an intercrop in the

Fig 72 *C. robusta*: young plantation intercropped with rice: mowing the stubble with a rotary mower (Courtesy: Capot)

Ivory Coast. There is obviously less competition than from larger interplanted crops but the shade from the coffee trees can possibly be detrimental to the pineapples in some areas.

Controlling pests and diseases

Pest and disease control practices will be studied later in Chapter 7. However, it should be mentioned here that it is necessary for the farmer to have a small reserve of current agro-chemicals, to enable him to deal with any infestation. The materials used for the various treatments are very diverse and there is a wide range of equipment adapted to both the type of chemical used and the methods of application. Lavabre has discussed this topic very thoroughly (see reference in Bibliography).

Replanting

Replanting an old coffee plantation with young shrubs becomes a necessity when access to new areas is not possible, or when the high costs of deforestation, clearing and land preparation need to be avoided. This operation may be carried out in a number of ways. The first method consists of uprooting the old shrubs, and replanting, after having marked the new rows in what were the original inter-rows. The young coffee trees develop satisfactorily, but there is a total halt to production for two or three years.

Another method consists of planting young coffee trees between the rows of existing coffee. They will either grow very slowly, or will tend to become etiolated due to a lack of light. The old coffee trees should be gradually uprooted to reduce the competition.

A third method consists of removing one out of two rows of old coffee trees and replacing them with young plants. As soon as the latter are well established, the remaining rows of old trees are removed and are in turn replaced by young ones. This method enables the planter to obtain some harvest during the transitional period.

Yet another method involves removing one row of coffee trees out of two or three and planting with young trees. The old coffee trees are pruned to leave a sap-drawer and two or three suckers are retained. The sap-drawer is removed after one harvest and shoots will be produced two years later. After three or four years, the old shrubs are removed and young ones planted. In the latter case, it is advisable to dig large holes ahead of the planting period, adding manure at the bottom (compost, fertiliser).

For old plantations, Haarer recommends uprooting the coffee trees in one operation, together with any shade trees, and redesigning the plantation based on modern principles and practices such as contour planting, erosion control measures, cropping on alternate strips and fertilisation.

Stereoscopic (three dimensional) **aerial photography** is used in coffee growing, particularly in Brazil. It provides information on such factors as soil types, the effects of erosion, the steepness of the slopes, detecting areas most susceptible to frost, the natural plant cover, the relief, and possibilities of mechanisation.

6 *Harvesting and yields*

General information

The time that elapses between the fertilisation of the flowers and the ripening of the fruits varies depending upon the species and variety. For the same species, this period may also be either accelerated or retarded by several factors. For example, flowering is triggered by the first rains which mark the end of the dry season but the periodicity of these rains may vary by several weeks from one year to the next. Some of the factors that have a more constant effect are:

- local climatic conditions;
- cropping methods (shade and pruning);
- the siting of the plantation.

Coffee trees, particularly *C. canephora*, flower over a period of several weeks. This is generally marked by a primary flowering followed by one or more secondary flowerings. The period of ripening may also occur over several weeks, which is beneficial if labour is in short supply.

However, in climates which have little seasonal variation, fruiting usually consists of a main harvest and secondary harvests spread out over a few months, so that the shrubs will bear flowers and fruits at all stages of development for a large part of the year. Such is the case with *C. canephora*.

Geneticists are often requested to create varieties that ripen either **early** or **late**, to coincide with the most favourable time of year, either from a climatic point of view, or in terms of labour availability.

Harvesting methods

Whatever the species cultivated, it is essential to harvest the fruits when they are fully ripe, to ensure the best possible quality. An indication of ripeness is their purplish-red colour. Fruits that are still green or just 'turning' are too often harvested in African, small-holder plantations, in order to avoid

(120)

damage from berry borer, or losses from stealing. The consequences of this practice are: a reduction in weight or about 10 to 20 per cent compared to ripe beans; a deterioration in total yield and organoleptic qualities, with the presence of many defective beans; and a reduction in the quality of flavour of the resulting coffee. Based on the results of a trial, Vaz and Baiao Esteves concluded that the taste of coffee became unacceptable when the proportion of beans from unripe fruit exceeded 10 per cent.

For wet processing of coffee, it is imperative to harvest choice arabicas when the fruits are fully ripe. This requires at least two or three harvesting periods.

Harvesting is usually carried out by hand. The fruits are separated from the branches singly and collected in various containers such as baskets, bags, and jerrycans. It is advisable to provide workers with two containers: one for ripe, healthy cherries, and the other for diseased, spotted or dried fruits. Harvesting is generally undertaken by women and children who are more skillful than men. They are paid at piece-work rates.

In some areas of Brazil, where coffee is grown on large plots of land where there is little available labour, the harvesting practice consists of stripping whole branches (por derrica). The cherries fall to the ground together with the leaves and twigs, whether they are ripe or not. They are picked up with a shovel and contain many impurities such as soil, stones, etc. To avoid picking up an excessive amount of foreign matter, the soil under the bushes may be briefly swept or alternatively the harvest is collected on sheets which are laid out under the coffee trees and moved from one tree to the other by the harvesters. Experiments have been conducted on the use of pre-emergence herbicides to ensure a weed-free soil prior to harvesting.

The sheets used for harvesting are generally either of canvas or plastic, and are placed around the base of the shrubs. They have proven to be effective in increasing the output of the harvesters, leaving both hands free for selectively picking the fruits as opposed to stripping the whole branch and therefore improving the quality of the harvest, mainly due to the absence of stones.

Regardless of the technique used, the harvested product must be cleaned and sorted when it arrives at the processing factory (Chapter 9). Despite this precaution, Brazilian arabica is generally not of the same high quality as that of other coffee-producing countries in South America.

Ladders have to be used during harvesting when the shrubs are tall and their branches are beyond the reach of the harvesters, as is often the case in Brazil. This eliminates the risk of breaking the branches in pulling them downwards to enable the fruit to be reached.

Individual harvesters' yields are a direct result of their dexterity and the yield per tree. As much as 100 kg of cherries may be harvested per day. However, the amount collected may not exceed 30 to 50 kg if harvesting conditions are less favourable, for example sparse fruiting or excessively dense shrubs which have not been pollarded.

Many manufacturers have attempted to design mechanical coffee harvesters. One such machine involved the vibration of the trunk and branches, but it was not satisfactory due to the damage inflicted on the tree. This damage was more serious on plants grown in lighter soil; the root system also being affected, and sometimes even resulted in the tree being uprooted. Another machine, inspired by a grape harvester design, and using vibrating 'fingers' between the branches, proved to be efficient and fast. However, it was not selective enough since the fruits removed were a mixture of ripe and unripe cherries plus various impurities; it was limited to harvesting only branches up to 2.5m in height. The slope of the land was also an impediment. Despite those technical problems and the high investment costs required to purchase it, this machine is being used on some commercial coffee farms in Brazil that are sited on relatively flat land, but are at a regional disadvantage in terms of the rarity and increasing cost of salaried labour.

Harvesting periods

Coffee-producing countries are located on both sides of the equator, and are so different ecologically that coffee is being harvested all over the world throughout the year. In the northern hemisphere, *C. arabica* generally flowers from February/March to May/June, which means that harvesting is carried out from September/October to December/January. *C. canephora* flowers from January/February and fruits ripen during the later months of the year.

In the southern hemisphere, where the seasons are reversed, flowering in *C. arabica* mostly occurs from August to October and harvesting is done from March until May. *C. canephora* flowers from August to November and the fruits are harvested from May to August.

The advantage of harvesting all the fruits from one branch at one time, either manually or mechanically, has given rise to research on a means of triggering the ripening process to induce uniform ripening. Products already known in the horticultural world have been used: gibberellic acid and Ethrel (2-chloroethane phosphoric acid). Experiments have been conducted with arabica and robusta in many countries using these two products. The results obtained in the Ivory Coast by the IFCC have been rather disappointing. In fact, the cherries developed the reddish colour, which is characeristic of ripe fruit, but this was found to be only a superficial change, and a 'false' ripeness. Beans that are fractionally either larger or smaller than average are insufficiently developed, and consequently there is a loss of weight and a decrease in the quality when these chemical ripening agents are used.

Yield

Fruiting is influenced by many factors for each coffee tree variety, some of which are: heredity, the age of the shrubs, planting density, ecological conditions (seasonal rainfall), cropping practices (shade, pruning, fertilisation, maintenance), damage by pests and diseases.

Moreover, the coffee tree, like many fruit tree species, is subjected to the phenomenon of biennial or alternate bearing, which is mostly a reaction of the shrub to the preceding harvest, and a sizeable harvest may only be produced every two or three years. The effect of this unfavourable characteristic is today overcome by using highly productive varieties and intensive cropping with large applications of fertiliser.

Nevertheless, it would be incorrect to calculate the profitability of a plantation based solely on the yield of one year. Estimates should be based on at least five consecutive years in order to be accurate.

The following information gives an indication of the yields that can be expected with *C. arabica* under normal growing conditions using unselected plant stock:

- 1st harvest (4 years) – 200 to 300 kg/ha;
- 2nd to 3rd harvests (5–6 years) – 600 to 800 kg/ha;
- subsequent harvests (annual average calculated over a period of 10 years) – 500 to 800 kg/ha.

Average yields in Brazil, calculated for several million hectares, are about 350 to 400 kg/ha. In its policy to revitalise coffee growing and diversify agriculture in coffee-growing regions, the State government estimated the profitability threshold to be seven bags or 420 kg of clean coffee/ha. In fact, many Brazilian farms, especially some of those most recently established in Paraña, have much higher production levels. On the other hand, there are still coffee plantations which are more or less exhausted and produce much less than the 350 to 400 kg/ha previously mentioned.

Yields of arabica plantations in other Latin American countries vary little from those of Brazil on average, but they are superior to those of Africa or Asia.

However, in addition to these very traditional farms, there are increasingly more coffee plantations where the use of selected plant stock and modern practices enable yields to be obtained that were seemingly inconceivable 20 years ago. In Brazil, extraordinary yields of 5 to 6 tonnes per hectare have been obtained with the 'Mundo Novo' variety, but more commonly 2 to 3 tonnes per hectare. Similar yields have been recorded in Costa Rica. Before the introduction of *Hemileia* in 1983, exceptional, record yields of 10 to 12 tonnes of clean coffee per hectare had been obtained in Colombia, with high density plantations of dwarf 'Caturra' coffee trees (10 000 to 30 000 trees per hectare), using very high quantities of fertiliser and sophisticated cultural techniques. It is now no longer unusual to harvest an average of 1000 to 1200 kg/ha annually with careful maintenance and appropriate fertilisation (Cameroon, Kenya).

Similar gains have been realised with *C. canephora*. Consequently annual yields, which were for a long time considered to be satisfactory at 800 to 1000 kg per hectare, can nowadays be easily increased by 50 per cent by making some investments, particularly in fertiliser use.

In Madagascar, the first clones selected from *C. canephora* (IFCC), which were grown on large plots, produced 2 or 3 tonnes per hectare. Later varieties showed more potential. Some other favourable factors include the fact that the first harvest of clonal material took place in the third year following planting and biennial bearing has been considerably reduced.

Techniques are undoubtedly evolving very rapidly in many of the major coffee-producing countries and conditions for coffee production will soon be greatly altered.

Average harvests of clean coffee for the other species, which are not as widely grown, are: 500–1000 kg/ha for *C. excelsa* and 300–600 kg/ha for *C. liberica*.

Harvest estimates

Methods of estimating coffee yields has given rise to research on both arabicas and canephoras. For the former, a Brazilian method entails choosing 200 coffee trees at random on a farm and determining the number of fruits borne by each tree. To facilitate the operation, a sample of 500 g is selected, the fruits counted, and the figure multiplied by the total number of samples of 500 g. A qualitative analysis must then be carried out to obtain a result that is closer to the commercial value. Four fruits out of 100 are removed at random and carefully examined. Healthy, normal beans are discarded, as are the peaberries, elephant beans, husks, etc. The operation is repeated several times to make it statistically valid.

The average weight of the beans must be known in order to estimate the tonnage. In Brazil, the weight was found to be almost constant from one year to the next, so figures taken from samples from the previous harvest are valid. An overall quantitative and qualitative estimate of the harvest can be made using statistical analysis.

This technique is obviously only applicable a few weeks before the harvest. Pochet estimates that a long-term yield forecast for *C. canephora* can be obtained from the following data:

a) Growth characteristics for a 20 month period prior to harvesting

In an equatorial climate, the branches formed during the short rainy season will produce most of the crop which will be harvested about 20 months later. The total rainfall during the months of March, April, and May must therefore be considered to be representative. If this value is below 440 mm, the result is likely to be a reduced harvest 20 months later.

b) Previous level of production

A high yield will exhaust the coffee tree and may adversely affect the following seasons crop. Pochet has reported that, over a period of 12 years, there was no indication that two low, or two large harvests occurred successively.

c) Intensity of the preceding flowering

This depends on two factors: the precipitation which occurs at the end of the long rainy season, and the existence of a pronounced dry season. The total precipitation threshold over the two months period prior to the dry season should be 230 mm for a good harvest; below this, flower bud initiation is poor and the harvest will be adversely affected. Precipitation during the dry season should amount to less than 70 mm for optimum flowering.

These data are obviously only valid for the Congolese region and regions with similar climates. They can be adapted to other situations and the general pattern is of interest.

On a national scale, coffee harvest estimates for a country are generally in the hands of a specialised service which is attached to a Ministry or State agency responsible for agricultural products. Two or three harvests are usually estimated, the last one just prior to the main harvest; the reliability of these estimates is approximately 2 to 5 per cent. This knowledge is very significant from a commercial point of view. It is kept highly confidential so that speculations may be avoided.

Productivity period

The longevity of coffee trees, together with their productivity, is related to the local ecological conditions and the general level of efficiency of maintenance. If ecological conditions are unsuitable, the shrubs will have difficulty overcoming the depressive phase that follows the initial harvest; they may even deteriorate and die. Each successive year it is necessary for the farmer to replace some of them. This situation should be given a great deal of attention, and the factors responsible should be identified and remedied if possible.

A coffee tree, when properly cultivated, may live for 30, 40, 50 years or more; 100-year old coffee trees are not unusual.

It is very important for the farmer to know the likely extent of the shrubs' production period, particularly the period of economic productivity, during which it is most likely to be profitable. Studies of production costs show that a coffee plantation with an average potential yield which has dropped below a certain level is no longer profitable from an economic point of view. The expenses that are incurred, even if they are depreciated, are no longer compensated for by the harvests. The example of Brazil previously mentioned illustrates this fact. At this stage, the only solution is to uproot, and if possible, replant the plantation with new stock, using new clonal material and techniques, or replacing the coffee with other suitable crops.

Generally, the profitable period of a coffee plantation does not exceed 15 to 20 or 25 years under optimum conditions. This seems to be the case in most countries. It must be stressed that it makes no sense to retain old, timeworn, decrepit coffee plantations. This is not economically viable, especially if they occupy fertile land that could be utilised more effectively.

The use of smaller varieties of arabica, planted at high densities, with shorter productive periods has been considered. This would provide only one vegetative cycle with intensive production for four or five years, before uprooting and replanting. However, the tendency is now towards the use of high density plantations and free-growth management. This system produces several cycles and three sizeable harvests, interspersed with total stumping. This rejuvenation plot by plot is then extended to the entire farm in successive blocks, so that an increased average yield and profitability justifies the use of the technical operations required by this very intensive cropping system.

However, considerable caution should be exercised before adopting these innovations, mainly, but not exclusively due to the sizeable investments necessary and the fact that the profitablility of the system has not yet been sufficiently proven.

7 Pests and diseases

General information

Two serious epidemics, one due to a disease, the other to a pest, have devastated coffee plantations over the past hundred years and are still doing considerable damage. The disease is *Hemileia vastatrix* or **rust**, a disease that is well known to pathologists and which is caused by a microscopic fungus. The other, *Hypothenemus hampei* Ferr. (*Stephanoderes hampei* Ferr.), commonly known as the **berry borer**, is an insect with infests the bean. In fact, *C. arabica* is no longer grown in Sri Lanka as a result of *Hemileia* attacks which are also quite severe in other coffee-producing countries. The berry borer, which is now encountered throughout the world, caused considerable damage to Brazilian harvests before chemical control was developed. It is still a cause of major concern in most coffee-growing countries.

New prevention and control treatments are now being developed, and increasingly powerful products are becoming available to farmers; these are helping to combat both rust and berry borer much more effectively. However, with the expansion of coffee growing, particularly in Africa, new diseases have appeared and new pests have proliferated. The numbers increase every year and this poses numerous problems to pathologists and entomologists, whose role is to study them and develop methods of control.

It is extremely fortunate that plant protection resources have considerably increased over the past 20 years. A wide range of synthetic products, such as organophosphates and systemic insecticides and fungicides is available to producers today.

However, producers should be aware that the effectiveness of these products depends essentially upon the conditions under which they are used. Choosing the appropriate product is most important, and it should be used strictly according to the manufacturer's instructions (quantity, method of use, time of year to apply, etc.). Negligence of any kind may detrimentally affect any chances of obtaining the desired results. It should also be noted that the effect of certain chemical products that are not sufficiently selective may have an undesirable effect by causing biological inbalances which favour the rapid proliferation of other pests which may have previously been considered to be of minor importance. The potential appearance of resistance to certain insecticides should also be considered, as well as the effects on beneficial predators of insect pests.

The effect of certain synthetic products on the organoleptic qualities of coffee is another consideration. An example is benzyne hexachloride (HCH), which gives the coffee an earthy, mouldy or 'bricky' flavour, the use of which is now prohibited. Lindane, its gamma isomer, which is also active, is currently used (under restricted use or banned in some countries) and does not have the same detrimental side-effects.

Finally, although it is far from recent, the use of biological control to offset the drawbacks of chemical control is very important. Although the results obtained in controlling the berry borer have not always been completely satisfactory in coffee growing, biological control techniques may still play an important role in the future protection of coffee plantations, perhaps in combination with chemical control, as in **integrated control** which consists of associating chemical with biological control techniques.

In this brief study, the main diseases and animal parasites that are potentially harmful to coffee trees will be examined. A more exhaustive study of diseases and pests of coffee has been written by Barat and Vayssiere.

Fungal diseases[1]

Introduction

The list of diseases which infect coffee is extremely lengthy. However, many of them are not serious and only four or five major diseases are of economic importance. Some of them may affect a limited geographical area, or have a very well-defined ecological specialisation, which limits their impact on the crop. The main diseases of coffee are:

- rots and fungal root rots;
- leaf rusts;
- coffee berry disease (*C. arabica*).

Other 'diseases', such as tracheomycosis or wilt disease, which once posed a serious threat to coffee plantations, have now practically disappeared. Most of the other diseases either have little economic impact or are considered to be physiological disorders which can be controlled by the use of appropriate agronomic or cropping practices.

It is interesting to note that the range of fungicidal remedies available is still rather limited for use against fungal diseases, since there has been much less progress made in this area than in the area of insecticides. However, effective control for most fungal diseases of coffee is available, although there is unfortunately still a lack of remedies for root diseases, which are

---

1. With the participation of R. Muller, Head of the Phytopathology service of the IRCC, Deputy Director General in charge of Scientific Affairs.

practically impossible to control chemically. Moreover, chemical control is costly and its use is only advisable for highly productive coffee growing.

Much research has been undertaken in view of finding a genetic solution for the major diseases. Some are still ongoing while the results of others are being practically applied, but are yet to be perfected.

Diseases of the roots and collar

Root rots

This group of major diseases are caused by higher fungi, mainly Basidiomycetes, but also some Ascomycetes. They may be found in different soil conditions, but the previous vegetation of the area (forests in particular) and the cropping method (shade trees) are important factors which may affect the occurrence of these diseases.

Wounds on underground organs that have been caused either by living organisms (white worms, nematodes, etc.) or have occurred during cultivation (roots cut during mechanical plantation maintenance) are factors that favour both the proliferation and continuation of these diseases.

The progression of these diseases from a central focus is generally slow. It mainly begins with the development of mycelial strands or **rhizomorphs** which spread from root to root. The first general symptoms are the withering of the foliage, which progressively dies, and the drying out of the branches. Death occurs soon after. The disease may be identified by examining the roots and the base of the trunk:

- **White rot,** due to *Leptoporus lignosus* (Kl.) R. Heim. Whitish filaments that are firmly attached to the roots can be observed (not to be confused with saprophytic filaments which are easily detached). The fruiting bodies of the pathogen appear later in groups at the base of the diseased stems;
- **Brown rot,** due to *Phellinus lamaoensis* (Murr.) Heim. (*Fomes lamaoensis* [Murr.] Petch.); also called root rot. The very fine mycelium of the fungus froms a brown crust, mixed with the soil, which adheres to the roots. The bark rots and the internal tissues of the taproot are streaked with black lines;
- **Black rot,** due to *Rosellinia bunodes* (B and Br.) Sacc. (Rosellinia root rot). Black mycelial strands can be observed on the roots, accompanied by bark rot which generally starts in the area of the collar, at soil level (often as a result of a wound);
- **Armillaria root rot** – one of the most serious and widespread root rots of coffee. There are three main agents: *Armillaria mellea* (Fr.) Karst.; *A. fuscipes* Petch; and *Clitocybe tabescens* (Fr.) (*Armillariella elegans* R. Heim, Bres.).

  The armillaria root rots can be recognised by a very characteristic symptom which is the longitudinal splitting of the diseased tissues, such as the roots (root splitting), collar (collar crack), or stems. The fruiting bodies of the pathogens arise from these cracks, which are caused by the development of mycelial invasions in the medullary rays.White mycelia can be observed under the bark (hyphae with many short branches); having the characteristic odour of fresh mushrooms. The rhizomorphs are small, black mycelial strands.

Armillaria mellea is very cosmopolitan. *Clitocybe tabescens* has caused serious damage in Madagascar and Reunion, but also in Cameroon in arabica plantations under shade.

Methods of controlling root rots

Control measures against root rots are difficult and costly, although they are less costly than the negligence which leads to the progressive destruction of the plantation. Planting replacement trees in areas which have been infected with root rot is risky: the young trees initially grow very vigorously, but generally die during the first fruiting season if not earlier.

The classic method of control is to surround the diseased area by a deep pit. All the trees within this area are uprooted, including shade trees, even if they appear to be healthy. All the lignified roots must be removed, even thin ones (less than one centimetre in diameter). Uprooting coffee trees using a winch attached to a goat produces satisfactory results and is cheaper than uprooting manually. It is advisable to incinerate all the trunks and woody debris which remain on the surface of the area.

The soil should not be left bare to reduce the risk of it becoming impoverished due to leaching and erosion. It is advisable to plant it with a herbaceous cover crop that will not harbour agents of root rots that are specific to woody plants. Annual fodder grasses are generally good, practical covers for this purpose. Almost all market garden crops can also be planted without risk. The area must not be replanted within three or four years of the removal. It is recommended to adjust certain soil factors during replanting, such as drainage, phosphate amendments, fertilisation and addition of green manure.

In regions where root rots occur, the best course of action is to take precautions in order to prevent large areas from being infected. A survey team must be trained to recognise the first signs of attack. Stumps of forest and shade trees are most likely to be infected, and must be destroyed before replanting. Diseased shade trees must be uprooted as soon as they are infected before they contaminate their neighbours through root contact. The coffee trees that surround them must also be uprooted. Major losses will be avoided if these precautions are taken.

Work undertaken in Cameroon by the IFCC (Blaha, 1970) has shown that fumigating the soil with methyl bromide, which diffuses deeply into the soil, greatly helps to eliminate the remaining mycelial debris. Although this practice cannot be recommended for large areas for economic reasons, it may be successfully applied to the initially infected area following the destruction of the plant stock, by allowing the gas to spread from a cartridge within a plastic covering buried in the ground.

Phthiriosis

This root disease, which is known throughout Africa, is caused by droppings of mealybugs (*Pseudococcus*) on which a fungus belonging to the Polyporaceae develops (*Polyporus coffeae* or *Bornetina coryum*). The fungus develops into a compact mycelial sleeve, forming a brownish, crusty sheath around the roots. The shrub, which has also been attacked by the mealybugs, is asphyxiated by the sheathing which isolates it from the soil. The vectors of the disease are ants (*Paratrechnina* sp. in Madagascar) which introduce and spread the mealybugs. Diseased trees display weakened, chlorotic vegetative growth, and invariably succumb to attacks by this fungus.

Contact insecticides are generally effective in controlling these diseases. The best formula contains Dieldrin (under restricted use) and is used as an emulsifiable concentrate which is abundantly applied using a sprinkler system around the base of the coffee trees (Lavabre).

Preventive measures in the infected regions consist of watering the planting holes and the surrounding area with an Aldrin solution (under resricted use) (20 g to 20 per cent per hole) or dipping the roots of young plants in an insecticidal solution.

Collar rot (Damping-off disease)

This disease, caused by *Rhizoctonia bataticola* (Taub.) Butler, is encountered in most tropical countries where it not only attacks all species of coffee tree but also tea, cocoa and rubber.

Its most spectacular manifestation gives it the name of damping-off disease. In the seedbed or nursery, more or less circular areas are observed where the seedlings have died. The infection is propagated much more rapidly when the soil is moist. Entire beds of small plants can succumb over a period of a few weeks. The attack occurs at the collar of the seedling and is characterised by a marked necrosis, which results in a circular blackening of the stem. The outer tissues of the stem are destroyed and the nutrition of the seedling is adversely affected. Full-grown trees are also reported to have been attacked.

As a preventive measure it is recommended to keep moisture to a minimum in the seedbeds and nurseries. Diseased and dead seedlings should be immediately uprooted and the soil disinfected as soon as the first symptoms appear. Good results are obtained using industrial formalin (containing 40 per cent formic aldehyde) at a concentration of 2 to 3 per cent (Saccas).

Diseases of the trunk
Tracheomycosis (**Carbunculariosis**)

Tracheomycosis is caused by the fungus *Fusarium xylarioïdes* (Steyaert) Heim and Saccas. It devastated West African coffee plantations from 1938 until

1945. This disease, which was previously unknown, seems to have started in the Congo, Kinshasa (Zaire), and Oubangui (Central African Republic) where it caused the deaths of almost all of the *C. excelsa* plantations. It then moved westwards and caused considerable damage to plantations of *C. excelsa* and related species such as *C. abeokutae*, particularly in Cameroon and the Ivory Coast. *Coffea canephora* var. *Kouilou* plantations were also highly susceptible. Only robusta coffees were considered to be resistant, although mainly in experimental stations; they were not observed to be resistant in every case.

The first symptoms of the disease are an abrupt cessation in growth. The young leaves turn yellow, followed by a drying of the branches. The shrub becomes rapidly defoliated. One of the characteristics of tracheomycosis is that the symptoms appear suddenly. The time taken for the shrub to die varies from a few weeks to a few months, but in general, the younger the plant, the more rapidly it succumbs.

The root system is not affected. However, under the bark, on the central vascular cylinder, blackish, brownish or violet streaks are observed. Saccas, who concentrated his studies on tracheomycosis, recommends the following treatment:

- total uprooting and incineration of dead or diseased trees;
- disinfection of wounds caused by pruning and lesions caused by insects, by spraying or swabbing with Bordeaux mixture.

Research has been concentrated on the selection of resistant varieties, given the seriousness of the disease and the difficulties encountered in applying chemical treatments in the African environment.

However, this disease has now almost completely disappeared after having attracted the attention of research workers and growers for several years. Cultivation of resistant robustas has been a significant factor in causing it to lose its economic impact.

Caution is still recommended, however, as it is difficult to predict the future of this type of disease, since there is always the possibility that mutation of strains of the pathogen may occur. It is particularly worth noting that it was detected in 1970 in Ethiopia on *C. arabica*, which was, until then, considered to be resistant. At the present time it does not seem to be causing significant damage to this species, but its very presence proves that the danger of its reappearance still exists.

In East Africa and Madagascar, *C. arabica* is affected by die-back caused by *Fusarium lateritium* Ness. This fungus causes the sudden death of whole parts of the plant. The leaves remain on the tree and become reddish-brown, as if they had been exposed to fire. Cutting back, mostly below the observed lesions, followed by the application of a protective coating, seems to be the only possible method of control. Multi-stem pruning should be adopted in all areas where the disease is present.

Root rots

Root rots, which have already been described, are likely to persist by infecting the bases of the stems.

Diseases of the branches and leaves

Rusts

There are two kinds of coffee leaf rust:

- **Common coffee rust** caused by *Hemileia vastatrix* Berk and Br.;
- **Grey coffee rust** caused by *Hemileia coffeicola* Roger and Maublanc.

Common coffee rust

First recorded in Ceylon in 1861, common coffee rust is the longest known disease of coffee. It is also the most widespread since it currently affects almost all of the coffee-producing countries following its appearance in Brazil in 1970. It is considered to be the most serious coffee disease, based on the fact that it led to the abandonment of coffee growing in Ceylon. However, that was in 1867, before Bordeaux mixture was discovered. The occurrence of this disease is highly variable, depending upon the species cultivated. *Coffea arabica* is the most sensitive, but there are also sensitive genotypes among the other species cultivated. Altitude also has some effect, as the disease is especially serious at low altitudes with a hot, humid climate. It is also affected by growing conditions.

Common coffee rust can be recognised by the white, circular lesions which first appear on the underside of the leaves. After about ten days they coalesce and become covered with a yellow-orange or bright orange powder which is composed of the fruiting bodies of the fungus. There are mainly kidney-shaped urediospores, covered with spines on half of their surface (hemileia = half smooth). They are referred to as sori. From the upper surface, these sori are seen in the form of 'oil spots'.

The urediospores are easily transported by moving vectors, particularly wind. It is thought that transatlantic air currents brought them from Africa to America.

The urediospores need water to germinate and epidemics are linked to the wet season since serious infections normally occur during periods of highest rainfall. Once the urediospores have germinated, the germinative filament penetrates the stomata and colonises the entire leaf. The abundant, highly branched mycelium is intercellular very small haustoria enter the cells.

The initial lesions, which can extend to 1 or 2 cm in diameter, coalesce to form an area that may cover most of the leaf surface. The damage afflicted is due both to the loss of photosynthetic activity in the diseased areas of the leaves, and to the premature leaf-fall which occurs. This defoliation can be massive in the case of major attacks and a die-back of the branches follows. Repeated attacks weaken the plant.

A great deal of work has been undertaken on control measures to combat this disease. Chemical control is possible by repeated applications of cupric compounds (two to five treatments depending upon the region). The first treatment must be applied just after the beginning of the rains, and the others at intervals of one month. Captafol has less effect than cupric compounds. However, this fungicide seems to have a stimulating effect on vegetative growth, unlike the cupric compounds, which have a depressive effect on growth when applied repeatedly in massive doses. The overall result is, however, positive. The most effective fungicide seems to be Triadimefon, which is systemic, preventive, curative, and antisporulant at the same time, therefore enabling the number of applications to be reduced.

For any given region, before adopting a chemical treatment policy that will inevitably be costly, it is advisable to evaluate the real damage and the spread of the epidemic. Studies carried out by the IRCC in co-operation with the Cadarache Nuclear Studies Centre (France), using very precise measuring methods, have shown that interruptions in the exchanges between the plant and the environment can only be discerned if at least 20 per cent of the leaves have been attacked. This implies that true damage to production only occurs as a result of more serious attacks.

Contrary to many theories, shade does not appear to be a factor which favours the spread of the disease. Although it is true that it may contribute to maintaining a moist atmosphere which favours the germination of urediospores, studies carried out at the Cadarache NSC appear to indicate also that light renders the plant sensitive to the effects of the pathogen. Since full exposure to light increases productivity, many recent observations have shown that high productivity is a factor related to sensitivity to the disease.

Cultural practices (high density planting, cyclical pruning, fertiliser application) which tend to increase productivity, must precede the application of chemical control measures to ensure that the latter are economically justified.

Genetic control has been the subject of many studies. Some of the most important investigations were carried out in Portugal, at the Centro de Investigaçao das Ferrugens do Cafeeiro (CIFC) of Oeiras which involved identifying virulent genes in the pathogen and relating them to genes controlling sensitivity in the host. Thirty-two physiological races of *Hemileia vastatrix* have been identified, corresponding to groups of sensitivity within the host.

Among the genes for resistance identified in arabicas, the SH_1 to SH_5 genes do not appear to be of much practical value. In fact, *Hemileia vastatrix* shows a high incidence of mutation and the resistance of these genes is rapidly being bypassed by the appearance of additive genes in the pathogen. Contrary to the classical theories, these mutations seem to be favoured by the use of 'multilines' (genotype mixtures), such as the composite variety 'Iarana', which was tried unsuccessfully in Brazil.

Of greater interest are the genes SH_6 to SH_9 (or SH_{10}) which come from *C. canephora* through the Hybrid of Timor, a spontaneous hybrid between *C. arabica* and *C. canephora* which is resistant to all currently known races of the pathogen.

The most exploitable result in the search for 'specific' or 'vertical' resistance has been the 'Catimor', a hybrid between the Caturra variety (dwarf bourbon arabica) and the Hybrid of Timor. However, using the Catimor hybrid is not without risk, as the use of resistant plants with a vertical resistance system exerts a selection pressure on the pathogen that favours mutants. In fact, many lines of Catimor include individuals that have lost one, some, or sometimes all of the genes of the Hybrid of Timor. This is a situation which favours successive monogenic mutations of the pathogen, and could lead to a loss of resistance by Catimor in the near future.

The 'Colombia' variety should be mentioned here. It was created in Colombia where it is already widely planted. This composite variety consists of about 70 per cent of the genotypes of the A group that are resistant to all races of rust known today, 25 per cent of the genotypes of groups 1, R, 2 and 3, and 5 per cent of the E group which has lost all the genes from the Hybrid of Timor.

However, although the loss of vertical resistance through successive monogenic mutations of the pathogen will lead to the emergence of races of the pathogen with an increasingly larger number of virulent genes, and is a real danger in terms of quality, it is less of a danger in terms of quantity. According to the most recent research work by the IRCC-Montpellier, the aggressive nature of the pathogen appears to be inversely proportional to the number of virulent genes it possesses.

Nevertheless, it is still preferable to use an incomplete resistance system of the 'horizontal' type, in other words, a 'non-specific', or 'general' system which is quantitative and multigenic, and which only exerts a reduced selection pressure on the pathogen. The incomplete resistance of coffee species to rust has been studied mainly by the IRCC, first 'in the field' in Cameroon, then in France in Montpellier, where the various components of resistance have been identified. Studies have also been undertaken in Brazil using *C. canephora* (mainly Kouilou), and *C. arabica*, to a lesser degree, within the framework of an FAO programme. The former studies, which were conducted with the collaboration of Colombian and Central American research scientists, specifically showed that genotypes with a high degree of incomplete resistance could be found in *C. arabica*, particularly in the Ethiopian stock collected during the ORSTOM and IRCC explorations in 1967. These genotypes should be exploited by associating them with the qualities of uniformity and productivity possessed by the best commercial varieties, such as Caturra, in hybridisation programmes.

Resistant varieties, whether they have vertical or horizontal resistance, can only be validly exploited by using vegetative propagation methods, particularly *in vitro* propagation techniques such as micropropagation and somatic embryogenesis.

In conclusion, the solution to the problem of coffee rust must be found in a combination of genetic, chemical, and agronomic measures. The seriousness of this disease must be not be underestimated and the areas and conditions where it is most harmful should be identified. Much of the research undertaken in this area in the major arabica-producing countries in Latin America has been inspired by the great fear that the disease has instilled, and is also one of the main reasons why coffee growing has been significantly modernised over the past two decades. For example, PROMECAFE, the Co-operative Regional Programme for the Modernisation and Protection of Coffee Growing in Central America, Mexico, Panama, and the Dominican Republic was created in 1979 within the Interamerican Institute for Agricultural Co-operation (IICA), based on the concept that a programme which is united in the areas of research, training, and extension of scientific knowledge would be best equipped to deal with the threat of rust in the Central American region.

Grey coffee rust
First recorded in Cameroon on *C. arabica* in 1929, grey coffee rust is caused by *Hemileia coffeicola*. It is easily distinguished from common coffee rust by its macroscopic and microscopic characteristics:

- instead of forming lesions in well-defined contours, the fruiting bodies appear in the form of a yellow powder spread over the entire underside of the leaf; these fruiting bodies are the first visible symptoms of the disease on the green surface of the leaves;
- the mycelium is scant and not branching, and consists mainly of two or three large filaments which develop below the sub-stomatal chamber (Figs 73 and 74). These filaments terminate in very large lobed haustoria which fully occupy the cell;
- the urediospores are covered with spines which are more sparse than those of *Hemileia vastatrix* (Fig 75).

This rust is more difficult to discern since it is microscopic, and also produces less defoliation. Farmers thus tend to minimise its effects which should really be taken much more seriously. Preliminary studies have shown that it reduces photosynthetic activity and phosphoric and carbonic assimilation. It is considered to be one of the major factors limiting production in Cameroon.

This rust was first encountered on arabica, but has since been found on robusta by Muller (1953), in Cameroon, also on Excelsa and on the so-called 'de la Nana' in the Central African Republic. It has also been found more recently on some species growing wild in the Ivory Coast. It spreads slowly and at present is only found in Central Africa (Cameroon, Nigeria, Sao Tomé, Angola), and in a few places in West Africa (Togo, Ivory Coast). This rust is less well known than *H. vastatrix*, and has inspired relatively few studies to date, with the exception of Cameroon where it has received some attention.

Like *H. vastatrix*, this rust is encouraged by conditions of extreme humidity. Infections follow the onset of the rainy season. Unlike *H. vastatrix*, *H. coffeicola* does not appear to have a propensity for specific ecological conditions. Although it is found growing in abundance in high altitude areas,

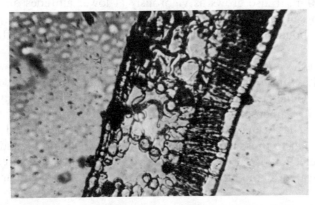

Fig 73   Mycelial filaments of *Hemileia coffeicola* in the mesophyll: cross-section of a leaf of *C. robusta* (Courtesy: Blaha)

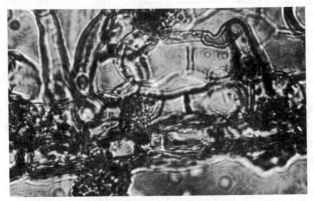

Fig 74   Mycelial filaments of *Hemileia coffeicola* in the leaf tissues: cross-section of a leaf of *C. arabica* (Courtesy: Blaha)

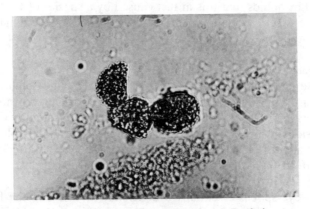

Fig 75   Urediospores of *Hemileia coffeicola* (Courtesy: Partiot)

above 1500 m, it also grows as vigorously at lower altitudes on arabica, as well as on sensitive genotypes of robusta at sea level, in hot and humid regions. It should thus be considered a potential danger for **all** coffee-growing regions.

Chemical control is feasible and cupric compounds are effective, as is captafol. Less information is available about the effectiveness of systemic fungicides. Genetic control systems have not yet been thoroughly explored. However, in Cameroon, a classification of genotypes based on a collection of *C. arabica* has been made, using on a quantitative scale of 'field resistance'. Studies similar to those carried out on *H. vastatrix* should be undertaken.

The selection of varieties which are resistant to the two coffee leaf rusts are complicated by the fact that the resistances are not of similar types.

American leaf disease (American leaf spot)
This disease is caused by *Omphalia flavida* Maublanc and Rangel, which is synonymous with *Stilbum flavidum* Cke.; *Stibella flavida* (Cke.) Linde; *Mycena citricolor* (Berk. and Curt.) Sacc. It owes its name to its localisation in Latin America and the West Indies on the leaves of all coffee species, but mainly on *C. arabica*. It also attacks many other plants from various families such as Compositae and Leguminosae. The main symptoms are the appearance of numerous, roughly circular, brown spots. The affected tissues die and dry out, leaving many holes in the diseased leaves which then die. The fruiting bodies of the fungus, which are yellow and mucilaginous, appear particularly on the upper side of the lesions.

This disease is generally limited to only a few trees in the plantations and therefore causes little damage. It may be controlled by applications of lead arsenate.

Mancha mantecosa
This is another disease that is limited to *C. arabica* grown on the American continent. It is also normally restricted to a few trees per plantation. It can be recognised by its oily leaf spots. It was first considered to be a viral disease transmitted by aphids, but it is in fact caused by a species of *Colletotrichum*. It is not very serious although it has been discussed at length in Latin American literature.

Brown eye spot
This disease, caused by *Cercospora coffeicola* Berk. and Cooke, affects the leaves of any age of coffee tree. However, it is particularly threatening to young plants in seedbeds or nurseries. Infection is indicated by the development of lesions, which are brownish-grey at the edges, light coloured in the centre, and about 1 cm in diameter. If the trees are severely attacked, the loss of leaves affects their vigour. The disease also attacks the fruits. *C. arabica* is much more sensitive than the other species.

Brown eye spot is essentially a deficiency disease and the fungus only emphasises a physiological imbalance. Observations made in Cameroon and more complete studies in Colombia have shown that the primary cause of this disease is a lack of nitrogen. The leaves of shrubs which have been attacked are always yellowish. In the nursery, inadequate shade increases the sensitivity of the plant to this disease.

Control is best achieved through good plantation management and applications of mineral fertilisers with a predominance of nitrogen.

The thread diseases

Three Basidiomycetes are encountered on mis-managed coffee trees, i.e. those that have suffered from a lack of pruning and have been subjected to excessive shade and moisture:

- **White thread disease** (Black rot) caused by *Pellicularia* (Corticium) *koleroga* Cke. was observed for the first time in India, but it exists all over the world. It is not specific to coffee trees, having been found on species of *Citrus* and *Ficus*. The development of the fungus, which is at first superficial, begins with a whitish-grey film on the affected parts (branches, leaves, fruits). It forms fine mycelial strands which often attach themselves to several leaves and branches. The disease then penetrates the tissue causing their death. The leaves are detached from the branches, but remain suspended by the filaments that surround them;
- **Spider web disease** is caused by *Marasmius scandens* Mas. (*M. pulcher* [B. and Br.] Petch) and resembles a white-grey mass comprising a group of mycelial filaments on branches and leaves. The dead leaves are retained by the mycelial threads;
- **Horse hair disease** is caused by *Marasmius equicrinis* (Muell), and is characterised by the presence of long, black filaments that develop on the leaves and branches and on which the fruiting bodies of the fungus form.

These three diseases, which are not particularly serious, require only good crop management to be successfully controlled.

Branch anthracnose (die-back)

The main symptom this disease is the drying out of the branches, beginning at the tips and descending progressively towards the older parts. The leaves and fruits subsequently dry and fall off.

Many fungi have been identified and associated with this disease, the most common of which is *Colletotrichum*, but it is not the true causal agent since it only develops on tissues which are already dying. It should be noted that this is not the *Colletotrichum* species which causes coffee berry disease of *C. arabica*.

The causes of this disease are often environmental or are related to cropping practices such as excessive exposure to light, alternating hot and cold temperatures, poor adaptation to a particular type of climate, inadequate fertiliser applications, severe rust attacks with defoliation, poor soil maintenance, in fact, any factor that could contribute to weakening the plant. the disease can therefore be controlled by effective crop management.

Fig 76   Necrotic spots on leaves of *C. robusta* due to attacks by *Colletotrichum coffeanum* (Courtesy: Carpentier)

This fungus is also found on leaves on which brown spots with yellow edges appear. This is only a symptom of a physiological disorder. Certain clones of *C. robusta* are particularly sensitive when young and should not be used for general distribution to planters because although they perform better when fully grown, they will require a lot of attention to achieve maturity (Fig 76).

Other branch and leaf diseases

Coffee leper is caused by a micro-alga, *Cephaleuros virenscens* Kze., and causes velvety, reddish-brown spots to appear on the leaves. These spots often turn green due to the combined presence of a lichen and a fungus. It is therefore not a true disease.

Sooty mould appears as a blackish coating on the leaves and is produced by a fungus that develops from the sugary secretions of mealybugs. This mould screen affects the efficient functioning of the chlorophyll. The sooty mould will disappear when the mealybugs are destroyed.

Pink disease is caused by *Corticium salmonicolor* B. and Br. and appears as a pink membrane or filament on the bark of the branches, causing the branches to wither. It must not be confused with the damage caused by a pest, the short-hole borer (*Xyleborus morstatti* Hag.).

Diseases of the fruit

Coffee berry disease

This disease is caused by the fungus *Colletotrichum coffeanum* Noack sensu Hindorf. It can destroy up to 80 per cent of the total coffee production depending upon the year and the location, was first discovered in Kenya in 1922. It then spread to neighbouring countries. It is called 'Coffee berry disease' or CBD by British authors. It is known in the eastern part of Zaire

(Kivu), in Uganda, Burundi, Tanzania and Angola. It spread to Cameroon in 1957, and was only transmitted to Ethiopia in 1971.

It is so far confined to the African continent, and is also strictly specific to *C. arabica*. It is found on fruits at all stages of their development, but a reliable diagnosis can only be made when based on the symptoms which appear on young, green fruit. There are two forms found on the young fruit:

- 'Scab' is characterised by yellowish-buff-coloured spots, which are slightly flattened and irregularly shaped, and which develop into small, black lesions. These are the acervuli of the fungus. They cause a dry rot of the pulp, which evolves slowly, and is not serious unless the lesions are located close to the peduncle of the fruit, causing the fruit to fall;
- An 'active' form, with darker lesions, bears larger and more numerous acervuli which are capable of liberating vast quantities of spores. This form causes a moist rot to develop in the pulp and the young beans; these develop rapidly and may lead to the total destruction of the fruit in just a few days. During the final stages, the fruits which are still attached to the branches appear as small, black, brittle shells which can easily be crushed between the fingers.

There are no typical symptoms on ripe fruit. The form known as 'brown blight' appears to be similar to that of other *Colletotrichum* species that develop on over-ripe fruit. At this stage, the lesions have no impact on production as the beans are not affected (Fig 77).

Coffee berry disease attacks the fruits borne by plants that show healthy vegetative growth, having unblemished green leaves and fruits. It should not, therefore, be confused with damage caused by *Cercospora coffeicola* which develops on the leaves and fruits of nitrogen-deficient trees and whose lesions are very different (see later description).

Fig 77 Mummified clusters of very young *C. robusta* berries, following attacks by *Colletotrichum coffeanum* (Courtesy: Carpentier)

Moreover, although almost all of the fruits may be affected, the branches and leaves remain perfectly healthy. There are no leaf spots or die-back. This is an important factor to be considered when identifying the disease.

Although it is specific to high altitude *C. arabica*-growing regions near the equator, normally above 1500 m, the disease may sometimes also occur at lower altitudes. In Cameroon, for example, the most sensitive varieties such as Caturra growing at 1000 to 1100 m may be affected, whereas other varieties remain unharmed.

Disregarding particular genetic sensitivities, one theory concerning the development of this disease is that the pathogen cannot reach epidemic proportions at low altitudes due to the great speed at which the fruits develop, compared with their slow development at high altitudes, particularly during their maturation phase. This would be the reason for the absence of the disease at lower altitudes.

The spores of the pathogen released from the surfaces of fruits are dispersed by the rain and transported by moving vectors in the plantations, although wind does not appear to play a role in this dissemination.

The initial development of an epidemic is dependent upon the rains because the spores need water in order to germinate. However, further development is influenced to a large extent by characteristics that are intrinsic to the fruit. Results of studies undertaken in Kenya that were confirmed by more in-depth investigations in Cameroon, have in fact shown that the fruits' sensitivity is variable during the various stages of its development. This sensitivity begins four to six weeks after flowering, reaches a maximum between 8 and 12 weeks, then diminishes and disappears towards the 22nd week, which also marks the end of its maturation phase. At this stage, the lesions no longer develop and there are no new infections despite favourable climatic conditions such as rain. If new lesions do appear at the time of pre-ripening and ripening during the dry season, which is less favourable for the spread of the pathogen, they are the result of infections which had occurred at the end of the maturation phase of the fruit but had remained latent.

For this reason the disease is at its most dangerous during the period which overlaps between the rainy season, being favourable to the activity of the pathogen, and the sensitive stages of the berries.

A specific control programme was proposed in Cameroon as a result of these findings. The flowers which will provide the year's fruit are initiated during the dry season, three months before the first rains in March, which induce the flowers to open. It has been shown that by artificially inducing flowering by irrigation during the dry season, a month and a half to two months before the rains, and by maintaining the growth of the fruits by regular applications of water until the arrival of the rains, their sensitive period is partially eliminated. By the time the rainy season starts, the sensitive stages of the fruit have passed and they are likely to escape the disease.

This control technique, which is integrated into intensive crop production practices, ensures the complete fulfilment of the floral potential, while decreasing the risks that often prevent the flowers from opening properly. If irrigation is applied during the dry season when there is maximum sunlight, the branches grow two or three times faster than under natural conditions, thus promoting maximum crop production for the following year. However, it has the disadvantage of stimulating leaf rust damage as it provides early stimulation to the pathogen on the diseased leaves remaining from the previous season, at approximately the same time as the vegetative activity of the plant is initiated. Early irrigation therefore induces abundant pathogens to gather prematurely, which are ready to develop the moment the rains begin. The result is an early renewal of the infection, with an acceleration of the epidemic phase.

Nevertheless, it has also been shown that rust attacks can be controlled with two or three applications of fungicide. Early irrigation certainly shows significantly increased possibilities of controlling CBD, considering that the only available chemical control for CBD requires between five and seven applications.

The origin of the primary inoculum of CBD has initiated much discussion in the past. According to Nutman and Roberts in Kenya, the non-lignified branches contained the pathogen without incurring any damage, although the spores emitted from this carrier are the source of contamination of the berries. A treatment schedule was established by measuring spore emission from the branches in the laboratory over a period of time. This programme consisted of applying pre-floral treatments during the dry season. However, the treatments were not applied efficiently, and studies showed that the spores emitted by the branches did not belong to the strain responsible for the disease. This system was subsequently abandoned for post-floral treatments such as those recommended in Cameroon. They had to be initiated just after flowering to keep pace with the increasing frequency and intensity of the rains during the first 20 weeks of fruit development. Seven applications of a cupric compound or five applications with a captafol base are necessary for conditions in Cameroon. In Kenya, where the two fruiting periods result from two flowerings (March and July) and overlap constantly, only two applications are necessary.

These treatments are generally successful. Captafol is the most effective fungicide and it also has a stimulating effect on vegetative growth. The systemics, which are of the benomyl type, have now lost their effectiveness through the emergence of resistant strains.

The primary source of contamination is obvious in Kenya, where the diseased berries produced from one of the two annual flowerings contaminate those from the second flowering. In countries where there is only one annual flowering as in Cameroon, it has been shown that the berries produced from interseasonal flowering and also the unharvested fruits serve as a bridge between the two seasons. When the diseased fruits fall to the ground, the fruit penduncles that remain on the tree are also sources of contamination.

Resistant varieties have been actively sought, but the search was disappointing until the arrival of the disease in Ethiopia. The non-specific 'horizontal' resistance system that was discovered in Ethiopia (Robinson and

Van der Graaf) enabled a quantitative scale to be established. This system is more attractive than vertical resistance because it undoubtedly leads to more durable resistance. Ethiopia is the centre of diversity for the species *C. arabica* and it was therefore relatively easy to find numerous resistant genotypes. Some of these genotypes, fruits of ORSTOM – IRCC explorations, also exist in Cameroon.

The work done in Kenya on resistant varieties should also be mentioned, where the 'vertical' oligogenic resistance system was investigated (Van der Vossen). Early sensitivity tests were also finalised in Kenya by inoculating the young seedlings at the 'small soldier' stage.

Other diseases of the fruit

- The so-called '**brown eye spot**' or '**leaf spot**' disease, caused by *Cercospora coffeicola*, can also attack fruits where it is known as '**grey blotch**'. This disease indicates a nitrogen deficiency, as with its presence on leaves. Its symptoms must not be confused with those of arabica coffee berry disease. A *Cercospora* infestation, which is only found on yellowing fruits, appears as dark brown lesions which are very flat. Their surface has a velvety-softness which is visible to the naked eye in direct light, and they are the fruiting bodies of the fungus;
- *Fusarium* **infections** or diseases are responsible for reducing coffee harvests in Brazil, Africa and other countries;
- **verrucose disease** caused by *Sclerotinia fuckeliana* (de Bar.) Fuck;
- **mealy pod disease** caused by *Trachysphaera fructigena* Tab. and Bunt. Reddish-brown spots are first observed on the fruits, a white or pinkish floury coating then develops and the fruit dries out.*C. liberica* and *C. abeokutae* appear to be the most sensitive species.

Physiological problems and nutritional deficiencies

Previously it has been shown that the development of an appreciation of the biology, physiology, and ecological requirements of coffee has helped to confirm that many of the losses attributed to specific diseases in association with micro-organisms can also be linked to physiological problems or poor nutrition, which are the primary causes of these ailments.

However, in addition to these types of disease, the direct effect of the environment on the growth and productivity of the plant should also be noted. Coffee should only be cultivated under suitable ecological conditions.

Many coffee varieties are cultivated in the world today. The wide range of choice facilitates the selection of those best adapted to a particular region. Conversely, the wrong choice may have serious consequences for the future of a plantation.

An example of the problems which may be encountered is illustrated by the case of planters in the Ivory Coast in regions with insufficient rainfall, about 15 to 20 years ago, who substituted robusta coffee, which was not adapted to that climate, for kouilou, which was sensitive to tracheomycosis. It must be stressed that the production potential of selected species can only be maximised by placing them in an environment which is suitable to them, and by giving them the appropriate care and attention. If not, there is a serious risk of failure and disappointment.

The effects of low temperatures should also be included with physiological problems. The catastrophic damage that was caused over a few years in Brazilian plantations of the Paraña State by temperatures just above 0°C is one example. Although not quite as serious, low temperatures have also affected *C. arabica* plantations of Latin America other than Brazil, and in Africa. Leaves and shoots are particularly sensitive to cold. The former show marginal necroses and may be completely 'scorched', resulting in leaf fall. The lesions in the bark of the young trunks or the branches caused by low temperatures also provide pathways to fungal agents.

At the opposite end of the spectrum, high temperatures in dry climates also affect coffee. The trees are sensitive in these areas, as they are naturally adapted to more moist environmental conditions. Plantations under shade are less exposed. Thus in Cameroon, *C. arabica* plantations on soils with volcanic ash and pozzolana, which are very permeable, become completely defoliated after a few months following the onset of the dry season. The same phenomenon occurs in the Ivory Coast during certain years with *C. canephora* in the forested regions bordering the savanna.

In many instances where the leaves turn yellow and the fruits fall prematurely (berry shedding), links must be sought with physiological or nutritional problems. A more thorough knowledge of the physiology of the coffee tree will enable the causes of these symptoms, which are perhaps too often attributed to diseases and pests, to be detected.

Finally, nutritional deficiencies have been the subject of extensive studies over the past few years, during the course of which their symptoms and effects have been determined. The easiest deficiency to discern has been nitrogen deficiency, the symptom of which is uniformly chlorotic foliage. This can be easily remedied by an appropriate application of nitrogen. Other deficiencies, such as those of potassium, phosphorus, calcium, and magnesium, can ony be detected with any certainty by foliar diagnosis or soil analysis. The same is true for trace element deficiencies such as iron, zinc, magnesium, copper, sulphur, etc., which must be dealt with by specialists.

Insects and other pests

The list of insect pests of coffee which have been recorded throughout the world is very long and has appeared in works by various specialists (see

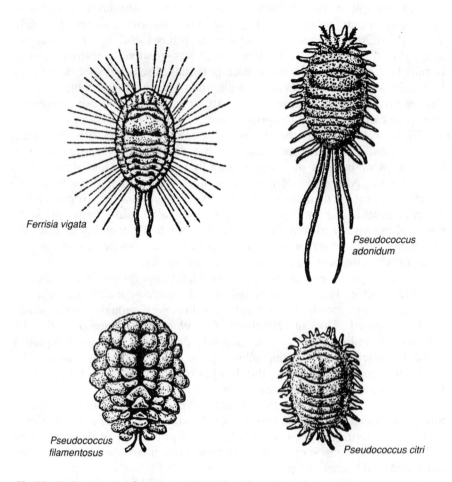

Ferrisia vigata

Pseudococcus
adonidum

Pseudococcus
filamentosus

Pseudococcus citri

Fig 78   Various scales found on coffee (after Green)

bibliography). The following section will concentrate on the most widespread pests that are responsible for the most serious damage in coffee plantations. The pests are listed according to the types of plant tissue which they attack.

·Pests which infest all plant tissues

Vayssiere reported that about 50 species of **scales** are known to infest the various parts of the coffee tree. The most important are: *Coccus viridis* Green, or **green scale**, which is yellowish-green, and is found in all the tropical regions of the globe. The damage it causes is mainly due to the presence of a toxin in its saliva. *Pseudococcus citri* Risso or **mealy bug** is just as widespread. The latter, like all Pseudococcinae, is covered with a waxy, floury coating (Fig 78). These two polyphagous insects attack all coffee species indiscriminately.

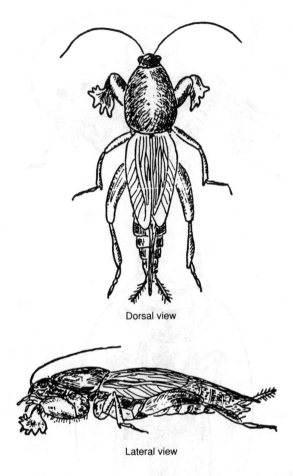

Dorsal view

Lateral view

Fig 79   Adult African mole cricket *Gryllotalpa africana* Beuv. (after Lavabre)

Control is nowadays more effective due to the use of systemic insecticides. It is also advisable to destroy the ants which are vectors of the scales (see phthiriosis).

Pests of the roots

Several species of **cricket**, including **mole crickets** (Orthoptera) are harmful to young coffee plants in nurseries or plantations. These include the African mole cricket (*Gryllotalpa africana* Beauv.) and *Brachytripes membranaceus* Drury.

The former species is very similar to the European garden cricket. It digs tunnels in the soil and severs any roots which it encounters in passing. It is brown, about 30 mm long, and its hind legs are powerful and well adapted to underground living (Fig 79). The latter is a large insect, 4 or 5

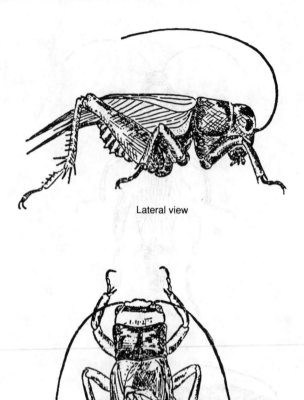

Lateral view

Dorsal view

Fig 80 *Brachytripes membranaceus* Drury. (after Lavabre)

cm long (Fig 80). It leaves the tunnels at night to collect its food, which consists mainly of young plants, severed at the base.

These insects can be destroyed by using poisoned bait. Lavabre recommends a mixture of equal parts of maize flour and rice bran, which is then mixed with 25 g of Lindane per 10 kg. The mixture is moistened and spread between the rows. The soil can also be treated by dusting with powders. Either Lindane or Dieldrin are recommended at a rate of 500 g of active material per hectare. The use of these pesticides are now prohibited in Europe, but they are still used overseas in special cases for the control of insects belonging to the order Orthoptera.

Termite populations (Isoptera) first attack the bark, then the wood of the coffee trees, entering through earthy tunnels which they excavate along the trunk and branches. To exterminate them, Lavabre recommends applying about 2 to 4 g of Lindane per tree or Aldrin at 10 to 20 g. These products are incorporated into the soil by hoeing.

Several species of **Nematode** attack the root systems of coffee trees. The microscopic larvae penetrate the roots, causing galls to form and the tissues to rot. The roots are eventually destroyed and as a reaction the coffee tree produces a mass of rootlets in the collar region. The nutrition of the shrub is at first retarded and finally stops; the foliage turns yellow and falls. According to Vayssiere, the following species of nematodes are most harmful to coffee: *Pratylenchus coffeae* Zimm., which is cosmopolitan and polyphagous; *Heterodera marioni* Conn. (*H. radicicola* Mueler) and *Tylenchus similis* Cobb. However, many other species are possibly present in some regions.

Nowadays many highly effective products are available to control these soil pests, namely Dieldrin, which is recommended by Lavabre, at 500 l/ha, or Etroprophos, which is much more toxic, at 10 kg/ha. The search for nematode-resistant varieties of canephoras and their hybrids is also an important selection criterion in South American research centres.

Pests of the trunk and branches

The trunk of the coffee tree may harbour many longicorn beetles, commonly referred to as **borers**. Vayssiere describes at least 60 species. The worst damage is caused by the following species:

Trunk borer (*Bixadus sierricola* White)

This trunk borer is not specific to the coffee tree. It is found extensively in afforested regions of West and Central Africa. The eggs are laid in the cracks of the bark, near the collar. The larvae penetrate the wood by digging a circular tunnel, which is at first horizontal, then vertical until it reaches the collar and further down to the taproot. Pupation occurs at one end of the tunnel. Development to maturity usually takes five to six months, but it can also take over a year and sometimes longer.

The larvae are approximately 5 cm long, yellowish-white with a brown head. The adults are between 20 and 28 mm long. Their body is brown, except for the antennae which are white at the base. A short, sharp spine is found on either side of the thorax (Fig 81).

Considerable damage to mature coffee trees is caused by rapid reproduction. There have been cases where coffee plantations have been destroyed

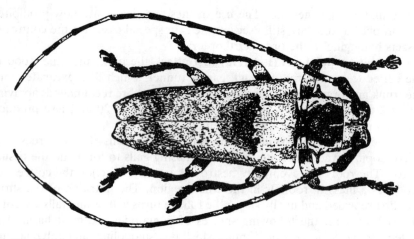

Fig 81 *Bixadus sierricola* White. (after Vayssiere)

by up to 50 per cent by massive attacks, in which some shrubs harboured over 20 borers. Nutritional problems caused by the girdling and the presence of numerous tunnels are the reasons for loss of harvests and the decline of affected trees. As a preventive and curative measure, Lavabre recommends a wash of residual insecticide applied with a brush to the trunk at a height of 0.50 m. This should contain 0.5 per cent Dieldrin emulsion (1 l of Dieldrin at 15 per cent in 29 l of water).

White stem borer (*Anthores leuconotus* Pasc.)

To the layman, this longicorn beetle looks very similar to the preceding one. Its biology is also comparable, but its geographical range is different. In fact, *Anthores leuconotus* is particularly widespread in the high altitude regions of East Africa, particularly Kenya, which are less humid than the West Coast. Similar methods of control are recommended.

Black stem borer (*Apate monachus* Fabr.)

The adults as opposed to the larvae of this Bostrychid do the most damage to coffee trees. The eggs are laid on open wounds and the adults excavate tunnels in the living tissue to feed on the wood. Their presence is discerned by small pellets of sawdust at the foot of the trees.

The adult is 10 to 19 mm long. Its cylindrical body is completely black and the elytra are ornamented with large spots in the creases (Fig 82). It is very widespread in West Africa. A related species, *A. terebrans* Pall, which is well known in Africa, has also been encountered in Jamaica.

Lavabre recommends the same Dieldrin-based treatment as specified for *Anthores leuconotus*.

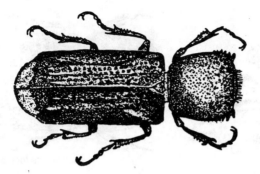

Fig 82   *Apate monachus* (after Lavabre)

Branchlet beetle (*Xyleborus morstatti* Hag., *Xylosandrus compactus* Eich.)

A certain number of related species are encountered in almost all the coffee-growing regions of the world. Vayssiere cites: *X. morigerus* (*X. coffeae*), Far East, East Africa, and Madagascar; *X. brasiliensis* Eg., Brazil; *X. discolor* Blan., Near East; *X. perforans* Woll., Surinam; *X. raripilis* Fauv., New Caledonia; *X. torquatus* Eich., South America.

Lavabre considers the beetle *X. morstatti* to be the most harmful of the *C. canephora* coffee pests in East Africa at the present time. He gives the following description:

> '**Adult**: the female *X. morstatti* Hag is 1.6 mm long on average; the male, which is smaller, is about 0.9 mm long. The females are shiny, oval-shaped and black and the males are light brown. They are covered with fawn-coloured soft hairs which can be clearly seen with a magnifying glass (Fig 83). The female has wings, the male is wingless (apterous).
>
> **Larvae**: the size varies depending upon the degree of development. They are about 2 mm to 2.3 mm long when completely developed, white, and without legs.'

The female is solely responsible for attacking the branches. She digs a circular tunnel less than 1 mm in diameter in the branch which penetrates the heartwood; she then tunnels in both directions. The eggs are laid at the end of this tunnel. The larvae (30 to 50 per egg-laying period) feed upon a fungus, *Ambrosia*. The spores, which adhere to the female's body, have been sown in the tunnel. The development cycle is 30 to 35 days.

Damage to the coffee trees is always very serious. It is apparent due to the presence of numerous dried, blackened branches. The orthotropous branches (suckers) are particularly sensitive. The nature of the attack is confirmed by making longitudinal cuts in affected branches and observing the tunnels excavated by the insect.

There is, as yet, no effective means of control. The removal and incineration of the dead branches has little effect if the attack is serious. Insecticides

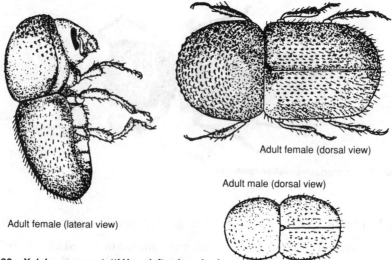

Adult female (dorsal view)

Adult male (dorsal view)

Adult female (lateral view)

Fig 83   *Xyleborus morstatti* Hag. (after Lavabre)

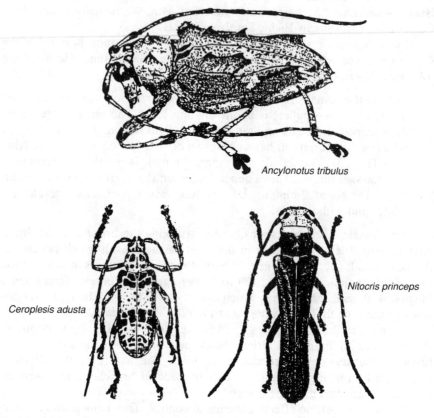

Ancylonotus tribulus

Ceroplesis adusta

Nitocris princeps

Fig 84   Other coffee tree borers (after Lepesme)

have not had satisfactory results, due to the difficulty of reaching the insects at any stage in the tunnels. The use of systemics has not been very successful, as the beetle feeds off the *Ambrosia* fungus and not the tissues of the coffee tree.

However, it seems that the establishment of the beetle is linked to the general nutritional status of the coffee tree. Cropping operations that may favour their establishment (mulch) may also help to eliminate them. Research is also being carried out on coffee trees that show some resistance.

Due to the general nature of this book, this study of coffee tree borers is limited to those species currently reputed to have the most harmful effects. However, Lavabre mentions some pests that are fairly prevalent in Africa. These are three other Cerambycid coleoptera: *Ceroplesis adusta* Serv., *Nitocris (Dyrphia) princeps* Jordan and *Ancylonotus tribulus* Cost. (Fig 84).

Pests of the leaves

The caterpillars of several Lepidoptera attack the leaves of the coffee tree. The most harmful seem to be the *Epicampoptera* or 'rat tail' caterpillars and leaf miners such as *Leucoptera coffeina* W.

Rat tail caterpillars (*Epicampoptera* spp.)

Several species of caterpillar of the genus *Epicampoptera* are found on coffee trees in tropical Africa: *E. strandi* Bryk in West and Central Africa; *E. marantica* Tams. in East Africa and Congo; *E. andersoni* Tams. in Central and East Africa; *E. vulvornata* Hering in the Congo.

The caterpillars are easily identified by their caudal, filamentous appendix, which is 1 to 2 cm long, and a semi-globulous green or multi-coloured bulge, located behind the head. The colour evolves from green to red-brown or yellow-green. They are between 35 and 45 mm long. The butterflies are grey and have a wing-span of 2 to 3 cm (Figs 85 and 86).

The brick red eggs are laid on the underside of the leaves, and are arranged in piles of 10 to 20 eggs. The caterpillars have a voracious appetite. They are estimated to absorb at least the equivalent of their own weight every day. It is obviously at this stage that the damage to the leaves is observed. In Africa (Central African Republic, Cameroon, etc.) entire plantations of several dozen hectares have been reduced to mere skeletons in a few weeks. The harvests are generally lost, and in the case of repeated attacks, the shrubs wither away. As the development cycle of the insect is about one month long, damage can be considerable (Fig 87).

DDT has been used in the past and was remarkably effective in controlling caterpillars. This insecticide, which is now banned from use for agricultural purposes, has been replaced by other equally effective products. One of the most effective of these is Endosulfan at 400 g ai/ha. Other effective products are: Dursban, Fenitrothion, Fenthion.

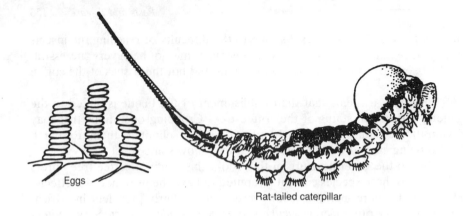

Eggs

Rat-tailed caterpillar

Butterfly

Fig 85 *Epicampoptera strandi* Bryk. (after Lavabre)

Fig 86 *Epicampoptera tamisi* caterpillars (Courtesy: Boulard)

Fig 87 *C. robusta* leaf eaten by *Epicampoptera strandi* (Courtesy: Boulard)

(154)

Experiments have also been carried out on biological control with a bacillus (*B. thuringiensis*). The use of new serotypes enables the extension of this method to be contemplated.

Coffee pyralid (*Dichocrocis crocodera* Meyr.)

The caterpillars of this moth are 25 to 30 mm long, and are initially grouped together between two leaves which are joined by threads, eventually becoming isolated in a folded or rolled up fragment of the leaf. Pupation occurs at the base of the trees. The adult butterfly has a wing-span of 20 to 30 mm. Its yellow wings are striped with ochre-coloured lines.

This pest exists in West Africa, but it is particularly widespread in the Congo, where it is found on all coffee species. The duration of the life cycle is about two and a half months and there may be four generations per year.

Lavabre gives the following advice for control: The most favourable time to control this pest is either when the caterpillars emerge, when they are about to join two young leaves, or at the time the colonies disperse. Suggested treatments applied as a spray are:

- 50 per cent Fenitrothion-based, 75 cc/100 l of water;
- 55 per cent Fenthion, 75 cc/100 l of water.

In the most severely infested parts of the plantation, it is necessary to clean the ground thoroughly and to burn the debris, as the caterpillars turn into pupae on the ground under the leaves and in the grass.

Leaf miners (*Leucoptera coma* Ghesq.; *L. meyrieki* Ghesq.; *L. caffeina* Wsh.)

The *Leucoptera* caterpillars dig tunnels in the parenchyma of the leaves, beneath the epidermis. Their presence is apparent due to the lighter colouring of the leaf along the course of the tunnels. The upper epidermis, which becomes isolated from the parenchyma, dries up and dies. The leaf becomes brown and curled. This decrease in the active photosynthetic surface of the leaf causes nutritional problems, which can be serious if the attack is severe.

This pest is found in all parts of Africa. In Latin America and the West Indies, a related species, *Leucoptera coffeella* Guer. Men. is responsible for the damage caused in *C. arabica* plantations.

Two insecticides, Parathion in powder form on the foliage, and Disyston, which is incorporated into the soil, control this pest effectively. However, these have since been largely replaced by synthetic Pyrethrins.

Coffee sphinx moth (*Cephonodes hylas* L.)

The caterpillars of this Lepidoptera also feed on the leaves of coffee. They are green with a blue dorsal line, and grow to about 6 or 7 cm in length when mature.

The butterfly has a wing-span of about 50 to 65 mm. Its body is a bright green colour, and its wings are transparent with brown edges (Fig 88). The damage caused depends on how extensively the pest has spread, but it is generally very localised. The sphinx is found in West Africa, Congo, the Far East and Madagascar.

The leaf skeletoniser (*Leucoplema* [= *Eplimema*] *dohertyi* Varr.)

The larvae of this Lepidoptera feed on the leaves of coffee, removing the lamina and leaving only the veins. It is a greyish caterpillar with numerous superficial protuberances, each of which is covered with hair. It lives for about two weeks on the underside of the leaves.

This pest attacks all coffee species. In East Africa it is considered to be one of the most serious pests of coffee. It can be controlled with products that have been recommended for other Lepidoptera.

Aphids

Vayssiere attributes the damage inflicted on coffee by aphids to a single species: *Toxoptera camelliae* Kalt (*Aphis coffeae* N., *T. aurantii* B. de F.). This aphid, which is very widespread, is polyphagous. In addition to coffee, it is found on tea, cocoa and citrus amongst others. It feeds on the sap of the plants which it attacks. Its punctures cause malformations, blisters on young leaves, and necroses on young branches.

The adults, both winged and wingless, are 16 to 17 mm long and have a brown body (Fig 89). The attacks of these small insects on coffee trees are rarely serious. They are controlled by dusting with Lindane, Parathion, and/or Diazinon powder (Lavabre).

Variegated grasshopper (*Zonocerus variegatus* L.)

This grasshopper, which has a foetid smell when crushed, is 45 to 55 mm. in length. Its body is a bright yellow-orange colour with multicoloured spots. The outer wings are green or yellowish (Fig 90).

Damage is caused at all stages of development. Young larvae at different stages and adults feed on leaves and young shoots. In very serious attacks, the coffee trees may be completely defoliated.

Lavabre advises insecticide treatments at the gregarious larval stage, which facilitates localised applications in small areas. The most efficient insecticides are Dieldrin in powder form (0.025 per cent) and Fenitrothion (0.1 per cent). Dieldrin at 100 g ai/ha or Fenitrothion should be used when larger areas need to be treated, as is necessary after the larvae have dispersed.

Thrips (*Diarthrothrips coffeae* Will and *Physothrips xanthocerus* Hood.)

These small insects which belong to the order Thysanoptera, are normally fairly harmless. However, they can become dangerous if allowed to multiply rapidly. In East Africa (Kenya and Uganda), they pose a permanent threat which planters need to be constantly aware of. They suck the sap from young

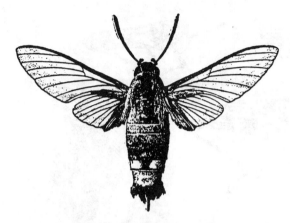

Fig 88   *Cephonodes hylas* L. (after Vayssiere)

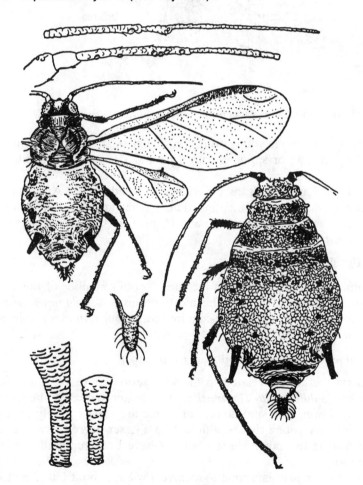

Fig 89   *Toxoptera camelliae*, coffee aphid (after Vayssiere)

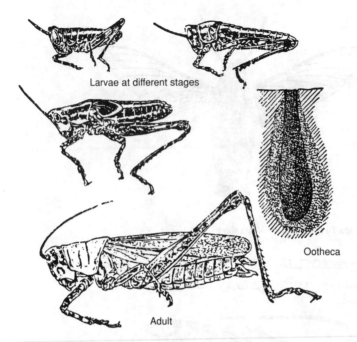

Larvae at different stages

Ootheca

Adult

Fig 90 *Zonocerus variegatus*, variegated grasshopper (after Lavabre)

shoots, leaves and even young fruit, causing them to dry out. They are controlled by dusting or spraying with Lindane, Diazinon, Fenitrothion or Fenthion.

Two other Hemipterous insects are encountered in East Africa and the Congo (Leo.), and should be mentioned here. They are *Habrochila ghesquieri* which feeds on leaves of arabica, and *H. placida* (Coffee lacebug) which feeds on robusta leaves.

Pests of the flowers and fruit

The Hemiptera (bugs and aphids) include a certain number of flower and fruit pests which affect coffee. The most serious are *Volumnus obscurus* Popp., *Lygus* spp. and the rainbow-coloured coffee bug (*Antestiopsis lineaticolis intricata* Ghesq. and Car.)

Mirids (*Volumnus obscurus* Papp. and *Lygus* spp.)

These insects are closely related to the very serious pests of young cocoa tree branches (*Sahlbergella, Distantiella*, etc.), better known by the name of capsids. The flower buds and flowers of coffee are most severely attacked, together with very young shoots, although to a lesser degree. These attacks cause the flowers to abort. Massive attacks have been reported in Gabon and Cameroon.

Volumnus obscurus is a small, green-yellow bug, about 6 to 7 mm long which thrives in humid, swampy regions where it multiplies. It migrates during the dry season, seeking food. These bugs can be controlled by spraying with Fenitrothion, Fenthion, or Pyrethrum, as is recommended for *Antestiopsis*.

Rainbow-coloured coffee bug (*Antestiopsis lineaticolis intricata* Ghesq. and Car.)

This insect, which was formerly classified in the *Antestia* genus, is one of the most formidable pests of arabica coffee in Africa and South East Asia. It causes considerable damage in East Africa (Kenya, Uganda, Tanzania).

The adult is about 7 mm long. Its body is brown or bronze with yellow-orange patterns (Fig 91). The eggs are laid on the underside of the leaves, in groups of 12 to 15, arranged in rows. According to Vayssiere, each female can lay an average of 10 to 14 batches of eggs. The young larvae, which are rainbow-coloured, are about 1 mm long, but at the fifth moulting they will have reached a length of about 3 mm (Fig 92). The total evolutionary cycle is about 8 to 10 weeks but may be noticeably shorter in hot regions.

Damage is caused both by larvae (at all stages) and adults. The young larvae pierce the young shoots and the flower buds, causing them to abort. More mature larvae and adults pierce the young berries, causing one or both of the ovaries of the fruits to abort.

Harvest losses can be very high (fruits are either atrophied, or have

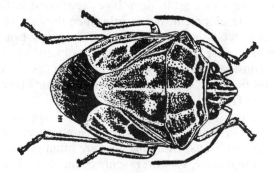

Fig 91   Female *Antestiopsis lineaticollis intricata* Ghesq. and Car.

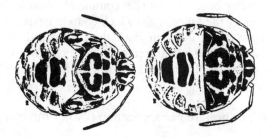

Fig 92   *Antestiopsis lineaticollis intricata* Ghesq. and Car. at the fifth moulting (after Carayon)

empty loculi). The growth problems caused by the damage to the buds and young shoots provoke a characteristic proliferation of branches (witches broom) with progressive degeneration, which also adversely affects productivity.

To control these insects, which prefer dense, shady foliage, the leaves should be thinned, to enable air and sunlight to penetrate more readily. When the level of infestation exceeds 1.5 bugs per tree, the use of pesticides is essential, either 50 per cent Fenitrothion or 55 per cent Fenthion, using about 75 cc in 100 l of water. Formulations with 6 per cent Pyrethrum are also effective.

Berry moth (*Thiliptoceras octoguttalis* Feld.)

The adult is a 10 to 15 mm long, silver-grey butterfly. It lays its eggs on flower buds or young fruit. The caterpillars penetrate the fruit, causing them to dry out, remaining attached to the branches by threads.

Berry borer (*Stephanoderes hampei* Ferr., beandorer, broca do café, etc.)

The coffee berry borer is undoubtedly the coffee pest that has caused and still causes the most damage to the crop. This insect, which is originally from Africa, is today almost cosmopolitan.

The adult measures about 1.5 mm in length, and is black-brown in colour. Its body is spiked with dark bristles. The larvae are whitish, crescent-shaped and without limbs. The evolutionary cycle lasts about one month.

The adult female lays its eggs in deep holes excavated in the fruits at various stages of their development, but mainly when they are three to four months old. The larvae feed on the endosperm of the young beans, through which they dig tunnels. One drupe may contain as many as five to eight larvae which cause considerable damage. The adult females leave the fruits after fertilisation and the cycle begins again, with new fruits being attacked by the next generation (Fig 93).

Damage to the harvests can be considerable. It is apparent from the considerable loss of yield (rotten, wasted fruit, empty beans, etc.) and a decrease in quality (pitted beans). National laws are often generally tolerant of such a shortcoming in quality. However, some countries such as the USA, enforce their laws more rigorously and the definition of flaws as well as the bean characteristic specifications, are more strictly regulated.

To control the berry borer, Lavabre recommends a preliminary harvest which involves collecting the fallen fruits which contain pests, and harvesting the infested fruits from the shrubs. These are then destroyed. To treat severe infestation, he recommends chemical treatments, which have now been standardised, the most effective of which is spraying (or fogging) with one of the following products:

- 800 g of Lindane per hectare per application (two or three applications at 10-day intervals);
- 700 g of Parathion per hectare per application (two to three applications at 10-day intervals).

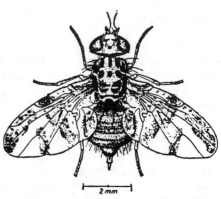

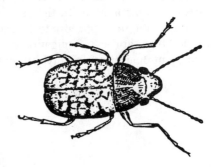

Fig 93 *C. robusta* berry attacked by
Stephanoderes hampei showing
larvae, nymph and imago (Courtesy:
Boulard)

Fig 94 *Ceratitis capitata* Wied. (after
Vayssiere)

Fig 95 *Araecerus fasciculatus* Deg.
(after Lepesme)

Endosulfan or Thiodan at 700 g of active ingredient per hectare gives
excellent results, which are even more effective than those of the preceding
formulations.

The berry borer attacks all coffee species, but *C. canephora* and
C. arabica are attacked much more severely than others. It is important to
note that the parasite can survive in beans in storage if the level of humidity
is above 12.5 per cent.

Biological control has been attempted on many occasions using several
hyperparasites and an entomophagous fungus. However, the results have not
yet been significant.

Fruit flies

Two species of fruit flies are commonly found in coffee fruits in Kivu and
East Africa. They are *Pterandrus fasciventris* Bez. and *Trirhithrunis coffeae*.
Ceratitis capitata Weid. (Fig 94) has been observed in East Africa. Eggs are
usually laid in the fruits as they begin to ripen. The larvae develop in the
pulp. These insects, along with some others like the *Antestiopsis* sp., are
responsible for the presence of a saprophytic bacteria in the cherries which
gives them a so-called 'earthy' or 'potato' taste.

Storage pests

Damage to stored coffee is usually due to the bruchid beetle, *Araecerus fasciculatus* Deg. The berry borer, *Stephanoderes hampei*, which is often thought to be responsible for the damage, is really a pest of the mature fruit. It can only survive in the beans for a few weeks if their moisture content is less than 12.5 per cent.

Araecerus fasciculatus Deg. (Fig 95) is a small, brown or black Coleopterous insect, about 2.5 to 4 mm long, and is somewhat similar to a bruchid beetle. It thrives in tropical regions where it attacks various stocks of foodstuffs including seeds of coffee, cacao and maize; into which it digs tunnels. Inadequately dried beans are particularly vulnerable to attack. The insect proliferates rapidly, the life cycle being 29 to 40 days in duration.

As a preventive measure, Lavabre strongly advises drying the beans thoroughly, keeping the stores clean, and ensuring the absence of potential sources of contamination. In the case of slight attacks, he advises spraying or dusting with the appropriate insecticides. Serious attacks can only be controlled by a thorough fumigation under a polyethylene cover or using low pressure equipment with methyl bromide.

8 *Horticultural improvement*

General information

Upon closely examining a coffee plantation, it is apparent that no two shrubs
are alike. This is particularly obvious with species other than *C. arabica*,
even to the undiscerning observer. Coffee trees can readily be distinguished
from one another by their macroscopic and morphological characteristics
such as size, leaf and fruit forms, length of the internodes, but closer examination and investigation reveals even more differences, including productivity, flowering and fruiting periods, resistance to epiphytes, percentage
of fruit components, pulp composition, thickness of the epicarp, size and
shape of the beans.

Some of these individual variations occur as a result of the natural
environment, such as microclimate and soil, or cropping practices used, such
as shade and fertilisation. These are known as **phenotypic characteristics**.
Others are inherited or **genetic** characteristics. Phenotypic characteristics are
not transmissible to the progeny and either evolve or disappear when the
factors that had first caused them to appear alter. On the contrary, genetic
characteristics are the expression of individual genes and may thus be handed
down to the progeny.

Apart from these minor variations, it is not unusual for isolated types
to appear in a plantation, which can be clearly distinguished from their
neighbours by very pronounced characteristics such as colour of fruits,
branching habit or leaf form. If the environment or cropping practices do
not appear to be the cause of these anomalies, they are most likely to be
mutants or **natural hybrids**.

The search for shrubs in a population that have certain desirable criteria,
studying them and their progeny (**selection**), creating new varieties that combine the characteristics possessed by two or more individuals (**hybridisation**),
and the artificial creation of mutants, are all within the realm of genetics,
which is the science used in the improvement of plant material.

The objective of this research, which is the work of plant breeders and
specialised agronomists, is to create new or improved varieties available to
farmers. These varieties should be able to adapt to different environments
and also combine high productivity with resistance to pests and diseases. An

(163)

improvement in the quality of the bean and beverage is also desirable. The ultimate aims are to lower the production costs of coffee and improve the product.

The importance of this research cannot be sufficiently emphasised, particularly with regard to periods of economic stagnation, which has been the case with coffee for a number of years. Producers can only confront such crises by **increasing yields** and **improving quality**. A poorly maintained coffee plantation may produce an average of 500 kg/ha of clean coffee, whereas a plantation with improved or selected plants, which are efficiently managed, may normally yield 1000 to 1500 kg, and even as much as 2 to 3 tonnes per hectare. Yields of this magnitude could reduce the production costs of coffee by between 33 and 50 per cent.

Methods of coffee improvement

The chromosome complement of coffee is well known from the results of Brazilian (Piza, Krug., Carvalho), and Dutch (Cramer) research workers. The basic (**haploid** or '**n**') chromosome number is 11. However, while most species, including *C. canephora*, are **diploids** with 2 n = 22 chromosomes, *C. arabica* is normally **tetraploid** with 4 n = 44 chromosomes. Nevertheless, although of little practical importance, there are some exceptions to this rule with **polyploid** varieties, such as *C. arabica*, var. *bullata* Cramer: 6 n = 66 and 8 n = 88, etc.

The genetic differences between the two main species, *C. arabica* and *C. canephora*, explain why it is practically impossible under natural conditions to create fertile hybrids between the two. In laboratory studies, geneticists resort to a technique which consists of doubling the number of chromosomes of the diploid species (2 n = 22) by treatment with colchicine, in order to facilitate crossings with tetraploid varieties of *C. arabica* (4 n = 44).

From a practical point of view, there is also a fundamental difference between the tetraploid *C. arabica* and all other species, in that it is, in fact, **self-fertile**, whereas *C. canephora*, like other diploid species, is **self-sterile** and must be **cross-pollinated**. In other words, *C. arabica* coffee flowers can be fertilised by their own pollen, while those of *C. canephora* have to be fertilised by pollen from flowers on other shrubs, in principle of the same species. This dominant trait involves the use of radically different methods for the improvement of the two main species of coffee. Some initial operations, however, are common to the two main species. For example, for the original parent material, the plant breeder must have a sample collection from all the trees found in regional plantations. If necessary, these plants may be subjected to observations for several years, depending upon the selection criteria being used. The operations that follow differ, depending upon whether a self-fertilising *C. arabica*, or other cross-pollinated species is being used as parent material.

Self-fertile coffee (*C. arabica*)

Productivity is obviously one of the most important criteria in coffee selection, if not the most important. Unfortunately, various experiments have shown that this characteristic has a complex heredity and a shrub chosen at random, even if it is not very productive, has as much chance as a specially selected shrub of producing a highly selective progeny. Through work carried out over a 13-year period at Mulungu Station, Snoeck and Petit have shown that the distribution for productivity of individual trees arising from a single mother tree is normal and complies with the law of Gauss. They are also of the opinion that instead of making observations over long periods of time, during which harvests are carefully weighed, it may be sufficient to make one large selection based on criteria, the heredity of which has already been established, for example, bean size, and to select, from the progeny, the most favourable lines, which would then be tested in comparative trials.

This finding enables the time required for a genealogical selection to be reduced. The steps involved in the procedure are as follows:

1 Choose the mother tree candidates.
2 Propagate the trees retained by seedlings.
3 Study the first progeny (F_1) (comparative trials) of the lines descended from the mother trees (six years).
4 Create seed tree orchards by vegetative propagation, using the mother trees retained.

It is therefore feasible to produce selected seedlings in about 12 years, compared to 25 years with the earlier techniques, based on the transmissability of the productivity characteristic.

However, improving *C. arabica* by this method may not lead to very favourable results, given the homogenous nature of the original plant material. The best results have been obtained with inter-varietal hybrids. Brazilian geneticists have worked extensively in this area. The sensational results obtained in the selection of the 'Mundo Novo' variety, which is a hybrid between two varieties of *C. arabica*: 'Bourbon' and 'Sumatra', are proof of this.

Mutations may also be potentially useful in the improvement of coffee trees. The success of selected lines of the 'Caturra' variety, which was considered to be a spontaneous mutant, should be noted in this context.

Self-sterile coffee trees (other species)

Two methods of selection may be adopted. One is the vegetative method, which favours selection of clones with desirable characteristics. The other is the generative method, the objective of which is to select clones that may produce favourable progenies when crossed. In the former method, the clones are perpetuated through the distribution of cuttings from selected clones. In the latter, selected seedlings are distributed from seed tree orchards made up of clones retained as parent trees.

The vegetative method achieves more rapid results, and has the advantage of faithfully conserving all of the characteristics observed in the clone, including those which show variation in the generative progeny, for example, productivity and resistance to various unknown factors. It has a disadvantage, however, in that it requires the appropriate equipment for cutting operations, and these are large and costly on a commercial scale.

- The fundamental advantage of the generative method, which takes longer than the vegetative method, is the distribution of the selected plant in the form of seedlings, which does not interfere with the planters' normal routine and is much less costly than distributing rooted cuttings. The IFCC (1963) proposed the following order of operations for both methods of selection:

Vegetative selection	Generative selection
	1 Compile collections
	2 Observe shrubs
3 Select elite plants as a source of cutting material	3 Select parent clones a) Carry out general compatability test for the combination (top cross)
4 Create plant collection as germplasm resource	
5 Carry out comparative trials in different locations	b) Carry out specific compatability test for the combination (test cross)
6 Choose selected clones	
	4 Establish biclonal or polyclonal seed tree orchards of selected seedlings

Some of the results obtained from the work on coffee improvement in Brazil, resulted in the selection of lines of *C. arabica* Bourbon Amarello and the identification of the mutant 'Caturra', and 'Mundo Novo', both exceptionally high producers. Numerous hybrids were also obtained from multiple combinations between the varieties of *C. arabica*, although this work is still at the experimental stage. Further results obtained include: in Kenya, the selection of the Kent variety which was imported from India, also of bronze-tipped types; in the former Belgian Congo, the selection of so-called INEAC lines; in India, selection and hybridisation of *Hemileia*-resistant types; and in Indonesia, the selection of hybrids of *C. congensis* × *C. robusta* or 'Congusta'.

Work undertaken by the IFCC in this area has been particularly successful. For example, in Madagascar, on large commercial plantations, the clonal progenies of certain selections of *C. canephora* and the hybrids *C. congensis* × *C. robusta* have produced between 2.5 and 3 tonnes per hectare of coffee, with large beans, representing a yield of more than 20 g for 100 beans. In the Ivory Coast, yields using the progenies of certain selected robustas and kouilous have been no less spectacular. The same holds true in the Central African Republic where certain robusta clones, which were established both there and in Cameroon, have a potential yield of over 2 tonnes per hectare.

These few examples illustrate the considerable advances made by teams of specialists in the area of plant improvement. The existing lack of a fundamental understanding of the cytology of species other than arabica, combined with the fact that the work was not properly implemented in the early stages, are the factors mainly responsible for the delay in the selection of canephoras.

Interspecific hybrids

In introducing this subject of interspecific hybridisation, the existence of a natural hybrid: *C. canephora* var. *Ugandae* × *C. congensis*, commonly referred to as 'Congusta' should be mentioned. This hybrid was first found in Java. It is very hardy and appears to be flood-resistant. Introduced into Madagascar for that reason, it is now widely cultivated in the valleys of the East coast which are subject to serious flooding during the rainy season.

Agronomists have sought a solution to the problems associated with climate encountered when growing interspecific hybrid forms of *C. arabica* in lowland, hot, very humid tropical zones, the most promising of these being the hybrid *C. arabica* × *C. canephora*.

The first attempts made in the 1950s were disappointing since the natural obstacle of chromosomal incompatability between the two species was not known at that time. The natural hybrid between *C. arabica*, a self-fertile tetraploid (4 n = 44 chromosomes) and *C. canephora*, a cross-fertilised diploid (2 n = 22 chromosomes) results in a triploid strain which has three sets of chromosomes, affecting meiotic division. As a result it is not very fertile or may even be sterile.

This problem was solved by the use of colchicine. The chromosomal duplication of *C. canephora* which resulted from the application of this technique made it possible to obtain tetraploid individuals of *C. canephora* that could be crossed with *C. arabica* to obtain fertile hybrids (Fig 30). Capot (1962) produced the first of these hybrids, which were given the name 'Arabusta'.

The characteristics of the first hybrids were not completely satisfactory. A long, meticulous selection and back-crossing operation was therefore undertaken. The main objectives were to increase fertility and the size of the beans, to reduce the percentage of peaberries, and to improve the quality of the processed beverage. Slow improvements over several years of diligent research work, have eventually resulted in Arabustas with commercially satisfactory quality and fertility.

The major problem in this work on improvement arises from the necessity to maintain a judicious balance between the different genetic components of the partners of the species concerned, perhaps at the expense, for example, of partially losing the aromatic contribution of *C. arabica* or reducing the resistance to diseases of *C. canephora* (particularly *Hemileia vastatrix*).

The team of geneticists working on arabusta with Capot were also confronted with other problems, for example, certain progenies showed sensitivity to shedding and an unacceptably high caffeine content. An adapted agronomic and technological concept was ultimately adopted with regard to a new form of coffee tree. A Research Centre, with 500 hectares of land, was established for this purpose by Ivorian authorities, who were anxious to reap the benefits of these new coffee trees.

It was only when a development programme for this crop had been established and entrusted to a State company, SATMACI, that other problems arose, such as the sensitivity of the hybrid to *Hemileia* and the presence of trunk, branch and flower bud pests, all of which required the intervention of expensive methods of prevention or control.

Highly satisfactory trials were conducted on the first harvests in Abidjan by the CAPRAL Company (Nestlé) for the production of instant coffee, which is now being manufactured on a large scale.

The sizeable aid that ORSTOM contributed to the IFCC programme in the Ivory Coast enabled an ambitious programme of interspecific hybridisation to be systematically developed in order to explore all possible combinations with diploid coffee trees such as *C. congensis, C. excelsa* and *C. liberica*. This programme is currently in operation.

The 'Icatu' variety, which was recently created in Campinas, Brazil is the result of crossings and back-crossings between hybrids of *C. canephora* × *C. arabica* and *C. arabica* 'Mundo Novo' and 'Catuai'. The objective was to obtain types which were resistant or tolerant to leaf rust (*Hemileia vastatrix*). Geneticists can now explore the potential of new hybrids by combining a large number of genes in a multitude of combinations of varying complexity that may eventually result in a significant improvement in coffee production and quality.

Genetic manipulations

Gene manipulation holds a great deal of promise today, not only in the area of quality improvement, but also with regard to most of the inherited factors which distinguish a species or a clone. The increase in the understanding of the genetic constitution of coffee which has taken place during the past few years certainly upholds this opinion. However, caution should be displayed regarding the success of these extremely difficult and delicate operations, and the length of time it takes to carry them out (Charrier, 1985). The most qualified specialists estimate that, based on the current state of knowledge and work, possibly 15 to 20 years or more may elapse before the first concrete results have been obtained. It should also be noted that at the plantation level, the real value of the new plant material must first be established through experiments conducted systematically in the field under realistic cropping conditions and under diverse ecological situations. Some of the important characteristics that need to be tested are potential yield, which will require a certain number of harvests, tolerance to the most harmful pests and diseases, classification of bean characteristics and, of course, the aromatic qualities of the processed beverage.

These investigations, which are essential, will take at least five, possibly 10 or 15 years and will thus increase the period of time that will elapse before the new coffee hybrids can eventually be exploited, for example the hybrid Arabusta.

The potential of genetic manipulation will undoubtedly also be involved in revolutionising coffee growing in the future. The high cost of research, together with the fact that results will not be available in the immediate future should not be discouraging.

New improvement programmes

Although the principles of established improvement programmes are valid, all the projects currently in progress emphasise the necessity to increase the variability of the *Coffea* species which are currently being cultivated, in order to obtain plants that satisfy increasingly demanding selection criteria. This includes ecological and agronomic adaptability, i.e. reaction to modern agronomic technology using herbicides, hormones and mechanical harvesting, also productivity, resistance to a wide range of pests and diseases, tolerance of environmental conditions, and commercial qualities.

This is clearly necessary for the self-fertile *C. arabica* species, which were originally selected from a number of limited strains (Typica-Bourbon and their hybrids and mutants), but is equally valid for the vegetative selection of diploid coffee trees, when a range of germplasm resources must be used in the search for elite forms.

Botanical explorations in the centres of origin have provided new plant material with characteristics that are of interest to geneticists. FAO and ORSTOM have, for example, organised missions to Ethiopia to collect *C. arabica* and search for varieties that are resistant to leaf rust, coffee berry disease, and/or are adaptable to growing in tropical, hot, humid, low-altitude zones. ORSTOM/IRCC have also sent exploratory missions to Kenya and Tanzania to find original rootstocks of *C. arabica* and Mozambico-coffee, and to Central Africa to collect diploid, ecologically original coffee species such as *C. congensis, C. canephora* var. de la Nana, *C. liberica* and *C. dewevrei.*

Joint research by the IFCC and ORSTOM in Madagascar, led by Charrier, on caffeine-free coffee species growing wild in the forest, and found exclusively on the Grande-Ile, was unfortunately interrupted in 1974. The in-depth studies on these species could, in fact, have culminated in the creation of hybrids that produce naturally decaffeinated coffee, and could also have contributed to an understanding of caffeinogenesis and ways of manipulating it.

Intra-varietal hybridisations in *C. arabica* and between clones among diploid varieties have also brought about a marked increase in the selection bases available in segregating populations of successive generations; also in the potential for hybrid vigour and rearrangement of the genetic base in the resulting hybrids. This is illustrated by the creation of the arabica cultivars, when a horizontal resistance to leaf rust and improved behavioural homogeneity in cross-fertilised coffee hybrids were revealed, mainly in specific crossings made after completion of the general compatability test.

The technique of **interspecific hybridisation** was initiated in the 1960s, together with the first genetic manipulations involving chromosomal duplication and fertility restoration in artificial tetraploids. This involved crossing individuals with widely differing chromosomal or genetic compositions, for example, tetraploid arabica and diploid robusta coffee, decaffeinated diploid Mascarocoffea and cultivated tetra or diploid coffee species. This resulted in one of the most interesting sources of variability being identified and it was immediately exploited.

Interspecific *Coffea* hybrids

The concept of combining the favourable agronomic or technological qualities of the most commonly cultivated coffee varieties by applying hybridisation techniques was exploited relatively early in experimental stations. It is, moreover, an accepted method of genetic improvement in self-sterile diploid species.

Plant breeders have only recently formulated a plan for combining the useful characteristics of related species. This became feasible due to advances made in general biological knowledge and the additional information which became available on the cytogenetics of *Coffea* and the techniques of genetic manipulation that control them.

For *Coffea* species, the characteristics sought in the genomes which are available involve either biological characteristics such as resistance to rust, coffee berry disease, berry borers, and/or nematodes; agrological characteristics such as the ability to adapt to drought or the humid heat of the lower altitude equatorial zones; or criteria of commercial interest such as bean size, flavour, caffeine or soluble solids content. The various combinations which are possible with these characteristics are so numerous that very different combinations could possibly lead to the creation of a hybrid with the same favourable constitution. Such is the case with hybridisations between *C. canephora* and *C. arabica*, which will be discussed in a later section.

Plant breeders first tried traditional methods of hybridisation due to a lack of knowledge of the biology of the species in question. Such is the case with hybrids produced in the Dutch West Indies between *C. arabica* and *C. liberica* (Arla) and *C. arabica* and *C. robusta* (Kawisari), which were created in an attempt to find leaf rust-resistant types, this disease having devastated the arabica plantations that had been established at the foot of Javanese volcanoes. Histological studies carried out before World War II showed that the infertility of these simple hybrids stemmed from their triploid nature which adversely affects meiosis. In fact, the instability produced prevented balanced chromosomal divisions from taking place during the division of the reproductive cells (gametes) and during the formation of the vegetative nucleus of the fertilised embryo.

However, these problems were then realised as a result of spontaneous chromatid rearrangements or induced chromosomal mutations. Fertile hybrids such as C387 were obtained, using parents of different species. This particular hybrid was found at the Campinas Agronomic Institute (Brazil), and was a result of a cross between *C. arabica* and *C. dewevreï*. At first treated as a botanical curiosity, it was later utilised in improvement projects, together with its parent, *C. arabica*.

The most popular of these interspecific natural hybrids remains the **Hybrid of Timor**, which was identified by Portuguese agronomists as a natural hybrid between arabica and canephora. Populations of this type, with equal numbers of chromosomes, are in fact relatively fertile. Its absolute resistance to the different types of rust which occur made it an essential choice in many back-crossing programmes using different varieties of arabica. The selection and development of elite progenies from these programmes is now in progress in Latin America.

The Brazilian 'Catimor' is the result of repeated crossings made between the Hybrid of Timor and the dwarf cultivar 'Caturra'. This product is remarkable for its rust-resistance, vegetative vigour and productivity, although it cannot yet compete commercially with roasted coffee beans prepared from good *C. arabica typica*, with its mutants and hybrids such as 'Mundo Novo' and 'Catuai', due to its poor bean size and shape.

Successive back-crossings with 'Caturra', up to the fifth generation, have produced an almost genetically stable cultivar in its country of origin, in the province of Minas Gerais. It has also been exploited extensively in the Pacific (New Caledonia) as well as in many Central and South American countries since the appearance of leaf rust.

The introduction of rust-resistance was also a major selection criterion in the creation of **completely artificial interspecific hybrids** through the inclusion of a diploid parent in the crossing. This was initially given the same level of ploidy as the tetraploid arabica parent through the use of colchicine. Colchicine was first applied to canephoras in 1947 by cytologists of the Campinas Agronomic Institute. The success of the chromosomal duplication was followed by a large number of improvement projects. These began in 1950, using tetraploid forms of *C. canephora* with more or less selected cultivars of *C. arabica*. The objective was to combine the characteristics of these two species and to produce F_1 hybrids, which were then vegetatively propagated after clonal selection. The **arabustas** were developed in this way by Capot at the IFCC Ivory Coast and similar programmes were later pursued by researchers from the same institute in Uganda, Cameroon, and Togo. Their intention was to create a plant from these two parents having intermediary agronomic and technological qualities. The objective was to offset the lack of success obtained in arabica growing in hot, humid zones of Africa, due mainly to virescence of the flowers, and to transfer certain characteristics of *C. canephora* such as resistance to rust, coffee berry disease, and nematodes to *C. arabica* through successive back-crossing with selections of arabica. Such was the aim of the Brazilian programme after 1970, the date rust was introduced in Brazil. This culminated with the synthesis of back-crossing at the BC3 level using selected coffee hybrids from the back-cross and Mundo Novo hybridisation programme. Plants were chosen from these new populations and were back-crossed with 'Catuai' and 'Catimor' cultivars, together with other combinations made using coffee trees with a smaller habit. Promising populations, from the point of view of hardiness and productivity, were thus created, which were then called **Icatu**, meaning 'bonanza' (prosperity or good luck in an Amerindian dialect of Brazil).

The use of polyploid-inducing agents such as colchicine on diploid, triploid, and sterile arabica × robusta hybrids enabled **hexaploid progenies** to be obtained. Coffee plants of this new hexaploid family have botanical characteristics that are somewhat similar to the arabusta tetraploids, although they differ in that their genetic constitution has many arabica characteristics, but is relatively lacking in canephora characteristics. Thus they are not rust-resistant, nor are they as fertile and adapted to lowland equatorial zones. Nevertheless, Arabusta-type programmes have become widespread, despite the problems encountered in the use of these hybrid populations, some individuals of which have inherited unfavourable parental characteristics such as shedding, poor technological yield, percentage of peaberries and empty loculi, although these are eliminated in the selection process. The positive results of the first interspecific hybridisations, such as the diversity of the populations created, their different characters such as productivity and ecological adaptability, the commercial quality of the fruit, disease and pest resistance, beverage quality, and caffeine content have all been encouraging factors. After tetraploidisation, the programmes will include various species of diploid coffee in the continuing hybridisations with arabica. Thus, depending upon the prevailing ecological, agronomic, or commercial requirements, the following may be combined: *C. congensis* for its ability to grow well under hydromorphic conditions; *C. stenophylla* for its resistance to leaf miners; de la Nana and *C. humilis*, for their dwarf habit; or *C. liberica, C. dewevreï* and *C. racemosa* for their tolerance to xerophytic conditions; finally Mascarocoffea for the absence of caffeine in its beans.

Artificial tetraploids

Initially, the objective of the chromosomal duplication of canephoras was to eliminate the chromosomal incompatability that existed between these two species (2 n = 22 chromosomes for canephoras; 4 n = 44 chromosomes for arabicas) in order to give them an improved potential for crossing and to create fertile hybrid lines. This was achieved by using colchicine in treating the actively growing seedlings (Capot) or the axillary buds (Berthou) of the clones selected as future parents in the interspecific hybridisation with *C. arabica*. This hypothesis was validated in the improvement programme already described.

However, it was observed that the use of first generation canephora tetraploids (TO) in these hybridisation programmes resulted in a large number of plants which produced excessively high percentages of incomplete fruits (peaberries and empty loculi). This problem was attributed to the still unstable constitution of the artificially induced tetraploid parent.

The first tetraploid canephoras were self-sterile, but as with their diploid parents, they also showed good floral compatability. Restoring the fertility of the pollen was therefore attempted, and achieved, using repeated reciprocal crossings. These led to the T 1 – T 2 – T 3 generations which were increasingly fertile and productive and also showed improved performance when crossed with the selected arabicas, successively generating so-called second and third wave progenies of Arabusta by increasing yields and the quantity of normal beans harvested (Fig 30).

The increased productivity of the T 3 canephora, the fertility of which has been restored, has demonstrated that many vegetatively propagated plants found in these tetraploid progenies achieve a production level that is just as high, if not higher than that of the original selected diploid canephora clones, with the additional advantage of exceptional bean characteristics, such as seed weights of more than 20 g per 100 beans.

The use of tetraploidy on normally diploid coffee species, followed by the restoration of fertility by interclonal tetraploid hybridisation, is a new and original way of improving these coffee trees. The potential should first be realised with canephora, and then extended to the other diploid species.

Other sources of ploidy in *Coffea*

The selection of diploid coffee trees by controlled hybridisation such as test crop trials or specific crossing trials following top-cross tests which reveal the general combining ability of the cutting source plants, leads to the production of selected hybrids. However, due to the pronounced heterozygosity of the parents, the performance of the hybrids never reaches the level of yield of the selected clones from which they originated, due to the heterogeneity of the individual trees that make up the population.

In an attempt to improve this situation, a means of obtaining homozygotic genotypes was sought, using the **haploid** form of the cutting source plants, after doubling the number of chromosomes in the haploid plants. Homogenous F_1 progenies could then be created by crossing the artificial diploids.

The haploid state of the clones being studied may be obtained either in their natural progenies, by selecting the seedlings in the nursery and using cytological examination of the young leaves. The weakest haploid plants, which are a very small percentage of the population i.e. 1.5×10^{-4}, can be kept alive by grafting, using grafted cuttings, or *in vitro* culture. They are then brought back to the diploid state by colchicine treatment, in order to restore the homozygosity of the desired characteristics. An alternative method is another culture, as *in vitro* culture with haploid tissue is still at the experimental stage.

By creating hybrids from these homozygotic parents, it is possible to obtain a phenotypic homogeneity in the first F_1 generation which is closer to the clonal progenies in terms of yield and other desirable criteria, particularly resistance to various factors or improved organoleptic characteristics.

Such di-haploid parents were being developed in the Ivory Coast (IRCC/Bingerville/ORSTOM/Man) at the beginning of the 1980s. Their great advantage, compared with classic, clonal selection lies in the establishment of bi-clonal seed orchards and the relative ease with which hybrid seeds can be distributed, in contrast to the relatively expensive production and distribution of cuttings.

Prospects for further improvement

Research work still needs to be carried out on selection and development following the creation of new stable or hybrid progenies, and promoting a new, highly efficient and profitable planting programme in rural areas.

With the introduction of Ivorian Arabustas, about 20 years elapsed between the time that Capot initiated the programme around 1962, the distribution of the material to planters, and their use in the manufacture of instant coffee. A long preparatory period was necessary. The tetraploid parents and the interspecific hybrid families were initially studied. Other studies then followed and individuals that did not conform to the selection criteria were eliminated. Collections of tree species were planted with the elite clones which were retained. Finally, additional studies were undertaken in such areas as food technology and marketing.

However, the ever-increasing knowledge of the cytogenetics of the inheritance system in *Coffea*, and the sophistication of the methods of genome analysis (by enzymology, biochemical analysis by mass spectrometry, gas chromatography, computer science, etc.) are reassuring to researchers working in the field of genetics, and new innovations are more likely to be successful. It thus becomes more practical to contemplate the provision of plant material which is adapted to the most diverse ecological and agro-economic conditions, directly to the planter. The aim is that this plant material will be flexible and adaptable enough to be used on the family farm as well as in the agro-industrial unit.

Moreover, the newly created strains would also benefit from the establishment of a method of conservation and a rapid system of propagation through tissue culture techniques, such as the ones previously described.

Through the use of *in vitro* cell culture and computer science, it will be possible to conduct early selection tests, and time and space will be conserved so that research workers may carry out the most complete comparative variety trials possible. The opportunities for this have, in the past, been much more limited.

The ease of transferring *in vitro* plant material in test tubes, which are totally safe from the phytosanitary point of view, will not only accelerate research, but will also facilitate its co-ordination at an international level. Efficiency, speed, economising in resources, a guarantee that studies will produce useful results, with improved opportunities to apply them, will be key factors for experiments in the area of coffee tree improvement in the future.

9 *Green coffee processing*

General information

The ripe fruits of coffee are normally processed in the production area. They go through a certain number of operations, the objectives of which are to extract the beans from their covering of pulp, mucilage, parchment and film, and to improve their appearance.

The following techniques are used to obtain clean coffee beans:

- **Wet processing** in which the fresh fruit is processed in three stages:
  a) Removal of the pulp (pulping) and mucilage (mucilage removal), washing,
  b) Drying of parchment coffee,
  c) Removal of the inner coverings, parchment, and film (hulling);
- **Dry processing** which consists of two stages:
  a) Drying of the fruit (coffee berries or cherry coffee),
  b) Removal of the dried coverings in a single mechanical operation (hulling).

Wet processing is always used for the choice arabica coffees produced in Central America, Colombia, etc., which are classifed as **mild** on the international market, as this method, which requires more care than dry processing, enhances the beans' appearance, thus rendering the batches more valuable. Any coffee, be it arabica or another type, that does not belong to this superior category but is still processed by the wet method, is qualified as **washed. Fully washed** is the name given to coffee prepared by wet processing that has been fermented. Canephoras (robustas) are sometimes prepared in this manner in countries such as Indonesia, India, Uganda, etc., in an effort to increase their value.

Dry processed coffee is called **hard coffee**. This includes about 80 per cent Brazilian arabicas and the largest fraction of African or Asian canephora coffees. Dry processing is used for the aforementioned coffees, unless wet processing is preferred due to local climatic conditions, and particularly when major tonnages produced by large farms are processed.

The two techniques both consist of a series of operations, the order of

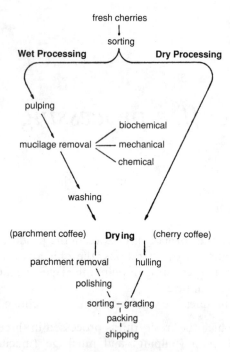

fresh cherries

sorting

Wet Processing   **Dry Processing**

pulping

biochemical

mucilage removal ⟨ — mechanical

chemical

washing

(parchment coffee)   **Drying**   (cherry coffee)

parchment removal   hulling

polishing

sorting – grading

packing

shipping

Fig 96   Succession of operations in the wet and dry processing of coffee

which is shown in Fig 96. It should be noted that the later steps apply to coffees processed by either method. In both cases, the ripe cherry, which is the product to be processed, has a 65–75 per cent water content, much of which must be eliminated during the course of the drying process.

Wet processing

The first operation, **pulping**, is often preceded by **sorting**, a basic cleaning, the objective of which is to eliminate plant debris such as leaves and pieces of branches, and foreign particles such as stones and earth, that have been collected during harvesting. This operation is particularly important in Brazil due to the primitive harvesting method used, called **strip picking**.

To facilitate processing and to obtain a better product, it is also advisable to separate the ripe and unripe cherries, or those that have dried out on the bush or the ground because of late harvesting. These operations can be manually undertaken for small quantities. For larger tonnages, mechanical equipment is used, such as separators with an oscillating framework or rotary sieves, or various types of washer, the most common of which is the **siphon-vat** arrangement.

This is a stone vat, shaped like a flattened cone, with a capacity of

1–2 m³. At its centre there is a large bent pipe, connected to the outside, which descends to within twenty centimetres of the bottom. The vat is filled with water to about four fifths capacity and supplied with a continuous flow of liquid, which transports the cherry coffee. A constant level of water is maintained by an overflow pipe, which enables the excess water to flow out. The cherries are sorted according to density. At the bottom of the vat are deposits of stones and soil; the healthy fruits settle above them, as they are slightly denser than water; and the impurities, including dry cherries and empty husks, which are less dense than water, float to the surface. The healthy cherries are carried along by the water current through a central tube to a nearby pulper. Slight impurities are sent to an adjacent tank, but the foreign particles, which are much more dense than water, are eliminated by releasing a hatch which opens a hole at the bottom of the vat.

Unfortunately, mechanical separators or washers cannot satisfactorily be used to separate the ripe and unripe cherries, which have very similar densities. The cherries should be harvested when fully ripe, but if this is not possible, the harvesters must sort them, separating the ripe and unripe fruits.

In Brazil, where the harvest includes a large proportion of more or less green cherries, the pulp must be softened by soaking the fruits for a period of one to three days to facilitate pulping. However, this practice is not recommended, as it may result in anaerobic, malodorous fermentations which may reduce the quality of the beans. Mechanised, colorimetric sorting using electronic sorters have been introduced and tested to eliminate these deficiencies, but the cost of the operation is very high.

Pulping

Pulp removal must be done as soon as possible after harvesting. A few hours usually elapse before this operation is carried out since the fruits that have been collected are gathered, transported, but may have to wait before processing, however this should not exceed 36 hours. Too long a wait might lead to the production of beans with a disagreeable taste and smell which are called **stinker beans**.

Pulping is achieved using special equipment called pulpers, even for small quantities of fruit. There are two types: the **cylinder** (or drum) **coffee pulper** and the **multidisk coffee pulper**, both of which are based on the same principle.

The former consists essentially of a rotary, metal cylinder coated with a thin, copper lining, having a raised surface (buttons) and an adjustable plate (breast) on one side of the equipment (Fig. 99). The cherries are carried along by the rotation of the equipment and are pressed between the cylinder and the breast. The pulp, which is shredded by the rough surface of the buttons, is carried out, while the beans that are held in a hollow of the channel of the breast are expelled through a lateral opening.

In the multidisk pulper, the rotary cylinder is replaced by one or more

Fig 97 'Anglia' pulper with cylinders and a vibrating seive for separating the small, unpulped cherries (Courtesy: Bentall)

disks with a stamped copper lining (more recent equipment has cast iron disks coated with stainless steel), mounted on a horizontal axle, which is driven by a rotational movement (120 turns/min). The pulp is removed by the progressive compression of the fruits which become caught between each disk and two lateral plates or transoms, located on either side of the upper part of the equipment. The pulp is separated by a knife, which has a fixed, adjustable blade and allows the pulp to pass through while retaining the beans (Fig. 98).

A considerable amount of water is required to operate these two types

Fig 98 Pulper with three discs
(Courtesy: Gordon)

of equipment properly, particularly the cylinder coffee pulpers. A minimum flow of one litre per kg of fruit is judged to be necessary. Wilbaux estimates that 40 m³ of water per tonne of clean coffee is the required amount for receiving the cherries, transporting them hydraulically in the pulping machine via the water current, removing the pulp, and sorting and repassing any cherries with residual pulp adhering to them. The speed of the rotation must be carefully adjusted to ensure that the pulp is properly removed. In other words, there shouldn't be too much pulp in the coffee parchment, or too many whole cherries among the pulp.

The output of the pulpers is proportional to the length of the cylinder in this type of equipment, and to the number of disks in the other type. In the cylinder pulper, it is dependent upon the number of openings which exist for the removal of the beans, on an approximate unit rate of 500 kg of cherries processed per hour. For the disk equipment, it is estimated that the capacity of a disk corresponds approximately to that of a cylinder pulper with two openings, or about 1000 kg of fruit per hour.

The energy required by any type of pulper is calculated on the basis of one horsepower for a cylinder with two openings, or per disk. Equipment built for use on large farms (or co-operatives) has a large output, with an hourly capacity of 2 to 3 tonnes of fruit.

Alternatively, small-scale planters can obtain manual equipment with an hourly capacity of 50 to 250 kg of cherries. This equipment is completely satisfactory if it is well maintained and supplied with enough water and ripe fruit. For these purposes, a disk pulper, which is more resistant to wear, is generally preferable to cylinder equipment.

Pulping equipment is robust and can endure long-term service. The copper linings of the cylinders and disks are the only parts that may deteriorate rapidly if foreign matter (stones, metal pieces, etc.) is introduced with the fruit. If this occurs, the metal relief buttons become flattened and the quality of pulping is reduced as a result. It is therefore important to have any damaged equipment relined, or to replace the worn disk or disks if necessary.

As satisfactory as the operations of the pulpers may be, a small percentage of fruit, generally the smaller than average cherries, is always carried out, unpulped, with the beans. These cherries must be recovered and recycled through a new round of pulp removal using more closely adjusted equipment (**pulper-repasser**). On large farms, the problem of faulty pulp removal is avoided by first briefly sorting and grading the fruit. This is imperative when the same equipment must process a heterogeneous collection containing fruits of different species and varieties.

A new type of pulper has recently been perfected in which the pulp is removed from the fruit as it passes between two fluted rollers. This is especially suitable for processing cherries with a leathery covering such as those of *C. liberica*.

Mucilage removal

When the coffee emerges from the pulpers, it is still coated with a mucilage that sticks to the parchment. This material is rich in pectin and is very hygroscopic, which renders it an obstacle to the rapid drying of the beans. It is eliminated by using one of the following techniques:

- Biochemical (fermentation);
- Chemical;
- Mechanical;
- Mechano-chemical combination.

Biochemical removal: fermentation

Fermentation involves placing the pulped coffee in appropriate environmental conditions, so that the pectin of the mucilagenous coating of the beans decomposes due to a lactic fermentation. However, secondary fermentations such as acetic, butyric or putrid, which are harmful to the quality of the product, should not be allowed to follow. The pectinolysis is accelerated by the presence of different micro-organisms such as yeast and bacteria.

When it emerges from the pulping machines, the parchment coffee is carried along by a water current to cement basins or tanks, having a slightly inclining bottom and rounded corners with a capacity of 1 to 10 m^3. The depth of these tanks should not exceed 1.5 m. After a thorough straining, enough time remains for the mucilage to soften and decompose; it can then be easily eliminated by washing (Figs 99, 100 and 101).

The operation is marked by a slight rise in the temperature of the mass of beans due to various fermentations, among which lactic fermentation

Fig 99   Array of fermentation tanks. San Salvador (Courtesy: Fritz)

Fig 100   Fermentation tanks.
Kenya (Courtesy: Coste)

Fig 101   Pulp removing station. Foreground: fermentation tanks and washing channels, Angola Coffee Institute (Courtesy: Gordon)

predominates. A very slight increase in the acidity (pH) also occurs from 6.5 to 6.8 at the beginning, to between 4.5 and 4.8 at the end of the operation. The rise in temperature is favourable to the effects of the fermentation, which includes the activity of the enzyme diastase on the pectins, but it must not be excessive since it may cause unpleasant flavours to develop. It is equally important to prevent harmful pathogenic species, such as moulds, from appearing. It is essential to stir the contents of the tanks two or three times so that fermentation is homogenous throughout.

At the end of the fermentation process, the beans will have lost their gluey coating, becoming rough to the touch. This is the sign that the fermentation is complete. Prolonging it will only result in harmful secondary fermentations, which may reduce the quality of the coffee, especially in low altitude areas where the ambient temperature is relatively high.

Removing the floating beans using a water current often precedes the removal of the mucilage. These beans generally ferment poorly and produce a coffee of lesser quality. This type of sorting is carried out in tubs with perforated bottoms, or better still in channels that have been designed for the purpose of separating the beans according to their densities. The two categories of coffee are then processed separately. The proportion of floating beans depends upon the quality of the harvest. It is normally 5 per cent, but can be much higher if the fruit has been seriously affected by pests. This practice is very popular with arabica planters in East Africa and Kivu. Sorting by density is also achieved mechanically in special equipment based on the 'jig' principle. The separation is accelerated by an underwater 'piston system' in an 'Aagard' coffee pre-grader. The heterogeneous material arrives on a sieve which is submerged in water and is agitated in such a way that it creates ascending and descending currents. The beans are suspended and resettle at each thrust of the piston.

The duration of the fermentation process is very variable. It depends upon the principal elements involved, such as the volume of the mass of beans, the species or variety of coffee, the maturity of the fruits, the ambient temperature and altitude. For arabicas, it is between 12 and 48 hours (Kenya: 12 to 18 hours; Indonesia: 18 to 24 hours; Mexico: 18 to 40 hours; Cameroon: 12 to 24 hours) and for robustas it is between 12 and 36 hours. Excelsa and liberica coffees, which are wet processed, may have to be fermented for 40 to 60 hours.

The effect of fermentation on the quality of coffee at consumer level is still being debated. In fact, many producers consider that if fermented correctly, it could indeed have a positive effect on the final beverage. However, ideas on this subject have lately become much more clear as a result of trials and experiments.

Many trials, conducted mainly in Kenya and Cameroon, have shown that the operation of fermentation, in addition to hydrolysing the mucilage, also allows the excretion of soluble products such as phenols and diterpenes which make the drink harsh and bitter. Whatever the methods of mucilage removal may be (biochemical, mechanical, or chemical), the organoleptic rating of the beverage is the same. However, it should be noted that for certain arabica coffees from Kenya, Kivu, etc., the slightly acid taste of the drink which is appreciated by consumers is obtained by using a relatively long fermentation period.

One technique, called **underwater fermentation**, is fairly commonly practiced in the arabica-growing regions of East Africa and Kivu. It consists of covering the coffee in the tanks with water. The decomposition of the mucilage is slower than in classical, 'dry' fermentation, but there is a higher level of acid formation, mainly lactic acid. Wilbaux estimates that this method slightly improves the quality of fine coffees.

Underwater fermentation, or better still, soaking the coffee after the mucilage has been removed, facilitates the excretion of soluble substances such as polyphenols and diterpenes. This refining technique helps to improve the quality, while reducing harshness and bitterness.

Mixed fermentation is also practiced. This entails an initial stage of dry fermentation, followed by underwater fermentation.

The most common causes of poor fermentation are:

- coffee remaining in the vats for too long: this causes alterations to occur in the beans, such as hydrolysis and germination, and the formation of **stinker beans**, which considerably reduce the value of the merchandise;
- use of dirty vats or containers: these may contain residues from earlier operations;
- parchment not adequately drained: this causes the mass to remain submerged and aerobic fermentation is halted;
- use of alkaline or polluted water;
- environment not being sufficiently moist: the tanks may be exposed to the sun.

Most of these problems are easily remedied. If for some reason draining is delayed, Wilbaux recommends submerging the mass of beans to halt the fermentation and avoid any further loss of quality.

It is not always easy to prepare small quantities of less than 100 kg of coffee properly. The difficulty is essentially due to the exceedingly small volume of the mass to be fermented. The temperature rise is both insufficient and irregular. One portion of the coffee remains more or less under-fermented, whereas the other portion may be over-fermented. The mixture results in a product of mediocre, indeed inferior, quality. Small-scale arabica producers are thus advised to group together in co-operatives, which would then produce tonnages that are large enough to ferment satisfactorily. Very interesting experiences of this type have been reported in the Caribbean and some Central American countries.

Independent, small-scale producers are advised to use containers (tanks, boxes, baskets) that are at least two-thirds full. They should have openings so that the excess water and juice resulting from the decomposition of the mucilage may run off. Producers are particularly advised to stir the mixture several times at regular intervals. Finally, they must cover the fermenting mass with bags or banana leaves, held firm by stones, and place the containers in a sheltered area, away from sun and rain.

Chemical removal

Several chemical products have been tested for removing the mucilage from coffee, mainly lime, which precipitates the pectins in the form of insoluble pectates which are then easily removed by washing. Alkaline carbonates have also been used.

This technique is still not widespread, despite its twofold advantage of speed and low cost. Interest in it was revived, however, a few years ago when the Inter-American Institute of Agronomic Sciences (Costa Rica) designed a machine in which mechanical action was combined with a chemical treatment.

Coffee prepared in this way is sometimes described as being 'chemically fermented'. When taste-tested by experts, no noticeable difference could be discerned when compared with coffee which had been traditionally fermented. Nevertheless, a lack of acidity was sometimes noticed, and this is a quality sought by certain consumers (see fermentation).

Mechanical removal

It has been demonstrated from experiments that fermentation does not have any beneficial effect on coffee except, of course, for the development of special flavours that are appreciated by a certain clientele. On the contrary, a poor or over-long fermentation may reduce the quality of the product. These factors have led to the conception of mechanical mucilage removal. The equipment used is the **'Raoeng' pulper and mucilage remover**, which first appeared on the market about 60 years ago. This equipment simultaneously pulps, removes the mucilage, and washes the coffee. It essentially consists of a long, cylindrical, perforated casing with a current of water running through it under pressure, in which a fluted cylinder turns rapidly (400 to 550 turns/min). The cherries, which are carried along by the water, are compressed between the cylinder and its casing. The shredded pulp and the mucilaginous material are separated from the beans and washed away by the water. (Figs 102 and 103).

This equipment works well if it is used to process ripe, homogenously sized cherries. If not homogenous, they must be first sorted. It also needs an adequate water output of 3–9 m^3 per hour, and a pressure of 4–6 atm., depending upon the model. Because of its large capacity (750 to 3000 kg of fruit per hour), the energy it requires is 8 to 25 horsepower. This, together with its high cost, means it can only be of interest to relatively large farms and processing co-operatives. However, it has one indisputable advantage for groups of small-scale producers, in that by eliminating the need to ferment numerous small batches of beans, it also eliminates one of the main reasons for the variation in quality that has been criticised in coffees of that origin, and is particularly common in arabicas.

Fig 102 The 'Aquapulper' pulper and mucilage remover (Courtesy: Bentall)

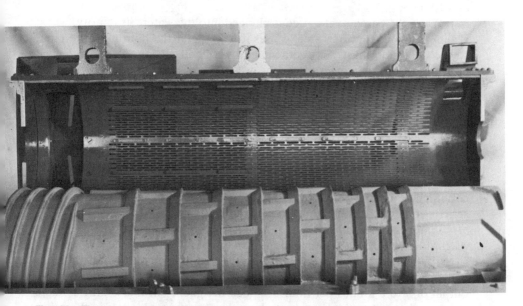

Fig 103 The 'Aquapulper' with the gearcase open to show the pulping drum
(Courtesy: Bentall)

However, the pulper-mucilage remover is more widely used by cane-phora coffee producers than arabica producers. Indeed, many of the latter are strongly attached to the traditional way of preparation.

It should be noted that with classical fermentation, a two per cent weight loss in dry matter is recorded, mainly due to the use of the 'Raoeng' machine. This does not occur with the other processes.

Mechano-chemical removal

Equipment known as the 'Cafépro' has been designed by technicians at The Inter-American Institute of Agricultural Sciences in Turrialba, Costa Rica. Its purpose is to combine mechanical and chemical actions in the mucilage removal operation. It consists of a long, fixed cylinder divided into two parts, within which an axle equipped with stirring rods turns. Wood ash is placed in the first part of the cylinder and a whitewash is placed in the second. In addition, the supply of water must be ensured. Mucilage removal is completed within less than an hour.

Washing

The objective of washing is to remove products formed during the course of fermentation, such as the debris from the pulp which remains adhered to the parchment, etc. Washing is generally carried out in large tanks, called washers, or by slowly moving the coffee through open-topped channels (Figs 104 and 105).

When the parchment coffee is plunged into the water, its density, which is slightly above that of water, causes it to settle at the bottom of the tank, so the operation must be accompanied by a good mixing. This is achieved either by rotary stirring rods in the washers, or by workers with wooden spades when the washing is carried out in channels.

Small-scale producers wash the beans very simply using semi-submerged baskets in running water in a creek, or even in tins or basins. The latter requires several changes of water.

Washing is completed when the water is as clear on leaving the channel or washtub as when it entered. Parchment coffee must be clean and free of all impurities; it must also be rough to the touch. Poorly washed parchment coffee may begin to ferment, producing alcohol; it may also heat up, with serious consequences to the quality of the beverage.

Water requirements are high: about 10 litres per kilogramme of coffee. Aagard has devised a system used in Kenya, based on water recycling.

Centrifugal equipment is currently being studied; particularly for use with parchment coffee. Continuous hydraulic equipment with a considerable output of 5 to 6 tonnes per hour has been designed, but this is only suitable for factories with a large output. Liquid pumps are also used, these are effective for recirculation.

Fig 104   Washing channels. Kenya.

Fig 105   Washing channels, Angola Coffee Institute (Courtesy: Gordon)

Fig 106   Drying parchment coffee on stretchers

(188)

Drying

After the parchment coffee has been washed and drained, it will have a moisture content of 50–60 per cent. The presence of parchment accounts for about 7–8 per cent. In order to lower the moisture content of the beans to about 12 per cent to ensure their conservation, about 100 kg of water must be eliminated from 200 kg of parchment coffee to obtain 100 kg of clean coffee.

The drying of the parchment coffee is promoted by thorough draining when it leaves the washing channels. During the course of this operation, the contact water accounting for 5–10 per cent is largely removed by gravity. Drainage towers are often used for these purposes.

Drying requires a lot of care and supervision, especially if artificial methods are used. If the procedure is careless, too rapid, or too lengthy, moisture from rain or dew may condense on the beans during the course of the operation, altering the quality of the beans: they may become discoloured, mottled, brown, or reddish-brown. This could have serious consequences on the commercial value of the product. It must not be forgotten that excessive drying leads to an additional weight loss which cannot be compensated for commercially. According to Wilbaux, drying induces a volumetric contraction of the bean of approximately 12 to 15 per cent.

Two main drying techniques are used: **natural (or solar) drying** and **artificial drying**. Sometimes both are used; referred to as **mixed drying**.

Solar drying

The simplest method of drying for use by small-scale producers is the **fixed** or **mobile raised screen**, which can be made very inexpensively using local materials. Each screen consists of a light, wooden frame, 2 m × 1 m, within which is a fine netting or woven sheet made of vegetable fibres. The screens are arranged side by side in an unshaded spot, on a rudimentary stand, 1 m from the ground. This ensures that farmyard animals cannot reach them, and also isolates the coffee from soil moisture. The screens should be of an easily portable size. At night, they are stacked in a store. To improve the efficiency of this drying method, a mobile roof may be installed which can be moved in case of rain. This is called a 'bus dryer' in Cameroon (Figs 106 and 107).

Superior dryers, with a greater output, consist of wooden screens mounted on small wheels. The use of a rail system enables them to be either exposed to the air or stored in a warehouse. The exchange from one to the other can be carried out rapidly. Similarly, **terrace-dryers** are set up under buildings with a mobile roof (Fig 108).

However, the most common drying method involves the use of a **cemented area**, the size of which depends upon the extent of the harvest. One square metre is generally estimated to hold 12 kilos of moist parchment coffee. The area is slightly inclined (1 to 2 per cent) so that rainwater may run off towards surrounding furrow drains. (Figs 109, 110, 111 and 112).

Fig 107   Drying parchment coffee on fixed screens. Kenya (Courtesy: Cours)

Fig 108   Drying parchment coffee: area under mobile roof. Colombia

Fig 109   Drying coffee: cemented area with shelter. Zaire

Fig 110   Brazilian fazenda: drying area. Background: coffee plantation

Fig 111   Coffee drying on a family-run farm. Madagascar

Fig 112   Drying area in Brazil. Background: *C. arabica* Mundo Novo

Fig 113 Transporting parchment coffee by small carts to the drying area of a large fazenda. Brazil

It is essential to have an alternative means of protecting the drying area from rain in countries where rain is likely during the drying period. Some methods of protection used are sheet iron or wooden panels. At the onset of rain, the coffee is rapidly piled into a heap. It is now common practice to use sheets of plastic, the edges of which are held down by stones. Another common system is the use of low, raised walls around the drying area. The coffee is piled at the base of the wall and is protected by sheets which are supported by the low wall and held in place by rafters or metal fastenings.

The coffee is either carried by hand to the area or transported in small carts via a rail network (Fig 113). In Brazil it is often transported by a water current in small open-topped channels.

The cost of constructing the cemented area is quite high, so small-scale planters sometimes use an area of packed earth as an alternative. Drying obviously takes more time with this method. It is also less even than on the cemented area, and the coffee emerges with a high level of impurities. The value of the product is definitely affected by the drying method used. Coffees of excellent origin can lose some of their quality if poorly dried.

Drying must be progressive, so that the parchment, or protective coating, remains intact for the entire period of exposure. The inner parts of the bean are also affected by the drying process. If they are not sufficiently dehydrated, water moves from the internal tissues to the superficial layers and this moisture migration may cause alterations in the physical composition of the bean and the appearance of discoloured spots and other unsightly variegations. On the other hand, a well-conducted drying process will produce beans of uniform colour and high quality.

Drying begins with the exposure to the sun of a thin layer of coffee beans which is stirred frequently. This removes the surface moisture that could potentially initiate a harmful post-fermentation reaction if allowed to remain. This inevitably occurs with coffees that are too moist, are spread out in too thick a layer, and are not adequately stirred (Wilbaux). As the bean dehydrates, the thickness of the layer may be gradually increased, and during the final stages there may be as much as 10 to 15 kg of moist parchment coffee per square metre, or a layer 3 to 4 cm thick. Once the coffee has reached the required degree of dryness, it is piled into a large heap, which is then covered with a canvas or polythene sheet, prior to transport to the storage silos.

The duration of the drying period depends primarily on the climate; the diurnal temperature, the sun's intensity, relative humidity, ventilation, and the nature of the material on which the coffee is exposed: screens, cement, tiles, bricks, earth, etc. In countries with a low relative humidity during the harvest period and very intense sunshine, as is the case in the region of São Paulo (Brazil), the drying of the parchment coffee may only take six to eight days. In less-favoured regions drying may take between 10 and 15 days.

Judging the right degree of dryness is very important. The beans are usually tested by biting them. If the teeth leave a mark on the beans, they are not dry enough. To obtain an approximate numerical indication of the moisture content, various types of moisture meters can be used to measure the moisture capacity or the dialectric constant.

Artificial drying

Artificial drying is necessary in very wet climates and when the drying operation needs to be accelerated due to the extent of the harvest.

The oldest technique uses the heated hearth of a **traditional stove**, which consists essentially of a hearthstone and a flat surface over which the coffee is spread. This is heated by a grid of tubes through which hot combustion gases circulate. This type of dryer is also used for cocoa and copra. The beans must be constantly supervised when they are being dried, due to the variability of the heating and the risk of fire. The output is low: about 25 kg of dried parchment coffee per square metre per day. The temperature should be between 75° and 80°C at the beginning of the operation, decreasing progressively to about 50°C (canephora).

Several specialised manufacturers designed **mechanical dryers** at the beginning of the century and the use of these are still very widespread. The most widely used are the 'Gardiola' or 'Okrassa' dryers, the main component being a cylindrical drum made from perforated sheet iron, which is slowly rotated at a speed of 2 turns/min around a tubular axle. The drum is divided into compartments so that the weight of the beans is equally distributed. The central tube is connected to a network of smaller tubes which span the compartments and open into an outside casing. Hot air produced by a boiler, circulates through the tube system, heating the mass of coffee which slowly loses its moisture. The temperature of the mass should not exceed 90°C at the beginning, falling to 65°–70°C during the final stages.

Many models of this type of rotary dryer exist, differing mainly in size and capacity (1 to 6 tonnes of moist parchment coffee). The drying period lasts between 20 and 30 hours, depending upon the initial moisture content of the coffee and the thermal capacity of the equipment. Arabica coffees are generally dried more slowly and at a lower temperature than the other species.

This equipment works well, but its output is relatively low and it is very expensive to purchase. It is only suitable for factories which process large tonnages.

There are many other types of coffee dryers. Some, which are either continuous or discontinuous, are similar to cereal or fodder dryers, while others are of the tunnel type. The use of hot air generators which use fuel oil and are easy to adjust has become popular during recent years. Entirely artificial drying is a delicate operation which can result in serious errors if not properly carried out.

Storing parchment coffee

No matter how carefully the coffee is dried, its moisture content is rarely evenly distributed. The size of the beans, the degree of ripeness of the fruit, etc., all effect the distribution of moisture. Some uniformity can be obtained by storing the parchment coffee for at least one week in silos with a capacity of a few cubic metres. This operation, which is commonly practiced with choice arabica, ensures that the market product will look more homogeneous, particularly with regard to colour, and that its intrinsic qualities will also be more uniform.

Hulling

The simplest equipment used for hulling parchment coffee is the pestle and mortar, which is still used in some countries for processing small quantities of coffee. 'Bonifiries' still exist in Guadeloupe, which are equipped with a pestle mounted on a camshaft, driven by a hydraulic wheel, above a mortar which contains the coffee. A type of rotary mill was used for some years in Central America, consisting of a circular trough, 2 to 5 m in diameter containing the coffee to be hulled, in which two millstones rotated. In Yemen, hand operated, horizontal millstones are still used, with one fixed and the other mobile.

These antiquated methods are now almost extinct, and are being replaced by **mechanical hullers**. These machines consist of a ribbed cast-iron cylinder, dirven by a rapid rotational movement mounted in a gearcase. The coffee circulates in the equipment, being transported by the ribbed surface of the cylinder. From the combined action of pressure and friction, the

Fig 114   Huller-polisher 'Okrassa' no. 2, Bentall (Courtesy: Bentall)

(196)

coating of the bean is broken, fragmented, and removed by a ventilating fan. The film, which is the inner coating, is mostly removed at the same time.

The complete removal of the film requires additional friction. This is achieved by machines called **polishers**, which differ from the hullers in the profile and nature of the phosphorous bronze cylinder. The polisher gives the bean a shiny appearance, which is popular with certain choice arabicas. A type of equipment, called the **huller-polisher**, carries out the two operations simultaneously (Fig 114).

This equipment is quite satisfactory provided the parchment coffee is very dry. If this is not the case the coffee 'chokes' the machine, causing parts of the machinery to overheat, and the beans are liable to be crushed. Small hand-operated hullers exist but they require a great deal of manual effort, which makes them rather unpopular.

A huller based on the force of impact of a centrifugal disk on the bean has recently appeared in the coffee industry. It requires very little energy, and one of its advantages is that it does not heat the beans.

Dry processing

In dry processing, the fresh fruits are dried immediately after they have been harvested. Once they are dried, the pulp, mucilage and parchment form a sort of husk enveloping the beans. The beans can then be removed simply by breaking the husk.

Although there are fewer operations involved in dry processing than in wet processing, this method is more time consuming. In fact, drying the cherries takes longer than drying the parchment coffee. The quantity of moisture that must evaporate is much greater because the fresh fruit has a moisture content of 60–75 per cent and the covering of the fruits is a major obstacle in the moisture transfer. For example, on the basis of a moisture content of 65 per cent, about 3 kg of water must evaporate to produce 1 kg of clean coffee.

Drying cherry coffee requires at least as much care as parchment coffee. The risks of secondary fermentations are even greater due to the presence of mucilage, a very hygroscopic material. The Brazilians have been preparing their coffees in this way for two centuries and have perfected a technique.

Drying
Natural drying

Similar methods are used for drying both cherry and parchment coffee: screens, mobile roofs, terraces, cemented areas. However, the area in which the coffee is spread out must be larger for the same tonnage of harvested beans. In Brazil, it is estimated that the equivalent of one twentieth of the number of coffee trees in production must be used in square metres, for example, 100 000 coffee trees ÷ 20 = 5000 m².

The thickness of the layer of fruit must not exceed 5 to 6 cm (about 40 kg of fresh fruit per square metre). If it does, there is a serious risk of mould developing, seeds germinating, and black beans forming.

The drying, which involves similar principles to those used in drying parchment coffee, takes much longer. It lasts an average of 10 to 20 days, and is complete when the covering of the bean (husk) is easily broken when pressed between the fingers.

Small-scale planters must be made aware of the loss in quality that can result from poor drying. The most serious situation occurs when rain falls during the drying period, causing it to be spread over several weeks. The beans change under these circumstances. Black beans, so-called coloured beans, and sometimes stinker beans may appear. However, some elementary precautions can be taken to prevent this deterioration:

- The coffee must be spread to dry in a thin layer when it is fresh and still very moist. The thickness of the layer is increased progressively, without exceeding 5 cm at the end of the operation;
- The operation must be supervised carefully so that the drying coffee is not exposed to rain or nocturnal dew. The harvest can either be protected with a covering on site or the screens placed under some kind of shelter;
- The drying coffee must be stirred several times a day;
- Only very dry cherry coffee must be placed in a store before hulling: it should not have a moisture content of more than 12 per cent.

Artificial drying

Similar equipment is used for artificially drying both cherry and parchment coffee. The former operation obviously takes longer and requires a higher energy consumption.

In Brazil, in the large 'haciendas', solar and artificial drying are often used alternately to simulate more closely the natural conditions which are favoured by producers. In accordance with this a slow-drying type of equipment for cherry coffee, the **Torres dryer** was designed and developed in Brazil. The **cereal type**, vertical dryer is also widely used, particularly in processing factories with a large capacity.

Hulling

The most basic hulling procedure consists of pounding the dry cherries in a mortar. It is still a common practice for small harvests, despite the drawback of having a high level of breakages.

Hullers ensure a better method with greater output. This equipment, namely the 'Engleberg system' consists of a cylinder mounted on a horizontal

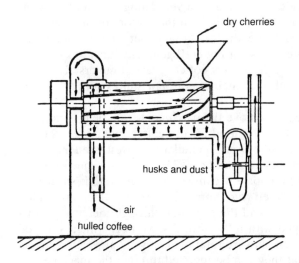

dry cherries

husks and dust

air

hulled coffee

Fig 115 Diagram of a coffee huller, 'Engleberg system'

Fig 116 Huller-parchment remover, type no. 1 'Africa' (Courtesy: Gordon)

axle with steel blades or knives attached at an angle to a surrounding cover or gearcase. The cylinder is driven by a motor at a speed of 400–500 turns/ min and rotates inside the gearcase, the lower part of which is pierced. The hulling blades are mounted inside the gearcase, and the distance of the blades or knives from the cylinder can be regulated. The coffee is carried along by the rotations of the cylinder and is violently thrown against the fixed blades. The husks break due to the repeated collisions (Fig 115).

The debris from the husk is expelled by a ventilating fan and the beans are collected when they drop out of the hole in the bottom of the machine.

Equipment capable of dealing with a rather large output is also manufactured (500 to 600 kg of coffee beans per hour). It generally functions satisfactorily if it is supplied with very dry cherry coffee. Manual hullers also exist, but they are not very successful since their operation requires a lot of manual effort.

Hullers can also be used to remove the parchment from beans and their output is greater than when they are used for dry coffee hulling (Fig 116).

Wilbaux draws attention to the Brazilian huller, the '**Descascador**', which performs excellently without heating the beans. It also has a much greater capacity (450 kg/hour). This equipment consists of a perforated, sheet iron cage within which a blade-covered rotor turns. The beans, which are hulled as they pass between the blades and the cage, fall through the cage perforations. The huller is equipped with a 'Sururuca' separator, which is a type of winnowing basket, having an outward rotational movement which recovers any unhulled cherries so that they can be recycled through the machine.

Other types of equipment with a greater output of 10 tonnes of cherry coffee per hour, are based on the same principle, using either sheet iron or barred cages.

It should be noted that dry processing must always be preceded by sorting prior to harvesting, the objective of which is to separate the impurities, the dry fruits, etc. This preliminary operation is achieved with the same methods as wet processing, using mechanical separators, washers, siphon-vats, etc.

New hulling techniques have been introduced over the past few years. In one type of equipment the cherry coffee is compressed between a rotating, grooved drum, and an adjustable breastplate composed of three sections, each of which is lined with detachable rubber sheets. The advantage of this machine is that it does not break or heat the coffee, and has a high work capacity but a relatively low energy output.

Pneumatic hulling is an original technique which has not yet had any commercial success. It entails breaking the husk by compression, followed by an abrupt decompression within a closed container; a valve rapidly reduces the pressure. Dry cherries which are riddled with holes due to insect attack (mainly the berry borer) are not sensitive to this difference in pressure and emerge from the huller unchanged. It is therefore easy to separate the damaged fruits from the healthy ones.

Operations common to dry and wet processing

After hulling, the coffee still contains impurities and a rather large proportion of defective, undesirable and/or broken beans. The export regulations in each country that define the criteria that the various graders must satisfy in order to be of export quality (processing rules) require that the producer, or merchant-exporter, carries out a certain number of complementary operations which include **cleaning, sorting, grading**, etc.

Cleaning

The simplest cleaning and dusting equipment in use is the **winnowing machine**, of which several models have been specially manufactured for coffee. It is slow and unreliable, but it is adequate for farm processing 'of small harvests, which are generally re-graded before being shipped. For larger quantities **cleaner-separators** equipped with vibrating and ventilated sieves are more practical.

A whole range of equipment is available for large outputs, particularly of Brazilian origin, which combine cleaning, sorting, and grading. These are only of interest to large farms or processing factories.

Cleaning with a winnowing machine must be complemented by efficient **stone removal** to eliminate as many stones as possible since these could damage equipment.

Sorting and grading

The objective of sorting is to remove misshapen, unsuitable, black, discoloured, or spotted beans, in addition to broken ones of which there is normally a rather high percentage. Both the appearance and the quality of the coffee is improved by this procedure, since some of these defects can give it an inferior flavour.

Fig 117   Sorting tables with mobile shutters in a factory, El Salvador (Courtesy: Fritz)

Unfortunately there is no completely satisfactory equipment for this operation. The effectiveness of most types depends on the differences in density which exist between healthy, normal beans and those which are aborted, unhealthy or pest infested. Machines can eliminate most of the impurities, also a fraction of the defective and undesirable beans, but most of the black, coloured, or spotted beans, which have virtually the same density as that of healthy coffee beans, cannot be separated. It is therefore necessary to sort them manually after processing. Although this operation is exacting, it is essential and must be very carefully executed, particularly when dealing with arabica coffee, which can be significantly down-graded by the presence of so-called colour flaws (Fig. 117).

Good mechanical sorting requires a preliminary size classification of the coffee. This is a prerequisite for good densimetric sorting. Manufacturers have also designed equipment in which the two operations of sorting and grading are combined: cylindrical sorters, oscillating or vibrating sorters, air-float or depression densimetric graders, catadors, etc.

The **catador** cleaning and grading equipment is of particular interest. This machine is very widespread due to its efficiency. It consists of a tall wooden or metal box, about 4 m high, divided longitudinally into two parts with a sieve or grating at the lower end which is connected to the outside. The top is closed with wire netting. At the base is a powerful fan, with one or two independently adjustable parts.

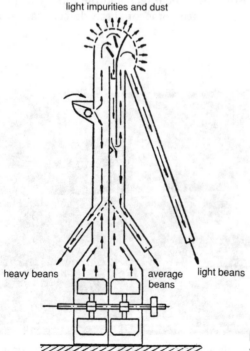

Fig 118   Diagram of a double ventilation type of catador

The coffee is poured into the hopper by a bucket elevator and is evenly dispersed by a distributor-roller. As the beans fall into the hopper, they encounter a violent air current produced by the fan. The denser components continue to fall until they reach the bottom grating and are carried outside. The remaining fractions are carried up in the airstream to where a double densimetric sorter is operating. The dust and smaller impurities are then removed from the equipment. This produces a cleaning operation which is comparable to that of a powerful winnowing machine with a time duration of a three-category grading. It is therefore possible to recirculate each fraction, and by appropriately adjusting the ventilation, to obtain a triple separation and grading. The output of a catador is 500–600 kg/hour and several types are available (Figs 118 and 119).

Large coffee processing factories and co-operatives are generally equipped with an array of catadors. However, this simple equipment now tends to be replaced by gravity flow or densimetric tables which are more efficient in separating the beans according to their densities. Nevertheless, as with catadors, this type of sorting must be preceded by sorting according to bean size.

Equipment is now available which can sort beans according to their colour. These **electronic sorters** are equipped with photo-electric cartridges. Several types of equipment adapted for use with raw coffee are now being manufactured. Some are monochromatic, othes are bichromatic. Their work is generally outstanding and improves the value of the coffee, particularly with regard to arabicas.

The latest models have been considerably improved. They are automated and their output is between 100 and 150 kg per hour per channel compared with only 35 to 40 kg, 30 years ago. However, their purchase price is high and the equipment requires skilled personnel to operate and maintain it. It should also be preferably housed in air-conditioned premises. The use of such equipment is therefore limited to large farms and co-operative factories (Figs 120 and 121). Sorting equipment which uses ultraviolet light is also currently being designed.

Equipment built by a German company will clean and remove the film from coffee beans simultaneously by stirring and friction, with or without water or an inert material such as moist sawdust. The objective of removing the film is to improve the appearance of the beans, making the colour more uniform.

At the end of these operations, the beans are **homogenised according to grade** if necessary. This is often referred to as 'bulking' and is an essential process in large-scale or co-operative factories for preparing samples of uniform quality. On a small scale, the piles of various types of coffee are spread out on canvas sheets and are mixed by shovelling them together until a fairly uniform sample has been produced. Alternatively equipment referred to as **mixers** is used for large quantities.

Coffee processing is now complete. The producer is now required to package his merchandise in accordance with current regulations.

Fig 119   Gordon micro-processor and catador for samples (Courtesy: Gordon)

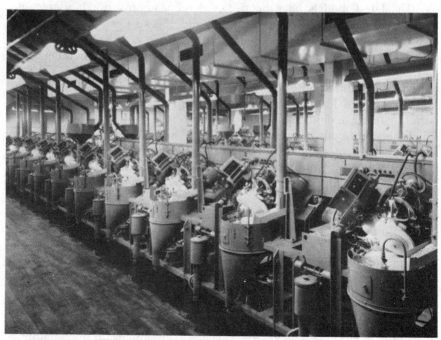

Fig 120   Array of electronic sorters in a factory, Ivory Coast

(204)

Fig 121   Electronic sorters, Illycafe Company, Trieste (Courtesy: Illy)

Fig 122   Coffee warehouse. Colombian port of Buenaventura

In Francophone countries, such as Brazil, Zaire, Venezuela, etc., the most common practice is to use new jute bags containing 60 kg of coffee. In Colombia, Guatemala and Mexico, the standard net weight is set at 70 kg; while in Costa-Rica, Indonesia, Haiti and Cuba it is 80 kg.

Before the bags are shipped, they must be stored in well-ventilated stores which are protected from high humidity. They should also be isolated from the ground or stone floor by a grating or pallet, and, if possible, treated with insecticide. It is advisable to thermally insulate the stores in order to reduce the effects of temperature and relative humidity variations in the store, since these are harmful to good conservation (Fig 122).

Composition of coffee fruits and clean coffee yields

1 Canephora coffee (Robusta):
100 kg of ripe cherries provide approximately:
a) Wet processing

74 kg of pulped coffee	44 kg of pre-dried coffee
52 kg of washed coffee	26 kg of parchment coffee
49 kg of dried coffee	22 kg of clean coffee

b) Dry processing
40–45 kg of dry cherries
22 kg of clean coffee
56–60 kg of fresh pulp
Sub-products
12–15 kg of dry pulp
3–5 kg of parchment
20 kg of husks
(Source: Knaus in R. Wilbuax)

2 Arabica coffee
100 kg of ripe fruit decompose into about:
39 kg of fresh pulp
(or 16 kg of dry pulp)
22 kg of mucilage
39 kg of moist parchment coffee
100 kg of moist parchment coffee provides about:
79 kg of dry parchment coffee
54 kg of dry clean coffee
1 kg of ripe fruit contains about 550 cherries.
1 m^3 of ripe fruit weighs about 620 kg.
1 m^3 of fresh fruit weighs about 420 kg.
100 kg of parchment provides about 3 kg of ash.
100 kg of parchment ash contains about 10 kg CaO, 23 kg K_2O.
(Source: R. Coste. *Les Caféiers et Cafés dans le Monde*, vol. II, p. 10.)

Technology for small farms and family-run plantations
Small farms

The equipment necessary for processing the production of a plantation of 30 to 50 ha, which may range from 150 to 250 tonnes of fresh fruit, may include:

For wet processing: a pulping workroom with siphon-vat equipment, a pulping machine with two openings which will pulp 1 tonne/hour of cherries, three to four fermentation vats and a drying area, an 18″ huller-polisher, a sorter-grader and winnowing machine. A 1–2 horsepower engine is powerful enough to operate the pulper; a more powerful engine of 3–5 horsepower will be required to operate the huller.

If possible, the operation should be sited on sloping land near to a water point. The fruits are transported to the siphon-vat, from where they fall into the pulper which is placed under the spout of the siphon-vat. Upon leaving the pulper, the parchment coffee should be carried by a water current to the fermentation tanks. From there it is conveyed by the wash water circulating in about 30 metres of channels. It is then brought to the entrance of the drying area. Operations of this 'cascade-type' are reduced in scale, compared with more commercial types of enterprise.

For dry processing: a washing basin or a siphon-vat, a drying area of about 200 m^2, a small huller which can also be used for parchment coffee, a rotating sorter-grader and a winnowing machine. The energy required is approximately 6–8 horsepower.

Family-run plantations

Only a very limited amount of equipment is required. For wet processing: a small hand pulper with a tank for the water supply, plus two cement tanks, or alternatively two boxes, each with a hole at the bottom to drain away the water from fermentation and washing, a number of mobile drying screens. For hulling, small hand-operated equipment should be used, or better still, a motor-driven collective huller. The impurities will be removed by winnowing in an air current, followed by hand sorting.

For dry processing: a good cement-floored drying area is essential, or a series of screens which give the best result in terms of bean quality.

The planter should seek advice or help from a company or a co-operative for the removal of the hulls of cherry coffee. It is also preferable to have the use of a store for the harvested beans which are being dried.

By-products from coffee processing

The pulp and hulls make an excellent fertiliser after they have been allowed to decompose, although they are often regarded as waste products of no value.

Layers of a mixture of pulp and hulls should be alternated in a compost pit with layers of soil and plant debris including household waste. If the mass is kept moist, by watering if rainwater is insufficient, the decomposition will be advanced enough after a year for the material to be usable. 15 to 20 kg of this compost buried around the base of each adult coffee tree is an excellent organic manure which should not be neglected.

Efforts have been made, with varying degrees of success, to use coffee pulp in tanning, in the preparation of ethyl alcohol, and in the extraction of pectin, etc. An original approach of using them in the preparation of combustible gas (methane) has been seen in India and the Central African Republic. Thirty kg of partially decomposed pulp added to 18 l of water and 2 kg of fermented manure gave 670 l of gas in 72 days, which was sufficient to raise the temperature of 30 l of water from 20°C to 70°C. One tonne of cherries provides about 400 kg of fresh pulp plus the mucilage, or 200 kg of partially decomposed pulp. This would be sufficient to provide a source of heat that would be 15 times greater. With an adult plantation of 50 hectares, producing 200 tonnes of fruit or 40 tonnes of partially decomposed pulp, the use of this heat source could provide a continuous supply of hot water for a household.

Carbonised coffee parchment provides a high quality form of charcoal which is odourless, smokeless and has a high calorific value. This 'Kahawa coal' is very useful for cooking food and is marketed in Kenya.

Using the hulls as fuel is only moderately successful as the technique is dificult to master, mainly due to the high levels of potassium and silica which they contain. They do, however, represent an enormous source of calorific energy which could be used for the artificial drying of many agricultural products.

It is also interesting to note that in certain countries such as India, Yemen and Bolivia, people have long been consuming an 'herbal tea' prepared with dried coffee pulp.

Reject material from sorting

There is currently an interest in the reject material obtained from sorting. This consists of black, dry, or broken beans, etc., which are not marketable and represent a sizeable loss for the producing countries. Studies are being carried out, mainly on serotonin and its derivatives, cafeic and chlorogenic acid, lipids, and certain diastases. At present, however, the potential use of these products appears to be very limited.

10 *Production costs and profitability*

General information

Calculating the production costs of an agricultural product is generally rather complex, especially with regard to a perennial species such as coffee. However, it is essential for any head of a fairly large farm to know his annual production costs, since this is the only way for him to determine the profitability of his enterprise. Moreover, if he discovers any weaknesses, he may then act accordingly, and may correct a situation that is burdened with debt due to management problems, or compromised by climatic, cropping, financial, or economic hazards.

Commercial farms

When calculating the production cost of a perennial species, **establishment** or **investment costs** which include clearing the site, laying out and planting the crop, and purchasing equipment, must be distinguished from the **annual costs** of running the farm, which include maintenance, harvesting and depreciation costs.

Establishment or investment costs

Establishment costs are the expenses required to establish the plantation and maintain it until production commences. From this period, it is possible to calculate the level of profitability and depreciation of the various components of the investment. Payment is divided up annually over a previously determined period of time, generally the supposed duration of the fully productive and most profitable period of the plantation. In theory, the amounts calculated each year as amortisation or depreciation, should accumulate and be available for establishing a new plantation once all accounts have been settled. Nevertheless, during a period of inflation, currency devaluation should be taken into account in the calculations, otherwise the planter may not benefit from the real value of the capital that he invested. This concept

(209)

complicates the accounting, but it is nevertheless a reality that should be considered.

The breakdown of the establishment costs for a sizeable commercial farm includes many very diverse items, particularly the purchase of land, hiring of labour, construction of buildings such as housing, workshops, stores, etc., construction of access and service roads, purchase of equipment and tools, nurseries, miscellaneous tasks such as clearing, staking, digging, planting, etc. and maintenance costs for planted plots such as weeding, cutting, disease and pest control. Those of most importance are described in greater detail in the following section.

Labour: Labour costs must be calculated taking into account the legal daily wage; social security (accident insurance, paid leave, medical expenses, etc.); benefits in kind: housing (estimated rent), supplies, etc.; recruitment costs per contract: transport, bonuses, food. These expenses can be calculated on the basis of 200 or 300 days of work per annum per worker.

Plants: Cost of seeds; plastic or other type of bags; nursery preparation (salaries, equipment); fertilisation; sowing and transplanting; maintenance and the purchase of planting material if necessary.

Fertiliser: Fertiliser costs for the plantation including transport costs.

Tractors and vehicles: Purchase price; depreciation calculated over a period of three years (or one third per year); insurance, maintenance, spares and repairs; fuel and lubricants; tyres, etc.

Agricultural machinery and equipment: Purchase price, depreciation, maintenance, servicing, repairs (spare parts), etc.

Estimate of establishment costs
Cost of buying or leasing the land
Labour and supplies

- Land preparation and planting;
- Clearing and windrowing of the felled trees; road and path construction; establishment of cover crop; marking out; digging planting holes;
- Plants: costs calculated according to previous section; Planting;
- Fertilisation: costs calculated according to previous section plus costs of fertiliser applications;
- Plant protection: application equipment, agro-chemicals, labour;
- Cropping and maintenance practices: equipment, labour, etc.

Annual expenses (administrative)

- Management and office expenses: travel, secretarial assistance, etc.; taxes; building maintenance and repairs, etc.

Interest on invested capital

- Interest is usually calculated at a reasonable rate, generally at 5 or 6 per cent, but it is not uncommon to have a higher rate.

For the first year, therefore, investments are the total of the following four items:

Land acquisition + Labour and supplies + Annual expenses + Interest on capital = **Total** _____

Calculations should be made in this way every year until the farm profits cover the expenses. For coffee, the pre-cropping period, excluding the first small harvests, is generally about four to five years, perhaps only three for plantations using polyclonal varieties.

If the separate expenses for the first year, second year, etc. are totalled, they represent the total amount of capital invested in the farm. If the plantation has a vigorous, healthy and uniform plant stock when it enters into production, its monetary value may largely exceed the investment made, but this is not always the case.

It is difficult to calculate the length of time necessary to achieve profitability in coffee growing during the first years of the farm's existence. It is reasonable, especially when prices are high, to estimate a productive life of 12 to 15 years, but it is not uncommon for this to extend to 20 years. With high-density plantations, profitability should be calculated on the basis of a shorter period, depending upon the type of farm.

Determining the production costs of coffee

The production costs of coffee can be established every year as follows:

I – Annual farm expense (or per season)

Nature of expenditure	Labour	Materials	Total expenses
Maintenance:			
Weeding			
Replanting			
Pruning			
Fertiliser			
Etc.			
Plant protection:			
Pest control			
Etc.			
Harvesting:			
Picking			
Internal transport			
Preparation of the coffee:			
Labour			
Bags, etc.			
Fuel			
Transport			
TOTAL			

II – General annual expenses

Management and administrative costs   _____
Taxes   _____
Insurance (buildings, harvests, etc.)   _____
Annual depreciation: _____
    Plantation capital (see above)   _____
    Buildings[1]   _____
    Equipment[2]   _____
    Land improvement[3]   _____
    General maintenance and repairs   _____
    Miscellaneous   _____

TOTAL   _____

1   Cement buildings may be depreciated over a 15 year period.
2   Equipment can be depreciated over a 3–5 year period, depending upon its nature and use.
3   Land improvement (drainage, irrigation, erosion control, access roads, etc.) may be depreciated over a 5–15 year period, depending upon their nature.

III – Interest on capital

Interest on invested capital   _____

Total annual expenses

I. Farming costs   _____
II. General costs   _____
III. Interest payments   _____

    GRAND TOTAL   _____

Profitability

The profitability of the farm takes into account the overall total of coffee sales, (deducting, if necessary, transport costs to the point of sale and when the coffee is sold externally, subtracting all fees such as customs, freight, insurance and brokerage).

Farm balance sheet (year or season)

Total farm profits   _____
Total farm expenses   _____

    END OF YEAR FIGURES   _____

The difference, which may be either positive or negative, represents the profit or loss of the farm during the year or season in question.

Estimating the production costs is more complicated with a farm which has mixed cropping (coffee, cocoa, etc.) as certain expenses apply to different items, and are often based on estimates.

If a farm is planted over a period of a few years, section by section, there is an advantage in establishing production costs for all of the plots having the same age. If not, general costs are included with the costs of the immature plots, producing a total which is too high.

Small-scale farms and family-run plantations

The concept of production costs in relation to small African or Malagasy non-commercial farms of 5 to 20 ha and family-run plantations, is very different from that for a commercial plantation for the following reasons: the land is generally not purchased; the infrastructure mainly consists of an access path or road; the equipment includes only essential agricultural tools and some agro-chemicals; the establishment comprises a store constructed of local materials and a drying area or screens (except when the coffee is prepared by wet processing, whereupon some additional expenses are required). If the farmer uses salaried labour, he must calculate the costs of this item as defined for commercial plantations (see page 211).

If the planter farms his coffee plantation without salaried labour, he must theoretically take into account the time that he and the other adults in his family spend working on the plantation or elsewhere. The number of days (or hours) worked, including the time it takes to travel to and from the place of work, should be noted and totalled at the end of the year, and estimated on the basis of the statutory cost of regional labour. In principle, the planter, and the members of his family who help him, must be reimbursed for their work from the income received from the sale of the coffee with an amount that at least equals what they would receive from a salaried job. The common misconception that the small-scale planter, African or not, has no expenses is totally erroneous and expenses must be calculated with regard to labour, particularly the number of work days devoted to maintaining the coffee plots.

Obviously the freedom that the small-scale planter enjoys, the opportunities he has to take part in many different types of activities, his family life, etc., are all advantages, the value of which is very difficult to estimate. However, this viewpoint should not encourage the head of the family to conclude that the profit he makes from the sale of his crop is total profit. The level of remuneration for the work done within the realms of the coffee plantation must be estimated, at least theoretically. Many trials aimed at calculating production costs have been based on this concept.

11 *Characteristics and composition of green coffee*

General information

The main botanical origins of coffee are two very different species: *C. arabica* and *C. canephora*. The former is almost exclusively cultivated in the Americas and the latter is widely grown in Africa and Madagascar. Production of both species is now expanding in Asia, particularly India and Indonesia. However, small tonnages of coffee from less common species, which are cultivated particularly in Africa, appear sporadically in European markets. These are mainly *C. excelsa* and *C. liberica*.

Each species comprises many different varieties, forms, and types and the specific characteristics of the beans varies. In addition to these botanical criteria there are also less obvious characteristics which occur as a result of various influences such as the ecological environment (sometimes the soil), cropping techniques, etc.

Some of these influences are genetic in origin, while others are phenotypic or environmentally related. They are manifested by pronounced differences in size, shape, colour, and even texture of the beans. These differences may therefore also appear in coffee harvested from shrubs with the same botanical affiliation, but which come from different regions.

The techniques used to process the coffee, the care taken during its processing, and the way the beans are stored before shipping also infuence the appearance of the beans, for example, more or less complete skin removal, and particularly colour, which may be affected by excess fermentation and insufficient or irregular drying.

Finally, aging changes the hue of the beans. This is easily recognised by merchants. The colouring of the beans becomes generally more subdued the longer they are stored.

These visible criteria are extremely important from a commercial pont of view. In a way they provide a key to any sample of beans: their botanical grouping, geographical origin, method of preparation, age, storage conditions etc. (Fig 123).

Naturally, the coffee is destined to be made into a beverage, so it may appear absurd to attach so much importance to the appearance of the beans. This belief may also be supported by the fact that merchant-retailers in France no longer display green coffee for the benefit of roasting companies.

However, the concern that green coffee should have a good appearance is still justified. The description of the product is not based solely on its botanical identity, or its genetic origins, but also on the attention that the producer has paid to sorting (elimination of abnormally coloured beans, mainly black, unripe beans that often give 'the cup' a bad taste, and impurities and broken beans that roast badly), grading (upon which the uniformity of the samples of beans depends, which is an important factor in good roasting) and last but not least, good preparation and packaging. The taste test then follows, so that the true organoleptic qualities of the beverage may be appreciated.

The subject matter of this chapter includes the examination of the characteristics of green coffee and the losses in quality which may result from poor preparation or inferior storage conditions.

Microscopic characteristics

The coffee bean is enveloped by a fine membrane, commonly called silverskin, which is actually the testa. It is thin, silvery, and shiny on *C. arabica*, thicker on *C. canephora*, papery on *C. excelsa*, and coarse and thick on *C. liberica*. According to Rabechault (1959), a microscopic examination of the skin does not show any particular anatomic characteristics. It consists of a regular layer of rounded sclerenchymatous cells, several strata of irregular polygonal cells with thin walls, and a layer of large rectangular cells.

The coffee bean, as described by Rabechault, has a hemispherical, semi-elliptical, or semi-ovoid shape. Its cross-section is, consequently, convex. An exceptionally rounded bean, without a flat side, is called a 'peaberry' (Fig 123c), which is developed in a unilocular fruit if one of the ovules aborts.

Whatever the shape of the bean, it always has a deep longitudinal furrow on the flat side, the other side being convex in outline. This furrow has many morphological characteristics in common with the bean itself (straight, sinuous, etc.). A transverse section of the bean shows the furrow to be not simply superficial, but a cleft that penetrates deep into the bean.

Examination of a cross-section of a bean reveals a gap in the tissues which can be discerned by a line which is discontinuous due to the presence of numerous lacunae. This lies on a symmetrical plane within the tissues. The embryo lies within this gap in the tissues, extending towards the base of the bean, with its tapering, cylindrical root and its cordate cotyledons. The embryo obtains its nutritional requirements from the endosperm during germination. This operation is facilitated by the presence of the lacunae, in

C. arabica typica

C. arabica var. laurina

C. arabica peaberries

C. canephora var. kouilou

Fig 123   Green coffee beans

C. liberica   *C. abeokutae* (Gros Indénié)

which the enzymes that are secreted by the embryo circulate more easily. The lacunae are linked together by thin cell walls, forming a tissue of mucilaginous nature.

The bean mass is predominately corneous endosperm, the cells of which contain protein, sugars, and lipids. In-depth studies on the structure of the coffee bean have been carried out by Dentan in particular, using improved investigative methods such as the electron microscope.

The beans ripen relatively quickly. Based on an experiment using *C. arabica* Catuai amarelo, Dentan estimated that the beans take 25 days to ripen, compared to 195 to 200 days for the development of the fruit. He also reported that for the first 100 days, the beans increase in volume and store starch. During the course of the next phase, reserve substances are stored (lipids, protein, polysaccharides). After 200 days, tryptophan deteriorates into aerotonin, and there is a migration of chlorogenic acids and mineral salts. Other research workers (see Bibliography) found that there was a change in the caffeoylquinic and decaffeoylquinic acid relations during this phase. These observations were taken up again by Dentan with regard to the unripe beans. They contain a certain quantity of tryptophan which may combine with other components during roasting and result in a deterioration of the taste. Excessive quantities of decaffeoylquinics in the bean would also produce an astringent taste and a decrease in the quality of the beverage.

Macroscopic characteristics

Based on macroscopic examinations, size differences are particularly marked between the two main cultivated species *C. arabica* and *C. canephora*. Arabica beans are larger and longer than those of canephora. The average length, for example of arabica originating from Brazil, is between 8 and 10 mm. The best achievements from arabica grown in Colombia or Central America are commonly 10 to 12 mm and the Maragogype variety can be as long as 14 to 15 mm.

C. canephora beans (robusta and Kouilou) are smaller (6 to 8 mm) and rounder. The median furrow tends to be more rectilinear than in the arabica bean. Moreover, the proportion of 'peaberries' encountered in an average sampling is generally higher among canephora, being 10 to 20 per cent compared to 5 to 10 per cent among arabica.

The *C. liberica* bean is larger than those of the two preceding species, its length often exceeding 15 mm.

With regard to density, there is a rather marked difference between the two main species: arabica beans have an average weight of 600 kg/m^3, whereas the canephoras weigh between 600 and 700 kg/m^3 (with the same moisture content). Apart from this factor, which is of genetic origin, the density of the beans may be affected by the ripeness of the fruit at the time of harvesting, or by pest attacks or disease infections.

The colour of the beans is of great commercial importance, especially for the choice arabicas. Preparation techniques have an essential role, particularly fermentation and drying. The colour varies between light yellow and intense green with a spectrum of intermediate shades: straw yellow, dark yellow, greyish yellow, light green, green blue, green bronze, and intense green.

The predominant colour of any sample varies according to its botanical origin, the nature of the soil of the region where it grows (presence or absence of certain mineral elements), cropping techniques (shade, fertilisation) and preparation (dry or wet processing, artificial or natural drying, skin removal). It may also vary, depending upon the length of time and conditions of storage.

Washed arabica beans are generally of a uniform colour: either a bright green, blue-green, or grey-blue. The canephoras have a less clear-cut colouring, and often have a greyish tinge as a result of poor skin removal.

In certain Central American countries, the good quality arabicas are sometimes artificially coloured in order to make them more attractive. This practice is generally tolerated provided the products used are non-toxic. The colouring, which is in the form of a very fine powder, is either mixed with the coffee at the time of polishing, or added to special equipment used in stirring.

So-called colour defects, meaning colour which is clearly different from the predominant colour of the sample, may occur. These may be caused by very diverse factors, such as harvesting either before or after ripening, fruits harvested that are fallen, diseased, or pest-infested, lack of care in the preparation, etc.

The **smell** of green coffee is very characteristic and the presence of mouldy or stinker beans in a sample is easily discerned by their smell. It is even more apparent during the roasting process or when the coffee is tasted. Certain coffees from the regions of Rio and Victoria in Brazil have a characteristic iodine-like aroma which is popular with some consumers ('Rio flavoured' coffees). Mouldy and rancid odours occur when the beans are moist.

Chemical or other odours may also result from storing the beans in substandard conditions near aromatic substances, either before or after they are shipped by sea. A particularly disagreeable odour may develop, for example, if the coffee is near skins and/or fertiliser based on animal substances, or if it is transported in vehicles that have contained such merchandise. These odours do not always disappear when the coffee is roasted.

The traditional method of packing green coffee in ordinary jute bags does not always give it adequate protection. It is better to use double polythene bags or containers which are now more commonly used.

The main defects of green coffee

Colour defects

Black beans

Any bean which is at least half black on the outside or inside is called a black bean. This is considered to be the main defect of green coffee, and is used as a standard in inspection tests. Recently, however, stinker beans have become more common in batches of certain origins, depreciating their value considerably (see aroma and taste deficiencies).

Black beans make the beverage taste bitter, disagreeable, and render it generally undrinkable. They lose less weight than normal beans when roasted (13 per cent compared to 18 to 20 per cent), and are easily distinguished by their sooty, dull appearance.

The reason for this serious defect must be attributed to the prolonged fermentation of fruits picked from the ground, which then undergo a poor drying process with intermittent periods of wetting. The presence of black beans is rare in wet processing, except where the fruit has been harvested from the ground, or if there are still some beans left from previous operations in the fermentation tanks and poorly cleaned washing channels.

Greyish or dark grey beans

There are several reasons for this colour defect: harvesting before the beans are ripe, initial fermentation of fruits in the heap, poor drying or repeated spells of wetting if stored under poor conditions, etc. Beans of this colour are classified as undesirable.

Foxy beans

The red colouring is essentially due to artificial drying which has been over-done. Reasons for this include too high a temperature, drying extended over too long a period of time, or the beans not having been sufficiently mixed. It may affect the tissues to varying depths. If the colouring is very superficial, it could be the result of excess fermentation coupled with loose pulp. In some cases it has been attributed to the adherence of a thin film of reddish soil from the drying area during hulling, if the soil has a high clay content.

Coated or murram-coloured beans

This colouring is imparted to the bean by the presence, either wholly or partially, of the skin. It is a defect of minor importance, except for extremely high quality arabicas.

White, opalescent, and glassy beans

These are generally beans that have been insufficiently dried or have reab-sorbed some moisture, within which internal enzyme reactions often appear. These beans are less dense than a healthy bean of the same volume. Glassy beans are the result of artificial drying using too high a temperature at the beginning, resulting in a rapid release of water vapour. They are considered undesirable.

Blotchy and spotted beans

Blotchy beans have spots of various colours due to incomplete or irregular desiccation. Spots appear on the beans due to the effect of oxidising agents which are present on the surface tissues following injuries. These develop particularly during the preparation of the beans, often during hulling, but certain lesions are induced by pest or disease infections.

Poor fermentation or the use of water with a high iron content (formation of black precipitates with the tannin from the beans) for wet processing can also give rise to spots. The presence of rather opaline, whitish spots reveals poor drying or the initiation of germination resulting in enzymatic reactions.

Defects in the aroma and taste
Stinkers

As soon as these beans are cut, they release a putrid, nauseating odour which is also rather volatile. A few hours after the bean has been cut, this odour will have disappeared. As the appearance of these beans is no different or only slightly different from that of healthy beans, it is very difficult to distinguish them. Unfortunately, their bad odour becomes apparent during roasting and the presence of a single stinker in a cylinder is enough to contaminate its entire contents. The taste comes through in the beverage and produces undrinkable coffee.

It has now been established that stinkers are caused either by excessively long fermentation or the use of unclean water. If it is a matter of only a few beans in a batch, the reason may be that the fermentation tanks or washing channels have been poorly cleaned and all the beans from the preceding operation were not removed.

One of the reasons for the occurrence of stinkers was believed to be the poor organisation of mechanical pulping operations in local installations while wet processing arabica beans, or alternatively inadequate equipment. Often, for various reasons, the berries remain in the heap or vat for several days after delivery before the pulp is removed. Fermentation occurs within the mass and reaches the butyric stage within certain fruits.

Whatever the cause, the presence of stinkers too often passes undetected until roasting, resulting in a significant loss to the buyer, and seriously discrediting the origin of the batch.

Rancid or acid beans

These beans have a rather dark brown colour and give off a disagreeable odour when cut. They are the result of poorly managed, excessively long fermentation and their defects are discernable in the beverage.

Musty beans

These beans are either partially or totally covered with mould. They give off a characteristic odour which does not disappear after roasting and is transmitted to the beverage. The presence of a few musty beans in a batch is enough to contaminate the total contents. It is usually the result of incomplete drying, or the reabsorption of moisture in the storage areas or during transport (wet bags).

Rio flavoured coffee

A slightly medicinal aroma is characteristic of certain coffees from the regions of Rio and Victoria in Brazil, due to the metabolic activity of bacteria in the soil, which produce an iodised substance which is absorbed by and transported within the coffee tree by the sap. However, it is not always regarded as a defect, as this very specific flavour is appreciated by some consumers, mainly in regions of Northern France.

Other abnormalities

Droughted beans

These arise from fruits that have been harvested several weeks before they are ripe. This practice has become more widespread in recent years, particularly in Africa, in an effort to combat the risk of the harvest being stolen from the trees. It may also be due to pressure from pickers in the bush who want to recuperate their advances. The unripe beans can be distingushed from the others by their smaller size, dull grey-green colour, and strong adherence of the skin. It is now known that they are either completely lacking in, or do not possess enough of the chemical substances that generate the distinctive aroma. Their organoleptic properties are nil or too low to give the beverage its traditional flavour. The effect of these beans on the quality of the beverage is obviously dependent upon the stage of ripeness of the berry when it is harvested; some berries being harvested as early as four to six weeks before they are fully ripe. The more unripe it is (ripeness being indicated by the dark red colour), the greater the loss of aroma. In extreme cases, there may even be a complete absence of aroma accompanied by a marked astringency and a poor flavour (Dentan and Illy, 1986).

Robusta harvests are likely to contain unripe beans. Certain batches have over 50 per cent unripe beans. Arabica harvests are also affected, but to a lesser extent. The increase of mechanised harvesting operations on the large estates of South America only exacerbates this problem. Agronomic research on mixed harvests of certain varieties must be finalised and applied.

Amongst the many known reasons for the deterioration of the quality of coffee, the high percentage of unripe beans in the batches is a major factor. The solution to this problem lies with the authorities responsible. It is their duty to alert the producers and if necessary to take all possible measures to dissuade them from this practice.

Broken beans

Any piece of bean which is smaller in size than an average half bean may reasonably be called a broken bean. The term 'truncuated bean' is reserved for those beans that have been damaged at one end. The term 'ear' refers to the convex part of a bean that has been broken into two pieces along the median furrow. The concave part is called the 'conch'. These fragments are the result of overly energetic preparation, either by using a pestle and morter or mechanical equipment. The beans become broken due to inadequate adjustment of the pulping equipment or hullers, or an excessively rapid rotation of the cylinders. Breakages most frequently occur during hulling when the coffee is too dry.

Broken beans are considered to be defective. They adversely affect the appearance of the batch, but more importantly they roast faster than whole beans, and tend to become charred. Their presence therefore has a negative effect on the quality of the beverage.

Crushed beans

These are rather flat beans, the median furrow of which has been laid open. They are the result of excessively severe pestling in the more basic method of preparation, or a blocking of the hullers or decorticators during mechanical treatments. Unlike broken beans, crushed beans are the result of processing insufficiently dried coffee.

Pitted beans

The surface of beans which have been infested by insects is more or less riddled with small, round holes such as those produced by the berry borer, *Stephanoderes coffeae*. Cutting them open reveals the galleries bored by the insect. When there are a great many perforations, they join together and give the bean a very characteristic latticed, gnawed appearance. The entrance of the opening is sometimes a greyish-green colour.

The berry borer is not the only insect responsible for pitted beans. *Araecerus fasciculatus* Gerr and various other pests attack coffee in storage: *Carpophilus dimidiatus* F. var. *mutilatus* Er., *Lophocateres pusillus* Klug.

Elephant beans

It is not unusual to find beans of this type among arabica, whereas they are less frequently found among robusta. These are large, deformed beans, consisting of several embryos enveloping the endosperm. Within a batch, they upset the uniformity of the bean size and are also a problem during roasting.

Wrinkled, aborted beans

These beans are smaller than normal. They are flat, often with a wrinkled, dull-coloured surface. They result from fruit that was harvested way before it was ripe, and also from fruits with aborted seeds. This can happen for several reasons, such as pest attacks, unfavourable rainfall regime, nutritional deficiencies, etc.

Wrinkled beans may result from artificial drying which was initiated at an excessively high temperature. They have little effect on the quality of the beverage.

Foreign matter

Whatever the precautions taken during harvesting and preparation of coffee, the batches are rarely free of foreign matter.

Foreign matter most frequently encountered is: soil and dust (trans-ported by the wind during drying); small stones (careless harvesting, drying on packed earth); pulp (poorly executed pulping) or parchment debris (incorrect adjustment of the huller's fan). Sometimes the beans are still in parchment (faulty huller operation) or dry cherries are present (great variation in the size of the fruit, huller poorly adjusted). Twigs and pieces of branches are also common.

The presence of soil and other related debris is revealed by handling the beans and observing the marks that they leave on the skin. It is easy to eliminate these impurities by passing the beans through a winnowing machine or a catador. Stones will be eliminated efficiently by this equipment which functions according to differences in density.

Pulp debris (skins) depreciates the value of the coffee, especially choice arabicas. The skins resemble large, dark brown fragments and give the beverage a bad taste.

Parchment debris is mostly small and very fragmented. It is eliminated mechanically by winnowing machine, catador or densimetric sorter.

Coffee beans in parchment or intact cherries are considered to be major defects because they give the green coffee a disagreeable appearance and are harmful to the roasting process.

Impurities such as twigs, leaf debris and wood fragments are very rarely found in well-prepared coffees. Also, their presence is often indicative, not only of a poorly executed harvest, but also of inefficient processing procedures, for example, using rudimentary methods. These foreign particles, which are very light, are easily disposed of by mechanical processing.

Coffee standardisation

Coffees must meet certain standards of quality in order to be exported from the producing countries. These conditions are listed in a set of 'coffee grading' rules that are applied by the appropriate authorities (administrative or not). The objective is to provide both the seller and the buyer with a guarantee as to the origin, nature, and quality of the merchandise. This facilitates commercial operations and enables forward transactions to be carried out in all the major international markets (New York, Antwerp, Hamburg, Amsterdam, Le Havre, Paris, etc.). It also makes it possible for official agencies to prohibit the export of coffee which, by its excessively low quality, poor appearance etc., does not conform to the standards, and could damage the good name of the producing country in question. Finally, the classification of coffees in standardised grades enables quality fluctuations during the course of a season or over several consecutive seasons, to be closely followed, based on statistical records and samples, and if necessary, production or trade may be influenced in order to remedy the situation.

Standardisation thus complies with legitimate commercial requirements, at both national and international levels, the general interest being to maintain, indeed to improve, the quality of the harvested beans.

For some considerable time, the rules of grading applied to coffee were limited to the guarantee of a 'dependable and marketable' quality. This very general and vague clause did not keep up with the considerable increase in coffee transactions throughout the world. It quickly became necessary to define the commercial, intrinsic, and often organoleptic qualities of exported coffees by specific criteria. Brazil was probably the first country to create a coffee standardisation system, certain clauses of which were then adopted by other countries.

Green coffee is divided into a certain number of standardised, statutory types that are defined by a tolerance to a certain percentage of foreign particles and a limited number of defects per 300 g sample. The estimate of the number of defects is achieved by using an equivalency scale. The most severely penalised defects are black beans, stinkers, cherries, coffee beans in parchment, so-called dry beans, etc. It is essential to revise this very old scale. The ISO (International Standard Organisation) has been working on such a revision for about twenty years. Various recommendations have been published (analytical techniques, evaluation of damage, storage and transport, etc.). There are also plans to harmonise European regulations within the framework of the EEC.

Basically, coffee beans must be healthy, they must not be altered in any way (mould, rot) and must have a moisture content which is generally accepted in international contracts, that is, a maximum of 13 per cent. French regulations actually limit this rate to 12.5 per cent for imported coffee.

Chemical composition of green coffee

This section has been written with the collaboration of J. C. Vincent, Director of the Laboratories of Chemical Technology of the IRCC in Montpellier.

Many analyses of green coffee have been published over the past hundred years, but most are somewhat incomplete. Thus Sklotta and Neisser (1938) proposed methods for measuring the main components. These methods were taken up again and improved wherever necessary by Hadorn and Suter. To establish the components of green coffee, the latter first determined the moisture and total lipid complex and divided the rest into two groups: water-soluble substances and insoluble substances (Table 17).

Navellier emphasises that these results make it clear that in the analysis of the various samples there is an unmeasured amount of about 10 per cent of soluble substances and about 2 per cent of insoluble substances, which can be made soluble by hydrolysis in a sulphuric medium. Knowledge has increased on several counts since this work was carried out, and in the last results, which were extremely satisfactory, the components of green coffee were published by Spiller based on results presented by Vitzthum. These results include the large classes of compounds: proteins, carbohydrates, lipids, also volatile and non-volatile acids, alkaloids, ash, water, and partially identified compounds.

A brief review of the main components
Water

Marketed green coffee generally has a moisture content of between 10 and 13 per cent. The legislation of coffee-producing countries, in accordance with those of coffee-consuming countries, specifies that the maximum level allowed is between 12 and 13 per cent. French law (Decree of 3 September 1965) has set this level at 12.5 per cent. Above this level, the storage of coffee is compromised, especially in a moist environment. Before long, the beans become mouldy and lose their colour. At the other extreme, coffee is rarely traded with a moisture content of less than 10 per cent. Indeed, producers who use sun-drying may have difficulty obtaining a drier product in a humid tropical environment, whereas those who use artificial drying methods expose their coffee to risks at the beginning of the roasting process, when the moisture content drops to below 10 per cent. Finally, considering current commercial trends, neither organisation has any interest in eliminating more water than is necessary to ensure the good conservation of the bean, and the state of dryness does not enter into the transaction process at this point.

Certain authors, such as Morris and Wood, have shown that slow chemical reactions affect the ability of moist coffee beans to provide tasty and aromatic roasted products. They estimate that this alteration can be avoided if the water content of the bean is below 10 per cent. It is also known that the berry borer, *Stephanoderes*, cannot survive in beans that contain 12.5 per cent water or less.

The moisture content of the bean has an effect on the roasting process. The drier the beans, the faster they are roasted. Navellier observes that during the course of this operation, green coffee loses more water than it apparently contains, and explains this phenomenon, which appears to be a paradox, in terms of the release of water molecules, the hydrogen and oxygen atoms of which are taken from transformed organic molecules. He calls this water 'chemical' water, which should be added to the 'biological' water contained in the green bean.

Determining the water content of green coffee analytically therefore assumes great importance. There are several laboratory methods, for example, evaporation in an oven at 105°C, or leaching, generally with toluene or by using various chemical methods (Fischer). Methods once under scientific investigation have now been standardised. They are now officially accepted in France (*J.O.* 6 October 1966) and have been examined by the 'coffee' group of the International Standard Organisation (ISO). The so-called reference method establishes the level of water loss, under reduced pressure, at 48°C, in the presence of a dehydrating agent (phosphoric anhydride): the practical method requires heating at 130°C to be carried out in two phases. Rapid practical methods are also used in trade and industry. They are less precise than laboratory methods, but with well-standardised equipment they are capable of giving sufficiently approximate results. These methods include, for example, the use of infra-red heating equipment, and electrical methods. The latter includes automatic equipment which functions per measure of the high frequency dielectric capacity. (Cedem, Foss-Electric).

Other, more sophisticated techniques are being investigated, such as the NMR (nuclear magnetic resonance) and infra-red reflectrometry, but they are too costly for most users.

Minerals

Green coffee contains an average of 3 to 4 per cent ash. This comprises mostly potassium, sodium, calcium, magnesium, phosphorous and sulphur. Numerous trace elements have also been found including iron, aluminium, copper, iodine, fluoride, boron, and magnesium.

Proteins

Green coffee contains a total of 1 to 3 per cent nitrogen, which is present in various combinations; the main ones being proteins and alkaloids. Several amino acids and certain sulphuric amino acids (particularly cystine and methionine) contained in coffee proteins play a major role in the formation of the aroma of roasted coffee, since they are involved in the Strecker reactions.

Alkaloids and other non-protein nitrogenous substances

The main alkaloid in coffee is **caffeine**. It is accompanied by other nitrogenous compounds in lesser quantities including choline and trigonelline.

Green coffee generally has a caffeine content of between 1 and 2.5 per cent. Arabicas contain the lowest amount of caffeine, with an average of 0.8 to 1.5 per cent, whereas with the canephoras, (Robusta, Kouilou) the content varies between 1.6 and 2.2 per cent. Some varieties contain 2.8 per cent and even exceed 3 per cent. Liberica and Excelsa coffees are in an intermediary position at about 1.5 per cent. Caffeine is also present in certain vegetable products such as tea (1 to 4 per cent), maté (1 to 4 per cent), the cola nut (2 to 3 per cent), cacao, etc.

In green coffee, the caffeine occurs as a double salt, caffeine chlorogenate and potassium.

The caffeine, or 1, 3, 7-trimethylxanthine, is a major counterpart of theobromine (3–7 dimethylxanthine). Its formula is $C_8H_{10}O_2N_4$ (anhydrous caffeine), but it crystallises with water in the form of a monohydrate, $C_8H_{10}O_2N_4H_2O$. Its improved formula is illustrated in Fig 124.

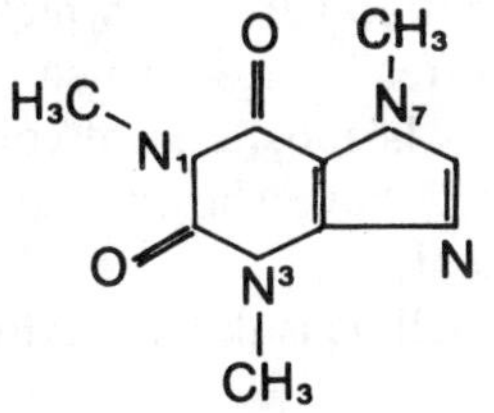

**Fig 124   Caffeine: 1, 3, 7-trimethylxanthine
(source: Ullman's Encyclopedia of Industrial
Chemistry, 1986 p. 317)**

Table 17 Chemical composition of green arabica and robusta coffees

Component	Content (% dry matter)	
	Arabica	Robusta
Kahweol	0.7 – 1.1	non-determined
Caffeine	0.6 – 1.5	2.2 – 2.7
Chlorogenic Acids	6.2 – 7.9	7.4 – 11.2
Saccharose and reducing sugars	5.3 – 9.3	3.7 – 7.1
Free amino acids*	0.4 – 2.4	0.8 – 0.9
Arabane	9 – 13	6 – 8
Mannane	25 – 30	19 – 22
Galactane	4 – 6	10 – 14
Other polysaccharides	8 – 10	8 – 10
Triglycerides	10 – 14	8 – 10
Proteins	– 12	– 12
Trigonellin	– 1	– 1
Other lipids	– 2	– 2
Other acids	– 2	– 2
Ash	– 4	– 4
Total	90 – 114	86 – 107

*Including active components from the Strecker reaction.
Source: Clifford and Wilson, *Coffee* (Croom Ed. London. 1985)

This compound looks like white, frayed, silky crystals which melt at 234°–237°C, but are slightly sublimated at about 100°C, and to a greater extent at 180°C. This partially explains the loss of aroma and flavour observed during roasting.

Navellier divides the methods used for assessing the amount of caffeine present into three categories: methods for weighing the caffeine, methods by which the alkaloid content increases after treatment with nitrogen, and finally, the recently developed methods which combine chromatographic separation and spectrophotometric measuring.

Chromatographic methods which use the gaseous phase (CMG) and high pressure liquid (HPLC) can now be added. These are favoured by analytical laboratories since the sample to be purified may be prepared quickly and easily.

Caffeine also exists in the other components of the fruit (pulp: 0.9 per cent) and in different tissues within the coffee plant. An analysis of dried arabica leaves has shown their caffeine content to be between 0.5 and 0.9 per cent, depending upon the season. The flowers contain 0.9 per cent, and the trunk contains 0.08 per cent (Wellman).

The coffee varieties which were grouped together by Chevalier as the Mascarocoffea series, which grow spontaneously in Madagascar and the Mascarenes Islands, do not contain caffeine. In addition, studies carried out at the IFCC have shown that only traces of the three associated alkaloids were present.

Trigonelline is the methylbeta form of nicotinic acid. Green coffee beans have a trigonelline content of 0.4–1.2 per cent. Navellier recalls that its decomposition during roasting is related to the appearance of nicotinic acid (vitamin PP or niacin) and various pyridinic components that may partially contribute to the development of the aroma.

Lipids

Coffee beans also contain fat. Some authors estimate that the presence of various lipids may affect the preservation of its organoleptic qualities. This, however, is much debated.

The fat is rich in unsaponified substances, which are not eliminated during the common refining procedures. This renders it unsuitable for certain uses, such as food. Its characteristics have been studied in the oil extracted from coffee grounds, and are as follows:

Iodine index	97.6
Saponification index	180.6
Free acidity in oleic acid	0.27%
Unsaponified substances	5.84%
Peroxide index	5.2

(Source: Kahn and Brown, quoted by Navellier.)

Poisson divides coffee lipids into three categories:

- fatty acids and their derivatives, glycerides and phospholipids;
- components of the unsaponified substances: carbides, sterols, di- and tri-terpenes, tocopherols;
- the components of the outer wax of the beans.

Arabicas are considered to be rich in oil (12 to 18 per cent). Robustas contain relatively less oil (9 to 14 per cent), but the significant variation of values reported in literature should be noted. The IRCC increased the rates to an oil content of about 42 per cent in *C. richardii* in the Mascarocoffea series.

Palmitic and linoleic acids are the most common, and, according to Folstar, the fatty acids appear not only in the triglycerides, which make up over 75 per cent of the lipoid content, but they are also present in the sterols and the terpenes of the unsaponified substances, as well as in the waxes.

Kaufman, quoted by Poisson, established the average composition balances of the lipids as follows:

Triglycerides	78.74%	75.2%
Diterpenic esters	15.0%	18.0%
Triterpenic, sterolic and methylsterolic esters	1.8%	1.4%
Free diterpenes	0.12%	1.2%
Free triperpenes and sterols	0.34%	–
Phosphatides	–	4.2%
Miscellaneous (carbides, etc.)	4.0%	–

Among the diterpenes, cafestol and kahweol are present in arabica coffee, whereas in robusta, kahweol appears to be absent. The differences between robusta and arabica regarding their $\triangle$ 5 Avenasterol content should also be mentioned. This could assist, for example, in the identification of the two species in ground, roasted coffees.

Carbohydrates

Carbohydrates represent more than half of the dry matter of green coffee beans. Among these, the polysaccharides are the most largely represented (over 40 per cent), whereas the content of oligosaccharides and monosaccharides is only 5 and 1 per cent, respectively. They do not appear to play an essential role in determining the qualities of the beverage, but they impart its 'caramel' colour and flavour which is also characteristic of other roasted products such as barley and chicory root.

Green coffee contains small quantities of free reducing sugars (especially glucose) and sucrose (5 to 8 per cent). Among the polysaccharides, Pictet reports the presence of hemicelluloses, starch, gums, mucilages, and pectins.

Aliphatic and polyphenolic acids

The coffee beans contain different organic aliphatic acids but especially phenolic acids which have the characteristics of tannins.

Vasco and Tabacchi have analysed the non-tannin phenols (simple phenols and flavonoids) and tannin phenols (condensed and hydrolysable tannins) in the pericarp of the fruit. Hydroxycinnamic acids are particularly common in the beans, especially in the form of chlorogenic acids (4 to 8 per cent) at double the chlorogenate level of caffeine and potassium. These components are mostly destroyed during roasting with the release of the alkaloid.

Other organic acids exist in coffee, and amounts of these can now be clarified using chromatographic methods. In addition to chlorogenic acids, the usual non-volatile and volatile organic aliphatic acids have also been identified including oxalic, malic, citric, tartric, and acetic acids.

Volatile principles and aromatic components

The volatile principles contained in green coffee are represented by water and 180 other substances, among which are methoxy-pyrazines, aliphatic hydrocarbons, carbonyls, acids, alcohols and thiols, puranes, pyreols, pyridins, quinolins, phenols, aromatic amines and carbonyls (Clifford).

The aromatic complex of roasted coffee is formed during roasting and develops from substances that are still largely unknown called 'precursors'.

The study of this complex, the isolation of the components, their identification and their amount constitutes a vast research programme, which has as yet, only been realised in part. The use of chromatography during the gaseous phase has helped to identify over 700 different substances that make up the aroma of coffee. However, none of them are solely responsible for the aroma.

12 Roasting and manufacturing coffee

Roasting and associated operations

The aromatic qualities of coffee only become apparent once the beans have been exposed to high temperatures during pyrolysis, which is still referred to as 'roasting' or 'grilling'. In addition to changes in its external appearance (colour, size and texture) during the course of this operation, the product is the centre of complex chemical changes, some of which generate the particular aroma and taste of coffee.

The roasting industry has developed extensively throughout the world over the past half century as a result of the increase in coffee consumption. In France, for example, the number of enterprises has increased from a few hundred in 1930 to almost three thousand in 1960. However, there are now only about 800 due to regrouping or competition. Among these 800, only about ten actually rate as major industrial establishments due to their size.

Coffee roasting is preceded by various operations including cleaning and dusting to remove the foreign matter from the beans (pieces of husk or parchment, stones, earth, string, nails, etc.). Many different types of equipment are suitable for this job, the most modern of which are the pneumatic separators. The beans are then stored in partitioned silos prior to roasting.

Progressive temperature increases have the following effect on coffee: at about 100°C, the beans begin to turn from green to yellow. The drying is accompanied by a loss of water vapour and the scent of toasted bread. Above 120°–130°C, the bean turns a chestnut brown which gradually darkens. At this stage (150°C) the coffee begins to give off an aroma like that of roasted seeds, before its characteristic aroma can be discerned. This only begins to develop at about 180°C, at which temperature the combustion gases appear in the form of bluish white curls, with a release of CO_2 and CO. The beans then turn brown and their volume increases. At a higher temperature, more gas of a darker colour is released. By this time the aroma has completely developed. The beans expand, crackle, and a shiny exudate collects on the surface. At about 270°C, the release of smoke is complete. The beans turn black and dull and cease to expand. At about 300°C they become black and sooty, and crumble at the slightest pressure. By this time the aroma has completely disappeared. At this extreme stage of roasting, the coffee is carbonised.

Specialists place the 'roasting zone' between 185° and 240°C, the optimum temperature being between 210° and 230°C. Above this temperature, over-roasting begins. Both the roasting temperature and the way the process is conducted have a considerable effect on the quality of the coffee.

The complexity of the phenomena that surround coffee during this pyrolitic process has been emphasised by Orosco. This author has determined through experimentation that four principal groups of reactions occur during roasting: dehydration, hydrolysis, desmolysis, and catalysis. The optimum intensity of each reaction occurs at well-defined temperatures. He has also found that some of these reactions overlap.

The most successful way to overcome the difficulties encountered during roasting is through experimentation. Indeed, in practice, roasting can only be a compromise between various requirements, the objective being to develop the maximum potential of the aromatic and organoleptic qualities of the bean according to the tastes of the clientele.

Roasting is still carried out very empirically in many 'roasting' plants. Professional methods, however, require an exact knowledge of green coffee characteristics, in order to identify not only the species, varieties, and types from all production areas, but also their particular characteristics, depending upon their origin, where they have been stored, their grade, the rate and nature of their impurities, etc. Each type will react differently to the various stages of the roasting process, such as length of time, rate of expansion, colour of the beans, weight loss, etc. The roaster must be familiar with these factors in order to obtain the maximum organoleptic qualities from each batch, with a minimal loss of substance.

The roasting process normally lasts for between 12 and 15 minutes. It is faster with certain types of equipment than others. For example, it can be completed in five minutes using the American **continuous roasting** technique. On the other hand, there are also **slow roasting** techniques, which require about 25 minutes. Recuperating the volatile aromatic substances released at the time of roasting and carried out with the hot gases has been the subject of several studies.

While roasting gives coffee its taste and aroma, it also changes the bean in certain ways. First of all, the bean **loses weight** (called a 'loss in the fire') due to the evaporation of water from the green coffee; the extreme limits of this evaporation are between 14 and 23 per cent. The amount of weight lost depends upon the level of moisture in the green bean, the botanical origin, the methods of preparation at the production site, storage conditions, the roasting method used, etc. With the **French roasting** method, which is very often used with canephoras, the loss of weight often exceeds 20 per cent. With lighter roasting methods, for example those used in Germany, the weight is somewhere between 15 and 16 per cent. Moisture evaporation is not the only element responsible. There is also the elimination of the silverskin (0.2 to 0.4 per cent) and the release of certain volatile elements.

French legislation allows a maximum weight loss of 22 per cent. On the other hand, customs regulations for green coffees that are temporarily admitted, and then re-exported, allow for a loss of only 20 per cent.

There is an **increase in volume** as the coffee is roasted. This phenomenon, which is due to the formation and expansion of gas between 180° and 220°C, also induces the endosperm to increase in volume. This is manifested in a volumetric increase of about 50 to 80 per cent (the extremes are between 30 and 100 per cent). The botanical origin, production area, amount of moisture present (Rabechault), and the roasting are all criteria that may affect the intensity of expansion. Whatever the cause, the potential for expansion is an important characteristic from a commercial point of view. Buyers are attracted by large, well formed beans, and are also rarely insensitive to the appeal of larger packages.

Bean colour is significantly affected by roasting. It is particularly dependent upon the intensity and duration of the operation. Cooling the beans fairly rapidly at the end of the roasting period can also make a slight difference. Waxing the beans, when allowed, also affects the colour.

Client preference is a major factor in determining the **aroma** and **flavour**: light (cinnamon or amber), medium, or dark (French or Italian) roasting are some of the roasting techniques that are accompanied by a particular aroma and taste. **Bean texture** is also significantly altered by roasting. The bean becomes porous and crumbles when pressure is applied.

Navellier (1959) defines the **chemical changes** as follows: Water evaporates, but more is then formed from the chemical decomposition of organic compounds, and the roasted coffee retains or absorbs a certain quantity of moisture.

The **minerals** do not change noticeably, but their relative content increases when the water and volatilised organic components disappear.

Almost the same proportion of **total nitrogenous substances** exist in roasted coffee as in green coffee. This observation indicates that the nitrogenous components which are metabolised are approximately proportional to the sum of the volatile constituents which are eliminated during the roasting process. It is therefore erroneous to deduce from the apparent stability of the level of total nitrogen that the nitrogenous components have not undergone any changes. Roasted coffee, which is porous, retains a few of the volatile components that are formed, through absorption. Traces of volatile nitrogenous substances that are produced during roasting make a valuable contribution to the aromatic complex.

The **fat** also maintains a reasonably stable relative level, which appears to increase at times, indicating that the loss of fat is proportionately lower than the total loss of original organic compounds. The fat also provides a small quantity of volatile principles.

The fat is released from proteolytic or carbohydrate complexes due to the heating process. Fat is exuded more rapidly from roasted coffee than from green coffee. This free fat acts as a solvent in absorbing various aromatic principles, due to a phenomenon that is analogous to that of enfleurage, which is used in perfume making. It also protects the aromatic principles from the oxidising reactions. Thus the fat is not responsible for the aroma of coffee, but probably only assists in absorbing and preserving it.

The **carbohydrates** are greatly affected by roasting. The largest molecules are broken down and the smallest are converted into volatile products. It is possible that a good part of the organoleptic components of roasted coffee come from the carbohydrates. However, the latter are also capable of providing volatile acids, aldehydes, and other components that affect the aroma very slightly.

The **acids** partially survive after roasting, but it should be noted that the content of soluble acids in coffee increases considerably during the course of this operation. Volatile acids make an important contribution to the aroma and taste of the beverage.

The **phenolic compounds** also deteriorate considerably. In addition to releasing the caffeine they previously contained, they also undergo a weight loss which probably coincides with the production of an equal quantity of volatile products.

The **alkaloids** undergo different changes: the caffeine is partially volatilised without decomposing, whereas the trigonelline is partially destroyed, and probably participates in the formation of pyridine and nicotinic acid.

It can therefore be concluded that the aromatic principles are derived from the organic compounds that are most affected during roasting.

Concerning the nature of the aroma, Navellier considers that the complexity of the mixture of the aromatic principles is such that it is no longer possible to discern which one dominates the odour. At the present time, no immediate principle is known which, when pure, smells like coffee and, on the other hand, alters the aroma of the coffee if removed.

The balance of the aromatic complex of roasted coffee is very precarious (Navellier). It takes very little time for a particularly volatile component to be lost or for the coffee to undergo a serious alteration if another component participates in the chemical reactions, for example if it is oxidised. These changes seriously depreciate the value of the product, which is said either to have aged or be stale.

Navellier states that the absence of a predominant aromatic principle, the extreme complexity of the mixture of the aromatic products, and the fragility of some of them, explain why it is taking so long to establish the list of components of the aromatic complex of coffee, and why the synthetic reconstitution of the aroma of an acceptable coffee is still out of reach.

Roasting equipment and techniques

There are two roasting techniques, heating by **convection** and heating by **conduction**, which differ in that in the former, the coffee is in contact with hot gases while in the latter it is in direct contact with a hot surface.

Heating by convection

This method has two variations: **hot air** roasting, where the beans are in contact with the hot air produced by a generator, and **flaming**, where the beans are directly exposed to a flame.

In the first variation, which is now the most common and widespread, the hot air is produced in a combustion chamber and is passed through the coffee by a blower. Gases are released from the coffee and mix with the air, which is then removed by a suction system. The silverskin is also released from the beans and removed by the air currents. The cylinder rotates slowly. Blades mounted in the cylinder ensure a thorough mixing of the beans and the diffusion of hot gases. A probe enables samples to be taken and helps monitor the operation. Temperatures are controlled by various types of measuring equipment. The coffee is removed by a large run-off valve, which is operated by a counter-weight.

The heating design varies depending upon the fuel used. With coke, a special oven is necessary; with gas or oil, special burners are normally required. The application of this technique has given rise to various systems and models of equipment.

With flaming, the coffee is subjected to the direct effect of a flame produced by the combustion of a gas conveyed by a duct mounted in a rotating axis in the roasting chamber. The beans are actively mixed by agitators to prevent some of them from being overheated. Although this technique is not as widespread as the one previously described, it is used in many countries.

Heating by conduction

This is the oldest method in use. It involves the transfer of heat by conduction. The cylinder or metal ball containing the coffee, is rotated either manually or by a motor above a firebox fueled by charcoal, gas or electricity. This technique is being used less and less, except for small family-run operations.

Whatever the method of roasting used, when the coffee has reached the desired level of roasting, it is poured out through the opening of the drum into a shallow cooling tank which has a large diameter. Here it is mixed by agitators, and a ventilating fan directs a cool current of air towards the lower part of the tank. The temperature decreases rapidly, thus eliminating any risk of over-roasting.

The capacity of the equipment varies from a few kg to 500 kg of raw coffee. The lower categories, with capacities of up to 25 kg, include the type of display equipment which is set up in retail outlets.

At one extreme are small sample coffee roasters, with a capacity of between 50 and 250 g. Other small types of equipment have a capacity of 50 to 150 kg. Equipment with a larger capacity (generally 150 to 250 kg) is used in large coffee-roasting plants. At the other extreme are large, continuous roasters which have an hourly output of between 2 and 4 tonnes.

Continuous roasting, which was perfected 30 years ago in the United States by Burns, has now made significant technical progress. The capacity of this equipment is between 2 and 4 tonnes per hour, with a roasting time of about 4 to 5 minutes. In this equipment, the coffee is carried along by blades and passes through a long, perforated, horizontal cylinder, which rotates slowly at a rate of four to six turns per minute. A hot air current blows through it, the temperature of which is rigorously controlled.

A very new roasting technique is now available, called the 'fluidised bed' system. Its novelty lies in the absence of any mobile piece of equipment

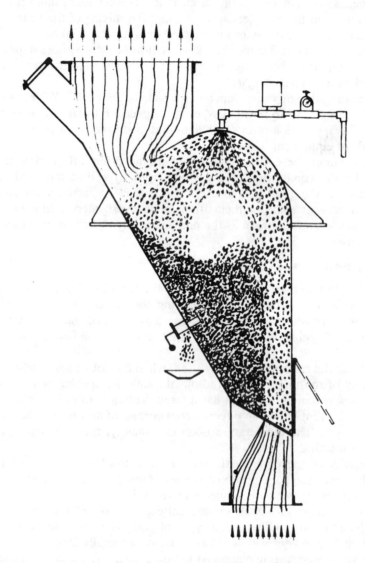

Fig 125   Diagram of a 'Neotherm' coffee roaster with a fluid bed (Courtesy: Neotec)

(agitator) in the roasting chamber. The coffee is suspended in this chamber by a vigorous hot air current. The roasting time is about 3 to 5 minutes depending upon the nature of the coffee and the degree and quality of roasting desired (Fig 125).

Finally, 'high yield' or 'super yield' roasters exist which enable the coffee to be roasted within a very short period of time: about a minute and a half

1	Sample roaster	10	Skin remover	17	Run-off pipes
2	Green coffee	11	Cooling sieve	18	Filling pipes
3	Passage design	12	Stone remover	19	Silos for roasted coffee
4	Green coffee silos	13	Ascending conduit	20	Filling pipes
5	Weigher-mixer	14	Recipient	21	Mobile weigher with scales
6	Green coffee supply	15	Fan motor	22	Packer
7	Conveyor	16	Rotary electrical distributor		
8	IDEAL-RAPID Roaster				
9	Combination fuel oil and coke stove				

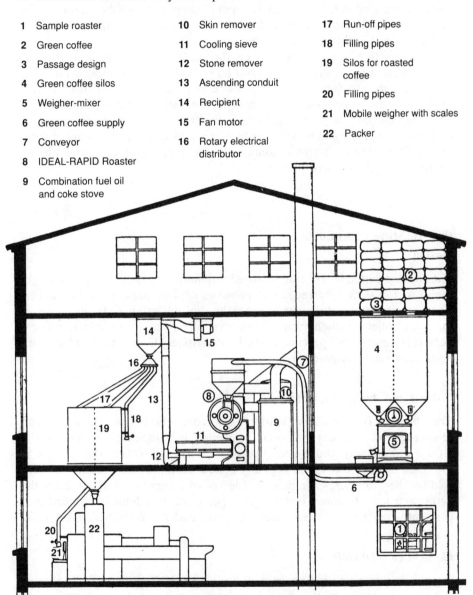

Fig 126 Simplified diagram of a typical roasting installation (source: Gothot, Maschinenfabrik at Emmerich, West Germany)

to three minutes. Their basic concept is that hot air at 300°C circulates at a high speed which considerably accelerates thermal transfer. With this ultra-rapid process, the volumetric increase of the bean is between 5 and 10 per cent, which is the same as with the traditional technique. In addition, much less moisture is lost during this procedure. Fig 126 illustrates a roasting installation with an Ideal Rapid roaster. The improvement in the quality of coffees processed in this way varies, depending upon the species and even the origins. Arabicas increase in acidity whereas robustas lose their bitterness. Opinions on this subject differ widely.

The roasting industry has progressed considerably over the past 10 years. At the present time, there are several large equipment-manufacturing firms which are able to satisfy all the possible requirements of clients, to give quotations, and supply equipment ranging from small-scale to complete factory installations, from storage containers and mixing tanks to packaging equipment, including automatic controls, and, of course, the essential computer. This allows electronic commands and equipment operations to be viewed on an illuminated display.

Post-roasting operations
Sorting

The roasted coffee is sometimes sorted to eliminate beans that are too light (pale) or too dark (charred). The presence of these decreases the quality. The occurrence of pale beans is generally, but not exclusively due to fruits that were collected when unripe. They give the beverage an unpleasant taste. Sorting is now normal practice in the United States, Germany, and Belgium, using electronic equipment.

Coating, polishing, or glazing

The objective of coating or polishing is to cover the beans with a thin film of non-hygroscopic material which is meant, in principal, to conserve the aroma and enhance the appearance of the bean. However, this method is too often used to conceal low quality coffees. Commercial preparations are sold for these purposes. French law (decree of 3 September 1965) limits the authorised use of coated material to 2 per cent. This limit is reduced to 1 per cent when applied to so-called 'superior' coffees, as defined in the text.

Flaws of roasted coffees

Defective, roasted coffee beans may be the result of either defective green coffee beans, or beans that have been damaged during the roasting process and other operations. These are normally black, charred, marbled or spotted, pale, pitted, and broken beans.

Commercial blends

Coffees can be divided into three groups according to their organoleptic characteristics:

- **So-called 'mild' coffees**, produced exclusively from *C. arabica*, which has been carefully prepared at the production site. Mostly Central American and South American coffees from Colombia, Costa Rica, El Salvador, Ecuador, Guatemala, etc., are thus included in this category. However, many arabicas from Africa or Asia are comparable (Mysore, Kenya, Tanganyika, Cameroon, Java, etc.), and although not commercially designated as such, they could be placed in the same category.
- **Brazilian coffees** (Santos, Rio, Victoria, Praña, etc.), display a considerable diversity despite having the same botanical origin (*C. arabica*). They are all generally characterised by having lower-grade organoleptic qualities. They are thus average quality arabicas.
- **Canephora coffees**, which are essentially of African robusta origin, have a neutral taste, and are less aromatic than the previous classes. However, they are appreciated for their individual qualities and are used for local consumption and in the manufacture of instant coffee.

Few coffees have all the characteristics necessary to provide the beverage with the ideal aroma and taste. In the roasting process, therefore, several specifically selected types must be blended so that their different qualities compliment each other. An average of three to five types of coffee may be associated in a blend, but it is not unusual to find even more in certain highly superior blends. Blending may be carried out before or after roasting. If the characteristics of the coffees are compatible (moisture content, grade, percentage of small beans and peaberries etc.) it may be carried out prior to roasting. Coffees are blended after roasting if there is too great a variation in type.

However, these are not the only considerations that guide the merchant. The price factor also helps to determine the choice of components, depending upon the purchasing potential of the clientele, as well as seasonal supplies.

Brazilian coffees, especially 'Santos' are generally used as a basis for most blends in almost all European countries, particularly in Scandinavia and Central Europe. In West Germany, Belgium, the Netherlands, Italy, Switzerland, etc., the range of varieties used is wider, including more 'milds'. In France, many African canephoras are used, particularly Robusta and Kouilou. The more 'milds' used, the better the quality of the blends, especially if superior quality beans from this category are used.

Packaging roasted coffee

Roasted coffees rapidly lose their flavour and aroma. The loss is very noticeable after two to three weeks. Later on, a rancid taste develops which persists.

Roasted coffee easily absorbs atmospheric moisture. Its qualities become rapidly altered when its moisture content exceeds 6 per cent. In order to avoid this, stock must be renewed regularly, at least for superior qualities. Alternatively, an expiration date must be displayed on the package or sufficiently airtight packaging should be used which can preserve the qualities of the coffee for a longer period of time.

Studies conducted to determine the factors responsible for the deterioration of the aroma of coffee have indicated that atmospheric oxygen is the main factor. It reacts with certain components, especially the fats. Experiments have shown that the quality of a batch of coffee which is deprived of air (including that retained in the tissue of the beans) remains preserved for a very long time.

The alteration is mainly due to oxidation of substances on the bean's surface. This is why some coatings inside the packages, which can absorb fats, have a harmful effect on the product. Packaging materials used for roasted coffee must therefore be odourless, impenetrable to water vapour and fats, and low in price.

Major progress has been made in this area over the past few years, using compound materials, combining glued or laminated products, plastic films, polythene, textiles, metal, (aluminium-cellulose compound), etc. Airtight vacuum-packaging or the inclusion of an inert gas in absolutely airtight containers (or packages) are the most satisfactory solutions in terms of conservation, provided the package is not opened. However, they are only used for certain categories of coffee, as they are rather expensive.

Another satisfactory solution is to pack the coffee in airtight packages fitted with a one-way valve, enabling excess CO_2 to be released without allowing oxygen from the air to enter.

Ground coffee

The market for ground coffee has greatly increased, in both the United States and Europe, particularly in France, where it currently represents 80 per cent of sales. French law is particularly strict with regard to ground coffee. It prohibits the use of residues from sorting and states that their use by a manufacturer is considered illegitimate and their sale fraudulent (Decree of 10 December 1965).

The use of ground coffee may be favoured by the housewife because it is less time-consuming to prepare, but it does not preserve the aromatic qualities of the product. In fact, as soon as the package is opened, the grounds are much more sensitive than the bean to the oxidation process (becoming rancid), due to their large surface area. The contents of the package should therefore be stored in a hermetically sealed container.

With this practice, the visual attraction of high quality beans has faded over the years in favour of ground coffee, the nature (except for the obliga-tory indication of the species), composition, and origins of which are poorly defined. This is a great pity.

Coffee with milk is sold by automatic vending machines in Japan, with great success. It is sold in metal containers or cans resembling beer cans, providing a hot drink in winter and a cold drink in the summer months.

Coffee as a beverage

Preparation

To prepare a good cup of coffee, certain conditions must be met, without which the principles that give the beverage its organoleptic qualities may be destroyed or extinguished.

An essential element in obtaining an aromatic cup of coffee is the **nature** of the coffee used. It is obvious that however perfect the preparation equipment used, and whatever care is taken in preparing the coffee, an aromatic beverage cannot be obtained from a low or mediocre quality coffee. By the same token, a top quality product will only produce a mediocre beverage if it is not prepared carefully.

Grinding

One important factor in obtaining a good cup of coffee is how finely the coffee is ground. If the coffee is ground too coarsely, the water will filter through too quickly and the beverage, which is not sufficiently charged with aromatic principles, will taste rather bland. On the other hand, if the powder is too fine, particles will be carried by the water and deposited at the bottom of the cup. Fine grinding also prolongs the filtering process and cools the water, rendering the beverage muddy and bitter.

Coffee should be ground somewhere between these two extremes, depending on the nature of the equipment used. Typical grounds are, for example: average ground for household coffee makers, finely ground for depression equipment, special ground for percolators, ultrafine ground for 'turkish' coffee, etc.

Illy (1980) divides grinding into two categories. The first category is very regular, made up of uniform particles of average size from which small, powdery particles have been separated. This is the type of coffee used with filters, percolators, and all equipment used to prepare a fairly diluted drink (50 to 65 g/l) which are subjected to the hydrolytic effect of hot water, since the beverage that has been prepared is not immediately consumed. The second category consists of grounds made up of particles of various sizes, and contains up to 50 per cent of very small, powdery particles (less than 0.02 mm) and 50 per cent medium-sized and larger particles. This type of ground is used to prepare 'espresso' coffee. It consists of particles that can aggregate, and consequently resist the high pressure of the equipment used, which is normally 9 to 10 bars.

The Coffee Brewing Institute was a former American interdisciplinary organisation (New York) with the objective of carrying out all scientific and technical research that could potentially improve the quality of coffee as a beverage. This organisation found through experimentation, that the level of extraction during filtering of 18 to 22 per cent of the weight of the grounds gave an optimum flavour and aroma to the beverage. Below 18 per cent, the coffee had a raw taste and above, it tended to become bitter.

Grinding equipment

The most simple grinding equipment is the classic hand-operated coffee grinder, in which the beans are crushed by an adjustable, articulated mill-stone.

Modern electrical equipment is based on the same principle using a millstone or on physical crushing by blades, which rotate at a high speed (10 000 to 25 000 turns/min) in a metal tank. The advantage of grinding mills (Fig 127) is that they do not heat the coffee, unlike the bladed equipment, which benefits from the speed of operation.

Large-scale equipment is particularly used in the manufacture of instant coffee (see Chapter 10) and generally consists of very small, metal grinding cylinders, which are assembled in pairs at adjustable distances depending upon the degree of fineness of the grind required. This equipment yields between 200 and 2000 kg/hour depending upon the model. In other types, the coffee is ground between two vertical disks that rotate in opposite directions at high speed or else between two articulating millstones, one of which remains stationary. Manufacturers have paid special attention to the ventilation of the grinding equipment in order to avoid excessive heating and a loss of aroma.

Coffee makers

There are many different models of coffee maker. They can be divided into three categories depending upon the way they operate: infusion, lixiviation, or decoction.

The equipment is often fitted with gadgets such as a suspended filter carrier, an optical reader for the water level, an anti-drip system, a heating plate, etc. Nevertheless, it should not be forgotten that the coffee-maker is merely an instrument for preparing coffee and that the quality of the beverage still depends on the nature and quality of the grounds used, regardless of the care taken in its preparation.

High-capacity equipment is used in restaurants and cafés, from the classic percolator to automatic 'espresso' machines, which operate under pressure from 10–15 bars. Two techniques are applied: either a hydraulic system which uses city water, with the addition of a differential piston with a multiplying effect, or an ingestion-compression system, with a pump incorporated and electronic equipment for measuring and regulating the temperature.

There are now many rather sophisticated models of household, espresso machines. Their capacity varies: some can make one or two cups simultaneously, while others make up to 12 to 15 successive cups.

The quality of the water used in preparing the coffee is an important element to take into consideration. The presence of certain salts or chemical substances (chlorine) is sufficient to affect the aroma. Water which is high

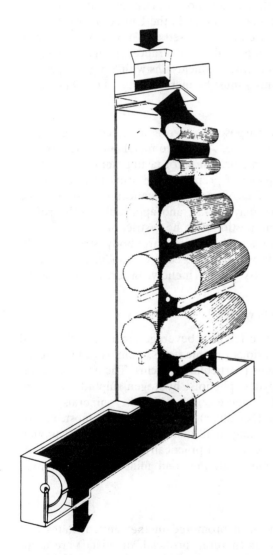

Fig 127   Industrial mill (Courtesy: Neotec)

in calcium (hard water) gives the coffee a bitter taste, as does chlorinated water. Some people use certain non-carbonated mineral waters. In conclusion, the water must be pure and free of mineral salts, organic impurities, and chemicals.

The use of calcium-free, soft water is essential with espresso equipment so that the piping and injectors do not get blocked (Grouard brothers, 1986). The liquid must be in contact with the ground coffee at **sub-boiling point**, approximately 87°–90°C. At a lower temperature, its effect is insufficient and a portion of the aromatic principles are not extracted from the powder.

The quality of the beverage with regard to its 'strength', also depends upon the **quantity** of coffee used. There is no standard amount; it depends entirely on the taste of the consumer. A survey in the United States revealed that an average of 8 g of ground coffee are used in 170 g of water, which makes approximately one large cup (150 g). In France, a survey taken by the 'Coffee Committee' gave comparable conclusions with 8.5 g. To prepare a 'strong' cup of coffee, the quantity must be increased by 10 to 20 per cent.

Sample tasting

Sample tasting for commercial purposes or agronomic, technological, or chemical research is a frequent practice. All coffee merchants, roasting factories and research stations have some provision for tasting samples of coffee.

The equipment must be capable of preparing the drink from the green beans, under strict conditions of cleanliness and uniformity, so that the judgement of the coffee samples may be fair and applicable to the coffee produced in the establishment in question with no restrictions.

The terms most often used in describing coffee are: body, strength, rich, poor, acidic or acidity, strong, harsh, neutral, earthy, woody, rank, bitter, sour or sourish, foul, stinker, grassy, fruity, mellow, bitter, musty, greasy, muddy.

The chemical composition of the beverage

The fundamental constituents of coffee as a beverage include: caffeine and trigonelline, chlorogenic acid, various organic acids, tannins, amino acids, sugars, salts, minerals and vitamins (particularly niacin). The aromatic components include: furfurol, aldehydes, phenols, hydrogen sulphide, mercaptans. The fat remains completely in the grounds with other minerals.

Coffee has a low food value (Navellier) since it retains at most, one or two grammes of dry matter containing small quantities of partially caramelised carbohydrates, traces of proteins, and practically no fat. Organic acids (mainly chlorogenic acids), tannins, caffeine, and minerals are the main constituents of this dry matter.

Flavoured coffees

Flavoured coffees have recently been promoted in the United States and Canada. A wide variety of flavours (natural, artificial, or mixed) are used: vanilla, walnut, various chocolates, almonds. They are reputed to complement the flavour of the coffee without concealing it. The flavour must also be absorbed by the beans. Aromatic substances are available either in spray or liquid form.

Instant coffee

The principals involved in producing instant coffee are relatively simple: a liquid concentrate of coffee is prepared with hot water, and is then finely pulverised in a hot, dry air current (atomisation). An anhydrous powder is precipitated (instant coffee), which, when diluted in water, re-constitutes the beverage. However, improvements made by the manufacturers to enhance the quality of the product are varied and relatively complex.

In a review of the manufacturing processes, Cambrony distinguishes six main operations: the selection of green coffee beans, roasting, grinding and filtering, extraction, evaporation, and packaging.

The first two steps are similar to those used in the usual preparation of roasted coffee. When grinding the roasted beans, special attention must be paid to the uniformity and the degree of grinding, which depends on the type of extractor used and the powder-solvent (water) ratio that is considered to be economical.

The extraction occurs under pressure which is either discontinuous in an array of percolators, or continuous, using a contraflow system.

These two processes result in the production of a solution of soluble material which is equivalent to 25 to 30 per cent of the weight of the ground coffee.

Hydrolysis may be used to facilitate drainage, using either a slightly acidic liquid (sulphuric or hydrochloric acid), or alternatively high pressure at a higher temperature. The extract is then clarified or purified using the technique, the extraction level could reach 40 per cent and above. The application of this technique in the second phase of production involves the use of appropriate equipment such as autoclaves and pressure extractors.

The dehydration of the coffee concentrate may be achieved by using atomisation (spray process), vacuum drying, or sublimation (freeze drying). The first process is the most frequently used. The last is less used on a commercial level because its cost is relatively higher, despite the high quality of the flavour of the instant coffee produced (Figs 128 and 129).

Instant coffee must be specially vacuum-packed in metal boxes, bottles or plastic bags due to its hygroscopic nature.

One tonne of green coffee yields about 240 kg of instant coffee; the loss during roasting being 20 per cent and level of extraction, 40 to 50 per cent. The grounds, which amount to about 560 kg per tonne of green coffee, have no use at this stage other than as compost.

The use of instant coffee is undoubtedly increasing throughout the world. The ease and speed with which one can prepare a cup of coffee, the quality of which continues to improve through technical progress, will guarantee its continued success.

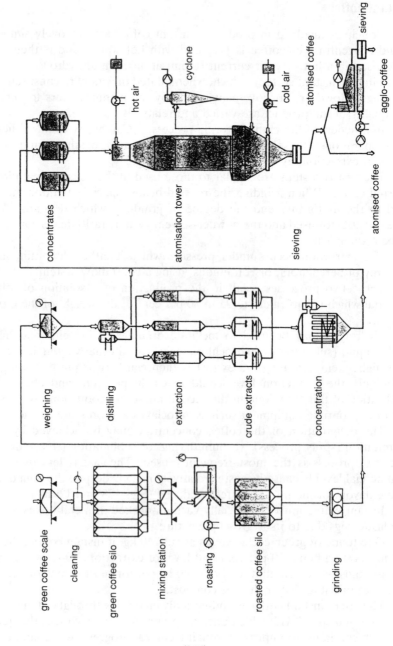

Atomised Coffee

weighing

distilling

extraction

crude extracts

concentration

green coffee scale

cleaning

green coffee silo

mixing station

roasting

roasted coffee silo

grinding

concentrates

hot air

cyclone

cold air

atomisation tower

sieving

atomised coffee

atomised coffee

sieving

agglo-coffee

Fig 128   Diagram showing the system for producing atomised coffee (source: Vabre)

Freeze-dried Coffee

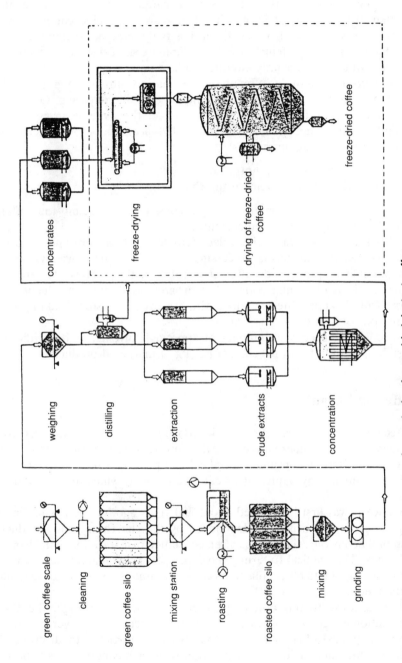

green coffee scale

cleaning

green coffee silo

mixing station

roasting

roasted coffee silo

mixing

grinding

weighing

distilling

extraction

crude extracts

concentration

concentrates

freeze-drying

drying of freeze-dried coffee

freeze-dried coffee

Fig 129 Diagram showing the system for producing freeze-dried, instant coffee (source: Vabre)

Decaffeinated coffee

French regulations specify that roasted, decaffeinated coffee must contain less than 0.1 per cent of its weight of anhydrous caffeine compared with the product when dry. This regulation is strictly adhered to, requiring that manufacturers of decaffeinated coffee eliminate almost all of the alkaloid content, without significantly altering the flavour.

The production of decaffeinated coffee has given rise to a great number of patents throughout the world. This number is still increasing. One of the most commonly used techniques is to extract the caffeine using organic solvents, mainly methyl chloride and ethyl acetate. Another technique involves the following operations:

- Caffeine extraction using hot water;
- Reabsorption of the caffeine using charcoal.

The most recently developed technique consists of extracting the caffeine with CO_2 at a supercritical temperature.

For some considerable time, decaffeinated coffees were known to lose much of their flavour during processing. This is less true nowadays, as it is now possible to produce decaffeinated coffee with qualities that are very similar to those of regular coffee. The progress made in its production will be particularly appreciated by those who are advised to stop drinking coffee for reasons of health.

French law specifies a number of approved solvents, and also the permissible quantity of residual solvent per kg of marketed product.

Coffee and health

Coffee has a physiological effect on the consumer, particularly with regard to the nervous and circulatory systems. It is also reported to stimulate cerebral activity, and is often consumed specifically to prolong wakefulness. It is also a heart stimulant, by nature of its caffeine content, which also has diuretic properties.

Since it was first introduced about 300 years ago, coffee has had many adversaries. It was originally denounced by the church as being conducive to amoral behaviour, since it was often consumed in association with alcoholic beverages. The medical fraternity have also, over the years, voiced several, seemingly legitimate objections to its consumption; often grossly exaggerated by the media.

In response to this potentially damaging media coverage, the ISCA (International Scientific Coffee Association) encouraged several eminent doctors and physiologists to carry out research in order to disprove the theories which linked coffee consumption with such conditions as hypertension and cardiac disorders.

These studies, which were backed by scientific and medical findings, suggest that reasonable, or moderate coffee consumption of four to five cups a day for an adult presents no danger. However, the surveys and experiments conducted thus far have not been sufficient enough to establish a rule.

Chicory

Chicory is worthy of some note in connection with coffee consumption. Originally used for medicinal purposes, it is referred to in the writings of several ancient cultures and was cultivated very early on in Europe, being manufactured industrially in the Netherlands before coffee was introduced. Its consumption has increased over the years to such an extent that it is now regarded as a foodstuff. In the early 1800s, limited supplies of coffee in Europe led to it becoming a commonly consumed drink, often added to coffee for economic reasons.

The shoots of chicory are now widely used as a vegetable, while the roots are processed for use as a beverage either in their own right, or with coffee.

In Northern France, where chicory is widely cultivated, the roots are harvested between October and December, depending on climatic conditions. They are carefully washed, cut into pieces and dried in an atmosphere of 13 per cent humidity to ensure their conservation. The roasting process follows, which allows the particular aromatic flavour of the chicory to develop. Various forms of processed chicory are available, mainly grains, ground, concentrated liquid extract and 'instant'.

Fresh chicory root contains about 72 per cent water, 25–28 per cent non-nitrogenous, dry matter (14 per cent of which is inulin), 1.5 per cent protein, 0.36 per cent lipids, and 1.4 per cent fibre. When processed, commercial chicory contains proteins, lipids, cellulose, 8 to 10 per cent levulose, 7 to 8 per cent inulin, and traces of intybin.

Ground coffee chicories are produced by coffee roasters containing various percentages of chicory. Powdered coffee chicories are also made by coffee roasters, either by adding chicory during the initial stages of coffee processing, or by mixing already made instant coffee and instant chicory. Mixtures of powdered coffee chicory tend to have a higher percentage of chicory than that of ground coffee chicory. French regulations state that the quantity of chicory should not be more than 10 per cent of the roasted coffee used.

An infusion made with chicory has a dark colour and a rather bitter taste, which is agreeable but very different from that of coffee. Prolonged use of chicory has a beneficial effect on the digestive tract, and especially on the liver, due to the presence of inulin and intybin. It is very popular in Northern France, Belgium, the Netherlands and Germany, and is also widely used in certain coffee-producing countries, for example India, where 18 000 tonnes are consumed per year.

Some of the world's main producers of chicory are: France, South Africa, India, Belgium, Poland, U.S.S.R., Czechoslovakia, Austria, Hungary, Romania, and Yugoslavia.

13 *Worldwide coffee production*

Francophone countries
General information

Before 1789, the French colonies (including Santo Domingo) were producing about 40 000 tonnes of coffee per year which constituted almost the entire coffee supply of Europe, national coffee consumption being only about 6000 to 8000 tonnes per year at that time. Over the years, production gradually declined for various social and economic reasons and coffee growing became largely replaced by sugar cane growing. At the end of the last century, the small amount of coffee produced by the French colonies came from Guadeloupe, Reunion, and the African colonies, where the planters had first settled. During this time, coffee growing was expanding considerably in Latin America and Brazil.

Between the wars (1920–1940), French coffee production increased considerably as a result of supportive measures taken by the government. However, the origin of coffee became mainly African, and canephoras largely replaced arabicas. Just before the last war, the French colonies were exporting about 60 000 tonnes of coffee, which were entirely consumed by the mother country. Production began again after a period of stagnation during the war, about 180 000 – 200 000 tonnes being produced at the time when coffee-producing countries were gaining independence.

Since then, despite the decrease in rates and newly imposed restrictions due to worldwide overproduction, production has increased to 500 000 tonnes, with the help of incentives provided by the governments of the new countries, represented by a multinational organisation, the OAMCAF. This amount may be taken to be their current potential.

The coffee-growing situation will be briefly examined first in French overseas departments and territories, followed by other independent francophone countries. Table 18 illustrates worldwide coffee production in 1985–6, with estimated figures for 1986–7.

Overseas departments

The West Indies

Arabica coffee was introduced in Martinique in 1723, and in Guadeloupe in 1726. From 1790 onwards, Guadeloupe was exporting 3710 tonnes of coffee annually.

Coffee from Guadeloupe enjoyed an excellent worldwide reputation for a long time. Its quality was comparable, if not superior to that of the best arabicas of Central America or Colombia. Depending upon the method of preparation used for export, it was classified as 'Improved' or 'Inhabitant' Guadeloupe.

Coffee plantations (essentially arabica) still occupy several hundred hectares of land in Guadeloupe (as opposed to 3200 in 1935), in the southern and western regions. There are also some old *C. liberica* and *C. excelsa* plantations. Production is limited to a few dozen tonnes per year and provides mainly for local consumption. A very small amount is exported. The same is true for Martinique, where the small amount of coffee produced is used for local consumption.

The French government is anxious to diversify production in an effort to combat the current trends away from coffee growing. Unfortunately, their efforts have not yet been as successful as had been hoped. The major agricultural products exported are still sugar cane (which is on the decline), bananas, and pineapples.

Reunion

Formerly called Bourbon Island, Reunion was one of Europe's main coffee suppliers 200 years ago. It exported about 3000–3500 tonnes per annum.

Coffee growing (*C. arabica*) was introduced there in 1718 (or 1715) with seeds from Arabia. However, the consequences of the Revolution, devastation by a disease due to *Hemilieia vastatrix* and severe damage by cyclones, were all extremely detrimental to coffee production.

Attempts to revive coffee growing had little success. The rural population had set great store by traditional sugar cane growing, which admittedly was better adapted to the local environment than coffee growing. Tea planting also failed for the same reasons.

Only a few tonnes of coffee are produced per annum in Reunion. It is of excellent quality and is consumed locally, together with a large amount of robusta coffee imported from Madagascar.

Overseas Territories

New Caledonia

Coffee growing began here with *C. arabica* around 1860. Later on, *C. liberica* was also grown and the indigenous species *C. canephora* was grown when

Table 18   Worldwide production of green coffee in 1985–86 (millions of tonnes)

Country	1985–86	1986–87*	Country	1985–86	1986–87*
Africa			**South America**		
Angola	11.4	13.9	Bolivia	8.0	8.9
Benin	0.7	1.1	Brazil	1 368.5	1 541.3
Burundi	32.0	35.0	Columbia	705.8	645.2
Cameroon	100.0	132.1	Ecuador	125.3	123.2
Cent. African Repub.	13.9	15.1	Paraguay	17.0	19.3
Congo	1.3	1.0	Peru	73.6	75.8
Ivory Coast	280.9	274.0	Venezuela	46.3	67.4
Ethiopia	170.0	178.4	TOTAL	2 344.5	2 454.1
Gabon	2.2	0.8			
Ghana	0.6	0.7	**Central America**		
Guinea	2.9	6.5	Costa Rica	79.5	158.3
Equatorial Guinea	1.9	0.5	Cuba	24.2	26.2
Kenya	121.9	111.1	Dom. Rep.	26.0	47.2
Liberia	3.7	4.3	Guatemala	158.0	176.5
Madagascar	58.2	59.8	Haiti	29.7	26.2
Malawi	3.7	5.5	Honduras	52.3	93.2
Nigeria	0.8	1.2	Jamaica	1.3	1.2
Uganda	165.5	170.8	Mexico	296.4	335.8
Rwanda	40.1	39.1	Nicaragua	42.5	46.0
Sierra Leone	6.7	5.9	Panama	8.8	11.8
Tanzania	49.0	41.3	Salvador	107.0	140.6
Togo	15.2	15.5	Trinid. & Tobago	1.5	1.9
Zaire	109.9	125.5	TOTAL	827.2	1 065.0
Zambia	1.0	1.0			
Zimbabwe	10.3	12.7	**Oceania**		
TOTAL	1 203.8	1 252.8	Pap. New Guinea	47.3	63.2
			Miscellaneous		0.2
Asia			WORLD TOTAL	4 961.3	5 474.1
India	94.2	129.2			
Indonesia	150.0	339.8			
Philippines	56.3	49.9			
Sri Lanka	6.2	2.3			
Thailand	31.6	27.8			
TOTAL	538.3	639.0			

* Estimates.
(Source: *Quarterly Statistical Bulletin*, OIC, Feb. 1988, in *Café, Cacao, Thé* no. 1, 1988.)

the disease *Hemileia* appeaared in 1911. Both *C. arabica* and *C. canephora* are sometimes grown together on the same land. The climate of the West coast is more favourable to arabica, while the wetter slopes of the East coast are more suitable for canephora. However, arabica growing is currently on the decline on the West coast, while the amount of robusta grown on the East coast is increasing.

Coffee growing is very small-scale. Plantations are family-run and the average size is between one and five hectares. Their yields are not very high, often due to lack of appropriate care. The main production centres on the East coast are: Canala, Houaïlou, Ponerihouen, and Hienghène. On the West coast they are: Bouloupari, La Foa-Moindou. Approximately 3000 hectares are planted with robusta. The coffee beans are largely dry processed due to labour and climatic problems, but are of a good quality.

Some 25 years ago the island was exporting a few hundred tonnes of coffee per annum to France. Production declined for various reasons and the island went from being a coffee exporter to an importer, as it was no longer producing enough to meet its own consumption needs. However, this situation has improved in the last ten years, with the encouragement and technical assistance (IRCC) given to planters. Robusta production is increasing every year and the country will soon be exporting again.

An experimental field station was established in Ponerihouen on the East coast under the direction of the IRCC. The work carried out there, and the results obtained, have greatly influenced the revival of coffee growing.

French Polynesia

The introduction of *C. arabica* in the Polynesian islands (particularly Tahiti) dates back to the beginning of this century on the initiative of colonists from Reunion who had settled in New Caledonia. Arabica is grown mostly in Tahiti (500 ha) and the southern islands (750 ha). The overall area of coffee plantations on the archipelago that makes up French Polynesia is about 1500 hectares.

The amount of coffee produced is relatively low and is consumed locally. Possibilities for expansion are limited to those islands which have the most favourable conditions due to the sparse population and the presence of two competitive products: copra and vanilla.

Vanuatu (formerly New Hebrides)

Arabica was among the crops grown by the first settlers, but it was abandoned in about 1910 after major damage had been caused by *Hemileia*. It was replaced almost entirely by robusta, which was imported from Java. The small amount of coffee produced is consumed locally.

Independent francophone countries

The major coffee producers of francophone Africa are the Ivory Coast, Madagascar, and Cameroon, all of which are former French colonies.

Ivory Coast

The Republic of Ivory Coast, the production of which, since 1963, largely exceeds 200 000 tonnes per year, sometimes amounting to as much as 300 000 tonnes, is one of Africa's leading coffee producers. It is the third largest producer in the world, after Brazil and Colombia.

The first plantations date back to 1881, when a settler first introduced *C. liberica* in Elima, after which time it spread throughout the region. However, production did not develop until after spontaneous and imported varieties of *C. canephora* were planted.

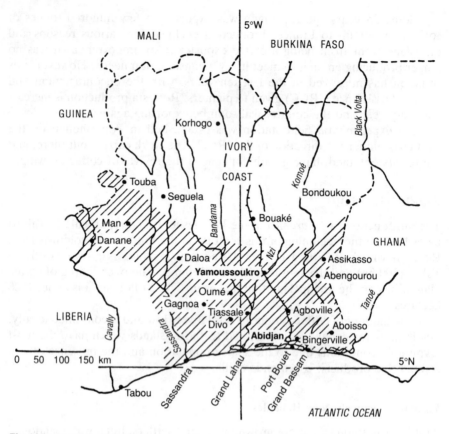

Fig 130   Republic of Ivory Coast, coffee-growing region

Canephora plantations can be found almost throughout the low altitude forested area (100–400 m), but particularly in the southern (Divo, Tiassale, Aboisso, Agboville and central (Dimbokro, Oumé, Gagnoa) regions. There are still a few plantations in the area to the west that borders Liberia, with the exception of the regions of Man and Danané. The total area cultivated is estimated to be about 1 300 000 hectares, almost all of which belongs to local farmers (Fig 130).

The predominant characteristic of this type of coffee farming is its extreme fragmentation. There are about 500 000 planters, more than 70 per cent of the coffee plantations having an area of less than 5 hectares, while only – per cent are larger than 25 hectares.

The main flowering period is February – March and harvesting takes place between October and March. Yields obtained by the African planters vary. They range from 100 – 600 kg/ha according to the level of maintenance carried out on the plantations, and may even exceed 1000 kg/ha when selected plant material is used.

Certain recommended techniques with regard to shrub maintenance, pruning, disease and pest control, harvesting methods, should be implemented in order to increase average yields. The IRCC has been striving to achieve this goal, with the support and participation of the French and Ivorian governments, through the selection of new varieties and by formulating expansion programmes which could help to increase yields and profitability. The encouraging results that have been achieved by young managers hired by the government in rural areas, may hopefully improve the current situation. The new hybrid *C. arabica* X *C. robusta*, or Arabusta, was created in Ivorian research stations.

All of the robusta produced in the Ivory Coast is dry processed in regional hulling factories, after which the majority of it is homogenised and packaged in large private factories in Abidjan. The Tombokro factory, which was first set up in 1973 in Central Ivory Coast by the SERIC, is a remarkable technological achievement, having a capacity of 40 000 tonnes of green coffee, and very up-to-date equipment.

Table 19 Principal destinations of coffees exported by the Ivory Coast in 1987

Destination	Tonnage
France	37 669
Italy	38 491
United States	28 559
Netherlands – Belgium – Luxembourg	9 162
United Kingdom	15 719
Japan	3 325
Federal Republic of Germany	3 444
TOTAL	136 369

(Source: *Le café* no. 440, March 1988)

Coffee exporting is regulated by legal measures (decree of 10 June 1981). They are enforced by the Department for the Supervision of Conditioning in the ports of Abidjan and San Pedro. Part of the production, which is made into instant coffee locally, is exported to neighbouring countries and the Middle East.

Ivorian robustas are appreciated for their neutral, clean taste both by instant coffee manufacturers and by those who consume it directly, either pure or mixed with arabica.

A stabilisation fund was established in 1955. Its intervention during difficult periods enabled planters to find ways of subsisting by selling coffee. The number of tonnes exported over the past few years and their destinations are illustrated in Table 19. It should be noted that France received 37 669 tonnes of Ivorian coffee in 1987 while the United States received 28 509 tonnes. Coffee sales form a major part of the budget of the Ivory Coast, amounting to between 25 and 30 per cent.

A sizeable coffee plantation regeneration operation has been in progress since 1985, initiated by a state-run company, the SATMACI, with technical assistance from the IRCC. It is hoped that nearly 500 000 hectares will have been regenerated by the year 2000. Its objective is to stabilise production at about 300 000 tonnes per year using multi-stem pruning to regenerate good, fruit-bearing branches on degraded trees that are still of a productive age. This programme also includes replanting and extension.

The IRCC, which has been widely represented in the Ivory Coast since its independence, greatly assists in the development of coffee growing and improving the quality of exported coffee. Its services have been established in several stations which are equipped with laboratories, mainly the Central Station in Divo, which is undoubtedly the largest station in the world entirely devoted to coffee and cocoa research.

A factory for the manufacture of instant coffee was established in 1962 (CAPRAL). Its initial capacity of 6500 tonnes (equivalent in green coffee) had doubled by 1978.

Madagascar

At the time of publication of the French edition of this book, Madagascar had not yet become reintegrated into the francophone region, hence its inclusion in this section. Coffee plantations are estimated to occupy about 200 000 hectares of land in Madagascar, 99 per cent of which are planted with *C. canephora* (robusta and Kouilou). The nationalised industrial plantations occupy about 20 000 hectares. There are approximately 400 000 Malagasy planters. Attempts at planting *C. arabica* have, as yet, been unsuccessful and* this species is only represented by small pockets totalling a few hundred hectares on the central high plateaux and in Ankaisina in the north, these being regions where the climate is favourable to the species.

Plantations of *C. canephora* are spread throughout the East coast, particularly in the great alluvial plains of coastal rivers at a distance of about 1200 km, between latitudes 13.5° and 24.5°. On the West coast, there is limited production in Sambirano and on the island of Nosy-Bé (Fig 131). Flowering occurs between August and November and harvesting is undertaken from May to October.

Malagasy planters achieve an average yield of 200–300 kg/ha, although on well-tended farms the yield is often easily maintained at 800 to 1000 kg/ha. The clones selected by the IFCC yield approximately 1500 to 2000 kg/ha on commercial farms.

With assistance and support from the French and Malagasy governments, the IFCC attempted to improve coffee growing in Madagascar through the selection of well-adapted plant material and the implementation of rational farming techniques. A sizeable renovation programme was undertaken in 1966. It was unfortunately interrupted in 1976 due to political upset. Since then, several programmes have been revived through various funding sources mainly FED and FAC), which are more or less integrated into an

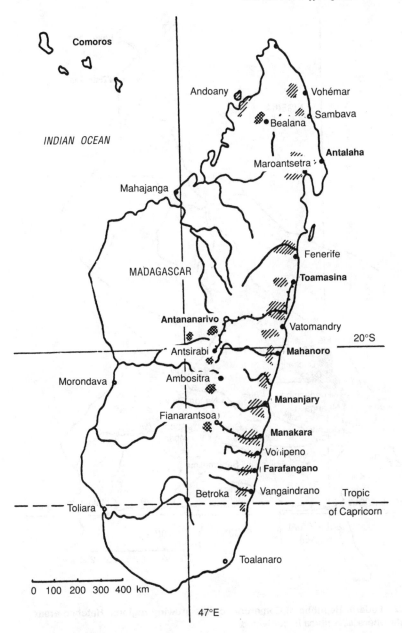

Fig 131 Malagasy Republic, coffee-growing regions. Hatched areas indicate where
***C. arabica* is cultivated**

ambitious agrarian reform plan. A so called 'arabica' operation was also
undertaken in the region of Lake Alaotra in 1979–80. A more recent operation which was called the 'Southeast Operation' concerned robusta coffee
production.

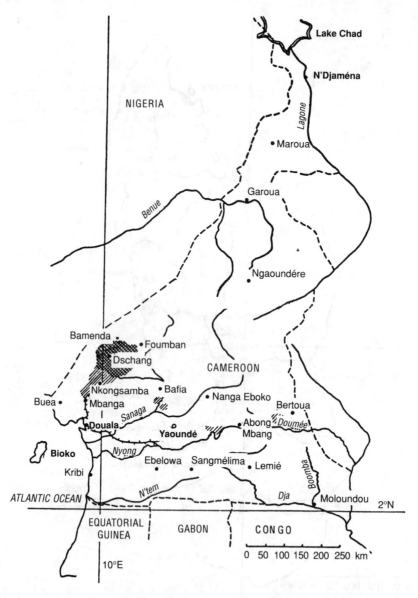

Fig 132   Federal Republic of Cameroon, coffee-growing regions. Hatched areas indicate where *C. arabica* is cultivated

Malagasy robusta and Kouilou coffees have a pleasing appearance and their neutral taste makes them popular for blending and for the manufacture of instant coffee. The arabica coffees, the export of which is limited to a few hundred tonnes, are of a good quality, but most of the production is consumed locally.

Coffee is shipped via the port of Toamasina (about 15 000 tonnes) and the harbours of Manakara (15 000 tonnes), Mananjary, Sambava, Nosy-Bé and Antalaha. A coffee stabilisation fund was established in 1957. It has helped to reduce the impact of low coffee rates on Malagasy planters, for whom coffee is the main means of support.

Coffee exports make up about 25 per cent of Madagascar's total export trade. This amounts to about 50 000 tonnes per year (1985–1986). The recipients are mainly France and the United States.

Federal Republic of Cameroon

The expansion of coffee growing in Cameroon dates back to 1925–35, with *C. arabica* on the high plateaux of Bamiléké and Bamoun, and *C. canephora* in the middle-altitude regions of the west. In later years, robusta growing expanded in the east in Abong Mbang (Fig 132).

At the present time, approximately 350 000 hectares are used for coffee growing, about 50 per cent of which is occupied by arabica.

The predominant characteristic of coffee growing in Cameroon is the general care taken, particularly in regions where arabica is grown. This is the result of a rather strict technical discipline which was imposed on the African planters when coffee first started to be grown in the country, and which has persisted. Yields are generally satisfactory. Before independence, a great many European planters made a considerable effort to increase the yields of their plantations. The various operations, including pruning, soil cover and fertilisation, are still being carried out and pre-harvest operations are constantly being improved. Several co-operatives operate satisfactorily, the oldest being the 'Co-operative of Bamoun Planters of Arabian Coffee', the headquarters of which is in Foumban. This co-operative was first established in 1932. The plantations belong to about 400 000 small-scale Cameroonian planters, with the exception of 3000 hectares of commercial farms.

The arabica coffee produced by Cameroon is of a superior quality and is very popular. It is comparable with that which originates from the highly favoured Central American provenances. All of the coffee produced is exported via the port of Douala.

Table 20   Main destinations of coffee exported from Cameroon in 1987

Destination	Tonnage
France	19 967
Netherlands	6 648
West Germany	7 761
Italy	20 617
United States	1 881
Japan	3 955
Belgium	2 532
United Kingdom	758
Switzerland	2 216
TOTAL	66 335

(Source: *Le Café* no. 440, March 1988)

Agronomic research in connection with coffee growing in Cameroon is carried out with the support and assistance of the French government, and also the IRCC, whose staff work in several national centres and stations.

The destinations and respective quantities of coffee exported over the past few years are illustrated in Table 20. They represent about 25 per cent of the overall export trade. A rate stabilisation fund was established in 1955. It provides financial assistance to planters, particularly during periods of crisis.

Other coffee-producing francophone countries

Central African Republic

Coffee is the major exported resource of this country, ranked even above the diamond in importance. Since 1980, annual production of robusta has varied between 11 000 and 18 000 tonnes.

Since 1970, there has been a progressive decrease in the contribution to production made by commercial plantations and a corresponding increase in the contribution made by family-run farms. In 1986, the commercial plantations, which numbered about 30, were producing as little as 3000–3500 tonnes of coffee. However, the profitability of some of them should help to revive the interest in coffee growing and serve as a model for future programmes.

The area occupied by family-run plantations has increased from 14 600 hectares in 1969 to over 50 000 hectares in 1986. The cultivation of Excelsa coffee, which was previously grown in the eastern part of the country, is now being abandoned.

A major Agronomic Coffee Centre (IFCC) previously operated in Boukoko (M'Baïki) but has since ceased all research activities.

Togo

Coffee is grown in Togo in the only area with a favourable climate, that being in the northwest part of the country (Klouto, K'Palimé, Atakpamé). There are approximately 35 000 hectares of coffee plantations, including old plantations of the Niaouli variety which are not very productive and are pest ridden, and a few hectares of *C. arabica* on the Dayes plateau.

Family-run plots make up the main production source which amounted in 1986 to about 15 000 tonnes per year, achieving a prospective 20 000 tonnes in 1990, as a result of government efforts and outside financial assistance. The IRCC provides technical support to Togo (Tové Central Station, near K'Palimé), whereas a national company (SRCC) assists the planters in their agricultural operations.

Robustas from Togo are of a high quality. They are exported via the port of Lomé. A state-run organisation, the OPAT, is responsible for commercial operations such as harvest prices. quality control, shipping and sales. Coffee represents 20–25 per cent of exported resources. It is the second largest export product of Togo; phosphates being the largest.

Other African Countries

Benin (formerly Dahomey): The coffee production of this country is minimal, amounting to only a few hundred tonnes per year. Robusta and Niaouli are grown there, especially in the Parakou-Abomey region.

Congo (People's Republic of Congo): Coffee is not widely grown in this country; a few thousand hectares of *C. robusta* being grown in Niari.

Gabon: Coffee growing was practically non-existent in this country until recent years, when a promotional campaign was carried out with technical support from the IRCC. Several thousand hectares of commercial plots have since been planted with Robusta.

Guinea: Coffee growing in Guinea appears to be fairly widespread according to available statistics. However, most of this area has actually been either neglected or abandoned. Based on export statistics, which indicate between 4000 and 6000 tonnes of coffee per year, the area actually farmed would be approximately 35 000 to 40 000 hectares in the forested area of Guinea, which would indicate a lower, average yield. Robusta is the main species cultivated, together with a few Excelsa plantations that have been spared by trachaeomycosis.

This limited production was most recently exported to Eastern Europe and the USSR as payment for old debts.

Non-Francophone countries

Africa

Angola

Angola was one of the top producers of robusta coffee before independence. Exports at the time were approximately 200 000 tonnes per annum. However, since then, various factors have had catastrophic consequences on the exploitation of coffee plantations. Only 15 000 to 20 000 tonnes have been exported annually over the past few years. It is unlikely that production will recover in the light of the country's present political status.

In the past, when Angola was a Portuguese province, Angolan coffee was sought after and much appreciated for its superior quality. Several agronomic stations, including a Research Institute in Luanda and a central station in Gabela, were responsible for carrying out research studies. Exports during the last years have been mainly to Portugal, DDR, FRD, the Netherlands and Poland.

Burundi

Burundi, a mountainous country, produces almost exclusively arabica coffee, particularly in the Buyenzi region near the Rwandan border (40 per cent of total production) and in the Muyinga and Guteza regions. Plantations are all

Table 21   Main countries of origin of Robusta coffees exported throughout the world

Country of origin	Tonnages		
	1980	1985	1987
Africa:			
Angola	47 500	18 600	16 140
Cameroon	93 000	96 600	84 480
Central African Republic	11 400	19 000	11 520
Congo	2 100	2 500	480
Ivory Coast	216 000	280 000	168 780
Gabon	600	2 200	780
Madagascar	65 100	44 000	48 300
Uganda	108 000	151 000	13 020
Togo	9 000	13 500	13 020
Zaire	59 000	70 000	103 440
TOTAL	611 700	697 400	596 880
Asia:			
Indonesia	217 000	273 000	272 640
Philippines	16 000	31 200	16 260
Sri Lanka	900	5 000	720
Thailand	2 100	20 500	22 680
TOTAL	236 000	329 700	312 300

family-run, their average size being half a hectare. They rise in terraces from the valley bottoms up to 2000 m and cover about 50 000 hectares.

A major effort to improve production has been undertaken over the past years, with French technical (IRCC) and financial assistance. It has concentrated on methods of increasing yields and quality improvement, with the establishment of several pulping installations and modern hulling-sorting factories.

About 35 000 tonnes of coffee are exported annually. The revenue obtained from these exports amounts to 80 per cent of the country's income. Arabicas from Burundi, which had previously been exported to the United States, are now mostly exported to Western Europe. A small amount of robusta is produced (1300 tonnes in 1985) on the Imbo plain, along the banks of Lake Tanganyika.

Ethiopia

C. arabica is thought to have originated from Ethiopia. Vast areas of forest contain major natural and semi-spontaneous stands of this species on the high plateaux of Kaffa (Jimma) and the region of Lake Tana. These are still being exploited to a certain extent.

C. arabica is grown exclusively in the regions of Kaffa, Sidamo, Illubaor, Harrar and Wollega. Plantations cover an area of about 700 hectares (not including forest stands), being located at altitudes of 1300 to 2000 m. These are mostly family-run plantations with an average size of less than two hectares. In the past, Ethiopian arabicas were mainly dry processed: wet processing being used almost exclusively on large plantations.

Several projects, some funded by the IDA, assisted in promoting the production of 'washed' coffees. This was mainly achieved through the use of proper equipment, provided at great expense. The designated regions are Kaffa and Sidamo (training managers, creating a road network in desert areas, installing pulping equipment). More recently, in 1980, the so-called Bebeka project organised the establishement of four, state-run farms. Each one was divided into 25 hectare plots with a water processing factory.

Ethiopia produces between 180 000 and 200 000 tonnes of coffee per annum and is the major producer of arabica and the second largest coffee producer among the East African countries. The export quota set by the ICO, which is much lower than these tonnages, takes into consideration the high local consumption.

Ethiopian coffees are exported via the ports of Djibouti (Afar and Issas), which is connected to Addis Ababa by rail (550 km), and to Assab by road. The quality of the coffee produced is generally high, although it can be variable at times and is not monitored. The 'Harrars' in particular are estimated to be among the best in the world.

Coffee is exported to the United States, West Germany, Switzerland, Italy, Saudi Arabia, France and Japan.

Kenya

European settlers were, at one time, the exclusive producers of *C. arabica* in Kenya. Since independence, Africans have become increasingly involved in coffee-growing.

Plantations of about 150 000 hectares exist, 60 to 70 000 of which are family-run. These are located in the Kiambu, Thika and Ruiru districts (Fig 133), and are remarkably well-maintained and technically advanced. However, yields are highly influenced by the annual rainfall pattern; some seasons being very dry. They are are generally between 600 and 1000 kg/ha, and sometimes over 1000 kg/ha in ecologically favoured regions.

Kenya coffees are carefully wet processed. They have a unique, slightly acidic taste that is favoured by many consumers. African producers are affiliated with co-operatives, all of which are grouped together in regional unions. Their harvests, like those of European countries, are selected and standardised in a central factory of the Coffee Board in Nairobi.

Between 105 000 and 110 000 tonnes of coffee are produced in Kenya per annum, the main recipients being the United Kingdom, the United States, Germany, Australia, Canada and Japan. Kenya coffee is sold by the board at the auctions in Nairobi.

A large National Coffee Research Station in Ruiru, which has a network of regional stations, is responsible for all agronomic problems that arise with regard to coffee growing in the country.

Fig 133   Kenya, Uganda and Tanzania, coffee-growing regions. Hatched areas indicate where *C. arabica* is cultivated

Uganda

Uganda, together with the Ivory Coast, is one of the main robusta coffee producers in the world. The climatic conditions of this high plateau (1100 to 1300 m) below the equator and the quality of the soils together make it an ideal country for this species (Fig 133).

The country's political problems, together with the difficulties encountered in transporting the coffee to Kenya for shipping from the port of
Mombasa, have resulted in a decrease in production. Before independence,
Uganda produced as much as 200 000 tonnes of coffee per annum, whereas
over the past few years its production has fallen to 150 000 to 170 000 tonnes.

Uganda also produces several thousand tonnes of arabica in the Buganda
and Mt. Elgon regions. Approximately 250 000 hectares are cultivated and
arabica is grown on approximately 25 000 hectares. These are divided into
about 500 000 plots, most of which are family-run.

Most of the harvests are dry processed in co-operatives and then taken
over by the Coffee Board in its central factory in Kampala, which is extremely
well-equipped. Only arabicas are wet processed. The Coffee Marketing
Board regulates the coffee trade. It operates via a certain number of
approved co-operatives and factories (curing works and scheduled hulleries).

About 160 000 tonnes of coffee are exported from Uganda per annum,
more than 95 per cent of which is robusta. It is shipped from the port of
Mombasa, Kenya, which is connected to the Ugandan capital, Entebbe,
by rail. In 1985, their contribution to the country's export trade was 92 per
cent.

Rwanda

Rwanda, like its neighbour Burundi, is a mountainous country and produces
arabica. The coffee plantations occupy about 30 000 hectares which are
divided amongst 500 000 smallholders. The harvests are wet processed.
About 45 000 tonnes of coffee are exported per annum. The coffee is transported by road to the port of Mombasa, Kenya.

Tanzania

Two main species of coffee are grown in Tanzania, with arabica being the
predominant species, occupying abut 200 000 hectares (7000 of which are
large plantations in the area south of Mt. Kilimanjaro) compared to only
about 20 000 hectares of robusta (Fig 133). The cultivation of arabica is
very localised in the districts of Arusha, Oldeani, and Moshi, south of Mt.
Kilimanjaro. Robusta is grown west of Lake Victoria (Bukoba).

African producers are governed by several dozen co-operative groups
that are assembled into unions, one of which, the KNCU (Kilimanjaro Native
Co-operative Union, Ltd.) obtained remarkable results with the Chagga
chiefdoms, with highly developed stands. The aim of several internationally
funded projects is to increase coffee production. It could potentially reach
75 to 80 000 tonnes per year. Two large processing factories have been built:
one in M'Bozi, the other in M'Bingo (Buvoma). There is also a coffee
research station in Lyamungu (Moshi).

The main recipients of Tanzania's coffee are the United States, West
Germany, Japan, the United Kingdom and France.

Zaire

Prior to the turbulent period that preceded independence in former Belgian Congo (1960), the coffee situation was as follows:

• European Plantations: 140 000 hectares (1/5 arabica);
• Congolese plantations: 80 000 hectares (2/5 arabica).

According to current estimates, the area cultivated is approximately 280 000 hectares, 230 000 of which is robusta, and 50 000 of which is arabica. There are approximately 300 000 to 350 000 small-scale Zairean farmers.

Robusta plantations are dispersed within the large expanse of the Congo basin. A few large stands exist regions of Stanleyville, Upper and Lower Uele, Tchuapa and Maniema. Arabica plantations are all located in high altitude zones in the east, mainly in Kivu.

The Belgian government had created several offices which were primarily concerned with marketing coffee. Among them the Robusta Office, with factories in Leopoldville (Kinshasa), played a major role in promoting coffee growing among rural populations. The high reputation of Congolese coffee was ensured by this office. Since independence, the Zairean Coffee Office (OZACAF) has taken its place.

The exports of the new country have increased to about 120 000 tonnes per year of which 15 000 tons are arabica. All the coffee is shipped via the port of Matadi, except for that which comes from the eastern part of the country, which is shipped from the Kenyan port of Mombasa. The main recipients are Italy, France, Belgium and Switzerland. Coffee is the third most important product exported from Zaire, after copper and cobalt.

A research organisation in Yangambi, Zaire, was started in 1933 by the Belgian government, and called the Congo National Institute for Agronomic Studies (INEAC). The remarkable results achieved there, mainly with regard to coffee trees, have had far-reaching effects at the international level. Unfortunately, this very important centre, which has since become specifically Zairean, being called the National Institute for Agronomic Studies and Research (INERA), no longer has the financial means which it had previously and its activities are thus limited. A revival project, funded by the FAO and the UNDP is currently being considered.

Other countries

Arabica-producing countries include Cape Verde (a few dozen tonnes per year), Malawi (2000–3000 tonnes), Zambia (1000 tonnes) and Zimbabwe (8000–12 000 tonnes, with an extension project). Robusta-producing countries are: Ghana (2000–3000 tonnes), Equatorial Guinea (500–1000 tonnes), Liberia (10 000–12 000 tonnes), Mozambique (a few hundred tonnes), Nigeria (2000–3000 tonnes), Sierra Leone (8000 to 9000 tonnes), Sao Tomé and Principe (a few dozen tonnes, a small quantity of which comes from Liberia).

The Americas

The main coffee producers of Latin America (exclusively *C. arabica*) are: Brazil, Colombia, Costa Rica, Guatemala, Mexico, San Salvador, Honduras, Equador, Peru, Venezuela, and the Dominican Republic. Panama and Nicaragua are secondary producers. Some countries, such as Cuba and Jamaica, consume a large proportion of their production. Others, such as Bolivia, Haiti, Paraguay and Puerto Rico, produce only a small tonnage or may even import coffee.

All of these countries, with the exception of Brazil, produce 'washed' arabica coffees that are generally of an excellent quality, and are classified as 'mild'. In Brazil, however, the harvests are dry processed and produce a product of inferior quality, with few exceptions.

Brazil

Brazil is the world's primary producer and exporter of coffee. Before the war, its exports amounted to two thirds of the tonnages exported by all the coffee producing countries combined. Since the development of coffee growing in other countries, mainly in Africa, this figure has fallen to 30 per cent. This privileged situation is made possible by climatic conditions that are very favourable to arabica, together with excellent soils. In 1985, coffee represented 44.3 per cent of Brazil's total exports.

The total area occupied by coffee plantations in 1986 was about 3 350 000 hectares, with a production potential of about 1 800 000 tonnes per year. This area has been reduced by about 650 000 hectares since 1975, when severe frosts were recorded in Paraña. Large, aging plantations that were either unprofitable or located in climatic zones prone to frost were abandoned or converted to other crops such as corn, soy beans, citrus and sugar cane. On the other hand, large areas were planted with coffee in states less exposed to frost, mainly Minas Gerais, which, with a current, annual potential of 600 000 tonnes per year, is now a primary producer. Coffee growing has also increased in the states of São Paulo, Bahia, and Espiritu-Santo. Plantations in the southern region are located in the state of Santa Catarina at a latitude of 27° south, just outside the tropical zone.

New plantations have been established using selected coffee trees. They are maintained carefully according to expert technical advice from development agencies.

Climatic hazards are frequently encountered by Brazilian coffee growers. In addition to frost, which is very serious in Paraña, there are also torrential rains in some years and long periods of drought and adverse weather. This may greatly affect production at certain times of the year.

Farming methods have evolved over the years. Hired daily labour is gradually being replaced by tenant farming with the farmer's family living on the property. Mechanisation is spreading rapidly, mainly for treatments to control *Hemileia vastatrix*. Mechanical harvesting is also becoming increasingly popular.

A new element has emerged recently in Brazilian coffee growing with the development of robusta (Conilon) in the Amazon region which is available to several million immigrants from the south. Several hundred thousand families have been granted plots of forest land which they farm. They sell wood and grow rice, coffee and cocoa. The results of this large project are rather debatable. The problems encountered when settling, together with drought and malaria, have caused many settlers to abandon the area. However, the harvest of Conilon (1986–1987) is estimated to be 150 000 tonnes, most of which is consumed locally and used to produce instant coffee. Nevertheless, the size of the plantations indicates that this production could increase in the near future to 300 000–400 000 tonnes.

Coffee growing is Brazil's main agricultural activity. It is practiced on 300 000 farms, and employs over 5 000 000 people. An additional 1 000 000 people work in the areas of transporting, storing, marketing, and exporting coffee. Virtually all the harvests are dry processed. Given the harvesting method of stripping, the quality of Brazilian coffee generally does not match that of Central American or Colombian coffees, which are harvested and wet processed very carefully. There are however, a few exceptions, such as the Sul de Minas, which are of excellent quality.

The Brazilian classification system for green coffee has preserved its traditional characteristics: species, origin, defects, bean size, colour, flavour. The black bean is always considered a major defect according to this type of classification, whereas unripe beans, which can seriously reduce the quality of the batch, are considered minor defects.

Coffees from the states of Rio de Janeiro and Minas Gerais have a unique, slightly iodised flavour, which is bacterial in origin (Rio flavour). This characteristic could potentially indicate a serious defect, but the coffees are highly favoured by certain consumers.

Coffee is exported via the ports of Santos (60 per cent), Rio de Janeiro, and Paranagua, the main recipients being the United States, Italy, West Germany, Sweden, France and Japan. A national organisation, the Coffee Institute of Brazil (CIB), was responsible for implementing production programmes and exporting coffee. It was to be dissolved in 1987, its substitute being a National Council for Coffee Policy with supposedly the same responsibilities. A research institute, the Centre for Agronomic Research of Campinas, which has enjoyed worldwide recognition for some time, is in charge of research studies on coffee.

A fair proportion of Brazil's coffee is processed into instant coffee (atomized and freeze-dried) for local consumption and export. Part of the harvest from Conilon is used for this.

Brazil is itself a great consumer of coffee. Betwen 450 000 and 500 000 tonnes are consumed per annum, or almost 4 kg per person per annum.

Table 22 Main countries of origin of coffee imports in 1987 in certain West European countries

Country of origin	Importing countries (tonnages)									
	West Germany	France	Italy	United Kingdom	Netherlands	Spain	Belgium and Luxemburg	Sweden	Switzerland	Austria
South America										
Brazil	41 685	56 251	71 208	10 397	26 317	43 086	18 992	41 320	17 487	20 169
Colombia	208 664	27 748	15 810	16 536	43 908	20 840	10 564	32 032	10 870	7 557
Ecuador	1 572	155	543	–	55	2 821	–	53	354	2 122
Central America										
El Salvador	27 232	2 059	608	628	1 974	7 614	135	685	1 350	3 540
Guatemala	13 041	2 903	6 751	3 186	4 409	1 459	1 851	3 718	7 591	2 517
Costa Rica	13 648	5 103	6 197	8 748	5 418	3 832	882	5 083	5 428	2 118
Mexico	4 286	4 074	1 213	491	3 012	3 189	729	940	1 992	3 107
Nicaragua	6 367	6 345	1 167	182	2 664	3 694	1 179	207	2 723	1 271
Honduras	2 529	2 031	4 941	1 149	1 225	1 677	1 585	488	4 234	2 545
Haiti	38	2 808	4 885	15	616	–	1 811	–	326	–
Africa										
OAMCAF*	12 408	89 591	67 792	16 846	15 580	15 087	9 098	75	4 021	1 279
Uganda	4 034	16 216	30 878	23 756	11 869	11 000	2 502	–	–	66
Zaire	5 982	34 884	45 924	3 098	2 318	5 704	3 425	–	287	522
Kenya	27 734	2 197	3 735	6 524	10 435	422	2 014	8 792	3 154	1 290
Tanzania	17 245	1 161	1 840	3 060	7 795	117	497	117	144	–
Angola	–	1 345	100	–	50	3 680	210	–	1 730	135
Ethiopia	18 194	5 981	2 912	590	250	–	1 228	–	1 016	226
Rwanda & Burundi	29 043	6 322	917	2 664	5 984	330	1 219	261	15	–
Asia and Oceania										
Indonesia	12 330	14 704	13 210	1 554	2 892	3 774	2 953	326	3 454	3 000
India	3 114	2 645	4 267	138	266	590	33	2 511	376	672
Papua New Guinea	24 538	211	511	4 452	321	–	–	20	31	486
Miscellaneous	12 735	12 286	11 243	2 551	7 907	23 767	27 204	250	4 756	6 320
TOTAL	486 419	297 020	268 852	106 565	155 465	152 765	88 668	94 400	73 485	58 646

*Ivory Coast, Cameroon, Madagascar, Central Africa, Togo, Benin, Congo, Gabon.
(Source: Coffee circular, Delamare, August 1988).

(269)

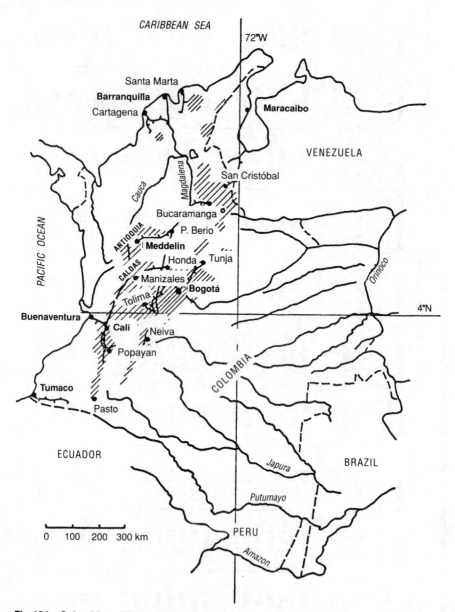

Fig 134   Colombia, coffee-growing regions

Colombia

Colombia is the second largest coffee producer in the world. It exports between 600 000 – 700 000 tonnes of coffee per year, having a value of 5 per cent (1980) of the Gross National Product. Arabica only is grown, as in Brazil, but careful harvesting and preparation ensure that the quality of most of the production is as good as coffees with superior origins.

Coffee is cultivated in areas located in the three mountain ranges that make up the hilly northwestern part of the country, at altitudes of 800 – 2000 m. The large production centres are in the departments of Caldas, Antioquia, Cauca, Cundinamarca, Tolima and Valle (Fig 134).

Coffee plantations occupy a total area of well over 1 000 000 hectares, belonging to more than 500 000 planters. There are very few large properties; most of the plantations being between 2 and 15 hectares and family-run. The plantations are well-maintained, fertilised, and pruned. Average yields are between 400 kg and 800 kg/ha, depending upon the region, with peaks above 1500 kg/ha in new coffee plantations. Wet processing is generally very carefully carried out.

The hilly relief of this part of the country presents major difficulties with transporting coffee from the production sites to river or sea ports. The ports used for export are Buena-ventura (Pacific Coast) for 90 per cent of the coffee, Cartagena, (Atlantic Coast) for 5 per cent, and Barranquilla (Atlantic Coast) for 5 per cent. Colombia's main recipients are the USA, West Germany, the Netherlands, France and Japan. About 100 000 tonnes of coffee per annum are also consumed locally.

The quality of the beverage made from Colombian coffees is excellent. They are categorised commercially as 'mild'. The main variety cultivated is Brazilian arabica caturra, a hybrid which is reputed to be rust-resistant (*Hemileia vastatrix*). It was created by crossing the hybrid Timor with caturra. Several thousand hectares have already been planted with this variety, often replacing older varieties. A major effort to modernise techniques has also been undertaken and the results have been favourably reflected in the yields, which, in certain plantations exceed 100 – 1200 kg/ha.

· A diversification programme was undertaken in coffee growing regions, the main objective being the elimination of 100 000 hectares of coffee trees. This measure was taken to tailor production to an export quota established by the ICO and thus avoid excessive stockpiling.

The success achieved by coffee growers in Colombia is due largely to a sponsor organisation, the National Federation of Coffee Planters of Colombia (FNC). This organisation has considerably influenced the promotion of coffee growing. It has established a large, modern research centre in Bogota which specialises in chemistry and technology.

Costa Rica

The coffee growing region of Costa Rica is located in the heart of the country on either side of the central plateau, in the provinces of San José, Cartago, Alajuela, Heredia (Fig 135). Coffee plantations cover about 100 000 hectares. The land belongs to more than 40 000 farmers, 20 000 of whom are small-scale farmers having less than five hectares.

The cultivation, harvesting, and preparation of the product are executed with great care. The coffee is of a high quality, particularly that which is grown in the Atlantic regions. Yields have increased to between 1200 and

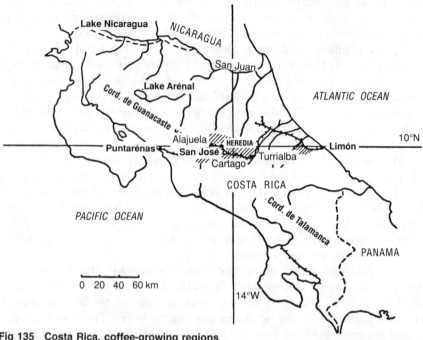

Fig 135   Costa Rica, coffee-growing regions

1500 kg/ha through the use of very modern practices such as high density planting (6000 to 8000 bushes per hectare) fertilisation, pruning and irrigation.

About 100 000 to 120 000 tonnes of coffee are exported, the 1985–86 harvest, which was approximately 170 000 tonnes being exceptional. Local consumption, which is high, is about 12 000 to 15 000 tonnes per annum, for 6 kg per person. Coffee is exported via the ports of Limón (Atlantic Coast) and Puntarenas (Pacific Coast).

The traditional recipients of these top quality coffees are the United States and West Germany. Secondary buyers are the Netherlands, Sweden, France and other countries.

An international agronomic research organisation is based in Turrialba: The Inter-American Institute for Agricultural Sciences. A great deal of their research is devoted to studying coffee trees.

Guatemala

Coffee is grown in an area that covers most of the southern part of Guatemala, which is traversed by many secondary ranges of the Andes Mountains. The main ʳroduction regions are those of San Marcos, Suchitepéque, Quezaltenango and Santa Rosa (Fig 136). Together this amounts to 250 000 hectares of coffee plantations, belonging to 60 000 planters. Some of these are either large estates, or properties owned by companies or foreign settlers.

Fig 136   Guatemala, coffee-growing regions

Guatemalan coffees are exported via the ports of Puerto Barrios (10 per cent), San Tomas de Castillo on the Atlantic Coast (80 per cent), and San José and Champerico on the Pacific Coast (10 per cent). The quality of the coffees is excellent, particularly those from the higher altitude regions.

Production is approximately 160 000 tonnes per annum. It has been greatly affected by both the political turmoil and civil war which have devastated the country over the past few years. Local consumption is about 20 000 tonnes per annum, or about 3 kg per person. Guatemalan coffee is very popular, some origins being classified among the best coffees in the world.

Fig 137   Mexico, coffee-growing regions

Mexico

Coffee growing regions in Mexico are located in the southern mountainous zone, particularly in the states of Oaxaca, Chiapas, and Veracruz (Fig 137). Plantations cover about 500 000 hectares and are divided into 100 000 plots of less than 10 hectares; there being few large estates. Yields are between 200 and 500 kg/ha, given the highly variable climatic conditions which prevail in these high altitude regions.

Sixty per cent of the production that is exported, which is about 300 000 tonnes/year, is bought by the United States. Amongst the European recipients are West Germany and Spain. Local consumption amounts to about 12 000 tonnes annually.

Mexican coffees are of an excellent quality; some of them being considered among the best in the world. For the most part, exports are transported by road (Laredo) to the United States (65 per cent) and the remainder via the Atlantic coast (Veracruz and Coatzacodleos).

El Salvador

Coffee plantations in El Salvador are located in the region that extends from the Pacific coast to the high plateaux. They cover about 180 000 hectares and are divided into about 50 000 plantations. There are many small-scale planters, but only a few hundred major landowners. The main production

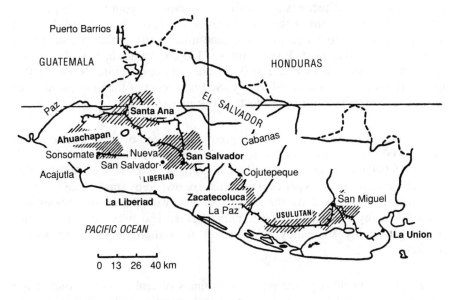

Fig 138 El Salvador, coffee-growing regions

areas are located in the departments of Santa Ana, Libertad, Usulutan and Sonsomate (Fig 148).

Production is currently about 120 000 tonnes of coffee per annum. Political troubles and the civil war have resulted in a decrease in coffee production, which had previously been as high as 170 000 to 180 000 tonnes per year. Local consumption is very high.

Exports are shipped via the ports of Acajutla (55 per cent), Cutuco (38 per cent) and Puerto Barrios in Guatemala (7 per cent). In 1965, they represented 50.8 per cent of total trade. The United States and West Germany are the major buyers of El Salvador's coffee.

Other countries

Honduras: The production of this country has risen considerably over the past 20 years. In 1965 it was 25 000 tonnes, whereas now it has increased to 100 000 tonnes, 12 000 of which are consumed locally.

The plantation area covers between 350 000 and 400 000 hectares, 80 per cent of which are divided into plots of less than 10 hectares. The production regions are mainly Santa Barbara, El Paraiso, Comayague and Cortès. Ninety five per cent of the exports are shipped via the port of Puerto Cortès (Atlantic Coast).

Ecuador: Ecuador is unique in that it produces both arabica (60 per cent) and robusta (40 per cent). It was possible to plant the latter species due to land improvements made for the oil palm in favourable, low altitude regions.

About 400 000 hectares are cultivated. Arabica accounts for 75 per cent and robusta 25 per cent. There are about 60 000 small farms which have an average area of 2 to 3 hectares. The amount of coffee produced fluctuates from one year to the next. Production was 120 000 tonnes in 1985–86, 85 000 tonnes the previous season and 90 000 tonnes the year before. About 18 000 tonnes of coffee are consumed locally. Sixty per cent of the arabicas are wet processed, whereas all of the robusta is dry processed.

Peru: Coffee production in Peru has greatly increased over the past 10 years from 50 000 tonnes in 1974–75, to 80 000 tonnes in 1985–86 and 1986–87. About 15 000 tonnes are consumed locally. About 140 000 hectares of coffee plantations exist, over 60 per cent of which are owned by small-scale planters.

Coffee is exported via the port of Callao, with the United States and West Germany being Peru's customary clients. The 'washed' arabicas are of a high quality and enjoy an excellent reputation on the international market.

Venezuela: Venezuela produced 60 000 tonnes of arabica coffee during the 1986–87 season and does not appear to have been affected by oil exploitation. Most of the production, which amounts to more than 50 000 tonnes, is consumed locally.

Coffee plantations occupy over 250 000 hectares which are divided up into small plots in high altitude zones (600 to 1500 m). The main port used for export is Maracaïbo, Venezuela's usual clients being the United States, West Germany and France.

Dominican Republic: The Dominican Republic increased its coffee production from 20 000–25 000 tonnes during the 1950s and 1960s, to about 50 000 tonnes during recent seasons, despite the devastation of the crops caused by several cyclones. The area cultivated is about 150 000 hectares, divided between approximately 60 000 small-holders. Local consumption is currently 18 000 tonnes per year.

Coffee is exported to the United States, Puerto Rico, Belgium, Italy and France. Coffees from some origins, such as Barahona, are of excellent quality.

Jamaica: Jamaica produces between 1500 and 2000 tonnes of arabica coffee per annum. This origin is particularly recognised as the 'Blue Mountain' variety, which has a worldwide reputation, and is currently the object of a government revival plan.

Asia and Oceania

Three countries in Asia have a sizeable coffee production.

Indonesia

Indonesia is now approaching the position of being the third largest coffee producer in the world, jointly with the Ivory Coast. Prior to 1938, about 400 000 hectares of coffee plantations existed, but they suffered from the political turmoil that preceded and followed the independence of the archipelago, which at the time was called the Dutch East Indies.

The lowest production figure was recorded during 1949 and 1950 (about 10 000 tonnes in Java, compared to 50 000 tonnes previously). The situation has improved progressively, following a long period of stagnation, and has today reached a production level of over 300 000 tonnes, with a view to increasing this to 400 000 tonnes in the very near future (350 000 tonnes in 1985–86). This increase is the result of intense government promotional measures including both the rehabilitation of large nationalised properties, which were more or less abandoned after independence, and the implementation of an ambitious plantation extension programme.

Coffee plantations are located in Sumatra, Java, and Sulawesi (formerly Celebes). They cover an area of over 600 000 hectares, nine tenths of which are farmed by small-holders. The rest belongs to the state or to private farmers. The two major species are grown, robusta largely predominating with 92 to 95 per cent of the harvests. A little over 5 per cent of the harvests is arabica. This is not likely to increase, due to a lack of favourable climatic conditions.

Robusta coffees are dry processed, with arabicas being 'washed' and 'natural'. The quality of the robustas is very variable and often poor. The arabicas, on the other hand, are much more consistent.

Most of the coffee is exported to the United States, the Netherlands, Italy and Japan. The government of Indonesia judged its export quota to be insufficient, considering its production, hense the country was obliged to sell more than 100 000 tonnes over and above its quota in 1984–85.

India

Coffee plantations are located in the southwestern part of the country, particularly in the states of Karataka (formerly Mysore), Kerala and Tamil Nadu (formerly Madras). High altitude zones (namely Chickmagalur and Nilgiris) are planted with arabica, while robustas predominate in other, lower altitude regions (Malabar, Salem, Coorg) (Fig 139).

The total area occupied by coffee plantations was 112 000 hectares in 1957. It is currently about 200 000 hectares, with slightly more arabica than robusta being grown. In 1957 there were 43 000 plots and estates, wheras currently there are almost 700 000, 85 per cent of which are less than 5 hectares.

Most of the coffees are dry processed. Some arabicas are specially treated in order to obtain 'monsoon', and are more or less comparable to coffees of that name from former times which had been shipped by sail for six months.

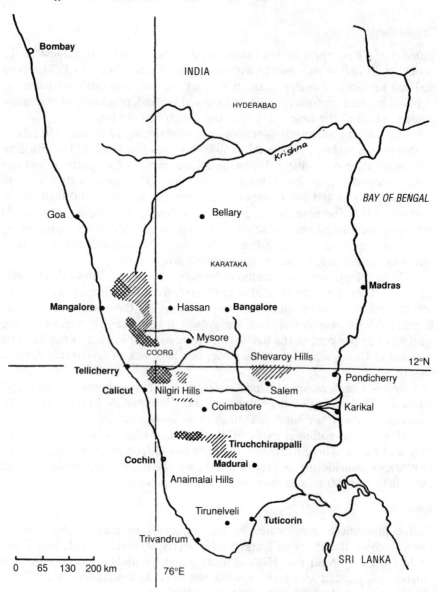

Fig 139 India, coffee-growing regions. Hatched areas indicate where *C. arabica* is cultivated

Production has risen to about 120 000 tonnes per annum, but local consumption absorbs more than half of this and continues to increase. The available quantities, considering the quotas, are shipped to Eastern Europe, the USSR and Italy. The government aims to increase the size and number of areas where the two species are grown, mainly by searching out potentially new regions.

Indian coffees are generally of average quality, but the 'monsoon' arabicas have a unique flavour, and the quality is highly appreciated.

The Philippines

Coffee production in the Philippines has greatly increased over the past few years. In 10 years, it rose from 35 000 tonnes (1975–76) to over 60 000 tonnes at the present time. This is the only country that still harvests small tonnages of Liberica and Excelsa for local consumption.

There are over 150 000 coffee plantations, but 25 per cent of these are not yet productive. Government projects include the extension of areas farmed by small-scale planters, particularly with arabica, in the mountainous regions of Benguet.

Robusta forms about 90 per cent of total production, which is about 65 000 tonnes. More than half of the production is consumed locally, and this amount is on the increase. The United States and Western Europe are the main clients for arabica. Roasted coffee is shipped to China and Taiwan while instant coffee is sent to Japan and neighbouring countries. Manila is the only port from which the coffee is exported.

Other countries

China: Production of coffee in China is very localised in the far south: Yunan, Kouang-Si, Hainan. Both species are grown, with robusta being largely predominant on the island of Hainan. Between 10 000 and 15 000 tonnes of coffee are produced per annum.

Viet Nam: Coffee plantations with robusta, arabica, and Excelsa (Chari) occupy about 40 000 hectares. These plantations formerly belonged to European settlers. After independence they were nationalised and divided into plots which were allocated to Vietnamese or made into collective state farms or co-operatives.

The main coffee growing regions are the former Annam (Dalat, Bam Me Thuot, Darlac), and the former Tonkin (Tuyen Quang, Co Nghia). The government is very keen to develop coffee growing.

The Vietnamese drink very little coffee; their main beverage being tea. The 300 to 400 tonnes of coffee harvested are for the most part exported to Japan and Eastern European countries.

Thailand: A few thousand hectares of plantations of Robusta coffee are cultivated in Thailand, often in association with other crops such as rubber and food crops. The 20 000 – 30 000 tonnes of coffee produced is not enough to satisfy consumption needs and instant coffee is imported. The government's aim is to increase production.

Yemen: Arabica, which was imported from Abyssinia (Ethiopia), has been grown in Yemen (north) since former times, dating back one or two thousand years. The plantations are all family-run and consist of small farmed areas in valley bottoms or terraces on mountain slopes. Irrigation (by gravity) is often commonly practiced to combat extended periods of drought. About 15 000 hectares are divided into a multitude of family plots.

Coffee is dry processed, often using rather archaic methods. A revival project, which is now being implemented, should enable 16 000 hectares of coffee plantations to be maintained.

The Yemenis currently use the husk of the fruit to make herbal tea, and even import sizeable quantities from Ethiopia. Yemeni coffees are well known throughout the world as 'Mocha' or 'Hudaydah', depending upon which of these two ports they are shipped from before being loaded at Aden. Coffee is exported to Saudi Arabia and Japan.

Papua New Guinea: Coffee growing in New Guinea has made considerable progress over the past few years. About 150 000 hectares of arabica are currently grown and the authorities hope to increase production from 50 000 tonnes to over 60 000 tonnes. The coffee is bought by Australia, the United States and Germany, with about 1000 tonnes per year being consumed locally.

Other producers: Other producers in this area worthy of note are Hawaii, with much modernised methods, Malaysia and Sri Lanka. Another attempt has recently been made to grow coffee in Australia (Queensland), on a few dozen hectares which have been maintained using very advanced techniques such as trickle irrigation, fertilisation and mechanised harvesting.

14 *Worldwide coffee consumption*

Western and Eastern Europe
General information

Western Europe imported over 2 000 000 tonnes of green coffee in 1987, compared to 1 000 000 tonnes in 1960 and 700 000 in 1955. West Germany is the major importer with 486 000 tonnes, followed by France with 297 000 tonnes. Italy is third with 270 000 tonnes. Great Britain is more modest with just over 105 000 tonnes, although it should not be forgotten that tea remains the favourite drink of the British, despite a noticeable and continuous increase in coffee consumption.

The Eastern European countries have doubled their imports over the past 20 years. They imported 120 000 tonnes in 1966, and 250 000 tonnes in 1986. East Germany has shown the most noticeable increase with 70 000 tonnes, compared to 25 000 tonnes.

Western Europe

With regard to the origin of the coffee imported, Western Europe uses mostly Brazilian coffees (about 25 per cent). Moreover, arabica coffees generally make up about 75 per cent of the shipments. Fifty per cent of the robustas from all origins, which totalled 570 000 tonnes in 1987, went to France (they constitute 57 per cent of the tonnages received). The rest is mostly consumed by Italy (124 000 tonnes, or 46 per cent of its imports), the Netherlands, (36 000 tonnes, or 23 per cent). However, the lack of success of this species of coffee among German, Swiss, and Scandinavian consumers should be noted (Table 23).

Tables 23, 24 and 25 show the global imports of green coffee and Robusta in Western Europe.

Table 23   Total imports of green coffee to Western Europe (tonnes)

	1980	1984	1986
France	310 000	281 000	282 200
West Germany	418 000	428 000	568 400
Italy	220 000	223 000	251 600
Netherlands	134 000	144 000	142 500
Spain	140 000	122 000	131 600
Great Britain	72 000	110 000	102 100
Belgium-Luxembourg	85 000	90 000	90 200
Sweden	91 000	92 000	93 300
Switzerland	60 000	59 000	61 300
Austria	41 000	52 000	62 500
Finland	67 000	69 000	57 900
Denmark	57 000	46 000	46 600
Norway	38 000	41 000	39 700
Miscellaneous	8 000	7 000	8 400
TOTAL	1 741 000	1 764 000	1 938 300

(Source: J. Louis Delamare Circulars, Le Havre, no. 332, 1981, no. 341, 1984, and Quarterly Statistical Bull., ICO June 1987)

Table 24   Imports of green robusta coffee in Western Europe (tonnes)

Recipients	1970	1980	1987	% of total imports
West Germany	37 000	33 800	30 800	6.3
Austria	–	6 000	5 600	9.5
Belgium-Luxembourg	16 450	16 700	20 400	22.7
Spain	27 600	36 000	49 200	32.2
France	156 000	180 000	155 000	52.2
Great Britain	55 500	43 500	46 200	43 4
Italy	33 000	100 000	124 200	46.1
Netherlands	37 150	40 000	36 000	22.8
Switzerland	16 800	15 200	12 600	17.3
Other countries	70 000	78 000	90 000	14.0
TOTAL	458 500	559 000	570 000	25.05

(Source: Coffee circulars. J. Louis Delamare, Le Havre)

According to available statistics, coffee consumption in Western Europe is almost wholly stationary or has risen only slightly over the past 10 years, being currently about 2 000 000 tonnes. Estimating the increase to be about 0.2 per cent per year, a figure given by some economists, it may be deduced that it is less than the population increase of 1.5 to 2.0 per cent, and has thus declined. This finding can be statistically proven for Denmark, the Netherlands, and even France. On the other hand, it has increased slightly in Belgium, West Germany, Greece, Italy, and Portugal. These trends must be carefully interpreted, taking into account the major changes that have occurred over the past years in the European coffee industry such as free circulation of merchandise within the EEC, stocks, development of processing techniques, standardisation of qualitites favouring exchanges of roasted or instant coffees.

Information from the ICO, which comes from better sources, is undoubtedly more reliable. It states that the consumption of all of these countries during the same year rose from 1 465 000 tonnes to 1 570 000 tonnes, or an increase of 0.7 per cent per annum.

Whatever may arise from this controversy, an attempt is made here to resolve the figures for the consumer countries, beginning with France.

France

Green coffee imports have evolved as follows in France since 1970:

1970	239 065 tonnes	1985	275 760 tonnes
1975	288 898 tonnes	1986	282 000 tonnes
1982	314 890 tonnes	1987	297 000 tonnes

With consumption running at about 5 kg *per capita* per year (adults only), its population ranks among the highest consumers in the world.

Robusta coffees represent about 52 per cent (1987), which is the highest proportion among the countries of the EEC. These figures theoretically indicate a relative stability in consumption, indeed a slight decrease considering the current demographic index of 1.8 per cent. Industrialists and merchants in the profession should heed this finding if it is confirmed. It would not be wise to run the risk of a loss in interest, as in the United States, where consumption has dropped considerably over the past 20 years.

The main criticism of coffee in France, excluding its price, which is sometimes considered excessive, pertains to its quality, which is judged rather harshly by many consumers. Young people seem to be particularly poorly informed about coffee and are more attracted to the flashy publicity of various alcoholic or non-alcoholic beverages.

Relaying information to those responsible for distribution, sales, and public services, as well as to consumers, is an area that has been explored very little so far, and has great potential. The French Coffee Committee concentrates on this type of activity as much as its financial resources will allow. More recently, a delegation of the ICO in Paris bravely tackled this problem, making it a priority to train instructors at teaching establishments, hotel management schools, and schools of domestic science. The Association Scientifique Internationale du Café (International Scientific Coffee Association) has been very thorough during the course of its international meetings, keeping attention focussed on these topics and promoting continuous scientific research on quality improvement. This is certainly a sizeable task, but the stakes are high, and every effort must be made in order to prevent the current situation from worsening.

About 200 000 tonnes of coffee are absorbed by France for domestic consumption. Fifty thousand tonnes become instant coffee and 40 000 tonnes

Table 25   Origin of green coffees imported by France (tonnes)

Country of origin	1970	1975	1982	1987
Americas				
Brazil	55 853	58 685	60 261	56 251
Colombia	2 951	10 891	17 120	27 747
Costa Rica	1 785	3 085	4 305	5 103
El Salvador	–	614	2 322	2 059
Ecuador	1 406	1 744	329	155
Guatemala	774	2 667	2 005	2 903
Haiti	2 802	4 314	3 139	2 808
Honduras	104	713	2 323	2 031
Mexico	1 274	5 020	5 549	4 074
Nicaragua	507	1 252	5 567	6 345
Peru	382	104	361	–
Dominican Republic	383	669	216	–
Venezuela	643	708	2	–
Others (Americas)	545	363	1 859	2 290
Total Americas	69 409	90 829	107 358	111 766
Africa				
Cameroon	17 254	29 412	26 353	19 967
Ivory Coast	89 625	96 643	81 014	37 669
Madagascar	23 586	25 344	16 223	25 280
Others OAMCAF	16 564	8 686	15 466	6 675
Burundi-Rwanda	272	4 546	1 743	6 322
Zaire	11 014	11 099	26 766	34 884
Kenya	211	1 333	1 830	2 197
Uganda	94	9 031	14 592	16 216
Tanzania	290	707	1 556	1 162
Angola	592	3 080	598	1 345
Ethiopia	1 933	1 743	7 432	5 981
Ghana	–	–	68	–
Sierra Leone	–	–	312	2 204
Others (Africa)	2 043	249	1 819	2 623
Total Africa	163 750	191 873	195 772	162 525
Asia and Oceania				
India	521	652	1 461	2 645
Indonesia	3 322	4 524	6 023	14 704
Malaysia	591	59	581	211
New Guinea	–	55	928	–
Others (Asia and Oceania)	1 397	701	1 939	4 205
Total Asia and Oceania	5 831	5 991	10 932	21 765
Miscellaneous and transhipments	75	205	828	964
GRAND TOTAL	239 065	288 898	334 890	297 020

(Source: J. Louis Delamare Circulars, August 1986 and *Le Café*, no. 439, February 1988, p. 22)

are consumed in restaurants and cafés. More than three quarters of the tonnages used in homes are sold by supermarkets and 20 per cent by traditional, small stores.

The coffees sold in France are mostly blends of arabica and robusta. The proportions of each species vary. The so-called high quality or 'high-grade' coffees are exclusively arabica and are generally sold under the mark of the country or countries of origin.

Their prices are naturally dependent upon their origin and their availability on the market.

The major port for importing coffee is Le Havre (180 000 tonnes in 1984 and 1985), which has just modernised its facilities for receiving and shipping bulk shipments. Marseille is used to a lesser extent, followed by Bordeaux and Dunkirk.

Since 1965, France has enforced very strict regulations (decree of 3 September 1965) concerning fraud prevention, the import of green coffee, the sale of roasted coffees, drinking coffee, coffee extracts, and decaffeinated coffees. These regulations have been modified by several circulars (see appendices). Tables 23, 24 and 25 give all the necessary information on the origin of the coffees imported by France since 1970, and on the amount coming from the francophone regions.

West Germany

In West Germany, coffee consumption has reached a high *per capita* rate of nearly 6 kg, which is constantly rising. Coffee imports have greatly exceeded 400 000 tonnes per year over the past few years. The main characteristic of the German market is the high quality of the coffees imported from Colombia, El Salvador, Kenya, Burundi and Tanzania (Table 22). These coffees are all arabicas and represent about 90 per cent of the tonnages. The shipments of robusta from Indonesia and West Africa (10 per cent) are used in particualr for manufacturing instant coffee.

The German importers are very particular with regard to coffee. For example, Saarland traditionally imports the best 'Maragogype'. Another example of their inflexibility is illustrated by the difficulties encountered in persuading them to accept the ultra-rapid roasted coffees. This is a new technique that was introduced in 1983, but its disadvantage is that it alters the normal taste of the coffee. Sales dropped an average of 8 per cent during the period that followed its marketing. Instant coffee consumption has decreased in recent years. It was 9 per cent in 1985, compared to 13 per cent in 1980.

Coffee is heavily taxed, which certainly affects consumption, and explains the success of chicory and coffee subsitutes in this country. The main port used for importing coffee is Hamburg. In West Germany, coffee is considered a fine drink and benefits from active promotion. Selling is often accompanied by sampling in stores.

Italy

Coffee imports in Italy have almost reached the same level as France, at nearly 270 000 tonnes. Imports have been increasing constantly by about 2 per cent per year over the past 10 years. Brazil is the main supplier (75 000 tonnes per year), followed by the Ivory Coast (15 per cent), Cameroon (6 per cent), Zaire (10 per cent), Indonesia, and Colombia. About 55 per cent of imported coffees are arabicas; the rest are robustas from various origins.

Most of the coffee is consumed in the form of 'espresso'. Consumption of instant coffee is negligible; being only about 3 per cent. However, there is some dissatisfaction among consumers. A recent study revealed that 14 per cent of all Italians had either stopped drinking coffee or decreased their consumption. The ever-increasing quantity of robusta in the blends may be one of the reasons for this.

Trieste is the main port used for importing coffee, followed by Genoa and Naples. Two-thirds of the coffee consumed in Italy pass through Trieste, which can thus be considered the major Mediterranean port. It is particularly well-equipped for receiving coffee in bulk, with the most modern electronic facilities and computers.

Netherlands

Coffee consumption *per capita* in the Netherlands is about 7.7 kg per annum. It doubled between 1960 and 1971, and has currently stabilised at around 7.5 kg. In 1987, 155 000 tonnes were imported, consisting of arabicas from Brazil, Colombia, Kenya and Tanzania. Robustas (23 per cent) come mainly from West Africa, Uganda and Indonesia. It should be noted that the percentage of arabica has increased noticeably in the past 20 years. Amsterdam is the main port used for importing.

United Kingdom

Coffee consumption in the United Kingdom has continued to increase over the past few years; currently standing at 2.5 kg *per capita*, compared with 2.15 kg in 1975. Despite this increase, tea still remains the most popular drink, with a level of consumption of 74 per cent, compared with 26 per cent for coffee. However, it is interesting to note that 25 years ago the ratio was six to one.

Imports exceed 100 000 tonnes per year (see Table 23), and are almost equally divided between the two species. The arabicas come mainly from Brazil, Colombia, Haiti and Kenya, while the robustas are supplied by West Africa, Uganda, Zaire and Indonesia. Most of the shipments are received at the port of London.

Belgium-Luxembourg

Belgium is one European country where coffee consumption *per capita* is particularly high, at over 7 kg. Its imports (89 000 tonnes in 1987) consist mostly of arabica (about 80 per cent) from Brazil, Colombia, Costa Rica,

Rwanda and Burundi. The robustas come mainly from the Ivory Coast and Zaire. Antwerp is the major coffee market, and large tonnages of coffee pass through here on their way to Western Europe.

Denmark, Finland, Norway, Sweden

These Scandinavian countries distinguish themselves by a very high *per capita* coffee consumption, the highest in Europe. To illustrate this statement, the figures are: 11.6 kg for Sweden, 10.5 kg for Norway, 10.2 kg for Finland. In Finland, consumption has even reached the record figure of 14.6 kg. These countries traditionally buy 90 per cent arabica, their suppliers being mainly Brazil, Central America (mostly Costa Rica for Finland), Kenya, Rwanda, and Ethiopia.

Switzerland

Coffee consumption in the Helvetian Federation has been relatively stationary for the past five years, with shipments of about 70 000 tonnes per annum (Table 23), which corresponds to about 6.2 kg *per capita*. The coffees (80 per cent arabica) come from Brazil, Colombia, Kenya and Central America. The robustas are imported from Indonesia, Ivory Coast and Angola.

Spain

Coffee consumption in Spain has been steadily rising over the past 20 years, and reached 3.5 kg *per capita* in 1985 (compared to 1.5 kg in 1965), with 152 000 tonnes imported in 1987. The main suppliers of arabica are Brazil, Colombia, and Central America. Uganda, Zaire, and Angola are the main suppliers of robusta, which amount to 32 per cent of the imports. The shipments are mainly received at the ports of Barcelona, Alicante, Cadiz, and Carthagena.

Austria

Austria is another European country where coffee consumption is rather high. The rate was 7.35 kg *per capita* in 1985. The importers prefer fine coffees, which is illustrated by a 92 per cent proportion of arabica in the shipments. Purchases of robusta are negligible. The main suppliers are Brazil, Colombia, Central America and Kenya.

Portugal

Coffee imports in Portugal have risen by 50 per cent over the past 15 years. They now exceed 20 000 tonnes, 70 per cent of which is robusta (Angola being the main supplier). The shipments arrive at Porto and Lisbon, except for those from the Central American countries which go via the Northern European ports.

Greece

Coffee consumption in Greece is about 20 000 tonnes per annum (1985), almost all of which is imported from Brazil. Robusta consumption is only about 1 per cent.

Eastern Europe

Coffee imports in Eastern Europe are increasingly slowly. They are currently between 250 000 and 300 000 tonnes per year. In the USSR, where tea is the national drink, imports have not increased noticeably since 1970. They amount to about 45 000 tonnes annually. On the other hand, in East Germany, where coffee is still popular, statistics indicate a major increase to about 70 000 tonnes, compared with 30 000 tonnes in 1970.

Yugoslavia also shows an increase in consumption with about 50 000 tonnes, following a peak of 60 000 tonnes in 1979. In other countries, consumption has not changed in 10 years, for example Poland consumes about 35 000 tonnes, Rumania 18 000 tonnes, Czechoslovakia 30 000 tonnes, Hungary 30 000 tonnes, and Bulgaria 3000 tonnes. There is little hope of increasing coffee consumption in these countries due to numerous constraints which provide obstacles to importing, and excessively high taxes.

The Americas

United States

The United States is by far the biggest coffee importer in the world. The evolution of consumption can be estimated by consulting some import statistics (see also Table 26):

1960	1 328 000 t	
1965	1 325 000 t	
1970	1 183 000 t	average:
1975	1 309 000 t	1 240 000 t
1980	1 045 000 t	
1981	993 000 t	
1982	1 045 000 t	
1983	987 000 t	average:
1984	1 034 000 t	1 050 000 t
1985	1 200 000 t	
1987	1 194 000 t	

These figures are highly indicative of a gradual decrease in consumption *per capita* over the past 25 years (1960–1985), especially considering the population increase.

Several studies have been conducted to define this decrease and analyse the cause(s). They have mostly been carried out through surveys, which have only served to confirm the decrease. However, the main factor appears to be the quality, which is not sufficiently taken into account by the roasters, with the second factor being the prices.

Consumption has thus dwindled from 5.62 kg per person per annum in 1975, to 4.65 kg in 1985. The percentage of the population that consumes coffee is also estimated to have fallen from 61.6 per cent in 1975 to 52.4 per cent in 1986. In addition, coffee is becoming markedly less popular with young people. In 1962, the level of consumers aged between 10 and 19 years was 25.1 per cent as opposed to only 4.6 per cent in this age group in 1986. In 1962, 81 per cent were between the ages of 20 and 29, as opposed to only 38.5 per cent in this age group in 1986. These figures are of considerable importance. They have understandably prompted a reaction from the ICO, which has begun an active campaign geared towards young people in coffee shops, on university campuses and the like.

This alarming decrease does not yet appear to be stopping, or even slowing down. In 1986, it dropped again. Expressed in cups per person per day, this corresponds to 3.32 in 1986, compared with 3.57 in 1985. Economists estimate that the decline will not be checked for several years although it may stabilise at a value between 4.5 kg and 4.0 kg *per capita* per year.

Soft drinks have been the major beverage consumed in the United States since 1985, when coffee was deposed by soft drinks for the first time (59.4 per cent compared to 54.9 per cent in 1985).

Roasting companies (mainly the large multi-national firms) are forced to react to this situation which could pose a problem for the future of their industry. Efforts are being made to offer high quality coffees (mainly Colombian) and to produce decaffeinated coffees and improved ground coffees, which meet consumers' needs. Moreover, the sale of coffee is being stimulated by increased advertising, which emphasises the quality and presentation of the product on the store shelves.

Consumption of instant coffee has also decreased somewhat. In 1975, it amounted to 35 per cent of consumption, compared with 20 per cent in 1986. On the other hand, decaffeinated coffee is quite popular; it amounted to 23 per cent of consumption in 1986, compared with 14 per cent in 1975. This is most likely to be as a result of the campaigns over the past few years which have emphasised the negative effects of caffeine on health.

The main suppliers of coffee to the United States are Brazil and Colombia, followed by Mexico and the majority of the Central American countries. In Africa, Uganda and the Ivory Coast are the main suppliers of robusta, whereas in Asia, Indonesia is the major supplier (Table 26). The main ports used for receiving coffee are New York, New Orleans, San Francisco and Houston.

Table 26   Main origins of green coffee imported to the United States in 1970–1987 (tonnes)

Country of origin	1970	1975	1980	1987
Americas				
Brazil	283 028	224 871	203 322	235 676
Colombia	149 826	204 024	102 576	152 937
Costa Rica	22 474	11 514	14 880	33 040
El Salvador	32 351	61 106	55 152	67 012
Ecuador	35 996	41 616	46 401	77 088
Guatemala	42 971	52 465	50 613	86 330
Honduras	12 809	24 033	13 255	30 512
Mexico	58 924	99 716	82 623	165 859
Peru	31 383	31 827	30 797	34 352
Dominican Republic	21 148	20 178	29 985	26 766
Venezuela	15 182	10 927	981	9 752
Miscellaneous	15 936	14 889	20 586	12 206
TOTAL	722 028	797 166	650 172	931 530
Africa				
Cameroon	25 176	–	13 985	1 881
Ivory Coast	73 993	57 932	59 852	28 559
Madagascar	18 483	19 114	9 232	384
Angola	83 075	72 124	3 796	156
Zaire	10 433	17 855	5 791	3 223
Burundi	16 316	15 665	2 678	19 910
Rwanda	20 647	10 810	3 630	–
Kenya	10 407	13 908	11 937	16 000
Uganda	55 412	57 502	73 736	35 197
Tanzania	16 898	16 594	2 812	1 732
Ethiopia	64 230	31 961	34 690	25 235
Miscellaneous	17 978	17 883	–	4 087
TOTAL	395 995	341 846	259 636	123 362
Asia-Oceania				
Indonesia	49 349	45 893	67 075	54 684
New Guinea	7 821	10 740	–	2 843
Miscellaneous	5 494	1 920	39 636	41 901
TOTAL	65 784	74 005	123 432	99 428
Miscellaneous and transhipments	96	4 293	11 697	40 036
GRAND TOTAL	1 183 903	1 309 220	1 044 937	1 194 356

Canada

Coffee consumption has greatly increased in Canada over the past half century. It now largely exceeds 100 000 tonnes per annum (115 000 tonnes in 1985), or 4.5 kg *per capita*. However, tea is still very popular. Consumption of instant coffee is rather high at about 30 per cent.

Canada imports its coffee mainly from Brazil and Colombia. The ports used for receiving the coffee are Montreal, Vancouver, Saint John, Halifax, and Toronto.

Brazil

Brazil deserves a special mention among the consumer countries. Although it is the major coffee producer, it is also one of the top consumers. With 450 000 to 500 000 tonnes consumed per annum amounting to about 4.0 kg *per capita*, it currently occupies second place.

Other countries

Coffee consumption in coffee-producing countries other than Brazil increases steadily every year. This is particularly noticeable in Colombia (120 000 tonnes per annum), Mexico (100 000 tonnes), Venezuela (50 000 to 60 000 tonnes) and Haiti (20 000 tonnes). Among the non-producing countries, Argentina (30 000 tonnes per annum) and Chile (60 000 tonnes) should be mentioned.

Africa

Coffee consumption in Africa is relatively high in the countries of the north-ernmost and southernmost parts of the continent. However, it is modest in the tropical countries which are generally producers.

Algeria imported 70 000 tonnes in 1984 and 78 000 tonnes in 1985. In **Morocco**, where tea is the national drink, 10 000 to 15 000 tonnes of coffee are consumed per annum. In **Tunisia**, coffee consumption is only about 3000 to 4000 tonnes per year as tea is also the national drink; the same holds true for **Egypt**.

Sudan receives about 20 000 tonnes per annum for its own consumption; its suppliers being Brazil, Kenya, and Ethiopia. **South Africa** is a modest coffee consumer; its imports amounting to only 2000 to 3000 tonnes per annum.

Coffee consumption per population of countries located in the inter-tropical zone is estimated by the ICO to be between 40 000 and 50 000 tonnes per annum.

Asia and Oceania

Japan

Japan occupies fifth place in the world among coffee-importing countries. Its imports have greatly increased over the past 15 years: 100 per cent between 1975 and 1983, and 40 per cent since 1980. They amounted to 260 000 tonnes in 1986, or 2.2 kg *per capita* (compared to 1.2 kg in 1975).

Coffee is the second most commonly consumed beverage, after green tea. This infatuation for coffee is due in particular to the extraordinary success of the sale of liquid coffee, which is sold ready to drink, in metal cans, by vending machines which provide hot drinks in winter and cold drinks in summer. Iced coffee has also recently become very popular.

Experts estimate that consumption has not yet reached its peak and may reach 2.6 kg *per capita* in 1991, which is an increase of 20 per cent compared with 1985.

Near and Middle East

Israel imports about 20 000 tonnes of coffee per annum. The Arab Emirates recorded a sizeable increase in their imports: 800 tonnes in 1979 and 20 000 tonnes in 1984. The imports of Syria and Lebanon are between 7000 and 8000 tonnes, and 10 000 tonnes per annum, respectively (1985). Those of Iran and Iraq have not been published for several years.

Far East

The main markets are South Korea, Hong Kong, Singapore, and Malaysia. South Korea has seen a major increase in its imports, from 300 tonnes in 1979 to nearly 25 000 tonnes in 1985. In China, imports of 600 tonnes were recorded in 1984 (compared with 25 tonnes in 1979). Singapore has a coffee import-export trade, which makes it difficult to calculate the country's consumption. India and Indonesia consume a sizeable part of their production.

Oceania

There are two coffee consuming countries that should be mentioned in Oceania, namely Australia and New Zealand. The former has been importing about 35 000 tonnes per annum since 1980 and the latter, 5000 to 6000 tonnes during the same period.

Bibliography

General reading

Coste, R. et al. (1955). *Les Caféiers et les Cafés dans le monde*, (Coffee trees and coffee throughout the world). Part **I**. Les *Caféiers*, 382 pp. (1955). Part **II**. *Les Cafés*, Vol. 1, 372 pp. (1959). Vol. 2, 397 pp. (1961). Ed. Larose, 15 R.V. Cousin, Paris.

References pertaining to particular chapters

Chapter 1
Page 11: Charrier, A. (1986). 'Progrès et perspectives de l'amélioration génétique des caféiers'. Onzième Colloque de l'ASIC, Lomé, Togo. 403–25.

Chapter 3
Page 31: Dentan, E. (1986) 'Étude microscopique du développement et de la maturation du grain de café'. Onzième Colloque de l'ASIC, Lomé, Togo. 381–98.

Chapter 4
Page 46: Cambrony, H., Dublin, P. (1984). 'Techniques de reproduction végétative *in vitro* et améliorations chez les caféiers cultivés'. *Café, Cacao, Thé.* vol. 28, **4**, 231–44.

Chapter 5
Page 64: Henao, A. U., Mestre-Mestre, A. (1980). 'Efecto de la densidad de poblacion y su sistema de manejo sobre la produccion de café'. *Cenicafé*, **1–4**, 29–51.

Henao, A. U., Arias, N. S. (1981). 'Distancias de siembra y dosis de fertilizante en la produccion de café'. *Cenicafé*, **3**, 88–104.

Kiara, J. M., Nsagi, S. B. C. (1982). 'The costs of establishing various coffee densities in Kenya'. *Kenya Coffee*, **556**, 173–83.

Page 65: Snoeck, J. (1987). Report for the 7th ASIC Colloquium, Montreux.

Page 111: Snoeck, J. (1987) 'Diagnostic pour la détermination des formules d'engrais minéraux pour les caféiers'. Com. Colloque ASIC, Montreaux.

Chapter 7
Page 128: Barat, H., Vayssière, P. in Coste, R. (1955). *Les caféiers et les cafés dans le monde*. Larose.

Page 145: Lavabre, E. (1962). *Protection des cultures de caféiers, cacaoyers et autres plantes pérennes tropicales*. IFCC, Paris, 92.

Chapter 8
Page 168: Charrier, A. (1985). 'Progrès et perspectives de l'amélioration génétique des caféiers'. ASIC Colloquium, Lomé, Togo. 422–3.

Chapter 11
Page 215: Rabechault, H. in Coste, R (1959) *Les caféiers et les cafes dans le monde*. Larose, Paris. 97–120.

Page 217: Dentan, E. (1980). 'Structure fine du grain de café vert'. VIII Colloque Scientifique International du Café. Ass. Scient. Inter. du Café, Salvador, Brazil. Larose, Paris. 59–64.

Dentan, E. (1985). 'Microscopic structure of the Coffee Bean' in Clifford, M. N., Wilson, K. C. *Coffee*. Croom Helm, London. 284–304.

Dentan, E. (1986). 'Etude microscopique du développement et de maturation du grain de café'. Onzième Colloque ASIC, Lomé, Togo. 381–98.

Page 217: Ohiokpehai, U., Brumen, G., Clifford, M. N. (1982). 'The chlorogenic acids content of some peculiar green coffee beans and the implication for beverage quality'. ASIC Tenth Colloquium, Salvador. 177–86.

Page 222: Dentan, E., Illy, A. (1986). 'Etude microscopique de grains de café matures, immatures et immatures fermentés Arabica Santos'. Onzième Colloque ASIC, Lomé, Togo. 341–68.

Chapter 12
Page 233: Navellier, P. in Coste, R. (1959). *Les caféiers et les cafés dans le monde*. 201–2.

Page 241: Illy, E. (1980) 'Facteurs qui influent sur la qualité de la tasse de café'. OIC, London. Promotion 83/80.

Page 244: Grouard (Brothers). (1986) 'Les CHR et le Café'. *Le grain de cafe*, **9**, 7–8.

Page 245: Cambrony, H. 'Le café soluble' in Coste, R. (1959). *Les caféiers et les cafés dans le monde*, vol. 1.

Publications after 1963[1]

Premier Colloque International sur la Chimie des Cafés Verts, Torréfiés et leurs Dérivés (First International Colloquium on the Chemistry of Green and Roasted Coffees and their Derivatives). (Paris, 20–22 May 1963). *Café Cacao Thé*, Paris 203 pp. **3** and **4** (1963).

Deuxième Colloque International sur la Chimie des Cafés Verts, Torréfiés et leurs Dérivés (Second International Colloquium on the Chemistry of Green and Roasted Coffees and their Derivatives). 262 pp. (Paris 3–7 May 1965). **4** (April 1966).

Troisième Colloque International sur la Chimie des Cafés Verts, Torréfiés et leurs Dérivés (Third International Colloquium on the Chemistry of Green and Roasted Coffees and their Derivatives). 442 pp. (Trieste, 2–9 June 1967). ASIC, Paris, (June 1968). **4**.

Le Pelley, R. H. (1968). *Pests of coffee*. 590 pp. Longmans, London.

Coste, R. (1968). *Le Caféier* (The coffee tree). 310 pp. Larose, Paris.

Krutzfeldt, H. H. (1968). *Coffea Curiosa* (Curious facts on coffee). 110pp. Verlag Gordian, Max Rieck GmbH, Hamburg.

Pintauro, N. (1969). Soluble coffee manufacturing processes. *Food Processing Review*, 254 pp. **8**, NDC, New Jersey.

Krug, C. A., Poerck R. A. (1969). Enquête mondiale sur le café. Etudes agricoles de la FAO (Rome) (Worldwide coffee survey). FAO Agricultural studies) 512 pp. **76**.

Quatrième Colloque International sur la Chimie des Cafés Verts, Torréfiés et leur Dérivés (Fourth International Colloquium on the Chemistry of Green and Roasted Coffees and their Derivatives). (Amsterdam, 2–6 June 1969). 264 pp. ASIC, Paris, (Oct. 1970). **4**.

Lavabre, E. M. (1970). Insectes nuisibles des cultures tropicales. (Insects that are harmful to tropical crops). *Techniques agricoles et productions tropicales (XX)*. 276 pp. Maisonneuve et Larose, Paris.

Geer, T. (1971). *An oligopoly. The world coffee economy and stabilisation schemes*. 323 pp. Dunellen, New York.

Sivetz, M. (1973). *Coffee, origin and use*. 500 pp. Coffee publications, 3635 N.W. Elmwood Dr., Corvallis, Oregon 97330, USA.

Cinquième Colloque International sur la Chimie des Cafés Verts, Torréfiés et leurs Dérivés (Fifth International Colloquium on the Chemistry of Green and Roasted Coffees and their Derivatives). (Lisbon, 14–19 June 1971). 436 pp. ASIC, Paris (1973). **4**.

Sixième Colloque International sur la Chimie des Cafés Verts, Torréfiés et leurs Dérivés (Sixth International Colloquium on the Chemistry of Green and Roasted Coffees and their Derivatives). (Bogota, 4–9 June 1973). 360 pp. Federaciòn Nacional de Cafeteros de Colombia, Bogota (December 1974). **4**.

Primeiro Congresso brasileiro sobre pragas e doenças do cafeeiro. (Vitória, 4–6 July 1973). 129 pp. IBC-GERCA, Rio de Janeiro.

Benoit-Cattin, M. (1973). Le café et le cacao dans l'économie de la Côte d'Ivoire (Coffee and Cacao in the Economy of Ivory Coast). Mém. pour l'obtention du dipl. d'ét. sup de sc. agron. University of Montpellier. 97 pp. Fac. Droit et Sc. écon. October 1973.

Secondo Congresso brasiliero sobre pesquisas cafeeiras. (Poços de Caldas, 10–14 Sept. 1974). 392 pp. IBC-GERCA, Rio de Janeiro.

Septième Colloque Scientifique International sur le Café (Seventh International Scientific Colloquium on Coffee). (Hamburg, 9–14 June 1975). 576 pp. ASIC Bremen (July 1976). **4**.

Terceiro Congresso brasileiro de pesquisas cafeeiras, (Curitiba/Paranã, 18–21 November 1975). 325 pp. IBC-GERCA, Rio de Janeiro.

Quarto Congresso brasileiro de pesquisas cafeeiras (Caxambu/M. Gerais, 23–26 November 1976). 314 pp. IBC-GERCA, Rio de Janeiro.

Instituto Brasileiro du Café. (January 1979) Manuel de recomendaçoes, 3rd ed.

Eichler, O. (1976). *Kaffee und Coffein* (Coffee and Caffeine). 491 pp. Springer Verlag, Heidelberg. 2nd Edition reviewed and corrected.

Quinto Congresso brasileiro de pesquisas cafeeiras, (Guarapari. E. S., 18–21 October 1977). 305 pp. IBC-GERCA, Rio de Janeiro.

Huitième Colloque Scientifique International sur le Café (Eighth International Scientific Colloquium on Coffee). (Abidjan, 28 November–3 December 1977). 572 pp. ASIC, Paris (Nov. 1979). **4**.

Sexto Congresso brasileiro de pesquisas cafeeiras, Ribeirão Prêto. (São Paulo, 24–27 October 1978). 414 pp. IBC-GERCA, Rio de Janeiro.

Guide concernant les limites maximales. Codex pour les résidus de pesticides. (1978). (Guide concerning maximal limits. Codex for pesticide residues). 223 pp. FAO-OMS, (Rome), GAC/PE.

Araxá. M.G. (1979). Sétimo Congresso brasileiro de pesquisas cafeeiras, 4–7 December. 395 pp. IBC-GERCA, Rio de Janeiro.

Deuse, J., Lavabre, E. M. (1979). Le désherbage des cultures sous les tropiques. (Weeding crops in the tropics). *Techniques agricoles et productions tropicales (38)*. 312 pp. Maisonneuve et Larose, Paris.

1 For earlier documentation, please refer to the author's publications in 1955, 1961 and 1968.

Jacques-Felix, H. (1979). *Le café* (Coffee). 'Que sais-je?' 126 pp. PUF, Paris.

Kolpas, N. (1979). *Coffee, etc.* 157 pp. John Murray, London.

Sivetz, M., Desrosier, N. W. (1979). *Coffee technology*. 736 pp. AVI Publishing Company, Inc., Westport, Connecticut.

Neuvième Colloque Scientifique International sur le Café (Ninth International Scientific Colloquium on Coffee). (London, 16–20 June 1980). 335 pp. ASIC, Paris, (Oct. 1981). **4**.

Oitavo Congresso brasileiro de pesquisas cafeeiras. Campos do Jordao/SP, (25–28 November 1980). 446 pp. IBC-GERCA, Rio de Janeiro.

Nono Congresso brasileiro de pesquisas cafeeiras. (Sao Lorenço/M. Gerais, 27–30 Oct. 1981). 471 pp. IBC-GERCA, Rio de Janeiro.

Maier, H. G. (1981). *Kaffee* (Coffee). 199 pp. Verlag Paul Parey, Berlin and Hamburg.

Jobin, P. (1982). *Les cafés produits dans le monde*. (Coffees produced throughout the world). 463 pp. P. Jobin et Cie, Le Havre. 4th Edition.

Dixième Colloque Scientifique International sur le Café (Tenth International Scientific Colloquium on Coffee). (Salvador, Bahia 11–14 October 1982). 649 pp. ASIC, Paris (October 1983). **4**.

Marshall, C. F. (1983). *The World Coffee Trade*, 254 pp. Woodhead-Faulkner, Cambridge.

Berthaud, J., Charrier, A., Guillaumet, J. L., Louarn, M. (1984). Les Caféiers (Coffee trees) in Pernes, J. *Gestion des ressources génétiques des plantes* (Management of the Genetic Resources of Plants). TIACCT, Paris. 45–104.

Clifford, M. N. and Wilson, K. C. (1985). *Coffee: Botany, biochemistry, and production of beans and beverage.* 458 pp. Croom Helm, London.

Onzième Colloque Scientifique International sur le Café. (Eleventh International Scientific Colloquium on Coffee). (Lomé, Togo 11–15 February 1985). 696 pp. ASIC, Paris (September 1986).

Clarke, R. J. and Macrae, R. (1985). *Coffee*, vol. 1: *Chemistry*, 306 pp.; vol. 2: *Technology*, 316 pp. (1987); vol 4: *Agronomy*. Elsevier Applied Science Publishers, London.

Viani, R. (1986). Coffee, in *Ullmann's Encyclopedia of Industrial Chemistry*, vol. A7, 315–39.

Anonymous. (1987). Coffee to 1991. Controlling a surplus. The Economist Intelligence Unit. *Special Report no, 1086*. 116 pp. (March 1987).

Periodicals and documents (Chronological listing 1968–1985)

Botanical and systematic classification

Dublin, P. (1968). Le rapport longueur pivot/ longueur hypocotyle des plantules de *Coffea racemosa* Lour. et de quelques autres espèces du genre. (The relationship between the lengths of the taproot and the hypocotyl in plantlets of *Coffea racemosa* Lour. and other species of the same genus). *Café Cacao Thé* (Paris) vol. 12, **2** (April-June) 127–34.

Ornano, M. d', Chassevent, F., Pougneaud, S. (1968). Composition et Caractéristiques chimiques de *Coffea* sauvages de Madagascar. (Chemical composition and characteristics of wild *Coffea* species in Madagascar). *Café Cacao Thé* (Paris), vol. 12, **2** (April-June) 144–56.

Friedman, F. (1970). Etude biogéographique de *Coffea buxifolia* Chev. (Madagascar). (Bic geographical study of *Coffea buxifolia* Chev. [Madagascar]). *Café Cacao Thé* (Paris), vol. 14, **1** (January-March) 3–12.

Janardhan, K. V., et al. (1971) Starch scoring by visual observation in fresh wood of coffee plants. *Indian Coffee* (Bangalore), vol. 35, **6**. (June 1971). 219–21.

Chassevent, F. (1972). Composition et caractéristiques chimiques des *Coffea* sauvages de

Madagascar. VII. Recherche de l'acide chlorogénique et de composés dans les graines de caféiers sauvages. (Chemical composition and characteristics of wild *Coffea* species of Madagascar. VII. The search for chlorogenic acid and related compounds in the wild coffee seeds). *Café Cacao Thé* (Paris), vol. 16, **2** (April-June 1972). 161–6.

Williams, J. A. (1972). A method for differentiating between *Coffea arabica* and *C. canephora* plants and their hybrids. *Turrialba* (San José), Vol. 22, **3**. (July-September 1972). 263–7.

Orozco, F. J., Cassalett, C. (1974). Relaciòn entre las caracterìsticas estomáticas y el número cromosómico de un híbrido interespecífico en café. (Relationship between the stomatal characteristics and the chromosomal number of an interspecific coffee hybrid). *Cenicafé* (Chinchiná), vol. 25, **2** (April-June 1974). 33–49.

Ducrouix, A., Hammonnière, M., Pascard, C., Poisson, J. (1975). Structure du mascaroside, hétéroside diterpénique de *Coffea vianneyi* Leroy (Structure of the mascaroside, the diterpenic heteroside of *Coffea vianneyi*

Leroy). *Café Cacao Thé* (Paris), vol. 19, **1**. (January-March 1975). 57–8.

Dublin, P., Parvais, J. P. (1975). Note sur les premiers haploïdes spontanés découverts chez le *Coffea canephora* var. *Robusta*. (Notes on the first spontaneous haploids discovered in *Coffea canephora* var. *Robusta*). *Café Cacao Thé* (Paris), vol. 19, **3** (July-September 1975). 191–6.

Charrier, A. Berthaud, J. (1975). Variation de la teneur en caféine dans le genre *Coffea*. (Variation of the caffeine content in the *Coffea* genus). *Café Cacao Thé* (Paris), vol. 19, **4**, (October-December 1975). 251–64.

Charrier, A. (1976) La structure génétique des caféiers spontanés de la région malgache (*Mascarocoffea*). Leurs relations avec les caféiers africains (*Eucoffea*). (The genetic structure of spontaneous coffee trees of the Malagasy region [*Mascarocoffea*]. Their relationship with African coffee trees [*Eucoffea*]). *Café Cacao Thé* (Paris), vol. 20, **4** (October-December 1976). 245–50.

IFCC-ORSTOM. (1978) Etude de la structure et de la variabilité génétique des caféiers: résultats des études et des expérimentations réalisées au Cameroun, en Côte d'Ivoire et à Madagascar sur l'espèce *Coffea arabica* L. collectée en Ethiopie par une mission ORSTOM en 1966. (Study of the structure and genetic variability of coffee trees: results of studies and experiments conducted in Cameroon, Ivory Coast and Madagascar on the species *Coffea arabica* L. collected in Ethiopia by an ORSTOM mission in 1966). 100 pp. Bulletin IFCC **14**, Paris (September 1978).

Berthaud, J., Guillaumet, J. L. (1978). Les caféiers sauvages en Centrafrique. Résultats d'une mission de prospection (janvier-février 1975). (Wild coffee trees in Central African Republic. Results of an exploration). *Café Cacao Thé* (Paris), vol. 22, **3** (July-September 1978). 171–86.

Lopes, C. R., Monaco, L. C. (1979). Chemotaxonomic studies of some species of the *Coffea* genus. *Journal of Plantation Crops* (Mangalore), vol. 7, **1** (June 1979). 6–14.

Berthaud, J., Guillaumet, J. L., Le Pierres, D., Lourd, M. (1980). Les caféiers sauvages du Kenya: prospection et mise en culture. (Wild coffee trees of Kenya: exploration and cultivation). *Café Cacao Thé* (Paris), vol. 24, **2** (April-June 1980). 101–12.

Leroy, J. F. (1980). Evolution et taxogenèse chez les caféiers (*Coffea* L., *Psilanthus* Hook. f. et *Nostolachma* Durand). Hypothèse sur leur origine. (Evolution and taxogenesis of coffee trees [*Coffea* L., *Psilanthus* Hook. f. and *Nostolachma*]. Hypothesis on their origin). Comptes rendus Acad. Sci. Paris,

Série D, vol. 291 (13 October 1980) 593–596.

Quijano Rico, M., Spettel, B. Determinación del contenido en varios elementos en muestras de cafés de diferentes variedades. (Determining the content of various elements in different varieties of coffee trees). Laboratorio de Investigaciones sobre la quìmica del café y de los productos naturales de la Federaciòn Nacional de Cafeteros de Colombia (LIQC), Bogotà, Colombia, T. P. –006, 23 pp.

Berthaud, J., Anthony, F. le Pierres, D. (1984). Les caféiers de la Nana (De la Nana coffee trees). *Café Cacao Thé* (Paris). Vol. 28. **1**, pp. 3–12.

Ecology and developmental physiology

Benac, R. (1969). Evolution de l'azote total, nitrique et ammoniacal d'échantillons de sols, de feuilles, et de fruits de caféier Arabica. (Evolution of nitric, ammoniacal, and total nitrogen in samples of soil, leaves, and fruits of the arabica coffee tree). *Café Cacao Thé* (Paris), vol 13. **2** (April-June 1969). pp. 116–30.

Boyer, J. (1969). Etude expérimentale des effets du régime d'humidité du sol sur la croissance végétative, la floraison et la fructification des caféiers Robusta. (Experimental study of the effects of the soil humidity levels on the vegetative growth, flowering and fruiting of robusta coffee trees). *Café Cacao Thé* (Paris), vol. 13, **3** (July-September 1969) 187–200.

Charrier, A (1971). Etude de la pollinisation des caféiers cultivés par marquage du pollen au phosphore (^{32}P) et au soufre (^{35}S) radioactifs. (Study of the pollination of cultivated coffee trees by marking the pollen with radioactive phosphorus (^{32}P) and sulphur (^{35}S). *Café Cacao Thé* (Paris), vol 15, **3** (July-September 1971) 181–90.

Beaudin Dufour, D., Muller, L. E. (1971). Effet de la radiation solaire et de l'age sur le contenu en caféine et en azote des feuilles et des fruit de trois espèces de caféiers. (Effect of solar radiation and age on the caffeine and nitrogen content of the leaves and fruits of three species of coffee trees). *Turrialba* (San José), vol. 21, **4** (October-December 1971) 387–92.

Gopal, N. H., Ramaiah, P. K. (1972). 'Studies on the physiology of germination of coffee seed. I. Observations on sprouting'. *Journal of Coffee Research*. (Chikmalagur), vol. 2, **1** (January 1972), 14–9.

Patel, R. Z. (1972). 'Radioisotopes and coffee research in Kenya. Distribution and functional roots of coffee'. *Kenya Coffee* (Nairobi), vol. 37, **441** (December 1972), 373–5.

Keller, H. *et al.* (1972). 'Kaffeinsynthese in Fruchten und Gewebekulturen von *Coffee arabica*'. (Synthesis of caffeine in the fruits and tissue cultures of *Coffea arabica*). *Plante* (Berlin), vol. 108, 339–50.

Andre, M. (1973). 'Observations sur l'orthotropisme et le plagiotropisme des rameaux chez *Coffea arabica* L.'. (Observations on the orthotropism and plagiotropism of the branches of *Coffea arabica* L.). *Café Cacao Thé* (Paris), vol. 27, **2** (April-June 1973) 125–8.

Browning, G. (1973). 'Flower bud dormancy in *Coffea arabica* L. I. Studies of gibberellin in flower buds and xylem sap and of abscissic acid in flower buds in relation to dormancy release'. *J. hort. sci.* (London), vol. 48 **1**, 29–41. II. 'Relations of cytokinins in xylem sap and flower buds to dormancy release'. *J. hort. sci.* (London), vol. 48, **3**, 297–310.

Barros, A. Santos, Maestri, M. (1974). 'Ritmo de crescimento do tronco do café'. (Growth rhythm of the trunk of the coffee tree). *Turrialba* (San José), vol. 24, **2**, (April-June) 127–31.

Reffye, Ph. de, (1974). 'Le contrôle de la fructification et de ses anomalies chez les *Coffea arabica*, Robusta, et leurs hybrides Arabusta'. (Controlling the fruiting and anomalies of *Coffea arabica* and robusta and their Arabusta hybrids). *Café Cacao Thé* (Paris), vol. 18, 4 (October-December) 237–254.

Orozco, C., F. J., Cassalette, D. C. (1974). 'Características anatómicas de la hojas y su relación con el posible ciclo fotosintético en café'. (Anatomic characteristics of the leaves and their possible connection with the photosynthetic cycle of the coffee tree). *Cenicafé* (Chinchiná), vol. 25, 4 (October-December) 104–12.

Looser, E., Baumann, T. W., Wanner, H. (1974). 'The biosynthesis of caffeine in the coffee plant'. *Phytochemistry* (Oxford), vol. 13, **11** (November) 2515–8.

Suryakantha Raju, K. (1975). 'Dimorphism in coffee'. *Turrialba* (San José), vol. 25, **1** (January-March) 88–9.

Browning, G. (1975) 'Shoot growth in *Coffea arabica* L. I. Responses to rainfall when the soil moisture status and gibberellin supply are not limiting'. *Kenya Coffee* (Nairobi), vol. 40, **473** and **474** (August-September) 259–69.

Reffye, Ph. de, Snoeck, J. (1976). 'Modèle mathématique de base pour l'étude et la simulation de la croissance et de l'architecture de *Coffea robusta*'. (Basic mathematical model for studying and simulating the growth and architecture of *Coffea robusta*). *Café Cacao Thé*. Paris. Vol. 20, **1** (January-March) 11–32.

Gopal, N. H., Vasudeva, N., Balasubramanian, A. (1976). 'Studies on absorption and translo-

cation of phosphorus using radioactive superphospate (^{32}P) in coffee plants'. *J. Coffee Res.* (Mysore), vol. 6, **3–4** (July-October) 69–75.

Reffye, Ph. de (1976). 'Modélisation et simulation de la verse du caféier à l'aide de la théorie de la résistance des matériaux'. (Modelling and simulation of the shedding of the coffee tree, with the help of the theory of material resistance). *Café Cacao Thé* (Paris), vol. 20, **4** (October-December) 251–72.

Sudhakara Rao, G., Ventkataramanan, D., Rao, K. N. (1977). 'Changes in the respiratory quotient of embryos of *Coffea canephora* 'S 274' with time'. *Turrialba* (San José), vol. 27, 4 (October-December) 419–20.

Tesha, A. J., Kumar, D. (1978). 'Some aspects of stomatal behaviour in *Coffea arabica* L. I. Effects of soil moisture, soil nitrogen, and potassium and air humidity'. *Kenya Coffee* (Nairobi), vol. 43, **512** (November) 339–43.

Gopal, N. H., Raju, K. I. (1978). 'Physiological studies on flowering in coffee under South Indian conditions'. VIII. Number of flower buds in relation to wood starch of cropping branches'. *Turrialba* (San José), vol. 28, **4** (October-December) 311–3.

Opile, W. R. (1979). 'Hormonal relationships in fruit growth and development of *Coffea arabica* L.'. *Kenya Coffee* (Nairobi), vol. 44, **520** (July) 13–21.

Vasudeva, N., Gopal, N. H. (1979). 'Physiological studies on flowering of coffee under South Indian conditions. IX. Effect of different irrigation treatments on blossom and yield of arabica coffee'. *Journal of Coffee Research* (Mysore), vol. 9, **3** (July) 74–9.

Tesha, A. J., Kumar, D. (1979). 'Effects of soil moisture, potassium and nitrogen on mineral absorption and growth of *Coffea arabica* L.'. *Turrialba* (San José), vol. 29, 3 (July-September) 213–8.

Raju, K. I., Gopal, N. H. (1979). 'Distribution of caffeine in arabica and robusta coffee plants'. *Journal of Coffee Research* (Mysore), vol. 9, 4 (October) 83–90.

Pochet, P. (1979). 'Une exception à la règle du dimorphisme des axes végétatifs dans le genre *Coffea*?'. (An exception to the rule of dimorphism of the vegetative axes in the *Coffea* genus?) *Café Cacao Thé* (Paris). Vol. 23, **4** (October-December) 271–6.

Kumar, D., Tieszen, L. L. (1980). 'Photosynthesis in *Coffea arabica* I. Effects of light and temperature'. *Experimental Agriculture* (Cambridge), vol. 16, **1** (January) 13–19. 'II. Effect of water stress'. *Ibid*, 21–7.

Brasil, O. G., Crocomo, O. J. (1980). 'Formacao de àcidos orgànicos, acucares e lipideos a partir de acetato ^{14}C em folhas de cafeeiero'. (Formation of organic acids, sugars and lipids from ^{14}C acetate in coffee leaves). *Turrialba*

(San José), vol. 30, **3** (July-September) 338–42.

Renard, C., Ndayishimie, V. (1982). 'Etude des relations hydriques chez *Coffea arabica* L. I. Comparaison de la presse à membrane et de la chambre a pression pour la mesure du potential hydrique foliaire (ψ)'. (Study of the water relationships of *Coffea arabica* L. I. Comparison between the membrane press and the pressure chamber for measuring the leaf water potential [ψ]) *Café Cacao Thé* (Paris), vol. 26, **1** (January-March) 27–30.

Reffye, Ph. de. (1981). 'Modèle mathématique aléatoire et simulation de la croissance et de l'architecture du caféier Robusta'. (Indeterminate mathematical model and simulation of the growth and architecture of the robusta coffee tree). 'I. Etude de fonctionnement des méristèmes et de la croissance des axes végétatifs'. (Study of the workings of the meristems and the growth of vegetative axes). *Café Cacao Thé* (Paris). vol 25, **2** (April-June) 83–104. 'II. Etude de la mortalité des méristèmes plagiotropes'. (Study of the mortality of plagiotropic meristems). *Ibid.*, **4** (October-December) 219–30. 'III. Etude de la ramification sylleptique des rameaux primaires et de la ramification proleptique des rameaux secondaires'. (Study of the sylleptic ramification of the primary branches and the proleptic ramification of the secondary branches). *Ibid.*, vol. 26, **2** (April-June) 77–96. 'IV. Programmation sur micro-ordinateur du tracé en trois dimensions de l'architecture d'un arbre. Application au caféier'. (Programming the three dimensional structure of the architecture of a tree on the micro-computer, applied to the coffee tree). *Ibid.*, vol. 17, **1** (January-March) 3–20.

Maestri, M. and Santos Barros, R. (1981). 'Scofisiologia de cultivos Tropicales'. *Café* IICA, Zona Norte.

Propagation

Rivas V., R. Morales Diaz, A. (1968). 'Aplicaciones foliares de nutrientes a plantas de café criadas en viveros e plena exposición solar'. (Foliar applications of nutrients to coffee trees grown in nurseries in full sunlight). *Agronomia Tropical* (Maracay), vol 18, **1** (January-March) 117–30.

Osorio B., J., Castillo Z., J. (1969). 'Influencia del tamano de la semilla en el crecimiento de la plantulas de café'. (Influence of seed size on the growth of coffee seedlings). *Cenicafé* (Chinchiná), vol. 20, **1** (January-March) 20–40.

Mondonero, J. R. (1970). 'Quick test with tetrazolium chloride on coffee seed viability'. *The J. of Agric. of the Univ. of Puerto Rico.* (Rio Pedras), vol. 14, **2** (April) 370–6.

Bouharmont, P. (1971). 'La conservation des graines de caféier destinés à la multiplication au Cameroun'. (The storage of coffee seeds to be used for propagation in Cameroon). *Café Cacao Thé* (Paris), vol. 15, **3** (July-September) 202–10.

Colonna, J. P. (1972). 'Contribution à l'étude de la culture *in vitro* d'embryons de caféiers. Action de la caféine'. (Contribution to the study of *in vitro* embryo culture of coffee trees. The effect of caffeine). *Café Cacao Thé* (Paris), vol. 16, **3** (July-September) 193–203.

Rabechault, H., Cas, G. (1973). 'Relations entre l'inhibition par la caféine de la croissance des embryons de caféiers et leur teneur en phénols totaux'. (The relationship between the growth inhibition of coffee embryos by caffeine and their total phenol content.) *C. R. Acad. Sc. Paris*, Série D, vol. 277 (17 December) 2697–700.

Boudrand, J. N. (1974). 'Le bouturage du caféier Canephora à Madagascar'. (The propagation of the canephora coffee tree in Madagascar). *Café Cacao Thé* (Paris), vol. 18, **1** (January-March) 31–48.

Carvalho, F. J. P. C., Carvalho, P. C. T., Crocomo, O. J. (1974). 'Cultura de tecido de explantes de cafés'. (Tissue culture of coffee explants). Segundo Congresso brasileiro sobre pesquisas cafeeiras. Poços de Caldas, (10–14 September), IBC-GERCA, Rio de Janeiro, 299–300.

Oyebade, I. T. (1975). 'Growth of *Coffea canephora* (Pierre ex Froehner) seedlings as influenced by gibberellic acid and ethrel (2-chloroethane phosphonic acid)'. *Turrialba* (San José), vol. 25, **1** (January-March) 49–53.

Bandel, G., Carvalho, F. J. P. C., Crocomo, O. J., Sharp, W. R., Gutierez, L. E., Carvalho, P. C. T. (1975). 'Aspectos citológicos da diferenciaçao de tecidos de cafeeiro cultivado *in vitro*'. (Cytological aspects of the differentiation of tissues of the coffee tree cultivated *in vitro*). *Anais da Escola Superior de Agricultura 'Luiz de Queiroz'* (São Paulo), vol. 32, AESQAW 32–1–724. 717–24.

Melo, M., Carvalho, A., Monaco, L. C. (1976). 'Contribuçao do porta-enxerto, no teor de cafeina em graos de café'. (Effect of the rootstock on the caffeine content of coffee beans). *Bragantia* (Campinas), vol. 35, t. I, **6** (February) 55–61.

Nsumbu, N., Bouharmont, J. (1977). 'Différenciation de racines et de tiges feuillées à partir de feuilles de *Coffea canephora*'. (Differentiation of roots and leafy stems from *Coffea canephora* leaves). *Café Cacao Thé* (Paris), vol. 21, **1** (January-March) 3–8.

Bouharmont, P. (1977). 'Expérimentation sur

le renouvellement de l'appareil végétatif du caféier par recépage des anciennes tiges. I. Le caféier Arabica'. (Experiments on the renewal of the vegetative apparatus of the coffee tree by stumping the old stems. I. The arabica coffee tree). *Café Cacao Thé* (Paris) vol. 21. **1** (January-March).

Sondahl, M., Sharp, W. (1977). 'Growth and embryogenesis in leaf tissues of *Coffea*'. Annual Meeting of the Am. Soc. of Plant Physiologists, Madison, Wisconsin (16–20 August)

Bouharmont, P. (1977). 'Expérimentation sur le renouvellement de l'appareil végétatif du caféier par recépage des anciennes tiges. II. Le caféier Robusta'. (Experiments on the renewal of the vegetative apparatus of the coffee tree by stumping the old stems. II. The robusta coffee tree). *Café Cacao Thé* (Paris). vol. XXI, **2** (April-June) 99–110.

Walyro, D. J., van der Vossen, H. A. M. (1977). 'Pollen longevity and artificial cross-pollination in *Coffea arabica* L.'. *Euphytica* (Wageningen), vol. 26, **1** 225–31.

Sondahl, M. R., Sharp, W. R. (1977). 'High frequency induction of somatic embryos in cultured leaf explants of *Coffea arabica* L.'. *Z. Pflanzenphysiol.* (Stuttgart), vol. 81, 395–408.

Monaco, L. C., Sondahl, M.R., Carvalho, R., Crocomo, O. J., Sharp, W. R. (1977). 'Applications of tissue culture in the improvement of coffee'. *Applied and fundamental aspects of plant cell, tissue and organ culture*. Springer-Verlag (Berlin) 109–29.

Vasudeva, N., Ratageri, M. C. (1979). 'Effect of certain chemicals and growth regulators on pollen germination in robusta coffee'. *Journal of Coffee Research* (Mysore), vol. 9, **2** (April) 46–8.

Nsumbu, N. (1979). 'Différenciation des tiges feuillées à partir des plants décapités de *Coffea canephora*'. (Differentiation of leafy stems from capped *Coffea canephora* plants). *Café Cacao Thé* (Paris), vol. 23, **3** (July-September) 171–4.

Nsumbu, N. (1979). 'Etude de plants et de méristèmes apicaux de *Coffea canephora* après traitement par la colchicine'. (Study of plants and apical meristems of *Coffea canephora* after treatment with colchicine. *Café Cacao Thé* (Paris), vol. 23, **4** (Oct-Dec) 255–66.

Couturon, E., Berthaud, J. (1979). 'Le greffage d'embryons de caféiers. Mise au point technique'. (Grafting coffee tree embryos. Perfecting the technique). *Café Cacao Thé* (Paris). vol. 23. **4** (Oct-Dec) 267–70.

Van der Vossen, H. A. M. (1980). 'Methods of preserving the viability of coffee seed in storage'. *Kenya Coffee* (Nairobi), vol. 45, **525** (January) 31–5.

Vasudeva, N. (1980). 'Effect of ascorbic acid on the growth of arabica coffee seedlings'. *Journal of Coffee Research* (Mysore), vol. 10, 1 (January) 1–3.

Couturon, E. (1980). 'Le maintien de la viabilité des graines de caféiers par le contrôle de leur teneur en eau et de la température de stockage'. (Maintaining the viability of coffee tree seeds by controlling their water content and the storage temperature). *Café Cacao Thé* (Paris), vol. 24, 1 (January-March) 27–32.

Dublin, P. (1980). 'Induction de bourgeons néoformés et embryogenèse somatique. Deux voies de multiplication *in vitro* de caféiers cultivés'. (Induction of neoformed buds and somatic embryogenesis. Two methods of *in vitro* propagation of cultivated coffee trees). *Café Cacao Thé* (Paris), vol. 24, **2** (April-June) 121–30.

Sondahl, M. R., Chapman, M.S., Sharp, W. R. (1980). 'Protoplast liberation, cell wall reconstitution and callus proliferation in *Coffea arabica* L. callus tissues'. *Turrialba* (San José), vol. 30, **2** (April-June) 161–5.

Lanaud, C. (1981). 'Production de plantules de *C. canephora* par embryogenèse somatique réalisée à partir de culture *in vitro* d'ovules'. (Production of *C. canephora* seedlings by somatic embryogenesis from *in vitro* ovule culture). *Café Cacao Thé* (Paris), vol. 25, **4** (October-December) 231–6.

Dublin, P. (1981). 'Embryogenèse somatique directe sur fragments de feuilles de caféiers Arabusta'. (Direct somatic embryogenesis on fragments of leaves from Arabusta coffee trees). *Café Cacao Thé* (Paris), vol. 25, **4** (October-December) 237–42.

Stemmer, W. P. C., van Adrichem, J. C. J., Roorda, F. A. (1982). 'Inducing orthotropic shoots in coffee with the morphactin chloro-fluorenol-methylester'. *Experimental Agriculture* (Cambridge), vol. 18, **1** (January) 29–35.

Nsumbu, N., Miafuntila, K., Ogula, M. E. (1982). 'Différenciation de racines et de tiges feuillées à partir de racines de *Coffea canephora*'. (Differentiation of roots and leafy stems from roots of *Coffea canephora*). *Café Cacao Thé* (Paris), vol. 26, **1** (January-March) 17–26.

Couturon, E. (1982). 'Obtention d'haploïdes spontanés de *Coffea canephora* Pierre par l'utilisation du greffage d'embryons'. (Obtaining spontaneous haploids of *Coffea canephora* Pierre by grafting embryos). *Café Cacao Thé* (Paris), vol. 26, 3 (July-September) 155–60.

Okelana, M. A. O. (1982). 'Rehabilitation of robusta coffee, *Coffea canephora* Pierre: Influence of stumping height and multiple shooting on flushing and cherry production'.

Café Cacao Thé (Paris), vol. 26 (October-December) 273–8.

Zok, S. 'Multiplication végétative *in vitro* du caféier (*C. arabica*) par culture de méristèmes et de sommets végétatifs'. (*In vitro* vegetative propagation of the coffee tree (*C. arabica*) by meristem and plant top culture). *Café Cacao Thé*, vol. 28, **4** 303–4.

Purushotham, K., Sulladmath, U. V. (1983). 'Influence of length of coffee cutting on rooting'. *Jnl. of Res.* (Chikmagalur), vol. 13, **3** 57–63.

Deuss, J. and Descroix, F. (1984). 'Le bouturage du caféier Robusta dans le programme de replantation de la caféière au Togo'. (The propagation of robusta coffee in the programme to re-establish coffee plantations in Togo). *Café Cacao Thé*, vol. 28 **3** 165–178.

Cultivation

Bouharmont, P. (1968). 'La taille du caféier Robusta dans la zone caféicole de l'Est du Cameroun'. (Pruning robusta in the coffee growing region of Eastern Cameroon). *Café Cacao Thé* (Paris), vol. 12, **1** (January-March) 13–27.

Austin, J. S. F. (1968). 'The possibility of minimal cultivation in coffee with Gramaxone'. *Tanganyika Coffee News* (Moshi), vol. 7, **4** (April-June) 109–12.

Mitchell, H. W. (1968). 'Grasses for mulching coffee'. *Kenya Coffee* (Nairobi), vol. 33, **393** (October) 327–35.

Boyer, J. (1968). 'Influence de l'ombrage artificiel sur la croissance végétative, la floraison, et la fructification des caféiers Robusta'. (The influence of artificial shade on the growth, flowering, and fruiting of robusta). *Café Cacao Thé* (Paris), vol. 12, **4** (October-December) 302–20.

Aduavi, E. A. (1971). 'A note on the nutritional effects of cuprous oxide sprays on *Coffea arabica*'. *Kenya Coffee* (Nairobi), vol. 36, **420** (January) 13 and 15.

Deuss, J. (1971). 'La régénération des caféières et les facteurs de production: couverture du sol, engrais'. (The regeneration of coffee plantations and production factors: soil cover, fertiliser). *Café Cacao Thé* (Paris), vol. 15, **2** (April-June) 115–28.

Dagg, M. (1971). 'Water requirements of coffee'. *Kenya Coffee* (Nairobi), vol. 36, **424** (June) 149–51.

Verlière, G. (1973). 'La nutrition minérale et la fertilisation du caféier sur sol schisteux en Côte d'Ivoire'. **I**. 'Etude de la nutrition minérale'. (Mineral nutrition and fertilisation of coffee trees on schistic soil in Ivory Coast. I. A study of mineral nutrition. *Café Cacao Thé* (Paris), vol. 17, **2** (April-June) 97–124.

II. 'Influence de la fertilisation minérale sur les rendements'. (Effect of mineral fertiliser on yield). **III**. 'Relation entre les rendements et la composition minérale des feuilles'. (Relationship between yield and the mineral composition of the leaves). *Ibid.*, **3** (July-September) 211–22. **IV**. 'Influence de la fertilisation minérale sur la composition du fruit'. (The effect of mineral fertiliser on the composition of the fruit). *Ibid.*, vol. 17, **4** (October-December) 269–80.

Patel, R. Z., Kabaara, A. M. (1975). 'Isotope studies on the efficient use of P – fertilisers by *Coffea arabica* in Kenya'. **I**. 'Uptake and distribution of P^{32} from labelled KH_2PO_4'. *Experimental agriculture* (London), vol. 2, **1** (January) 1–11.

Muller, R. A. (1975). 'L'irrigation précoce, assurance pour une production régulière de haut niveau du caféier Arabica'. (Early irrigation, a guarantee for high-level, regular production of arabica). *Café Cacao Thé* (Paris), vol. 19, **2** (April-June) 95–122.

Browning, G., Fischer, N. M. (1975). 'Shoot growth in *Coffea arabica* L. **II**. 'Growth flushing stimulated by irrigation'. *Kenya Coffee* (Nairobi), vol. 40, **476–477** (November-December) 355–65.

Ramakrishnan Nayar, T. V. (1976). 'Cultures intercalaires entre jeunes caféiers Robusta'. (Intercropping between young robusta coffee trees). *Indian Coffee* (Bangalore), vol. 40, **2** and **3** (February-March) 70–1.

Snoeck, J. (1977). 'Essai d'irrigation du caféier Robusta'. (Irrigation trial with robusta coffee). *Café Cacao Thé* (Paris), vol. 21, **2** (April-June) 111–28.

Fisher, N. M., Browning, G. (1978). 'The water requirements of high density coffee'. **I**. 'Response to irrigation and plant water stress measurements'. *Kenya Coffee* (Nairobi), vol. 43, **503** (February) 43–6.

Bouharmont, P. (1978). 'L'utilisation des plantes de couverture dans la culture de caféier Robusta au Cameroun'. (The use of cover crops in the cultivation of robusta coffee in Cameroon). *Café Cacao Thé* (Paris), vol. 22, **2** (April-June) 113–38.

Carvalho, M. M. de, Duarte, G. de S., Ramalho, M. A. P. (1978). 'Efieto da composiçao de substrato no desenvolvimento de mudas de cafeeiro (*Coffea arabica* L.)'. **II**. 'Esterco de galinheiro'. (The effect of the composition of the substrate on the development of coffee tree seedlings [*Coffea arabica* L.]). **II**. 'Fientes de poulet'. *Ciência e practica* (Escola Superior de Agricultura de Lavras, Minas Gerais), vol. 2, **2** (July-December) 224–38.

Kumar, D. (1978). 'Investigation into some physiological aspects of high density plantings of coffee (*Coffea arabica* L.)'. *Kenya Coffee*

(Nairobi), vol. 43, **510** (September) 263–72.

Snoeck, J., Duceau, P. (1978). 'Essais d' engrais minéraux sur *Coffea canephora* en Côte d'Ivoire: production et rentabilité'. (Trials with mineral fertiliser on *Coffea canephora* in the Ivory Coast). *Café Cacao Thé* (Paris), vol. 22, 4 (October-December) 285–302.

Bouharmont, P. (1979). 'L'utilisation des plantes de couverture et du paillage dans la culture du caféier Arabica au Cameroun'. (The use of cover crops and mulching in the cultivation of arabica coffee in Cameroon). *Café Cacao Thé* (Paris), vol. 23, 2 (April-June) 75–102.

Akunda, E. M. W., Imbalba, S. K., Kumar, T. (1979). 'High density plantings of coffee. Adaptive changes in some plant characteristics'. *East Afr. Jnl.* (Nairobi), vol. 45, 2 133–36.

Raju, T. Dhruvakumar, H. K., Krishnamurthy Rao, W. (1980). 'Compatability of nitrogenous fertilisers with alkaline Bordeaux mixture'. *Journal of Coffee Research* (Mysore), vol. 10, 1 (January) 12–7.

Tubelis, A., Foloni, L. L., Nascimento, F. J. L. do, Villa Nova, N. A., (1980). 'Temperatura do ar em cafezal'. (The air temperature in a coffee plantation). *Turrialba* (San José), vol. 30, 1 (January-March) 9–15.

Taleisnik, E., Pacheco, R. (1980). 'Evaluación del efecto de dosis crecientes de nitrato sobra la actividad de la reductasa del nitrato; nitrógenio derivado del fertilizante en cafeto'. (An evaluation of the effect of increased quantities of nitrate on the activity of reductase nitrate; nitrogen derived from the fertiliser in the coffee tree). *Turrialba* (San José), vol. 30, 1 (January-March) 29–34.

Narain, K. V. (1980). 'Used coffee powder for organic manure'. *Indian Coffee* (Bangalore), vol. 44, **5** (May) 83–4.

Snoeck, J. (1980). 'Evolution du chimisme du sol dans des essais d'engrais minéraux sur *Coffea canephora* en Côte d'Ivoire'. (The development of the chemism of the soil in mineral fertiliser trials with *Coffea canephora* in the Ivory Coast). *Café Cacao Thé* (Paris), vol. 24, 3 (July-September) 177–88.

Nascimento, F. J. L. do, Tubelis, A. (1980). 'Estimativa do inicio da formaçao deorvalho em cafezal por meio dos perfis verticais de umidade absoluto do ar'. (Estimate of the beginning of dew formation in a coffee plantation with the help of vertical profiles of absolute air humidity). *Revista Ceres* (Viçosa), vol. 27, **153** (September-October) 526–34.

Mwakha, E. (1980). 'Intercropping dry beans in high density arabica coffee'. II. 'Response to bean rows and nitrogen fertiliser'. *Kenya Coffee* (Nairobi), vol. 45, **536** (November) 319–24.

M'Itungo, A. M., Van der Vossen, H. A. M. (1981). 'Nutrient requirements of coffee seedlings in polybag nurseries: the effect of foliar feeds in relation to type of potting mixture'. *Kenya Coffee* (Nairobi), vol. 46, **543** (June) 181–7.

Uribe-Henao, A., Salazar-Arias, N. (1981). 'Distancias de siembra y dosis de fertilizante en la producción de café'. (Plantation spacing and quantities of fertiliser to be applied in coffee production). *Cenicafé* (Chinchiná), vol. 32, 3 (July-September) 88–105.

Bouharmont, P. (1981). 'Expérimentation sur les dispositifs et les densités de plantation du caféier Arabica au Cameroun'. (Experimenting with designs and densities of arabica coffee plantations in Cameroon). *Café Cacao Thé* (Paris), vol. 25, 4 (October-December) 243–62.

Cestac, Y., (1981). 'Etude des possibilités d'utilisation de nouvelles formulations d'herbicides dans des caféières de Robusta adultes en Côte d'Ivoire'. (A study of the possibilities of using new herbicide formulas on mature robusta plantations in the Ivory Coast). *Café Cacao Thé* (Paris), vol. 15, 4 (October-December) 269–76.

Bouharmont, P. (1982). 'La plantation du caféier Arabica au Cameroun'. (Planting arabica in Cameroon). *Café Cacao Thé* (Paris), vol. 16, 1 (January-March) 3–16.

Krishnamurthy Rao, W. Ananda Alwar, R. P. (1982). 'Availability of sulphur as influenced by the use of complex fertilisers and straight fertiliser mixtures'. *Journal of Coffee Research* (Chikmagalur), vol. 12, **2** (April) 31–7.

Cestac, Y., Snoeck, J. (1982). 'Les essais de densités, de dispositifs de plantation et de taille sur caféiers Robusta en Côte d'Ivoire. Résultats et perspectives'. (Trials on plantation density and design, and pruning with robusta coffee in Ivory Coast. Results and prospects). *Café Cacao Thé* (Paris), vol. 16, 3 (July-September) 183–98.

Snoeck, J. 'Méthodologie des recherches sur la fertilisation minêrale du caféier Robusta en Côte d'Ivoire. L'analyse du sol pour l'étude des besoins en engrais minéraux'. (Research methodology on the mineral fertilisation of robusta coffee in the Ivory Coast. Soil analysis for the study of mineral fertiliser requirements). *Café Cacao Thé*, vol. 28, 4 267–78.

Afolani, C. A., Papolamt, C. A. (1985). 'An economic appraisal of N; P, and K fertiliser use on mature robusta coffee at Isuada plantation, Nigeria. *Café Cacao Thé*, vol. 29, 1 31–6.

Bouharmont, P., Lotode, R., Awemo, S., Castaing, X. (1986). 'La sélection gén érative du caféier Robusta au Cameroun. Analyse des résultats d'un essai d'hybrides diallèle partiel implanté en 1973'. (The generative selection of the robusta coffee tree in Cameroon. Analysis of the results of a trial with partially diallel hybrids planted in 1973). *Café Cacao Thé*, vol. 30, **2** 93–112.

Pavan, M. A., Chaves, J. C. D., Mesquita Filho, L., (1986). 'Manejo da adubaçao para formaçao de lavouras cafeeiras'. *Pesquisa Agropecuaria Brasileira*, vol. 21, **1** 33–42.

Diseases and pests

Flechmann, C. H. W. (1967). 'Os ácaros do cafeeiro'. (Acarid parasites of the coffee tree). *Anais da Escola Supoerior de Agricultura 'Luiz de Queiroz'* (Piracicaba), vol. 24, 91–5.

Ondieki, J. J., Kabaara, A. M. (1968). 'Foliar spraying of calcium superphosphates to control coffee berry disease in Kenya'. *Kenya Coffee* (Nairobi), vol. 32, **384** (January) 23–7.

Baum, J. (1968). 'The coffee root mealybug complex'. *Kenya Coffee* (Nairobi), vol. 33, **388** (May) 175–8.

Bruneau de Mire, Ph. (1969). 'Note taxonomique à propos de *Sphaerocrema dewasi* agent causal de la défoliation en mannequin d'osier du caféier Robusta au Cameroun'. (Taxonomic notes on *Sphaerocrema dewasi*, defoliating agent, turning the robusta coffee tree into a 'wicker basket' in Cameroon). *Café Cacao Thé* (Paris), vol. 13, **1** (January-March) 55–6.

Lopez-Duque, S., Fernandez-Borrero, O. (1969). 'Epidemiologia de la mencha de hierro del cafeto (*Cercospora coffeicola* Berk. and Cook.)'. *Cenicafé* (Chinchiná), vol. 20, **1** (January-March) 3–19.

Ingram, W. R. (1969). 'Cherry fall in robusta coffee: pest damage and frequency of picking'. *East African Agric. and For. J.* (Nairobi) (April) 464–7.

Saccas, A. M., Charpentier, J. (1969). 'L'anthracnose des caféiers Robusta et Excelsa due à *Colletotrichum coffeanum* Noack en République Centrafricaine'. 84 pp. (Coffee berry disease in robusta and Excelsa due to *Colletotrichum coffeanum* Noack in the Central African Republic). *Bulletin IFCC* **9**, Paris (April).

Saccas, A. M., Charpentier, J. (1969). 'L'anthracnose des caféiers Robusta et Excelsa due à *Colletotrichum coffeanum* Noack en République Centrafricaine'. (Coffee berry disease in robusta and Excelsa due to *Colletotrichum coffeanum* Noack in the Central African Republic). *Café Cacao Thé* (Paris), vol. 13, **2** (April-June) 131–49, and **3** (July-September) 221–30.

Schieber, E., Grullon, L. (1969). 'El problema de nemátodos que attacan al café (*Coffea arabica*) en la República Dominicana'. (The problem of coffee nematodes (*Coffea arabica*) in the Dominican Republic). *Turrialba* (San José), vol. 19, **4** (October-December) 513–7.

Muller, R. A. (1970). 'Evolution de l'anthracnose des baies du caféier d'Arabie (*Coffea arabica*) due à une forme de *Colletotrichum coffeanum* Noack au Cameroun'. (Development of coffee berry disease on *Coffea arabica* berries due to a form of *Colletotrichum coffeanum* Noack in Cameroon). *Café Cacao Thé* (Paris), vol. 14, **2** (April-June) 114–29.

Valencia, A. G. (1970). 'Estudo fisiológico de la defoliación causada por *Cercospora coffeicola* en el cafeto'. (Physiological study of the defoliation of the coffee tree caused by *Cercospora coffeicola*). *Cenicafé* (Chinchiná), vol. 21, **3** (July-September) 105–14.

Saccas, A. M. Charpentier, J. (1971). 'La rouille des caféiers due à *Hemileia vastatrix* Berk. et Br.'. (Coffee rust due to *Hemileia vastatrix* Berk. and Br.) *Bulletin IFCC* **10**, Paris, (February) 124 pp.

Muller, R. A. (1971). 'La rouille du caféier (*Hemileia vastatrix*) sur le continent américain'. (Coffee rust [*Hemileia vastatrix*] on the American continent). *Café Cacao Thé* (Paris), vol. 15, **1** (January-March) 24–30.

Waller, J. M. (1971). 'The weather and CBD'. *Kenya Coffee* (Nairobi), vol. 36, (April-May) 119–24.

Lavabre, E. M. (1972). 'La lutte contre les mauvaises herbes en cultures caféières par l'emploi judicieux des plantes de couverture'. (Controlling weeds in coffee plantations through the appropriate use of cover crops). *Café Cacao Thé* (Paris), vol. 16, **1** (January-March) 44–7.

Saccas, A. M. (1972). 'La rouille "farineuse" des caféiers due à *Hemileia coffeicola* Maub. et Rog. (Grey coffee rust due to *Hemileia coffeicola*). Bulletin IFCC, **11**, Paris (July) 68 pp.

Pereira, J. L. (1972). 'The influence of fungicide spray volumes on the control of coffee diseases'. *Turrialba* (San José), vol. 22, **4** (October-December) 409–14.

Steiner, K. G. (1973). 'Wechselwirkung zwischen Witterung, Wirt, Parasit und Fungiziden bei der Kaffeekirschenkrandheit (*Colletotrichum coffeanum* Noack)'. (Interaction between the climate, the host, the parasite and fungicides in coffee berry disease due to *Colletotrichum coffeanum* (Noack). Thesis defended 25 April 1973, Univ: J. Liebig of Giessen, 154 pp.

Mogk, M. (1973). 'Untersuchungen zur Epidemiologie von *Colletotrichum coffeanum* Noack *sensu* Hindorf in Kenia, eine Analyse der Wirt-Parasit-Umwelt-Beziehungen'. (Research on the epidemiology of *Colletotricum coffeanum* Noack *sensu* Hindorf in Kenya, analysis of host-parasite-environment relationships). Thesis defended 19 June 1973, University J. Liebig of Giessen, 163 pp.

Snoeck, J. (1973). 'Essais de désherbage chimique de jeunes caféiers Robusta en Côte d'Ivoire'. (Chemical weeding trials with young robusta coffee trees in the Ivory Coast). *Café Cacao Thé* (Paris), vol. 17, **3** (July-September) 223–30.

Pereira, J. L. *et al.* (1973). 'Redistribution of fungicides in coffee trees'. *Experimental Agriculture* (London), vol. 9, **3** (July) 209–18.

Muller, R. A. (1973). 'L'anthracnose des baies due caféier d'Arabie (*Coffea arabica* L.) due à une forme virulente de *Colletotrichum coffeanum* Noack'. (Coffee berry disease in *Coffea arabica* L. due to a virulent form of *Colletotricum coffeanum* Noack). **I**. 'Variations de la sensibilité des fruits au cours de leur développement'. (Variations in the fruits' sensitivity during the course of their development). **II**. 'L'irrigation, méthode préventive de contrôle de la maladie'. (Irrigation, preventive method for controlling the disease). *Café Cacao Thé* (Paris), vol. 17, **4** (October-December) 281–312.

Suryakantha Raju, K., et al. (1974). 'Effect of some common insecticides on the germination of urediospores of *Hemileia Vastatrix* B. et Br.'. *Journal of Coffee Research* (Chikmagalur), vol. 4., **1** (January) 13.

Saccas, A. M. (1975). 'Les pourridiés des caféiers en Afrique tropicale'. (Root rots afflicting coffee trees in tropical Africa). Bulletin IFCC, **13**, Paris, (January) 172 pp.

Abasa, R. O. (1975). 'A review of the biological control of coffee insect pests in Kenya'. *East Afric. Agric. and Forestry J.* (Nairobi), vol. 40, **3** (January) 292–9.

Decazy, B. (1975). 'Contribution à l'étude biologique et écologique du "tigre du caféier", *Dulinius unicolor* Sign., à Madagascar'. (Contribution to the biological and ecological study of the 'coffee bug' *Dulinius unicolor* Sign., in Madagascar). *Café Cacao Thé* (Paris), vol. 19, **1** (January-March) 19–34.

Delabarre, M., Snoeck, J. (1975). 'Résultats de deux essais de triage d'herbicides sur caféiers Robusta en Côte d'Ivoire'. (Results of two trials for grading herbicides using robusta coffee in the Ivory Coast). *Café Cacao Thé* (Paris), vol. 19, **1** (January-March) 41–4.

Bakala, J., Bompeix, G., Muller, R. A. (1975). 'Culture *in vitro* de *Hemileia vastatrix* Berk. and Br. (*In vitro* culture of *Hemileia vastatrix*). *Café Cacao Thé* (Paris), vol. 19, **4** (October-December) 291–2.

Murakaru, G. N. W. (1976). 'Influence of age of coffee seedlings on infection by *Colletotrichum coffeanum* Noack (*Glomerella cingulata* Stonen Spauld and von Schrenk)'. *Kenya*

Coffee (Nairobi), vol. 41, **479** (February) 53–7.

Okioga, D. M. (1976). 'The recognition and the control of *Pseudomonas syringae*, the bacterial blight of coffee in Kenya'. *East African Agricultural and Forestry Journal* (Nairobi), vol. 42, **2** (October) 191–7.

Van der Vossen, H. A. M., Cook, R. T. A., Murakaru, G. N. W. (1976). 'Breeding for resistance to coffee berry disease caused by *Colletotrichum coffeanum* Noack (*sensu* Hindorf) in *Coffea arabica* L.'. **I**. 'Methods of preselection for resistance'. *Euphytica* (Wageningen), vol. 25, **3** (November) 733–45.

Massaux, F., Tarjot, M., Misse, C., Tchiendji, C., Lacroix, M. (1978). 'Contribution à l'étude des relations hôte – parasite entre la rouille farineuse (*Hemileia coffeicola*) et le caféier *Coffea canephora* var. *robusta* au Cameroun'. (Contribution to the study of host-parasite relations between grey coffee rust and the *Coffea canephora* var. *robusta* coffee tree in Cameroon). *Café Cacao Thé* (Paris), vol. 22, **1** (January-March) 37–56.

Blaha, G. (1978). 'Un grave pourridié du caféier Arabica au Cameroun: *Clitocybe (Armillariella) elegans* Heim.'. (A serious coffee rot afflicting arabica coffee in Cameroon: *Clitocybe (Armillariella) elegans* Heim.) *Café Cacao Thé* (Paris), vol. 22, **3** (July-September) 203–16.

Baeza-Aragon, C. A. (1978). 'Parasitismo de *Bacillus penetrans* en *Meloidogyne exigua* establecido en *Coffea arabica*. (Parasitism of *Bacillus penetrans* in *Meloidogyne exigua* which is present in *Coffea arabica*). *Cenicafé* (Chinchiná), vol. 29, **3** (July-September) 94–7.

Jaenh, A., Lambert, N. S. (1978). 'Uso de torta de mamona como nematicida em viveiro de café'. (Using ricin oilcakes as a nematicide in coffee tree nurseries). Sexto Congresso brasileiro de Pesquisas. Riberao Prêto, São Paulo, (24–27 October) IBC-GERCA (Rio de Janeiro) 151–4.

Vermeulen, H. (1979). 'Coffee berry disease in Kenya'. PhD thesis, College of Agriculture, Wageningen, 28 February 1979, 113 pp.

Tarjot, M., Lotode, R. (1979). 'Contribution à l'étude des rouilles orangée et farineuse du caféier au Cameroun'. (Contribution to the study of common coffee rust and grey coffee rust in Cameroon). *Café Cacao Thé* (Paris), vol. 23, **2** (April-June) 103–8.

Maithia, A. S. K. (1979). 'Effect of oil suspended fungicides on coffee berry disease and yields'. *Kenya Coffee* (Nairobi), vol. 44, **521** (August) 19–23.

Cardenas Morales, J. A. (1979). 'Fluctuación poblacional del minador de la hoja del cafeto (*Leucoptera coffeella* Guer. Men. 1842), en el Campo experimental de Ixtacuaco, Ver.'. 64 pp. (Fluctuations in the population of the coffee leaf miner [*Leucoptera coffeella* Guer. Men. 1842] at the experimental station of Ixtacuaco, Ven.) Thesis in Agronomy with an emphasis on parasitology. Autonomous Univ. of Chapingo (Chapingo, Mexico).

Muller, R. A. (1980). 'Contribution à la connaissance de la phytomycocénose constituée par *Coffea arabica* L., *Colletotrichum coffeanum* Noack *sensu* Hindorf, *Hemileia vastatrix* B. et Br., *Hemileia coffeicola* Maublanc et Roger'. 175 pp. (Contribution to the knowledge of the phytomycocenosis formed by *Coffea arabica* L., *Colletotrichum coffeanum* Noack *sensu* Hindorf, *Hemileia vastatrix* B. and Br., *Hemileia coffeicola* Maublanc and Roger). Bulletin IFCC, **15**, Paris, (September).

Montoya, R., Chaves, G. M. (1981). 'Influencia de la temperatura˙y de la luz en la germinación, infectividad y periodo de generación de *Hemileia vastatrix* Berk. y Br.'. 33 pp. (Influence of the temperature and light on germination, the power of infection, and the time of generation of *Hemileia vastatrix* Berk. and Br.). *Promecafé*, IICA, Zona Norte, Serie de Publicaciones Miscelaneas, San José, Costa-Rica **278** (March).

Saccas, A. M. (1981). 'Etude de la flore cryptogamique des caféiers en Afrique centrale'. 522 pp. (Study of the cryptogamic flora of coffee trees in Central Africa). Bulletin IFCC **16**, Paris, (May).

Pavan, M. A., Bingham, F. T. (1982). 'Toxidez de metais em plantas'. **II**. 'Caracterizaçao da toxidez de niquel em caffeeiros'. (The toxicity of metals for plants. II. Characterisation of the toxicity of nickel for coffee trees). *Pesquisa agropecuaria brasileira* (Brasilia), vol. 17, **2** (February) 323–8.

Kannan, N. Muthappa, B. N. (1982). 'Tip blight disease of young coffee plants in the nursery'. *Journal of Coffee Research* (Chikmagalur), vol. 12, **2** (April) 38–41.

Penagos D. H., Flores, J. C. 'Hábito y tiempo de penetración de la broca del café *Hypothenemus hampeii* (Ferrari) al fruto'. (Procedure and penetration time of the berry borer *Hypothenemus hampeii* (Ferrari) in the fruit). *Revista Cafetalera, Anacafé* (Guatemala), **137** 5–15.

Muller, R. A. (1984). 'Quelques réflexions à propos de la sélection de variétés résistantes à la rouille orangée (*Hemileia vastatrix* B. et Br.)'. (Some thoughts regarding the selection of rust-resistant varieties [*Hemileia vastatrix* B. et Br.]). *Café Cacao Thé*, vol. 28, **1** 17–42.

Mignucci, J. S., Hepperly, P. R., Ballester, J., Rodriguez-Santiago, C. (1985). 'Anthracnose and berry disease of coffee in Puerto Rico'. *Jnl. of Agr.; Un. of Puerto Rico*, vol. 69, **1** 107–18.

Leguizamon, J. (1985). 'Contribution à la connaissance de la résistance incomplète du caféier Arabica (*Coffea arabica* L.) à la rouille orangée (*Hemileia vastatrix*)'. 124 pp. (Contribution to the knowledge of the incomplete resistance of arabica coffee [*Coffea arabica* L.] to coffee rust [*Hemileia vastatrix*]). Bulletin IRCC, **17** (April)

Harvest: yields and yield estimates

Vincent, J. C. (1968). 'Influence de la maturité des fruits sur la qualité du café Robusta'. (Effect of the maturity of the fruits on the quality of robusta coffee). *Café Cacao Thé* (Paris), vol. 12, **3** (July-September) 240–9.

Monroe, G. E., Wang, J. K. (1968). 'Systems for mechanically harvesting coffee'. Transactions of the ASAE (Michigan), vol. 11, **2** 270–2, 278.

Phillips, A. L. (1970). 'Evaluation of performance of coffee harvesters'. *The J. of Agric. of the Univ. of Puerto Rico* (Rio Pedras), vol. 14, **2** (April) 320–7.

Souza, G. I. D., Venkataramaiah, G. H., et al. (1970). 'Investigations on side effects of BHC on coffee in South India'. *Indian Coffee* (Bangalore), vol. 34, **II** (Nov.) 296–302.

Carvalho, A., *et al.* (1970). 'Occorência dos principais defeitos do café em varias fases de maturaçao dos frutos'. (The appearance of coffee's main flaws during the various phases of fruit maturation). *Bragantia* (Campinas), vol. 29, 207–20.

Bierhuizen, J. F. (1970/1). 'Estudos sobre a productividade do cafeeiro'. **I**. 'Efecto da luz, temperatura et concentraçao de CO_2 na fotossíntese et transpiraçao de *Coffea arabica*'. **III**. 'Diferenças na fotossintese de quatro variedades de caffeeiro' (Study of the productivity of the coffee tree. I. The effect of light, temperature, and soil humidity on the photosynthesis and transpiration of *Coffea arabica*. III. Differences in the photosynthesis of four varieties of coffee trees). *Estudos Agrónomicos* (Lisbon), vol. 11–12 (January 1970, December 1971) 15–25, 27–35, 39–42.

Browning, G., Cannell, M. G. R. (1970). 'Use of 2-chloroethane phosphonic acid to promote the abscission and ripening of fruit of *Coffea arabica* L.'. *Journal of Horticultural Science*, London, vol. 45, 223–32.

Janardhan, K. V., Gopal, N. H., Ramaiah, P. K. (1971). 'Carbohydrate reserves in relation to vegetative growth, flower bud formation and crop levels in arabica coffee'. *Indian Coffee* (Bangalore), vol. 35, **4**, (April) 145–8.

Oyebade, I. T. (1971). 'Effect of pre-harvest sprays of ethrel (2-chloroethane phosphonic acid) on robusta coffee (*Coffea canephora* Pierre) berries'. *Turrialba* (San José), vol. 21, **4** (October-December) 442–4.

Cannell, M. G. R. (1972). 'Use of gibberellic acid to change the seasonal fruiting pattern of arabica coffee in Kenya'. *Kenya Coffee* (Nairobi), vol. 36, **432**, (March) 91–101 and *Horticultural Science*, vol. 46, 289–98.

Upegui L. G., Valencia A. G. (1972). 'Anticipación de la maduración de la cosecha de café, con aplicaciones de Ethrel'. (Speeding up the maturation of the coffee harvest by applying Ethrel). *Cenicafé* (Chinchiná), vol. 23, **1** (February-March) 19–26.

Patel, R. Z., Kabaara, A. M. (1973). 'Effect of fruiting load on the functions of roots of coffee in Kenya'. *Kenya Coffee* (Nairobi), vol 39, **446** (April) 122–6.

Snoeck, J. (1973). 'Adaptation d'une méthode de groupement de la maturation des fruits de caféier Robusta. Essai préliminaire avec l'étéphon'. (Adaptation of a grouping method for the maturation of the fruits of the robusta coffee tree. Preliminary trial with etephon). *Café Cacao Thé* (Paris), vol. 16, **2**, (April-June) 129–36.

Adenikinju, S. A. (1975). 'A preliminary study of the influence of chemical sprays on fruit set and abscission in robusta coffee (*Coffea canephora*) Pierre ex Froehner'. *Turrialba* (San José), vol. 25, **4** (October-December) 414–17.

Oyebade, T. (1976). 'Influence of pre-harvest sprays of Ethrel on ripening and abscission of coffee berries'. *Turrialba* (San José) vol. 26, **1** (January-March) 86–9.

Snoeck, J., Bernard-Coffre, P., Pechereau. (1976). 'La récolte mécanique du café à l'aide d'un fouetteur'. (Mechanical harvesting using a beater). *Café Cacao Thé* (Paris), vol. 20, **4** (October-December) 297–300.

Snoeck, J. (1977). 'Essais de groupement de la récolte des fruits du caféier Canephora à l'aide de l'étéphon'. (Trials for grouping the fruit harvests of canephora using etephon). *Café Cacao Thé* (Paris), vol. 21, **3** (July-September) 163–78.

Raw, A., Free, J. B. (1977). 'The pollination of coffee (*Coffea arabica*) by honeybees'. *Tropical agriculture* (Guildford), vol. 54, **4** (October) 365–70.

Opile, W. R. (1977). 'Effect of gibberellic acid on yield of arabica coffee in Kenya'. *Kenya Coffee* (Nairobi), vol. 42, **501** (December) 395–403.

Sudhakara Rao, G., Venkataramanan, D. Partha, T. S., Rao, K. N. (1978). 'Ethylene-induced changes in the chemical composition of coffee mucilage'. *Turrialba* (San José) vol. 28, **2** (April-June) 153–5.

Gomide, M. B., Hostalacio, S., Duarte, C. de S. (1978). 'Efeito de dosagens e numeros de aplicaçoes de Ethrel na formaçao de mudas de cafeeiro (*Coffea arabica* L.) cultivar Mundo Novo'. (Effect of the doses and the number of applications of Ethrel on the formation of seedlings of *Coffea arabica* L., Mundo Novo cultivar). *Ciência e Practica* (Escola Superior de Agricultura de Lavras, Minas Gerais), vol. 2, **2** (July-December) 214–23.

Opile, W. R. (1978). 'Influence of fruit stage on the use of (2-chloroethyl) phosphonic acid (CEPA) in Kenya'. *Kenya Coffee* (Nairobi), vol. 43. **511** (October) 301–9.

Walyaro, D. J., Van der Vossen, H. A. M. (1979/80). 'Early determination of yield potential in arabica coffee by applying index selection'. *Euphytica* (Wageningen), vol. 28, **2** (June 1979) 465–72; and *Kenya Coffee* (Nairobi), vol. 45, **526** (January 1980) 25–9.

Uribe-Henao, A., Mestre-Mestre, A. (1980). 'Efecto de la densidad de población y su sistema de manejo sobre la producción de café'. (Effect of the population density and the farming system on coffee production). *Cenicafé* (Chinchiná), vol. 31, **1** (January-March) 29–51.

Srinivasan, C. S. (1980). 'Association of some vegetative characters with initial fruit yield in coffee (*Coffea arabica* L.)'. *J. of Coffee Research* (Mysore), vol. 10, **2** (April) 21–7.

Rothfos, B. (1980). *Coffee production*. 366 pp. Gordian-Max Rieck GmbH, Hamburg.

Snoeck, J. (1981). 'Facteurs du rendement influencés par les apports d'azote chez le caféier Robusta en Côte d'Ivoire'. (Yield factors affected by applications of nitrogen to robusta coffee in the Ivory Coast). *Café Cacao Thé* (Paris), vol. 25, **3** (July-September) 173–80.

Coffee improvement

Capot, J., Dupautex, B., Durandeau, A. (1968). 'L'amélioration du caféier en Côte d'Ivoire. Duplication chromosomique et hybridation'. (Coffee tree improvement in the Ivory Coast. Chromosomal duplication and hybridisation). *Café Cacao Thé* (Paris), vol. 12, **2** (April-June) 114–26.

Carvalho, A., Monaco, L. C. (1968). 'Relaciones genéticas de especies seleccionadas de *Coffea*'. 19 pp. (Genetic relations between selected species of *Coffea*). *Café* (Lima), (Oct-Dec) vol. 9, **4**.

Castillo Z. J., Quinceno, G. (1970), 'Comparación de lineas de *Coffea arabica* L. por su resistencia a *Ceratocystis fimbriata* (Ell. Halst.) Hunt'. (Comparison of lines of *Coffea arabica* L. for their resistance to *Ceratocystis fimbriata* [Ell. Halst.] Hunt). *Cenicafé* (Chinchiná). vol. 21, **3** (July-September) 95–104.

Goujon, M. (1971). 'Considérations à propos de la résistance des plantes. Le cas particulier des caféiers attaqués par les rouilles orangée et farineuse'. (Considerations regarding plant resistance, in particular the case of coffee trees attacked by grey coffee rust and common coffee rust). *Café Cacao Thé* (Paris), vol. 15, **4** (October-December) 308–28.

Capot, J. (1972). 'L'amélioration du caféier en Côte d'Ivoire. Les hybrides "Arabusta" '. (Coffee tree improvement in the Ivory Coast. The 'Arabusta' hybrids). *Café Cacao Thé* (Paris), vol. 16, **1** (January-March) 3–18.

Charrier, A., (1972). 'L'intercompatibilité des clones de caféiers cultivés sur la Côte Est Malgache'. (The intercompatibility of coffee tree clones grown on the east coast of Madagascar). *Café Cacao Thé* (Paris), vol. 16, **2** (April-June) 111–22.

Kammacher, P., Capot, J. (1972). 'Sur les relations caryologiques entre *Coffea arabica* et *Coffea canephora*'. (Caryological relationships between *Coffea arabica* and *Coffea canephora*). *Café Cacao Thé* (Paris), vol. 16, **4** (October-December) 289–94.

Louarn, J. (1972). 'Introduction à l'étude génétique des *Mascarocoffea*: nouvelles déterminations de leurs nombres chromosomiques'. (Introduction to the genetic study of *Mascarocoffea*: new conclusions on their chromosomal numbers). *Café Cacao Thé* (Paris), vol. 16, **4** (October-December) 312–6.

Chinnappa, C. C. (1974). '**B** chromosomes in *Coffea arabica*'. *Journal of Coffee Research* (Balehonnur), vol. 4, **3** (July) 61–6.

Reffye, Ph. de. (1974). 'La recherche de l'optimum en amélioration des plantes et son application à une descendance F_1 de caféiers hybrides Arabusta'. (The search for the optimum in plant improvement and applying it to an F_1 progeny of hybrid Arabusta coffee trees). *Café Cacao Thé* (Paris), vol. 18, **3** (July-September) 167–78.

Carelli, M. L. C., Lopes, C. R., Monaco, L. C. (1974). 'Chlorogenic acid in species of *Coffea* and selections of *C. arabica*'. *Turrialba* (San José), vol. 24, **4** (October-December) 398–401.

Capot, J., Ake Assi, L. (1975). 'Un nouveau caféier hybride de Côte d'Ivoire'. (A new hybrid coffee tree of the Ivory Coast). *Café Cacao Thé* (Paris), vol. 19, **1** (January-March) 3–4.

Partiot, M. (1975). 'La résistance horizontale du cacaoyer au *Phytophthora* sp. Méthodes d'évaluation précoce'. (Horizontal resistance of the cocoa tree to *Phytophthora* sp. Methods of early detection). *Café Cacao Thé* (Paris), vol. 19, **2** (April-June) 123–36.

Orozco-Castano, F. J. (1975). 'Inactivación de la auto-incompatibilidad en *Coffea canephora* por tratamiento al pistilo'. (Inactivation of self-incompatibility in *Coffea canephora* by treatment of the pistil). *Cenicafé* (Chinchiná), vol. 26, **2** (April-June) 101–5.

Berthou, F. (1975). 'Méthode d'obtention de polyploides dans le genre *Coffea* par traitements localisés de bourgeons à la colchicine'. (Method of obtaining polyploidies in the *Coffea* genus by localised treatments of buds with colchicine). *Café Cacao Thé* (Paris), vol. 19, **3** (July-September) 197–202.

Grassias, M., (1975). 'Observations sur la conjugaison chromosomique de *Coffea arabica* L.'. (Observations on the chromosomal conjugation of *Coffea arabica* L.). *Café Cacao Thé* (Paris), vol. 19, **3** (July-September) 177–90.

Louarn, J. (1976). 'Hybrides interspécifiques entre *Coffea canephora* Pierre et *C. eugenioides* Moore'. (Interspecific hybrids between *Coffea canephora* Pierre and *C. eugenioides* Moore. *Café Cacao Thé* (Paris), vol. 20, **1** (January-March) 33–52.

Dublin, P., Parvas, J. P. (1976). 'L'haploïdie spontanée liée à la polyembryonie chez le *Coffea arabica* L.'. (Spontaneous haploidy linked to polyembryony in *Coffea arabica* L.). *Café Cacao Thé* (Paris), vol. 20, **2** (April-June) 83–90.

Berthaud, J. (1976). 'Etude cytogénique d'un haploïde de *Coffea arabica* L.'. (Cytogenic study of a *Coffea arabica* L. haploid). *Café Cacao Thé* (Paris), vol. 20, **2** (April-June) 91–6.

Capot, J. (1977). 'L'amélioration du caféier Robusta en Côte d'Ivoire'. (Improvement of robusta coffee in the Ivory Coast). *Café Cacao Thé* (Paris), vol. 2, **4** (October-December) 233–44.

Berthaud, J. (1978). 'L'hybridation interspécifique entre *C. arabica* et *C. canephora* P. Obtention et comparaison des hybrides triploïdes, Arabusta et hexaploïdes. Première partie'. (Interspecific hybridisation between *C. arabica* and *C. canephora* P. Obtaining and comparing triploid, Arabusta, and hexaploid hybrids. Part I). *Café Cacao Thé* (Paris), vol. 22, **1** (January-March) 3–12. 'Deuxième partie'. (Part II). *Café Cacao Thé* (Paris), vol. 22, **2** (April-June) 87–112.

Noirot, M. (1978). 'Polyploïdisation de caféiers par la colchicine. Adaptation de la technique sur bourgeons axillaires aux conditions de Madagascar. Mise en évidence de chimères périclines stables'. (Polyploidisation of coffee trees by colchicine. Adapting the technique to axillary buds in the conditions of Madagascar. Proof of stable pericline chimera). *Café Cacao Thé* (Paris), vol. 22, **3** (July-September) 187–94.

Lanaud, C. (1979). 'Etude de problèmes génétiques posés chez le caféier par l'introgression de caractères d'une espèce sauvage (*C. kianjavatensis: Mascarocoffea*) dans l'espèce cultivée *C. canephora (Eucoffea)*'. (A study of the genetic problems in the coffee tree caused by the introgression of characteristics of a wild species [*C. kianjavatensis: Mascarocoffea*] in the cultivated species *C. canephora* [*Eucoffea*]). *Café Cacao Thé* (Paris), vol. 23, **1** (January-March) 3–28.

Bouharmont, P. (1980). 'La sélection végétative du caféier Robusta au Cameroun. Lère partie Programme de sélection'. (Vegetative selection of robusta coffee in Cameroon. Part 1. Selection programme). *Café Cacao Thé* (Paris), vol. 23, **4** (October-December) 227–54. '2ème partie. Diffusion du matériel végétal'. (Part 2. Dissemination of the plant material). *Café Cacao Thé* (Paris), vol. 24, **1** (January-March) 3–18.

Cadena-Gomez, G., Buritica-Despedes, P. (1980). 'Expresión de resistencia horizontal à la roya (*Hemileia vastatrix* Berk. y Br.) en *Coffea canephora* variedad Conilón'. (Horizontal resistance to rust [*Hemileia vastatrix* Berk and Br] in *Coffea canephora* var. Conilón). *Cenicafé* (Chinchiná), vol. 31, **1** (January-March) 3–27.

Grassias-Hubault, M. (1980). 'Etude de la fertilité et du comportement méiotique des hybrides interspécifiques tétrapoloïdes Arabusta *Coffea arabica* × *C. canephora*'. 98 pp. (Study of the fertility and meiotic behaviour of the tetraploid interspecific hybrids Arabusta *Coffea arabica* × *C. canephora*). PhD. dissertation, specialising in Plant Improvement, Univ. of Paris Sud, Centre d'Orsay, 8 July.

Lanaud, C., Zickler, D. (1980). 'Premières informations sur la fertilité des hybrides pentaploïdes et hexaploïdes entre *C. arabica* (*Eucoffea*) et *C. resinosa* (*Mascarocoffea*)'. (First information on the fertility of the pentaploid and hexaploid hybrids between *C. arabica* [*Eucoffea*] and *C. resinosa* [*Mascarocoffea*]). *Café Cacao Thé* (Paris), vol. 24, **3** (July-September) 169–76.

Van der Vossen, H. A. M., Walyaro, D. J. (1980). 'Breeding for resistance to coffee berry disease in *Coffea arabica* L. **II**. Inheritance of the resistance'. *Euphytica* (Wageningen), vol. 29, **3** (November) 777–91.

Dublin, P. (1984). 'Techniques de reproduction végétative *in vitro* et amélioration chez les caféiers cultivés'. (Techniques of *in vitro* vegetative propagation and improvement in cultivated coffee trees). *Café Cacao Thé* (Paris), vol. 28, **4** 231–44.

ASIC (1986). 'Les biotechnologistes et les caféiers. – Table ronde'. (Biotechnologists and coffee trees – Round Table). *Café Cacao Thé*.

ASIC-IRCC, Montpellier.

Couturon, E. (1986). 'Le tri précoce des haploides d'origine spontanée de *C. canephora*'. (Early selection of haploids of *C. canephora* of spontaneous origin). *Café Cacao Thé.* (Paris), vol. 30, **3** 171–82.

Processing technology

Levabre, E. M., Decazy, B. (1968). 'Contribution à l'étude des problèmes posés par le stockage des cafés dans les pays de production. Premières données sur le comportement de l'*Araecerus fasciculatus* à température et humidité contrôlées'. (Contribution to the study of problems caused when coffee is stored in the country where it is produced. First facts on the behaviour of *Araecerus fasciculatus* under controlled temperature and humidity). *Café Cacao Thé.* (Paris), vol. 12, **4** (October-December).

Rolz, C., Menchu, J. F. et al (1968). 'La tostación continua del café en cama fluida'. (Continuous roasting of coffee on a fluidized bed). *Café* (Lima), vol. 9, **3** (July-September) 3–19.

Ghosh, B. N. (1968). 'Recent advances in the mechanisation of wet coffee processing'. *Kenya Coffee* (Nairobi), vol. 38, **395** (December) 397–400.

Wooton, A. E., Verkade, F. A., Mitchell, H. W. (1968). 'Sun-drying arabica coffee'. *Kenya Coffee* (Nairobi), vol. 33, 261–71.

Gopalakrishna Rao, N. et al. (1969). 'Moisture variations in coffee beans during storage under different climatic conditions'. *Indian Coffee* (Bangalore), vol. 33, **1** (January) 21–31.

Northmore, J. M. (1969). 'Stinkers (Over-fermented beans)'. *Kenya Coffee* (Nairobi), vol. 34, **396** (January) 26–30.

Brandenberger, H. et al. (1969). 'Über die Decoffeinierung von Kaffee mit Trichlorâthylen'. (Decaffeinating coffee using trichloroethylene). *Zeitsch. f. Lebensm. Unters. u. Forsch*, vol. 139, **4** (March) 211–19.

Vincent, J. C. (1969). 'Essais de préparation du café Robusta par voie humide au Cameroun'. (Trials on wet processing robusta coffee in Cameroon). *Café Cacao Thé.* (Paris), vol. 13, **3** (July-September) 211–9.

Wilbaux, R., Richar, M., Hahn, D. (1970). 'Essai de stockage de café vert en silo métallique hermétique'. (Trial on storing green coffee in an airtight metallic silo). *Café Cacao Thé.* (Paris), vol. 14, **2** (April-June) 141–4.

Durichen, K., Heiss, R. (1970). 'Physikalische Überlegungen zur Verpackung von Röstkaffee in Weichpackungen'. (Physical considerations of packing roasted coffee in soft packaging). *Kaffee und Tee Markt* (Hamburg), vol. 20, **15** (August) 5–11.

Vincent, J.C. (1971). 'Essais comparatifs de méthodes rapides de préparation du café Arabica'. (Comparative trials on rapid methods of preparing arabica coffee). *Café Cacao Thé* (Paris), vol. 15, **1** (January-March) 49–54.

Corte dos Santos, A. (1971). 'Etude de l'évolution de plusieurs caractéristiques d'un café Arabica au cours d'un stockage expérimental effectué à cinq humidités relatives différentes'. (A study of the evolution of several characteristics of an arabica coffee during experimental storage at five different relative humidities). *Café Cacao Thé*. (Paris), vol. 15, **4** (October-December) 329–40.

Stessels, L., Fridmann, M. (1972). 'Utilisation de l'énergie solaire pour la conservation du café en région tropicale humide'. (The use of solar energy for storing coffee in tropical moist regions). *Café Cacao Thé* (Paris), vol. 16, **2** (April-June) 135–48.

Stessels, L. (1973). 'Utilisation de l'énergie solaire pour la conservation du café en région tropicale humide. Projet de magasin industriel de stockage'. (The use of solar energy for storing coffee in tropical moist regions. Project for an industrial store). *Café Cacao Thé* (Paris), vol. 17, **2** (April-June) 142–58.

Ballion, P., Hahn, D., Vincent, J. C. (1973). 'Etudes comparatives des méthodes de criblage sur café vert'. (Comparative studies on methods of grading green coffee). *Café Cacao Thé* (Paris), vol. 17, **3** (July-September) 231–40.

Stirling, H. G. (1974). 'The effects of temperature and moisture content on the quality of parchment arabica coffee during a 12 month sealed storage trial'. *Kenya Coffee* (Nairobi), vol. 39, **456** (March) 73–9.

Multon, J. L. (1974). 'Evolution de plusieurs caractéristiques d'un café Arabica au cours d'un stockage expérimental effectué à cinq humidités relatives et quatre températures différentes'. (Evolution of several characteristics of an arabica coffee during experimental storage using five different relative humidities and four different temperatures). *Café Cacao Thé* (Paris), vol. 18, **2** (April-June) 121–32.

Stirling, H. G. (1975). 'Further experiments on the factors affecting quality loss in stored arabica coffee'. *Kenya Coffee* (Nairobi), vol. 40, **446** (January) 28–35.

Colombo, A. J., Aquarone, E., Baruffaldi, R. (1975). 'Influences des conditions de chauffage sur l'élimination de l'eau des extraits de café au cours de la lyophilisation'. (The effect of heating conditions on the elimination of water from coffee extracts during freeze-drying). *Café Cacao Thé* (Paris), vol. 19, **1** (January-March) 45–6.

AFNOR (1975). 'Analyse granulométrique des fèves de café vert par tamisage en laboratoire (traduction du document ISO/TC 34/SC 8/GT 2N 306E)'. 5 pp. (Granulometric analysis of green coffee beans by grading in the laboratory – Translation of document ISO/TC 34/SC 8/GT 2N 306E). (Paris), (September).

Barel, M., Challot, F., Vincent, J. C.(1976). 'Contribution à l'étude des fèves de cafés défectueuses'. (Contribution to the study of defective coffee beans). *Café Cacao Thé* (Paris), vol. 20, **2** (April-June) 129–34.

Challot, F. (1976). 'Recherches sur l'origine des fèves puantes chez *Coffea arabica*'. (Research on the origin of stinkers in *Coffea arabica*). *Café Cacao Thé* (Paris), vol. 20, **3** (July-September) 201–8.

Madison, B. L., Kozarek, W. J., Damo, C. P. (1976). 'High pressure liquid chromatography of caffeine in coffee'. *Journal of the AOAC* (Baltimore), vol. 59, **6** 1258–61.

Fernandez Urpi, M. (1977). 'Evaluación de los sistemas para tratar las aguas residuales del beneficio de café'. 24 pp. (Evaluation of the systems used for processing the residual waters from coffee processing). Departamento de estudios técnicos y diversificación, Oficina del Café (San José, Costa Rica).

AFNOR (1977). 'Café vert en sacs. Echantillonnage'. 6 pp. (Green coffee in bags. Sampling) (Paris), NF VO3–300, (July).

AFNOR (1977). 'Café vert. Détermination des matières étrangères et défectuosités'. 2pp. (Green coffee. Determining foreign matter and defects). (Paris), NF VO3–309, (July).

AFNOR (1977). 'Café vert. Examens olfactif et visuel'. 2pp. (Green coffee. Olfactory and visual tests). (Paris), NF VO3–306, (July).

AFNOR (1977). 'Café vert. Analyse granulométrique, tamisage manuel'. 5pp. (Green Coffee. Granulometric analysis, manual sieving). (Paris), NF VO3–308, (July).

AFNOR (1977). 'Café vert. Détermination des fèves endommagées par les insectes'. 8pp. (Green Coffee. Determining insect-damaged beans). (Paris), NF VO3–312, (July).

AFNOR (1977). 'Café vert. Détermination de la masse de 1000 grains'. 2pp. (Determining the mass of 1000 beans). (Paris), NF VO3–307, (August).

Arjona, J. L., Roche, G., Rios, Gibert, H., Vincent, J. C. (1977). 'Torréfaction du café en couche fluidisée gazeuse'. (Roasting coffee on a gaseous fluidised bed). *Café Cacao Thé* (Paris), vol 21, **4** (October-December) 263–72.

Arjona, J. L., Rios, G. M., Gibert, H., Vincent, J. C. (1979). 'Torréfaction due café en couche fluidisée gazeuse'. (Roasting coffee on a gaseous fluidised bed). *Café Cacao Thé*, (Paris) vol 23, **2** (April-June) 119–28.

Shin, H. K. (1979). 'Étude de l'épuration des

gaz émis en cours de torréfaction du café en vue de la récupération des arômes'. 108pp. (Study of the purification of gas emitted during coffee roasting in view of recovering the aromas). Doctoral Thesis in Food Sciences with an option in Food Technology and Engineering – Fermentations. Technical and Scientific University of Languedoc, Montpellier, 5 November 1979.

ISO (1980).'Café vert. Examens olfactif et visuel, et détermination des matières étrangères et des défauts'. 2pp. (Green coffee. Olfactory and visual tests, and determining foreign matter and defects). International Standard 4149, First edition, (February).

Cros, E., Fourny, G., Guyot, B., Rouly, M. Vincent, J. C. (1980). 'Evolution d'n café Arabica torréfié stocké dans quatre emballages modèles. Analyse sensorielle. Evolution de la fraction volatile. Comparaison par rapport à un témoin. Limite de l'utilisation optimale'. (Development of a roasted arabica coffee stored in four model packages. Sensory analysis. Development of the volatile fraction. Comparison with a control. Limit of the optimal use). *Café Cacao Thé* (Paris), vol. 24, **3** (July-September) 203–26.

Shin, H. K., Crouzet, J. (1981). 'Récupération de l'arôme du café en cours de torréfaction. **I.** Piégeage des émissions gazeuses par condensation et absorption'. (Recuperating the aroma of the coffee during roasting. I. Trapping the gas emissions by condensation and absorption). *Café Cacao Thé* (Paris), vol. 25, **2** (April-June) 127–36.

Shin, H. K., Crouzet, J. (1981). 'Récupération de l'arôme du café en cours de torréfaction. **II.** Elimination des matières grasses'. (Recuperating the aroma of the coffee during roasting. II. Elimination of fat). *Café Cacao Thé* (Paris), vol. 25, **3** (July-September) 191–6.

ISO (1981). 'Café vert. Analyse granulométrique. Tamisage manuel'. 5pp. (Green coffee. Bean size analysis. Manual sieving). Norme internationale 4150, Première édition (August).

Jallel, S. A., Sreekantiah, K. R. (1984). 'Application of fungal pectic enzymes in coffee curing'. *Jnl. of Food Sc. and Technology* (Mysore), vol. 21, **21** 5–8.

Green coffee – roasting – legislation

Thier, H. P. *et al.* (1968). 'Scopoletin, ein Bestandteil des Rohkaffees'. (Scopoletin, an element of raw coffee). *Zeitschr. Lebensm. Unters, u. Forsch.* (Munich), vol. 137, **1** (April) 1–4.

Ornano, M. d', Chassevent, F., Dalger, G. (1968). 'Note sur la détermination de la teneur en eau du café lyophilisé par spectrophotométrie dans l'infrarouge'. (Report on determining the water content of freeze-dried coffee using spectrophotometry in infrared light). *Café Cacao Thé* (Paris), vol. 12, **3** (July-September) 250–60.

Fritz, W. (1968). 'Zur Bildung cancerogener Kohlenwasserstoffe bei der thermischen Behandlung von Lebensmitteln. **II** Das Rösten von Bohnenkaffee und Kaffee-Ersatzstoffen'. (Formation of carcinogenic hydrocarbons during thermal processing of foodstuffs. II. Roasting coffee and its replacement products). *Die Nahrung* (Berlin), vol 12., **8** 799–804.

Fritz, W. (1969). 'Zum Lösungsverhalten der Polyaromaten beim Kochen von Kaffee-Ersatzstoffen und Bohnenkaffee'. (Rendering polyaromatic hydrocarbons soluble when boiling coffee and coffee substitutes). *Dtsch. Lebensm. Rdsch.* (Stuttgart), **3** (March) 83–5.

Harms, U. Wurziger, J. (1969). 'Beiträge zum Genusswert und Bekömmlichkeit von Röstkaffee. Phenolische Substanzen im Kaffeewachs von Rohkaffees verschiedener Art und Herkunft'. (Contribution to the study of the stimulating value and digestibility of roasted coffee. Phenolic substances of the wax of raw coffee of different types and origins). *Kaffee u. Tee Markt* (Hamburg), vol. 19, **6** 6–9.

Biggers, R. E., Hilton, J. J., Gianturco, M. A. (1969). 'Differentiation between *Coffea arabica* and *Coffea robusta* by computer evaluation of gaz-chromatographic profiles. Comparison of numerically derived quality predictions with organoleptic evaluations'. *J. Chrom. Sci.* (Clinton), vol. 7, **8** 453–72.

Rostolan, J., de Poisson, J. (1970). 'Structure partielle de la cafamarine'. (Partial structure of cafamarine). *Café Cacao Thé* (Paris), vol. 14, **1** (January-March) 47–9.

Sanint, O. B., Valencia, G. A. (1970). 'Actividad enzimática en el grano de café en relatión con la calidad de la bebida. **I.** Duración de la fermentación'. (Enzyme activity in the coffee bean in relation to the quality of the beverage. I. Length of fermentation time). *Cenicafé* (Chinchiná), vol. 21, **2** (April-June) 59–71.

Thaler, H. (1970). 'Untersuchungen an Kaffee und Kaffee-Ersatz. Polysaccharide der grünen Bohnen von (*Caffea canephora* var. *robusta*'. (Studies on coffee and its substitutes. Polysaccharides of the green beans of *Coffea canephora* var. *robusta*). *Zeitschr. f. Lebensm. Unters. u Forsch.* (Munich), vol. 143, **5** (August) 342–8.

Washuetti, J., Bancher, E., Riederer, P. (1970). 'Eine neue Dünnschichtchromatographische Methode zur Bertimmung des Coffeingehaltes in gerösteten Kaffeebohnen'. (A new method of quantitative analysis of caffeine in roasted coffee using chromatography on a thin layer). *Zeitschr. f. Lebensm. Unters. u. Forsch.* (Munich), vol. 143, **4** (August) 253–6.

Paris, R. R., Motohiro Ninshio. (1970). 'Sur la séparation des acides chlorogéniques du café vert: *Coffea robusta* Lind.'. (Separation of the chlorogenic acids of green coffee: *Coffea robusta* Lind.) *C. R. Acad. Sc. Paris*, vol. 270, **11** 1465–7.

Gal, I., Bekes, I. (1971). 'Schnellmethode zur orientierenden Bestimmung von Coffein in Röstkaffee'. (A rapid method for estimating the amount of caffeine in roasted coffee). *Zeitschr. f. Lebensm. Unters. u Forsch* (Munich), vol. 147, **1** (September) 10–3.

Mohr, E. (1971). 'Mikrobiologische Untersuchungen an Rohkaffee, Röstkaffee, Flüssigkaffee und Extraktkaffee'. (Microbiological studies of green and roasted coffee, and liquid and solid extracts). *Kaffee und Tee Markt* (Hamburg), vol. 21, **17** (September).

Hahn, D., Vincent, J. C. (1972). 'Essais de mesures spectroréflectrométriques sur cafés vert et torréfié et sur cacao'. (Trials on spectroreflectrometric measures of green and roasted coffee and cacao). *Café Cacao Thé* (Paris), vol. 16, **2** (April-June) 149–60.

Jardin, C. (1972). 'Le café et le consommateur. Normes, réglementations, et contrôle'. (Coffee and the consumer. Standards, regulations, and control). *Café Cacao Thé* (Paris), vol. 16, **3** (July-September) 243–59.

Bucko, A. (1972). 'L'importance du café pour l'organisme de l'intellectuel'. (The importance of coffee for the organism of the intellectuel). *Minerva Medica* (Turin), vol. 63, **64** (suppl.) (September) 44–53.

Baiao Esteves, A., Santos Oliveira, J. (1973). 'Contribution à l'étude des caractéristiques des cafés d'Angola'. (Contribution to the study of the characteristics of coffee from Angola). *Café Cacao Thé* (Paris), vol. 17, **1** (January-March) 46–52.

Chassevent, F., Dalger, G. (1972). 'Détermination de la teneur en eau des extraits de café en poudre soluble par spectrophotométrie dans le proche infrarouge, la méthode de Karl Fischer et les méthodes d'étuvage'. (Determining the water content of coffee extracts in soluble powder by spectrophotometry in close infrared light, the method of Karl Fischer and oven-drying). *Café Cacao Thé* (Paris),vol. 16, **1** (January-March) 49–61.

Mohr, E. (1972). 'Untersuchungen Über Fettphase von Roh- un Röstkaffee'. (Studies on the fat content of raw and roasted coffee). *Kaffee und Tee Markt* (Hamburg), vol. 22, **5** 3–4.

Wurziger, J. (1973). 'Les éléments constitutifs nouveaux récemment découverts dans le café et leur importance pour l'appréciation des infusions du café.' (Basic new elements recently discovered in coffee and their importance for the appreciation of coffee drinking). *Annales des falsifications et de l'expertise chimique* (Paris), vol. 66 **707** (January-March) 1–18.

ISO/TC (1973) 'Measurement of methyl chloride residue in roasted coffee beans'. 4 pp. 34 SC/8/WG2. Special task group of test methods concerning roasted and soluble coffee, (July).

Baltes, W. et al. (1973). 'Die Remissionspektralphotometrische Bestimmung von Trigonellin und Coffein in Kaffee'. (Determining trigonellin and caffeine in coffee by remission spectrophotometry). *Z. f. Lebensm. -Unters. u. Forschung* (Munich), vol. 152, **3** 145–6.

Schilling, P., Gal, S. (1973). 'Gaschromatographische Bestimmung von Coffein in Kaffee'. (The quantitative analysis of caffeine in coffee by gas chromatography). *Z. F. Lebensm. -Unters. u. Forschung* (Munich), vol. 153, **2** 94–96.

Chassevent, F., Dalger, G., Gerwig, S., Vincent, J. C. (1974). 'Contribution à l'étude des *Mascarocoffea*. Etude des fractions lipidique et insaponifiable. Relation éventuelle entre les teneurs en caféine et en acides chlorogéniques'. (Contribution to the study of *Mascarocoffea*. Study of lipidic and unsaponifiable fractions. Possible relationship between caffeine content and chlorogenic acids). *Café Cacao Thé* (Paris), vol. 18, **1** (January-March) 49–58.

AFNOR (1974). 'Cafés. Détermination de la teneur en caféine.' 4 pp. (Coffee. Determining the caffeine content). (Paris), NF VO5–251. (February).

AFNOR (1974). 'Café soluble. Dosage de l'eau (Méthode pratique)'. 2 pp. (Instant coffee. Quantitative analysis of water [Practical method]. (Paris), NF VO5–221, (February).

AFNOR (1974). 'Cafés et dérivés. Vocabulaire'. 7 pp. (Coffee and derivatives. Vocabulary). (Paris), NF V00–101, (February)

Mohr, E., Lahne, R. (1974). 'Leitsubstanzen des Kaffee-Aromas'. (Main substances in the aroma of coffee). *Kaffee u. Tee Markt* (Hamburg), vol. 24, **9** (May) 10–4.

Lopes, M. H. C. (1974). 'Caractéristiques chimiques et technologiques des cafés *Racemosa* du Mosambique'. (Chemical and technological characteristics of *Racemosa* coffees in Mozambique). *Café Cacao Thé* (Paris), vol. 18, **4** (October-December) 263–76.

Hamonnière, M. (1974). 'Contribution à l'étude d'un principe amer cristallisé isolé des graines du *Coffea vianneyi* Leroy'. (Contribution to the study of an isolated bitter crystallized element in seeds from *Coffea vianneyi* Leroy.

Café Cacao Thé (Paris), vol. 18, **4** (October-December) 277–9.

Wurziger, J. (1974). 'Über Farbreaktionen mit Kaffeeinhaltsstoffen sur Untersuchung und Bewertung von Rohkaffee. **I**. Farbreaktionen zur Unterscheidung zwischen Arabica- und Robusta-Rohkaffee'. (Colourimetric reactions with the components of coffee for the study and evaluation of raw coffee. I. Colourimetric reactions to differentiate between raw arabica and robusta coffees). *Kaffee- u. Tee-Markt* (Hamburg), vol. 24, **23** (December) 3–4 and 6–7.

Wurziger, J. (1974). 'Über Farbreaktionen mit Kaffeeinhaltsstoffen zur untersuchung und Bewertung von Rohkaffee. **II**. Farbreaktionen zum Nachweis und zur Bewertung von Qualitäts-Veränderung an Rohkaffees durch Aufbereitung un Lagerungseinflüsse'. (Colourimetric reactions with components of coffee for the study and evaluation of raw coffee. II. Colourimetric reactions for studying and evaluating the variation in quality of raw coffee due to processing and storage). *Kaffee- u. Tee-Markt* (Hamburg), vol. 24, 23, (December) 7–8 and **24** (December) 5–9.

Van de Voort, F., Townsley, P. M. (1974). 'A gas chromatographic comparison of the fatty acids of the green coffee bean, *Coffee arabica*, and the submerged coffee cell culture'. *J. Inst. Can Sci. Technol. Aliment.* (Ottawa), vol. 7, **1** 82–5.

Vitzthum, O. G., Barthels, M., Kwasny, H. (1974). 'Schnelle gaschromatographische Coffeinbestimmung in Coffeinhaltigem und Coffein freim Kaffee mit dem Stickstoffdetektor'. (Rapid determination of caffeine in caffeinated or decaffeinated coffee by gas chromatography with a nitrogen detector. *Z. f. Lebensm. Unters. u. Forsch.* (Munich), vol. 154, **3** 135–40.

Townsley, P. M. (1974). 'Production of coffee from plant cell suspension cultures'. *Can Inst. Food Sci. Technol. J.* (Ottawa), vol. 7, **1** 79–81.

Wurziger, J. (1974/5). 'Über Farbreaktionen mit Kaffeeinhalsstoffen zur Untersuchung und Bewertung von Rohkaffee. **III**. Farbreaktionen zum Nachweis und zur Bewertung von Bearbeitungseinflüssen bei Arabica- und Robusta-Rohkaffees'. (Colourimetric reactions with the components of coffee for studying and evaluating raw coffee. III. Colourmetric reactions for studying and evaluating the effects of processing of raw arabica and robusta coffees. *Kaffee- u. Tee-Markt* (Hamburg), vol. 24, **24**, (December 1974) 9 pp.; vol 25, **1** (January 1975) 6–9; vol. 25, **3** (February 1975) 22–24.

Arcila P., J. (1975). 'Efecto del etephon en la calidad de la bebida del café'. (The effect of etephon on coffee quality). *Cenicafé* (Chinchiná), vol. 26, **1** (January-March) 49–52.

Simon, D., Yen, S., Cole, P. (1975). 'Coffee drinking and cancer of the urinary tract'. *J. Nat. Cancer Inst.* (Bethesda), vol. 54, **3** (March) 587–91.

Van de Voort, F., Townsley, P. M. (1975). 'A comparison of the unsaponifiable lipids isolated from coffee cell cultures and from green coffee beans'. *Can. Inst. Food Sci. Technol. J.* (Ottawa), vol. 8, **4** 199–201.

Buckland, E., Townsley, P. M. (1975). 'Coffee cell suspension cultures: caffeine and chlorogenic acid content'. *Can. Inst. Food Sci. Technol. J.* (Ottawa), vol. 8, **3** 164–5.

Lara, W. H., Toledo, M. de, Takahashi, M. Y. (1975/6). 'Teores de cobre em café torrado et moido e em café babida'. (Copper content of roasted and ground coffee and the beverage). *Revista do Instituto Adolfo Lutz* (São Paulo), vol. 35/36, (single issue) 17–22.

Amorim, H. V., Legendre, M. G., Amorim, V. L., Saint-Angelo, A. J., Ory, R. L. (1976). 'Chemistry of Brazilian green coffee and the quality of the beverage. **VII**. Total carbonyls, activity of polyphenol oxidase, and hydroperoxides'. *Turrialba* (San José), vol. 26, **2** (April-June) 193–5.

ISO (1976) 'Cafés et dérivés. Vocabulaire'. 11pp. (Coffee and derivatives. Vocabulary). Norme internationale 3509, 1st edition, (June).

Eichler, O. (1976). *Kaffee und Coffein*, 492 pp. (Coffee and caffeine). Springer-Verlag, Berlin, New York.

Promayon, J., Barel, M., Fourny, G., Vincent, J.C (1976). 'Essais de détermination de la teneur en chicorée dans les mélanges solubles de café et de chicorée'. (Trials for determining the chicory content in powdered mixtures of coffee and chicory). *Café Cacao Thé* (Paris), vol. 20, **3** (July-September) 209–18.

Folstar, P. (1976). 'The composition of wax and oil in green coffee beans'. 65 pp. *Agricultural Research Reports* 854, Pudoc (Wageningen).

Vitzthum, O. G. (1976). 'Chemie und Bearbeitung des Kaffees', in *Kaffee und Coffein* (Coffee and caffeine) par Eichler, O. Springer-Verlag ed., Berlin, 3–38.

Miya, E. E., Shirose, I. (1977), 'Fraudes do café e influência na qualidade da bebida'. (The effect of coffee frauds on the quality of the beverage). *Boletim do Instituto de Tecnologia de Alimentos* (Campinas, São Paulo), **49** (January-February) 123–49.

Wurziger, J., Capot, J., Vincent, J. C. (1977). 'Über Untersuchungen an Arabusta-Rohkaffees'. (Research on raw Arabusta coffee). *Kaffee und Tee Markt* (Hamburg), vol. 27, **12** (June) 3–8.

Maier, H. G., Krause, H. G., (1977). 'Zur

bindung flüchtiger Aromastoffe an Pulverkaffee. I Bindung kleiner Mengen'. (Relationship between volatile aromatic substances of powdered coffee. I. Relationship between small quantities). *Kaffee und Tee Markt* (Hamburg), vol. 27, **13** (July) 3–6.

Dias, F. M., Louharanu, Vokac, L. (1977). 'Flavour and taste changes on irradiated coffee beans'. 20pp. International symposium on food preservation by irradiation. Wageningen, Netherlands, 21–25 November 1977, IAEA-SM 221/5.

Bernardes, B., Lima, A. L., Pinho, S. M., Loharanu, S. (1977). 'Short term toxicity studies of irradiated coffee (*Coffea arabica*)'. 11 pp. Institut de la Santé publique – Institut vétérinaire (Rio de Janeiro, Brazil).

ISO (1978). 'Café vert. Détermination de la teneur en eau (Méthode de référence fondamentale)'. 5 pp. (Green coffee. Determining the water content [A fundamental method of reference]). Norme internationale (International standard) 1446, First Edition.

Folstar, P., Van der Plas, H. C., Pilnik, W., Schols, H. A., Melger, P. (1979). 'Liquid chromatographic analysis of NB-alkanoyl–5-hydroxytryptamine (C–5-HT) in green coffee beans'. *J. Agric. Food Chem.* (Washington), vol. 27, **1** (January-February) 12–5.

Fabre, J. C. L., Spitalier, F., Estienne, J. (1979). 'Automatisation du dosage de la caféine'. (Automatization of the quantity of caffeine). *Ann. Fals. Exp. Chim.* (Paris), vol. 72, **773** (March 133–9.

Cros, E. Guyot, B., Vincent, J. C. (1979). 'Profil chromatographique de la fraction volatile du café. Différence entre cafés verts sain et puant. Influence de la torréfaction sur le grain et la boisson'. (Chromatographic profile of the volatile fraction of coffee. The difference between healthy raw beans and stinkers. Effect of roasting on the bean and the drink). *Café Cacao Thé* (Paris), vol. 23, **3** (July-September) 193–302.

Vasudeva, N., Ratageri, M. C., Venkataramanan, D., Raju, K. I. (1981). 'Caffeine, carbohydrates and protein in spent coffee from commercial blends'. *Journal of Coffee Research* (Chickmagalur), vol. 11, **2** (April) 49–51.

Diaz Santanilla, J., Fritsch, G., Muller-Warmuth, W. NMR (1981). 'Untersuchungen Über innere Bewegungen und Über den Einbau von Wasser in Roh- und Röstkaffee'. (Nuclear magnetic resonance research (NMR) on internal movements of water contained in green and roasted coffee). *Zeitschr. f. Legensmitteluntersuchung und Forschung* (Munich), vol. 172, **3** 173–7.

Ndjouenkeu, R., Clo, G., Voilley, A. (1981). 'Influence des conditions de préparation du café boisson sur la concentration en méthylxanthines dosées par chromatographie liquide haute performance'. (The effect of conditions of preparing coffee on the concentration of methylxanthines measured out by high performance liquid chromatography). *Science des Aliments* (Paris), vol. 1, **3**, 365–75.

Maier, H. G., Ollroge, I., Balcke, C. (1982). 'Freie Monosaccharide im Kaffee'. (Free monosaccharides in coffee). *Kaffee und Tee Markt* (Hamburg), vol. 32, **8** (April) 3–7.

Grimseh, A. (1982). 'Über Chlorogensäuren im Kaffee'. 95 pp. (Chlorogenic acids in coffee). Thesis presented at the Naturwissenshaftlichen Fakultät der Technischen Universität Carolo-Wilhelmina zu Braunschweig.

Guyot, B., Lahmy, S., Vincent, J.C. (1982). 'Dosage du 3–4 benzopyrène dans le café torréfié et ses sous-produits de torréfaction'. (Amount of 3–4 benzopyrène in roasted coffee and its sub-products from roasting). *Café Cacao Thé* (Paris), vol. 26, **3** (July-September) 199–206.

Wurziger, J., Drews, R., Suche, B. (1981). 'Ein Beitrag zur Qualitätsbeurteilung von Arabusta-Kaffee'. (Contribution to the improvement of the quality of Arabusta coffee). *Kaffee und Tee Markt* (Hamburg), vol. 31, **18** (September) 3–8.

Guyot, B., Cros, E., Vincent, J. C. (1982). 'Caractérisation et identification des composés de la fraction volatile d'un café vert Arabica sain et d'un café vert Arabica puant'. (Characterisation and identification of the components of the volatile fraction of a healthy raw arabica coffee and a green arabica stinker). *Café Cacao Thé* (Paris), vol. 26, **4** (October-December) 279–90.

Picard, H., Guyot, B., Vincent, J. C. (1984). 'Etude des composés stéroliques de l'huile de café (*C. canephora*)'. (Study of the sterolic components of coffee oil [*C. canephora*]). *Café Cacao Thé*, vol. 28, **1** 47–62.

Duplatre, A., Tisse, C., Estienne, J., (1984). 'Contribution à l'identification des espèces Arabica and Robusta par l'étude de la fraction stérolique'. (Contribution to the identification of arabica and robusta species through the study of the sterolic fraction). *An. Fals. et Exp. Ch.* Paris, **828**, 259–70.

Gervais, P., Voilley, A., Ndjouenkeu, R. (1984). 'Influence du tassement de la mouture sur l'extraction de café boisson par filtration'. (The effect of compressing the grind on the extraction of the coffee by filtering). *Science et Aliments* (Paris). **3**, 161–7.

Physiological effects

Coste, R. (1979) 'Une accusation injustifiée: la responsabilité du café dans certains troubles de la santé'. (An unjustified accusation: the responsibility of coffee for certain health problems). Et. bibliographique. *Café Cacao Thé*, vol. 23, **4**, 300–2.

Pozniak, P. C. (1985). 'The carcenogenicity of caffeine and coffee'. *Jnl. of Am. Dietetic Ass.* (Mount Morris), vol. 85, 1127–33.

Ruschenburg, U., Jahr, D. (1986). 'Teneurs en benzo-a-pyrène du café et de certains autres produits alimentaires'. (Content of benzopyrene in coffee and other food products). *Café Cacao Thé*, vol. 30, 7–10.

Elias, P. S. (1986). 'Current biological problems with coffee and caffeine'. *Café Cacao Thé*, vol. 30, **2**, 121–38.

Martin, J. B., Heyden, S. (1986) 'Caffeine consumption and mortality among 10 000 hypertensives'. *Café Cacao Thé*, vol. 30, **4**, 281–8.

Debry, G. (1988). Le café. 'Sa composition, sa consommation, ses incidences sur la santé'. 232 pp. (Coffee. Its composition, consumption, and affect on health). Monography from the Centre of Human Nutrition, Nancy.

Processing by-products

Tango, J. S. (1971). 'Utilizaçao industrial do café e dos seus subproductos'. (Industrial use of coffee and its sub-products). *Boletim do Instituto de Tecnologia de Alimentos* (Campinas), **28** (December) 49–73.

Jarquin, R., et al. (1973). 'Pulpa y pergamino de café. **II**. Utilización de la pulpa de café en la alimentación des ruminants'. (Coffee pulp and parchment. II. Using the coffee pulp to feed ruminants). *Turrialba* (San José), vol. 23, **1** (January-March) 41–7.

Franco, C. A., Gallo, A. C., Lopez, R. A. (1973). 'Efecto de la pulpa de café en el aumento de peso de los cerdos'. (The effect of the coffee pulp on increasing the weight of pigs). *Cenicafé* (Chinchiná), vol. 24 (April-June) 33–46.

Jarquin, R. et al. (1974) 'Pulpa y pergamino de café. **IX**. Uso de la pulpa de café en la alimentación de cerdos en la fase de crecimiento y acabado'. (Coffee pulp and parchment. IX. Using the coffee pulp to feed pigs during their growth and finishing phase). *Turrialba* (San José), vol. 24. (October-December) 353–9.

Balogun, T. F., Koch, B. A. (1975). 'Coffee grounds replacing sorghum grains in pig rations'. *Tropical Agriculture* (Guildford), vol. 52, **3** (July) 243–9.

Mestre-Mestre, A. (1977). 'Evaluación de la pulpa de café como abono para almácigos'. (Evaluation of the coffee pulp as fertiliser for nurseries). *Cenicafé* (Chinchiná), vol. 28, **1** (January-March) 18–26.

Sivetz, M. (1977). 'How and why spent grounds can be used as fuel'. *Tea and Coffee Trade Journal* (New York), vol. 141, **8** (August) 20–2.

Jarquin, R., Bressani, R. (1977). 'Evaluaciòn nutricional, en cerdos, de la pulpa de café sometida a varios procesos de almacenamiento'. (Evaluation of the nutritional value for pigs of coffee pulp that has been stored in various ways). *Turrialba* (San José), vol. 27, **4** (October-December) 385–91.

Coffee pulp: Composition, technology and utilization. 95 pp. Under the direction of J. E. Braham and R. Bresani. Ed. International Development Research Centre (Ottawa), 1979.

Boopathy, R., Mariappan, M. (1984). 'Coffee pulp. A potential source of energy'. *Jnl. of Coffee Res.* (Chickmagalur), vol. 14, 108–16.

Orue, C., Bahar, S. (1985). 'Utilisation of solid coffee waste as a substrate for microbial protein production. *Jnl. of Food Sc. and Tech.* (Mysore), vol. 22, **1**, 10–6.

Documentation of the ASIC

There is a wealth of documentation available on coffee trees and coffee, provided by the Proceedings of the Colloquia organised by the Association Scientifique Internationale du Café (ASIC) – International Scientific Coffee Association. These publications currently total over 5000 pages of text on all disciplines of research and agrotechnology, including the last and 12th Montreux Colloquium (Switzerland). They are an original source of information of exceptional scientific and technical value on coffee production and processing.

There are over 1000 such reports, interested parties, therefore, should contact the Association's headquarters at 42 rue Scheffer, Paris 75116. Telephone: (1) 47 04 32 15, for information.

Appendices

I Coffee price stabilisation

This book is essentially technical and has very limited economic content. However, it would appear to be appropriate to touch briefly on certain topics pertaining to the stabilisation of coffee prices, which is extremely important for producers.

The price of coffee on the major international markets, like those of many tropical products such as cacao, cotton and suger, fluctuates considerably as a result of statistical adjustments that are made between production estimates and consumption. These are arrived at by the organisations concerned and are based on the information they receive, which may or may not be accurate.

This situation can place producers at a disadvantage and may also prove difficult for the economies of the countries concerned. Consequently, in 1954, organisations responsible for regulating prices were created in francophone African countries. They were assisted as necessary by French national funding. At the international level, a major institution, the International Coffee Organization (ICO) was created; which was based in London.

Stabilisation funds

The Stabilisation Funds (Product Organisations) operate in the same way as State Companies under an administrative or pluri-ministerial sponsorship. Their objective is to ensure that planters will receive a guaranteed price, which is fixed for the entire length of the harvest season. In this way they are protected from market fluctuations and dissuaded from storing the harvests for too long, often under poor conditions. Their effectiveness is based on the fact that they compensate for high and low prices. It is possible, when prices are favourable (at their peak) to set up financial reserves so that an adjustment may be made upwards when they are low. They supervise all commercial operations on which they have the exclusive monopoly. They are also responsible for ensuring transportation and selling of the products.

The organisations undoubtedly provide producers with certain benefits which have evolved through the years with the establishment of the sometimes quite sizeable reserve funds. These have not escaped the attention of government authorities who have coveted them. It must be said that in most cases, the obligatory amount taken by the authorities represents a major source of revenue for public finances, and may represent an additional budget. Nevertheless, planters, as normal citizens, are indirect beneficiaries of the facilities that they finance in their region, such as roads, access paths, schools, hospitals and agronomic research. They also receive assistance for the purchase of small-scale equipment, fertilisers, phytosanitary treatments and selected plants, thanks to their liquid assets.

Whatever the criticisms of these funds may be, the considerable role they have played in agricultural development should not be overlooked, particularly that which concerns coffee growing in francophone countries.

II   Major international organisations

The International Coffee Organization (ICO)

This organisation was created in 1963 to apply the first International Coffee Agreement (1962), which was renegotiated several times in 1968, 1976 and 1983. The latter expired on 30 September 1989. The ICO currently associates 50 producer countries and 24 consumer countries.

The first International Coffee Agreement was implemented in 1954, with the creation of a Special Coffee Commission, which was responsible for planning a study on the worldwide situation and its strategy for the future in anticipation of an international agreement.

The resumption of the demand for coffee at the end of the Second World War caused prices to rise substantially as production was not very high. These prices made coffee growing considerably more popular, and there was a sizeable increase in the areas planted. A crisis period then followed due to overproduction.

This situation argued in favour of the establishment of an international agreement, despite the marginal position of the United States, which had always been in favour of a free market of supply and demand.

The period between 1957–1962 was marked by several limited agreements for the Latin American producer countries. Despite a serious drop in prices, none of the agreements were effective. Nevertheless, a Permanent Group for the Study of Coffee was created in 1958, with the participation of the United States, as the situation was worsening due to a saturated market. The group's essential objectives were to conduct a survey, to gather statistics, and to seek a compromise for the creation of an international agreement between producer countries.

The Latin-American Accord of October 1958 was thus a major milestone in this effort, as it introduced a system for establishing export quotas for the first time. However, these measures were not sufficient to prevent prices from dropping, because production, namely in Brazil, continued to increase.

The consequence of this alarming situation was that several countries joined together, including those of the French community, representing 85 per cent of world production, to make a new agreement under the name 'International Short-Term Agreement on Coffee'. Extended from year to year, the agreement was finally invalidated in 1963. However, the positive results, namely with regard to prices, enabled the foundations of an even greater International Agreement to be laid, to which all producer and consumer countries adhered.

This agreement was signed for a five-year period in November 1962, with the 54 producer and consumer countries as members. Its objective was thus defined: 'to achieve a logical balance between supply and demand under conditions that will ensure that consumers will have their supply and the producers will have sufficient outlets at fair prices'. This entailed adjusting exports by using a quota system and a pricing policy, which enabled the market to be stabilised by adjusting the quotas.

Applying these measures, particularly the control of quotas, posed serious problems. The agreement mapped out a system of certificates of origin and re-exportation which was not satisfactory in practice. Stamps were thus substituted, and these were found to be more effective.

The responsibility of implementing the international agreement was entrusted to an organisation created for this purpose, the International Coffee Organization (ICO).

On 30 September 1968, when the agreement expired, a new one succeeded it. The latter came into effect on 1 October 1968, with 53 member countries (34 exporters and 19 importers).

The objectives defined by the new agreement were identical to those of the preceding one, but many articles were modified, namely the basic quotas, the exemption policy, the price-regulating mechanism, the new markets, processed coffee, and others. An important point to emphasise in these new measures concerned the production objectives of member countries and the setting up of a diversification fund, both of which would ensure production control, so that a better balance between supply and demand could be achieved.

The period that followed was marked by violent turbulences in the market, essentially due to the crisis that followed the serious frosts in Brazil in 1975, which created a shortage syndrome among consumer countries. However, a new agreement was concluded in 1976, which was valid until 1 October 1982. The price increase that followed the events of 1975, and the euphoria felt by producer countries, obliged the ICO to suspend the application of certain measures based on an export quota system. The objective was to bring production figures closer to consumption figures in order to keep the prices within a margin that was acceptable to everybody.

This period is marked by some price instability. First the prices dropped, which was unavoidable after the spectacular take-off of 1976 and 1977, they then rallied moderately. The same period was also affected by numerous difficulties for the ICO, mainly with the proliferation of the so-called 'orphan' or 'tourist' coffees, or others that are sold fraudulently despite the regulations, and the initiative of the Latin American producers to create a group in an attempt to stabilise prices, called the 'Bogota Group'. In spite of these setbacks, the agreement was extended for one year, until 1 October 1983.

A new agreement was negotiated in 1983, which was to be applied as of 1 October. It had serious problems, mainly with regard to export quotas. These had been re-established according to the new measures, in an attempt to stabilise the market, which is too oriented towards the fall in prices due to worldwide over-production and the considerable inventory. A serious crisis was avoided in 1987 during discussions held in London (ICO) on revising export quotas as demanded by several producer countries. The agreement that was arrived at, after long deliberations, in October of the same year, attested once again to the conviction of the producers and consumers, that their interest lay in seeking a compromise within the framework of an international agreement. This opinion was confirmed at the Yamossoukro Conference (Ivory Coast), a few weeks later.

Dr. A. Fontana Beltrao, current Executive Director of the ICO, took up the position in 1968, with the signature of the Agreement the same year. The former President of the Pan-American Coffee Bureau, he succeeded M. J. Oliveira Santos. Since then he has assumed these difficult and delicate duties very competently, using diplomacy in all situations. These qualities have undoubtedly enabled the ICO to solve many problems and to overcome many obstacles very satisfactorily.

The African and Malagasy Coffee Organisation (OAMCAF)

The necessity of co-ordinating the marketing of coffee from coffee-producing franco-phone countries led to the creation of a Liaison Committee for the Coffee Stabilisation Fund involving the new producer countries (Ivory Coast, Cameroon, Madagascar, Central African Republic, Togo, Dahomey) in 1960. In 1963, with the membership of Congo and Gabon, the African and Malagasy Coffee Organisation (OAMCAF) was born, which represents the total production of francophone Africa (former French colonies).

The OAMCAF then became a group within the International Coffee Organiz-ation (ICO), which was created in the same year. Its members, who maintained their individual responsibilities as members of the ICO, accepted that the protection of their common interests be entrusted to the group, which gave them even greater authority. The OAMCAF is the only group of this type within the ICO.

The objectives of the OAMCAF are clearly defined in Article 1 of its statutes (25 February 1969). They are:

- to study together all problems pertaining to coffee, mainly with regard to pro-duction, processing, and marketing;
- to co-ordinate policies on the world markets, so that an optimum price level may be ensured;
- to achieve this goal, the Organisation will co-operate with regional or international organisations that pursue similar goals.

The OAMCAF is directed by a management committee in which all member countries are represented. The committee elects its president every year. This committee is invested with all powers necessary for the execution of its mandate. The operations of the Organisations are ensured by the Secretary General who is appointed by the Director.

The activities of the OAMCAF are twofold. It promotes and encourages co-operation between member countries and represents them in negotiations at the ICO. It also allocates each country with its quota. The OAMCAF ranks as third among world coffee producers, after Brazil and Colombia. Its exportable production in 1985–86 was about 500 000 tonnes.

STABEX (Stabilisation system for export earnings)

This organisation was set up by the Lomé Convention I. It puts the first agreement between industrialised and developing countries into concrete form. Its objective is to partially stabilise the economies and resources of producer countries by acting on harmful effects or abrupt drops in earnings caused by fluctuations in world markets or variations in production.

Green coffee and coffee extracts have been included from the very beginning in the list which entails 44 agriculture-based products and sub-products.

International Scientific Coffee Association (ASIC)

The ASIC was created in 1966, following two of the first colloquia on coffee organised in Paris by the French Coffee and Cocoa Institute (IFCC). It meets the unanimous need expressed by participants at these meetings to have a perennial organisation which could periodically gather specialists throughout the world of all vocations who are interested in coffee, so that their work might be studied and compared.

This association was thus officially established as a 'non-governmental' organisation on the initiative of some individuals and with the patronage of the IFCC, according to the French law of 1 July 1901 on French and foreign associations.

The objective of the ASIC is defined as follows according to Article 1 of its statues: 'to establish an inventory of scientific, technical, and applied knowledge, and to encourage, realise and co-ordinate research which may contribute to a better exploitation of coffee and its derivatives and the improvement of its quality in the common interest of the producers, merchants, manufacturers, and consumers.'

Of the 12 colloquia organised since 1963 on the initiative of the ASIC (Paris, 1963; and 1965; Trieste, 1967; Amsterdam, 1969; Lisbon, 1971; Bogota, 1973; Hamburg, 1975; Abidjan, 1977; London, 1979; Bahia, 1982; Lomé, 1985; Montreux, 1987); the first two dealt with all the problems of coffee research, including all the steps from production to consumption. Only the main disciplines concerned will be mentioned here, in order to avoid too long a listing: agronomy, analytical techniques of green and roasted coffee and their derivatives, chemical composition at various stages, study of the aromas, roasting, physiological effect, conservation and storage and packaging. The proceedings of the colloquia, published by the ASIC, contain the texts of all the reports presented *in extenso*, with comments and discussions.

This documentation gathers 600 reports on some 5000 abundantly illustrated pages. They constitute an original source of information on coffee production and processing of exceptional technical and scientific value which is indispensable to scientists and professionals alike.

This organisation is, in fact, the only one in the world which is totally independent, the scientific vocation of which is specifically devoted to coffee production and processing. It is the only one which offers specialists of all disciplines the possibility to meet through periodical international colloquia, in order to become familiar with the others' work, and to exchange views on research objectives.

French National and International Organisations

International Coffee Organization, ICO, 22 Berners Street, W1P 4DD, London, United Kingdom.
Association Scientifique International du Café (ASIC), 42 rue Scheffer, 75016, Paris, France.
Organisation Inter-africaine du Café, (OIAC), B.P. 210 Abidjan, Ivory Coast.
Organisation Inter-africaine et Malgache des Cafés (OAMCAF), 27, quai Anatole France 75007, Paris, France.

The main French national organisations
Fédération National du Commerce due Café, 3, rue de Copenhague, 75008, Paris.
Fédération Nationale des Syndicats de Torréfacteurs de Café, 3, rue de Copenhague, 75008, Paris.
Chambre Syndicale des Torréfacteurs de France, 35, rue des Belles-Feuilles, 75016, Paris.
Syndicat National de l'Industrie et du Commerce des Cafés, 17 rue de Constantinople, 75008, Paris.
Chambre Syndicale des Décaféineurs, 51–53, rue Fondary, 75015, Paris.
Syndicat National des Cafés Solubles, 140, boulevard Haussmann, 75008, Paris.
Comité Français du Café, 3, rue de Copenhague, 75008, Paris.
Institut de Reoherche du Café, du Cacao et autres plantes stimulantes, IRCC, CIRAD, 42, rue Scheffer, 75116, Paris. Laboratoires de recherches, Agropolis, B.P. 5035, 34060 Montpellier. Nombreuses implantations et présences outre-mer.

III   Coffee legislation in France (Decree of 3rd September 1965)

This text was the subject of a circular dated 22 November 1965. Several circulars then followed, elaborating on specific points.

Article 1: It is prohibited to possess products, other than those defined in the present decree, with the purpose of selling, or offering for sale under the name of 'coffee', with or without qualification, or under a description containing only the word 'coffee', or a derivitive, or the name of a species, a variety, or an origin.

This legislation applies mainly to so-called 'broken' and 'sorted' products. It does not contest the use of the word 'coffee' in conformity with the public administration regulations applied from Article 11 of the law of 1 August 1905 and the regular use for trade when it is a matter of foodstuffs and beverages other than those meant in the present decree, which was written to include the initial state of coffee.

Green coffee

Article 2: The name 'green coffee' or 'raw coffee' is reserved for the whole, healthy seeds (beans) that come from fruits of plants of the *Coffea* genus that are free of the parchment and at least part or all of the silverskin. Moreover these coffees must:

1 Belong to one of the following species: *C. arabica* (arabica), *C. canephora* (robusta and Kouilou), *C. liberica* (liberica), *C. dewevrei*, var. *excelsa* (Excelsa), *C. abeokutea* (Indenié) and other cultivated species of the *Coffea* genus;
2 **a)** Not have had any of their principle components removed, nor have been altered or contaminated, either from rot or mould;
  b) Not give off any foul odour or an odour that is foreign to coffee, mainly due to stinkers. The name stinker applies to beans which release a very disagreeable odour when cut, often putrid or rum-like; these beans may be either tobacco-brown or brownish, and are sometimes waxy in appearance;
3 **a)** Not contain over 0.5 per cent stones and other foreign matter;
  b) Not contain over 120 flawed beans per 300 g of coffee.
    The description of flawed beans and the scale by which to calculate the defects are provided in the decree drawn up by the Minister of Agriculture and the Minister of Finance and Economic Affairs, the Ministerial Delegate in Charge of Co-operation, and the Minister of State in Charge of Overseas Departments and Territories. This decree also limits the quantity of black beans, cherries, pitted beans or beans attacked by the berry borer, and broken beans;
4 Be retained by a sieve with round holes of 4.76 mm diameter (screen no. 12), with 6 per cent of the beans going through this sieve, these beans being subsequently retained by a sieve with round holes of 3.97 mm diameter (screen no. 10);
5 Consist of beans of a single botanical species. This measure does not concern the direct sale when roasted, decaffeinated, or consumed;
6 Not contain more than 12.5 per cent moisture;

Roasted coffee

Article 3: With regard to roasted coffee, the name 'coffee' is reserved for the product resulting from the roasting of the green coffee, from which none of the principal components have been removed. Moreover, these coffees must:

1 Not give off a foul odour nor have a bad taste, mainly as a result of stinkers;
2 **a)** Not contain over 0.2 per cent stones or other foreign particles;

b) Not contain flawed roasted beans exceeding either 8 per cent in weight, or in number, more than that which corresponds to 40 flaws per 100 g.

This description of flawed roasted beans and the scale by which to estimate them are specified in the joint decree of the Minister of Agriculture, the Minister of Finance and Economic Affairs, the Ministerial Delegate in Charge of Co-operation, and the Minister of State in Charge of Overseas Departments and Territories. This also limits the quantity of black, charred, and broken beans.

3 Not contain more than 5 per cent moisture. However, with the exception of so-called 'superior' coffees mentioned in Article 4 of the present decree, this measure is not applicable to coffees intended for retail sale in small pre-prepared packages, under the twofold condition that the quantity of dry matter contained in each packet represents at least 95 per cent of the net weight indicated on the label of the package and that the moisture content is below 10 per cent of the product sold;

4 Not contain over 2 per cent coating material. The list of authorised coating materials is given in the joint decree of the Minister of Agriculture and the Minister of Public Health and Population.

Article 4: Indications of superior quality cannot be used unless they pertain to roasted coffees, the characteristics of which are listed hereafter and the roasting date of which is indicated on the label or package. However, this date may be replaced by the expiration date for sale to the consumer under conditions specified by the decree of the Minister of Agriculture. In addition to the conditions previously specified in Article 3, the so-called 'superior' coffees must:

1 Not contain cherries;

2 Not contain flawed beans in a quantity exceeding either 2 per cent in weight, or in number, more than that which corresponds to 10 flaws per 100 g sample, calculated according to the scale specified by the decree in Article 3 (2) of the present decree;

3 Be completely free of stones and other foreign matter;

4 Not contain more than 3 per cent moisture;

5 Not contain more than 1 per cent authorised coating material under the conditions specified in Article 3 (4) of the present decree;

6 Be sold in airtight packaging.

Article 5: The name 'ground coffee' is reserved for the product obtained by grinding the roasted coffee as previously defined in Article 3. This product must be packed in airtight packages as soon as it has been ground. It must not contain more than 5 per cent moisture.

Supplement

Applications of decree no. 65–763 of 3 September 1965 regarding coffee and the establishment of the description of flawed beans and the scale for estimating the flaws in raw and roasted coffees.

The Minister of State for Overseas Departments and Territories, the Minister of Agriculture, the Minister of Economy and Finance, and the Secretary of State of Foreign Affairs, in charge of Co-operation, Declare:

Section I

Green coffee

Article 1: The morphological and organoleptic characteristics of flawed beans of raw coffees are as follows:

- Over-ripe dry bean: mossy or verdigris bean;
- Cherry: dried fruit consisting of all or part of its outer coverings with its seed/s;
- Black bean: a bean, half or more of which is black, outside or inside;
- Sour bean: a waxy-looking reddish brown bean that releases a slightly disagreeable odour when cut which is different from that of the healthy green bean;
- Bean in parchment: a bean that is entirely or partially covered in its parchment;
- Half black bean: a bean that is half black in colour, either internally or externally;
- Spongy white bean: a white or whitish bean, with a spongy consistency, like cork. The tissues of which cave in at the slightest pressure from a finger nail;
- Dry bean: a wrinkled, light, greyish or blackish bean;
- Immature bean: a greenish or greyish bean that is not ripe, and generally has a wrinkled surface;
- White bean: a white, very light bean, with a much lower density than a healthy bean of the same size;
- Undesirable bean: a bean that is malformed or altered inside and does not match any of the definitions given in the present article.
- Insect-infested bean: a bean attacked by insects, with:
  - at least two small holes or tunnels caused by the berry borer (*Stephanoderes*) or any other pest or;
  - a large hole caused by a bruchid beetle (*Araecerus*);
- A husk (ear): a malformed bean with a cavity or the outer part of an empty bean;
- Broken: any part of a bean that is smaller than half of a bean of the same size;
- Large skin or husk: fragment of the outside covering of the fruit;
- Small skin or parchment: fragment of the covering of the bean;
- Large piece of wood: a twig of about 3 cm in length;
- Average size piece of wood: a twig of about 1 cm in length;
- Small piece of wood: a twig of about ½ cm in length.

Article 2: The scale for estimating the flaws of green coffee is established as follows:

	Flaws		Flaws
1 over-ripe dry bean	2	5 undesirable beans	1
1 cherry	1	5 husks	1
1 black bean	1	5 broken beans	1
1 sour bean	1	10 insect-infested beans	1
2 beans in parchment	1	or beans attacked by the berry borer	1
2 half black beans	1	1 large skin or husk	1
5 white spongy beans	1	3 small skins or parchment	1
5 dry beans	1	1 large piece of wood	2
5 immature beans	1	1 medium-sized piece of wood	1
5 white beans	1	3 small pieces of wood	1

Article 3: In conformity with the clauses of Article 2 of the decree of 2 September 1965 regarding coffee, the quantity of flawed beans in raw coffee may not exceed 120 flaws per 300 g.

This clause notwithstanding, the number of flaws due to the presence of black beans, cherries, broken beans or insect-infested beans cannot exceed per 300 g:
- 5 flaws in the form of black beans;
- 5 flaws in the form of cherries;
- 15 flaws in the form of broken beans;
- 15 flaws in the form of beans attacked by insects or the berry borer.

However, until the date specified in the conditions stated in Article 16 of the decree of 3 September 1965 and in conformity with the clauses of that article, the quantity of flawed beans allowed in green coffee is a maximum of 180 flaws per 300 g; the number of flaws in the form of black beans should not exceed eight and the number of flaws due to the presence of beans attacked by pests should not exceed 30.

Section II

Roasted coffee

Article 4: Flawed, roasted coffee beans are the result either of flawed green coffee beans, or of beans that have been altered during roasting and additional operations.

Their outside appearance, after eliminating the coating if necessary, and often their inner structure clearly contrast with those of healthy beans.

The morphological and organoleptic characteristics of flawed beans are as follows:

- Black bean: an originally black, sooty-looking bean, which is dull due to the absence of any coating, with a generally granular surface;
- Charred or carbonised bean: a blackish bean, having a charcoal-like texture and easily crushed between the fingers, reducing it to fine particles;
- Cherry: dried-out fruit with all or part of its outer covering with its bean or beans;
- Bean in parchment: a bean that is completely or partially covered in its parchment;
- Half-black bean: a bean that is at least half sooty-looking;
- Marbled or spotted bean: a roasted bean that shows irregularities in its superficial colouring, which is generally brittle, and has a bad flavour;
- Undesirable bean: a bean that looks flawed, which can be easily cut without powdering, and does not correspond to any of the definitions given in the present article. It is easily found when reintroduced in the refined part of the sample;
- Pale bean: a yellow to light brown bean. It can sometimes give off a bad odour when crushed, or be of a non-brittle and insufficiently roasted consistency;
- Insect-attacked bean: a bean that has been attacked by pests and has at least:
  – two small holes or tunnels excavated by the berry borer or any other pest or;
  – a large hole caused by a bruchid beetle (*Araecerus*);
- Shell: a bean containing a cavity or an outer part of an empty bean;
- Broken bean: any part of a bean that is smaller than half a bean; one distinguishes between those retained by the sieve module 36, defined by the standard NF X 11–501 (diameter of the holes: 4 mm) and those which pass through this sieve;
- Thick skin or husk: a fragment of the outer covering of the fruit;
- Small skin or parchment: a fragment of the covering of the bean;
- Large piece of wood: 3 cm long twig;
- Average size piece of wood: 1 cm long twig;
- Small piece of wood: ½ cm long twig.

Article 5: The scale for calculating the flaws of roasted coffee has been established as follows:

	Flaws		Flaws
1 black bean	1	10 insect-attacked beans	1
1 charred bean	1	10 shells	1
1 cherry	1	10 broken beans > 4 mm	1
1 bean in parchment	1	0.2 g of small broken beans < 4 mm	1
2 half black beans	1	1 thick skin or husk	1
2 marbled or spotted beans	1	1 large piece of wood	2
2 undesirable beans	1	1 average size piece of wood	1
2 pale beans	1	3 small pieces of wood	1

Article 6: In conformity with the clauses in Article 3 of the decree of 3 September 1965 regarding coffee, the quantity of flawed beans contained in the roasted coffee cannot exceed either 40 flaws per 160 g sample or 8 per cent in weight. This clause notwithstanding, this quantity is fixed either in number or percentage or weight, and the number of flaws due to the presence or black of charred beans cannot exceed, for 100 g:

In number	In weight
3 flaws in the form of black or charred beans	0.6%
8 flaws in total breakages	1.6%

However, until the date specified in the conditions stated in article 16 of the decree of 3 September 1965 and in conformity with the measures specified in this article, roasted coffees may contain a quantity of flawed beans not exceeding 60 flaws per 100 g sample or 12 per cent in weight.

The number of flaws due to the presence of black or charred beans or the presence of breakages cannot exceed, for 100 g:

In number	In weight
5 flaws in the form of black or charred beans	1 %
12 flaws in total breakages	2.4%

Section III

General measures

Article 7: If a flawed bean corresponds simultaneously to several definitions given either in Article 1 for green beans, or Article 4 for roasted coffees, this bean should only be classified in the category responding to the most serious flaw, according to the scales specified in Articles 2 and 5, respectively.

The calculation, either of flaws, the maximum number having been established in Articles 2, 3, 4, and 16 of the decree of 3 September 1965, or certain flaws the number being limited by Articles 3 and 6 of the present decree, must be done in consideration of this classification.

Article 8: The head of the department of fraud prevention and quality control, under the authority of the Director General of Production and Markets at the Ministry of Agriculture, the Director General of Customs and Indirect Law at the Ministry of Economy and Finances, the Secretary General in charge of the administration of Overseas Departments and the Director of Overseas Territories at the Ministry of State in charge of Overseas Departments and Territories are responsible for implementing the present decree, each one in his own field. The decree will be published in the *Official Journal of the French Republic* (JORF).*

Paris, September 8, 1966

* A new and much simplified regulation was adopted by the French Government: Decree of 3rd April 1991, published in the *Official Journal of the French Republic*, 8–9th April 1991.

Index

acid beans 221
acids 230, 234
administrative expenses 210
aerial photography 119
Africa, coffee imports 291
African and Malagasy Coffee
  Organisation 250, 317
agobiada 87
aliphatic acids, green coffee
  230
alkaloids 227, 234
altitude, and maturation 32
Amarelo Coffee 2
American leaf disease 138
Angola, coffee production 261
*Antestiopsis lineaticolis
  intricata* (rainbow-coloured
  coffee bug) 159–60
Anthores leuconotus (white
  stem borer) 150
Apate monachus (black stem
  borer) 150
aphids 156
apical meristem culture 47–8,
  52
arabica *see Coffea arabica*
arabustas 15–16, 167, 171–2
Araecerus fasciculatus
  (bruchid beetle) 162
arcure 87
Armillaria root rot 129–30
aroma 220–1, 231, 234
  see also organoleptic quality
artificial drying 194–5, 198
ASIC (International Scientific
  Coffee Association) 317–18
Australia, coffee imports 292
Austria, coffee imports 287
auxin/cytokinin balance 54

back-crossing 171–2
banks, protective 79
bare-root planting 67–9
bayonet pruning 86
beans
  aborted 223
  acid 221
  black 198, 215, 219
  colours 214, 218–20
  homogenised 203
  sizes 218

stinkers 177, 183, 198, 219,
  220–1
  storage 162, 219
bean colour, in roasting 233
beetles 151, 153, 162
Belgium-Luxembourg, coffee
  imports 286–7
bench grafting 59
bending method 45–6, 87
Benin, coffee production 261
berry borer 127, 160, 162, 223,
  226
berry moth 160
biennial bearing 123
biological pest control 128
Bixadus sierricola (trunk
  borer) 149–50
black beans 198, 215, 219
black rot 129
black stem borer 150
blending 239
blotchy beans 220
Blue Mountain coffee 276
Bogota Group 316
borers 149–50 *see also* berry
  borer
Bourbon Amarello 4, 166
Boyer 27, 28, 73
branch anthracnose 139–40
branchlet beetle 151, 153
Brazil
  climatic hazards 13, 14–15,
    267, 316
  coffee consumption 291
  coffee production 267–8
  coffee standards 225
  harvesting 121
  yields 123
Brazilian coffee blends 239
broken beans 222
brown blight 141
brown eye spot 138–9
brown rot 129
bruchid beetles 162
buds, micropropagation 49–50
bugs 158–61
Burundi, coffee production
  262
by-products 207–8

Cafépro 186

caffeine content
  C. canephora 5
  green coffee 227
caffeine-free coffee 10, 169
calcium 107
callus 41, 47
callus phase 48, 52–3
Cambrony 29, 30, 46–7, 245
Cameroon 142–4, 259–60
Canada, coffee imports 290
canephora *see Coffea
  canephora*
Capot 30, 93, 96, 167–8, 172
carbohydrates 230, 234
catador grader 202–3
Catani 103–4
catch crops 117–18
caterpillars 153–6
Catimor 134–5, 171
Catuai 4, 36, 62
Caturra 63, 123, 165, 166
CBD (coffee berry disease) 5,
  140–4
Central African Republic,
  coffee production 260
Cephaleuros virenscens
  (coffee leper) 140
Cephonodes hylas (coffee
  sphinx moth) 155–6
Cercospora coffeicola (brown
  eye spot) 138–9, 144
charcoal 208
Charrier 11, 168
chemical control 128
  CBD 143
  Hemileia coffeicola 138
  Hemileia vastatrix 134
cherries 2, 177, 179
cherry coffee 197–200
chicory 249
China, coffee production 279
chromatographic separation
  228, 230
chromosomes, in coffee 164
CIB, herbicides 113
clean weeding 72, 77, 112
cleaning 201
climatic factors 12–17, 25, 99
Clitocybe tabescens (root rot)
  129–30
clonal nursery 45